Assessment of Children and Youth

Assessment of Children and Youth

LIBBY G. COHEN
University of Southern Maine

LORAINE J. SPENCINER
University of Maine at Farmington

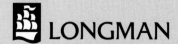

An Imprint of Addison Wesley Longman, Inc.

New York • Reading, Massachusetts • Menlo Park, California • Harlow, England
Don Mills, Ontario • Sydney • Mexico City • Madrid • Amsterdam

Acquisitions Editor: Virginia L. Blanford
Associate Editor: Arianne Weber
Design Manager: Wendy Fredericks
Cover Designer: Rubina Yeh
Cover Illustration: Betty Pinette/Spindleworks Artists Cooperative
Art Studio: Burmar Technical Corporation
Electronic Production Manager: Su Levine
Senior Manufacturing Manager: Willie Lane
Electronic Page Makeup: Stratford Publishing Services, Inc.
Printer and Binder: Maple-Vail Book Manufacturing Group
Cover Printer: Coral Graphic Services, Inc.

Library of Congress Cataloging-in-Publication Data
Cohen, Libby G.
    Assessment of children and youth / Libby G. Cohen, Loraine J.
  Spenciner.
       p.   cm.
  Includes index.
  ISBN 0-8013-1802-5
    1. Psychological tests for children. 2. Child development—
Testing. 3. Youth—Psychological testing. 4. Adolescence.
5. Behavioral assessment of children. 6. Behavioral assessment of
teenagers. 7. Educational tests and measurements. I. Spenciner,
Loraine J. II. Title.
  BF722.C638   1998   97-15010
  371.26—dc21   CIP

ISBN 0-8013-1802-5

Please visit our website at http://longman.awl.com

4 5 6 7 8 9 10 MA 03 02 01 00

Contents

Preface   xi

CHAPTER 1

Looking at Assessment

Overview   1
Chapter Objectives   2
What Shapes Our Views   2
Federal Mandates Regarding Assessment
    Practices   2
Confidentiality and Informed Consent   8
Assessment Questions, Purposes, and
    Approaches   8
Assessment Steps and Purposes   9
Snapshot: Cory   16
Preparing to Administer an Assessment
    Instrument   18
Responding to Diversity   19
Avoiding Assessment Bias   19
Professional Standards and Ethical
    Considerations   20
Preferred Practices   20
Extending Learning   21

CHAPTER 2

Involving Families and Being Responsive to Diversity

Overview   23
Chapter Objectives   24
What Shapes Our Views   24
Responding to Diversity   25
Federal Legislation and the Role of Parents   29

The Assessment Process for Families of Young
    Children, Birth to Age 5   31
Snapshot: Questions Concerning Juan's
    Physical Development   31
How Parents of Children and Youth Ages 5
    Through 21 Are Involved in the Assessment
    Process   40
Snapshot: Questions About Alexandra's
    General Academic Work   40
Snapshot: Using the Prereferral Model—
    Questions About Jimmy's Academic
    Work   41
Snapshot: Questions About Elaina's
    Behavior   43
Techniques for Listening to and Understanding
    Parent Perspectives   47
Snapshot: La Donna Harris, a Comanche
    Woman   50
Preferred Practices   51
Extending Learning   51

CHAPTER 3

Reliability and Validity

Overview   53
Chapter Objectives   53
Correlation   54
Correlation Coefficient   54
Reliability   55
Validity   59
Snapshot: Prentice Dillon and Erin
    Gates   60
Responding to Diversity: Fairness in
    Assessment   62
Snapshot: Prentice Dillon and Erin Gates
    Continue Their Conversation   63

Preferred Practices   65
Extending Learning   66

CHAPTER 4

Norms and Test Scores

Overview   67
Chapter Objectives   67
Standardized Tests   68
Scales of Measurement   70
Snapshot: Activity Levels   71
Frequency Distribution and Normal Curve   72
Measures of Central Tendency   73
Types of Scores   74
Snapshot: Deciding When to Use Measures of
    Central Tendency   75
Snapshot: A Conversation Between Lincoln
    Bates and Sari Andrews   79
Basal and Ceiling Levels   80
Standard Error of Measurement and
    Confidence Intervals   81
Snapshot: Confidence Intervals   82
Scoring Guidelines   82
How Should Assessment Approaches Be
    Evaluated?   87
Preferred Practices   88
Extending Learning   89

CHAPTER 5

Observation, Interview, and Conferencing Skills

Overview   91
Chapter Objectives   91
What Shapes Our Views   92
General Guidelines for Planning
    Observations   92
Recording Methods   93
Snapshot: Maria   103
Observing the Classroom Environment   104
Snapshot: Stoney Brook Elementary and
    Lincoln High Learning Environments   111

Observing the Student   115
Snapshot: Observations of Jon   119
Reliability of Direct Observations   119
Calculating Interobserver Reliability   121
Validity of Direct Observations   122
Developing Informal Norms   122
Interviewing   124
Conferencing and Collaborating   125
Preferred Practices   126
Extending Learning   126

CHAPTER 6

Achievement: Overall Performance

Overview   129
Chapter Objectives   129
What Shapes Our Views   130
Responding to Diversity   130
Standardized Instruments   132
Published Achievement Tests   135
Snapshot: A Special Education Teacher's
    Comments   147
Curriculum-Based Assessment   150
Criterion-Referenced Tests   151
Published Criterion-Referenced
    Tests   152
Connecting Instruction with Assessment:
    Alternative Assessment   152
Self-Assessment   158
Peer Assessment   158
Report Card Grades as Measures of
    Achievement   158
Observing the Student Within the
    Environment   159
Preferred Practices   162
Extending Learning   162

CHAPTER 7

Performance-Based Assessment

Overview   167
Chapter Objectives   167

What Shapes Our Views   168
Assessing Performance   168
Authentic Assessment   170
Portfolio Assessment   172
Snapshot: Linking Daryl's IEP with Portfolio
   Assessment   177
Exhibitions   178
Responding to Diversity   178
Developing Scoring Systems   179
Ensuring Technical Adequacy   182
Preferred Practices   184
Extending Learning   190

CHAPTER 8
Reading

Overview   193
Objectives   193
What Shapes Our Views   194
Reading Theorists   194
Instructional Approaches   196
Assessment Principles   196
Standardized Instruments   198
Concerns About Standardized Reading
   Tests   203
Connecting Instruction with
   Assessment   204
Self-Assessment   217
Peer Assessment   217
Observing the Student Within the
   Environment   217
Preferred Practices   223
Extending Learning   223

CHAPTER 9
Written Language

Overview   225
Chapter Objectives   225
What Shapes Our Views   226
Purposes and Approaches   227
Standardized Tests of Written Language   227

Concerns About Standardized Tests of Written
   Language   234
Connecting Instruction with
   Assessment   235
Snapshot: Seth   241
Scoring   242
Self-Assessment   245
Peer Assessment   245
Observing the Student Within the
   Environment   246
Preferred Practices   246
Extending Learning   246

CHAPTER 10
Oral Language

Overview   249
Chapter Objectives   249
What Shapes Our Views   250
Understanding Speech and Language
   Disorders   251
Snapshot: Bethany   252
Snapshot: Eugene   253
Responding to Diversity   253
Speech and Language Assessment   254
Assessment Questions, Purposes, and
   Approaches   256
Standardized Tests of Oral Language   256
Concerns About Standardized Tests   271
Connecting Assessment with Instruction   271
Observing the Classroom Environment   272
Snapshot: Nina   273
Students with Severe Communication
   Disorders   274
Preferred Practices   276
Extending Learning   276

CHAPTER 11
Mathematics

Overview   279
Chapter Objectives   279

What Shapes Our Views   280
Evaluating Mathematical Power   282
Responding to Diversity   286
Standardized Instruments   286
Snapshot: Kara   292
Connecting Instruction with
    Assessment   294
Rubrics   303
Self-Assessment   303
Peer Assessment   303
Observing the Student within the
    Environment   305
Preferred Practices   305
Extending Learning   309

CHAPTER 12
Development of Young Children

Overview   311
Chapter Objectives   311
What Shapes Our Views: The
    Children   312
Federal Legislation Affecting the Assessment
    of Young Children   312
Screening   313
Snapshot: Luiz and His Mother Visit the
    Community Screening Clinic   316
Limitations of Screening   318
Comprehensive Developmental
    Assessment   321
Snapshots: Special Challenges   322
What Shapes Our Views: Developmental
    Assessment   322
Choosing Appropriate Developmental
    Assessment Instruments   323
Concerns Regarding the Assessment of Young
    Children   326
Snapshot: Bennie Knight   327
Snapshot: The Hodgkin Family   328
Working with Families   330
Transition and Assessment   330
Assessing School Readiness   332
Preferred Practices   334
Extending Learning   334

CHAPTER 13
Cognitive Development

Overview   337
Chapter Objectives   337
What Shapes Our Views   338
Intelligence Tests as Samples of
    Behavior   338
Responding to Diversity   339
Standardized Instruments   341
Snapshot: Andres   370
Preferred Practices   376
Extending Learning   378

CHAPTER 14
Adaptive Skills

Overview   381
Chapter Objectives   381
What Shapes Our Views   382
Responding to Diversity   382
Informants   384
Maladaptive Behavior   384
Standardized Instruments   385
Snapshot: Jean   396
Preferred Practices   397
Extending Learning   397

CHAPTER 15
Behavior in the Classroom

Overview   399
Chapter Objectives   399
Types of Problem Behaviors Observed in the
    Classroom   400
Snapshot: Mr. Norford's Seventh Grade
    Class   400
What Shapes Our Views   401

What Contributes to Problem Classroom
    Behaviors? 405
Responding to Diversity 405
Classroom Behaviors Within an Intervention
    Context 405
Snapshot: Mr. Wing's Classroom 407
Observing the Student Within the
    Environment 407
Questions, Purposes, and
    Approaches 409
Working with Other Professionals in Assessing
    Problem Behaviors 409
Standardized Instruments for Assessing
    Problem Behaviors 412
Observing the Student 424
Other Assessment Approaches 424
Preferred Practices 425
Extending Learning 426

CHAPTER 16
Sensory and Motor Abilities

Overview 429

SECTION 1
Identifying and Assessing Students
Who Are Blind or Who Have
Visual Impairments 430

Section Objectives 430
Understanding Blindness and Other Visual
    Impairments 430
Signals of Visual Problems 431
Screening Instruments 432
Interpreting a Vision Report 432
Snapshot: Working with Other
    Professionals at Millbrook Middle
    School 436
Assessments Specific for Students with Visual
    Impairments 436
Preferred Practices 438

SECTION 2
Identifying and Assessing Students Who Are Deaf
or Who Have Hearing Impairments 439

Section Objectives 439
Understanding Hearing Impairments 439
Signals of Hearing Impairments 440
Measuring Hearing Loss 440
Categories of Hearing Impairments 442
Assessments Specific for Students with
    Hearing Impairments 443
Preferred Practices 443
Snapshot: Chad 445

SECTION 3
Identifying and Assessing Students
with Physical Disabilities 445

Section Objectives 445
Understanding Difficulties and Disabilities in
    Motor Development 445
Signals of Motor Difficulties 446
Common Assumptions Concerning Motor
    Development 447
What Shapes Our Views 447
Assessments Specific for Students with
    Physical Disabilities 448
Snapshot: Richie 450
Assessment of Academic and Social
    Skills 451
Preferred Practices 451
Extending Learning 451

CHAPTER 17
Youth in Transition

Overview 453
Chapter Objectives 453
What Shapes Our Views 454
Transition Services 454

Purposes of Transition Assessment   461
Snapshot: Tiffany   461
Published Instruments   462
Connecting Instruction with
    Assessment   474
Preferred Practices   476
Extending Learning   476

CHAPTER 18

Interpreting Tests and Writing Reports

Overview   479
Chapter Objectives   479
What Shapes Our Views   480
Responding to Diversity   481
General Principles for Report Writing   481
Types of Assessment Reports   483
Snapshot: Observation Report on John
    Diamond   486
Comprehensive Assessment
    Reports   489
Writing the Report   489
Snapshot: Gina's Comprehensive Assessment
    Report   492
Evaluating the Report   494
Sharing Assessment Results with
    Others   494
Computer-Generated Reports   498
Preferred Practices   499
Extending Learning   499

CHAPTER 19

Implementing Program Evaluation

Overview   501
Chapter Objectives   502
Introduction to Evaluation   502
When Does Evaluation Happen?   503
What Shapes Our Views   503
Planning an Evaluation of a Specific Student's
    Program   504
Snapshot: The Nelson Early Childhood
    Team   505
Responding to Diversity   507
Planning an Evaluation of a Program   508
Snapshot: Reaching Out to Family
    Members   509
Snapshot: An Informal Method for Identifying
    Needs at the Waverly School District   510
Issues in Designing and Conducting
    Evaluations   513
Participating in an Evaluation of Your Program
    by Others   513
Preferred Practices   514
Snapshot: Evaluating Special Education
    Services at Sandy Brook Public School   515
Extending Learning   515

Glossary   517

Index   523

Preface

The purpose of this book is to provide future and experienced educators and other professionals with a fundamental understanding of traditional and contemporary perspectives on the assessment of children and youth, ages 3 through 21. New developments in cognitive psychology, school reform, and research on teaching and learning have had an impact on current thinking about assessment. The changing composition of our society has also influenced assessment practices. The traditional family unit now includes a much broader definition of "family." By the year 2000, individuals in the United States will be from increasingly diverse cultural and linguistic backgrounds.

FEATURES

This book features broad coverage of traditional and contemporary assessment approaches. Individual tests are discussed at length and various assessment approaches are explained in detail. A format for evaluating traditional and contemporary approaches is included. Snapshots (case studies) illustrate the use of tests and assessment approaches.

This text is accompanied by a World Wide Web site (WWW) (http://longman.awl.com/AssessNet/) that provides students and instructors with numerous activities and ideas to extend learning. Students may follow the Snapshots in the textbook for additional activities on the WWW or they may choose WWW learning activities linked to individual chapters. Snapshots that have a computer icon 💻 indi-

cate a related web activity. Some web-based activities allow students to collaborate in team activities between and across classes. Instructors can use the WWW site to download transparencies, link to teacher education sites, or add additional resources through one of the pages in the instructor's area. *Assessment of Children and Youth* can be used independently of the WWW, as the text stands alone, although many instructors may wish to take advantage of the special capabilities that this technology adds to learning.

Major topics covered in this book are:

- Individuals with Disabilities Act Amendments of 1997
- description of professional standards
- the role of families in the assessment process
- issues of diversity
- assessment of the physical, learning, and social environments
- observation techniques
- performance-based assessment
- standardized instruments
- criterion-referenced testing
- curriculum-based assessment
- informal assessment
- contemporary approaches to the assessment of mathematics and literacy
- transition assessment
- assessment of sensory and motor abilities
- the role of technology in gathering, synthesizing, interpreting, and reporting information
- interpreting tests and writing reports
- program evaluation

ORGANIZATION

Several themes are common throughout the book. Each chapter begins with a set of objectives. We hope that the reader will use these objectives as guideposts in learning. Most chapters begin with a section titled What Shapes Our Views. This section links the topic of the chapter to one or more theoretical perspectives. Assessment questions, purposes, and approaches are described for each assessment area. The WWW strand may be followed throughout the text by locating icons within the book that signal web-based material. Diversity is addressed in the chapters in a section titled Responding to Diversity. Observing the physical, learning, and social environments of students is discussed throughout the book. Each chapter includes case studies and a section called Preferred Practices in which we summarize key points from the chapter and highlight best professional practices. Finally, at the end of each chapter, we offer a group of questions for reflection.

ACKNOWLEDGMENTS

We dedicate this book to current and future teachers—we admire, respect, and salute you for your dedication to improving the lives of children and youth. We extend our sincere appreciation to the many people who helped and supported us in the development of this book. We are very grateful to the University of Maine at Farmington and to the University of Southern Maine for the sabbatical leaves granted to us to complete this work. We extend a very special thank you to Debbie Albert, Dale Blanchard, Jen Button, Jen Gehrke, Viki Hellgren, Richard Holmes, Nancy Lightbody, Cathy Morris, Linda Nerbak, Christine Perez, Toni Rees, Ron Robert, Carole Seamon, Emily Taliento, Sue Thorson, Pearl Wuthrich, and B. K. We deeply appreciate the help and support of the editorial and production staff at Addison Wesley Longman—thank you to Ginny Blanford, Arianne Weber, and Tyler Steben.

We extend grateful appreciation to the manuscript reviewers who provided us with thoughtful and insightful reviews: Mary R. Adair, Slippery Rock University; Paul Beare, Moorhead State University; V. K. Constenbader, Rochester Institute of Technology; Laurie U. deBettencourt, University of North Carolina at Greensboro; Bill Evans, University of West Florida; Dan Fennerty, Central Washington University; Janice Ferguson, Western Kentucky University; James E. Gilliam, University of Texas at Austin; Ted Gloeckler, University of Akron; Robert G. Harrington, University of Kansas; Randy Kamphaus, University of Georgia; Nancy E. Marchand-Martella, Eastern Washington University; Martha J. Meyer, Butler University; Clyde Shepherd, Keene State College; and Robert J. Wright, Widener University.

We also extend grateful appreciation to Betty Pinette, who created the artwork that appears on the cover. Betty Pinette is an artist living in Brunswick, Maine. She joined the Spindleworks Artists Cooperative in 1978 where she is presently involved in a variety of artistic pursuits including painting, weaving, poetry writing, printmaking and art quilts. Betty's work has been in numerous shows including the Walt Kuhn Gallery, the University of Maine and the Portland Museum of Art. The Spindleworks Artists Cooperative is funded through the Maine Department of Mental Health and Mental Retardation.

Finally, we are especially grateful to our families, Les, Seth, Jay, Amy, Dave, Dina, and Ruth—we appreciate your continued support and good humor.

Libby G. Cohen
Loraine J. Spenciner

Looking at Assessment

OVERVIEW

A teacher shares concerns with another teacher about a new student in the classroom. A mother calls to discuss questions that were raised during a meeting about her child. Teachers and other professionals who work with students with disabilities not only raise questions but must work with others to respond to concerns and make decisions about students. They must be able to observe, collect, record, and interpret information about students with disabilities. As members of a school team, they plan, monitor, and evaluate individualized education programs.

This chapter begins with a discussion of federal law that relates to the assessment of children and youth with disabilities. These laws and court cases have had profound effects on assessment practices. Since this is an area that continues to change, we will examine resources that regularly provide updated information.

Next, assessment questions that guide the process of collecting information and the steps and purposes of the assessment process are introduced. Selecting assessment approaches begins with a careful consideration of the assessment questions and purposes. Throughout the chapters in this book, you will find detailed discussions of specific assessment questions, purposes, and approaches.

Professional standards and ethical considerations provide a foundation for assessment. Standards have been developed by the American Psychological Association, the Council for Exceptional Children, and the National Association for the Education of Young Children and are discussed later in this chapter. These standards will serve to guide your work with students and their families.

Finally, sections of this chapter begin themes that you will see throughout this book. You will find in the section What Shapes Our Views a discussion of the theories, perspectives, and conceptual frameworks; in Assessment Questions, Purposes, and Approaches an examination of the assessment questions and appropriate assessment approaches; in Physical, Learning, and Social Environments an exploration of various aspects in classrooms that affect student performance; and in Responding to Diversity a probing of issues in sensitivity and responsiveness to students and the uniqueness of their families.

CHAPTER OBJECTIVES

After completing this chapter, you should be able to:

Explain the general requirements for assessment as mandated by federal laws.

Provide a rationale for the participation of families in the assessment process.

Explain the requirements for confidentiality and for family rights.

Identify assessment questions and describe the different steps and purposes for assessment.

Describe how to administer an assessment instrument.

Discuss issues related to assessing students who come from diverse cultural, ethnic, racial, and linguistic backgrounds; geographic regions of origin; gender; disability; and economic groups.

Apply professional standards and ethical considerations.

WHAT SHAPES OUR VIEWS

Assessment is an integral aspect of instruction. Assessment enables educators to gather and interpret information about students and to make decisions. Assessment provides information about what individual students can and cannot do, know and do not know. School-wide assessments help administrators and school board members determine the success of school programs.

Assessment is a major focal point in education reform. In addition to quizzes, tests, and exams, teachers use other assessment approaches to provide regular feedback to students regarding their performance and to give them opportunities to improve. Teachers connect instruction with assessment and use this information to change or modify teaching and learning activities.

Teachers also use assessment approaches to answer questions regarding student achievement, abilities, behavior, development, and skills. Is there a possibility that the student has a disability? Should the student be referred for further assessment? By observing, collecting, and recording information, classroom teachers work with other educators and school personnel to interpret the information, answer questions, and make decisions about students. Some of these students may have disabilities.

Questions about students with disabilities bring assessment to another level. Assessment in the field of special education involves not only these general assessment aspects but legal aspects as well. Does the student have a disability? Federal and state laws specify assessment requirements that must be followed. Special educators and other personnel working with students with disabilities must comply with these requirements.

In the following section, we will examine the federal mandates regarding assessment practices. These mandates address the assessment process that will be conducted. The term **assessment approach** is used to describe the way information is collected.

FEDERAL MANDATES REGARDING ASSESSMENT PRACTICES

Children and youth with disabilities have been able to receive special education services in their local schools since the passage of federal legislation (P.L. 94–142) in 1975. P.L. 94–142 has been reauthorized and updated several times. In 1990, the reauthorization (P.L. 101–476) was known as the Individuals with Disabilities Education Act, or IDEA. In 1997, the Individuals with Disabilities Act Amendments of 1997 specified special education services under two parts: Part B specified special education services for children and youth ages 3 through 21; Part C described early intervention services for infants and toddlers, birth through age 2. The 1997 reauthorization of IDEA continues the mandated requirements relating to the assessment process that teachers and test examiners must know and understand. These requirements form the legal basis for identifying and providing services to children and youth with disabilities.

Locating Children and Youth

Identifying children and youth who need early intervention or special education services is a collaborative effort among teachers in the schools and personnel who work in agencies that serve children and families.

Child Find

Child Find is an identification process for locating and evaluating children with disabilities. As part of Child Find activities, public schools and other state and local agencies alert parents of preschool children to the availability of screening services in their community.

Children and Youth Who Are Eligible for Special Education

IDEA guarantees that children and youth with disabilities have the right to a free, appropriate public education (**FAPE**). Children and youth are supported in their education program by receiving special education services if their disability adversely affects their educational performance and if these special services would allow them to benefit from the education program. Figure 1.1 describes the areas of eligibility according to IDEA.

Special Considerations for Young Children from Ages 3 Through 9

Practitioners who work with young children have voiced concerns over (1) the potential detrimental effects of labeling a child at a young age, (2) the lack of adequate assessment tools for young children, and (3) the belief that some of the disability categories used with older children may not be appropriate (Figure 1.1). IDEA allows state personnel to include the term **developmental delay** in state regulations so that children ages 3 through 9 can receive education and related services without being labeled according to specific disability category (Figure 1.2). Developmental delay is also used with infants and toddlers in determining eligibility for early intervention services.

Although young children vary greatly in their rate of development, this term was designed to reflect a significant delay in development. The term refers to:

> a condition which represents a significant delay in the process of development. It does not refer to a condition in which a child is slightly or momentarily lagging in development. The presence of developmental delay is an indication that the process of development is significantly affected and that without special intervention, it is likely that educational performance at school age will be affected (McLean, Smith, McCormick, Schakel, and McEvoy, 1991, p. 2).

Procedures for Ensuring the Rights of Students and Families

IDEA specifies procedures that ensure that the rights of parents and children are protected during the assessment process and the delivery of services. These procedures are referred to as **due process** requirements and specify that:

- Parents must be provided written notice whenever there is a proposal to initiate or change the identification, evaluation, or educational placement of their child.
- Parents have the right to review their child's records regarding the assessment and educational placement.
- Parents may obtain an independent evaluation of their child by a qualified examiner who is not employed by the school. The evaluation is at no cost to the parent and is paid for by the public school.

Autism: a child with autism has a developmental disability that significantly affects verbal and nonverbal communication and social interaction, typically observed before age 3, and that adversely affects the child's educational performance. (If a child manifests characteristics of autism after the age of 3, the child can still be eligible for services under this definition if these criteria are satisfied.) Other characteristics that are often associated with autism include: engagement in repetitive activities and stereotyped movements, resistance to change in the environment or during daily routines, and unusual responses to sensory experiences. The term does not apply if a child's educational performance is adversely affected primarily due to a serious emotional disturbance.

Deaf-blindness: a child with deaf-blindness exhibits concomitant visual and hearing impairments that together cause such severe communication and other developmental and educational problems that they cannot be accommodated in special education programs solely for children with deafness or children with blindness.

Deafness: a child who is deaf has a hearing loss so severe that with or without amplification the child is unable to process language through hearing. The condition adversely affects the child's educational performance.

Hearing impairment: a child has a hearing impairment, whether permanent or fluctuating, if it adversely affects the child's educational performance but is not included under the definition of deafness.

Mental retardation: a child with mental retardation functions significantly below average in intellectual functioning concurrently with deficits in adaptive behavior that are manifested during the developmental period. The child's educational performance is adversely affected.

Multiple disabilities: a child has multiple disabilities (such as mental retardation–blindness, mental retardation–orthopedic impairment, etc.), the combination of which causes such severe educational problems that they cannot be accommodated in special education programs solely for one of the impairments. This term does not include deaf-blindness.

Orthopedic impairment: a child has a severe orthopedic impairment that adversely affects educational performance. The term includes impairments caused by congenital anomaly (e.g., clubfoot, absence of some member, etc.), impairments caused by disease (e.g., poliomyelitis, bone tuberculosis, etc.), and impairments from other causes (e.g., cerebral palsy, amputations, and fractures or burns that cause contractures).

Other health impairment: a child with a health impairment shows limited strength, vitality, or alertness due to chronic or acute health problems such as heart condition, tuberculosis, rheumatic fever, nephritis, asthma, sickle cell anemia, hemophilia, epilepsy, lead poisoning, leukemia, or diabetes that adversely affect a child's educational performance.

Serious emotional disturbance: a child with a serious emotional disturbance exhibits one or more of the following characteristics over a long period of time and to a marked degree that adversely affects a child's educational performance:

1. an inability to learn that cannot be explained by intellectual, sensory, or health factors;
2. an inability to build or maintain satisfactory interpersonal relationships with peers and teachers;
3. inappropriate types of behavior or feelings under normal circumstances;
4. a general pervasive mood of unhappiness or depression;
5. a tendency to develop physical symptoms or fears associated with personal or school problems.

The term includes schizophrenia. The term does not apply to children who are socially maladjusted, unless it is determined that they have a serious emotional disturbance.

Specific learning disability: a child with a specific learning disability exhibits a disorder in one or more of the basic psychological processes involved in understanding or in using language, spoken or written, that may manifest itself in an imperfect ability to listen, think, speak, read, write, spell, or to do mathematic calculations. The term includes such conditions as perceptual disabilities, brain injury, minimal brain dysfunction, dyslexia, and developmental aphasia. The term does not apply to children who have learning problems that are primarily the result of visual, hearing, or motor disabilities, of mental retardation, of emotional disturbance, or of environmental, cultural, or economic disadvantage.

Speech or language impairment: a child with a speech or language impairment has a communication disorder such as stuttering, impaired articulation, a language impairment, or a voice impairment that adversely affects the child's educational performance.

Traumatic brain injury: a child with traumatic brain injury has an acquired injury to the brain that was caused by an external physical force resulting in total or partial functional disability or psychosocial impairment, or both, that adversely affects a child's educational performance. The term applies to open or closed head injuries resulting in impairments in one or more areas, such as cognition; language; memory; attention; reasoning; abstract thinking; judgment; problem-solving; sensory, perceptual and motor abilities; psychosocial behavior; physical functions; information processing; and speech. The term does not apply to brain injuries that are congenital or degenerative, or to brain injuries induced by birth trauma.

Visual impairment including blindness: a child has an impairment in vision if, even with correction, it adversely affects the child's educational performance. The term includes both partial sight and blindness.

FIGURE 1.1

Children and Youth Who Are Eligible for Special Education and Related Services

A developmental delay is a delay in one or more of the following:
- Physical development including fine and gross motor
- Cognitive development
- Communication development
- Social or emotional development
- **Adaptive development**
(*Federal Register,* 1992, sec. 300.7)

FIGURE 1.2

Definition of Developmental Delay

- Due process also insures that parents, schools, or agencies have a right to an impartial hearing conducted by a hearing officer when disagreements occur. A hearing can be requested by either a parent or a school district.

Multidisciplinary Teams

Teachers and other professionals who assess students with disabilities can represent various disciplines, depending on the needs of the student. For example, individuals may come from the fields of medicine, occupational therapy, physical therapy, psychology, social work, speech-language pathology, or therapeutic recreation in addition to special education. Professionals involved in the assessment of students with disabilities should be knowledgeable of the general requirements of assessment (Figure 1.3).

For a student with a disability who has been evaluated for the first time, a member of the evaluation team, or someone who is knowledgeable about the assessment approaches used with the student and the results of the assessment, must be present at an individualized education program meeting (*Federal Register,* 1992, sec. 300.344).

Early Childhood Teams

The **early childhood team** is a **multidisciplinary team** that includes parents, the family ser-

vice coordinator, and other team members from various disciplines. This team assesses, implements, and evaluates early childhood intervention services. Early childhood teams focus on children with disabilities from birth through age 2. In some states, early childhood teams cover children from birth to school age 5.

The general requirements differ for young children and school-age students in several main areas (Table 1.1). Some differences involve the emphasis and focus of the assessment. Other requirements involve differences in time lines.

General Requirements of Assessment. Assessment procedures must be fair and equitable for all children and youth (*Federal Register,* 1992, Sec. 300.532):
- The test be administered in the student's native language or other mode of communication.
- The test be validated for the purpose that it is being used.
- The test be administered by trained personnel in conformance with instructions from the test publisher.
- The assessment yield not merely an intelligence quotient but addtional information about the student's educational needs.
- The assessment of students with impaired sensory, manual, or speaking skills be completed with tests that are selected and administered to reflect the student's aptitude or achievement level (or other factor) accurately. The tests should not reflect the student's impaired sensory, manual, or speaking skills (except where these skills are the factors that are being measured).
- No single test be used to determine a student's eligibility for special education services.
- The student be assessed in all areas related to the suspected disability, including, where appropriate, health, vision, hearing, social and emotional status, general intelligence, academic performance, communicative status, and motor abilities.
- The assessment be made by a multidisciplinary team, including at least one team member with knowledge in the suspected area of disability.

FIGURE 1.3

General Requirements of Assessment

TABLE 1.1   Assessment for Young Children and School-Age Students and Youth

Federal requirement	Children birth through age 2 and preschoolers who receive services under an IFSP	Children and youth ages 3 through 21 who receive services under an IEP
Emphasis	child and family focus	student focus
Assessment team	early childhood team	IEP team or student assistance team (for prereferral model)
Prereferral (optional)	none	student assistance team (SAT) develops interventions and strategies before referral to the IEP team
Referral	parent, practitioner, or teacher identifies questions and concerns	parent, teacher, or student identifies questions and concerns
Assessment focus	adaptive, cognitive, communication, physical, and social emotional domains	academic skills, adaptive skills, cognitive ability, emotional or problem behaviors, health, motor ability, speech and language, transitional assessment and vision or hearing.
Parent permission for assessment	required before all assessments	required before most assessments
Assessment must be completed	45 days after referral	60 days after referral (unless indicated sooner by state laws)
Plan for services	Individualized Family Service Plan	Individualized Education Program
Parent permission for services	required before child participates in early intervention or special education services	required before student participates in special education services
Review of service plan	6 months	12 months
Reevaluation	1 year	3 years (based on IEP team's determination)

The Individualized Education Program

Each child or youth who receives services must have an **individualized education program** (IEP). This written document is based on a comprehensive assessment and is developed by the **IEP team.** Figure 1.4 describes the specific assessment information that must be included in the IEP.

The IEP team conducts a reevaluation at least every three years by first reviewing existing assessment information. Using the review and input from the parents, the team determines what additional assessment is needed.

The Individualized Family Service Plan

An **individualized family service plan** (IFSP) is written for children age birth through age 2. Children who are 3 to 5 years of age may have an IFSP rather than an IEP as long as (1) the IFSP is consistent with state policy, and (2) the parents concur (*Education of the Handicapped Act Amendments,* 1986, sec. 677[d]; *Individuals with Disabilities Education Act Amendments,* 1991, sec. 14 [c]). Similar to an IEP, the Individualized Family Service Plan includes information about the child's level of functioning, the goals or outcomes for the child, and the services

Assessment information required in the IEP includes:
- Names of tests used to assess the student
- The student's current level of education performance
- Measurable annual goals as well as benchmarks or short-term objectives
- A statement regarding the specific special education and related services to be provided and the extent to which the student will be able to participate in the regular education program
- A statement of any individual modifications in the administration of state or districtwide assessments
- The projected dates for the beginning of services and the anticipated length of services
- Information as to how the student's progress will be assessed and when the assessment will occur (*Federal Register,* 1992, Sec. 300.346; *Federal Register,* 1997, Sec. 614)

FIGURE 1.4

Assessment Information Required in the IEP

that will be provided. The services described in the plan can include some for the family as well as for the child. Figure 1.5 lists the required components of the IFSP related to assessment.

Team members need to be aware that the assessment of each child (including the needs identified by the family) must be completed within 45 calendar days from the time the child is referred to the team. The law also provides that the team, with the consent of the parents, can begin early intervention services before the assessment has been completed if an interim IFSP is written.

The Individualized Transition Plan

When a student reaches the teen years, the **IEP team** must write an **individualized transition plan** (ITP). Beginning at age 14, a statement of

1. A statement of the child's present level of development, including physical, cognitive, communication, social-emotional, and adaptive (self-help skills) descriptions, based on acceptable objective criteria.
2. An optional statement of the family's concerns, resources, and priorities related to enhancing their child's development. This information, called family-directed assessment, is gathered only with parental permission.
3. A statement of the major outcomes expected to be achieved for the child and family, and the criteria, procedures, and time lines used to document progress.
4. A statement of specific early intervention services necessary to meet the needs of the child and family, including the frequency, intensity, and method of delivering services.
5. A statement of the natural environments in which early intervention services will be provided.
6. The projected dates for the beginning of services and the anticipated duration.
7. The name of the family service coordinator who will

be responsible for the implementation of the plan and coordination with other agencies and persons.
8. The date for periodic review of the IFSP (usually at 6-month intervals or more frequently when appropriate) and the date for reevaluation (at 12 months or more frequently when appropriate).
9. The steps to be taken supporting the transition of the toddler to preschool or into other appropriate placement(s) if the child is no longer eligible for intervention services. (In some states there is a difference between the eligibility criteria for toddlers and for preschoolers.)
10. The contents of the plan will be fully explained to the parents or guardian, who must give written consent prior to provision of services described in the plan. If consent is not provided with respect to a particular early intervention service, then early intervention services to which consent is given will be provided.

Education of the Handicapped Act Amendments, 1986, sec. 677[d]; *Individuals with Disabilities Education Act Amendments,* 1991, sec. 14[c].

FIGURE 1.5

Assessment Information Required in the IFSP

transition service needs is written. The ITP must describe the services that the student needs during the transition from school to adulthood as determined by the IEP team. Transition assessment and the ITP are described in Chapter 17.

CONFIDENTIALITY AND INFORMED CONSENT

Professionals who are involved with the gathering of information about a student have both a legal and an ethical responsibility to ensure that the information is maintained and used appropriately. These individuals need to agree that the information that is shared is for the purposes of enabling the family and assisting the student through individualized educational services. Teachers and other practitioners should discuss a particular student and family only with those professionals who have a legitimate interest in the information and with whom the family has consented to share information.

Family Educational Rights and Privacy Act of 1974

The **Family Educational Rights and Privacy Act** (FERPA) of 1974 (P.L. 93–380), commonly referred to as the "Buckley amendment," states that no educational agency may release student information without written consent from the student's parents. This consent specifies which records are to be released, the reasons for such release, and to whom. A copy of the records to be released should be sent to the student's parents.

FERPA allows families and students over 18 years of age access to and the right to inspect any of their records that are held at any education institution, including preschool, elementary and secondary schools, community colleges, and colleges and universities that accept federal money. Parents also have the right to challenge and correct any information contained in these records. Professionals will want to ensure that only materials relevant to the student have been filed in the student's folder. Irrelevant information about the personal lives of families or information that is at best subjective and impressionistic has no place in a family's record.

ASSESSMENT QUESTIONS, PURPOSES, AND APPROACHES

Assessment Questions

Assessment is a global term for observing, gathering, recording, and interpreting information to answer questions and make legal and instructional decisions about students. What types of questions do teachers and parents have? Teachers of young children and parents wonder if the child is developing typically in one or more of the following developmental areas:

Communication. Should Jaleh be talking more now that she is 4 years old?

Cognitive development. Is Katie experiencing difficulty performing many activities that the other children can do quite easily?

Physical development. Does Sammy have difficulty seeing? Hearing? Does he have problems with fine and gross motor activities?

Adaptive development. Should Luis be able to feed himself and take care of toileting needs?

Social-emotional development. Sonia has difficulty getting along with other children. Will she "outgrow" this?

Teachers and parents of older children frequently have questions about a student's achievement, ability, or skills in one or more areas:

Academic area. Does Elliot have a reading problem?

Overall achievement. Why isn't Bill doing better in school?

General intelligence. Will Joy be able to learn how to compute a math problem?

Social-emotional status. Daryle has difficulty making friends. How can he be helped? Sabrina seems sad and depressed. What is causing this behavior?

Physical development. Can Norweeta hear students speaking during class discussions? Joey frequently walks on tiptoes. Does this indicate a problem?

Communicative status. Bradley can hear the speaker but doesn't seem to understand. What could be the cause of his difficulty?

Assessment Steps and Purposes

In working with students with disabilities or who may have disabilities, there are specific questions and decisions to be made during each of the assessment steps: screening, referral, determining eligibility, program planning, program monitoring, and program evaluation (Figure 1.6).

As Figure 1.6 illustrates, the steps are sequential and progressive. Decision points allow the team to use the information to make decisions regarding the needs of the student.

Assessment Approaches

Educators use a variety of assessment approaches to gather information about the student and about the classroom environment. A teacher may administer a test that consists of a set of questions given to a student to determine the individual's knowledge or skill(s). The results are reported in one or more types of scores. However, **testing** of students is only one approach. Some approaches can be used to answer many different questions about a student, while other approaches are useful for gathering information for a specific purpose (Table 1.2). Be sure that the approach will yield the type of information that you need.

Table 1.2 illustrates the assessment questions, steps and purposes, and approaches.

The assessment questions guide each of the steps and purposes during the assessment process. Various assessment approaches can be used to gather information.

The IDEA amendments of 1997 specify that information provided by the parent may be included in the assessment. Best practice suggests that parents be encouraged to participate in the assessment to the degree that they choose to be involved. Team members can suggest assessment approaches for parents to use. Table 1.3 illustrates some of the questions that parents have and the tools that they can use in helping to answer assessment questions.

ASSESSMENT STEPS AND PURPOSES

Step 1. Screening

The assessment question focuses on "Is there a possibility that the student may have a disability?" The purpose of **screening** is to determine whether students may have disabilities and to refer them for further assessment. Screening is designed to assess large numbers of students efficiently and economically. Based on the information collected during screening, evaluators decide whether to refer the student to the team for further assessment. Screening approaches differ, depending on whether the student is a preschooler or of school age.

Preschool Children

In many communities, children under age 6 come to the assessment process as a result of Child Find activities. Child Find directs parents to screening services in their community that are open to infants, toddlers, and preschoolers and that are free of charge.

Comprehensive screening of young children includes several components: parent concerns; medical history (often given through parental report or completed by parents using a checklist); vision and hearing tests; and the use of commercial screening instruments and obser-

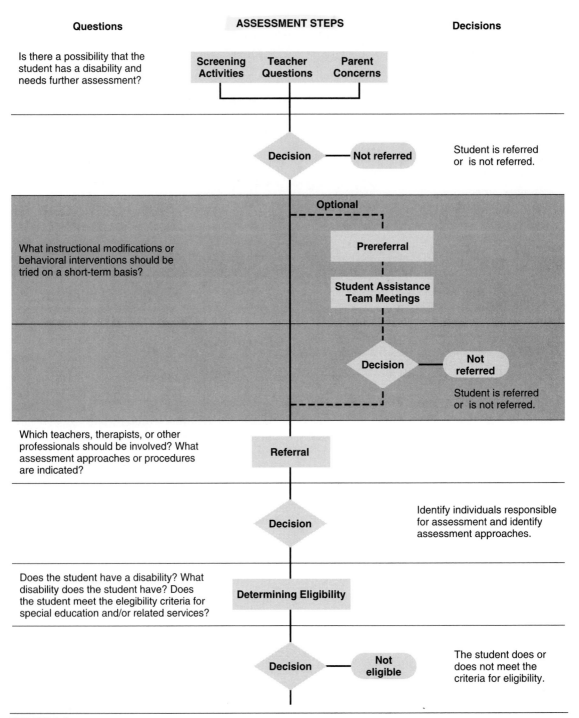

Questions	ASSESSMENT STEPS	Decisions

Is there a possibility that the student has a disability and needs further assessment?

Screening Activities **Teacher Questions** **Parent Concerns**

Decision — Not referred

Student is referred or is not referred.

Optional

What instructional modifications or behavioral interventions should be tried on a short-term basis?

Prereferral

Student Assistance Team Meetings

Decision — Not referred

Student is referred or is not referred.

Which teachers, therapists, or other professionals should be involved? What assessment approaches or procedures are indicated?

Referral

Decision

Identify individuals responsible for assessment and identify assessment approaches.

Does the student have a disability? What disability does the student have? Does the student meet the elegibility criteria for special education and/or related services?

Determining Eligibility

Decision — Not eligible

The student does or does not meet the criteria for eligibility.

FIGURE 1.6

The Steps in the Assessment Process

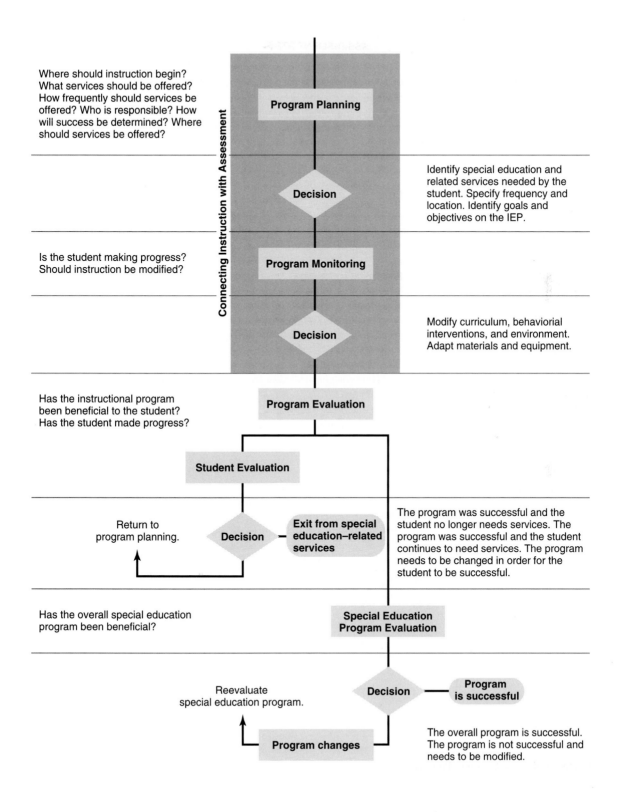

Where should instruction begin?
What services should be offered?
How frequently should services be
offered? Who is responsible? How
will success be determined? Where
should services be offered?

Connecting Instruction with Assessment

Program Planning

Decision

Identify special education and
related services needed by the
student. Specify frequency and
location. Identify goals and
objectives on the IEP.

Is the student making progress?
Should instruction be modified?

Program Monitoring

Decision

Modify curriculum, behaviorial
interventions, and environment.
Adapt materials and equipment.

Has the instructional program
been beneficial to the student?
Has the student made progress?

Program Evaluation

Student Evaluation

Return to
program planning.

Decision

**Exit from special
education–related
services**

The program was successful and the
student no longer needs services. The
program was successful and the student
continues to need services. The program
needs to be changed in order for the
student to be successful.

Has the overall special education
program been beneficial?

**Special Education
Program Evaluation**

Reevaluate
special education program.

Decision

**Program
is successful**

Program changes

The overall program is successful.
The program is not successful and
needs to be modified.

TABLE 1.2   Assessment Questions, Purposes, and Approaches

Assessment questions	Steps and purposes	Approaches
	Screening	
Is there a possibility of a disability?	To determine whether students *may* have a disability and should be referred for further assessment	Norm-referenced instruments Curriculum-based assessment Criterion-referenced assessment Observations Checklists
	Referral	
Who are the teachers, therapists, or other professionals who should be involved? What approaches are indicated?	To determine the professionals who should be involved and the assessment approaches that are indicated	
	Eligibility	
Does the student have a disability? What disability does the student have? Does the student meet the criteria for services? What are the strengths and weaknesses? What is the student having trouble doing? What does the student understand?	To determine if there is a disability To determine the need for special education and related services To compare the student's performance with the performance of the peer group To determine specific strengths and weaknesses To understand why the student is having difficulty	Norm-referenced instruments Curriculum-based assessment Criterion-referenced assessment Observation Probes Error analysis Interviews Checklists Student, parent, and/or teacher conferences Performance assessment

CONNECTING INSTRUCTION WITH ASSESSMENT

	Program Planning	
What types of special education and related services should be provided? What classroom modifications and adaptations should be implemented? What does the student not understand? Where should instruction begin?	To determine the locations and type of services(s) to be received To assess the physical, learning, and social classroom environments To understand what the student knows and does not know To determine where instruction should begin To plan the student's program To determine instructional approaches	Norm-referenced instruments Curriculum-based assessment Criterion-referenced assessment Observations Probes Error analysis Interviews Checklists Student, parent, and/or teacher conferences Performance assessment

vation reports in the areas of general development, abilities, and skills. Screening instruments are generally inexpensive and are designed to be completed in a short amount of time, 30 minutes or less. Specific screening instruments are discussed in Chapter 12.

School-Age Students

Children entering public school for the first time, or who are transferring to a new school, must be screened. Screening is conducted by one or more individuals such as the special education or general education teacher and in-

TABLE 1.2   (Continued)

Assessment questions	Steps and purposes	Approaches

CONNECTING INSTRUCTION WITH ASSESSMENT

	Program Monitoring	
Once instruction begins, is the student making progress? Should the instruction be modified?	To understand the pace of instruction To understand what the student knows prior to and after instruction To understand the strategies and concepts the student uses To monitor the student's program	Curriculum-based assessment Criterion-referenced assessment Observations Probes Error analysis Interviews Checklists Student, parent, and/or teacher conferences Portfolios Exhibitions Journals Written descriptions Oral descriptions
	Program Evaluation	
Has the student met the goals of the IEP? Has the instructional program been successful for the student? Has the student made progress? Has the instructional program achieved its goals?	To determine whether the IEP goals have been met To determine whether the goals of the program have been met To evaluate program effectiveness	Curriculum-based assessment Criterion-referenced assessment Observations Probes Error analysis Interviews Checklists Student, parent, and/or teacher conferences Portfolios Exhibitions Journals Written descriptions Oral descriptions Surveys

volves various approaches. An educator often begins by reviewing past work and test scores of the incoming student. The new student may be asked a set of questions. In the classroom, teachers observe and collect information about the student's work and performance. Teachers may observe that the student is having trouble seeing a computer screen, understanding and following directions, working with others, reading and comprehending. Parents utilize screening approaches too. They may have concerns about their child when they see their child in relation to other children in the neighborhood or when they compare their child to their knowledge about growth and development.

School personnel conduct a variety of other screening activities. The school nurse arranges for students to have a regular vision and hearing screening. Educators review student attendance records and follow up on students who are not attending school on a regular basis. Classroom teachers administer group tests of school achievement, and student scores are screened to identify those students who show they are hav-

TABLE 1.3   Parent Involvement in the Assessment Process

Assessment step	Questions parents may raise	Assessment tools used by parents
Screening	Is Juan developing like other children?	Parent report form Parent observation
Prereferral	What can we do? Will Jimmy fall behind his class?	Observation sheet Monitoring sheet
Eligibility	Does Alexandra's behavior indicate a need for special services?	Parent historical report of student's behavior Parent observation
Program Planning	*What are our priorities for Elaina? Where would be the most appropriate setting for services? How will we evaluate the services? Who will coordinate the services?	Parent report form
Program Monitoring	How is the plan working?	Parent-made video or audiotape
Evaluation of Student	Do we feel that our child has made progress?	Parent questionnaire Parent-made videotape
Evaluation of Student's Program	Does the program meet our child's needs?	Parent questionnaire

* Children who have an IFSP

ing difficulty. When young children or school-age students are identified by the screening process as needing further assessment, the evaluator, teacher, or parent completes a referral form.

Step 2. Making a Referral

Teachers or parents identify their questions and concerns and request further assessment by completing a written **referral** (Figure 1.7).

The route that the written referral travels differs, depending on school policy. Some schools have a policy in which the written referral goes directly to the IEP team (Referral Decision). Other schools use a prereferral step before the referral is sent to this team (Prereferral Decision) (Figure 1.6).

Prereferral Decisions

Questions about a student are referred to an **assistance team,** which usually is comprised of regular classroom teachers and special educators in the school building. The team may be known as the student assistance team (SAT), teacher assistance team, or intervention assistance team. In addition to questions about individual student behaviors or academic work, this team enables teachers, both regular and special education, to help one another with general academic or discipline concerns including adapting and modifying the curriculum. Although these **prereferral** procedures are not required by law, they represent good professional practice.

Referral Decisions

The IEP team, which is different from the assistance team, receives the written referral form. Based on the referral information about the student, the team may recommend specific assessment approaches or assessment instruments to be used in **determining eligibility.**

Step 3. Determining Eligibility

The assessment questions focus on "Does the student have a disability? What disability does

MEMORIAL SCHOOL

Referral Form

Student's Name: _Cory Young_   Date of Birth: _9/7/xx_

Grade: _5_   Teacher: _Ms. Leslie_

Parent/Guardian: _Joseph Davis_

Address: _Harris Lane_
Columbia

Source of referral: _Joanne Leslie, classroom teacher_

Designated school official accepting referral: _Ralph Townsend, principal_

Reason for referral: _Cory has a lot of difficulty organizing his work. His reading and math skills are below grade level. He is highly distractible. His written work is weak— mechanics, story line, and topic development below average._

Procedures, tests, records or reports used as a basis for the referral:

Iowa Tests of Basic Skills: reading 3.0, language/writing 2.8, spelling 2.5, math 3.1. Even with alternative seating, Cory gets little accomplished.

Other relevant factors involving the referral:

He wears glasses inconsistently.

FIGURE 1.7

A Teacher's Referral Form

the student have? Does the student meet the criteria for services?" The purpose of this step is to examine the assessment information to make a determination regarding the student's eligibility for special education and related services according to state and federal guidelines (Part B services) or early intervention (Part C) services for infants and toddlers.

As specified in IDEA, assessment for the purposes of eligibility must be conducted by a multidisciplinary team. Thus, a student who is suspected of having a specific disability usually undergoes several different types of assessment, including physical, psychological, educational, and vocational, to determine the nature and extent of the disability. For exam-

SNAPSHOT

Cory

Cory is a fifth grade student at Memorial School. Although he has never been referred for special education services, Cory has had considerable difficulty in school. This year, his teacher, Joanne Leslie, has become increasingly concerned about his lack of academic progress and his difficulty in organizing his work. Cory is very distractible in class and has a short attention span. Because his reading and math skills are weak, he has difficulty in keeping up with assignments.

Ms. Leslie decided to examine Cory's records to determine what had been done last year to help him be more successful. She found that Cory had been assigned special seating near the teacher to help with attention deficit issues and that a teacher assistant had worked with him in spelling. The teacher had noted that Cory still had problems completing assignments and the teacher assistant was not always available. Miss Leslie examined his most recent achievement scores. Compared to other students in fifth grade, Cory's reading and math scores were low. After consulting with Cory's parents, she completed a referral form for special education services (Figure 1.7).

ple, a student who is nonverbal may have a multidisciplinary evaluation that includes being seen by (1) an audiologist to determine the extent, if any, of a hearing loss; (2) a speech and language pathologist to assess understanding of language (receptive language) and communication skills; (3) a special educator to assess academic and functional skills; (4) a vocational rehabilitation counselor to identify interests and abilities; and (5) a psychologist to determine intellectual functioning. Various approaches will be used, including, for example, observations, norm-referenced instruments, and performance assessments. All of these evaluators work together to view and analyze the assessment information, with all contributing expertise from their respective disciplines.

The assessment information is shared during the IEP meeting, and team members determine whether or not the student is eligible to receive special education and related services.

Because decisions are based on assessment information, appropriate assessment approaches must be chosen and used carefully.

Evaluators must have appropriate training, take responsibility in evaluating the adequacy of the approach, follow professional standards and ethical principles, and be knowledgeable about the limitations of specific approaches. In the chapters that follow we will discuss these approaches in more detail.

Step 4. Program Planning

In **program planning,** the assessment questions focus on "What should be included in the student's individualized program? What types of modifications should be made to the curriculum? Where should instruction begin?" The purposes are to: 1) determine the student's current level of functioning, and 2) plan the instructional program. Much of the information gathered in Step 4 will be useful in planning the instruction and developing realistic goals.

What Should Be Included in Program Planning?

Program planning includes assessing the student's current level of functioning and determining where instruction should begin. Members of the IEP team identify the special education and related services to be included in the student's program. The team plans adaptations and modifications to the curriculum and to the classroom environment. Team members utilize commercially published norm-referenced and criterion-referenced tests, checklists, observations, or curriculum-based assessments, as well as other assessment approaches.

Connecting Assessment with Instruction

Connecting assessment with instruction is part of program planning and Step 5, **monitoring individual progress.** Connecting assessment with instruction provides rich information about a student's current level of achievement, which allows the teacher to make informed decisions regarding the student's instructional program. A teacher uses this type of assessment in planning daily teaching and learning activities to address the special needs of students. "Good classroom assessment tells us more than 'Knows it; doesn't know it.' It also tells us why" (Shepard, 1996). Connecting assessment with instruction is one of the most important aspects of the assessment process. In later chapters we will examine a variety of assessment approaches that link instruction with assessment.

Step 5. Monitoring Individual Progress

The purposes of this step are to determine: 1) if the student is making progress and 2) whether instruction should be modified if the student is not making progress. The student's progress should be assessed frequently. Teachers use several different approaches to gather information; these are described in the following chapters. Information from this assessment step allows the IEP team members to modify interventions, teaching procedures, or materials if the student is not progressing as expected.

Step 6. Evaluating the Program

Evaluating the program consists of several types of questions. One type focuses on the student's program described in the IEP. The emphasis is on whether the student is making progress and meeting the goals of the individualized education program.

Another type addresses the overall evaluation of special education services. These questions focus on the progress, as a group, of student participants in the program, the degree of satisfaction with the program as expressed by teachers, administrators, and parents, and the effectiveness of the program. The following section examines these two types of evaluation questions in more detail.

Student Evaluation

This type of assessment is used to make decisions about the success of the instructional program for individual students. The IDEA Amendment of 1997 requires a reevaluation of the student's performance and educational needs at least every three years. For children receiving services under an IFSP, the program must be reviewed every six months (or more frequently, if appropriate), and the full evaluation must be conducted annually.

1. Annual review. The purpose of the review is to determine whether or not the IEP goals have been met. Teachers may use a variety of assessment approaches to answer questions about the success of the individualized program.

2. Reevaluation. The IEP team reviews existing assessment information and considers the following questions: Does the student continue to need special education and related services? What is the student's present level of performance and educational need? On the basis of the review, and with input from the student's parents, the IEP team decides what additional information is needed and the assessment approaches to be used.

Program Evaluation

Program evaluation involves evaluating the overall services provided to groups of students or programs. Educators need to examine the success of programs offered to students. Strong programs need to be replicated; programs that are not effective need to be changed or eliminated. Evaluation questions include: Is the program successful? Are goals being met? Do parents feel satisfied with the services? Information is collected in a variety of ways including: aggregating assessment results of students who participate or have participated in the program; asking teachers, students, and parents to complete checklists or rating scales; interviewing current students in the program and their parents; or asking graduates of the school or program and their employers to complete questionnaires. We will study program evaluation in more detail in Chapter 19.

PREPARING TO ADMINISTER AN ASSESSMENT INSTRUMENT

Preparing to administer an assessment instrument begins with careful planning.

Before the Testing Begins

Before the testing session begins, the examiner should:

1. Understand the purpose(s) of the assessment (as stated in the test manual).
2. Read the test manual thoroughly.
3. Carefully review the test items.
4. Know the administrative procedures. Some examiners find that it is helpful to mark the different sections in the manual with a paper clip or self-stick note for easy reference.
5. Organize the necessary materials and check to see that none are missing.

6. Reexamine the scoring procedures and verify that the answers can be recorded correctly. By ensuring that student responses can be recorded efficiently, the test administration will go more smoothly.

When the Student Arrives

When the student arrives, the examiner should:

1. Establish and maintain rapport. Some students may be nervous and anxious about the testing; other students may have little motivation to participate or to do their best. Plan to spend enough time in making the student feel comfortable before beginning the session.
2. Convey a sense of confidence about the student's performance and avoid statements such as, "This is going to be a difficult test." The examiner can say, for example, "This test may have some items that you will find easy and some items that will be more difficult."
3. Once the testing begins, be aware of changes in lighting or noise level. Watch for signs of student fatigue or hunger. A test break may be needed or an additional session may be scheduled.
4. During the testing, maintain neutrality. Be careful about providing the student with information about the correctness of responses. Remember that not only words but facial expressions and other body language convey information. Students might ask if an answer is correct. Phrases such as "I see that you are trying hard" provide encouragement to students without violating testing procedures.
5. Carefully record student responses in the appropriate spaces on the test form.
6. Be sensitive to the needs of the student. Some students may need more time to explore test materials or share an interesting thought that has nothing to do with the test items!

After the Testing Is Completed

After the testing session has been completed:

1. Thank the student for participating.
2. Once the student leaves, finish recording any additional information. Observations of the student should be noted.
3. Compute scores.
4. Interpret results.
5. Write report.

Chapters 4 and 18 discuss calculating scores, analyzing results, and report writing in detail.

RESPONDING TO DIVERSITY

Students and their families have diverse cultural, ethnic, racial and linguistic backgrounds, come from different geographic regions of origin and gender, disability, and economic groups. They bring with them various perspectives, values, knowledge of native languages, and attitudes about the roles and responsibilities of the family, society, education, and professionals. The perspectives and values that students bring to the assessment situation can affect the student's attitudes toward the testing environment and performance, the examiner, and the purposes of the assessment (Sattler, 1988).

Sometimes perspectives and school expectations work in opposing directions. For example, educational expectations of the classroom developed by members of the majority culture tend to focus on the individual work of the student and competitiveness between students, whereas the educational expectations held by some families place an importance on group affiliation rather than individual accomplishment. These diverse perspectives may conflict with aspects of special education services and assessment practices in which assessment is focused on building student independence and intervention services are individualized.

Sensitivity

Sensitivity involves concern and respect for others, and it begins by learning about yourself, your beliefs, and your family heritage. Sensitivity grows by meeting other peoples, listening to who they are, and discovering their traditions, beliefs, and values. In working with families, knowledge should be balanced with an appreciation for that particular family, their experience of culture, their levels of acculturation, and the changing nature of culture itself (Dennis and Giangreco, 1996).

AVOIDING ASSESSMENT BIAS

Assessment approaches are considered biased if they ". . . project only predominant values and attitudes and do not reflect the linguistic and cultural experiences of minority groups" (Padilla and Medina, 1996, p. 6). There are few tests available that have been developed for use with students who come from culturally and linguistically diverse backgrounds. Table 1.4 contains a summary of litigation relating to bias in the assessment of individuals with disabilities. Failure to comply with the legislation and subsequent court rulings can result in serious penalties for school districts.

Students from nondominant groups may be less familiar with testing and less test-wise than other students. There may be a lack of motivation to participate in certain assessment approaches, and that lack of motivation prevents the student from performing to the best ability.

There are special considerations for students whose primary language is not English. Translating a test into another language does not mean that its content, difficulty, reliability, and validity are the same. A word in one language can have a different meaning, a different frequency of use, and a different difficulty level than in another language (American Educational Research Association, and American

TABLE 1.4 Litigation Relating to the Assessment of Culturally and Linguistically Diverse Individuals

Litigation	Ruling
Diana v. *State Board of California* (1970)	Placement of a Spanish-speaking student in a special class for children with mental retardation was found to be inappropriate because the placement was on the basis of intelligence tests given in English. The State of California agreed that: • All children whose primary language is not English should be tested in their primary language and in English. • All Mexican-American and Chinese-American students enrolled in classes for students with mental retardation should be reevaluated in their primary languages and in English to eliminate unfair verbal items.
Larry P. v. *Riles* (California, 1979)	Placement of African-American students in special education classes was found to be inappropriate because of unfair testing. The court ruled that intelligence tests cannot be used as the sole basis for placing students in special classes.
Parents in Action on Special Education (PASE) v. *Hannon* (Illinois, 1980)	Certain intelligence tests are not biased against African-American children.

Psychological Association, and National Council on Measurement in Education, 1985).

minimal competencies for educational diagnosticians (Table 1.5).

PROFESSIONAL STANDARDS AND ETHICAL CONSIDERATIONS

Individuals who conduct assessments must know and understand professional standards. According to authorities in the field (American Educational Research Association et al., 1985; Bredekamp and Rosegrant, 1992), educators and test examiners who administer tests should have the training and experience necessary and should follow professional standards and ethical procedures. Educators and examiners should not attempt to evaluate students whose age, disability, linguistic, or cultural backgrounds are outside the range of their academic training or supervised experience.

The Council for Educational Diagnostic Services (1995), a division of the Council for Exceptional Children, has published a list of

PREFERRED PRACTICES

Assessing students involves preparation and a variety of skills on the part of the examiner. The examiner should be knowledgeable regarding federal mandates and the requirements for assessing students with disabilities. The examiner needs to understand a variety of assessment approaches and must be able to select those approaches that are appropriate for each of the purposes in the assessment process. The examiner must use only those approaches in which the examiner has received thorough training in administering and interpreting. The examiner must follow ethical procedures and adhere to the highest professional standards.

An examiner must develop good interpersonal skills for working with students and their families. These skills include being sensitive and

---

TABLE 1.5 Minimum Standards for Educational Diagnosticians

THE EDUCATIONAL DIAGNOSTICIAN MUST HAVE KNOWLEDGE OF:

---

1. Laws, regulations, and policies, including those at the federal, state/provincial, and local levels related to diagnosis, assessment, placement, and due process;

2. Ethical issues and standards of professional practice, including confidentiality, training standards for particular instruments and procedures, limitations of one's own competence, and a willingness to pursue continuous professional development;

3. The criteria for technical adequacy of instruments as well as the limitations and appropriate use of each type of assessment procedure.

THE EDUCATIONAL DIAGNOSTICIAN MUST HAVE KNOWLEDGE OF AND SKILLS IN:

---

4. Collection of assessment data, including the selection, administration and accurate scoring of instruments and procedures appropriate to the areas of concern, such as basic academic skills, perception, language, adaptive behavior, and classroom behavior. Knowledge and skill in a wide variety of observation techniques is also essential. Throughout the process, an educational diagnostician must conduct these procedures in a manner that demonstrates respect for the individual;

5. Assessment strategies for culturally diverse groups that include a selection of approaches that encourage nonbiased assessment and take into consideration the influence of English as a second language;

6. Appropriate use of assessment information to make classification and instructional planning recommendations;

7. Communication, both oral and written, including development of assessment reports that convey results to parents and other professionals in a manner that is understandable, conveys the importance of the assessment process, and includes any reservations regarding the assessment procedures.

Adapted from Council for Educational Diagnostic Services (1995). Knowledge and skills needed by educational diagnosticians: A policy statement. *CEDS Communique* 23(1, Fall), 2.

---

responsive to diversity. Some of these skills will be areas that an examiner needs to develop; other skills may come more naturally for the examiner because of previous experience.

An examiner must be aware of and sensitive to the family's feelings about their child's academic performance or problem behaviors. Family members have much information about their child and may wish to share this knowledge. The examiner should appreciate individual preferences. One family is comfortable with a minimal level of involvement, whereas another family would like to be involved fully with the process. These individual preferences need to be recognized and appreciated.

As a member of a multidisciplinary team, an examiner can differ from other team members in philosophy and in amount and type of training. Teams are often comprised of members from various agencies and programs with different job responsibilities and schedules. The way in which team members work together affects the success of the assessment process.

EXTENDING LEARNING

1.1 You have been asked to make a presentation to the new members of the school board regarding the requirements for assessment as mandated by the IDEA amendments of 1997. Prepare an outline for your talk.

1.2 What are the purposes in assessment and how do they differ from one another?

1.3 Make a list of various assessment approaches that you have experienced. Which approaches were the most effective for you? Why?

1.4 Make arrangements to visit two different school districts and discuss the process used in screening new students and in referring students for further assessment. What types of forms do they use? Compare and contrast the approaches.

1.5 The Family Educational Rights and Privacy Act (FERPA) applies to any student who attends a school that receives federal funds. How do these regulations apply to your college or university?

1.6 Contact your State Department of Education. What information resources does it provide on assessment of students with disabilities?

1.7 Being responsive to diversity begins with sensitivity to others. Make a list of ways that have been helpful to you in developing sensitivity toward others and identify the ways that have been most effective. Share your list and discuss your findings with the class.

1.8 Begin to develop your own list of resources. Locate several professional journals that regularly publish articles on assessment in special education. Develop a list of Web sites and share them with other students. You might begin with the Education Law site, which contains the full current text of basic legal information for special education. The location is:

http://www.access.digex.net/~edlawinc/

REFERENCES

American Educational Research Association, American Psychological Association, and National Council on Measurement in Education (1985). *Standards for educational and psychological testing.* Washington, D.C.: Author.

Bredekamp, S., and T. Rosegrant, eds. (1992). *Reaching potentials: Appropriate curriculum and assessment for young children.* Vol. 1. Washington, D.C.: National Association for the Education of Young Children.

Council for Educational Diagnostic Services (1995). Knowledge and skills needed by educational diagnosticians: A policy statement. *CEDS Communique* 23(1, Fall), 2.

Dennis, R. E., and M. F. Giangreco (1996). Creating conversation: Reflections on cultural sensitivity in family interviewing. *Exceptional Children* 63(1), 103–116.

Education of the Handicapped Act Amendments, Report 99–860. Washington, D.C.: U.S. Government Printing Office, September 22, 1986.

Federal Register (Vol. 42, No. 163, pp. 42474–42518). Washington, D.C.: U.S. Government Printing Office, August 23, 1977.

Federal Register (Vol. 57, No. 189, pp. 44794–44852). Washington, D.C.: U.S. Government Printing Office, September 29, 1992.

McLean, M., B. J. Smith, K. McCormick, J. Schakel, and M. McEvoy (1991). *Developmental delay: Establishing parameters for a preschool category of exceptionality.* (CEC Position Paper). Reston, Va.: Council for Exceptional Children.

Padilla, A. M., and A. Medina (1996). Cross-cultural sensitivity in assessment: Using tests in culturally appropriate ways. In *Handbook of multicultural assessment,* edited by L. A. Suzuki, P. J. Meller, and J. G. Ponterotto. San Francisco: Jossey-Bass.

Sattler, J. (1988). *Assessment of children.* 3d ed. San Diego, Calif.: Jerome M. Sattler.

Shepard, L. (1996). Classroom testing and external accountability. Paper presented at the annual meeting of the American Educational Research Association, April, New York, N.Y.

Involving Families and Being Responsive to Diversity

OVERVIEW

Educators work closely with family members in identifying student strengths and needs, in planning the education program, and in assessing progress. Within each family, adult members may have similar or very different priorities for their children. They may wish to be involved in their child's program in a variety of ways. Family members are often at different points in their understanding and acceptance of their child's disability. For example, one parent wants to assist the team by sharing medical reports and discussing the child's diagnosis; another parent looks to team members for help and explanations. In working with families, you will need to identify the extent to which families wish to be involved in their child's assessment process and in the development of the individualized plan as well as the preferred methods of home and school communication.

Working with diverse family groups involves many skills: listening carefully, understanding and being responsive to various perspectives, sharing meaningful information, and planning together to develop an appropriate education program. Each family unit is unique. The uniqueness of families includes such diverse aspects as culture, disability, economic status, ethnicity, gender, geographic region of origin, language, and race. Professionals who work with families must be sensitive to and responsive to all elements of diversity. This chapter will give you a foundation in these skills.

CHAPTER OBJECTIVES

After completing this chapter, you should be able to:

Define the term *family* and describe areas that are important to consider in working with families.

Identify the important issues in being responsive to family diversity.

Discuss special considerations for working with families of young children from birth to age 5.

Identify areas important for working with families of students ages 5 to 21.

Describe the role of families in the assessment process as outlined by federal law.

Discuss the ways families are involved in each of the various assessment steps.

Compare assessment tools designed for parent use.

Use techniques for listening to and understanding parents.

Discuss important components of conferencing with parents.

WHAT SHAPES OUR VIEWS

Our definition of the term **family** continues to undergo changes. Today, the term reflects our understanding of the increasing diversity of family patterns and structures. Although there continues to be much debate regarding the definition, many agree that a family consists of two or more individuals who may or may not be related but who have extended commitments to each other.

Although families can include many or only a few members, each family unit is affected by four major factors. Turnbull and Turnbull (1990) developed a family systems model to assist in organizing concepts about these important factors:

1. A family's interaction system
2. Family functions
3. Family characteristics
4. A family's life cycle

The first component, a family's interaction system, is the center of the model and involves the interactions of individual family members on a daily and weekly basis. There are four major subsystems of interaction: adult and adult; parent and child; child and child; and extended family, friends, neighbors, and professionals.

The second component, family functions, or the needs of the family, are met by tasks that fall into seven broad categories:

1. Economic
2. Daily care
3. Recreation
4. Socialization
5. Affection
6. Self-definition
7. Educational/vocational

Certain functions or needs are more important for some families than others because of personal desires or cultural traditions.

The third component, family characteristics, includes not only the individual characteristics of family members but the characteristics of the family as a unit as well. For example, the number of family members, their cultural background(s), and their socioeconomic status all affect family characteristics. A child's disability, including any special challenges the child's disability presents, affects family characteristics too.

Finally, much like individuals, families, too, have life cycles. During a lifetime, an individual experiences a series of transitions as the individual progresses through different stages of growth. These stages of the life cycle may be characterized by changing interests and needs. Similarly, all families go through periods of transition during their passage through different stages as the family unit's needs and interests change. For example, a young family's immediate needs may be finding a job and a place to live. The family may be coping with any number of related problems, including poverty, illiteracy, and lack of job skills. Young children make many demands, both physical and emotional, just when parents would rather spend time finding friends for themselves or perhaps someone to assist with child care.

As children grow older, the role of parents shifts from one of meeting children's needs to one of assisting them to become independent. Families in this stage become more involved in their child's schooling and in planning for their future. Families of various backgrounds approach these roles differently. Family traditions can become an issue as parents develop an understanding of their own roles and adjust their dreams for their children. As children move into adulthood, families will experience other challenges and needs, such as accepting decisions of adult children and encouraging them in their chosen vocations.

For families that include a child with a disability, there will be additional considerations at each of these stages. Young families with an infant with special needs frequently must adjust a dream about their child's future. The child they envisioned running and skipping may never walk, hear, or speak. Grandparents who had looked forward to the birth of a grandchild may also need help in their acceptance of the infant with special needs. Later on, families with a pre-teen-ager find that they have to arrange for continued supervised child care. They will need to find time to attend team meetings at school and to meet with their child's teacher. Eventually, families with a young adult must make decisions regarding independent housing and moving from the familiar education system to a new service system. Educational services will be replaced by rehabilitative services, which often have different criteria for eligibility. Families eventually need information about guardianship, estate planning, and wills.

Thus, in many ways, the basic life-cycle experience is common, whether or not the family unit includes a child with special needs. For most families, though, the special challenges that the disability presents create additional demands. Different expectations for their child and different concerns during the family life cycle frame different perspectives for families who have recently moved to this country, who come from poverty, who speak a home language different from the majority group, or who represent a nondominant group.

RESPONDING TO DIVERSITY

An important aspect in working to meet the needs of families with children with disabilities is the the importance of understanding and being responsive to culture, disability, economic status, ethnicity, gender, geographic region of origin, language, and race. Professionals need to be sensitive to assumptions members of the dominant group can carry, and they must have the ability to make accommodations for members of less dominant groups. For example, the birth of a child with an hereditary disorder does not deter an Amish couple from having more children. A child with a disability is accepted as "God's will," and genetic counseling is inappropriate for an Amish family (Waltman, 1996). Individuals working with this family will need to accept and respect the family's decisions and to reassure them that professionals can work cooperatively with the family and not in opposition.

Often, professionals assume that because a family has lived in this country for many years that they have become acculturated. Some families deliberately avoid adopting the "American way" in an effort to retain their cultural uniqueness. Thus, several generations may grow up not holding the values of the dominant culture.

Cultural heritages, values, and beliefs may dramatically affect the family's perception of and participation in the assessment process

(Haney and Knox, 1995; Hanson, Lynch, and Wayman, 1990), development of the intervention, and plans for the future. Other aspects of diversity may affect a family's cooperation. Key areas of importance include the following:

Aspirations

A family's hopes for their child may range from appropriate to elevated or depressed expectations. Family aspirations have an impact on the levels of involvement that families choose, from making the referral for assessment to participating in the assessment process to helping develop a plan for services. Family aspirations can be influenced by certain cultural or regional expectations as well. For example, residents in some regions place a high value on family and community. A family from this region may hope that after completing school their child will join the family business.

Assistance

The family may actively seek help from others; or the family may view its needs and problems as private matters to be addressed only within the family. For example, residents in some rural areas place a high value on personal independence and self-sufficiency. They may be reluctant to ask for additional assistance.

Authority of the School

Cultural beliefs, such as feelings about school authority in decision making (Turnbull and Turnbull, 1990) or respect of authority (Alper, Schloss, and Schloss, 1994), often affect the level and types of involvement family members choose. Some families have difficulty with the joint decision-making process of parents and professionals working together. They consider professionals authority figures to be respected and obeyed. Such family members may try to avoid confrontation in discussions, or they may reject school authority altogether.

Child Rearing

Families approach child rearing from various perspectives too. In some families there is much close physical contact between mother and child, and communication is characterized more by touch than by vocal stimulation. Other families spend much time in talking with children. Some families do not encourage their child to participate in gross motor activities for safety concerns. Other families of young children promote independent exploration and travel.

Communication

Communication involves active listening and responding to both verbal and nonverbal communication. Being sensitive and responsive to family diversity includes appreciating that family groups may have unique communication patterns. For example, some regional and cultural groups support and value assertiveness in making needs and wishes known to others; some groups view assertiveness as rude and avoidable.

Communication styles can help or hinder family members' efforts to seek services. For example, to receive services, family members have to make an initial referral, make follow-up phone calls, complete paperwork, and deal with a service system with various requirements and eligibility procedures. The variety of communication and interpersonal skills needed to negotiate the service system can create barriers for some families in obtaining services.

Some family groups have unique nonverbal communication patterns; for example, avoiding eye contact with elders to signify respect. The art of communication may take on a special significance to some groups. For instance, a focus on relationships rather than on tasks can mean it is more important to continue a conversation with a friend than it is to be on time for an appointment to discuss a child's assessment.

For families newly arrived in this country, communication that involves technologies can create additional barriers. For example, families may not be acquainted with the procedure of operating a digital phone to negotiate a computer-assisted telephone call or using a telephone answering machine.

Disability

Perceptions of disability encompass a range of emotions for family members: embarrassment and shame, guilt and blame, grief and acceptance. Some groups may view a person with a disability as having second-class status. Family members may believe that there are social or physical barriers because their child has a visible disability. Parents may lack knowledge about their child's disability and have difficulty in locating information to develop realistic expectations. Various issues relating to the acceptance of the disability involve the parents, the extended family, and the community. The extended family's perceptions and the cultural community's acceptance of the disability often play a critical role for the immediate family.

Legal Status

Families may lack knowledge of their rights regarding services for their children. Parents who have an illegal status commonly fear government and school officials and are reluctant to have their child assessed.

Literacy and Language

Some family members may not have the ability to speak, read, or write English. Other family members may have poor literacy skills in their native language. Even families who have strong literacy skills may be limited by the availability of materials in their native languages or dialects.

Identifying translators and their availability is critical for families so that they can participate in the assessment process. The challenge of translating exact meanings between two languages is often difficult. For families who speak a dialect different from the translator's, this challenge sometimes becomes a barrier.

Few standardized assessment instruments are written in languages other than English. Many standardized instruments do not include representative samples from cultural, racial, ethnic, and linguistic groups. To compound the problem, examiners can lack familiarity with family diversity.

Meetings and Support Groups

These groups are often helpful for family members who would like assistance; yet, the group discussion format is more difficult for some individuals than others. Shapiro (1994) describes how the problems can be overcome in support groups among Latino families. Approaches that are beneficial include the development of ethnically competent group facilitators (who have a familiarity with Latino ethnic history and culture), the involvement of community leaders, outreach using the Latino media, repeated personal contact, attention to making the group culturally relevant, and meeting in a neutral or culturally significant location.

Parental Roles

In many cultures, the person who makes the decisions is the principal male family member. This could be the father, grandfather, uncle, or brother-in-law. Although the mother or other female family representative might attend all meetings regarding the child, she may refuse to make any decisions or sign any papers. The male figure may never attend any of the meetings; yet the decisions are his to make. This decision-making process can be frustrating to the team; however, if the team has knowledge

TABLE 2.1   Considerations in Responding to Family Diversity

Area of consideration	Issues in being responsive to diversity
Aspirations	A family's hopes for their child may range from appropriate aspirations to elevated or depressed expectations.
	Family aspirations affect the level of involvement families choose in making the referral, in participating in the assessment process, in helping to develop a plan of services. Family aspirations are influenced by culture, economic status, gender, or geographic regional expectations.
Assistance	Family members may actively seek help or they may view needs and concerns as private matters. Family views are influenced by one or more aspects of diversity.
Authority	Some families wish to participate in parent professional partnerships. Families from some cultural communities naturally defer to authority.
Children	Families approach child rearing from various perspectives, including independence, communication, and physical contact.
Communication	Some families use an assertive style in their verbal communication that assists them in referring their child and in entering the service system. Other families naturally defer to authority figures and do not pursue issues.
	Some families use nonverbal communication, including eye gaze and gestures to communicate important wants or needs.
	Communicating takes on a special significance to some groups. Finishing a conversation is more important than being on time.
	Communication that involves technology may be a barrier for some families.
Disability	A disability may be viewed as shameful, or the person with a disability may be viewed as having a second-class status.
	A disability can present social or physical barriers. These barriers may be perceived, or they may be actual barriers of access.
	Issues of acceptance involve one or more of the following groups: parents, extended family, community.
Legal status	Families may lack knowledge of their rights.
	Families with illegal status often fear government authorities or school officials.
Literacy and language	Family members may not have literacy skills in their own language or in English. Information and materials are seldom available in the family's native language. Translators may not be available.
	Standardized instruments often lack a representative norming sample.
	Examiners may not be familiar with aspects of diversity.
Medical practices	Medical practices differ and can cause misinterpretation between families and school personnel.
Meetings and support groups	The format of group discussions can cause difficulty for families of some communities.
Transient status	Families that are homeless or move frequently have difficulty entering the service system.

of the parental roles beforehand, additional attempts can be made to accommodate the male family member's schedule.

Transient Status

Some families move frequently from one residence to another, and some can be homeless for periods of time. Locating children and providing services is challenging when families move from one service area to another.

Medical Practices

Medical practices differ across cultures and can cause misinterpretation by school personnel.

One example of a traditional practice that has led to misunderstandings in the American culture is the use of coin rubbing. This massage treatment is utilized by the Vietnamese community to treat disorders such as headaches and colds. Coin treatment, or *Cao Gio,* literally translates to "scratching the (bad) wind out of the body." The treatment involves the massaging of chest and back with a medicated substance, like Ben-Gay, and the striking or scratching of the skin with a coin or spoon. This process leaves superficial bruises and, when spotted by professionals who are unaware of the techniques, has often resulted in a referral for child abuse. This practice provides a clear example of differences and also dramatically underscores the issues in diagnosis and interpretation when the various cultures meet. (Hanson et al., p. 122)

Table 2.1 summarizes the important considerations in working with families and developing a sensitivity to diversity. Understanding and being responsive to diversity is a complex process. The skills involved require you to be thoughtful and reflective in practice. You must exercise care not to promote stereotypes by making generalities about cultural groups. A key point to remember in working with families is ASK. Asking families to determine preferences and needs avoids stereotypical assumptions as well as careless regard to family heritage.

FEDERAL LEGISLATION AND THE ROLE OF PARENTS

The role of parents has long been recognized in federal legislation that regulates the provision of services to children and youth with disabilities. One of the most important aspects of this legislation is the defining of parent and guardian rights. These rights are described in the Individuals with Disabilities Education Act (IDEA) amendments of 1997, under the broad term due process. Due process refers to the legal safeguards that must be followed during the assessment process and the delivery of services. These safeguards ensure that the rights of families and their children are protected.

Guaranteed Rights

The child's parent(s) or guardian must be notified of any assessment procedure (*right of notice*) and provide consent (*right of consent*) for the assessment of their child. Before the assessment process begins, school personnel must send the parents a written form that describes the types of assessments to be conducted. The parent provides consent by signing and returning the form. However, the parent can revoke consent at any time during the assessment process by notifying the school. The parent can request that a full assessment of all areas associated with the disability be completed. This assessment must include multiple measures, must be conducted by a multidisciplinary team, and, for children ages 3 through 21, must be completed within 60 days of referral. Sixty days is the maximum number of days; some states have passed legislation that specifies a 45-day maximum. Teachers and examiners should check with your state department of education to determine the laws in your state.

Infants and toddlers, ages birth through 2, and preschoolers who will have an individualized family service plan must have assessment procedures completed 45 days after the initial referral (*right of evaluation*). Parents may request a reevaluation or obtain an independent evaluation if there are any questions or concerns regarding the evaluation (*right to an independent evaluation*). These and other important rights are described in Table 2.2.

TABLE 2.2   The Rights of Parents and Guardians According to IDEA

	BEGINNING THE ASSESSMENT PROCESS
Right of parents and guardians	*Definition*
Right of notice	The parent must receive a notification of the proposed assessment in the family's native language or principle mode of communication.
Right of consent	The parent must give consent before the child is assessed to determine eligibility for special education services.
Right of evaluation	The assessment must include multiple measures, be conducted by a multidisciplinary team, and be completed within 60 days of referral for special services. For young children who will have an IFSP, the assessment must be completed within 45 days of the initial referral.
Right to an independent evaluation	The parent has a right to request an evaluation by an independent evaluator if there are questions or concerns regarding the child's evaluation conducted by school personnel.
	USING THE ASSESSMENT INFORMATION
Right of participation	The parent must be invited to participate in the writing of the child's educational plan (an individualized family service plan or an individualized educational program).
Right of notice	The parent must receive a notification of the proposed changes in the education program, which must be in the family's native language or principle mode of communication.
Right of access	The parent must be allowed access to all educational records.
Right to confidentiality	The educational records are confidential. The parent must give consent to have the child's records released to other institutions or agencies. The parent has the right to refuse disclosure of information contained in the records to other professionals or agencies.
Right to hearing	The parent has the right to a hearing with an impartial hearing officer. The parent has a right to present evidence and to cross-examine school staff.
Right to mediation	The parent has the right to a process, called mediation, which attempts to resolve differences with school personnel before going to a hearing.
Right to resolve differences	If the parent is not satisfied with the decision of the hearing officer, a second step, the right to appeal to the state court system, can be implemented.

THE ASSESSMENT PROCESS FOR FAMILIES OF YOUNG CHILDREN, BIRTH TO AGE 5

In this section we will examine some of the questions and decisions that parents make concerning the assessment of young children. Many teachers and other professionals who work with families of young children from birth to age 5 provide services within the context of a **family-focused philosophy.** A family-focused philosophy requires that teachers and therapists attempt to create opportunities for families to acquire the knowledge and skills necessary to strengthen the functioning of the family. A family-focused philosophy supports the belief that families need to be able to choose the services that will benefit them. Thus, families are not merely recipients of services but rather active participants in the assessment, implementation, and evaluation of special services.

Parents of young children have questions about their child's development; parents of school-age children have academic concerns.

Some parents have questions about their child's behavior. Addressing the concerns of parents of preschool children and parents of children enrolled in school involves two distinct processes. First, we will examine the process for young children before their enrollment in school. This process includes the questions parents of young children may have, the answers through assessment to these questions, and the procedure for making decisions.

Initial Questions and Decisions

During the early years of a child's growth, parents and other family members may develop concerns about their child's development. In fact, parents are often the first to question or to observe areas of difficulty for their child, much as happened in Juan's family. Parents sometimes share their concerns with someone close to their child, such as a teacher or child care provider.

Teachers and child care personnel should listen to parents and encourage discussions about their children. They should inform parents

SNAPSHOT

Questions Concerning Juan's Physical Development

Juan was born $3\frac{1}{2}$ months premature and is now 4 years old. He lives at home with his mother, father, maternal grandmother, and two younger brothers. Every day his grandmother takes him for a ride in his red wagon when she goes down to the corner store. He enjoys watching the activities at a construction site along the way. His grandmother and his father have some concerns about Juan's development. He was slow to walk and talk, and his speech is still difficult to understand. He prefers to play alone or to watch cartoons on television.

His grandmother shared her concerns with a neighbor who works at the community child care center. The staff at the center had recently completed an inservice workshop on child development. The neighbor listened sympathetically and then suggested that the grandmother could take Juan to the child center for a free community screening on the first Monday of the month.

about neighborhood screening activities and encourage them to have their children screened periodically. Assisting parents and other adults to become aware of screenings, programs, and services for children with special needs is called Child Find. Preschool teachers, public health nurses, social workers, and doctors are some of the professionals involved with Child Find. Personnel from state agencies that work with children and families conduct a variety of Child Find activities throughout the year. For example, radio and television announcements or newspaper articles describe community screenings and dates screenings will be held. Brochures distributed in public places explain ways to observe a young child's development and list common questions that arise for parents. These printed materials also contain information about community screenings. Families with questions about their child may decide to take advantage of these free screenings, or families may decide to discuss their concerns with their primary medical provider.

Screening Questions for Families

Parents are encouraged to share their observations and concerns during screening. A social worker, nurse practitioner, or educator usually meets with the parent(s) to discuss their questions and concerns and to record information about their child's development. The discussion during the screening process focuses on problems or concerns. The assessment question is: Does this child have a problem that requires further assessment?

Parents are asked to complete a checklist or parent report form concerning various milestones in their child's development. Many standardized screening tools provide a parent report form as an integral part of the screening profile (Table 2.3).

One example of a standardized screening tool, the *AGS Early Screening Profiles* (Harrison, Kaufman, Kaufman, Bruininks, Rynders, Ilmer, Sparrow, and Cicchetti, 1990), provides a comprehensive parent questionnaire (Figure 2.1).

This questionnaire is designed to provide information in four developmental areas: communication, daily living skills, socialization, and motor skills. The parent rates whether or not the child does different activities within each of these four areas by indicating "always or almost always," "sometimes or partially," and "never or almost never."

Screening Decisions for Families

If there are concerns after all the information about the child has been collected, the screening results are forwarded to a team of professionals known as the early childhood team. The child's parent(s) will be invited to participate and, together, team members decide what additional assessment information is necessary.

Questions Regarding Eligibility

As members of the early childhood team, parents have the opportunity to identify their concerns and participate in the team process in determining whether or not their child is eligible for special services. Parents can provide valuable information based on their child's developmental history or their observations of their child at home. The key question the team must address is, "Does this child and family meet eligibility requirements for special services?" In Chapter 1 we described this process in detail and how IDEA defines these areas of eligibility for students ages 3 through 21.

Decisions Regarding Eligibility

Decisions regarding eligibility are based primarily on standardized testing. However, parents can add valuable information to this decision by taking an active role during the assessment process. For example, parents can provide information informally through discussions or they can complete a parent report form from a standardized instrument (Table 2.4). Parents of young children often choose to

TABLE 2.3   Selected Standardized Screening Instruments that Incorporate a Parent Report

Screening instrument	Age range of child	Parent involvement	Scoring
AGS Early Screening Profiles (Harrison et al., 1990)	2 yrs. through 6 yrs. 11 mos.	Home survey	Descriptive categories of above average, average, below average.
		Health survey	Information is not scored but integrated into the recommendations.
		Self-help/social profile	Percentile ranks.
Brigance® Preschool Screen (Brigance, 1985)	3 through 4 yrs.	Parent rating form	Categories of yes, no, uncertain. Parents may include explanations in writing.
Early Screening Inventory–3 (Meisels, Henderson, Marsden, Browning, & Olson, 1991)	3 through 4 yrs.	Parent questionnaire	Not scored; assists in providing an overview of the child's development.
Early Screening Inventory (Meisels & Wiske, 1988)	4 through 6 yrs.	Parent questionnaire	Not scored; assists in providing an overview of the child's development.
FirstSTEP (Miller, 1992)	2.9 through 6.2 yrs.	Parent/Teacher Scale	Descriptive categories of always/usually, some of the time, rarely, or never. Raw score is converted to scaled score. Information is integrated into the child's record form.

be present in the room so they can add their observations of their child's behavior. They may be able to provide feedback regarding whether or not the skills that their child demonstrates are typical of what they feel their child can do. Parents can supplement information about their child. For example, they may offer to share a videotape of their child in different settings.

Assessment procedures focus on one or more of the following developmental domains: adaptive, such as self-help; cognitive; communication; physical, including gross and fine motor skills; and social-emotional development.

Early childhood team members should be aware that assessment of each child (including the needs identified by the family) must be completed within 45 calendar days from the time the child is referred to the team.

Questions and Decisions in Planning the Program

If the team decides that the child is eligible for special services, the next step involves questions and decisions regarding the child's program. What are the family's priorities and resources? **Family-directed assessment** focuses on information that family members

SOCIALIZATION DOMAIN

1. Labels happiness, sadness, fear, and anger in himself or herself; for example, says "I'm happy." _____ 2 1 0

2. Identifies people by characteristics other than name; for example, says "That's Tony's sister." _____ 2 1 0

3. Has a best friend of the same sex. _____ 2 1 0

4. Has a fairly regular group of friends. _____ 2 1 0

5. Plays at least one game or activity with others; for example, tug-of-war or hide-and-seek. _____ 2 1 0

6. Takes part in elaborate make-believe activities alone or with others; for example, plays "school" or "house." _____ 2 1 0

7. Follows rules of simple games. _____ 2 1 0

8. Shares toys or possessions without being told to do so. _____ 2 1 0

9. Watches television or listens to radio for information about a particular area of interest; for example, a sports hero or a wild animal. _____ 2 1 0

10. Uses appropriate table manners without being told; for example, chews with mouth closed, says "please," and doesn't reach in front of others. _____ 2 1 0

11. Responds appropriately when introduced to strangers; for example, says "Hi, it's nice to meet you." _____ 2 1 0

12. Ends conversations appropriately; for example, says "See you soon." _____ 2 1 0

13. Follows time limits set by parents or teachers. (If the child cannot tell time, score 0.) _____ 2 1 0

14. Apologizes for unintentional mistakes; for example, says "Excuse me" after bumping into someone. _____ 2 1 0

15. Avoids asking questions or making statements that might embarrass or hurt others; for example, doesn't say "You look terrible." _____ 2 1 0

Please continue to the next column.

MOTOR SKILLS DOMAIN

1. Walks as primary means of getting around. _____ 2 1 0

2. Walks down stairs with alternating feet. _____ 2 1 0

3. Runs smoothly, with changes in speed and direction when necessary; for example, playing tag or running to catch a ball. _____ 2 1 0

4. Jumps over small objects. _____ 2 1 0

5. Climbs on and off high play equipment; for example, jungle gyms. _____ 2 1 0

6. Hops forward on one foot with ease. _____ 2 1 0

7. Catches small ball thrown from a distance of ten feet. _____ 2 1 0

8. Screws a lid onto a jar and unscrews it. _____ 2 1 0

9. Builds three-dimensional structures, such as a house or bridge, using at least five blocks. _____ 2 1 0

10. Completes jigsaw puzzle of at least six pieces. _____ 2 1 0

11. Opens door by turning doorknob. _____ 2 1 0

12. Opens lock with key. _____ 2 1 0

13. Marks with pencil, crayon, or chalk on appropriate writing surface. _____ 2 1 0

14. Draws at least two recognizable objects, such as an animal or a house. _____ 2 1 0

15. Uses scissors to cut out complex items; for example, pictures from magazines. _____ 2 1 0

This is the end of the questionnaire.

Please check to make sure you responded to every item.

FOR OFFICE USE ONLY	
DOMAIN	**Raw Score***
Communication	
Daily Living Skills	
Socialization	
Motor Skills	

*Sum of all 1 and 2 scores.

FIGURE 2.1

Sample Items from the AGS Early Screening Profile and Parent Questionnaire

Source: From Early Screening Profile by Patti Harrison, Alan Kaufman, Nadeen Kaufman, Robert Bruininks, John Rynders, Steven Ilmer, Sara Sparrow, and Domenic Cicchetti. © 1990. American Guidance Service, Inc., 4201 Woodland Road, Circle Pines, MN 55014. Reprinted with permission of the Publisher. All rights reserved.

BOX 2.1	
AGS EARLY SCREENING PROFILES	

Publication Date: 1990

Purposes: A screening test that measures the following areas of development: cognitive/language, motor, articulation, and self-help/social. The battery also contains additional checklists that may be completed by the parent or the child's teacher.

Age/Grade Level: Ages 2 years through 6 years, 11 months.

Time to Administer: 15–30 minutes.

Technical Adequacy: The instrument was standardized in 1987–88 and needs to be re-standardized to reflect changes in the diversity of the U.S. population.

Suggested Use: May be used as part of an overall screening procedure.

choose to share with other team members regarding family resources, priorities, and concerns. Family-directed assessment relates to children ages birth through 2 and, in some states, to children ages 3 to 5. Families are not required by law to participate in family-directed assessment but families must be given the opportunity. Table 2.5 lists the assessment areas in family-directed assessment and illustrates information that a family may share. Thus, parents not only participate in the process of identifying child-related strengths and needs, but they may exchange information with practitioners regarding family-based needs. The focus of family-directed assessment is on the process that encourages families to identify needed services rather than on the assessment of families to determine which services to deliver.

A teacher or other professional may support

TABLE 2.4   Selected Standardized Instruments that Incorporate a Parent Report

Areas of concern	Instrument	Age	Reliability	Validity
Behavior	Behavior Rating Profile, Second Edition (Brown & Hammill, 1990)	6 yrs. 6 mos. to 18 yrs. 6 mos.	adequate	not adequate for eligibility decisions
Behavior	Child Behavior Checklist (Achenbach, 1991)	4 yrs. to 18 yrs.	adequate	adequate
Behavior	Conners' Parent Rating Scales (Conners, 1990)	3 yrs. to 17 yrs.	adequate	adequate
Behavior	Revised Behavior Problems Checklist (Quay & Peterson, 1987)	6 yrs. to 18 yrs.	adequate	adequate
Development	Battelle Developmental Inventory (BDI) (Newborg, Stock, & Wnek, 1988)	birth to 8 yrs.	adequate	adequate
Development	Bayley Scales of Infant Development (Bayley, 1993)	birth to 42 mos.	adequate	adequate
Development	Child Development Inventory (Ireton, 1992)	15 to 72 mos.	adequate for younger children	not adequate for eligibility decisions

TABLE 2.5   Family-Directed Assessment: Hearing the Family's Concerns, Resources, and Priorities

Areas that comprise family-directed assessment	Sample comments by family members during a family-directed assessment
Family concerns	"How can I learn more about my child's disability?"
	"How will my child get along in school?"
Family resources	"We have reliable transportation."
	"Our child's relatives live nearby."
Family priorities	"We want to know how to communicate with our child."
	"We would like some help with toilet training."

family-directed assessment by assisting the family in identifying information or by helping the family complete a written form, rating scale, or other standard procedure. The Family Information Summary (Figure 2.2) is an example of an instrument used in family-directed assessment. This information will be used by the early childhood team in the development of the individualized family service plan (IFSP).

What are the outcomes, or goals, that the team believes that the child should accomplish? What type(s) of special services should be provided in order for the child to achieve the outcome(s)? Table 2.6 lists the 16 types of special services that can be offered to the child and family.

The team must decide where the services should be provided and how frequently. Young children and families can receive services in their home, a clinic, a child care center, a nursery school or Head Start Center, or a school-based program. Family members are important team participants in these decisions. A professional who is responsive to diversity understands that some families prefer to have services in their home while other families prefer to take their child outside the home for services.

The services are described in the child's individualized plan. Infants and toddlers (birth through 2 years of age) have an Individualized Family Service Plan (IFSP). Children who are 3 to 5 years of age may have an IFSP rather than an individualized education program (IEP) as long as the IFSP: (1) is consistent with state policy, and (2) the parents concur. A sample of an IFSP can be found in Chapter 12.

Questions and Decisions in Monitoring the Special Services

Once the IFSP is implemented, teachers, therapists, other service providers, and parents monitor the program. The monitoring questions should relate to the measurable goals. Team members check the plan on a regular basis, noting progress or lack of progress.

FAMILY INFORMATION SUMMARY

Child's Name _____

Date _____

What is important for people who help us to know about us?

Important people in our family (names, ages, relationships):

Others who are important to us:

Important events for us:

Some of our family's strengths:

We are concerned about or need:

FIGURE 2.2

Family Information Summary

Source: From Turbiville, V., I. Lee, A. Turnbull, and D. Murphy (1993), *Handbook for the development of a family-friendly individualized family service plan (IFSP),* p. 39. Lawrence, Kan.: Beach Center on Families and Disabilities, University of Kansas. Reprinted with permission.

TABLE 2.6 Early Intervention Services for the Child and Family According to IDEA

1. Assistive technology devices and assistive technology services	An assistive technology (AT) device means "any item, piece of equipment, or product system . . . that is used to increase, maintain, or improve the functional capabilities of children with disabilities" (IDEA, 1991). The AT service includes evaluating the needs of the child, purchasing or otherwise providing acquisition of the device, and training in its use. The training may include not only the child but the family.
2. Audiology	This service includes identifying the hearing loss, determining the need for amplification, and providing auditory training, aural rehabilitation, speech reading, and other services.
3. Family training, counseling, and home visits	Social workers, psychologists, and other trained personnel assist the family in understanding the special needs of the child and enhancing the child's development.
4. Health	These services may include clean intermittent catheterization, tracheostomy care, tube feeding, and the changing of dressings.
5. Medical	Medical services are only for diagnostic or evaluation purposes.
6. Nursing	These services include assessment of health status for the purpose of providing nursing care, provision of nursing care to prevent health problems or to restore or improve function, and administration of medications.
7. Nutrition	Some of these services include individual assessment and developing and monitoring feeding skills and problems.
8. Occupational therapy	These services are designed to improve the child's functional ability to perform adaptive skills in home, school, and community settings.
9. Physical therapy	These services improve, prevent, or alleviate movement dysfunction.
10. Psychological	Planning and managing a program of psychological services may include psychological counseling for children and parents, family counseling, consultation on child development, parent training, and education programs.
11. Service coordination	A service coordinator is assigned by the team to ensure that services are coordinated and that the plan is carried out.
12. Social work	A social worker may make home visits to evaluate the living conditions and the patterns of parent-child interaction. These services also include individual and family-group counseling with parents and other family members and appropriate social skill-building activities with the child and parents. The social worker may also identify, mobilize, and coordinate other community resources.
13. Special instruction	Special instruction services may include not only working with the child but with the family as well. An important aspect of this service is to provide families with information, skills, and support related to enhancing the skill development of the child.
14. Speech-language pathology	This area includes identifying needs and providing services in the development of communication skills.
15. Transportation	These services consist of the reimbursement of travel costs incurred when the child and family receives other early intervention services.
16. Vision, orientation, and mobility services	These areas include evaluating visual functioning, referral, and training.

Questions and Decisions in Evaluating Special Services

Evaluating special services that are provided to children with disabilities has two different aspects: first, the child's progress must be evaluated, and second, the program must be evaluated. Parents should be provided the opportunity to assist in both of these types of evaluations.

Evaluating Progress: The Six Month Review

At the end of 6 months, or sooner if indicated, the team must meet to discuss progress and review the IFSP. Parents must receive written notification of the IFSP meeting. Parents participate in the evaluation by completing checklists, providing videotapes and parent reports, and making observations. Let's examine some specific examples of information that family members share during team meetings:

- An aunt provides a list of information regarding what her nephew can do independently around the house.
- A grandfather makes a videotape of his granddaughter reading to her stuffed animals
- A father completes the parent checklist on a recently standardized instrument.

If the information collected during the assessment process indicates that there is little progress, then the team will examine whether or not they believe that the program needs to be modified. Changes to the IFSP are based on team decision making.

TABLE 2.7   **Selected Early Education Program Evaluation Instruments that Incorporate a Parental Report**

Instrument	Purpose	Reliability	Validity
*Family-Centered Program Rating Scale, 2nd ed. (Murphy & Lee, 1991)	Parents and staff rate the degree to which an early education program is family-centered.	adequate	needs additional study
Project Dakota Parent Satisfaction Survey (Kovach & Jacks, 1989)	Parents rate their child's early education program in five areas: 1) program and staff responsiveness; 2) growth in knowledge and skills for helping your child; 3) growth in understanding normal behavior and problems; 4) utilization of community resources; and 5) building a support system.	needs additional study	needs additional study
Family-Focused Intervention Scale (Mahoney, O'Sullivan, & Dennebaum, 1990)	Family members rate the degree of family-focused services they receive. The scale also includes parents' perception of intervention program benefits.	adequate	adequate

*Spanish form available

Reevaluation: The Annual Review

Young children who receive special services must be reevaluated each year, or more often if the team feels it is necessary. Again, parents must be sent a notification of the reevaluation and they are invited to the team meeting to discuss the assessment results and write the new IFSP. If the information collected during the assessment process indicates that there are substantial gains, then the team will discuss whether or not special services are still required. If the team decides that the child and family continue to be eligible for services, then the next step is to write the new IFSP.

Evaluating the Program

Does the program address the family's needs? Through the use of informal feedback, parents are asked to provide feedback. For example, a letter sent to all families participating in an early childhood special education play group serves as an effective informal evaluation instrument. Included in the letter is a postcard with several questions for families to answer and return by mail.

Teachers and other school staff may decide to use commercial program evaluations (Table 2.7) in soliciting parent feedback, many of which focus on the evaluation of early education programs. Commercial program evalua-

tions should provide information regarding the standardization and technical characteristics of the instrument.

HOW PARENTS OF CHILDREN AND YOUTH AGES 5 THROUGH 21 ARE INVOLVED IN THE ASSESSMENT PROCESS

Screening Questions and Decisions

Screening is mandated by law for all students enrolling in school for the first time. Children are screened upon entering school at age 5 and students who move into a new school district are screened soon after they enroll in the new school. During the child's school career, teachers will contact parents regarding their concerns or parents can contact school personnel with their questions. Physicians, too, refer a student for evaluation.

Teachers should encourage parents to discuss any questions or concerns that they have throughout the school year. Teachers can assist parents by asking informal questions such as, "What would be helpful for me to know about Alexandra?" or leading questions such as, "Tell me what Alexandra likes to do at home."

SNAPSHOT

Questions About Alexandra's General Academic Work

Mrs. Balinsky is worried about her daughter's grades. She remembers with pride how Alexandra put a puzzle together when she was only 2 years old. Later, in elementary school, she always brought home report cards with A's. But now, in ninth grade, Alexandra seems to have lost interest in schoolwork and good grades. She barely passed English and math last year. Why could there be such a change in Alexandra? Mrs. Balinsky decides to contact the school with her questions and concerns.

School staff handle parent questions and concerns in different ways. Some schools use a prereferral model; others may not. The prereferral model is not mandated by law, but many schools find that this model is helpful in addressing questions and concerns.

Prereferral Model: Addressing Parent Questions and Concerns in Other Ways

In Chapter 1 we discussed a prereferral system that is used before the student is referred for special education services. You may recall that in this model questions about a student are referred to an assistance team, which consists of regular classroom teachers and special educators in the school building. The team follows a problem-solving approach to addressing questions about a student's behavior or academic work. Thus, when a parent or teacher has questions about the student, the team meets to discuss the concerns and plan a process for gathering information.

The team also develops intervention strategies. During the implementation of the intervention, the teacher or, when appropriate, the parent carefully records its effectiveness. If the first intervention is not successful, the team will develop and implement additional interventions and record the results. Although these prereferral procedures are not required by law, they can be helpful in addressing some questions and concerns. The Snapshot of Jimmy illustrates the use of the prereferral model.

In the prereferral model, Jimmy's teacher and other educators who make up the Bennington Middle School Student Assistance Team (the SAT) will meet with his mother to discuss concerns and to devise a plan. Some examples of strategies that Jimmy's teacher or the SAT might suggest include teaching Jimmy a self-monitoring strategy when doing his homework and working with the parent to assist in monitoring homework. Figure 2.3 shows an example of one of these strategies, a parent-student monitoring sheet. Jimmy, his teacher, and his mother developed this sheet together.

Jimmy's mother agrees to let him work at the kitchen table because other family members usually watch television in the living room each evening. She agrees to remind him of the time they have set for evening homework. Jimmy's teacher suggests she can assist Jimmy in organizing his materials. The SAT agrees that she will help him decide where to keep school supplies such as pencils, dictionary, and

SNAPSHOT

Using the Prereferral Model—Questions About Jimmy's Academic Work

Fourteen-year-old Jimmy, a ninth grader at Bennington Middle School, seems to struggle with completing his homework. After supper, he looks forward to watching his favorite television program before beginning his algebra and English assignments. After the program finishes, Jimmy sits down to work on the couch; yet, his mother has noticed that he usually gets up frequently and wanders around the house to find an assignment, a pencil, or a book. He becomes distracted easily and usually forgets what he has set out to find. He rarely finishes his work before bedtime.

JIMMY'S DAILY HOMEWORK CHECK

September 13, 19xx
Six checks for extra hour of TV

	Parent checks	Comments
Quiet area for homework	_____	
Study hour starts at 7:30 pm	_____	
School supplies available	_____	

	Jimmy checks	Comments
Working on homework 1–15 minutes	_____	
Working on homework 16–30 minutes	_____	
Working on homework 31–45 minutes	_____	
Working on homework 46–60 minutes	_____	

FIGURE 2.3

Parent-Student Monitoring Sheet

paper. During the homework hour, Jimmy records his progress on the monitoring sheet. If he receives six checks out of a possible seven areas, he can choose a previously agreed-upon reward.

Perhaps for Jimmy these interventions will address the problem, and the assessment process will end. However, when assistance team members think that a student requires more extensive remediation, they provide a formal referral to the special services team.

Referral

When questions about a student persist, the student assistance team completes a written referral form and forwards the referral to the coordinator of the special services team. This team consists of the student's parents, school personnel, and the student, when possible. The team may be known as the IEP team or child study team.

Decisions for the Team

The special services team receives the formal referral delineating questions about the student, which comes directly from the child's parents, teachers, student assistance team, or a student may self-refer. The special services team makes decisions regarding assessment procedures and develops an assessment plan. This plan describes questions the team is trying to answer about the student's special needs, the tests and procedures that will be used, and the individuals who will complete the assessments. The parent or guardian must sign a written permission before the assessment process begins. As team members, parents can choose to be an active part of this process, although this is not mandated by law. They provide copies of medical records and/or educational reports. Parents frequently add observations of the student at home and in the community. They also assist the team in gathering information by using informal tools such as checklists, rating scales, or videotape or audiotape recordings.

Eligibility Questions and Decisions

In this step of the assessment process the team addresses the following question: Does the student meet the criteria for a disability? Does the student need special education to learn and to develop? Parents and other team members must decide if the student's special needs meet the eligibility requirements as described in IDEA, which was discussed in Chapter 1. For example, the assessment process may focus on one or more of the following areas to determine eligibility:

- Academic skills such as math, reading, writing, and spelling
- Adaptive behavior such as self-help and independent skills
- Behavior, social, or emotional issues

- Health and orthopedics
- Learning abilities
- Listening skills
- Speech and language
- Vision or hearing
- Vocational assessment

Decisions regarding eligibility are based on information collected during the assessment process. Parents can provide information to which other team members do not have access. Elaina's mother can share information regarding her behavior at home and in the community. Further, parents are often the only team members who can provide an historical perspective. In Alexandra's case, this information is necessary to develop a more comprehensive picture of the assessment questions.

Parents can provide information informally through discussions or contribute information on a standardized instrument. There are numerous instruments that solicit parent information as part of the profile. An example of one of these instruments, the *Child Behavior Checklist* (Achenbach, 1991), is illustrated in Figure 2.4.

SNAPSHOT

Questions About Elaina's Behavior

Ten-year-old Elaina's mother is discouraged. Some days, Elaina seems to argue constantly with her sisters and neighborhood friends. She comes running into the house, slams the screen door, and screams that she hates everyone. Her mother has tried to talk with her, but Elaina usually ends up crying and locking herself in the bedroom. Her mother feels that the other children are becoming resentful and don't want to include Elaina in their plans.

Elaina's mother contacts the school and arranges to meet with Elaina's teacher and guidance counselor. During the meetings, the guidance counselor suggests several strategies to try at home. Elaina's teacher agrees to follow up in the classroom. However, as the months go by, the mother becomes more concerned with the lack of progress. She again contacts the school and fills out the referral form.

Below is a list of items that describe children and youth. For each item that describes your child **now or within the past 6 months**, please circle the **2** if the item is **very true** or **often true** of your child. Circle the **1** if the item is **somewhat** or **sometimes true** of your child. If the item is **not true** of your child, circle the **0**. Please answer all items as well as you can, even if some do not seem to apply to your child.

0 = Not True (as far as you know)   **1 = Somewhat or Sometimes True**   **2 = Very True or Often True**

0 1 2	1.	Acts too young for his/her age	0 1 2	31. Fears he/she might think or do something bad
0 1 2	2.	Allergy (describe): _____		
		_____	0 1 2	32. Feels he/she has to be perfect
			0 1 2	33. Feels or complains that no one loves him/her
0 1 2	3.	Argues a lot		
0 1 2	4.	Asthma	0 1 2	34. Feels others are out to get him/her
			0 1 2	35. Feels worthless or inferior
0 1 2	5.	Behaves like opposite sex		
0 1 2	6.	Bowel movements outside toilet	0 1 2	36. Gets hurt a lot, accident-prone
			0 1 2	37. Gets in many fights
0 1 2	7.	Bragging, boasting		
0 1 2	8.	Can't concentrate, can't pay attention for long	0 1 2	38. Gets teased a lot
			0 1 2	39. Hangs around with others who get in trouble
0 1 2	9.	Can't get his/her mind off certain thoughts; obsessions (describe): _____		
			0 1 2	40. Hears sounds or voices that aren't there (describe): _____
		_____		
0 1 2	10.	Can't sit still, restless, or hyperactive		_____
			0 1 2	41. Impulsive or acts without thinking
0 1 2	11.	Clings to adults or too dependent		
0 1 2	12.	Complains of loneliness	0 1 2	42. Would rather be alone than with others
			0 1 2	43. Lying or cheating
0 1 2	13.	Confused or seems to be in a fog		
0 1 2	14.	Cries a lot	0 1 2	44. Bites fingernails
			0 1 2	45. Nervous, highstrung, or tense
0 1 2	15.	Cruel to animals		
0 1 2	16.	Cruelty, bullying, or meanness to others	0 1 2	46. Nervous movements or twitching (describe):
				_____
0 1 2	17.	Day-dreams or gets lost in his/her thoughts		
0 1 2	18.	Deliberately harms self or attempts suicide	0 1 2	47. Nightmares
0 1 2	19.	Demands a lot of attention	0 1 2	48. Not liked by other kids
0 1 2	20.	Destroys his/her own things	0 1 2	49. Constipated, doesn't move bowels
0 1 2	21.	Destroys things belonging to his/her family or others	0 1 2	50. Too fearful or anxious
			0 1 2	51. Feels dizzy
0 1 2	22.	Disobedient at home		
			0 1 2	52. Feels too guilty
0 1 2	23.	Disobedient at school	0 1 2	53. Overeating
0 1 2	24.	Doesn't eat well		
			0 1 2	54. Overtired
0 1 2	25.	Doesn't get along with other kids	0 1 2	55. Overweight
0 1 2	26.	Doesn't seem to feel guilty after misbehaving		
				56. Physical problems without known medical cause:
0 1 2	27.	Easily jealous	0 1 2	a. Aches or pains (**not** headaches)
0 1 2	28.	Eats or drinks things that are not food — **don't** include sweets (describe): _____	0 1 2	b. Headaches
			0 1 2	c. Nausea, feels sick
		_____	0 1 2	d. Problems with eyes (describe): _____
0 1 2	29.	Fears certain animals, situations, or places, other than school (describe): _____	0 1 2	e. Rashes or other skin problems
			0 1 2	f. Stomachaches or cramps
			0 1 2	g. Vomiting, throwing up
		_____	0 1 2	h. Other (describe): _____
0 1 2	30.	Fears going to school		

Please see other side

FIGURE 2.4

Sample Items from the Child Behavior Checklist (Ages 4–18)

Source: Copyright T. M. Achenbach. Reproduced by permission.

Questions and Decisions in Planning Services

If the team decides that the student is eligible for special services, the next step involves questions and decisions regarding the student's program and writing the IEP. One of the rights of parents is to participate with other team members in planning the special education services that their child will receive. During the IEP meeting, the team addresses several questions: What types of special education services should be provided? Where should the services be delivered? How should the services be coordinated and evaluated?

Some team members may conclude that the student should be placed in the regular classroom with the special education teacher providing consulting services. On the other hand, some parents may question whether or not their child will receive as much support in the regular classroom as in the resource room. Parents and other team members will need to discuss these difficult questions and make decisions based on the assessment process. The IEP team has 30 days to complete the writing of the IEP after the student qualifies for special education.

Questions and Decisions in Monitoring Services

Once the plan is implemented, communication between home and school is very important in monitoring services. The assessment questions during this step include: Is the student making progress? Does the program need to be modified? Teachers and parents will monitor student progress by observing the student's work and behavior or by completing informal assessments. For example, parents, as well as the student's teachers, can use a log book to enter comments about daily or weekly progress. Figure 2.5 illustrates information provided by the parent. These informal tools that parents utilize are helpful to the team in monitoring the student's individualized program.

Questions and Decisions in Evaluating Services

Evaluating the special education services that are provided to students with disabilities involves two types of decision making: first, the team addresses questions regarding the student; and second, school personnel focus on questions regarding the overall program. Parents

---

October 5, 19xx

Jenny had an appointment with the doctor this afternoon. The doctor told us that she wants to change the dosage of her medication. This morning Jenny began the increased amount. The doctor said it may take her a few days to adjust.

Mrs. Williams

FIGURE 2.5

Entry from a Traveling Log Book

May 15, 19xx

Dear Parent,

We are evaluating your child's reading program this spring, and we would appreciate your help. Please take a few minutes to answer the following questions. If possible, could you please return this letter in the enclosed stamped envelope by Friday.

Thank you,
Sandy Files
W. G. Willard School

	Yes	Sometimes	No
1. My child brings home books from the school library.	_____	_____	_____
2. My child likes to read out loud to other family members.	_____	_____	_____
3. My child enjoys reading activities at school.	_____	_____	_____
4. I feel that my child is making progress in reading.	_____	_____	_____
5. My child completes homework assignments in a reasonable amount of time.	_____	_____	_____

6. Please add additional comments or suggestions:

Thank you for your help!

FIGURE 2.6

A Teacher-Developed Program Evaluation Form

should be provided the opportunity to assist in both types of evaluations.

Evaluating Student Gains Annually

At least once a year, the team must meet to review the student's current program and develop a new IEP. Parents or school personnel can request IEP meetings at other times, if needed. Parents must receive written notification of the IEP meeting. The team will address questions regarding whether or not the student is making gains or if the program needs to be changed. The part of the IEP form that lists the annual goals and objectives and the evaluation procedures will assist the team in these decisions. Teams will need to consider whether or not the student still requires special service(s) to benefit from the education program. Parents may actively participate in the evaluation of student gains by completing checklists, videotapes, and parent reports, or other recording sheets. Let's examine some specific examples of information that parents share during team meetings:

- A father shares information with the team regarding his son's behavior after school and on the weekend, while the teacher shares information regarding her observations of the student in the lunch room and on the playground.
- A grandmother records by audiotape information about homework habits and other behaviors at home.
- A mother and special education teacher report information that they have, together, compiled using observations of the student.

The Three-Year Review

Students must be reevaluated every three years, or more often if the parent(s) or school believes it is necessary. The IEP team meets to review existing evaluation data and identifies what additional data is needed. Once the reevaluation has been completed, parents are invited to the team meeting to discuss the assessment results. Based on the reevaluation assessment information, team members make a decision about the student's eligibility for special education. If the team makes the decision that the student is no longer eligible, then the student exits the special services system. If the team makes the decision that the student continues to be eligible for special services, then the next step is to write the new IEP.

Evaluating the Education Program

As consumers, parents can contribute valuable information in this assessment step because they are most familiar with the day-to-day operation of the program. Parents commonly provide feedback to school personnel through the use of informal instruments, such as the teacher-made questionnaire illustrated in Figure 2.6.

Teachers and other school staff can decide to use commercial program evaluations in soliciting parent feedback. Commercial program evaluations should provide information regarding the standardization and technical characteristics of the instrument. We will study program evaluation in more detail in Chapter 19.

TECHNIQUES FOR LISTENING TO AND UNDERSTANDING PARENT PERSPECTIVES

Parents and other family members have a wealth of knowledge about their child. Some people are more comfortable in sharing this information by filling out a form or checklist. Others prefer a more personal approach. Interviews and family stories allow families who are comfortable in talking to others to share valuable information.

In using these techniques, the first step is to acknowledge that you want to hear what parents are saying (Cohen and Spenciner, 1994). Careful listening ensures that your own biases do not overshadow what is being related to you. Listening to families requires complex skills, such as sensitivity and respect.

Interviews

The interview format allows different family members to talk and to share their individual perspectives. An interview that is a face-to-face meeting is usually much more conducive to sharing information than an interview conducted over the telephone. Like other forms of assessment, the interview should be responsive to diversity. Create a positive tone by your respect, acceptance, support, and warmth. Set aside your own beliefs and judgments. You will need to focus on listening carefully and not let personal bias be a source of error.

Be sensitive in your probing. Respect parents' right to share only the information that they wish. Some parents are not ready to discuss some areas initially, or they do not want to confront a topic at certain periods of time.

Conducting an interview with the family (Dunst, Trivette, and Deal, 1988) includes several steps: planning the interview, meeting the family, listening to family members, and completing the interview.

Planning the Interview

When you contact the family, be sure to state the purpose of your visit. For example, "I'd like to visit with you and Alexandra's father to talk further about your concerns."

Decide on a mutually convenient place and time. Some families prefer a meeting in their home where they feel more comfortable in talking about their concerns in familiar surroundings. Other families prefer meeting in the home due to a strong sense of duty or cultural tradition to entertain a guest in their home. Some families are more comfortable meeting in a community setting, perhaps a quiet coffee shop or at the school.

Meeting the Family

Three important aspects help to ensure that the interview will go well. The first is to acknowledge each family member who is present and thank each person for taking the time to be there. Next, establish rapport with family members by showing a genuine interest in what the family has to say. Finally, repeat the purpose of your visit. "I know that you have some concerns about Alexandra and I hope that from our visit I can better understand them."

Listening to Family Members

Ask questions and rephrase statements to help family members clarify important points. Many professionals find it helpful to prepare a few questions in advance. Prepared questions can help family members in "getting started." As you think about the types of questions that would be helpful, consider the wording of the questions and the type of answer that might result.

For example, a question such as, "Could you tell me about some of the difficult times during the day for Alexandra?" encourages an extended response. Leading questions such as, "Tell me more about . . . " are helpful too. Asking "What time of day is most difficult for Alexandra?" will likely lead to a word or phrase response, whereas "Is getting ready for school in the morning a difficult time for Alexandra?" will probably result in a minimal response (yes or no). These latter types of questions serve to stop or limit the discussion.

Completing the Interview

Remember that family members have many obligations and that they have probably made special arrangements to be present. Generally, interviews should not exceed an hour in length. Conclude the interview by summarizing the discussion and by thanking each of the family members present.

Family Stories

Sharing a "family story" can be the easiest and the least intimidating assessment technique for family members. Family stories represent events and people that are important to the family. Family stories often include valuable information regarding how others in the household relate to the child with special needs. By listening to family stories, you learn about the family's cultural values and practices, attitudes, habits, and behaviors. Family stories give us a good idea of how families see themselves and how they want others to see them.

In preparing to conduct a family story, the following guidelines have been developed based on work by Atkinson (1992).

1. Choose the appropriate setting: The setting should be quiet and comfortable.
2. Explain the purpose of the family story: Family members should understand that the information to be shared is valuable and will help you in understanding the child and in developing the education program.

3. Use open-ended interview techniques: Questions that encourage extended responses will assist the storyteller. Encourage family members to remember stories and events. Try to focus your questions around certain areas:

Their child
   a. How would you describe your child's growth and development?
   b. What do you think your child inherited from you?
   c. Who are the important family members or people in the community?

Family traditions
   a. What beliefs or ideals do you want to pass on to your child?
   b. What holidays or celebrations are important to your family?

Social factors
   a. How does your family like to spend free time together?
   b. What does your child like to do during these times?

Education
   a. What do you hope your child will learn in school?
   b. How would you like me to contact you . . . by telephone . . . by mail . . . or. . . ?

Photographs, drawings, and other material are helpful in assisting the storyteller.

4. Be a good listener: Build trust and show that you care about what is being shared. At times you will want to ask follow-up questions, probe for details, and be responsive.

5. Look for connections: Family stories frequently provide useful information about the child's early years and present skills and competencies. Family stories are especially helpful in learning about family diversity in your classroom. Storytellers may become classroom resources to assist you in planning special events or celebrations.

The snapshot on page 50 illustrates the importance of "family" to the Comanche people as told by this family story. After reading this snapshot, consider the following questions: What are some important themes in this family story? How might these themes affect the assessment process?

Planning Parent Conferences

Parent-teacher conferences can be effective ways to share information with parents and to learn more about the student from the parent's perspective. In addition to sharing and receiving information, parents and professionals can develop a rapport and a better ability to cooperate in preventing and solving problems (Turnbull and Turnbull, 1990). However, the key to successful conferences is planning. During parent-teacher conferences, the teacher typically has a limited amount of time scheduled for meetings. Parents, too, often have made several special arrangements to come to the school at the scheduled conference time.

Planning the Conference

Planning the conference consists of notifying the parent(s) and preparing the conference agenda. Notify the parents of the date and purpose of the conference. Many schools routinely schedule conference days at the beginning of the year and send written notices. If the meeting is to be an IEP conference, a written notice must be sent prior to the meeting.

Families generally appreciate a follow-up telephone call. However, be sure to check with the parent if you have called at a convenient time. If not, ask when a better time would be for you to call back. The telephone conversation allows the parent to ask questions about the conference and to decide on which family members should attend. Families may want to decide whether or not the student with a disability should be present at the conference.

Planning the conference also includes identifying the agenda items. Notify other professionals who are working with the student and who may not be aware of the scheduled conferences. For example, the speech therapist,

SNAPSHOT

La Donna Harris, a Comanche Woman

(This snapshot includes excerpts from her speech, given a few years ago at the first Comanche training session [Harris, n.d.]).

I am the daughter of Lily Tabbytite, the granddaughter of Wakeah, and the great-granddaughter of Kotsepeah, who was the daughter of Maria, a Spanish captive. My grandfather was Tabbytite, son of Hohwah and Tsa-ee.

I do this so that you will know how we are related; if not by blood, then by extended family, the "Indian Way." It not only shows our relationship, but it shows me how I should behave toward you. Tribal governments and tribal societies were built on relationships and kinships; how you were related showed you the etiquette of how you should behave to one another. In a tribal society, one would never openly criticize a relative. There were other ways of doing it. There were only certain people that could do the criticism or the correcting—not necessarily criticism—but they could show you the way to behave properly. When we try to make tribal societies work like western societies, sometimes it doesn't fit and creates a lot of stress in our community.

The first time that I went to tribal council, I remember Edgar Monetachi. Because he was such an eloquent speaker, people would ask him to speak for them, even if they disagreed with his position. He had a responsibility to those relatives and talked for them because he had the power and medicine to be able to be a good speaker.

It was always amazing to me when kaku and papa would go downtown to Walters and we would run into an old Comanche lady. The old lady would call me sister or daughter and they would chat for a while. Afterward, I'd say, "I didn't know that we were related to her" and kaku would trace it back to some wonderful thing that happened between families that made us kin—not between her and that other old lady, but between families. Those relationships made me feel strong and gave me a feeling of belonging to everybody. . . .

occupational therapist, or physical therapist may want to be present.

Review the student's folder and gather samples of the student's work. Plan a tentative agenda of areas or items to be covered. Consider where you will be meeting. Several chairs placed at a small round table look inviting and less threatening than chairs placed around your desk.

Conference Time

To establish rapport, talk informally with parents and other family members before beginning the conference. Express your gratitude that family members have been able to make arrangements to attend the conference. Have an interpreter or translator present for families, if needed.

Begin with the student's accomplishments. Provide examples of student work or share classroom anecdotes. Discuss areas of growth and areas of concern. Encourage parents to ask questions or to make comments. Ask for clarification when you are unsure of the information that families have shared. Use good communication skills, including jargon-free language. Remember that, as well as the words you speak, body posture and head nods are important ways of showing your interest in what families have to say.

At the close of the conference, summarize the important points. End the meeting on a positive note and thank family members for coming.

Completing Postconference Activities

After the conference is over, there are two activities that need to be completed. First, a brief summary of the conference should be recorded as soon as possible after the meeting. These notes should include the date, the participants, highlights of the meeting, and any decisions made. These notes are particularly important if there is a due process hearing at some future time. If the conference were an IEP or IFSP meeting, a copy of the minutes of the meeting must be mailed to the parents.

Next, whether or not the student attended the conference, set aside time to talk about the meeting with the student. Briefly summarize the meeting and any decisions that were made. The student may have questions about the conference that should be answered.

PREFERRED PRACTICES

Parents have an important role in the assessment process. If their child is identified before age 5, the focus of the assessment will be on the child and family. If their child is identified after age 5, then the focus of the assessment will be directed to their child. Family priorities will probably change over time. Always check to see if family members feel that the information they have provided in the past is current.

Involve families to the extent that they wish to be involved in the assessment process and accept the wishes of family members as to their levels of participation. Individual family members can differ in their preferences: one member will be more comfortable in just talk-

ing; another family member will prefer to provide information by completing a questionnaire or a rating scale.

Be open to issues in working with families different from your own. Family diversity can include issues of culture, disability, economic status, gender, geographic region or origin, and race. Avoid stereotypical assumptions. Work to become familiar with families in your community. When in doubt, ask families to determine preferences and needs.

EXTENDING LEARNING

2.1 Think about your own family based on the concepts identified by a family systems model. How does this help you in understanding the complexity of the family unit?

2.2 Obtain two or more of the commercial instruments described in this chapter to preview and compare. Which one would you choose to use? Why?

2.3 Interview a family with a child. In thinking about your conversation, did the family identify family needs and priorities for their child? Did they mention resources important to the functioning of their family? Which interview questions were most helpful? What questions might you include in another interview?

2.4 Using one of the Snapshots in this chapter, develop a simulation of a parent-teacher conference. Students can take on the roles of parent, teacher, and administrator. Assign one student the role of observer. The observer should be prepared to report observations made during the simulation.

2.5 Begin a list of resources to help you become responsive to diversity. What books would you include? What journals regularly publish helpful articles? What families in your area would be willing to be a resource?

2.6 Attend a meeting of a parent organization. What were some of the issues discussed? In what ways was the meeting informative?

REFERENCES

Achenbach, T. M. (1991). *Child behavior checklist/4–18*. Burlington, Vt.: Center for Children, Youth, and Families.

Alper, S. K., P.J. Schloss, and C.N. Schloss (1994). *Families of students with disabilities*. Boston: Allyn & Bacon.

Atkinson, R. (1992). *The life story book from autobiography to personal myth*. Gorham, Maine: University of Southern Maine, Center for the Study of Lives.

Bayley, N. (1993). *Bayley scales of infant development*. 2d ed. San Antonio, Tex.: The Psychological Corporation.

Brigance, A. H. (1985). *Brigance® preschool screen for three- and four-year-old children*. North Billerica, Mass.: Curriculum Associates.

Brown, L., and D. D. Hammill (1990). *Behavior rating profile, second edition*. Austin, Tex.: Pro-Ed.

Cohen, L. G., and L. J. Spenciner (1994). *Assessment of young children*. White Plains, N.Y.: Longman.

Conners, C. K. (1990). *Conners' rating scales manual*. North Tonawanda, N.Y.: Multi-Health Systems, Inc.

Dunst, C., C. Trivette, and A. Deal (1988). *Enabling and empowering families*. Cambridge, Mass.: Brookline.

Haney, M., and V. Knox (1995). *Project unidos para el bienestar de los ninos y de su famila* (Project UBNF). Paper presented at the Zero to Three Conference, December, Atlanta, Ga.

Hanson, M. J., E. W. Lynch, and K. I. Wayman (1990). Honoring the cultural diversity of families when gathering data. *Topics in Early Childhood Special Education* 10(1): 112–131.

Harris, L. (n.d.). Summarized version of the speech given by LaDonna Harris at the first Comanche training session. Unpublished manuscript.

Harrison, P. L., A. S. Kaufman, N. L. Kaufman, R. H. Bruininks, J. Rynders, S. Ilmer, S. S. Sparrow, and D. V. Cicchetti (1990). *AGS Early screening profiles*. Circle Pines, Minn.: American Guidance Service.

Ireton, H. R. (1992). *Child development inventory*. Minneapolis, Minn.: Behavior Science Systems.

Kovack, J., and R. Jacks (1989). *Program evaluation using the Project Dakota parent satisfaction survey: A manual for administration and interpretation of findings using a validated instrument*. Eagan, Minn.: Project Dakota.

Mahoney, G., P. O'Sullivan, and J. Dennebaum (1990). Maternal perceptions of early intervention services: A scale for assessing family-focused intervention. *Topics in Early Childhood Special Education* 10(1): 1–15.

Meisels, S. J., L. W. Henderson, D. B. Marsden, K. G. Browning, and K. A. Olson (1991). *Early screening inventory-3*. Ann Arbor, Mich.: University of Michigan, Center for Human Growth and Development.

Meisels, S. J., and M. S. Wiske (1988). *Early screening inventory*. New York: Teachers College Press.

Miller, L. J. (1992). *FirstSTEP: Screening test for evaluating preschoolers*. San Antonio, Tex.: The Psychological Corporation, Harcourt Brace.

Murphy, D. L., and I. M. Lee (1991). *Family-centered program rating scale*. Lawrence, Kans.: Beach Center on Families and Disabilities University of Kansas.

Newborg, J., J. R. Stock, and L. Wnek (1988). *Battelle developmental inventory*. Allen, Tex.: DLM.

Quay, H. C., and D. R. Peterson (1987). *Revised behavior problem checklist*. Odessa, Fla.: Psychological Assessment Resources, Inc.

Shapiro, J. (1994). Educational/support group for latino families of children with down syndrome. *Mental Retardation,* 32(6): 403–415.

Turbiville, V., I. Lee, A. Turnbull, and D. Murphy (1993). *Handbook for the development of a family-friendly individualized family service plan (IFSP)*. Lawrence, Kans.: Beach Center on Families and Disabilities, University of Kansas.

Turnbull, A. P., and H. R. Turnbull, III (1990). *Families, professionals, and exceptionality: A special partnership*. 2d ed. Columbus, Ohio: Merrill.

Waltman, G. H. (1996). Amish health care beliefs and practices. In *Multicultural awareness in the health care professions,* ed. M.C. Julia, Boston, Mass.: Allyn & Bacon.

Reliability and Validity

OVERVIEW

The measurement concepts discussed in this chapter are central to an understanding of assessment. The use of these concepts can be compared to the construction of a house in which the foundation forms the basis for the framework. Reliability and validity form the foundation of assessment. An assessment approach that has a sturdy foundation will be much more useful than one in which reliability and validity are weak.

This chapter continues the discussion on responding to diversity. Being responsive to diversity means that assessment procedures are fair. Fairness in assessment indicates that assessment methods are equitable, free of bias, adapted for students with disabilities, sensitive to diverse groups of students, and based on contemporary views of growth and development, aptitude, cognition, learning, behavior, and personality.

CHAPTER OBJECTIVES

After completing this chapter, you should be able to:

Define the concept of correlation and show how this concept is closely related to reliability and validity.

Define reliability and describe the different types of reliability.

Explain ways in which errors in measurement can be taken into consideration.

Define validity and describe the different types of validity.

Describe the application of the concepts of reliability and validity as they apply to all forms of assessment.

Discuss the concept of true score.

Explain why assessment approaches should be responsive to diversity.

CORRELATION

A **correlation** indicates the extent to which two or more scores vary together. It measures the extent to which a change in one score has a relationship with a change in another score. For example, in general, the higher a student's intelligence score, the higher will be the student's score on a vocabulary test. In general, students with higher intelligence quotient (IQ) scores tend to have higher vocabulary scores and students with lower IQ scores will probably have lower vocabulary test scores. We can say that IQ and vocabulary level correlate with each other. However, caution must be used when interpreting relationships; just because two scores correlate does not mean that one score causes a change in the other score. The correlation between shoe size and reading achievement is an example of a strong correlation but lack of causation. As shoe size increases, reading achievement also increases!

CORRELATION COEFFICIENT

A **correlation coefficient** quantifies a relationship and provides information about whether there is a relationship, the direction of the relationship, and the strength of the relationship.

Direction of a Relationship

The direction of a correlation can be determined by the presence of a + or − sign. A + sign indicates that a relationship is positive; and a − sign indicates that a relationship is negative. (When positive correlation coefficients are written, the + is usually omitted.) When one test score increases as another test score increases, the relationship is positive. However, when one test score decreases while the other test score increases, the relationship is negative. In a positive relationship, the scores either increase together or decrease together. The relationship between IQ and vocabulary achievement is a positive relationship, because both of these variables usually increase together. The relationship between thumb sucking and age of a child is usually a negative relationship, because as children get older thumb sucking decreases.

Strength of a Relationship

The value of a correlation coefficient can vary from +1.00 to −1.00. The closer the correlation coefficient is to 1.00, either +1.00 or −1.00, the stronger the relationship. The closer the correlation coefficient is to 0.00, the weaker the relationship. For example, a coefficient of .89 is stronger than a coefficient of .15 because .89 is closer to 1.00, just as a coefficient of −0.54 is stronger than a coefficient of .45 because −0.54 is closer to −1.00.

Positive Relationship

If there were a perfect relationship between IQ level and vocabulary achievement, the correlation would be expressed as either +1.00 or 1.00. If for every increase in IQ score there is a corresponding increase in vocabulary scores, we can say that the relationship between IQ and vocabulary level is 1.00. However, because there are so many other variables that influence both IQ and vocabulary achievement, this relationship will never be a perfect 1.00. Figure 3.1 illustrates this relationship.

Negative Relationship

A perfect negative relationship is indicated by −1.00. The relationship between level of achievement and the number of errors that are made is a negative relationship. As the achievement increases, the number of errors that an individual makes decreases. Figure 3.2 illustrates this relationship.

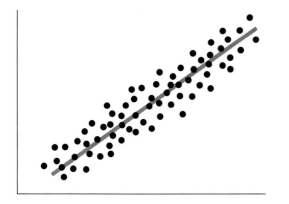

FIGURE 3.1

Scatter Plot of a Positive Relationship

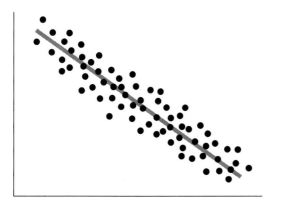

FIGURE 3.2

Scatter Plot of a Negative Relationship

Zero Relationship

The relationship between an individual's score on an intelligence test and the height of that individual is zero. When arranged on a scatter plot, most of the intelligence test scores and the height measurements are not associated with each other; the scores do not vary with each other. Figure 3.3 illustrates this relationship.

We will now consider how the knowledge about correlations is used to describe the reliability and validity of tests.

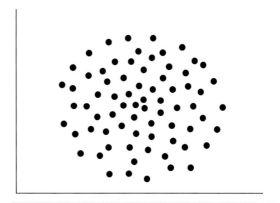

FIGURE 3.3

Scatter Plot of a Zero Relationship

RELIABILITY

Reliability and validity can be compared to the construction of a foundation for a house. The underlying foundation of a test must be solid and strong so that the test can be administered with minimal errors and the performance of students can be interpreted with confidence. How do we know whether tests are useful? How do teachers know that the performance of students is consistent? How do we know that a test measures what the authors say it measures? Reliability and validity help us to determine the answers to these questions.

Teachers should evaluate the reliability and validity that are reported in test manuals. While there are some books and journal articles that report evaluations of tests, tests are not given "seals of approval." To be useful, they must meet certain standards.

Reliability describes the stability or consistency of test performance. The teacher needs to know that a student's test performance is stable over time and over different test items that have similar objectives. If a student is administered a test on a given day, the teacher wants to have some assurance that the test scores of the student, if retested on the following day, will be about the same as the scores that were obtained on the first test. Or, if a student takes one form or version of a test, the teacher needs to know that the test scores of the student, if tested with a similar form of a test, will be about the same. Of course, it is impractical and unnecessary for a student to take a test every day.

Reliability provides an estimate of the consistency of test results when a test is administered under similar conditions. All types of reliability are expressed as the consistency or agreement between sets of test scores. This consistency or agreement is described by a correlation coefficient. Some test manuals use the term *reliability coefficient* in place of the term *correlation coefficient*.

In a test manual, a lowercase r designates a reliability or correlation coefficient. For example, if a test manual reports that r = .92, we know that the reliability for this test is .92 and that because this value is close to 1.00, the teacher can have some confidence that the test has adequate reliability. For guidance in evaluating correlation coefficients, Nitko (1996) recommends that when major educational decisions are made, a reliability coefficient of at least .90 is the preferred standard.

Sources of Error

Many sources of error can be associated with the process of assessment. Errors in measurement can stem from the testing environment, the student, the test, and the examiner. Sources of error in the testing environoment include:

Noise distractions

Poor lighting

Uncomfortable room temperature

Sources of error associated with the student include:

Hunger

Tiredness

Illness

Difficulty in understanding the test instructions

Sources of error associated with test administration include:

Unclear directions

Poorly worded test items

Ambiguous scoring

An examiner who is not prepared or who interprets administration or scoring guidelines incorrectly

Reliability can be thought of as consisting of the student's **true score** and an error score. The true score is the score an individual would obtain on a test if there were no measurement errors. The **obtained score** is the score that a student achieves on a test. This is the best estimate we have of a student's performance. If all testing conditions were perfect and there were no errors of measurement, the obtained score and the true score would be the same. But, since error is always present, we can never know the true score. We can, however, estimate an individual's true score by using the formula

$$X = T + E$$

where the student's obtained or observed score X equals the true score T plus the errors that are associated with measurement, represented by E, the error score.

Because of the possibility of error, the test publisher should provide estimates of reliability. Three professional organizations, the American Educational Research Association, the American Psychological Association, and the National Council on Measurement in Education, have issued a guidebook titled *Standards for Educational and Psychological Testing* (1985). These professional standards are very important. According to these standards

Reliability refers to the degree to which test scores are free from errors of measurement. A test taker may perform differently on one occasion than on another for reasons that may or may not be related to the purpose of measurement. A person may try harder, be more fatigued or anxious, have greater familiarity with the content of questions on one test than another, or simply guess correctly on more questions on one occasion than on another. For these and other reasons, a person's score will not be perfectly consistent from one occasion to the next. Indeed, an individual's scores will rarely be the same on two forms of a test that are intended to be interchangeable. Even the most careful matching of item content and difficulty on two forms of a test cannot ensure that an individual who knows the answer to a particular question on Form A will know the answer to a matched counterpart on Form B. (p.19)

Types of Reliability

There are five types of reliability: test-retest, alternate form, split-half, internal consistency, and interscorer-interobserver-interrater reliability. Each type of reliability has several advantages and disadvantages. Test publishers should tell how they obtained the samples of students, individuals, or observations on which their reliability coefficients are determined. Typically, a test manual will report several reliability coefficients, and it is preferable that at least two *types* of reliability should be specified: reliability coefficients that describe the consistency of the test and reliability coefficients that describe the stability of the test.

Test-Retest Reliability

Test-retest reliability can be estimated when the same test is administered to the same student twice. The scores obtained on the first and second administrations can be correlated and a reliability coefficient obtained. This coefficient is an index of the stability of the test score. Because the same test is ad-

ministered twice, it is very important to know the time interval between the two administrations of the test. Too short an interval will cause the reliability coefficient to be inflated. When the time interval is too long, a student may experience developmental changes that will affect the reliability coefficient. Anastasi (1982) recommends that when estimating test-retest reliability a short interval be used in order to avoid the influence of developmental changes.

There are several drawbacks to this type of reliability. Having been exposed to the test items and to the directions for taking the test over two test administrations, it is possible that the student will obtain a higher test score on the second testing. Also, as mentioned earlier, maturation, growth, and development of the student may artificially inflate the reliability coefficient.

Alternate Form Reliability

Alternate form reliability is also known as equivalent form or parallel form reliability. Frequently, there is a need for two forms of a test that contain different test items but that evaluate the same knowledge and skills. This procedure is especially useful when tests are used to pretest and posttest students. The two forms have different designations. For example, some forms are designated A and B; others may be labeled X and Y or L and M.

Like test-retest reliability, alternate form reliability has several disadvantages. It is difficult to develop two parallel forms of a test. In addition, as with test-retest reliability, the reliability coefficient can be inflated by a shorter interval between test administrations, the effect of practice on similar test items, and maturation, growth, and development of the students. When test publishers report alternate form reliability coefficients, the *Standards for Educational and Psychological Testing* (American Educational Research Association et al., 1985) recommends that test publishers state the order in which the alternate forms were administered, the time interval between the two administrations, and the reasons for choosing the particular time interval.

Split-half Reliability

Split-half reliability is expressed by a coefficient that is obtained by administering a test to a group of students, dividing the total number of test items in half to form two tests, and correlating the scores on the two halves of the test. For example, suppose a test has 20 items. We could administer the entire test to a group of students and then divide the test into two halves, each containing 10 items. Different methods can be used to break a test into two halves: by separating the first half from the second half or by separating the even numbered items from the odd numbered items. The items on the two halves can then be correlated.

Dividing a test into a first half and a second half can cause problems in determining the reliability. Fatigue, practice effect, failure to complete the test, and print quality can affect the reliability coefficient (DeVellis, 1991). Assuming random order of the test items, the test could be divided by odd-even items or by balancing the halves. Balancing halves could involve item length, response type, or another characteristic that is appropriate for the test. The most appropriate method of splitting the halves of a test will depend on the test and the testing situation (DeVellis, 1991).

With the split-half procedure, the test is administered only once. Therefore, reliability coefficients obtained through this procedure are a measure of internal consistency, not of the temporal stability of test performance.

Internal Consistency Reliability

This type of reliability is similar to the split-half method. **Internal consistency reliability** is an estimate of the homogeneity or interrelatedness of responses to test items. The test is administered only once. Usually one of the Kuder-Richardson formulas is used to find the average coefficient obtained by calculating all the possible split-half coefficients. The more similar the test items are to each other, the higher will be the reliability coefficient. Like split-half reliability, internal consistency reliability does not provide an estimate of the stability of the test over time.

The advantage of using internal consistency instead of the split-half method is that internal consistency provides the average split-half correlations based on all possible ways of dividing the test into two halves. The split-half method allows only one division of the test in half.

Interscorer/Interobserver/ Interrater Reliability

This type of reliability is a measure of the extent to which two or more scorers, observers, or raters agree on how a test should be scored. **Interscorer/interobserver/interrater reliability** is important when errors in scoring or differences in judgment can affect the test outcomes. Interscorer/interobserver/interrater reliability measures the agreement between examiners. This type of reliability should be reported when:

1. There is a possibility that errors can be made in computing the test score(s).
2. A test item can have more than one answer.
3. A response to a question can have more than one interpretation.
4. Observations are made about the behaviors of one or more students.
5. Interviews are used to collect information.

Factors That Influence Reliability

Several factors can affect the reliability of a test (Mehrens and Lehmann, 1991; Sattler, 1988):

1. Test length. Generally, the longer a test is, the more reliable it is.
2. Speed. When a test is a speed test, it is inappropriate to estimate reliability using internal consistency, test-retest, or alternate form methods. This is because not every

student is able to complete all of the items in a speed test. In contrast, a power test is a test in which every student is able to complete all the items.

3. Group homogeneity. In general, the more heterogeneous the group of students who take the test, the more reliable the measure will be.

4. Item difficulty. When there is little variability among test scores, the reliability will be low. Thus, reliability will be low if a test is so easy that every student gets most or all of the items correct or so difficult that every student gets most or all of the items wrong.

5. Objectivity. When tests are scored objectively, rather than subjectively, the reliability will be higher.

6. Test-retest interval. The shorter the time interval between two administrations of a test, the less likely that changes will occur and the higher the reliability will be.

7. Variation with the testing situation. Errors in the testing situation (e.g., students misunderstanding or misreading test directions; noise level; distractions; and sickness) can cause test scores to vary.

VALIDITY

The **validity** of a test is the extent to which the test measures what it says it measures. Expressed in another way, a test is valid if it measures what it is intended to measure. According to *Standards for Educational and Psychological Testing* (American Educational Research Association et al., 1985), "Validity is the most important consideration in test evaluation. The concept refers to the appropriateness, meaningfulness, and usefulness of the specific inferences made from test scores" (p. 9).

Reliability is a prerequisite of validity. Reliability must be demonstrated before evidence of validity can be considered. A test that is reliable is not necessarily valid. There are several types of validity: content, criterion-related (which includes concurrent and predictive validity), construct, and face validity. A correlation coefficient (r) is commonly used to report criterion-related and construct validity. From our discussion of reliability, you will recall that r is also used to report measures of reliability.

Types of Validity

Content Validity

Content validity measures the extent to which the test items reflect the instructional objectives of a test. Content validity is important for all educational and psychological tests (Salvia and Ysseldyke, 1995). It is the most important type of validity for achievement tests.

An estimate of the content validity of a test is obtained by thoroughly and systematically examining the test items to determine the extent to which they reflect the instructional objectives and the content that was intended to be tested. Content validity is usually evaluated by a panel composed of curriculum experts and specialists in tests and measurements who determine the extent to which the test items reflect the test objectives. Cronbach (1971) has written that, over time, tests become unrepresentative of curriculum and that test users must determine the extent to which a test retains content validity.

To facilitate the determination of content validity, test developers should document: 1) the test objectives, 2) the items that are measured by specific objectives, 3) the number of items for each objective, 4) the format and response type of the test items, and 5) the role of the curriculum or content experts in the development of the test items.

Most norm-referenced tests are constructed to represent the curricula that are taught in various geographic regions of the United States. Because these tests are so broad, they inadequately represent the curricula that are taught in many schools. Thus, as a rule, the content validity of norm-referenced tests must be thoroughly evaluated before a teacher can be confident that a particular test is appropriate in this respect.

SNAPSHOT

Prentice Dillon and Erin Gates

After all the students had been dismissed from school for the day, Prentice Dillon decided that he needed to review the test manual for a test that his school had recently purchased. He read the initial chapters in the manual that described the test and the administration procedures. Okay so far.

Dillon began the chapter that described the reliability of the test. The section that described internal consistency reliability said, "The reliability coefficients for the composite scores are greater than the reliability for the subtest scores." Prentice asked himself, "Why were the reliability coefficients of the composite scores higher than the reliability coefficients of the individual

subtests?" Prentice decided to see what Erin Gates, the other special educator in his building, knew about this test.

After reading the reliability section of the manual, Erin explained that it was not unusual for composite scores to have higher reliability coefficients than individual subtests. Composite scores sample a broader range of items than do individual subtests. In other words, more test items are used to calculate the reliability cofficients associated with composite scores than with individual subtests. The reliability coefficients associated with composite scores, in general, should be higher than the reliability coefficients associated with individual subtests.

Criterion-related Validity

Criterion-related validity refers to the extent to which scores obtained on one test or other measure relate to scores obtained on a test measuring another outcome or criterion. When determining criterion-related validity, test developers compare their test with another measure or criterion: another test, school grades, or observations.

Standards for Educational and Psychological Testing (American Educational Research Association et al., 1985) states that test developers should include: 1) information on the group of individuals that were used in the development of the test (known as the *standardization sample*); and 2) the statistics used when describing studies conducted in establishing criterion-related validity. In addition, the criterion measures (e.g., other tests, school grades, observations) and the justification for using them

should be described. When assessing the criterion-related validity of a test, it is important to verify that the criterion measure itself is valid as well. Concurrent and predictive validity are two types of criterion-related validity.

Concurrent Validity. Concurrent validity is the extent to which the results of two different tests administered at about the same time correlate with each other. To obtain concurrent validity two different tests are administered within a brief interval and the correlation between the scores obtained on the tests is calculated. This method of estimating validity is especially useful when a new test has been constructed. Suppose we were developing a new way to test the hearing abilities of students. We would administer our new test and also a standard hearing test. Next, we would establish concurrent validity by examining the relationship between the scores obtained on the two tests. The test authors want to know the extent to which a known instrument and a new test measure the same objectives. If the new test correlates highly with the established instrument, we can conclude that the new test is valid and that it has an acceptable level of concurrent validity. Evidence of concurrent validity is important when tests are used for achievement, diagnostic, and certification purposes (American Educational Research Association et al., 1985).

Predictive Validity. How accurately can current performance predict future performance or behavior? **Predictive validity** is the standard used when a test score aids in making forecasts about student performance or behavior. Although predictive validity, like concurrent validity, uses a criterion measure to determine validity, concurrent validity should never be substituted for predictive validity.

Be careful not to confuse concurrent validity with predictive validity. There are some important differences. While concurrent validity is a measure of the extent to which two sets of test scores relate to each other, predictive validity is an estimate of the extent to which one test accurately predicts future performance or behavior. When scores on one test accurately predict performance on another test or criterion, we can say that there is high predictive validity. Screening tests such as those used in preschool screening should have high predictive validity.

Construct Validity

Construct validity is the extent to which a test measures a particular trait, construct, or psychological characteristic. Reasoning ability, spatial visualization, reading comprehension, sociability, and introversion are "referred to as constructs because they are theoretical constructions about the nature of human behavior" (American Educational Research Association et al., 1985, p. 9). In determining construct validity, the test developer describes the con-

struct, indicating how it differs from other constructs and how it relates to other variables. In addition to the conceptual nature of the construct, the test developer must also take care when specifying the test format, test administration, and other facets of test construction (American Educational Research Association et al., 1985).

Construct validity is the most difficult type of validity to establish. A long period of time and numerous research studies are needed before construct validity can be verified for a particular test. Zeller (1988) compares the establishment of construct validity to a detective's search for clues. Evidence is accumulated bit by bit. The clues assist the test developer in determining the consistency of the evidence in the interpretation of construct validity. If the evidence falls into a systematic pattern, then the test developer can have confidence in the validity of the construct.

Face Validity

Face validity is the extent to which a test looks valid to the test users and test takers; that is, face validity has to do with the format and appearance of a test. Anastasi (1982) has written that "face validity concerns rapport and public relations" (p. 136). Although some experts discount the importance of face validity, Anastasi (1982) believes that face validity is a useful feature. Face validity should never be substituted for other types of validity, however.

Consequential Validity

Consequential validity is the extent to which an assessment instrument promotes the intended consequences (Linn and Baker, 1996). This type of validity has been used to describe performance-based assessments. Performance-based assessment, which is discussed in Chapter 7, provides information about what a student can do with knowledge in real-life, real-world settings rather than with isolated bits of knowledge. Domains such as dance and music have long used performance-based assessments to evaluate students. Performances are far more appropriate for evaluating how students dance or play musical instruments than are multiple-choice questions.

One of the primary reasons for using performance-based assessments is to improve student learning. The extent to which performance-based assessment improves student learning can be described as consequential validity. Factors that can affect student learning, and thus impact consequential validity, include school reform activities, instructional improvements, staff development activities, levels of student achievement, and accountability systems (Linn and Baker, 1996).

Factors that Influence Validity

Since validity is a measure of the extent to which a test measures what it says it measures, validity is affected by a number of factors:

1. Reliability. Reliability is a prerequisite of validity. However, just because a test is reliable does not mean that it is valid.
2. Item selection. A test is valid to the extent that it measures a student's exposure to the content that is being tested.

For example, when an achievement test is administered, it is assumed that the student has been exposed to the content relating to the test items. To the extent that the student was not exposed to the content, the validity of such a test is lower (Salvia and Ysseldyke, 1995).

RESPONDING TO DIVERSITY: FAIRNESS IN ASSESSMENT

Assessment has a great influence on the curriculum, instruction, classroom and school organization, and on opportunities for students in education and careers. Fairness in assessment means that all assessment approaches, including standardized tests, performance assessment, portfo-

lio assessment, and informal measures, are free from bias and that methods of student assessment are equitable and sensitive to diverse student populations (Maine's Curriculum Framework, 1995). Assessment should be fair to all students so as not to limit students' present education and their future opportunities (National Forum on Assessment, 1995). Fairness in assessment means that assessment methods are:

- Equitable
- Free of bias
- Adapted for students with disabilities
- Sensitive to diverse student populations
- Based on contemporary views of growth and development, aptitude, cognition, learning, behavior, and personality
- Administered by responsible professionals who have considered the adverse consequences to students of any applicable assessment devices

Equity

Differences in test results may be due to differences in educational opportunities, resources, or cultural expectations. This is especially true when considerations about culture, ethnicity, race, language, geographic region of origin, gender, disability, or economic status are a concern. Equity in assessment means that assessment is approached in a fair, impartial, and just manner. Assessment tools must be more than reliable and valid. Valid assessments can be made only when the assessment is *fair*. Fair assessments mean that all students have access to and can participate in a variety of assessment approaches.

Nonbiased Assessment

Assessment tools must be nonbiased. Tests may be biased when groups know approximately the same amount of material but one group scores consistently higher than another group on a test. One example of bias is seen in tests that portray individuals in stereotypic ways or in which the test problems contain ref-

SNAPSHOT

Prentice Dillon and Erin Gates Continue Their Conversation

Prentice continued reading the manual of the new test that his school had purchased. After finishing the reliability section, he decided to tackle the validity section. The manual said, "The achievement subtests were correlated with the cognitive subtests and the coefficients ranged from .20 to .65." Prentice knew that coefficients that approaching +1.00 indicated that there was a very close relationship. But, when evaluating the validity of a test, what did correlations between .20 and .65 mean?

Erin Gates was still in her classroom when Prentice asked if she could help him understand validity. Erin explained that the authors of the test manual were presenting evidence for the construct validity of their test. Construct validity is the extent to which a test measures a particular trait, construct, or psychological characteristic, such as achievement and cognitive ability. In determining construct validity, the test author describes the construct, indicating how it differs from other constructs.

Erin told Prentice that the correlations between .20 and .65 indicate that there is, in fact, some relationship between achievement and cognitive ability because achievement and cognitive ability are actually two different, but not totally separate, constructs. In fact, if the correlations were close to 1.00, for example, .90, .93, or .95, it would mean that the achievement subtests and the cognitive subtests were too closely related and that they were measuring the same constructs!

erences to only males, to only middle-class individuals (AAUW, 1992), or to topics that carry status with only those groups. When evaluating student behavior, some behaviors considered aberrant in one culture may be proper in another culture.

Types of alternative or **authentic assessment** such as portfolios, performance assessment, open-ended tasks, observation, interviews, and group work are generally thought of as being able to provide equitable assessment. The assumption underlying authentic assessment is that these tests create opportunities for a student to demonstrate learning regardless of culture, gender, race, socioeconomic status, or disability. However, these types of assessment instruments cannot be assumed to be free of flaws. They can be subject to bias, errors of reliability, and poor validity.

Linguistic Diversity

There are important considerations when testing students who are nonnative speakers of English or who speak languages other than English. Translation of an assessment tool or the use of an interpreter is not always appropriate (American Educational Research Assocation et al., 1985). Translation alone does not ensure that an assessment procedure is comparable in content, difficulty level, reliability, and validity to the original version.

Another important concern when assessing students who are nonnative speakers of English and who come from various racial, cultural, or ethnic backgrounds is that test developers and publishers use appropriate standardization samples. A standardization sample is the group of individuals that is actually tested during the development of the test. A test that is to be used with students from Cambodia or from Central America should include appropriate samples of these student groups in the standardization group. If the test is intended to be used with students who are nonnative speakers of English and who come from various backgrounds, the test publisher must provide appropriate information concerning the administration and interpretation of test performance (American Educational Research Association et al., 1985).

The following standards (American Educational Research Association et al., 1985) have been developed for testing linguistically diverse individuals:

1. For nonnative English speakers or for speakers of some dialects of English, testing should be designed to minimize threats to test reliability and validity that may arise from language differences.
2. Linguistic modifications recommended by test publishers should be described in detail in the test manual.
3. When a test is recommended for use with linguistically diverse test takers, test developers and publishers should provide the information necessary for appropriate test use and interpretation.
4. When a test is translated from one language or dialect to another, its reliability and validity for the uses intended in the linguistic groups to be tested should be established.
5. When it is intended that the two versions of dual-language tests be comparable, evidence of test comparability should be reported (pp. 74–75).

Adaptations for Students with Disabilities

Assessment activities must be accessible to students and must be designed to provide evidence about what the student knows. This means that students with disabilities should be able to participate in instruction and respond to assess-

ment tasks. For example, test developers should provide ways in which students who are physically disabled, blind, deaf, or who have other disabilities can participate in testing.

Tests that are administered to students with disabilities may be adapted or modified, depending on the needs of the individual student. There are ways in which tests can be modified (American Educational Research Association et al., 1985; Salvia and Ysseldyke, 1995). These are described in Table 3.1.

Despite the practice of modifying tests for students with disabilities, there are several major problems to consider. Many experts believe that unless a test has been normed using specific modifications, the test is invalid. When a test is administered in a different way than the one used when it was standardized, comparisons between students are not fair (American Educational Research Association et al., 1985). *Standards for Educational and Psychological Testing* (American Educational Research Association et al., 1985) states that unless tests have been validated for students with disabilities, test publishers should be judicious in making interpretations about performance.

Another criticism is the reporting of test scores or test performance when the modification is not identified. Some experts believe that not identifying modifications is misleading. Persons with disabilities have countered that modifying test procedures provides opportunities to demonstrate their abilities and that not modifying test procedures is unfair (American Educational Research Association et al., 1985).

Sensitivity to Diversity

Good practice requires that a variety of assessment tasks be used. Opportunities should be provided for students to answer in other languages, to demonstrate their abilities and skills in various forms, to use materials from various cultures, and to accommodate alternative ways of responding.

Consideration of Adverse Consequences

Some students do not perform well on assessments simply because they lack the background or experiences with certain methods of assessment. Teachers can try to ameliorate this by providing all students with instruction and practice in the assessment approaches that are used in evaluations.

Assessment developers and users must actively avoid assessment approaches, instruments, and techiques that may have adverse consequences on groups that currently are targets of discrimination or have previously been the targets of discrimination. Assessment is properly used when it assists in providing learning opportunities for students rather than

in placing students in tracks or limiting educational opportunities (National Forum on Assessment, 1995).

PREFERRED PRACTICES

Test manuals provide information about reliability and validity. However, teachers, test examiners, and administrators should review tests and test manuals and satisfy themselves that each test has acceptable levels of reliability and validity. Test users must be skilled examiners as well as informed consumers of tests.

Fairness in assessment means that teachers use only those assessment approaches judged

TABLE 3.1 Test Modifications

Type of modification	Example of modification
Location of the test administration	Test is administered in the special services room.
	Test is administered in a separate area of the classroom.
	Test is administered while child is sitting in a bean bag chair.
Presentation mode	Examiner reads items out loud.
	Examiner paraphrases the directions.
	Examiner uses prompts.
	Braille form of the test is used.
	Test directions and items are signed.
	Test directions and items are interpreted.
	The lighting is changed for students with visual impairments.
	A specific examiner may be chosen who is able to develop (or who already has) rapport with the student.
	Test is administered individually rather than in a group.
Response mode	Teacher or helper marks the responses as indicated by the student.
	Student gives the responses verbally rather than in writing.
	Student uses a voice synthesizer.
	Student is allowed to use a computer or calculator.
	Time limits for responding are extended or modified.
Test content	Nonvisual items are substituted for students with visual impairments.
	Items that are not dependent on the hearing of specific sounds are substituted for students who are hard of hearing or deaf.

to be reliable and valid. Fairness also means that bias has been minimized, that the assessment is equitable, and that the measures are sensitive to diverse populations. In the next chapter, you will learn about several other measurement concepts that will help you in evaluating the usefulness of assessment measures.

EXTENDING LEARNING

3.1 The director of testing has asked you to evaluate the reliability and validity of a test that is being considered for purchase. What standards of reliability and validity will you use when evaluating this measure?

3.2 Working with a small group of other students, review a test manual. Identify the types of reliability and validity that are reported. Explain the meaning of these two terms, using your own words.

3.3 Imagine that the following excerpt was found in a test manual: "The authors of the test determined that the achievement test lacks evidence of validity but has high reliability. The reliability coefficient is 1.15." What are two problems with this excerpt?

3.4 Yizhong, who recently moved to this country from Asia, is suspected of having a learning disability. What must the examiner consider when deciding which tests to use when assessing Yizhong?

3.5 A test publisher is in the process of developing a new measure of cognitive ability. What advice can you give the publisher about making sure that the instrument is fair?

REFERENCES

American Educational Research Association, American Psychological Association, and National Council on Measurement in Education (1985). *Standards for educational and psychological testing.* Washington, D.C.: American Psychological Association.

Anastasi, A. (1982). *Psychological testing.* New York: Macmillan.

Cronbach, L. J. (1971). Test validation. In *Educational measurement,* ed. R. Thorndike, 443–507. Washington, D.C.: American Council on Education.

DeVellis, R. F. (1991). *Scale development.* Newbury Park, Calif.: Sage.

Linn, R. L., and E. L. Baker (1996). Can performance-based student assessments be psychometrically sound? In *Performance-based student assessment: Challenges and possibilities,* eds. J. B. Baron and D. P. Wolf, 84–103. Chicago, Ill.: University of Chicago Press.

Maine Mathematics and Science Alliance. (1996). *Maine's curriculum framework.* Augusta, Maine: Author.

Mehrens, W. A., and I. J. Lehmann (1991). *Measurement and evaluation in education and psychology.* Fort Worth: Holt, Rinehart & Winston.

National Forum on Assessment (1995). *Principles and indicators for student assessment systems.* Cambridge, Mass.: National Center for Fair and Open Testing.

Nitko, A. (1996). *Educational assessment of students.* 2d ed. Upper Saddle River, N.J.: Prentice-Hall.

Salvia, J., and J. Ysseldyke (1995). *Assessment.* Boston, Mass.: Houghton-Mifflin.

Sattler, J. (1988). *Assessment of children.* San Diego, Calif.: Jerome M. Sattler, Publisher.

Zeller, R. A. (1988). Validity. In *Educational research, methodology, and measurement: An international handbook,* ed. J. P. Keeves, 322–330. Oxford: Pergamon.

Norms and Test Scores

OVERVIEW

This chapter begins a discussion of scoring, interpreting, and reporting test performance. Norm-referenced standardized assessment tests, scores, scoring procedures, and norms will be described. Because it is up to the test user to evaluate the usefulness of a test, we will also discuss how you can determine whether a test is worthwhile. In the following chapters we will return to this discussion as assessment approaches are presented.

CHAPTER OBJECTIVES

After completing this chapter you should be able to:

Describe norm-referenced standardized assessment.

Compare different ways of presenting and interpreting test scores.

Discuss the advantages and disadvantages of using different types of test scores when interpreting test performance.

Compare the application of the concepts of standard error of measurement and confidence intervals.

Describe how to evaluate the usefulness of tests.

Use test scoring procedures.

STANDARDIZED TESTS

Standardization Sample

When a test is administered to a student, the teacher can compare the performance of that student with the scores obtained by the sample of students who participated in the normative sample. To do this, however, it is very important to know the characteristics of the standardization sample. A **standardization sample** is a subgroup of a large group that has been selected to be representative of the large group. When a test is developed, it is this subgroup that is actually tested. The **population** is the larger group from which the sample of individuals is selected and to which individual comparisons are made regarding test performance. The terms *normative sample* or *norm sample* are also known as the standardization sample.

It is essential that the standardization sample be representative of the population of students. The standardization sample should include, in appropriate proportion, students from various geographic regions of the country, males and females, students who represent various racial, ethnic, cultural, and linguistic populations, and students from various economic strata. Some samples may even include the occupational categories and educational levels of the parents of the students. The best way for a test publisher to determine the appropriate proportions of representative groups (e. g., males, females, race, ethnicity, native language, etc.) that should be included in the standardization sample is to refer to the most recent census data and base the selection of the standardization sample on those percentages. Figure 4.1 shows how one test publisher illustrated the communities in the United States that participated in a national standardization of the test.

Norms

Norm-referenced test performance compares a student's test performance with the test performance of a sample of similar students who have taken the same test. **Norms** are the scores obtained by the norm or standardization sample on the test. These norms are published in the test manual.

Norm-referenced Tests

A **norm-referenced test** is a test that compares a student's test performance with that of similar students who have taken the same test. After a test has been constructed, the test developers administer it to a standardization sample of students using the same administration and scoring procedures for all students. This makes the administration and scoring "standardized." The test scores of the standardization sample are then converted to norms, which include a variety of types of scores.

Once a norm-referenced test has been standardized, it can be administered to students with characteristics that are similar to the norm group and the scores of these students can be compared with those of the norm group. Norm-referenced standardized tests can be based on local, state, or national norms. Because of the comparison of scores between a norm group and other groups of students, a norm-referenced test provides information on the relative standing of students.

Standardized Tests

Tests in which the administration, scoring, and interpretation procedures are prescribed in the test manual and must be strictly followed by the test examiner are known as **standardized tests.** Standardized tests are usually norm-referenced. Examiners must follow exact adminstration procedures when using standardized tests. When examiners fail to follow these procedures, the reliability, validity, and interpretation of the results are compromised.

Standardized norm-referenced tests can be both individual and group administered. Examples of standardized norm-referenced tests include *Woodcock-Johnson Psychoeducational*

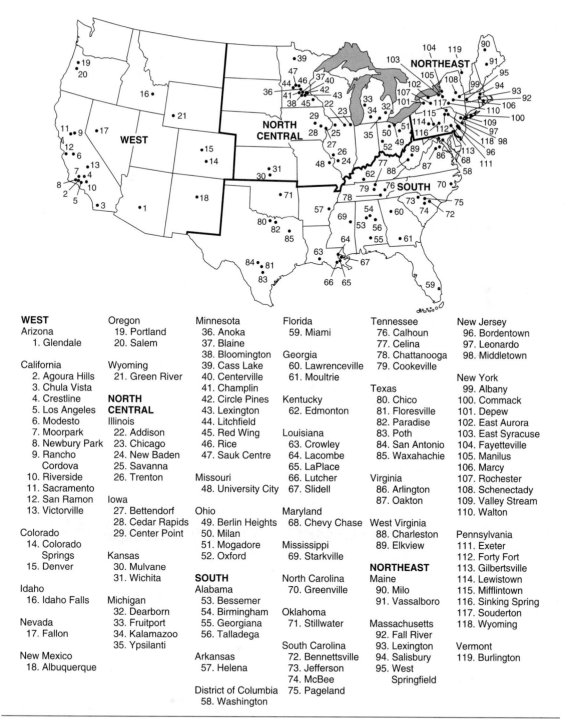

WEST

Arizona
1. Glendale

California
2. Agoura Hills
3. Chula Vista
4. Crestline
5. Los Angeles
6. Modesto
7. Moorpark
8. Newbury Park
9. Rancho Cordova
10. Riverside
11. Sacramento
12. San Ramon
13. Victorville

Colorado
14. Colorado Springs
15. Denver

Idaho
16. Idaho Falls

Nevada
17. Fallon

New Mexico
18. Albuquerque

Oregon
19. Portland
20. Salem

Wyoming
21. Green River

NORTH CENTRAL

Illinois
22. Addison
23. Chicago
24. New Baden
25. Savanna
26. Trenton

Iowa
27. Bettendorf
28. Cedar Rapids
29. Center Point

Kansas
30. Mulvane
31. Wichita

Michigan
32. Dearborn
33. Fruitport
34. Kalamazoo
35. Ypsilanti

Minnesota
36. Anoka
37. Blaine
38. Bloomington
39. Cass Lake
40. Centerville
41. Champlin
42. Circle Pines
43. Lexington
44. Litchfield
45. Red Wing
46. Rice
47. Sauk Centre

Missouri
48. University City

Ohio
49. Berlin Heights
50. Milan
51. Mogadore
52. Oxford

SOUTH

Alabama
53. Bessemer
54. Birmingham
55. Georgiana
56. Talladega

Arkansas
57. Helena

District of Columbia
58. Washington

Florida
59. Miami

Georgia
60. Lawrenceville
61. Moultrie

Kentucky
62. Edmonton

Louisiana
63. Crowley
64. Lacombe
65. LaPlace
66. Lutcher
67. Slidell

Maryland
68. Chevy Chase

Mississippi
69. Starkville

North Carolina
70. Greenville

Oklahoma
71. Stillwater

South Carolina
72. Bennettsville
73. Jefferson
74. McBee
75. Pageland

Tennessee
76. Calhoun
77. Celina
78. Chattanooga
79. Cookeville

Texas
80. Chico
81. Floresville
82. Paradise
83. Poth
84. San Antonio
85. Waxahachie

Virginia
86. Arlington
87. Oakton

West Virginia
88. Charleston
89. Elkview

NORTHEAST

Maine
90. Milo
91. Vassalboro

Massachusetts
92. Fall River
93. Lexington
94. Salisbury
95. West Springfield

New Jersey
96. Bordentown
97. Leonardo
98. Middletown

New York
99. Albany
100. Commack
101. East Aurora
102. East Syracuse
103. Fayetteville
104. Fayetteville
105. Manilus
106. Marcy
107. Rochester
108. Schenectady
109. Valley Stream
110. Walton

Pennsylvania
111. Exeter
112. Forty Fort
113. Gilbertsville
114. Lewistown
115. Mifflintown
116. Sinking Spring
117. Souderton
118. Wyoming

Vermont
119. Burlington

FIGURE 4.1

Map of a Standardization Sample

Source: Oral and Written Language Scales by Elizabeth Carrow-Woolfolk. © 1996. American Guidance Service, Inc., 4201 Woodland Road, Circle Pines, MN 55104-1796. Reproduced with permission of the Publisher. All rights reserved.

Battery–Revised, Kaufman Assessment Battery for Children, and the *Metropolitan Achievement Tests.*

Informal Tests

The term **informal tests** is an older term for a broad category of assessment approaches that do *not* include standardized tests. Informal tests include the current approaches of performance-based assessment, portfolios, exhibitions, and some teacher-developed tests.

Criterion-Referenced Tests

Instead of comparing a student's performance to a norm group, **criterion-referenced tests** measure a student's performance with respect to a well-defined domain such as reading or mathematics (Anastasi, 1982; Berk, 1988). While norm-referenced tests are constructed to discriminate between the performance of individual students on specific test items, criterion-referenced tests provide a description of a student's knowledge, skills, or behavior in a specific range of test items. This specific range is referred to as a **domain.** Test items on criterion-referenced tests are frequently tied to well-defined instructional objectives (Salvia and Ysseldyke, 1995). Criterion-referenced tests, instead of using norms, provide information on the performance of a student with respect to specific test items. The results of criterion-referenced tests are not dependent on the performance of other students, as are norm-referenced tests. An example of a criterion-referenced test is the Brigance® Diagnostic Inventory of Essential Skills.

Distinguishing Norm-Referenced Tests from Criterion-Referenced Tests

There are several characteristics that distinguish norm-referenced tests from criterion-referenced tests. One of these is mastery. Performance on a criterion-referenced test provides information on whether the student has attained a predetermined level of mastery. Sometimes, performance can be interpreted as mastery, nonmastery, or intermediate (Anastasi, 1982). While it is possible to construct a test that is both norm-referenced and criterion-referenced, caution must be used when interpreting the results of these tests, because it is difficult to combine both types of tests in one instrument.

Another distinction is the breadth of the content domain covered by the test (Mehrens and Lehmann, 1991). Typical norm-referenced tests survey a broad domain, while criterion-referenced tests usually have fewer domains but more items in each domain. Criterion-referenced tests typically sample the domain more thoroughly than norm-referenced tests (Mehrens and Lehmann, 1991).

Criterion-referenced tests can also be very useful in helping to make instructional planning decisions. Since criterion-referenced tests frequently cover a more restricted range of content than norm-referenced tests, they can provide more information about a student's level of performance.

SCALES OF MEASUREMENT

Student performance can be estimated using test scores. Test scores are based on different types of measurement scales. The description of a student's performance depends on the measurement scale that is used. There are four different scales used in measurement: nominal, ordinal, interval, and ratio.

Nominal Scale

A **nominal scale** represents the lowest level of measurement. It is a naming scale. Each value on the scale is a name, and the name does not have any innate or inherent value. Hair color, students' names, and numbers on football jerseys are all examples of nominal scales. Although there are numerals on football uniforms, there is no inherent rank or value to the numerals. A numeral is just associated with the name of the football player. A teacher may use a nominal scale to distinguish between groups 1, 2, and 3. The numbers 1, 2, and 3 have no intrinsic value; they are simply used to label

the groups. Because nominal scales merely represent names, they have limited usefulness. They cannot be added, subtracted, multiplied, or divided. They are rarely used in reporting test performance.

Ordinal Scale

An **ordinal scale** is the next level of measurement. An ordinal scale orders items in a scale or continuum. Ordering students according to class rank is an example of an ordinal scale (Table 4.1).

Interval Scale

An **interval scale** is similar to an ordinal scale but it has several important advantages. Interval scales order items on a scale or continuum, as do ordinal scales, but unlike ordinal scales, the distance between the items is equal. Because of this characteristic, ordinal scales can be added, subtracted, multiplied, and divided.

Interval scales have another interesting characteristic. Interval scales have a zero. However, the zero is placed at an arbitrary point along the measurement scale; it is not an absolute zero. For example, a Fahrenheit scale is an equal in-

TABLE 4.1   Ordinal Scale

Student	Rank
Jean	10
Mia	9
Mura	8
Melissa	7
Chris	6
Ruth	5
Lisa	4
Mei	3
Dan	2
David	1

SNAPSHOT

Activity Levels

Suppose a teacher is observing a student with a high activity level. The teacher wants to rank the activity level of the student from 1 to 10, with 10 being the most active and 1 the least active, like this:

The distance between each of the ranks 1, 2, 3, and so forth is not equal. That is, the same increase in activity may not be required, in the teacher's judgment, to raise a ranking from 3 to 4 as from 7 to 8. Because of this limitation, ordinal scales cannot be added, subtracted, multiplied, or divided.

Activity level	1	2	3	4	5	6	7	8	9	10
Classroom										
Playground										

terval scale; there is an equal distance between the degrees of temperature. The zero point, however, was arbitrarily established by Daniel Fahrenheit when he developed the temperature scale. Intelligence quotient scores are also based on equal interval scales. Although there is an equal distance between the scores, an IQ of zero cannot be measured. Another example of a test that uses an interval scale is the *Scholastic Aptitude Test* (SAT). SAT scores range from 200 to 800 points. There is no zero!

Ratio Scale

A **ratio scale** has all the characteristics of ordinal and interval scales and, in addition, it has an absolute zero. Height and weight measurements are examples of ratio scales. Teacher-developed tests, such as classroom spelling or arithmetic tests, frequently are based on the ratio scale. The total number of test items that a student answers correctly, or the **raw score,** is based on a ratio scale. Some observation and rating scales are also ratio scales. Because the ratio scale has an absolute zero, the scores can be used in mathematical operations. If we are recording the number of times students raise their hands, we may conclude that one student exhibits this behavior two or three times more than another student.

FREQUENCY DISTRIBUTION AND NORMAL CURVE

Frequency Distribution

A **frequency distribution** is a way of organizing test scores based on how often they occur. To create a frequency distribution, arrange the test scores in a column from high to low. Next to each test score, record the number of students who obtained that score. The frequencies are added to find the total number of students who took the test (Table 4.2). Next, a frequency polygon can be constructed (Figure 4.2).

TABLE 4.2   Frequency Distribution

Score	Frequency
100	3
90	2
80	5
70	4
60	6
50	5
42	3
30	1

Total number of students: 26

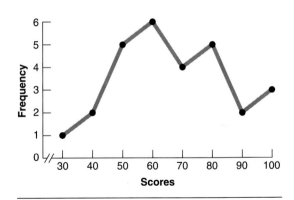

FIGURE 4.2
Frequency Polygon

Normal Curve

Frequency distributions can have different shapes. The shape represents how students' scores are grouped. In a **normal curve** most scores fall in the middle, and fewer scores occur at the ends of the distribution. The normal curve is a symmetrical, bell-shaped curve (Figure 4.3).

There has been considerable debate about whether human characteristics are distributed in a normal curve. While there is some evi-

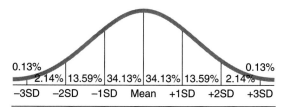

FIGURE 4.3

Normal Distribution

dence that physical characteristics such as height and weight are normally distributed, there has been active discussion about whether other characteristics, such as intelligence, development, and achievement, are normally distributed. While it is less likely that the performance of small groups of children will be normally distributed on a specific characteristic, the test results from large norm samples will probably be more normal in appearance (Mehrens and Lehman, 1991).

Skewed Distributions

Sometimes, the majority of scores occur at one end of the curve. These scores show **skewed distribution.** Positively skewed distributions contain only a few high scores, with the majority of scores occurring at the low end. Negatively skewed distributions have few scores at the low end and a majority of scores at the high end. When distributions are either positively or negatively skewed, the measures of central tendency—that is, the mean, median, and mode—shift. Figure 4.4 shows the placement of the mean, median, and mode in skewed distributions.

MEASURES OF CENTRAL TENDENCY

Measures of central tendency are used to describe the typical test performance of a group of students using a single number. The number that results from the calculation of a measure of central tendency represents the typical score obtained by the group of students (Gay, 1985).

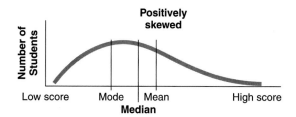

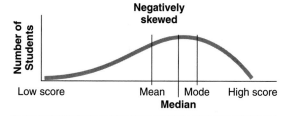

FIGURE 4.4

Skewed Distributions

The mean, mode, and median are measures of central tendency.

Mean

The **mean,** or the average score, is the most frequently used measure of central tendency. It is computed by adding all of the scores and dividing by the total number of scores (Table 4.3). Because all the scores in a distribution are taken into account when the mean is calculated, the mean is affected by extreme scores.

Median

Another measure of central tendency is the **median.** It is the point on a scale above which and below which 50 percent of the cases occur. The median is an excellent measure of central tendency when most of the scores cluster together but a few scores lie at the extreme ends of a distribution.

Mode

The **mode** is the score that occurs most frequently in a list of scores. In a distribution of scores, the mode is the most commonly occurring score. However, a distribution of test

TABLE 4.3   Finding the Average (Mean)

Score	Frequency	Frequency × score
100	1	100
98	2	196
90	2	180
85	4	340
70	6	420
50	5	250
42	3	126
30	2	60
25	1	25
Number of scores: 26		Sum of scores: 1697

$$\frac{\text{Sum of scores}}{\text{Number of scores}} = \text{Mean} \qquad \frac{1697}{26} = 65.26$$

$$\text{Mean} = 65.26$$

scores can have more than one mode. If a teacher wanted to know which test or test item was most frequently answered correctly, the teacher would look at the mode. However, the mode is infrequently used because it is not very helpful when describing the performance of an individual child or of a group of students. In a normal distribution, the mean, median, and mode all occur at the same point (Figure 4.3).

Standard Deviation

The **standard deviation** (SD) tells the degree to which various scores deviate from the mean. It is a unit of measurement, just as an inch and a foot are units of measurement. Scores can be expressed in the number of standard deviation units that they deviate from the mean.

The standard deviation is useful when comparing several sets of scores. It can be helpful when interpreting the test performance of one student or a group of students. When compar-

ing scores, the larger the standard deviation, the more variable is the performance; the smaller the standard deviation, the less variable is the performance of the students.

In a normal distribution, the percentage of scores that can be expected to fall within the first, second, and third standard deviations above or below the mean are shown in Figure 4.5. For example, when a group of scores is normally distributed, 34.13% of the scores can be expected to occur between the mean and the +1 SD, and 34.13% of the scores also occur between the mean and −1 SD. Approximately 14% of the scores fall between the +1 SD and +2 SD, and 14% of the scores fall between the −1 SD and −2 SD. Just over 2% of the scores occur between the first and second standard deviations and 0.13% of the scores occur between the second and third standard deviations.

For most tests, publishers provide information about the mean and the standard deviation in test manuals. You will not have to calculate the standard deviation. For example, the manual for the third edition of the *Wechsler Intelligence Scale* (WISC-III) reports that this test has a mean of 100 and a standard deviation of 15. This represents that approximately 34.13% of students have intelligence quotients (IQs) between 100 and 115. Similarly, approximately 68% of students have IQs between 85 and 115. Many states mandate specific guidelines for identification and placement of students. For example, some states may require that school-age students who are labeled mentally retarded have IQs that are at least two standard deviations below the mean. In this example, you will have to subtract 30 (2 times the standard deviation of 15) from 100 to obtain an IQ of 70.

TYPES OF SCORES

There are many ways of reporting test performance. A variety of scores can be used when interpreting students' test performance.

SNAPSHOT

Deciding When to Use Measures of Central Tendency

Brendan Strout, the special education consultant at Washington School, was preparing to meet with Ken Brown, the sixth grade classroom teacher. Brendan was examining the test scores of a group of students from Ken's classroom. Brendan wanted to be able to describe the performance of the students in order to assist Ken in making instructional decisions. Here are the scores of Ken's students:

90
82
81
80
79
75
75
75
20

Brendan summarized the scores in three ways.

1. He calculated the mean, or average, by adding up all of the scores and dividing by 9, the total number of scores

    90

    82

81
80
79   Median
75 ⎫
75 ⎬   Mode
75 ⎭
20

$657 \div 9 = 73$ This is the mean, or average score.

2. Next, Brendan arranged the scores from high to low and found the score that separates the top 50 percent of students who took the test from the bottom 50 percent of students. This score is 79.

3. Finally, Brendan found the score that occurred the most often in the group of scores. This score is 75 and is the mode.

Which measure of central tendency—the mean, median, or mode—should Brendan use in his discussion with Ken? (The answer can be found at the end of the "Extending Learning" section at the conclusion of this chapter.)

Raw Scores

The **raw score** is the number of items a student answers correctly without adjustment for guessing. For example, if there are 15 problems on an arithmetic test, and a student answers 11 correctly, then the raw score is 11. Raw scores, however, do not provide us with enough information to describe student performance.

Percentage Scores

A **percentage score** is the percent of test items answered correctly. These scores can be useful when describing a student's performance on a teacher-made test or on a criterion-referenced test. However, percentage scores have a major disadvantage: we have no way of comparing the percentage correct on one test with the percentage correct on another test. Suppose a child earned a score of 85% correct on one test and 55% correct on another test. The interpretation of the score is related to the difficulty level of the test items on each test. Because each test has a different or unique level of difficulty, we have no common way to interpret these scores; there is no frame of reference (Anastasi, 1982).

To interpret raw scores and percentage-correct scores, it is necessary to change the raw or percentage score to a different type of score in order to make comparisons. Raw scores and percentage-correct scores are rarely used when interpreting performance because it is difficult to compare one student's scores on several tests or the performance of several students on several tests.

Derived Scores

Derived scores are a family of scores that allow us to make comparisons between test scores. Raw scores are transformed to derived scores. Developmental scores and scores of relative standing are two types of derived scores. Scores of relative standing include percentiles, standard scores, and stanines.

Developmental Scores

Age and grade equivalents are **developmental scores.** Developmental scores are scores that have been transformed from raw scores and reflect the average performance at age and grade levels. Thus, the student's raw score (number of items correct) is the same as the average raw score for students of a specific age or grade. Age equivalents are written with a hyphen between years and months (e.g., 12-4 means that the age equivalent is 12 years, 4 months old). A decimal point is used between the grade and month in grade equivalents (e.g., 1.2 is the first grade, second month).

Developmental scores can be useful (McLean, Bailey, and Wolery, 1996; Sattler, 1988). They are easily interpreted by parents and profess-

ionals and the performance of students is placed within a context. Because of the ease of misinterpretation of these scores, they should be used with extreme caution. They have been criticized for a number of reasons.

For a student who is 6 years old and is in the first grade, grade and age equivalents presume that for each month of first grade an equal amount of learning occurs. But, from our knowledge of child growth and development and theories about learning, we know that neither growth nor learning occurs in equal monthly intervals. Age and grade equivalents do not take into consideration the variation in individual growth and learning.

Teachers should not expect that students will gain a grade equivalent or age equivalent of one year for each year that they are in school. For example, suppose a child earned a grade equivalent of 1.5, first grade, fifth month, at the end of first grade. To assume that at the end of second grade the child should obtain a grade equivalent of 2.5, second grade, fifth month, is not good practice. This assumption is incorrect for two reasons: 1) the grade and age equivalent norms should not be confused with performance standards; and 2) a gain of 1.0 grade equivalent is only representative of students who are in the average range for their grade. Students who are above average will gain more than 1.0 grade equivalent a year, and students who are below average will progress less than 1.0 grade equivalent a year (Gronlund and Linn, 1990).

A second criticism of developmental scores is that underlying them is the idea that because two students obtain the same score on a test they are comparable, that they will display the same thinking, behavior, and skill patterns. For example, a student who is in second grade earned a grade equivalent score of 4.6 on a test of reading achievement. This does not mean that the second grader understands the reading process as it is taught in the fourth grade. Rather, this student just performed at a superior level for a student who is in second grade. It is incorrect to compare the second grader to a child who is in fourth grade; the comparison should be made to other students who are in second grade (Anastasi, 1982; Sattler, 1988).

A third criticism of developmental scores is that age and grade equivalents encourage the use of false standards. A second grade teacher should not expect all students in the class to perform at the second grade level on a reading test. Differences between students within a grade mean that the range of achievement actually spans several grades. In addition, developmental scores are calculated so that half of the scores fall below the median, and half fall above the median. Age and grade equivalents are not standards of performance (Anastasi, 1982).

A fourth criticism of age and grade equivalents is that they promote typological thinking. The use of age and grade equivalents causes us to think in terms of a typical kindergartner or a typical 10-year-old. In reality, students vary in their abilities and levels of performance. Developmental scores do not take these variations into account.

A fifth criticism is that most developmental scores are interpolated and extrapolated. When a test is normed, students of specific ages and grades are included in the norming sample. However, not all ages and grades are included. **Interpolation** is when scores are estimated within the ages and grades that were tested. **Extrapolation** means that estimates of the performance of students outside the normative sample are made.

$$\frac{\text{Developmental age 144 months}}{\text{Chronological age 144 months}} \times 100 = 100$$

$$\frac{144}{144} \times 100 =$$

$$\frac{1}{1} \times 100 =$$

$$1 \times 100 = 100$$

But, suppose another student's chronological age is also 144 months and that the developmental age is 108 months. Using the formula, this student would have a developmental quotient of 75.

$$\frac{\text{Developmental age 108 months}}{\text{Chronological age 144 months}} \times 100 = 75$$

$$\frac{108}{144} \times 100 =$$

$$.75 \times 100 = 75$$

Developmental quotients have all of the drawbacks associated with age and grade equivalents. In addition, they may be misleading because developmental age may not keep pace with chronological age as the individual gets older. Consequently, the gap between developmental age and chronological age is larger as the student gets older.

Developmental Quotient

A **developmental quotient** is an estimate of the rate of development. If we know a student's developmental age and chronological age, it is possible to calculate a developmental quotient. For example, suppose a student's developmental age is 12 years (12 years $\times$ 12 months in a year = 144 months) and the chronological age is also 12 years, or 144 months. Then, using the following formula, we arrive at a developmental quotient of 100.

Percentile Ranks

A **percentile rank** is the point in a distribution at or below which the scores of a given percentage of students fall. Percentage correct is not the same as percentile. Percentage correct refers to the percent of test items answered correctly. Percentiles provide information about the relative standing of students when compared with the standardization sample. Look at the following test scores and their corresponding percentile ranks.

Student	Score	Percentile rank
Delia	96	84
Jana	93	81
Pete	90	79
Marcus	86	75

Jana's score of 93 has a percentile rank of 81. This means that 81 percent of the students who took the test scored 93 or lower. Said another way, Jana scored as well as or better than 81 percent of the students who took the test.

A percentile rank of 50 represents average performance. In a normal distribution, both the mean and the median fall at the 50th percentile. Half the students fall above the 50th percentile and half fall below. Percentiles can be divided into quartiles. A *quartile* contains 25 percentiles

or 25 percent of the scores in a distribution. The 25th and the 75th percentiles are the first and the third quartiles. In addition, percentiles can be divided into groups of 10 known as deciles. A *decile* contains 10 percentiles. Beginning at the bottom of a group of students, the first 10 percent are known as the first decile, the second 10% are known as the second decile, and so on.

The position of percentiles in a normal curve is shown in Figure 4.5. Despite their ease of interpretation, percentiles have several problems. First, the intervals they represent are unequal, especially at the lower and upper ends of the distribution. A difference of a few percentile points at the extreme ends of the distribution should be taken more seriously than a difference of a few points in the middle of the distribution. Second, percentiles cannot

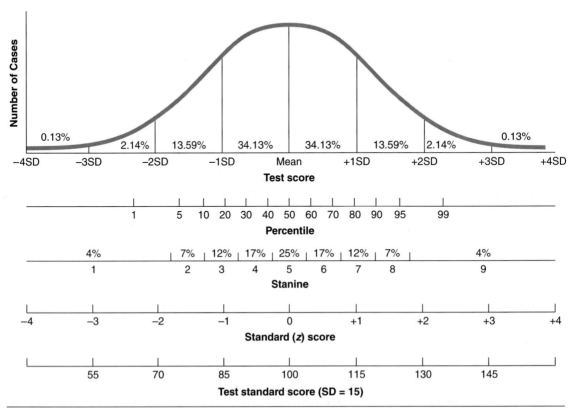

FIGURE 4.5

Normal Curve with Types of Scores

SNAPSHOT

A Conversation Between Lincoln Bates and Sari Andrews

Just after school started in September, Lincoln Bates, a seventh grade teacher of mathematics, reviewed last spring's test results for Karen Anderson, one of his students. He noticed that the results were reported using several types of scores:

STUDENT'S NAME: KAREN ANDERSON
AGE: 13 YEARS 5 MONTHS

TEACHER: J. PLANTE

GRADE: 6

Subtest	Grade Equivalent	Age Equivalent	Percentile Rank
Mathematics	4.1	9-6	9
Reading Comprehension	10.2	13-0	75
Spelling	6.4	12-0	45

Lincoln was unsure how to interpret Karen's scores on the mathematics achievement subtest. He decided to ask Sari Andrews, the school's test examiner. Lincoln said, "I'm not sure how to interpret the age equivalent and grade equivalent scores. Even though I used to teach fourth grade, I don't think that Karen approaches mathematics in the same way that a typical fourth grader does."

Sari explained, "Just because Karen earned a grade equivalent of 4.1 in mathematics does not mean that her thinking, behavior, and skill patterns are the same as other students who are in the fourth grade. The same holds true for her age equivalent score of 9-6. Age and grade equivalent scores can be misleading. I prefer to use percentile rank or standard scores as a way of interpreting her performance." What do you think?

be used in mathematical calculations (Gronlund and Linn, 1990). Lastly, percentile scores are reported in one hundredths. But, because of errors associated with measurement, they are only accurate to the nearest 0.06 (six one-hundredths) (Rudner, Conoley, and Plake, 1989). These limitations require that caution be used when interpreting percentile ranks. Confidence intervals, which are discussed later in this chapter, should be used when interpreting percentile scores.

Standard Scores

Another type of derived score is a **standard score.** Standard score is the name given to a group or category of scores. Each specific type of standard score within this group has the same mean and the same standard deviation. Because each type of standard score has the same mean and the same standard deviation, standard scores are an excellent way of representing a child's performance. Standard scores allow us to compare a child's performance on several tests and to compare one child's performance to the performance of other students. Unlike percentile scores, standard scores can be used in mathematical operations. For instance, standard scores can be averaged.

Figure 4.5 compares standard scores with the other types of scores we have discussed. As can be seen, standard scores are equal interval scores. The different types of standard scores, some of which are discussed in the following subsections, are:

a. z-scores: have a mean of 0 and a standard deviation of 1.
b. T-scores: have a mean of 50 and a standard deviation of 10.
c. Deviation IQ scores: have a mean of 100 and a standard deviation of 15 or 16.
d. Normal curve equivalents: have a mean of 50 and a standard deviation of 21.06.
e. Stanines: standard score bands that divide a distribution of scores into nine parts.

Deviation IQ Scores

Deviation IQ scores are frequently used to report the performance of students on norm-referenced standardized tests. The deviation scores of the *Wechsler Intelligence Scale for Children–III,* and the Wechsler Individual Achievement Test have a mean of 100 and a standard deviation of 15, while the *Stanford-Binet Intelligence Scale–IV* has a mean of 100 and a standard deviation of 16. Many test manuals provide tables that allow conversion of raw scores to deviation IQ scores.

Normal Curve Equivalents

Normal curve equivalents (NCEs) are a type of standard score with a mean of 50 and a standard deviation of 21.06. This score has been used in the evaluation of federally funded projects. When the baseline of the normal curve is divided into 99 equal units, the percentile ranks of 1, 50, and 99 are the same as NCE units (Lyman, 1986). Normal curve equivalents are not reported for some tests. One test that does report NCEs is the *Battelle Developmental Inventory*.

Stanines

Stanines are bands of standard scores that have a mean of 5 and a standard deviation of 2. As illustrated in Figure 4.5, stanines range from 1 to 9. Despite their relative ease of interpreta-

tion, stanines have several disadvantages. A change in just a few raw score points can move a student from one stanine to another. Because stanines are a general way of interpreting test performance, caution is necessary when making classification and placement decisions. As an aid in interpreting stanines, descriptors can be associated with each of the 9 values:

9–very superior
8–superior
7–very good
6–good
5–average
4–below average
3–considerably below average
2–poor
1–very poor

BASAL AND CEILING LEVELS

Many tests, because they are constructed to be used with students of differing abilities, contain more items than are necessary. To determine the starting and stopping points for administering a test, test authors designate basal and ceiling levels. (Although these are really not types of scores, basal and ceiling levels are sometimes called *rules* or scores.) The **basal level** is the point below which the examiner assumes that the student could obtain all correct responses and, therefore, it is the point at which the examiner begins testing. The **ceiling level** is the point above which the examiner assumes that the student would obtain all incorrect responses if the testing were to continue; it is, therefore, the point at which the examiner stops testing.

Basal and ceiling rules differ from one test to another. The test manual will designate the point at which testing should begin. For example, a test manual states, "Students who are 13 years old should begin with item 12," or, "Students who are in seventh grade should begin with item 3." Consult the test manual to determine the basal and ceiling rules for each test. For example, to determine a basal level, a manual may state, "Continue testing when three items in a row have been answered correctly. If three items in a row are not answered correctly, the examiner should drop back a level." To determine a ceiling, a manual may read, "Discontinue testing when three items in a row have been missed."

In individual tests basal and ceiling rules are generally the same. However, rules can vary from one test to another. For example, the basal rule may be to continue testing after three correct responses, while the ceiling rule may be to stop after three incorrect responses. Once the basal level has been established, the examiner begins testing and continues until three incorrect responses are obtained. This is the ceiling level, and the point at which testing should stop.

A false ceiling can be reached if the directions for determining the ceiling level are not followed exactly. Some tests require that a page of test items be completed to establish the ceiling level. The *Woodcock-Johnson Psychoeducational Battery–Revised* is an example of this type of procedure.

If a student fails to obtain a basal score, the examiner must drop back a level or page on the test. Let's look at the example of the student who is 9 years old. Although the examiner begins testing at the 9-year-old level, the student fails to answer correctly three in a row. Thus, the examiner is unable to establish a basal level at the suggested beginning point. Many manuals instruct the examiner to continue testing backwards, dropping back one item at a time, until three correct items are obtained. Some test manuals instruct examiners to drop back an entire level, for instance to age 8, and begin testing (Overton, 1992). When computing the student's raw score, items below the basal point are included as items answered correctly. Thus, the raw score includes all the items the student answered correctly plus the test items below the basal point.

STANDARD ERROR OF MEASUREMENT AND CONFIDENCE INTERVALS

Standard Error of Measurement

The administration of a test is subject to many errors: errors can occur in the testing environment, the examiner may make errors, the examinee may not be exhibiting the best performance, and the test itself may not able to evoke the best performance from the examinee. All these errors contribute to lowering the reliability of a test.

The **standard error of measurement** (SEM) is related to reliability and is very useful in the interpretation of test performance. The standard error of measurement is the amount of error associated with individual test scores, test items, item samples, and test times. From Chapter 3 we know that the true score is the score an individual would obtain on a test if there were no measurement errors. (The obtained score is the score that a student gets on a test.) Figure 4.6 shows the distribution of the SEM around the estimated true score.

If it is expected that the reliability or the standard error of measurement will differ for different populations, SEMs should be reported for each population for which the test will be used. *Standards for Educational and Psychological Testing* (American Educational Research Association et al., 1985) cautions that reliability

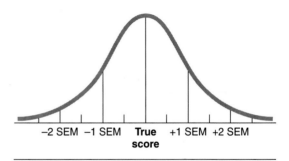

FIGURE 4.6

Standard Error of Measurement

coefficients that are obtained from a sample of students from several grades usually produce an inflated reliability coefficient. Therefore, reliability coefficients and SEMs should be reported for each grade level.

When the SEM is small, we can be more confident of a score; when the SEM is large, there is less confidence in the score. Thus, it follows that the more reliable a test is, the smaller the SEM and the more confidence we can have. The less reliable a test, the larger the SEM, and the more uncertainty we have in a score.

Confidence Intervals

Although we can never know a student's true score, we can use the concept of confidence intervals to give us a range within which the true score can be found. Because it is inadvisable to present a student's score as an exact point, the concept of **confidence intervals** is an important one to use when reporting a student's test score.

We can determine the probability that a student's score will fall within a particular range. The range can be described using three equivalent terms: band of error, confidence interval, and confidence band. The higher the probability level, the more confidence we can have that a student's score falls within a specific range. The lower the probability, the less confidence we have that a score falls within a particular range. For instance, we can be 50, 68, 90, 95, 98, or 99 percent confident that a student's true score can be found within a range of scores. The percent of confidence that is chosen depends on the preference of the test examiner. However, we prefer to use 90 percent level or higher.

SCORING GUIDELINES

After you have administered the test, you must carefully score it. If you have used a standardized test, you must use the specific procedures for scoring described in the test manual. Score

SNAPSHOT

Confidence Intervals

Jean Dubois, the special education consultant, had just finished administering the Comprehensive Form of the Kaufman Test of Educational Achievement (K-TEA) to Cindy, a 7-year-old who was suspected of having a learning disability. After Jean had marked the raw scores and the standard scores on the front of the Comprehensive Form (Figure 4.7) she was ready to write down the confidence interval. Jean decided to use the 90 percent level of confidence. Like many tests, the developers of the K-TEA have calculated the confidence bands so that test administrators do not need to make the calculations themselves. Jean, us-ing the K-TEA manual, found the tables that listed the bands of confidence for Cindy's standard scores (Table 4.4).

When Jean met with Cindy's family she was able to report her scores in this way: "I am very confident when I say that Cindy's performance on the Battery Composite on the K-TEA showed that her score was 88 ± 3. This means that her true score is between 85 and 91. It is more accurate to report her performance within a range of scores because test scores tend to fluctuate or change. There may be small changes in her scores if I were to retest her within a short time interval."

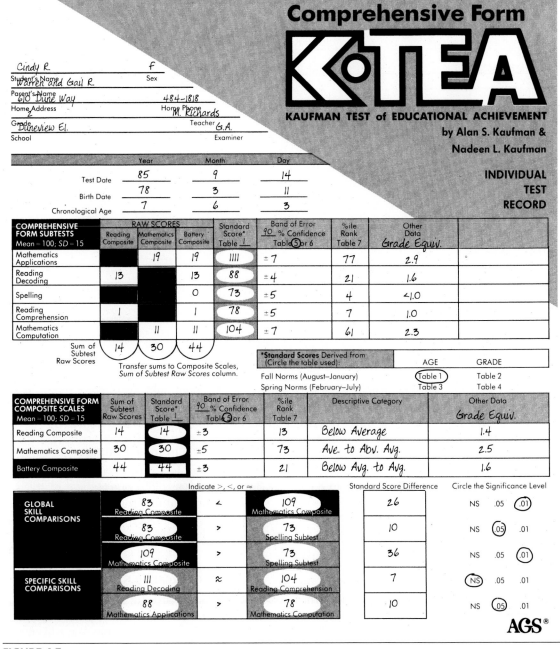

FIGURE 4.7

Kaufman Test of Educational Achievement (K-TEA) Record Form

Source: From Kaufman Test of Educational Achievement (K-TEA) by Alan S. Kaufman and Nadeen L. Kaufman.
© 1985. American Guidance Service, Inc., 4201 Woodland Road, Circle Pines, MN 55104-1796. Reproduced
with permission of the Publisher. All rights reserved.

TABLE 4.4 Average Bands of Error for Comprehensive Form Subtests and Composites at the 90 Percent Level of Confidence, by Grade and by Age

	AVERAGE BAND OF ERROR AT 90% CONFIDENCE LEVEL	
Subtest of composite	*Grades 1 to 12 (grade norms)*	*Ages 6 to 18 (age norms)*
Reading Decoding	± 6	± 5
Reading Comprehension	± 7	± 6
Reading Composite	± 5	± 4
Mathematics Applications	± 8	± 7
Mathematics Computation	± 8	± 7
Mathematics Composite	± 6	± 5
Spelling	± 7	± 6
Battery Composite	± 4	± 3

Source: Kaufman, A., & N. Kaufman (1985). K-TEA. Circle Pines, MN: American Guidance Service. Reprinted by permission.

the test as soon as possible after it has been administered. Be sure to allot sufficient time so that you do not feel rushed. Scoring must be accurate. All calculations should be carefully checked. Many tests have computer programs that will calculate the test scores for you. These can be very helpful in avoiding errors in computation.

Completing the Test Record Form

Biographical Information

The test record form contains a section for the examiner to complete biographical information about the student (Figure 4.7). Usually, this section can be found on the front of the test record form. The following information, in general, will be needed: student's name, gender, name(s) of parent(s), home address, home telephone, grade in school, age when tested, date of birth, student's homeroom teacher,

name of school, and examiner's name. If the student needs to use corrective lenses or a hearing aid, this should also be noted.

Chronological Age

Often it is necessary to calculate the student's chronological age, the precise age of the student in years and months. If testing took place over several days, use the first test date to calculate the chronological age. Figure 4.8 shows the steps in calculating chronological age.

Calculating Raw Scores

The raw scores are the number of items that the student answered correctly. Directions for computing the raw score may vary from one test to another. Within each subtest you will need to add the total number of items the student answered correctly. Each test will have its own system for indicating the student's correct and incorrect answers. Following the directions

EXAMPLE 1

Begin with the right column and subtract days, then months, and finally years. In this example no borrowing is required.

	Year	Month	Day
Test Date	1996	6	15
Birth Date	1981	3	13
Chronological Age	15	3	2

EXAMPLE 2

If the day for the test date is smaller than the day for the birth date, it is necessary to borrow one month (30 days) from the month column and add the 30 days to the day column. When borrowing one month always borrow 30 days.

	Year	Month	Day
Test Dates	1996	5	33
		~~6~~	~~3~~
Birth Date	1981	3	13
Chronological Age	15	2	20

EXAMPLE 3

If the month for the test date is smaller than the month for the birth date, it is necessary to borrow one year (12 months) from the year column and add the 12 months to the month column.

	Year	Month	Day
Test Dates	1995	14	15
	~~1996~~	~~2~~	
Birth Date	1981	3	13
Chronological Age	15	11	2

In general, chronological age is reported in days and months. If the number of days exceeds 15, add 1 month. If the number of days is equal to or is smaller than 15, do not change the months

FIGURE 4.8

Three Examples of Calculating Chronological Age

given in the test manual or on the test record form, the examiner will designate the correct answers by marking either a plus sign (+) or by designating points (e.g., 1, 2, or 3 points) for each correct answer. When calculating the raw score, the examiner will need to follow the test manual directions for calculating basal and ceiling scores.

After calculating the raw scores, the examiner writes these scores on the test form. These scores should be transferred to the section that summarizes the student's scores. For many test forms, this section can be found on the front of the test form.

Transforming Raw Scores to Derived Scores

You will remember from our previous discussion that derived scores are a family of scores that are obtained from raw scores. Derived scores allow us to make comparisons between test scores. Developmental scores and scores of relative standing are two types of derived scores. Scores of relative standing include percentiles, standard scores, and stanines.

Test manuals have norm tables that allow the examiner to convert raw scores to one or more types of derived scores. Some test manuals contain tables for age and grade norms for tests conducted during the fall, winter, or spring; other test manuals will have norm tables for tests administered at any time during the year. You may need to use more than one of the norm tables in the test manual. This will depend on the type of derived score that is required on the section of the test form that summarizes the student's scores.

Indicating Confidence Intervals

All test performance, you will recall, is prone to errors of measurement. Confidence intervals indicate the probability that a student's true score will fall within a particular range. Many test manuals provide tables of the bands of error for standard scores. In fact, because the standard score is not an exact score, a confidence interval should always be used when reporting standard scores. The test record form often requires the examiner to record the band of error, indicated by a plus sign (+) and minus sign (−) on the test record form. It is up to the examiner to determine the specific level of confidence, 50, 68, 90, 95, 98, or 99 percent, that should be used. For most assessment decisions, we recommend a confidence level of 90 percent or higher.

Graphing Scores

Many test record forms allow the examiner to plot a graph or profile of the student's test scores. A graph allows the examiner to depict test scores visually and assists in the interpretation of test performance. To develop a graph, the examiner transfers the student's scores to the designated section of the test record form and creates a graph. Some record forms also allow bands of error to be plotted.

Interpreting Test Performance

Conclusions and interpretations made about a student's performance based on the results of one test, measure, or observation are limited. A student's performance on only one measure indicates a narrow slice of information about the student. Because many sources of variability and error are present in any assessment situation and because many of the assessment approaches have limitations, we recommend that examiners use several *different* sources of assessment data. Sources of assessment data include: standardized measures; portfolio assessment; performance-based assessment; interviews with family members, teachers, and the student; and observations in classrooms, playground, cafeteria, and the student's home, if appropriate.

When making interpretations about a student's performance, include observations of the behavior of the student and observations of the environment.

Behavioral Observations

Describe the student's behavior during formal and informal testing. The examiner will want to note whether the student was cooperative, dis-

tractible, attentive, tired, shy, or exhibited other behaviors. What was the student's behavior at the beginning of the testing? during the testing? at the end? To a certain extent the testing situation is artificial, and this must be considered when drawing conclusions about a child's behavior (Sattler, 1988). A child's behavior can vary in different settings and with different examiners. Systematic observations, as discussed in Chapter 5, can be important sources of information.

The following list of behaviors is a starting point for discussion (Sattler, 1988, p. 728):

- physical appearance
- reactions to test session and to the examiner
- general behavior
- typical mode of relating to the examiner
- language style
- general response style
- response to failures
- response to successes
- response to encouragement
- activity level
- attitude toward self
- attitude toward the examiner and the testing process
- visual-motor ability
- unusual habits, mannerisms, or verbalizations
- the examiner's reaction to the child

Observations of the Environment

Note any factors in the environment such as interruptions, excessive noise, or unusual temperature that may affect the student's test performance and behavior. Approaches to assessing the environment will be discussed in Chapter 5.

Discussion of Results

When reporting the results of standardized tests, use the same types of scores throughout.

Standard scores, percentiles, or stanines are preferred. Report two or more types of scores, such as standard scores and percentiles. If a graph of the student's performance is available, be sure to use it.

HOW SHOULD ASSESSMENT APPROACHES BE EVALUATED?

Many concepts have been discussed in this chapter. It is important for you to understand these concepts when using a test. Table 4.5 can be helpful when determining the adequacy of assessment approaches.

Before using individual tests, professionals are urged to consult independent reviews. There are numerous resources available that provide independent evaluations of tests. The *Mental Measurements Yearbooks* (MMY) and *Tests in Print,* which are published by the Buros Institute of Mental Measurements at the University of Nebraska–Lincoln (University of Nebraska at Lincoln, Lincoln, Nebraska 68588), are probably the best-known sources of test reviews. *Test Critiques,* published by the Test Corporation of America (4050 Pennsylvania, Suite 310, Kansas City, Missouri 64112), is another source.

The Internet provides a wealth of information. A World Wide Web (WWW) site has been established for this textbook. At this site, you will find activities that help to extend your learning, test simulations, interviews, supplementary materials, and links to additional Internet resources on testing and assessment. The address for this Web site is

http://longman.awl.com/assessnet/

The ERIC Clearinghouse on Assessment and Evaluation can be accessed through the World Wide Web at

http://www.cua.edu/www/eric_ae

This site provides access to the ERIC database on tests and measurement, newsletters on tests and measurement, descriptions of tests, information on locating tests and test reviews, research studies and essays, and links to numerous Internet resources on tests and measurement. The Buros Institute of Mental Measurements WWW site has information on locating tests and test reviews. The WWW address for the Buros Institute of Mental Measurements is

http://www.unl.edu/buros/home.html

Other Internet resources include:

United States Department of Education
http://www.ed.gov/index.html
National Center for Research on Evaluation, Standards, and Student Teaching (CRESST)
http://cresst96.cse.ucla.edu/index.htm
National Association of Test Directors
http//www.natd.org

Many journals contain reviews of tests. Journals that may be of particular interest to special educators include: *Diagnostique, Exceptional Children, Journal of Early Intervention, Journal of Learning Disabilities, Journal of Reading, Journal of School Psychology, Journal of Special Education, Mental Retardation, Remedial and Special Education,* and *Topics in Early Childhood Special Education.*

Finally, test publishers provide catalogues that describe their products. Catalogues provide overviews of tests as well as information about how to purchase tests, record forms, and technical materials. Remember that the primary goal of test publishers is to sell tests. It is essential that independent reviews of tests, such as those contained in MMY, *Tests in Print, Test Critiques,* and various journals, be examined.

TABLE 4.5   Evaluation of a Test or Other Assessment Approach

NAME OF ASSESSMENT TEST OR APPROACH
AUTHOR(S)
PUBLISHER   DATE OF PUBLICATION

About the Assessment Test or Approach

  1. Purpose(s) (according to the manual)
  2. Extent to which individual items or tasks match the purpose(s)
  3. Length of time for test administration
  4. Group or individual

About Administration Requirements

  1. Education and experience of examiner requirements
  2. Additional training requirements

About the Student

  1. Considerations/adaptations for disability
  2. Considerations/adaptations for language
  3. Considerations/adaptations for culture/race/ethnicity

About the Technical Aspects

  1. Norms, goals, standards, outcomes. If relevant, indicate:
     a. Type
     b. Age, grade, language, culture, gender
     c. Representativeness
     d. Relevance of sample to student(s) tested
     e. Method of selection of sample
     f. Date of development of norms, goals, standards, outcomes
  2. Reliability
     What are the coefficients and how were they determined?
     a. Test-retest
     b. Alternate form
     c. Split-half
     d. Internal consistency
     e. Interscorer/interrater/interobserver

PREFERRED PRACTICES

When using standardized, norm-referenced tests, educators must determine whether consistent student performance is being measured and whether tests measure what the authors describe as the purpose of the tests. Test manuals provide information about technical aspects of tests, including the development of norms and test scores. Teachers, test examiners, and administrators need to carefully review tests before using them to satisfy themselves that each test has acceptable levels of reliability and validity. The technical concepts that have been discussed in this and previous chapters should be applied to the various tests, assessment approaches, and techniques discussed in this book.

TABLE 4.5   (Continued)

3. Validity
   What is the justification for each type of validity?
   a. Content
   b. Concurrent
   c. Predictive
   d. Construct
   e. Consequential validity

About the Results and Aids to Interpretation

1. Types of scores
2. Interpretation aids

About Fairness

1. Is the norm or comparison group appropriate?
2. Are considerations made for race, culture, gender, language, socioeconomic status, or disability?

About the Usefulness of This Test or Approach

1. Is it appropriate for the student(s)?
2. Is it fair?
3. Is it technically adequate?
4. Report from an independent source (*The Mental Measurements Yearbooks, Tests in Print, Test Critiques,* journal article, or Internet)

Conclusions

1. Overall strengths
2. Overall weaknesses
3. Summary and recommendations

About References

1. List of references consulted
2. List of other sources consulted

EXTENDING LEARNING

4.1 What are the advantages of using norm-referenced tests?

4.2 Imagine that you are the director of testing for a large metropolitan school district and that you will be giving a one-day workshop to your staff. What topics should be discussed relating to the technical adequacy of tests? Why did you choose each of these topics?

4.3 Clara received a score of 64 on an achievement test. How can the special education teacher use the concept of confidence intervals to explain Clara's performance to her family?

4.4 Several different types of test scores are discussed in this chapter. Which ones do you prefer to use? Why?

4.5 Obtain two or more test manuals and read the sections pertaining to the standardization samples. Compare and contrast the development of two tests, based on these descriptions. How closely does the norm sample of each test represent students in the community in which you live? What conclusions can you make?

(On p. 75 we asked: Which measure of central tendency—the mean, median, or mode—should Brendan use in his discussion with Ken? Answer: Brendan should use the median score of 79 because most of the scores in the class cluster around this score. The score represents the division between the top 50 percent of students and the bottom 50 percent of students. The mean score of 73 should not be used. Notice how this score was strongly influenced by the bottom score of 20.)

REFERENCES

American Educational Research Association, American Psychological Association, and National Council on Measurement in Education. 1985. *Standards for educational and psychological testing.* Washington, D.C.: American Psychological Association.

Anastasi, A. (1982). *Psychological testing.* New York: Macmillan.

Berk, R. A. (1988). Criterion-referenced tests. In *Educational research, methodology, and measurement: An international handbook,* ed. J. P. Keeves, 365–370. Oxford: Pergamon.

Cronbach, L. J. (1971.) Test validation. In *Educational measurement,* ed. R. Thorndike, 443–507. Washington, D.C.: American Council on Education.

DeVellis, R. F. (1991). *Scale development.* Newbury Park, Calif.: Sage.

Gay, L. R. 1985. *Educational evaluation and measurement.* Columbus, Ohio: Merrill.

Gronlund, N., and R. L. Linn (1990). *Measurement and evaluation in teaching.* New York: Macmillan.

Lyman, H. 1986. *Test scores and what they mean.* Englewood Cliffs, NJ: Prentice-Hall.

McLean, M., D. B. Bailey, and M. Wolery (1996). *Assessing infants and preschoolers with handicaps.* Columbus, Ohio: Merrill.

Mehrens, W. A., and I. J. Lehmann (1991). *Measurement and evaluation in education and psychology.* Fort Worth: Holt, Rinehart & Winston.

Overton, T. (1992.) *Assessment in special education.* New York: Merrill.

Rudner, L. M., J. C. Conoley, and B. S. Plake (1989). *Understanding achievement tests: A guide for school administrators.* Washington, D.C.: ERIC Clearinghouse on Assessment and Evaluation. (ERIC Document Reproduction Service, no. ED 314 426).

Salvia, J., and J. Ysseldyke (1995). *Assessment.* Boston, Mass.: Houghton-Mifflin.

Sattler, J. (1988.) *Assessment of students.* San Diego, Calif.: Jerome M. Sattler.

Zeller, R. A. (1988). Validity. In *Educational research, methodology, and measurement: An international handbook,* ed. J. P. Keeves, 322–330. Oxford: Pergamon.

Observation, Interview, and Conferencing Skills

OVERVIEW

Conducting observations, interviews, and conferences with others are valuable techniques that are used in conjunction with other assessment approaches. Observations focus on the student, teacher, and environment; they often provide information not easily obtained by other means. Interviews are used to gather information about the individual perspectives of students, parents, colleagues, and professionals. Observing and interviewing usually involve conferences and collaboration with other professionals as information is gathered and results are shared. This chapter provides information on how to plan and design observations and interviews and how to build skills in working with others.

CHAPTER OBJECTIVES

After completing this chapter, you should be able to:

Provide a rationale for planning and conducting observations.

Compare and contrast the use of anecdotal records, running records, event recordings, duration recordings, intensity recordings, latency recordings, interval recordings, category recordings, rating scales, checklists, and questionnaires.

Conduct observations.

Describe concerns relating to reliability and validity.

Describe the process for planning and conducting interviews.

Apply skills in conferencing and collaborating with others.

WHAT SHAPES OUR VIEWS

Direct observation is the systematic process of gathering information by looking at students and their environments. How independently is the student functioning? Does the student use age-appropriate skills? Does the student socialize with students without disabilities in a non-structured setting? What factors in the classroom environment provide guidelines for appropriate behavior? Does the learning environment support the student's special needs? How does the classroom environment encourage collaboration and a feeling of well-being among students?

Direct observations provide a rich amount of information; planning an observation involves selecting the information that is important for answering the assessment questions. Observations of the student and the environment provide valuable information during screening, prereferral, referral, determining eligibility, program planning, monitoring progress, and conducting evaluations.

Observations of a student provide information about achievement levels, growth, development, characteristics, social skills, and behaviors. Student observations involve looking at students and recording their behaviors, responses, characteristics, and products of their play and work. Using observations, professionals can collect information about the physical arrangement of the classroom, student groupings, teacher expectations, classroom procedures, and many other aspects of the learning and social environments.

GENERAL GUIDELINES FOR PLANNING OBSERVATIONS

Planning observations involves identifying the assessment question(s), defining the event or behavior to be observed, specifying the loca-

tion(s) for the observations, and deciding the method to use in recording observation data. Planning should address the accuracy of the observations as well as how the information will be integrated with other assessment information. In the following section we will examine each of these areas in more detail.

Observation Questions

Observations can be used to answer assessment questions during each of the steps of the assessment process. The observation may focus on the environment, or on one or more students. Since there are many events going on in a classroom at one time, the observer needs to focus on specific areas that will help respond to the assessment question. The question should be clearly stated. For example, "How independently is the student functioning in the regular classroom?"

Event or Behavior

The event or behavior should be defined in observable terms so that the observer will know when to record an observation. A definition that is detailed helps ensure that the recordings are reliable. For example, "We will define the student's independent functioning as behaviors that require only a verbal prompt."

Teachers need to collect observation information over a period of time; that is, observations should take place on several different occasions. Reliability is thereby increased and, as the information is synthesized, trends can be observed.

Location

Observations take place in the classroom, cafeteria, playground, other school settings, or in the home. Teachers and parents can usually observe students without disrupting routines. However, when an observer is not a usual part of the setting, the presence of the outsider can change aspects of the environment or of the students' behavior. Additional equipment, such as a video camera, can adversely affect the results of the observations.

Recording

There are many different ways of recording information: anecdotal records, running records, event recording, duration recording, latency of behavior, interval recording, category recording, checklists, and rating scales. Observers can audiotape or videotape the observations, although the equipment can be intrusive and disrupt activities. The preferred format (or formats) for recording observations is selected during planning.

Accuracy

Recording information takes skill and practice. Some of the important considerations include: Are your observations accurate? Are your findings consistent with what you might observe tomorrow? Do your findings agree with others who conduct the same observation? Methods of ensuring accuracy and consistency when using observation assessments are discussed in detail later in this chapter.

Integration

Observation data will need to be integrated with other assessment information that has been gathered. A process for integrating assessment information is described in Chapter 8.

RECORDING METHODS

There are a number of different methods from which to choose in planning observations. These methods allow for collecting and recording data in various formats. The method chosen is influenced by the type of behavior that will be observed (Table 5.1). Let's examine the different types of recording methods and some of the advantages as well as disadvantages of these methods.

Anecdotal Record

An **anecdotal record** is a brief narrative description of an event or events that the observer felt was important to record. Anecdotal records are recorded after the events have occurred and are usually written, although they

TABLE 5.1   Selecting a Method for Observation

RECORDING FORMAT			WHEN THE BEHAVIOR IS				
	Clear begin/end	Frequent	Infrequent	Brief	Lengthy	Unanticipated	Sequential
Anecdotal recording						X	
Duration recording				X	X		
Event recording	X	X	X	X			
Interval recording	X	X		X			
Running record							X

Adapted from Sulzer-Azaroff, B., and R.G. Mayer, (1991). *Behavior analysis for lasting change.* Fort Worth: Holt, Rinehart, & Winston.

Date: October 15	Time period: 1:00–1:50
Student: Leo B.	Class activity: Science
Leo worked in a small group with two other students for the first part of the period. The group used the classroom computer in locating information about bats for their presentation next week. Leo typed in much of the search information on the computer and worked well with the other two students. However, when they returned to their desks, he had trouble settling down. He asked to go to the bathroom twice, broke his pencil three times, and then spent the remainder of the class period with his head on the desk.	*Comments* L. seems to be very interested in this topic. Today was the first time he has worked for a steady 20 minutes. Is it the topic or use of computer? Or medication change? Tomorrow try having his group use other materials for searching for information.

FIGURE 5.1
An Anecdotal Record

can also be taped. The writer notes the date, time, and place of the event and, as accurately as possible, records the event as it took place. Verbal and nonverbal cues and direct quotations are also recorded. The observer should be as objective as possible, describing what was observed rather than interpreting the event or behavior (Sattler, 1988). Interpretive comments should be recorded separately from the description of the episode.

Let's consider a question that came before a student assistance team. Leo's parent had contacted the school to inquire whether the classroom teacher would observe any changes in behavior over the next two weeks. The physician planned to change Leo's level of medication and wanted to monitor any effects, both at home and at school. The student assistance team met to plan aspects of the observation. The team decided that the classroom teacher should complete a daily anecdotal record. Figure 5.1 is an example of the anecdotal record that Leo's classroom teacher logged.

There are several advantages to maintaining anecdotal records:

1. The observer requires little special training.
2. Unanticipated events can be recorded.

3. Actual behavior in a natural setting is described.
4. A check on other types of assessment is provided.

However, there are several disadvantages to this technique:

1. The recording of anecdotal records is dependent on the memory of the observer.
2. Bias may occur if the observer selects only certain aspects or incidents to be recorded.
3. The technique may not completely describe specific behaviors.
4. There are difficulties associated with validating narrative recordings.
5. The recording of the behavior can be time-consuming.
6. Records of several anecdotal observations may be difficult to summarize (Beaty, 1994; Gronlund and Linn, 1990; Sattler, 1988).

Gronlund and Linn (1988) provide the following suggestions for recording anecdotal records:

1. Before observing, decide what behaviors to observe.

2. When observing, watch out for any unusual behaviors that should also be recorded.
3. Observe and record the complete incident. This includes any precipitating behaviors as well as behaviors that occur as a consequence of the incident.
4. As soon as possible after the observation, record the incident.
5. Individual incidents should be recorded in separate anecdotal records.
6. The anecdote should just be a record of what was observed; any interpretations are kept separate from the description of the behavior.
7. Be sure to record both positive and negative behaviors.
8. Before making inferences about a student's behavior, record a number of anecdotes. It is difficult to generalize from one or two observations.
9. Training and practice in writing anecdotes are important.

Running Record

A **running record,** sometimes called a continuous record, is a description of events written as they occur. Unlike an anecdotal record in which the events are recorded sometime after they occur, a running record describes events while they are taking place. A running record provides a rich description of events and is helpful in analyzing the behavior of students. Unlike the anecdotal record, which is a selective record of events, the running record includes everything that is observed; it is a comprehensive, detailed account of events.

Let's examine an example: A special education teacher was gathering information about Sami's progress in preparation for the annual IEP meeting. One of the questions that the team was likely to raise was how Sami functioned in homeroom. The special education teacher decided to use a running record to gather information about Sami's interactions with other students during this time (Figure 5.2).

When recording information, the observer must carefully describe the events. It is much better to provide a factual, detailed account than to be judgmental. Factual accounts are less likely to be influenced by observer bias. The observer strives to write not only accurate but detailed descriptions of the observed events. Instead of simply recording, "the student moved toward the doorway," the observer can write:

ran toward the doorway

skipped to greet the teacher

cautiously avoided the boxes on the floor

Beaty (1994) describes several disadvantages of running records:

1. Writing a running record can be time-consuming.
2. Recording all the events that are observed is difficult; some details may be overlooked.
3. This technique is useful when observing individual students but is difficult when observing a group or groups of students.

One of the major disadvantages of anecdotal records and running records is that they are subject to observer bias and judgment. In addition, while they can provide rich descriptions of events, it is difficult to quantify behaviors. For these reasons, other types of recording systems have been developed.

Event Recording

Event recording is a procedure in which a behavior is recorded each time it occurs during an observation period. For example, if an observation lasts for 20 minutes, the observer records each occurrence of the behavior during

Date: May 10	*Student: Sami G.*
Period: Homeroom	*Focus: Sami's interactions with other students during free time*

7:45 Sami enters the room with two other students. One student grabs Sami's hat and turns it around backward. Sami grins and says "haaay."	*Observer comments:* Students entering the classroom. Several students seated; about 15 students standing around.
7:47 Sami wanders toward the back of the classroom and stops at JR's desk.	
7:48 JR asks "How's the man?"	
7:49 Sami gives him a high five.	
7:50 The homeroom teacher enters and asks everyone to take their seats.	
7:52 Sami heads for his desk but stops to watch Joe and Mark arm wrestle.	About 7 of the 25 students are milling around.
7:55 The teacher again asks everyone to take their seats.	
7:56 Sami makes his way to his desk and sits down. He looks at Jen (sitting to his left) and asks her if she watched HBO last night.	Sami is the only student not in his seat.
7:59 The teacher takes attendance and asks students to indicate if they are taking hot lunch. Sami raises his hand.	
8:05 Bell for first period rings.	

FIGURE 5.2
A Running Record

the 20-minute period. The observer must pay close attention to the student and precisely tally the number of times that the behavior occurs. In addition, before beginning event recording, the observer must carefully define the behavior to be observed. It is important to describe the beginning of a behavior and the end of the behavior so that there is no ambiguity about whether the behavior occurred or not. Event recording is useful for behaviors that occur very frequently or very infrequently. Event recording is sometimes referred to as frequency recording or event sampling.

Several different procedures can be employed for recording events. The simplest one is a tally. Each time the behavior occurs—for

example, each time the student raises her hand—a line is drawn on the page and then the number of lines are totaled:

///// ///// //   12

Event recording is used frequently to answer questions about students with disabilities. For example, an IEP team wondered if modification to the classroom environment had helped Pedrico feel more comfortable in volunteering in class. An event (or frequency) recording was used to gather this information (Figure 5.3).

In monitoring another student's individualized education program, the IEP team wondered to what degree the regular classroom en-

Date: Dec 1		Student: Pedrico G.
Class activity: Reading		Focus: Responds in class discussions by either raising hand or speaking out
Observer: Jake Orone		

Time	Frequency	Comments
:00		Beginning of class discussion. Teacher calls on P. and after P.'s comment says, "That's an interesting idea about why the author wrote that."
:05	/	
:10		
:15	//	P. raised his hand twice but teacher did not call on him.
:20		

FIGURE 5.3
An Event Recording

vironment was providing opportunities for Tia to communicate with her peers. Tia's personal aide completed an event recording form to document Tia's communication with peers during her daily schedule (Figure 5.4).

Sometimes it is helpful to know the rate of behavior over time. With event recording, the rate of occurrences of the behavior can be calculated. This is helpful when more than one observation is conducted, when observation times vary, when behaviors before and after an intervention are evaluated, or when the behaviors of various students are compared. For example, suppose the teacher wanted to know the effectiveness of the teaching strategy used to decrease Stacy's disruptiveness in class. Two months ago, an observer counted that Stacy engaged in shouting 30 times during a 15-minute period. To obtain a rate of occurrence we divide the number of occurrences of the behavior by the length of time observed. The calculation can be done as follows:

$$\frac{N}{T} = \text{Rate of occurrences}$$

where N = the number of occurrences of the behavior

T = the length of time of the observation

$$\frac{30 \text{ occurrences}}{15 \text{ minutes}} = 2 \text{ occurrences of shouting per minute}$$

In a recent observation, Stacy engaged in shouting 15 times during a 10-minute observation. What is the rate of occurrence? Would you say that there has been an improvement in Stacy's behavior? The answer is found at the end of this chapter in the Extending Learning section.

Event recording has several advantages (Beaty, 1994; Sattler, 1988):

1. The behavior or event is kept intact, thus facilitating analysis.
2. Behaviors that occur infrequently can be monitored.
3. Changes in behavior over a period of time can be recorded.

Despite the advantages, event recording also has several disadvantages (Beaty, 1994; Sattler, 1988):

1. Because the event is taken out of context, it may be difficult to analyze events that preceded the behavior.

Student: Tia Blackwell

Date: Week of September 5 to September 16

Assessment Question: Are mainstream environments providing opportunities for Tia to communicate with her peers?

Behavior: Communication. (Verbal communication)

Observer: T. Morrill, personal aide.

Schedule	Time	9/5	9/6	9/7	9/8	9/9	9/12	9/13	9/14	9/15	9/16
*Homeroom	7:30–7:45	0	0	0	1	1	0	2	0	1	0
*Art/music rotation	7:50–9:00	1	0	0	0	1	1	0	0	1	2
Functional life skills	9:10–10:20	3	0	1	2	1	0	1	3	2	0
*Physical education	10:30–11:40	2	1	3	1	2	3	3	0	2	3
*Cafeteria/lunch	11:50–12:20	0	0	1	2	1	0	2	2	1	1
Vocational training	12:30–1:50	2	0	1	2	3	1	1	3	2	2
Leisure	2:00–2:20	1	0	0	1	1	1	2	1	2	2
Prepare for departure/Bus	2:30–2:45	1	1	2	3	2	0	3	2	3	3

*Mainstream settings

FIGURE 5.4
Observations of Tia's Communication with Peers (Event Recording)

2. Patterns of behavior may not be detected.
3. Behaviors that are not easily defined cannot be recorded.
4. Reliability between observers is difficult to establish.
5. Unless the length of the observation periods across the sessions is constant, it is difficult to make generalizations.

Duration Recording

Duration recording is a measure of the length of time a specific event or behavior persists. For example, in developing instructional goals, the teacher wants to know how long a tantrum lasts or how long a student works independently. Duration recording is used when it is important to know the length of time the behavior or event lasted rather than whether it occurred.

The duration of a behavior or event can be hard to measure; because of the difficulties involved with this method, it should be used only when information about duration is essential. Before the observer begins duration recording, precise definitions for the beginning and ending of the behaviors must be specified. For example, the definition of when independent play begins could be when the child begins to look at the object, when the child approaches the object, or when the child actually picks up the object. Once the observer has determined how to define the beginning and ending of a behavior or event, a stopwatch can be used to time the length of the event.

Besides recording the duration of a behavior or event, there are two other methods of analyzing the data. The observer can determine the percentage of time a behavior or event occurs or calculate the average length of the behavior or event (Sattler, 1988). An observer may want to know the percent of time that the behavior or event occurs. This is known as the percentage duration rate.

To calculate the percentage duration rate, or the percent of time Ian worked independently, the observer divides the total duration of the behavior or event by the total time of the observation and multiplies this answer by 100 to obtain a percentage.

$$\frac{d}{t} \times 100$$

where d = the total duration of the behavior or event

t = the total length of the observation period

For example, in planning Ian's program, the IEP team is interested in determining his ability to work independently. The observer, using a stopwatch, watches Ian for a 30-minute interval, and records the information (Figure 5.5). The observer records that Ian worked independently during two time periods, of 8 minutes and 4 minutes for a total duration of 12 minutes.

To calculate the percent of time Ian worked independently during this time period, the numbers are inserted into the formula:

$$\frac{12}{30} \times 100 = 40\% \text{ of the observation period}$$

Intensity Recording

Intensity recording is a measure of the degree of a behavior. Since the degrees are usually defined as high, medium, or low, the observer's judgment can be very subjective and unreliable. Before using an intensity recording, specify the ways in which the various levels are differentiated.

For example, Carlos' IEP team wanted to know if the classroom strategies for including students with and without disabilities were enabling him to generalize the skills to other set-

Date: October 12	Comments
Student: Ian B.	
Purpose: to observe Ian working independently	
Class:	
Observer:	
Time:	
10:00–10:08	works independently
10:08	asks for help in reading paragraph
10:15	returns to seat
10:16	drops pencil, gets up to sharpen pencil
10:20	returns to seat
10:22	starts working
10:23–10:27	works independently
10:28–10:30	glances around room

FIGURE 5.5
A Duration Recording

tings. The team asked the special education teacher to observe Carlos' behavior on the playground during informal play and games. The teacher decided not to use event recording because the information needed (level of involvement) went beyond whether or not Carlos participated in outdoor games with students without disabilities. The teacher defined the degrees of involvement in the following ways:

High involvement: The target student participated fully in the activity and showed great interest through interactions with other students, body language, and general overall affect.

Medium involvement: The target student joined the other students in the activity but showed little interest in the progression of the activity, either by lack of interactions or affect.

Low involvement: The target student primarily watched the other students, occasionally shouting words of encouragement or added comments to the activity.

No involvement: The target student ignored the activity.

Using these descriptors, the teacher was able to complete an accurate, reliable recording.

Latency Recording

Latency recording is a measure of the amount of time between a behavior or event (or request to begin the behavior) and the beginning of the prespecified or target behavior. For example, suppose we wanted to know the length of time that elapsed between the moment Darcy was encouraged to use a switch to select an activity and when she depressed the switch. Using a stopwatch, the observer can determine the amount of time that elapses between the initiation of the request and when Darcy begins the requested behavior. In a variation of latency recording, instead of recording the time it takes to begin the requested behavior, the observer records the time between the initial request and the completion of the behavior (Alessi and Kaye, 1983).

Latency recording can be difficult to measure (Alessi and Kaye, 1983). The observer must carefully define the stimulus behavior (the behavior that actually signals the request to initiate behavior), the beginning of the target behavior, and the end of the target behavior.

Interval Recording

Interval recording is an observational method that involves the recording of specific events or behaviors during a prespecified time interval. Interval recording is effective when behaviors can be easily seen and occur frequently.

The period of observation is divided into equal time segments, and in each time slot the observer records the presence or absence of the behavior. Generally, the length of the time interval ranges from 5 seconds to 30 seconds. During each interval the observer records whether the behavior has occurred. The observer proceeds from one interval to the next until the observation period is finished.

An easy way to set up interval recording is to indicate time intervals on graph paper. For example, intervals of 30 seconds each can be drawn on graph paper using a ruler. If the observer will be watching for 10 minutes, there will be twenty 30-second intervals; for a 20-minute observation period, there will be forty 30-second intervals (Alessi and Kaye, 1983).

Figure 5.6 illustrates a combination of interval recording and event recording. If the behavior occurs during an interval, the letter *X* is marked. If the behavior does not occur, the letter *O* is written. The observer proceeds from one 30-second interval to the next, until the observation period is completed (Alessi and Kaye, 1983).

Establishing a Recording Interval

Sometimes it is difficult for the observer to continue to observe while recording. Proceeding from one interval to the next can be especially demanding when the observation interval is very brief, the behavior to be observed is complex, or the observer is recording the behaviors of a number of students. To help alleviate this problem, the observer can establish a recording interval. With this technique, the student is observed for a time interval, such as 5 seconds, and then the observer records the data during the next time interval, which could be 2 sec-

Example of event record with one-minute intervals. Top part shows event data for throwing behaviors counted within each interval for two children, R and C. Bottom part shows same data as scored by interval-only method. By comparison one can see that interval scoring is not as sensitive to the dynamics of the high rate of behavior as is the event within interval record. With the event (top) record one can see a sudden increase in rate of throwing after minute 9; the interval record is insensitive to this change. Likewise, the discrepancy between the two children is greater as measured by the actual rate (event) measure, and under-estimated by the interval (bottom) measure.

SOURCE: Adapted from Alessi and Kaye (1983).

BEHAVIORS	Total	Ch.	1	2	3	4	5	6	7	8	9	10	11	12	13	14	15
1. Objects thrown	30	R	1	3	1	1	2	2	1	1	1	3	3	3	2	3	3
by event	9	C	0	0	0	0	0	0	3	0	0	0	3	0	2	0	1
record		T															
		R															
		C															
		T															
2. Objects thrown	15	R	X	X	X	X	X	X	X	X	X	X	X	X	X	X	X
by interval	4	C	0	0	0	0	0	0	X	0	0	0	X	0	X	0	X
record		T															

FIGURE 5.6

Event and Interval Recording

Source: Cohen, Libby G., and Loraine J. Spenciner (1994). *Assessment of Young Children.* White Plains, N.Y.: Longman Publishers. Reprinted with permission.

onds. The observer then proceeds from one interval to the next, observing, recording, observing, and so on. This type of recording can be helpful in comparing the behavior of several students (Figure 5.7).

Category Recording

Category recording is a system of recording behavior in discrete groupings. Figure 5.8 shows two different observation instruments that use category recording. Category recording can be as simple as two categories (e.g., on-task and off-task) or complex enough to contain many categories (e.g., compliant, requests assistance, resists help, verbalizes need for assistance). As with other types of observations,

the behaviors must be discrete, be carefully defined, and have an observable beginning and end.

Rating Scales

Rating scales can help answer questions about the learning environment or about one or more students. Environmental rating scales are used to measure the degree to which the setting meets a certain criterion. These rating scales assist team members in problem solving around issues of a particular learning environment or of the teaching strategies currently in place. Environmental rating scales can be helpful when conducting program planning and when identifying the environment that will meet the student's needs.

Student	o	r	o	r	o	r	o	r	o	r	o	r	o	r	o	r	o	r	o	r	o	r	o	r	o	r	o	r
Anna																												
Maria																												
Nan																												

o = observe
r = record

FIGURE 5.7

Comparison of On-Task Behavior (Recording Interval Form)

Two-category instrument

	1	2	3	4	5	6	7	8
On-task	X				X	X	X	
Off-task		X	X	X				X

Observation period

Four-category instrument

	1	2	3	4	5	6	7	8
Uses words to express needs	X		X				X	X
Raises hand to signal teacher for help	X							X
Regards speaker		X	X	X		X		X
Complies with requests			X				X	

Observation period

FIGURE 5.8

Category Reporting

Student rating scales measure the degree to which a student exhibits a prespecified behavior. These scales are useful when they are combined with other types of assessment, such as with data obtained from interval recording, event recording, and the results of standardized testing. Rating scales can help to evaluate the quality of the behavior of one student or many students.

While rating scales can be useful, they have been criticized as being impressionistic, lacking interrater reliability, and being affected by the subjectivity of the observer (Sattler, 1988). Reliability is increased if descriptors are

SNAPSHOT

Maria

Maria's teacher, Mr. Ramsdell, feels that she is hyperactive and is unable to attend in the classroom. He discusses his concerns with the special education teacher, who team teaches with him several mornings a week. They decide to plan and conduct several observations of Maria and two other students who were selected because Mr. Ramsdell identified them as typical students. The purpose of the observation is to provide a brief picture of Maria's behavior compared to other students in her classroom and to answer questions regarding her hyperactivity. The teachers decided that because the observation would focus on several students, a recording interval form (Figure 5.7) should be used to allow the observer time to record multiple data.

Behavior	1	2	3	4
Student participates in small group activity	Student regards others who are talking	Student regards others who are talking and participates in group discussion	Student uses materials to assist in group activity and all of #2	Student evaluates own role in group activity and all of #3
Student shows respect for personal boundaries.	At school, student keeps hands to self.	At school, student maintains personal space when speaking with others and keeps hands to self.	Student identifies behavior appropriate to the environmental setting (school, home, community) and all of #2.	Student displays behavior appropriate to the setting (school, home, community).

FIGURE 5.9

An Example of Descriptors in a Rating Scale

added to the numerical ratings of these scales (Figure 5.9). Descriptors provide detailed information regarding each of the levels of the rating scale.

Checklists

Checklists are similar to rating scales and are used in observing the environment or in observing one or more students. While rating scales help to evaluate the degree or frequency of an item or a behavior, checklists usually require a simple yes or no response. A checklist is a list of characteristics or behaviors arranged in a consistent manner that allows the evaluator to check the presence or absence of the characteristic or behavior.

Checklists can be used to assess behaviors as well as products of one or more students. Some checklists provide space for comments or descriptions. Checklists are fairly easy to develop. The following guidelines can be used when developing checklists (Beaty, 1994; Gronlund and Linn, 1990):

1. Checklist items should be brief, yet detailed and easily understood.

2. Parallel word construction must be used. That is, the word order, subject, and verb tense should be the same for all items.
3. The items are nonjudgmental.
4. The checklist should stress positive behavior. Emphasis is placed on what the student *can* do as opposed to what the student cannot do.
5. Do not repeat items in different parts of the checklist.
6. The items should be representative of students' behavior.
7. Arrange the items in the order in which they are expected to appear.
8. A procedure must be provided for indicating each behavior as it occurs (e.g., check mark, yes-no, plus or minus sign).

Checklists, like rating scales, have greater utility when they are combined with other assessment approaches. Checklists can supplement the information obtained from observations, can help to evaluate a student's behavior, and can be used with one or more students. They have been criticized for lacking interrater reliability and for being affected by the subjectivity of the rater. In addition, they may miss behaviors, are limited to the presence or absence of behaviors, and do not provide information about the quality of the behavior (Beaty, 1994).

OBSERVING THE CLASSROOM ENVIRONMENT

How should I deal with Katya's behavioral outbursts? What can I do to help Timmy, a student with disabilities, feel a part of our classroom? How can we assist Boyanna in becoming more independent? The interaction of student learning and behavior is complex. The classroom environment can affect learning and behavior adversely, or the environment can be structured to enhance positive conduct and self-esteem. Teachers need to address environmental contexts as well as the needs of the individual student in a comprehensive assessment.

Three aspects of the classroom environment affect the student's learning and behavior: the physical environment, the learning or instructional environment, and the social environment. Rating scales and checklists are the most common ways of gathering information about the classroom environment. In the following sections, we will examine both teacher-constructed tools and commercial instruments for observing these three aspects of the classroom environment.

Physical Environment

The physical environment consists of seating arrangements, lighting, noise level, distractions, temperature, overall atmosphere, and general layout of the classroom. Some of the areas to consider in planning an observation of the physical environment include:

1. *Seating*
   - positioning
     Do the height and size of the chair give the student proper support?

     Are the student's feet supported (either resting flat on the floor or supported by a footrest)?

     Is the student seated in close proximity to other students?

     Does the student's position allow full view of the board, teacher, and other students?

     Does the student's position readily allow communication with the teacher and other students?
2. *Lighting*
   - lighting intensity
     Is the degree of lighting appropriate?

     Is the board or screen free from glare that might make reading difficult?
   - type of lighting
     Is fluorescent lighting used?

     Is natural light available?

3. *Noise*
   - minimum noise level

     Is the noise level of student work groups appropriate?

4. *Distractions*
   - visual

     Does the room have displays that are visually distracting?

   - sound

     Is there noise distraction (such as a clock ticking or a radiator pinging)?

   - events and activities

     Are there activities in the room that are distracting to the student?

5. *Temperature*

   Is the temperature level of the classroom comfortable?

6. *Overall atmosphere*

   Is the classroom atmosphere warm and accepting?

   Does the student appear to be comfortable?

7. *General layout*
   - the layout of the room and the type and placement of furniture, equipment, and materials

     Are all areas of the classroom accessible to the student?

     Are classroom materials accessible to the student?

   - the amount and type of space

     Is there enough space to meet the student's needs?

     Is there an accessible place to store adapted materials and equipment?

     Can the student easily move between areas of the room?

The amount of physical space and how it is arranged affects student functioning. For example, desks that are grouped in sets of three or four encourage students to discuss and share ideas. The placement of furniture, equipment, and materials is critical for students with disabilities. Furniture and adaptive equipment need to maximize the student's potential for independent participation. The availability of accessible space allows students with physical disabilities full classroom access. Differences in texture or color of carpet between centers enable students who are blind or have multiple disabilities to increase orientation and independent travel (mobility) skills. An organized environment helps students learn appropriate storage of materials. Accessible storage of materials assists students with disabilities in locating and using materials independently.

Figure 5.10 illustrates a teacher-made checklist for observing the physical environment. Information collected about the physical layout of this kindergarten classroom proved very helpful. The drawing helped the teaching team to think about the classroom layout and how they might improve learning opportunities. The teachers decided to try moving the science and mathematics center closer to the block area to allow children to use the blocks in various mathematics and science activities. The teachers also discussed how the location of adjacent areas contributed to difficulties that they had experienced during circle time. They decided to move the circle area away from the block center, which was distracting to Terry and Chris. They changed the center of the room to accommodate space for circle activities and added individual carpet squares to the area to help children understand individual space and reduce the likelihood of disruptive behavior. Figure 5.11 represents the rearranged environment.

An environmental rating scale is helpful to teachers in that it identifies the important components in a quality program. The rating scale provides a structured way of recording observations; items are organized in specific categories. While a checklist can indicate whether or not an item is present, a rating scale provides a judgment on the degree of an item. Teachers may use rating scales to identify the

Scaled drawing of classroom, including student seating arrangement.
Furniture and equipment that cannot be moved are underlined.

	Yes	No
Are all areas of the classroom large enough to be accessible?	_____	_____
Can the student with disabilities see and participate in classroom activities? (Appropriate positioning)	_____	_____
Is the student with disabilities positioned so that other students and teachers may readily interact with the student?	_____	_____
Does the classroom have sufficient computer(s) for student use?	_____	_____
Is the lighting appropriate?	_____	_____
Does the classroom have natural lighting available?	_____	_____
Is the noise level minimal?	_____	_____
Is the temperature comfortable?	_____	_____
Does the room provide appropriate stimulation? (Neither over- nor understimulation)	_____	_____
Does the classroom have a minimum of interruptions?	_____	_____

FIGURE 5.10

Kindergarten Teacher–Made Drawing and Checklist for Observing the Physical Environment

areas of strength in the classroom as well as the areas that need improvement.

Commercial Rating Scales

Commercial rating scales provide teachers with an identified list of items by which to measure the environment. Usually these scales have been standardized, and information concerning their reliability and validity is described in the examiner's manual. One example of a commercial environmental rating scale for preschool and developmental early education programs in public school is described in the following section.

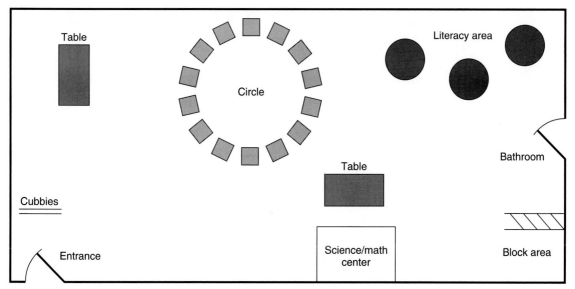

Scaled drawing of classroom, including student seating arrangement.
Furniture and equipment that cannot be moved are underlined.

FIGURE 5.11

Rearranged Physical Environment

Early Childhood Environment Rating Scale (ECERS)

The Early Childhood Environment Rating Scale (ECERS) (Harms and Clifford, 1980) is designed to be used in a variety of settings, including Head Start programs, parent cooperative preschools, private preschools, playgroups, and kindergarten programs. The purpose of the scale is to examine the quality of the environment currently being provided in a center or school and to offer a background for planning improvements.

Administration

This scale should be used by a trained observer. Each of the 37 items is rated according to a 7-point **Likert scale.** On Likert scales, the lowest rating (generally 1) indicates, for example, that the item never occurs, and the highest rating (in this case, 5) indicates that the item always occurs. A small amount of space after each item allows the observer to record additional information.

Scores

Each item includes descriptions of the possible numeric ratings. Information about the items is then tallied for a subtotal of each category. This instrument includes a profile sheet on which each category subtotal is recorded. The profile allows the user to quickly identify areas, or subcategories, of strength and weakness, as seen in Figure 5.12.

Standardization

The final version of the *ECERS* was field-tested in 25 classrooms in 17 child care centers in St. Louis. Additional information, including details about the environments in which this rating scale was used, would be helpful.

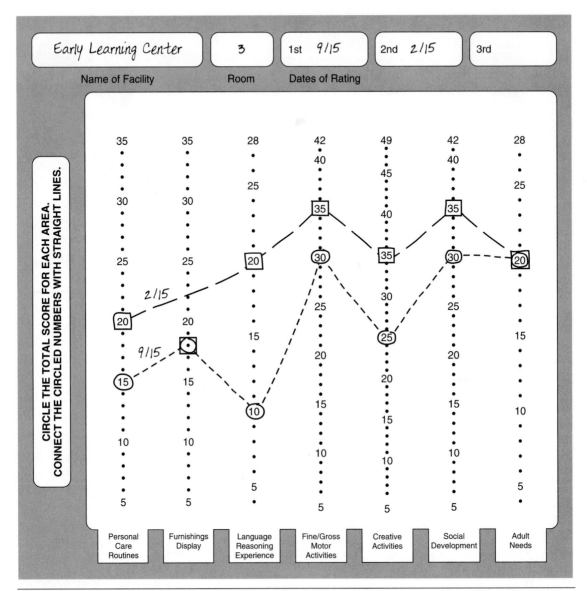

FIGURE 5.12

Early Childhood Environmental Rating Scale

Source: From *Early Childhood Environment Rating Scale* by Thelma Harms and Richard M. Clifford. Reprinted by permission of the publisher. (New York: Teachers College Press. © 1980 by Thelma Harms and Richard M. Clifford. All rights reserved), p. 18(d).

Reliability and Validity

The manual reports three measures of reliability: interrater reliability by item, interrater reliability by classroom, and internal consistency. Internal consistency data indicate problems with a few of the subscales. The authors note that although the subscales can be useful in providing information about the environment, they should not be used for evaluation purposes. Total scale scores, however, are adequate (Harms and Clifford, 1980, p. 39). Validity is adequate.

Summary

The Early Childhood Environment Rating Scale can be used in a variety of programs that serve young children birth through age 6. The information provided in describing each of the items is very helpful for several steps of the assessment process, including planning and evaluating the program. This scale is also very useful in understanding the quality of the physical environment. Given the philosophical differences among early childhood programs, the potential user should examine this scale to ensure that it will be valid for a given program.

BOX 5.1

EARLY CHILDHOOD ENVIRONMENT RATING SCALE

Publication Date: 1980
Purposes: Useful in assessing early childhood program environments
Age/Grade Levels: Most appropriate for preschool programs; some aspects may be helpful to primary grades.
Time to Administer: Need to observe greeting and departure activities; 10–15 minutes for other information.
Technical Adequacy: Adequate.
Suggested Use: Valuable tool to assist teachers in designing a classroom environment that supports children's development.

Learning Environment

What are the expectations of the classroom? How can the classroom be adapted to accommodate the student's learning needs? The learning or instructional environment consists of the teaching strategies that the teacher uses and the materials that are available for student use. Observing the learning environment involves examining the instructional materials as well as the methods of instruction. Some of the areas to consider in planning an observation of the learning environment include:

1. *Materials*
   - variety
     Do students have access to a variety of materials?
   - format
     Is the format of the materials appropriate?

2. *Manipulatives*
   Are manipulatives available?
   Are manipulatives appropriate?

3. *Learning Activities*
   - instructional methods
     Does the teacher use a variety of instructional methods?
   - opportunities to make choices
     Does the classroom teacher provide students opportunities to make choices during learning activities?
   - opportunities to share ideas
     Are student comments and questions respected and encouraged?

4. *Instructional Demands*
   - clear instructions for completing the assignments
     Does the teacher provide clear instructions and check for student understanding before students begin assignments?
   - assignments that are appropriate in difficulty and in length
     Are students assigned work that is appropriate in difficulty and length?

- assignments that are relevant to the students

  Do students perceive that the work is useful?

  Can students use a variety of materials?

5. *Modifications*
   - changes in furniture, equipment, or materials

     Is there easy and convenient access to furniture and equipment?

     Can students use the materials or is there a need for modification?

6. *Grouping*
   - grouping of students

     Do students complete some work independently?

     Can students work with a peer?

     Do students have opportunities to work cooperatively with others?

7. *Instruction*
   - adjustments

     Are the instructional strategies appropriate or is there a need for revision?

     Is there a variety of instructional methods in use?

   - pace of instruction

     Is the pace of instructional delivery appropriate?

   - adequate levels of assistance

     Does the teacher (or teaching assistant) provide prompts and other types of assistance on an as-needed basis to students?

     Is assistance faded as soon as possible?

8. *Expectations*
   - demands placed on students

     Are the teacher's expectations appropriate?

9. *Student Involvement*
   - teacher support

     Does the teacher encourage student involvement?

Is the student actively involved in learning activities?

Does the student participate in classroom discussions?

- peer support

  Do other students interact with the student?

  Does the student interact with other students?

10. *Assessment*
    - tools

      Is there a variety of assessment tools used in assessing student instructional needs and progress?

    - format

      If appropriate, are alternative formats used?

    - feedback

      Are students given feedback and suggestions for improvement?

11. *Curriculum*
    - reform standards

      Does the curriculum reflect recent reform standards and contemporary views?

12. *Schedule*
    - predictability of the daily schedule

      Does the classroom teacher follow a regular schedule?

      Is the schedule posted for students to see?

      Is there a minimum of interruptions?

13. *Transitions*
    - preparation and follow-through

      Does the teacher prepare students for the transition from one subject activity to another?

      Does the teacher provide time for students to transition?

Teacher expectations, teaching methods, and student requirements may be very different from one classroom to the next. These differences vary from the materials and equipment that are available to assist students in

SNAPSHOT

Stoney Brook Elementary and Lincoln High
<u>Learning Environments</u>

Stoney Brook Elementary School has three fourth-grade classrooms. The school has adopted a literacy curriculum, and all fourth graders must demonstrate competency in researching and writing a paper about a topic of their interest. The fourth-grade teachers approach the teaching of skills in researching information in different ways. In one classroom, the teacher invites an author to come in and talk with students. The author shares resource materials and shows how his or her information was researched. The author's enthusiasm for writing sparks the children's interest. In a second classroom, the teacher makes arrangements to take the students to the library, where the school librarian gives them a tour of the library's resources and discusses ways to find information in the on-line catalogue. Later, the children will be divided into small work groups and

return to the library to use the materials. In the third classroom, the children already use the computer daily to search and download information from the Internet. Their teacher will encourage them to use their skills independently in locating information for their individual papers.

The teachers in the English and history classes at Lincoln High have different teaching styles. The English classroom has several computers available for student writing and editing, including a word processing program with a word prediction feature. The teacher uses individual conferences and small-group peer editing. Much of the work is individualized. Next door in the history class, the teacher lectures and requires the students to take notes. The teacher assesses student learning by short-answer tests that cover the textbook and classroom lectures.

their work to teaching methods that may require different skills from the students. The snapshot above describes these various learning environments.

These examples at Stoney Brook Elementary and Lincoln High illustrate the variety of teaching methods, materials, and demands that may be placed on students in the same grade. Students with disabilities at Stoney Brook or Lincoln High may experience difficulties in one or more of these classrooms.

The Instructional Environment System-II (TIES-II)

The Instructional Environment System-II (TIES-II) (Ysseldyke and Christenson, 1993) is a

comprehensive tool for assessing the environment and designing interventions to address concerns about an individual student. Information from *TIES-II* is useful in a prereferral intervention, where the student is helped indirectly by modifying the learning environment. Other purposes for this scale include planning the program and monitoring individual progress.

TIES-II consists of 12 components that involve not only the physical environment but the learning and social environments as well. These components include:

- instructional match
- teacher expectations
- classroom environment

INSTRUCTIONAL PLANNING

- Instructional Match
- Teacher Expectations

How are the student's performance and behavior affected by instructional planning?

_____

_____

_____

_____

_____

INSTRUCTIONAL MANAGEMENT

- Classroom Environment

How are the student's performance and behavior affected by instructional management?

_____

_____

_____

_____

_____

INSTRUCTIONAL DELIVERY

- Instructional Presentation
- Cognitive Emphasis
- Motivational Strategies
- Relevant Practice
- Informed Feedback

How is the student's performance and behavior affected by instructional delivery?

_____

_____

_____

_____

_____

INSTRUCTIONAL MONITORING AND EVALUATION

- Academic Engaged Time
- Adaptive Instruction
- Progress Evaluation
- Student Understanding

How are the student's performance and behavior affected by instructional monitoring and evaluation?

_____

_____

_____

_____

_____

FIGURE 5.13

TIES-II Observation Record

Source: Reprinted with permission from Ysseldyke, J. and S. Christenson (1993). _The Instructional Environment System-II: A System to Identify a Student's Instructional Needs._ Longmont, Colo.: Sopris West. All rights reserved.

- instructional presentation
- cognitive emphasis
- motivational strategies
- relevant practice
- informed feedback
- academic engaged time
- adaptive instruction
- progress evaluation
- student understanding

Administration

TIES-II involves the gathering of information from five sources: a structured classroom observation, a student interview, a classroom teacher interview, a parent interview in order to understand the student's support for instructional needs in the home, and an instructional needs checklist. *TIES-II* includes an intervention planning form to assist team members in developing intervention strategies that include both classroom and home support.

Scores

After completing a classroom observation and student and teacher interviews, the examiner synthesizes the information and rates the extent to which each of the 12 components is present in the student's instructional environment, indicated by the terms *strongly agree, agree, disagree,* and *strongly disagree*. The results are then used to make decisions regarding intervention recommendations. Suggestions for improving instructional environments that have received low scores are provided in the manual. Figure 5.13 illustrates a section of the classroom observation form.

Standardization

TIES-II is a structured system that gathers qualitative information. It is not a norm-referenced instrument.

Reliability and Validity

Interrater reliability and content validity are adequate.

BOX 5.2

INSTRUCTIONAL ENVIRONMENT SYSTEM-II (TIES-II)

Publication Date: 1993

Purposes: Used to assess various aspects of the classroom environment and to identify interventions that may help individual students.

Age/Grade Levels: K–12. Some areas may not be appropriate in preschool or primary settings.

Time to Administer: Not stated.

Technical Adequacy: Interrater reliability and content validity are very good.

Suggested Use: A valuable instrument for collecting information about the physical, learning, and social environments in order to plan interventions for students who are having difficulties in being successful.

Summary

TIES-II measures 12 different aspects of the student's environment. These 12 constructs are fully defined, with many descriptors included for each component. This information on factors that are important in the teaching and learning process is very helpful as stand-alone information for the beginning as well as the experienced teacher.

Data are gathered through structured observations and interviews with the teacher, parent, and student. Because the examiner is required to use several sources of information in rating the environment, the examiner must be both very familiar with the constructs and skilled in synthesizing information.

Questionnaires

Questionnaires consist of a set of questions designed to gather information. Fuchs, Fernstrom, Scott, Fuchs, and Vandermeer (1994)

■ CLASSROOM RULES

	SPECIAL EDUCATION	REGULAR EDUCATION
1. During class are there important rules? (Yes or No)	_____	_____
2. If yes, how are they communicated? (for example, written or oral)	_____	_____
3. If class rules are *not* posted, what are they?	_____	_____
	_____	_____
	_____	_____
	_____	_____
4. If a rule is broken, what happens? What is the typical consequence?	_____	_____
5. Who enforces the rules? (teacher, aide, students)	_____	_____

■ TEACHER BEHAVIOR

	SPECIAL EDUCATION	REGULAR EDUCATION
1. a. Is homework assigned? (Yes or No)	_____	_____
b. If so, indicate approximate amount (minutes) of homework, and	_____	_____
c. the frequency with which it is given.		

*Directions for #2 - #4: Using a 3-point scale (1=**Often**, 2=**Sometimes**, 3=**Never**), rate each item according to frequency of occurrence in class. Place an asterisk (*) in the righthand margin to indicate important differences between the special and regular education classrooms.*

	SPECIAL ED	REGULAR ED			SPECIAL ED	REGULAR ED
2. Assignments in Class			b. Classroom punishment includes:			
a. Students are given assignments:			• time out		____	____
• that are the same for all			• loss of activity-related			
• that differ in amount or type	____	____	privileges (example, loss of free time)		____	____
• to complete in school			• teacher ignoring		____	____
at a specified time	____	____	• reprimands		____	____
• that, if unfinished in school, are			• poorer grade, loss of star, etc.		____	____
assigned as homework	____	____	• extra work		____	____
b. Evaluation of assignment:			• staying after school		____	____
• teacher evaluation	____	____	• physical punishment			
• student self-evaluation	____	____	(example, paddling)		____	____
• peer evaluation	____	____	5. To what extent do each of the following			
3. Tests			contribute to an overall grade? *Estimate*			
a. Tests are			*the percentage for each so that the*			
• presented orally	____	____	*total sums to 100%.*			
• copied from board	____	____	• homework		____	____
• timed	____	____	• daily work		____	____
• based on study guides given			• tests		____	____
to students prior to test	____	____	• class participation		____	____
• administered by resource teacher	____	____	6. Please list skills that have been taught			
b. Grades are:			since the beginning of the school year			
• percentages (example, 75%)	____	____	(Regular Education Teacher Only):			
• letter grades (example, B+)	____	____	Skill		Will Reteach Later?	
• both	____	____			(Yes or No)	
4. Academic/Social Rewards						
a. Classroom rewards or			_____		_____	
reinforcement include:						
• material rewards (example, stars)	____	____				

FIGURE 5.14

Classroom Ecological Inventory

Source: From the Classroom Ecological Inventory by D. Fuchs, P. Fernstrom, S. Scott, L. Fuchs, and L. Vandermeer. *Teaching Exceptional Children* 26(3), 11–15. Copyright 1994 by The Council for Exceptional Children. Reprinted with permission.

describe the *Classroom Ecological Inventory* (Figure 5.14), a questionnaire that special and regular education teachers can use to identify areas that increase integration efforts for students with disabilities.

This inventory and questionnaires like it are helpful to teachers in gathering information about teaching methods and materials.

Questionnaires are helpful to special educators who are consulting with regular education teachers. A discussion with another colleague centered around a questionnaire helps to provide structure to the conference. Using standard questions can help to keep the conversation more neutral. When sharing the form with the teacher, the observer may say, "Here are some items that one author feels are important. Let's look them over and see if they give us some ideas." Working with classroom teachers regarding the learning environment requires particular sensitivity to collaborative teamwork. In the latter part of this chapter, we discuss conferring with other professionals in more detail.

Social Environment

The social environment consists of the general classroom atmosphere as well as the relationships among students and between students and teachers. The overall atmosphere or classroom climate is important for student success. In planning and implementing observations of the social environment, educators must take care to build bridges with colleagues. Diplomacy and good interpersonal skills are critical for success. Some of the areas to consider when planning an observation of the social environment include:

1. *Teacher–student interactions*
   - respect for oneself and others

     Are all students valued for themselves?

     Does the teacher expect students to respect others?

   - supportive

     Are interactions warm and friendly?

   - interactions

     Does the teacher know how to communicate with students with disabilities?

     Does the teacher encourage students to interact appropriately with the teacher?

2. *Distractions*

   Are distractions kept to a minimum?

3. *Behavioral interventions*
   - positive behavioral supports

     Does the teacher use positive teaching strategies in helping students learn appropriate behavioral expectations?

   - behavior management

     Are behavior management strategies effective?

     Are expectations of behavior posted?

4. *Peer interactions*
   - student-to-student interactions

     Do students know how to communicate with students with disabilities?

     Do students interact appropriately with each other?

     Are students courteous, respectful, and supportive of learning?

5. *General atmosphere*
   - positive classroom climate

     Does the teacher have high expectations for all students?

     Is there an atmosphere of enthusiasm and support for students?

     Does the student appear to be comfortable in the social environment?

Figure 5.15 illustrates a teacher-developed checklist to assist in observing the learning and social environments of the regular classroom.

OBSERVING THE STUDENT

How independently is Sheila functioning? Does Jesse communicate with peers? Does Andre socialize with others? How prevalent is Ennio's

Classroom:	Check	Suggested modification
Does the teacher provide opportunities for making choices?		
Does the teacher require students to take notes?		
Does the teacher require students to copy material from the board?		
Does the teacher highlight important information on the board?		
Does the teacher expect students to work independently?		
Is the student required to respond to information orally?		
Is the student required to respond to information in writing?		
Is the student seated near distractions, such as the classroom door?		
Is the student required to memorize material?		

FIGURE 5.15

Teacher-Designed Checklist for Observing the Learning Environment of Middle and Secondary Students

Adapted from Turnbull, Turnbull, Shank, and Leal, 1995, p. 159.

TABLE 5.2   Questions and Methods of Observation

Assessment question	Recording methods
How independently is the student functioning?	Anecdotal record Latency recording Category recording Rating scale Checklist
How does the student communicate with peers?	Anecdotal record Running record Duration recording Rating scale Checklist
Does the student socialize with students without disabilities in a nonstructured setting?	Running record Event recording Interval recording Category recording

behavior? Conducting observations of a student is one of the best methods for obtaining specific information regarding a student's behavior (Turnbull, Turnbull, Shank, and Leal, 1995). Observers use a variety of recording methods in collecting information about assessment questions (Table 5.2).

For the observer who is sensitive and responsive to diversity, these observations create a picture of the uniqueness of the student. Some of the areas to consider in planning an observation include:

1. *Work habits*
   - time

     How long does it take the student to get started?

     How long is the student able to stay on task?
   - levels of assistance needed

     What can the student do independently?

     How frequently does the student need prompting?

     What types of prompts are helpful (physical, verbal, gestural)?
   - reinforcements used

     What types of reinforcement are effective?

     How does the student react to the reinforcement?

2. *Interactions with others*
   - other students

     Does the student have a variety of ways to communicate?

     Do other students communicate with the student?

     Does the student socialize with other students?
   - teacher

     Does the student have a variety of ways to communicate?

     Can the teacher communicate with the student?

Is the student given opportunities to demonstrate competence?

3. *Facial expression and affect*

   Does the student make eye contact with others?

   Does the student have appropriate affect?

4. *Body movements*

   Does the student have independent mobility skills?

   Is the quality of gross and fine motor responses adequate (not jerky)?

5. *Adaptive skills*

   Can the student eat independently?

   Does the student use appropriate grooming skills?

   Does the student dress in an age-appropriate manner?

6. *Participation in play and games*

   Does the student participate in unorganized play (free time, recess)?

   Does the student understand the rules of the game?

   Does the student play cooperatively?

Steps in Planning and Conducting Student Observations

Conducting observations is more than just watching the student and writing down impressions of what you have seen. An observation is a systematic procedure that involves informed attention and focused recording of what you witness. There are several steps to be completed in planning and conducting observations.

1. First, identify the purpose of the observations. What information is needed?

Rebecca is a 17-year-old student who attends the Life Skills Program at Central High School. Two of her IEP goals focus on increasing independent functioning and increasing prosocial behavior skills. The purpose of the observation is to collect information regarding the IEP goals in preparation for the annual review.

2. Second, define the behavior in terms that are observable and measurable.

Independent functioning is defined as an ability to complete a task without prompting.

The second goal of increasing prosocial skills was discussed in more detail by the IEP Team. One of the impediments to prosocial skills has been Rebecca's angry outbursts. An observer was asked to note Rebecca's angry outbursts during the lunch period and in homeroom. What is meant by "angry outbursts"? In planning the observation, the behavior must be defined. Angry behavior could be defined by physical and/or verbal aggression. Sometimes anger is not expressed. An individual may suppress angry feelings or show them in unexpected ways. The observer asked the teacher to give some examples of Rebecca's angry outbursts, and subsequently, they developed this definition: "screeching and screaming and hitting others." They decided that the observation should include both the verbal outbursts (screeching and screaming) as well as the physical contacts (hitting others).

Rebecca's behavior to be observed includes verbal outbursts (screeching and screaming) as well as the physical contacts (hitting others).

3. Third, identify where the observations will occur. Observations of the student may take place in any number of settings, depending on the assessment question:

- in the classroom
- in the resource room
- in the cafeteria
- on the playground
- in the community
- at home

The observations of Rebecca will be conducted in the classroom and in the cafeteria. The details of the observations can include:

- the physical setup of the cafeteria line
- the arrangement of tables
- the types of assistance from other students
- the types of assistance from teachers or cafeteria monitors
- the methods Rebecca uses to approach other students
- the initiations of other students talking to Rebecca

A direct observation such as this example may focus on the student or on the student interacting with others and involves careful recording of the target student's behavior. The recording is often completed on structured observation forms available commercially; however, teacher-developed forms may be the most useful. Several observations are conducted to ensure consistency or reliability of results.

4. Fourth, plan how the behavior will be recorded. Depending on the assessment question, student behaviors can be recorded by frequency, duration, magnitude, or latency. We discussed earlier in this chapter several ways in which various forms could be developed.

5. Finally, integrate the results with other information that has been gathered. After completing an observation, obtain feedback from the classroom teacher. You will need to know if the class time that you observed was typical or not. If there is no opportunity to talk, you may leave a brief form with the teacher that requests the following information: How typical was today's class? In what ways was it different?

SOURCES OF ERROR IN RECORDING OBSERVATIONS

Three types of errors affect the accuracy of observations: 1) errors of omission, 2) errors of commission, and 3) errors of transmission. Familiarity with these sources of error will help reduce the possibility of their occurrence.

SNAPSHOT

Observations of Jon

Jon is a 10-year-old student with autism. He has a number of self-abusive behaviors, including biting his wrists and banging his head. His teacher, concerned that the incidence of these behaviors is increasing, decided to conduct a series of classroom observations. The first observation was conducted during lunch in the cafeteria. Jon was observed as he entered the cafeteria and chose a seat at one of the tables. An-

other student sat down beside him at the table. Jon quickly opened his lunch box and began eating while the observer was momentarily distracted when two students briefly obstructed the view. Jon began to slap his head with his hand, and the behavior escalated until the teacher assistant noticed the self-abuse and went over to speak to Jon.

Errors of Omission

To leave out information that is helpful or important to understanding a student's behavior is an error of omission. Adding comments that provide a more complete picture of the observation is helpful in preventing errors of omission. Consider the above snapshot of Jon.

This observation could be recorded in terms of the number of minutes that Jon was in the cafeteria before he began the self-abusive behavior (that is, a latency recording), or the teacher could record the magnitude or degree of the behavior (intensity recording). However, these recordings would be incomplete. One important event has been omitted; namely, what happened when the student joined Jon. The question remains, "Did he affect Jon's behavior?"

Missing part of the sequence of events, even by a temporary distraction, jeopardizes the accuracy of an observation. In this case, the student who joined Jon may have sat too close or acted in a way that disturbed Jon. Perhaps Jon's abusive behavior was a communication attempt in response to the other student. Errors of omission can result from simply missing behaviors that occur.

Errors of Commission

Including information that did not actually occur is an error of commission. Errors of commission frequently occur when the observer is not able to take complete notes during the observation but must rely on memory to record the information at a later time.

Errors of Transmission

An error of transmission occurs when behaviors are recorded in an improper sequence. Since many behaviors are related and the order in which they occur is important, make precautions to guard against this type of error. Errors of transmission can be reduced by recording the time at which a particular behavior is observed or by recording the number of times that a particular behavior begins or ends.

RELIABILITY OF DIRECT OBSERVATIONS

Reliability is an important concern when discussing direct observations. Reliability is the consistency or stability of the observations.

When conducting direct observations, determining interobserver reliability is very important. Repp, Neiminen, Olinger, and Brusca (1988) discuss several factors that affect the accuracy of observers. These include reactivity, observer drift, recording procedure, location of the observer, reliability checks, observer expectancy, and the characteristics of the student.

Reactivity

Reactivity refers to the changes that individuals make in behaviors during an observation. Teachers may alter their instructions, give additional prompts, or increase the amount of feedback when they are being observed. Students may improve behavior because of the "visitor," or they put on a good "show." These changes in behavior are threats to the accuracy of an observation. The use of videotapes and audiotapes also increases reactivity.

Observer Drift

Observer drift occurs when the observer shifts away from the original objectives of the observation. Usually, the observer is not aware of this alteration. To prevent this phenomenon from occurring, the observer needs to periodically check the established purposes and criteria for conducting the observation.

Procedures

The type of recording procedure that is used can affect the accuracy of an observation. In summarizing previous research, Repp et al. (1988) found that 1) the use of partial intervals can overestimate continuous recording; 2) the use of whole intervals can underestimate the occurrence of the behavior; and 3) momentary time sampling is reliable. These authors recommend that small intervals be used but that the interval size should allow for only one response per interval.

Reliability Checks

The conduct of reliability checks can also affect the accuracy of observations. If an observer is aware that the accuracy of an observation is being monitored, the observer may change the usual methods of conducting the observation. Reliability of observations tends to increase when an observer is aware that the observations are being checked.

Predetermined Expectations

Bias can occur if the observer has a predetermined expectation about the observation. For example, if an observer knows that the student who is to be observed has been referred for aggressive behavior, the observation may be influenced by expectations of this behavior by the observer.

Student and Setting Characteristics

Certain characteristics associated with the student and the setting can influence the accuracy of an observation. The gender of the student, the complexity of the behaviors to be observed, the predictability of the student's behaviors, and the observer's familiarity with the setting can all affect accuracy.

Thus, reactivity, observer drift, recording procedure, location of the observer, reliability checks, observer expectancy, and the characteristics of the student and the setting can all affect the accuracy of observations. To minimize these threats, Repp et al. (1988) recommend that:

1. Observers be well trained.
2. Uncomplicated codes be used to record observations.
3. Observations be conducted by both male and female observers.
4. Interaction between observers be avoided.
5. Accuracy of observations be checked against a criterion.
6. Both observers and students be given a period of time in which they can adapt to each other.

7. Observations be conducted as unobtrusively as possible.
8. Permanent products (audiotapes, videotapes, student's drawings) be used, whenever possible.
9. Observations be conducted frequently and systematically.

CALCULATING INTEROBSERVER RELIABILITY

There are several ways of determining reliability of observations (Alessi and Kaye, 1983; Frick and Semmel, 1978). To calculate reliability it is important that 1) all data be collected independently, 2) at least two observers conduct observations, and 3) the observers look at the same phenomenon. If it is not possible for two observers to be present at the same time, a videotape or audiotape can be used for the second observer (Alessi and Kaye, 1983).

Event Recording

One way of determining interobserver reliability for event recording is to determine the percentage of agreements between the observers (Alessi and Kaye, 1983). The following formula can be used:

$$r = \frac{a}{a + d} \times 100$$

The number of times that the observers agreed with each other (a) is divided by the total number of times that the observers agreed (a) and disagreed (d) with each other. This number is then multiplied by 100 to give the percentage of agreements between the observers. For example, suppose two observers were using event recording to observe the number of times a student interrupted other students. The observers agreed 10 times and disagreed 4 times. Using the formula:

$$r = \frac{10}{10 + 4} \times 100$$

$$r = \frac{10}{14} \times 100$$

$$r = 71\%$$

Thus, the percentage of agreement between the observers in this example is 71%.

Duration Recording

Computing interobserver reliability for duration recording is similar to calculating interobserver reliability for event recording. The formula for duration recording is:

$$\% \ A_{dr} = \frac{t_1}{t_2} \times 100$$

where $\% \ A_{dr}$ = percentage agreement for duration recording

t_1 = time recorded by the observer with the smaller time duration

t_2 = time recorded by the observer with the larger time duration

For example, suppose two observers are recording the length of time a child plays independently. One observer records 180 seconds; the other observer records 190 seconds. Using the formula:

$$\% \ A_{dr} = \frac{180}{190} \times 100$$

$$\% \ A_{dr} = 95\%$$

In this example, there is 95% agreement between the observers.

Rating Recording

When computing agreement between two raters or observers, the following formula can be used (Sattler, 1988):

$$\% \ A_r = \frac{A_r}{A_r + D} \times 100$$

where $\% \ A_r$ = percentage agreement for rating recording

A_r = number of items for which observers agreed on the rating

D = number of items for which observers disagreed on the rating

For example, suppose two observers, using a 15-item rating scale, agree on the ratings for 12 of the 15 items. Using the formula, we have:

$$\% \ A_r = \frac{12}{12 + 3} \times 100$$

$$\% \ A_r = 80\%$$

In this example, there is 80% agreement between the two observers.

VALIDITY OF DIRECT OBSERVATIONS

The validity of observational measures is a very important concern. Validity is the extent to which an instrument measures what it is intended to measure. Validity standards depend on the observability of behaviors, the objectivity of the instrument, observer variability, and the representativeness of instrument items of the behaviors that are observed (Herbert and Attridge, 1975). While there is some evidence of validity for some observational instruments, the validity of many instruments is either unsubstantiated or questionable.

Hoge (1985), who makes several recommendations for assuring validity, advises that existing instruments be used when possible. Using existing instruments has several advantages: 1) time and effort are saved; 2) reliability and validity information are often available; and 3) information about the use of these instruments can lead to the development of sounder measures. Hoge cautions that care must be taken to assure that the instrument be reliable. Finally, he believes that instruments that broadly define behavior (e.g., on-task, off-task) are more likely to be valid than instruments that categorize behaviors into numerous subskills and categories. Remember that although it may be more difficult to determine the validity of observational measures, validity is a very important area of concern.

DEVELOPING INFORMAL NORMS

Developing informal norms will help to evaluate the behavior that is to be observed. The behavior of one or more students in the group can serve as the norm or comparison group for the student who is to be observed. In this instance, the other students in the group are known as the norm group, and the student who is to be observed is referred to as the target student. If informal norms are not developed, it is difficult to determine if the target student's behavior is atypical or abnormal (Alessi, 1980; Sattler, 1988).

There are three ways to develop informal norms. The first is to use several students or a group of students as the norm sample. The scan-check method is used with this approach. The observer scans the sample group of students for several seconds every few minutes and counts the number of students who are exhibiting the behavior that is to be observed. For example, every 3 minutes an observer scans a group of students for 5 seconds and counts the number of students who are working independently. After this scan-check, the observer can watch the target student for 5 seconds and observe to see whether the student is working independently. Figure 5.16 is an example of the scan-check method. This example can be used for interval or momentary time sampling recording.

The second method of establishing an informal norm sample is to ask the teacher to identify a student whose behavior is typical or representative of the behavior of the students in the group. By watching the behavior of the typical student, the observer can use the scan-check method to compare the typical student's behavior with that of the target student.

A third way to develop an informal norm is to compare several observations of the behavior of the target student that were conducted during separate observation periods. In this way, the behavior of the target student is compared with previous observations of that same behavior (Alessi, 1980; Sattler, 1988).

Record of Preschool Observation

Child's name: P. A.	Observer: N. T.
Age: 4-2	Date: May 3, 19xx
School: Applegate	Teacher: L. S.

Reason for Observation: To determine the extent P.A's behavior differs from her peers.

Activity Observed: circle time

Observation Techiques Used (e.g., interval, time sample):
30-second interval for P. A.   1 minute interval for class scan.

Behavior Codes	Grouping Codes	Teacher and Peer Reaction Codes
T On-task	L Large group	AA Attention to all
O Off-task	S Small group	A+ Positive attention
P Passive	O One-to-one	A- Negative attention
M Motor activity	C Cooperative	NA No attention
	P Parallel	NT Neutral attention
	F Free-time	

Time	Child	Comp. Child	Class Scan	Anecdotal Notes	Group	Tchr	Peer
9:16	P	T		not attending to teacher	L	NT	NA
	M	T	80%	walks away	L	A-	NA
9:17	M	T			L	NA	NA
	M	O	83%	walks to block area	L	NA	NA
9:18	M	T			L	NA	NA
	M	T	76%		L	NA	NA
9:19	T	O		attends to teacher	L	NA	NA
	T	T	80%		L	A+	NT
9:20	T	T			L	A+	NT
	P	T	80%		L	NA	NA
Sum-mary	3/10 30%	8/10 80%	80%		L=10	NT=1 A-=1	NA=8 NT=2

FIGURE 5.16

Scan-Check Method

Source: Alessi and Kaye (1983).

INTERVIEWING

The interview allows a face-to-face meeting in which participants discuss and share their individual perspectives. Interviews may be conducted with students, parents, colleagues, and other professionals. In Chapter 2 special considerations in interviewing parents and other family members were discussed.

Interviewing consists of asking the right questions and listening carefully to what the other person is saying. This skill demands that you know yourself and not let your own biases overshadow what is being told to you. If you use this technique, you must *want* to hear what the other person is saying. Being a good listener is a complex skill that calls for sensitivity and respect for others. Skillful interviewing requires training and practice.

The interview makes certain assumptions about the give and take of the communication process between individuals. Professionals need to be sensitive to assumptions that members of the dominant group hold about this communication process; these assumptions may not be the same for members of less dominant groups.

Planning and Conducting Interviews with Teachers and Other Professionals

In Chapter 2 we discussed planning and conducting interviews with family members. These steps are similar to those that are followed in working with other teachers and professionals. We will briefly review these steps but applied to fellow professionals.

Planning the Interview

In preparing to conduct an interview, contact the individual and state the purpose of the meeting. Plan a convenient time and place to meet.

1. State the purpose of the interview. The purpose may be to follow up on a student referral: "I'd like to sit down and talk further about your concerns about Sharda."

2. Arrange a convenient time and meeting place: "Do you have some time in the next few days that we could meet?" Since information shared during the interview may be confidential in nature, care needs to be taken to arrange a meeting place that can ensure confidentiality. Locations that are public gathering spots, such as the cafeteria or teachers' lounge, may not be appropriate.

Beginning the Interview

Establish rapport with the individual. Some interviewers spend a few minutes talking about a shared activity of mutual interest before sitting down to work. Acknowledge the fact that the individual has set aside time for the meeting. Begin the interview with broad questions and gradually ask more specific and focused questions (Nitko, 1996).

Conducting the Interview

1. Show a genuine interest in what the individual has to say. Create a positive tone by your respect, support, and warmth.

2. Ask questions and rephrase statements to help clarify important points. Many professionals find it helpful to prepare a few questions in advance. As you think about the types of questions that would be helpful, consider the wording of the questions and the type of answers that may result. Open-ended questions are usually more helpful. For example, ask "What have you tried?" or "What are you thinking about doing?" Too often the teacher or other professional requesting assistance is posed questions in the form "Have you tried *x?*" This line of questioning may be met with a single-word response and a sense of frustration.

3. Listen not only to hear but to understand what the individual is saying.

Completing the Interview

Generally, interviews should not exceed an hour in length. Conclude the interview by summarizing the discussion.

Conducting Interviews with Students

Interviews with students are helpful both when students are having academic difficulties and when students are doing well. The interview provides information about a student's perspective in a wide variety of areas, and is especially productive in giving insight into the student's overall patterns of behavior (Salvia and Ysseldyke, 1995) and self-concept. Student interviews are helpful in making adjustments to the classroom environment.

Interviews should be used with caution, however, as they can present difficulties for students with disabilities and for students from some cultural and ethnic groups. The interview technique requires skills in understanding and speaking the language of the interviewee. For example, students with processing difficulties, who in many cases take longer to compose a response, can inadvertently be cut off by the interviewer. Students who are not proficient in English can experience difficulty, even when a translator is present. The translator may or may not be proficient in the student's dialect. Translations can be misinterpreted because the nuances in the language do not transfer.

Steps in Conducting Student Interviews

Merrell (1994) describes the steps in conducting a student interview:

1. Begin by asking some general questions about why the student thinks she or he is being interviewed. Allow time for discussion of the student's interests and attitudes.
2. Lead the discussion toward a specific probing of the problem. For example, the interviewer might ask the student to describe what happens just before she or he gets involved in a fight.
3. Ask the student to describe his or her behavioral assets.
4. Obtain the student's perspective on what positive and appropriate behaviors she or he can marshall as well as a description of likes and dislikes.

5. Use this information along with other assessment information to develop a plan for addressing the problem behavior.

CONFERENCING AND COLLABORATING

Conferencing

Conferencing involves meeting with parents, teachers, therapists, or professionals in other agencies to share information, concerns, and ideas regarding common issues.

Collaborating

Collaborating is a more active process than meeting with others to discuss common issues. Collaboration involves a commitment on an individual's part to work cooperatively with others toward a common goal.

Building expertise in conferencing and collaborating begins with good interpersonal skills. Some individuals seem to have strong interpersonal skills; others need to develop and practice these faculties. Professionals improve interpersonal competence by working with others who demonstrate a strong commitment to teamwork and collaboration. Let's examine some of the characteristics of effective interpersonal skills:

- Individuals with strong interpersonal skills communicate in a positive, genuine manner. They are interested in what others are saying and in the ideas that others have.
- Interpersonal skills involve both verbal and nonverbal communication. Verbal communication refers not only to the words that are spoken but to the tone and pitch the speaker uses. Nonverbal communication consists of facial expression, body language, and gestures. Nonverbal customs can send strong messages to the speaker. For example, one of the expected norms in communication among some groups is that the speaker makes eye contact with the listener

and that a good listener indicates interest by returning the eye contact. Professionals must be aware that expected norms typical for members of the dominant group may not be held by professionals who are members of less dominant groups. In some cultural groups, the "lack" of eye contact is a scruple, a behavior that signifies respect for the speaker rather than lack of interest.

- Listen and hear the speaker out. Don't interrupt when a colleague is talking. Knowing all the answers is not important—or possible. Working together to create solutions is critical.

- Use everyday language and eliminate the use of jargon. The field of special education is filled with initials, numbers, and acronyms. Professionals from other disciplines may not be familiar with many of the terms that special educators use frequently.

Conferring with other professionals involves either meeting with others one-to-one or in a small group. The key aspects of conducting conferences are:

1. Setting a meeting time and location
   - Find a time and location that is convenient for each person.
2. Identifying and clarifying the situation
   - Describe the areas of concern: "I understand that Roberto has been having a difficult time. Could you describe what has been happening?"
   - Ask questions or restate what has been said, if you are unsure of the issues.
   - Determine the history and the frequency of the problem.
3. Generating ideas
   - Work together to brainstorm a list of interventions.
   - Write down each idea.
4. Making decisions
   - Identify possible solutions.
   - Build consensus.
5. Keeping focused
   - The meeting should have a purpose, and participants should feel that progress is

being made. Don't waste time by letting the meeting become sidetracked with other conversations or interruptions.
6. Developing a time line
   - Write down a time line for activities and interventions that will be tried.
   - Clarify the responsibilities of each member.
   - Schedule a follow-up meeting.
7. Keeping track of improvements
   - Share ideas of good experiences and solutions that have worked.

(Adapted from Ferguson, 1994; Heward, 1996)

PREFERRED PRACTICES

In conducting observations, the examiner needs to be aware of the sources of error that affect the accuracy of observations. Care should be taken to ensure that observations are both reliable and valid. Precautions are always taken to avoid bias.

Information gathered in observations is synthesized and integrated with other assessment data to assist the team in answering the assessment questions during one or more steps of the assessment process. This data includes observations of the student and of the environment.

Observing and interviewing involve working closely with other professionals. Conferencing and collaborating entail strong interpersonal organizational skills. Being sensitive to these skills and having opportunities to practice them in working with others are the first steps in becoming a skillful practitioner.

EXTENDING LEARNING

5.1 Darcy is a new student in your classroom who is frequently aggressive to others. The aggression is sometimes physical and sometimes verbal. You plan to ob-

Assessment questions	Type of observation
1. How often does Tia interact with her classmates? (Interact is defined as "makes eye contact.")	Frequency or latency
2. How can I help Ben settle down? (Settle down is defined as_____)	Duration
3. MJ is always late to class.	
4. Carla is so disruptive and has a high activity level. (Disruptive is defined as "talking when someone else is speaking.")	
5.	Latency
6. Can Harold complete the job application form in a reasonable amount of time?	

FIGURE 5.17

Linking Assessment Questions with Observation

serve Darcy's behavior for instances of aggression to find out what kinds of situations make her upset. Describe how you would proceed in planning and conducting the observation. Design or adapt an observation form to assist you in collecting information.

5.2 The assessment team has asked you to gather information regarding the degree to which a student is independent of others. You need to know examples of situations in which the student works independently and does not seek direction or assistance from others. Select three different time periods during the day to observe the student. Adapt one of the observation forms to assist you in collecting the information. Use your form to conduct the observation. What would you report back to the team?

5.3 Figure 5.17 illustrates the link between the assessment question and the decisions in planning this step of the observation. Sometimes more than one type of recording can be made. Can you complete the figure?

5.4 Select two students to observe using the event sampling technique. Record their responses to others in terms of affect and expression. Complete an interpretation of your observations, including a summary of the responses of each student and a comparison of the range of responses and intensity of expression.

5.5 Sometimes teachers assess out-of-seat behavior. Explain why the data should be collected using duration recording rather than event recording. (Hint: Are all out-of-seat behaviors equivalent as time away from the student's desk?)

5.6 Interview a teacher to learn about one or two learning or behavior problems in the classroom. Identify questions or additional information that would be helpful in addressing the problem. Based on these question(s), construct a checklist to help you gather this information.

5.7 Plan to conduct a student interview regarding the student's interests and school work. Use the steps in conducting an interview to plan your meeting. After you have conducted the interview, write an evaluation of the interview process. What aspects went well? What would you do differently next time?

5.8 Choose one of the schools described in the Snapshot of Stoney Brook Elementary and

Lincoln High. How might the methods, materials, and demands affect a student who is experiencing academic problems?

5.9 College professors often use group assignments to foster skills in collaboration. Consider a situation in which you have worked together with a group of classmates on a problem or assignment. Was the group project successful overall? Did members encounter difficulties in working together? Define what the problems were and discuss possible solutions.

(On p. 97 we asked if Stacy's behavior had improved after a two-month interval. The answer is:

$$\frac{15 \text{ occurrences}}{10 \text{ minutes}} = 1.5 \text{ occurrences per minute}$$

This represents an improvement.)

REFERENCES

Alessi, G. J. (1980). Behavioral observation for the school psychologist: Responsive-discrepancy model. *School Psychology Review* 9: 31–45.

Alessi, G. J., and J. H. Kaye (1983). *Behavior assessment for school psychologists.* Kent, Ohio: National Association of School Psychologists.

Beaty, J. (1994). *Observing development of the young child.* 3d ed. New York: Macmillan.

DeVellis, R. F. (1991). *Scale development.* Newbury Park, Calif.: Sage.

Ferguson, D. L. (1994). Magic for teacher work groups. *Teaching Exceptional Children* 27(1): 42–47.

Frick, T., and M. I. Semmel (1978). Observer agreement and reliabilities of classroom observational measures. *Review of Educational Research* 48: 157–184.

Fuchs, D., P. Fernstrom, S. Scott, L. Fuchs, and L. Vandermeer (1994). Classroom ecological inventory. *Teaching Exceptional Children* 26(3): 11–15.

Gronlund, N. E., and R. L. Linn (1990). *Measurement and evaluation in teaching.* New York: Macmillan.

Harms, T., and R. M. Clifford (1980). *Early childhood environment rating scale.* New York: Teachers College Press.

Herbert, J., and C. Attridge (1975). A guide for developers and users of observation systems and manuals. *American Educational Research Journal* 12: 1–20.

Heward, W. L. (1996). *Exceptional children: An introduction to special education.* 5th ed. Englewood Cliffs, N.J.: Merrill, an imprint of Prentice Hall.

Hoge, R. D. (1985). The validity of direct observation. *Review of Educational Research* 55: 469–483.

Merrell, K. W. (1994). *Assessment of behavioral, social, and emotional problems: Direct and objective methods for use with children and adolescents.* White Plains, N.Y.: Longman.

Nitko, A. J. (1996). *Educational assessment of students.* 2d ed. Englewood Cliffs, N.J.: Merrill, an imprint of Prentice Hall.

Repp, A. C., G. S. Nieminen, E. Olinger, and R. Brusca (1988). Direct observation: Factors affecting the accuracy of observers. *Exceptional Children* 55: 29–36.

Salvia, J., and J. E. Ysseldyke (1995). *Assessment.* 6th ed. Boston: Houghton Mifflin.

Sattler, J. (1988). *Assessment of children.* 3d ed. San Diego: Jerome M. Sattler.

Turnbull, A. P., H. R. Turnbull, M. Shank, and D. Leal (1995). *Exceptional lives: Special education in today's schools.* Englewood Cliffs, N.J.: Merrill, an imprint of Prentice Hall.

Ysseldyke, J. E., and S. L. Christenson (1993). *The instructional environment system-II.* Longmont, Colo.: Sopris West.

Achievement: Overall Performance

OVERVIEW

Achievement testing is the assessment of past learning that is usually the result of formal and informal educational experiences. This chapter is concerned with approaches that are used to assess the achievement of students. Several other chapters in this book also address aspects of the assessment of achievement. Chapter 7 is devoted to a discussion of performance-based assessment, Chapters 8 and 9 examine the assessment of reading and written language, and Chapter 11 examines the assessment of mathematics.

CHAPTER OBJECTIVES

After completing this chapter you should be able to:

Describe assessment questions, purposes, and approaches relating to the assessment of achievement.

Explain the integral link between instruction and assessment.

Compare approaches to the assessment of achievement, including norm-referenced standardized tests, criterion-referenced assessment, curriculum-based assessment, performance-based assessment, self-assessment, and peer assessment.

Describe how the assessment of the physical, learning, and social environments influences achievement.

WHAT SHAPES OUR VIEWS

The assessment of achievement occurs regularly throughout students' school careers. **Achievement** tests are designed to be administered to groups of students or to individual students in order to assess their formal and informal learning experiences. The questions, purposes, and approaches used in the assessment of achievement are described in Table 6.1.

RESPONDING TO DIVERSITY

The assessment of achievement must be sensitive to an individual's culture, ethnicity, race, language, geographic region of origin, gender, disability, and economic status. Assessment approaches, including standardized tests, performance-based assessment, and the other approaches described in this chapter, must be free from bias. There are several ways in which

TABLE 6.1 Assessment Questions, Purposes, and Approaches

Assessment questions	Steps and purposes	Approaches
	Screening	
Is there a possibility of a disability in achievement?	To determine whether students *may* have a disability and should be referred for further assessment	Norm-referenced instruments Curriculum-based assessment Criterion-referenced assessment Observations Checklists
	Eligibility	
Does the student have a disability? What disability does the student have? Does the student meet the criteria for services? What are the strengths and weaknesses? In what areas is the student having difficulty? What does the student understand?	To determine if there is a disability To compare the student's performance with the performance of the peer group To determine specific strengths and weaknesses To understand why the student is having difficulty	Norm-referenced instruments Curriculum-based assessment Criterion-referenced assessment Observations Probes Error analysis Interviews Checklists Student, parent, and/or teacher conferences Performance assessment
CONNECTING INSTRUCTION WITH ASSESSMENT		
	Program Planning	
What does the student not understand? Where should instruction begin?	To understand what the student knows and does not know To plan the student's program To determine instructional approaches	Norm-referenced instruments Curriculum-based assessment Criterion-referenced assessment Observation Probes Error analysis Interviews Checklists Student, parent, and/or teacher conferences Performance assessment

achievement tests can be biased (Howell and Rueda, 1996):

- format of the test
- test directions are too technical or do not translate easily into another language
- content of achievement tests can differ in importance across cultures
- examinee test-taking behaviors vary from one culture to another
- examiner personality characteristics can influence the examinee's responses

- the underlying psychological construct of the test may not be universal
- the individual examinee may not be represented in the norm group

Using a variety of approaches when assessing achievement reflects sensitivity to the student as well as a thorough attempt to understand what the student has learned. The assessment of achievement includes standardized testing in addition to a variety of these other approaches:

- curriculum-based assessment
- criterion-referenced assessment

TABLE 6.1   Assessment Questions, Purposes, and Approaches (Continued)

Assessment questions	Steps and purposes	Approaches
Program Monitoring		
Once instruction begins, is the student making progress? Should the instruction be modified?	To understand the pace of instruction	Curriculum-based assessment
	To understand what the student knows prior to and after instruction	Criterion-referenced assessment
		Observations
		Probes
		Error analysis
	To understand the strategies and concepts the student uses	Interviews
		Checklists
	To monitor the student's program	Student, parent, and/or teacher conferences
		Portfolios
		Exhibitions
		Journals
		Written descriptions
		Oral descriptions
Program Evaluation		
Has the student met the goals of the IEP?	To determine whether the IEP goals have been met	Curriculum-based assessment
Has the instructional program been successful for the student?	To determine whether the goals of the program have been met	Criterion-referenced assessment
		Observations
Has the student made progress?	To evaluate program effectiveness	Probes
Has the instructional program achieved its goals?		Error analysis
		Interviews
		Checklists
		Student, parent, and/or teacher conferences
		Portfolios
		Exhibitions
		Journals
		Written descriptions
		Oral descriptions
		Surveys

- alternative forms of assessment, such as systematic observations, anecdotal records, interviews with family members and the students themselves, samples of students' work, videotapes, audiotapes, performances, portfolios, and exhibitions.

STANDARDIZED INSTRUMENTS

Standardized tests of achievement are tests in which the procedures for administration, scoring, and interpretation are strictly established and followed. A standardized test is usually norm-referenced. A **norm-referenced test** (NRT) is a measure that compares a student's test performance with that of similar students who have taken the same test. The construction of a standardized test is often a lengthy and costly project that involves considerable research and development.

Steps in the Development of a Standardized Achievement Test

1. Test developers create specifications for the test.
2. Test items are written.
3. An item tryout is conducted in which the initial draft items are tried out on a large group of individuals.
4. The results of the item tryout are analyzed. Some items are discarded or modified; new items may be created. Methods of scoring and interpretation are developed.
5. Test developers conduct a national standardization of the test. A national standardization sample is selected that is representative of the United States, based on the results of the most recent census data. The standardization sample is structured so that the participants are selected according to balanced criteria for age, socioeconomic status, geographic region, urban/rural/suburban residence, race, eth-

nicity, and gender. Additional variables can be included, depending on the purposes of the test.
6. The data from the national tryout are analyzed and norm tables are developed. Norm tables are used to help compare the performance of individual students with the performance of the students' peers.
7. Final test materials are prepared, including test manuals, answer sheets, and scoring guides.

Benefits

The benefits of using standardized tests are that the test materials describe the development of the tests in detail, including the test content, administration, norms, reliability, validity, scoring, and interpretation. Because standardized tests are usually norm-referenced, comparisons can be made between the performance of an individual student, the student's peers, and the students in the sample on whom the test has been standardized. In addition, comparisons can be made between a student's performance on several subtests or on several separate tests in order to identify relative strengths and weaknesses. Depending on the test, standardized achievement tests can be used for screening, determining eligibility, program planning, monitoring progress, and program evaluation.

Disadvantages

Although standardized achievement tests have a number of advantages, they also have many disadvantages for students with special needs:

- tests assume that all students have been exposed to the content tested.
- many tests assume that students come from a homogeneous culture.
- many tests are biased against students with disabilities, females, certain cultures, ethnic groups, and economic groups.

- many tests do not test what has been taught in schools.
- many tests do not measure or consider creativity, interest, initiative, motivation, and values.
- many tests result in labeling or mislabeling of students.
- tests encourage teachers to teach toward the test.
- tests result in competition among students, teachers, and schools.
- tests generate fear (Nitko, 1996).
- test standards usually require that students be able to read and write independently.

Steps and Purposes of Achievement Testing

Screening

One frequent use of standardized achievement tests is to identify students who perform below, at the same level, or above their peers. That is, the utility of achievement test results in the screening process is in identifying students who need further assessment. Examples of achievement tests that can be used for screening are the *Iowa Tests of Basic Skills* and the *Peabody Individual Achievement Test–Revised.*

Determining Eligibility

Standardized achievement tests, when used in conjunction with other types of tests, can help to determine eligibility for services. For example, the *Wechsler Individual Achievement Test,* when used with a measure of cognitive ability, can help to determine eligibility for services.

Program Planning

Program planning and monitoring student progress connect instruction with assessment. Achievement tests can aid in instructional planning and can be helpful in identifying what the student knows and can do. Two tests often used in program planning are the *Peabody Individual Achievement Test–Revised* and the *KeyMath–Revised.* The teacher can also utilize other assessment approaches discussed in this chapter to assist with program planning.

Monitoring Progress

Students' progress in literacy, mathematics, and other academic content areas should be monitored with regularity. Norm-referenced tests may not be as useful in monitoring progress as are other assessment approaches because they are not sensitive to small changes in performance. Frequent monitoring assists the teacher in modifying instruction to meet the needs of the student. As with program planning, the teacher may also use other assessment approaches discussed in this chapter.

Program Evaluation

Achievement tests are employed to conduct two types of program evaluation. Individual student programs as specified in an IEP can be evaluated using achievement tests. In addition, when a school district is interested in examining the progress that a class, grade, school, or the school district itself has made over a period of time, achievement tests can be used as a measure. Program evaluation is discussed further in Chapter 19.

Group Tests

Group tests of achievement are usually administered to groups of students in classrooms. Students with special needs who are in regular classrooms frequently participate in group achievement testing. The purposes of group achievement tests are to: 1) assist in screening students, 2) evaluate the relative performance of students when compared with their peers, 3) describe the relative effectiveness of methods of instruction, and 4) evaluate curricula. The IDEA Amendments of 1997 require students with disabilities to be included in general state and district-wide assessments, with appropriate accommodations where necessary.

Most group tests must be administered using scripted directions provided by the test publisher. The tests usually have booklets that contain test items and separate answer sheets. Scoring is most often done by hand, although some publishers either provide or require that the answer sheets be returned for machine scoring. A variety of types of scores are reported, including standard scores, percentiles, stanines, and age and grade equivalents. Profiles can be generated, thus facilitating the comparison of students, classrooms, individual schools, and school districts.

Benefits

Group testing with standardized tests permits the testing of large groups of students using the same administration, scoring, and interpretation procedures. While group tests can be administered to individual students, it is not appropriate to administer individual tests to groups.

Disadvantages

Group testing has several disadvantages for students with special needs. The tests routinely require that students read and write independently. Further, many group achievement tests have separate test booklets that contain the test items and separate answer sheets. Some students may be able to correctly answer the questions but have difficulty transferring their answers to the answer sheet. Finally, many group achievement tests have multiple-choice answers. Students with disabilities as well as students from various culture or ethnic groups may have difficulty using this format.

There are a number of group achievement tests published. Table 6.2 presents a comparison of commonly used tests.

TABLE 6.2   Group Tests of Achievement

Test	Grade
Aprenda: La Prueba de Logros en Español (1990) Coordinated with Stanford Achievement Test Series	K through 13
California Achievement Tests/5 (CTB/Macmillan/McGraw Hill, 1993)	K through 12
Iowa Tests of Basic Skills (Hoover, Hieronymous, Frisbie, and Dunbar, 1993)	K through 9
Iowa Tests of Educational Development (Feldt, Forsyth, Ansley, and Alnot, 1993)	9 through 12
Metropolitan Achievement Tests (7th ed.) (Balow, Farr, and Hogan, 1992)	K through 12
SRA Achievement Series (Naslund, Thorpe, and Lefever, 1985)	K through 12
Stanford Achievement Test (9th ed.) (Harcourt Brace Educational Measurement, 1996)	K through 13
Tests of Achievement and Proficiency (Scannell, Hough, Loyd, and Risinger, 1993)	9 through 12

*Spanish form

TABLE 6.3   Individual Tests of Achievement

Name	Ages/grades
Basic Achievement Skills Individual Screener (BASIS) (Sonnenschein, 1983)	grades 1 through 12 & post–high school
Bateria Woodcock Psico-Educativa en Español (1996) Co-normed test of cognitive ability and achievement; normed on 800+ Spanish-speaking subjects from five countries	ages 4.0 through 20 years
Diagnostic Achievement Battery-2 (DAB-2) (Newcomer, 1990)	ages 6.0 through 14.0
Diagnostic Achievement Test for Adolescents-2 (DATA-2) (Newcomer and Bryant, 1993)	grades 7 through 12
Kaufman Test of Educational Achievement (K-TEA) (Kaufman and Kaufman, 1985)	grades 1 through 12 ages 6.0 to 18.11
Peabody Individual Achievement Test–R (PIAT–R) (Markwardt, 1989)	grades K through 12 ages 5.0 to 18.11
Wide Range Achievement Test 3 (WRAT3) (Wilkinson, 1993)	ages 5.0 to 75.0
Wechsler Individual Achievement Test (WIAT) (Harcourt Brace Educational Measurement, 1992)	grades K through 12, ages 5.0 to 19.11
Woodcock-Johnson Psychoeducational Battery–Revised, Tests of Achievement (WJ–R ACH) (Woodcock and Johnson, 1989)	grades K through 12 ages 2 to 90

*Spanish form

Individual Achievement Tests

When testing individual students, achievement tests provide the examiner with the opportunity to get to know students. Rapport can be established between the student and the test examiner, and the examiner can help the student feel at ease. Individual testing allows the examiner to observe the student's appearance, adjustment to the testing, cooperation, effort, motivation, attitudes, speech patterns, anxiety level, activity level, flexibility, impulse control, fine and gross motor abilities, distractibility, and mood (Sattler, 1988). The examiner can individualize the test administration according to the needs of the student. For example, if a student is tired or hungry test administration can be paused so that the student can take a break. A list of published individual achievement tests can be found in Table 6.3.

PUBLISHED ACHIEVEMENT TESTS

Basic Achievement Skills Individual Screener

The *Basic Achievement Skills Individual Screener (BASIS)* (Sonnenschein, 1983) measures skills in reading, mathematics, spelling, and writing and is intended for students in grades 1 through 12 and post–high school students. The test is both criterion-referenced and norm-referenced and produces scores that range from grades 1 to 12.

The items in each of the following content areas are arranged in grade level clusters:

Reading. The items in this cluster range from readiness through grade 8. The purpose of this subtest measures reading comprehension by asking upper-grade students to read graded passages and supply the missing words. This is known as the *cloze technique.*

Mathematics. The items in this cluster range from readiness through grade 8. The student is asked to solve computational problems using a pencil. Word problems are dictated by the examiner.

Spelling. The items in this cluster range from grades 1 through 8. The student is asked to write words that are dictated by the teacher.

Writing. The writing subtest is optional. After being assigned a topic by the examiner, the student writes for 10 minutes. The sample is scored holistically and is compared with average writing samples for students in grades 3 through 8.

Administration

The subtests are administered individually by the examiner. The test is untimed and administration time is less than one hour. There is one form.

Scoring

The subtests are hand scored. Both normative and criterion-referenced scores are available. The following normative scores are available: percentile ranks, stanines, standard scores, age equivalents, and grade equivalents. Criterion-referenced scoring involves evaluating the student's performance on clusters of items.

Standardization

The *BASIS* was standardized in the fall of 1982. The sample selected was representative of students in grades 1 to 12, based on the 1970 U.S. Census.

Reliability

The reliability appears to be adequate. Test-retest reliabilities are greater than .80. Internal consistency reliability is acceptable.

Validity

Content validity is based on the selection of items in the construction of the test. A number of validity studies were conducted on special populations of students, such as students who were learning disabled, gifted, mentally retarded, emotionally disturbed, and hearing impaired. However, the samples were small and additional research should be conducted to determine the usefulness of this instrument with special populations.

Summary

The *BASIS* is an individually administered test of reading, mathematics, spelling, and writing. The examiner is encouraged to determine the appropriateness of the test items by comparing them with the student's curriculum. The test is probably best used as a screening instrument rather than a test of achievement in content areas.

Diagnostic Achievement Battery-2

The *Diagnostic Achievement Battery-2 (DAB-2)* (Newcomer, 1990) measures achievement in the areas of listening, speaking, reading, writing, and mathematics. The test is intended for use with students ages 6 through 14. The test has four purposes: 1) to identify students who perform significantly below their peers in spoken language, written language, and mathematics; 2) to determine a student's strengths and weaknesses in skill development; 3) to

---

BOX 6.1

BASIC ACHIEVEMENT SKILLS INDIVIDUAL SCREENER (BASIS)

Publication Date: 1983
Purpose: A criterion-referenced and norm-referenced individual test that measures skills in reading, mathematics, spelling, and writing.
Age/Grade Levels: Students in grades 1 through 12 and post–high school students.
Time to Administer: 20 minutes to less than an hour.
Technical Adequacy: Reliability is adequate. The teacher is encouraged to examine the test items to determine the extent to which they measure the curriculum that the student has been taught.
Suggested Use: Screening

---

record student progress; and, 4) to assist in research studies. There are 12 subtests:

Story Comprehension. The student answers questions about a story that the examiner reads aloud.

Characteristics. The student answers yes-or-no questions after listening to the examiner read brief statements about characteristics of common objects.

Synonyms. The student provides synonyms for words that are read aloud by the examiner.

Grammatic Completion. The student completes sentences that are read aloud by the examiner.

Alphabet/Word Knowledge. The student identifies letters and words in isolation.

Reading Comprehension. After reading short stories silently, the student answers questions that are posed by the examiner.

Capitalization. After writing a series of sentences, the student must indicate the correct placement of capital letters.

Punctuation. This subtest is administered along with the Capitalization subtest. The student must indicate the appropriate use of punctuation.

Spelling. The student writes words that are dictated by the examiner.

Writing Composition. After looking at three pictures, the student writes a story that is evaluated for vocabulary and content.

Math Reasoning. After the examiner presents pictures (for young children) or problems (for older students) orally, the student solves the problems orally.

Math Calculation. The student solves basic mathematics problems that are presented on a worksheet.

Administration

The *DAB-2* is individually administered. The time to administer the test is less than one hour.

Scoring

Raw scores are converted to standard scores, percentile ranks, and grade equivalents.

Standardization

The standardization sample is a combination of 1983 data from the original *DAB* and data obtained for the *DAB-2*. The standardization sample consisted of 2,623 students who were from forty states. According to the manual, the combined standardization sample is representative of 1985 Census Bureau data. However, detailed information about the demographic characteristics of the sample is lacking.

Reliability

For the most part, the reliability of the *DAB-2* is based on the reliability of the *DAB*. A small internal consistency reliability study was done. Test-retest reliabilities were computed for a small sample. The coefficients were adequate for both types of reliability.

Validity

Content, criterion-related, and construct validity are described. Adequate evidence of validity is presented.

Summary

The *Diagnostic Achievement Battery-2* is an individually administered test of overall achievement in listening, speaking, reading, writing, and mathematics. While the test claims to be "diagnostic," it is best used as an overall measure of achievement. The standardization sample is both questionable and dated. Additional evidence of reliability is needed.

Kaufman Test of Educational Achievement

The *Kaufman Test of Educational Achievement (K-TEA)* (Kaufman and Kaufman, 1985) is an individually administered test of achievement for students in grades 1 through 12. Renorm-

ing was completed in 1996. The age-based norms range from 6 years 0 months to 18 years 11 months (18.11). The *K-TEA* has two forms, the Comprehensive Form and the Brief Form. Although the forms are not interchangeable, they do have overlapping uses. The applications listed for the Brief Form are: contributing to a battery, screening, program planning, research, pretesting and posttesting, making placement decisions, student self-appraisal, use by government agencies, personnel selection, and measuring adaptive functioning. The Comprehensive Form has all of these uses except screening. In addition, the Comprehensive Form is recommended for analyzing strengths and weaknesses and for analyzing errors. There is some overlap of items between the *K-TEA* and the *Kaufman Assessment Battery for Children (K-ABC)*.

Description of the Subtests in the Comprehensive Form

The Comprehensive Form consists of five subtests: Reading Decoding, Spelling, Reading Comprehension, Mathematics Applications, and Mathematics Computation. The Brief Form consists of three subtests: Reading, Mathematics, and Spelling.

Mathematics Applications. The examiner presents the items orally while using pictures and graphs as visual stimuli. The items assess the application of mathematical principles and reasoning.

Reading Decoding. The items assess the ability to identify letters and to pronounce words that are phonetic and nonphonetic.

Spelling. The examiner pronounces a word and uses it in a sentence. The student is asked to write the word. If students are unable to write, they are allowed to spell the word orally.

Reading Comprehension. The child is asked to read a passage and to respond either gesturally or orally to the items that have been presented.

BOX 6.2

DIAGNOSTIC ACHIEVEMENT BATTERY-2 (DAB-2)

Publication Date: 1990
Purposes: Measures overall achievement in listening, speaking, reading, writing, and mathematics
Age/Grade Levels: Ages 6 through 14.
Time to Administer: Less than one hour.
Technical Adequacy: The standardization sample is dated. Additional evidence of reliability is needed.
Suggested Use: While the test claims to be "diagnostic," it is best used as an overall measure of achievement.

Mathematics Computation. The student is asked to use a paper and pencil and to solve written mathematical problems.

Description of the Subtests in the Brief Form

Mathematics. This subtest measures basic computational skills and the application of mathematical principles and reasoning.

Reading. The items assess both decoding, by asking the child to read words, and reading comprehension, by requiring the child to read statements.

Spelling. The items consist of words that are read by the examiner and used in a sentence. The student is asked to write the word or to spell it orally, if the student is unable to write.

Administration

The *K-TEA* can be administered by persons who have had training in educational and psychological testing as well as by persons who have had limited training in these areas. For children in grades 1 through 3, the Comprehensive Form takes from 20 minutes to 1 hour to administer; the Brief Form requires from 10 to 35 minutes to administer.

Scoring

Raw scores can be converted to standard scores, with a mean of 100 and a standard deviation of 15. These are available for both fall and spring testing by grade level or by age. In addition, percentile ranks, stanines, normal curve equivalents, age equivalents, and grade equivalents can be obtained. Methods of interpreting *K-TEA* scores described in the manual are: the size of the difference and the significance of the difference between subtests and between composite scores, analyzing strengths and weaknesses, and identifying errors.

Standardization

Both the Comprehensive and the Brief Forms of the *K-TEA* were renormed between October 1995 and November 1996. Stratification of the standardization sample was done according to age, gender, region, race, ethnicity, and economic status as estimated by parental education. The standardization sample of the *K-TEA* was linked to the standardization samples for the Peabody Individual Achievement Test–Revised (PIAT-R), KeyMath-R, and the *Woodcock Reading Mastery Tests–Revised (WRMT-R).* For the *K-TEA,* the renorming sample consisted of students who were in grades 1 through age 22. The linking sample was developed by having the test examinees in the norm sample take one of the complete test batteries and one or more subtests from another battery. This linking approach permits the making of comparisons of test performance across batteries.

Reliability

The reliabilities of the Comprehensive Form's five subtests range from .90 (Mathematics Computation) to .95 (Reading Decoding). For grade levels, the reliability of the Battery Composite range from .97 to .98; for age groups, reliability ranges from .97 to .99. The reliability for the Reading Composite and Mathematics Composite extend from .93 to .98.

Test-retest reliability coefficients for the Comprehensive Form are high. Reliabilities of the three subtests of the Brief Form range from .85 (Mathematics) to .89 (Reading) for all grades and extend from .87 (Mathematics) to .91 (Reading) for all ages. The reliability of the Battery Composite is high.

Although the Comprehensive Form and the Brief Form "are not alternate forms in the true sense" (Kaufman and Kaufman, 1985, p. 189), for the purpose of reliability testing, the two forms were treated as alternate forms. The computed average intercorrelations between the Comprehensive Form and the Brief Form by grade level were .84 (Mathematics), .80 (Reading), .88 (Spelling), and .92 (Battery Composite). The average intercorrelations between the Comprehensive Form and the Brief Form by age level were .85 (Mathematics),

.83 (Reading), .90 (Spelling), and .93 (Battery Composite).

Validity

The validity of the Comprehensive Form and the Brief Form were estimated using similar procedures. Content validity was established through consultation with curriculum experts in each subject area. Three national tryouts were conducted during the fall of 1981 and the spring of 1982. The final selection of the items emerged from these tryouts.

Construct validity was estimated by showing that subtest and composite scores increased across age and grade levels. Criterion-related validity was demonstrated by correlating the results of the *K-TEA* with the results of other tests given to the same students. These tests included the *Kaufman Assessment Battery for Children (K-ABC), Wide Range Achievement Test (WRAT), Peabody Individual Achievement Test (PIAT),* and other tests.

Summary

The *Kaufman Test of Educational Achievement* is an individually administered test of achievement for students in grades 1 through 12 whose ages range from 6 years 0 months (6.0) to 18 years 11 months (18.11). The *K-TEA* has two forms, the Comprehensive Form and the Brief Form. Although the forms overlap in content, they are not interchangeable. Evidence for the technical adequacy of the test is sufficient. The reliability and validity of both forms is adequate. As with all achievement tests, educators must evaluate the content validity to determine how well it measures what has been taught.

Peabody Individual Achievement Test—Revised

The *Peabody Individual Achievement Test–Revised (PIAT-R)* (Markwardt, 1989) is an individually administered, norm-referenced test for students in grades kindergarten through grade 12 (5 years 0 months to 18 years 11

BOX 6.3

KAUFMAN TEST OF EDUCATIONAL ACHIEVEMENT (K-TEA)

Publication Date: 1985

Purposes: The Comprehensive Form measures: Reading Decoding, Spelling, Reading Comprehension, Mathematics Applications, and Mathematics Computation. The Brief Form consists of three subtests: Reading, Mathematics, and Spelling.

Age/Grade Levels: Grades 1 through 12; ages range from 6 years 0 months to 18 years 11 months.

Time to Administer: 20 minutes to approximately one hour.

Technical Adequacy: Renorming was completed in 1996. The reliability and validity of both forms is adequate. As with all achievement tests, educators must evaluate the content validity to determine how well it measures what has been taught.

Suggested Uses: The Comprehensive Form can be used to measure overall achievement. The Brief Form should be used for screening.

---

months). The manual states that the *PIAT-R* has the following uses: individual evaluation, program planning, guidance and counseling, admissions and transfers, grouping students, follow-up evaluation, personnel selection, and research. The manual also describes the following limitations: 1) the *PIAT-R* is not a diagnostic test; 2) it does not provide highly precise measurement of achievement; 3) it was not designed to sample the curriculum of individual schools, rather, it represents a representative curriculum of schools in the United States; and 4) the background and qualifications of the test administrator can have a varying influence on the interpretation of the test.

The test assesses achievement in six areas:

General Information. This subtest measures general knowledge. The examiner reads the open-ended questions aloud and the child answers orally.

Reading Recognition. The initial test items consist of ability to recognize the sounds associated with letters. Later test items consist of isolated words. The student is asked to reproduce the sounds and to read the words orally.

Reading Comprehension. The student reads a sentence silently and then is asked to identify the one picture out of four that best depicts the sentence.

Mathematics. Using a multiple-choice format, knowledge of basic facts and applications is assessed. The examiner reads all of the test items to the student. For the first 50 items, the child sees only the responses and not the test items. For items 50 to 100, the student sees the printed questions and the response choices.

Spelling. The format for the responses is multiple choice. The items at the beginning of this subtest measure the student's ability to distinguish a printed letter from an object and to recognize letters after hearing their names or sounds. Later items assess the child's ability to identify the one correctly spelled word out of four that the examiner pronounces.

Written Expression. This subtest has two levels. Level I can be administered to children in kindergarten or first grade and assesses copying and writing letters, words, and sentences that the examiner dictates. Level II is administered to children in grades 2 through 12. The student is asked to write a story in response to one of two picture prompts. A time limit of 20 minutes is allowed for a child to complete Level II.

Administration

The manual distinguishes between the qualifications of individuals who administer the *PIAT-R* and those who interpret the results. According to the manual, almost anyone can learn to administer the test. Persons who provide an interpretation are expected to have an understanding of psychometrics and curricula. Depending on the number of items that are administered, it takes approximately 30 minutes to an hour to administer the total test.

Scoring

For all of the subtests except Written Expression, the test items are either correct or incorrect. Raw scores can be converted to standard scores, percentile ranks, grade and age equivalents, stanines, and normal curve equivalents. A separate scoring guide is in the manual for the Written Expression subtest.

Three composite scores can be obtained. The Total Reading composite is derived from the performance on the Reading Recognition and the Reading Comprehension subtests. The Total Test composite is a composite score that is developed from the performance on the first five subtests. There is an optional Written Language composite, which is developed from the Written Expression and the Spelling subtests.

Standardization

The *PIAT-R* was renormed between October 1995 and November 1996. Stratification of the standardization sample was done according to age, gender, region, race, ethnicity, and economic status as estimated by parental education. The standardization sample of the *PIAT-R* was linked to the standardization samples for the *K-TEA, KeyMath-R,* and the *Woodcock Reading Mastery Tests–Revised.* For the *PIAT-R*, the renorming sample consisted of students who were in grade kindergarten through age 22. The linking sample was developed by having the test examinees in the norm sample take one of the complete test batteries and one or more subtests from another battery. This linking approach permits the making of comparisons of test performance across batteries.

Reliability

Split-half reliability coefficients were calculated by age and grade for all of the subtests, excluding Written Expression. The coefficients range from .92 (Reading Comprehension) to .97 (Reading Recognition). The split-half reliability coefficients for the composites are .97 (Total Reading) and .98 (Total Test).

Internal consistency reliability coefficients were computed by grade and age for all of the subtests, except Written Expression. With few exceptions, the coefficients were in the mid to high .90s. Internal consistency reliability for Written Expression was estimated. The resulting reliability coefficients for Level I were .61 (kindergarten spring testing), .60 (kindergarten fall testing), and .69 (grade 1). Internal consistency reliability coefficients were calculated for Level II of the Written Expression subtest. For Prompt A the coefficient was .86; for Prompt B the coefficient was .88.

In order to estimate test-retest reliability, approximately 50 children from grades 2, 4, 6, 8, and 10 were randomly selected and retested within a two to four week interval. Median test-retest reliability coefficients for the subtests, excluding Written Expression, ranged from .84 (Mathematics) to .96 (Reading Recognition).

Several interrater reliability studies were conducted on the scoring of the Level II Written Expression subtest. In one study, the median interrater reliabilities were .58 for Prompt A and .67 for Prompt B. In another study, intercorrelations between trained scorers and typical scorers ranged from .66 to .85.

Validity

The manual reports that content validity was established through the development process. Content area experts, tests reviewers, and others were consulted. As with any achievement test, however, the teacher should review the test to determine the extent to which the test has content validity.

Construct validity was estimated by showing that subtest and composite scores increased across age and grade levels. Concurrent validity was demonstrated by correlating the results of the *PIAT-R* with the *PIAT* and the *Peabody Picture Vocabulary Test–Revised (PPVT-R)*. Additional evidence is needed before concluding that construct validity has been demonstrated.

Summary

The *Peabody Individual Achievement Test–Revised* is an individually administered, norm-referenced test that can be administered to children in grades kindergarten through 12. The test assesses achievement in six areas: General Information, Reading Recognition, Reading Comprehension, Mathematics, Spelling, and Written Expression. The standardization and the reliability are acceptable. As with all standardized achievement tests, the teacher should evaluate the content validity of this test.

Wechsler Individual Achievement Test

The *Wechsler Individual Achievement Test (WIAT)* (Harcourt Brace Educational Measurement, 1992) is an individually administered achievement test for students who are in grades kindergarten through 12, ages 5 years through 19 years, 11 months. One of the major purposes for the development of the *WIAT* was to develop a test that corresponded with the federal requirements in P.L. 101–476, the Individuals with Disabilities Education Act (IDEA), for determining a learning disability. This law states that students with learning disabilities have a severe discrepancy between ability and achievement in one or more of the following areas: oral expression, listening comprehension, written expression, basic reading skill, reading comprehension, mathematics calculation or mathematics reasoning.

Three of the eight *WIAT* subtests, Basic Reading, Mathematics Reasoning, and Spelling,

---

BOX 6.4

PEABODY INDIVIDUAL ACHIEVEMENT TEST–REVISED (PIAT-R)

Publication Date: 1989

Purposes: Measures overall achievement in the areas of General Information, Reading Recognition, Reading Comprehension, Mathematics, Spelling, and Written Expression.

Age/Grade Levels: Grades K through 12; 5 years, 0 months to 18 years, 11 months.

Time to Administer: Approximately 30 minutes to one hour.

Technical Adequacy: The standardization sample and the reliability are acceptable. As with all standardized achievement tests, the teacher should evaluate the content validity of this test.

Suggested Use: Screening; measure of overall achievement in reading, mathematics, spelling, and written expression.

---

form the Screener. Figure 6.1 shows the organization of the *WIAT* subtests as they appear on the test record form.

The following is a description of the eight subtests:

Basic Reading. This subtest assesses word-reading ability. The first series of items contain pictures and the student must point to the correct responses. Later items contain printed words and the student must respond orally to each word.

Mathematics Reasoning. This subtest assesses the ability to reason mathematically. Many items are presented with a visual stimulus. The examiner reads the problem orally and, for many problems, the student is able to read along on a student's page. A variety of types of responses are required.

Spelling. Letters, sounds, and words are dictated. The student is required to write the responses.

Reading Comprehension. After reading brief passages, the student must answer comprehension questions orally.

Numerical Operations. A series of problems assess the ability to write dictated numbers and to solve basic mathematical calculations (addition, subtraction, multiplication, and division). The student writes the responses in a response booklet.

Listening Comprehension. The subtest items assess listening comprehension skills. Early items assess the student's ability to point to one of four pictures that corresponds to a word the examiner presents. Later items assess the student's ability to answer questions that are presented after the examiner reads a brief passage orally.

Oral Expression. The student must respond orally to directions that the examiner gives that relate to a series of items that are presented.

Written Expression. This subtest is administered only to students who are in grades 3 through 12. The examinee is asked to write in response to one of two writing prompts.

Administration

The *WIAT* is administered individually. The starting point for administration depends on the student's grade in school. The *WIAT* takes approximately 30 to 50 minutes to administer to students who are in kindergarten through grade 2. For older students, it takes about 55 minutes.

Scoring

Items on the Basic Reading, Mathematics Reasoning, Spelling, and Numerical Operations subtests are scored either correct or incorrect. The items on the Reading Comprehension, Listening Comprehension, Oral Expression, and the Written Expression subtests require some

Record Form

Summary

Child's Name		Sex		Year	Month	Day
School		Grade	Date Tested			
Teacher	Examiner		Date of Birth			
Referral Source			Age			
Reason for Referral						

Behavioral Observations

WIAT Subtests

☐Age ☐Grade	Raw Scores	Standard Score	Confidence Interval ▨%	Percentile	Other ___ ☐ Equivalent ☐NCE
Basic Reading			–		
Mathematics Reasoning			–		
Spelling			–		
Reading Comprehension			–		
Numerical Operations			–		
Listening Comprehension			–		
Oral Expression			–		
Written Expression			–		

Composites

☐Age ☐Grade	Reading	Mathematics	Language	Writing	Total Composite
Sum of Raw Scores	⬭ +	⬭ +	⬭ +	⬭ =	⬭
Standard Score					
Confidence Interval ▨%	–	–	–	–	–
Percentile					
Other ___ ☐Equivalent ☐NCE					

FIGURE 6.1

Wechsler Individual Achievement Test Record Form

Source: Wechsler Individual Achievement Test. Copyright © 1992 by The Psychological Corporation. Reproduced by permission. All rights reserved.

judgment by the examiner. The manual does provide general guidelines for scoring these subtests. The Written Expression subtest is scored both analytically and holistically. Raw scores are converted to grade-based standard scores. Percentiles, age and grade equivalents, and normal curve equivalents are also available. The discrepancy between *WIAT* standard scores and *Wechsler Preschool and Primary Scale of Intelligence–Revised (WIPPSI-R)* standard scores or *Wechsler Intelligence Scale for Children-III (WISC-III)* standard scores can be determined.

Standardization

The sample was stratified according to age, grade, gender, race/ethnicity (White, Black, Hispanic, Native American, Eskimo, Aleut, Asian, Pacific Islander, Other), geographic region, and the education of the parent(s) or guardian(s) based on 1988 data from the U.S. Census Bureau. The *WIAT* standardization sample was composed of 4,252 individuals, ages 5 to 19 years, who were in grades kindergarten through 12. The standardization sample overrepresents individuals whose parents are in the higher education levels. In addition, students in the southern United States are overrepresented. Weighting was used to adjust race/ethnicity proportions to those in the census data.

According to the manual, approximately 6 percent of the sample consisted of students who were categorized as learning disabled, speech/language impaired, emotionally disturbed, or physically disabled. Separate norms are not provided for these groups.

Several small studies were conducted with students in various disability groups, including students with mental retardation, emotional disturbance, learning disabilities, attention-deficit hyperactivity disorder, and hearing impairments. One of the major purposes for the development of the test was to aid in the identification of students with learning disabilities. However, the manual reports only one study that was conducted with a sample of 91 stu-

dents who were learning disabled. The publisher should be encouraged to conduct or sponsor additional studies so that more information can be gathered about the performance of students with disabilities on the *WIAT*.

Reliability

Split-half reliability coefficients for the subtest and composite standard scores were computed for each grade. In general, the coefficients are in the .80s and .90s. Test-retest reliability was calculated for a separate group of 367 students, in grades 1, 3, 5, 8, and 10, who were tested twice. For students who were in grade 1 the reliability coefficients for the subtest and the composite standard scores ranged from .80 (Oral Expression) to .95 (Spelling, Reading Composite, Screener). Interscorer agreement was calculated for 50 test protocols that were randomly selected from the standardization sample. For the Reading Comprehension and Listening Comprehension subtests, the average correlation was .98. For Oral Expression the average coefficient was .93; the average coefficients for Written Expression were .89 (Prompt 1) and .79 (Prompt 2).

Validity

Content validity was assessed by a panel of reviewers. Criterion-related validity was determined by correlating the *WIAT* with individual- and group-administered tests of achievement and ability. There is some evidence of construct validity. However, as with all tests, independent validity studies should be conducted in order to obtain additional information about the construct validity of the *WIAT*.

Summary

The *WIAT* is an individually administered test that assesses achievement in students in grades kindergarten through 12. Additional studies investigating the validity of the *WIAT* and the use of this test with students with disabilities must be conducted. As with all achievement tests, caution must be used and the test items carefully examined to determine

BOX 6.5

WECHSLER INDIVIDUAL ACHIEVEMENT TEST (WIAT)

Publication Date: 1992

Purposes: Measures strengths and weaknesses in oral expression, listening comprehension, written expression, basic reading skill, reading comprehension, mathematics calculation or mathematics reasoning.

Age/Grade Levels: Grades K through 12; ages 5 years through 19 years, 11 months.

Time to Administer: Approximately 55 minutes.

Technical Adequacy: The standardization sample, reliability, and validity are very good.

Suggested Uses: Measure of overall achievement; identifies academic strengths and weaknesses.

the degree to which they correspond with the curriculum that the student has been taught.

Wide Range Achievement Test 3

The *Wide Range Achievement Test-3 (WRAT-3)* (Wilkinson, 1993) was developed to measure the "codes which are needed to learn the basic skills of reading, writing, spelling, and arithmetic" (p. 10). This purpose is the same as the purposes in the previous editions of this test. The meaning of the word "codes" is unclear, although it is generally assumed that it refers to basic academic skills that are essential in reading, spelling, and arithmetic. The *WRAT-3* has three subtests:

Reading. The student is asked to recognize individual letters and words in isolation.

Spelling. The student is asked to copy marks, write his/her name, and to write single words that are dictated by the examiner.

Arithmetic. The student is asked to read numerals, solve problems that the examiner presents verbally, and to compute arithmetic problems using pencil and paper.

Administration

The *WRAT-3* is individually administered and can be used with individuals ages 5 to 75. There are two forms.

Scoring

The *WRAT-3* is hand scored and six types of scores are available: raw, absolute, and standard scores, percentiles, normal curve equivalents, and grade equivalents.

Standardization

The standardization sample of the *WRAT-3* was based on the 1990 U.S. Census and consisted of 4,443 individuals. The sample was stratified by age, region of the country, gender, and ethnic group.

Reliability

Reliability appears to be adequate. Internal consistency coefficients are reported for 23 age groups for each form of the test. The coefficients range from .85 to .91. Alternate form reliability is acceptable and median coefficients are: Reading, .92; Spelling, .93; and Mathematics, .89.

Validity

The examiner is strongly encouraged to examine the content of the test items. Content validity is highly questionable because it is unclear how well the test items assess the content areas of reading, mathematics, and spelling. Additional research studies are needed to substantiate the construct validity of this instrument.

Summary

The *Wide Range Achievement Test-3* is an individually administered test of reading, spelling, and mathematics achievement. The format of

SNAPSHOT

A Special Education Teacher's Comments

Patricia is in fourth grade. She has received special education services since kindergarten because of speech and language difficulties. When she was in third grade concerns about Patricia's behavior in the classroom were raised by her teacher, and Patricia's parent was asked at that time to seek a medical opinion about the possibility that Patricia had an attention-deficit hyperactivity disorder. The parent did not follow this advice, and the school did not follow up. Her current fourth grade teacher has raised these concerns again and she was referred for further evaluation.

As part of the evaluation, I administered the Wechsler Individual Achievement Test (WIAT). Patricia came willingly to the testing room. She seemed to listen carefully while I explained that some of the questions would be easy but would get harder since this was a test that could also be given to older children. We proceeded through the subtests.

When we came to the Spelling subtest I noticed an immediate change in her behavior and attitude. As soon as I gave her the spelling sheet and a pencil and asked her to write the words given to her, she became restless and silly. Her pencil grip seemed unsteady and she wiggled in her seat. She repeated every word slowly and talked to herself throughout this subtest.

After the Spelling subtest we took a short break, and then I proceeded to administer the remaining subtests in the WIAT. The restlessness was still present. When we were finished, I thanked Patricia and walked her back to her classroom.

I returned to my room and scored the test. An analysis of Patricia's performance showed that she had specific strengths and a number of weaknesses. I was very concerned about Patricia's behavioral changes when faced with tasks that involved writing.

Patricia's literacy instruction is based on the whole language approach, and a student who is exposed to a whole language curriculum is usually more comfortable with writing tasks, even those requiring spelling unknown words, because of the nature of the curriculum. I wondered if Patricia's behavior was an attempt to hide her perceived discomfort. In preparation for the IEP meeting, I summarized Patricia's performance and asked her teacher to bring samples of Patricia's classroom work and homework to the meeting. I also asked the teacher to bring samples of students who were performing "typically" so that the team would be able to compare Patricia's performance with the performance of students who were performing at this standard. Finally, I arranged for the consultant to conduct systematic observations of Patricia's behavior in her classroom.

the test has not significantly changed since it was first published. Although the standardization and reliability are acceptable, validity is questionable. This instrument is best used as a screening instrument, if at all.

Woodcock-Johnson Psychoeducational Battery—Revised, Tests of Achievement

The *Woodcock-Johnson Psychoeducational Battery–Revised (WJ-R)* (Woodcock and Johnson, 1989) is an individually administered battery that assesses cognitive and academic abilities in individuals ages 2 years through adulthood. The battery consists of two tests: *Woodcock-Johnson Tests of Cognitive Ability (WJ-R COG)* and the *Woodcock-Johnson Tests of Achievement (WJ-R ACH)*. Each part is comprised of a Standard Battery and a Supplemental Battery. Standard batteries can be administered alone or with the supplemental batteries. The *WJ-R COG* is described in Chapter 13.

The *WJ-R* has the following purposes: 1) diagnosis, 2) determination of psychoeducational discrepancies, 3) program placement, 4) indi-vidual program planning, 5) guidance, 6) assessing growth, 7) program evaluation, and 8) research. There are two parallel forms of the *WJ-R ACH* Standard Battery, each containing nine subtests. The subtests can be combined to form five clusters in reading, mathematics, written language, and knowledge (science, social studies, and humanities). A description of the subtests can be found in Table 6.4.

Administration

The time to administer the *WJ-R ACH* varies from approximately 20 minutes to over an hour, depending on whether both the Standard Battery and the Supplemental Battery are used. Raw scores can be converted to age and grade equivalents, percentile ranks, and standard scores. The scoring can be cumbersome and it is advisable to use a computer scoring program.

Norms

The *WJ-R* was standardized on 6,359 individuals in over 100 communities. The preschool sample consisted of 705 children who were 2 years to 5 years of age and not enrolled in kindergarten. There were 3,245 individuals in the kindergarten through grade 12 sample. The rest of the standardization sample consisted of individuals who were in college or not in school. The sample was stratified according to region, community size, sex, race—Caucasian, African American, Native American, Asian Pacific, Hispanic (non-Hispanic, Hispanic), and other—funding of college/university, type of college/university, and occupation of adults. The norms are continuous-year norms, that is, the norms were collected throughout the year.

Reliability

For the *WJ-R ACH,* only one type of reliability, internal consistency, is reported. The internal consistency reliabilities for the subtests are reported by age and not by grade. The reliabilities for ages 2, 4, and 6 range from .74 to .93. For the clusters, the reliabilities ranged from

---

B O X   6 . 6

WIDE RANGE ACHIEVEMENT TEST-3 (WRAT-3)

Publication Date: 1993
Purposes: Measures reading recognition, spelling dictated words, and basic arithmetic skills.
Age/Grade Levels: Ages 5 through 75.
Time to Administer: 15 to 30 minutes.
Technical Adequacy: Standardization and reliability are acceptable, validity is questionable.
Suggested Use: This instrument is best used as a screening instrument, if at all.

TABLE 6.4   Woodcock-Johnson Psychoeducational Battery–Revised, Tests of Achievement

---

There are two parallel forms of the WJ-R ACH Standard Battery, each containing nine subtests.

The subtests can be combined to form five clusters in reading, mathematics, written language, knowledge, and skills.

Letter-Word Identification. Assesses the ability to identify letters and words in isolation.

Passage Comprehension. Measures the ability to read a short passage and to identify the missing word.

Calculation. Assesses the ability to solve mathematical calculations using a booklet in which the child can respond in writing.

Applied Problems. Measures the ability to solve practical mathematical problems.

Dictation. Assesses the ability to respond in writing to questions about letter forms, punctuation, spelling, capitalization, and word usage.

Writing Samples. Measures the ability to respond in writing to various response demands.

Science. Measures knowledge relating to biological and physical science.

Social Studies. Measures knowledge relating to history, geography, government, economics, and other areas.

Humanities. Assesses the ability to recall knowledge in art, music, and literature.

The WJ-R ACH Supplemental Battery consists of five subtests.

Word Attack. Assesses the ability to apply the rules of phonic and structural analysis to read unfamiliar and nonsense words.

Reading Vocabulary. Assesses the ability to supply one-word synonyms and antonyms after reading words.

Qualitative Concepts. Measures knowledge of mathematical concepts and vocabulary.

Proofing. Measures the ability to identify a mistake in a passage and to indicate how to correct the error. The mistakes are in punctuation, capitalization, word usage, and spelling.

Writing Fluency. Assesses the ability to write simple sentences in seven minutes.

Spelling. Selected items contained in the Dictation and Proofing subtests are used to obtain the score for this subtest.

Usage. Selected items contained in the Dictation and Proofing subtests are used to obtain the score for this subtest.

Handwriting. The child's responses from the Writing Samples are compared with a ranked scale of handwriting. An informal checklist can be completed.

.91 to .97. Of special interest is that reliabilities for young children are only reported for ages 2, 4, and 6. No reliability information is provided for ages 3, 5, 7, or 8. Users of this battery must be cautious in interpreting the reliability information.

Validity

The manual reports a number of validity studies for the achievement battery. In general, there is evidence to support content, concurrent, and construct validity. The achievement portion of the battery reflects a skills-oriented approach to assessment. The extent to which various subtests reflect students' abilities depends on the instructional orientation of the teacher and the school curriculum.

Summary

The Tests of Achievements of the *Woodcock-Johnson Psychoeducational Battery–Revised* assess academic abilities in individuals ages 24 months through adulthood. The battery is norm-referenced and individually administered. Reliability information is lacking. A student's performance on the achievement subtests may be a reflection, in part, of the curriculum that has been taught.

BOX 6.7

WOODCOCK-JOHNSON PSYCHOEDUCATIONAL BATTERY–REVISED, TESTS OF ACHIEVEMENT (WJ-R ACH)

Publication Date: 1989

Purposes: Measures overall achievement in reading, mathematics, written language, and general knowledge in science, social studies, and humanities.

Age/Grade Levels: Ages 2 through 90.

Time to Administer: 20 minutes to over one hour.

Technical Adequacy: Reliability information is lacking. Validity is adequate; however, the teacher should determine content validity by comparing the test items with the curriculum that the student has been taught.

Suggested Uses: Measure overall achievement; may be used to indicate general areas of strength and weakness.

CURRICULUM-BASED ASSESSMENT

Curriculum-based assessment (CBA) is an approach to linking instruction with assessment. CBA has three purposes: 1) to determine eligibility, 2) to develop the goals for instruction, and 3) to evaluate the student's progress in the curriculum. Based on the performance on a CBA instrument, instructional goals can be specified. Because there is such a close link between assessment and instruction, CBA can be conducted frequently in order to determine if any changes in instruction or the curriculum need to be made. Data collection, interpretation, and intervention are all integral parts of CBA. Other terms used to describe CBA are: curriculum-referenced measurement, curriculum-embedded measurement, frequent measurement, continuous curriculum measurement, and therapeutic measurement. The

characteristics of CBA include (Choate, Enright, Miller, Poteet, and Rakes, 1995):

- links curriculum and instruction
- helps the teacher determine what to teach
- can be used frequently
- assists in the evaluation of student progress and program evaluation
- can be reliable and valid
- assists in improving student achievement

Developing a Curriculum-Based Assessment Instrument

While commercially published CBA instruments exist, there are advantages for teachers to develop their own. One important reason for this is that the curriculum may not correspond to the content of existing instruments. By constructing a CBA instrument, teachers can specify goals, build into the instrument any special adaptations for test administration, and help to ensure that the CBA instrument is valid.

Step 1: Identify the Purpose(s)

The instrument may be used to determine eligibility or entry into a curriculum, to develop the goals for intervention, or to evaluate the student's progress in the curriculum. Sometimes, one instrument can serve multiple purposes. For example, the CBA instrument that is used to develop goals can also be used to evaluate the student's progress.

Step 2: Analyze the Curriculum

Determine what is being taught. Determine the specific tasks that the student is being taught.

Step 3: Develop Performance Objectives

Determine if a student has demonstrated what has been taught. Behaviors should be specified that the student must demonstrate in order to indicate he or she has learned what has been taught.

Step 4: Develop the Assessment Procedures

In this step, specific test items that correspond with the performance objectives are developed. Different types of items can be developed. For example, the teacher can observe the student, request the student perform specific actions, specific academic tasks, demonstrate particular behaviors, or answer particular questions.

The scoring procedures must be delineated. You will have to specify how you will determine how well the student performs.

Considerations about reliability and validity are important. The CBA instrument must be valid. It must have a close correspondence with the curriculum.

Step 5: Implement the Assessment Procedures

Once the assessment procedures have been developed, information can be collected. How the teacher decides to record and keep track of the information will be important.

The way in which students are assessed must be consistent each time. Recording sheets will be helpful in keeping track of the information that is collected.

Piloting, or trying out, the CBA items before actual implementation is a good idea. Although a great deal of thought has gone into the development and construction of the items, it is always a good practice to try out the items before using them to assess students. CBA items should be administered according to the methods that have been developed.

Step 6: Organize the Information

Summarize the information that has been collected. Tables, graphs, or charts can be useful.

Step 7: Interpret and Integrate the Results

Integrate the CBA information with information that has been collected from standardized tests, observations, anecdotal records, and other forms of assessment. This is the point in the assessment process where the link between instruction and assessment is made. The decision-making process continues as educators, along with the team, decide where, when, and how instruction should proceed.

CRITERION-REFERENCED TESTS

A **criterion-referenced test** (CRT) measures a student's performance with respect to a well-defined domain (Anastasi, 1988; Berk, 1988). While norm-referenced tests are constructed so as to discriminate between the performance of individual students on specific test items, criterion-referenced tests provide a description of a student's knowledge, skills, or behavior in a specific range of well-defined instructional objectives. This specific range is referred to as a domain. Criterion-referenced tests, instead of using norms, provide information on the performance of a student with respect to specific test items. The results of criterion-referenced testing are not dependent on the performance of other students, as with a norm-referenced test.

There are several characteristics that distinguish CRTs from norm-referenced tests. One of these is *mastery*. Performance on CRTs provides information on whether students have attained a predetermined level of competence or performance, called mastery. Performance can be interpreted as mastery, nonmastery, or intermediate mastery (Anastasi, 1988). While it is possible to construct a test that is both norm-referenced and criterion-referenced, caution must be used when interpreting the results of these tests because it is difficult to combine both types of tests in one instrument.

Another distinction between criterion-referenced and norm-referenced tests is the breadth of the content domain that is covered by the test (Mehrens and Lehmann, 1991). Typical norm-referenced tests survey a broad domain, while CRTs usually have fewer domains but more items in each domain. CRTs typically sample the domain more thoroughly than norm-referenced tests (Mehrens and Lehmann, 1991).

CRTs can also be very useful in helping to make instructional planning decisions. Since they frequently cover a more restricted range of content than norm-referenced tests, they can provide more information about a student's levels of performance.

Teacher-Developed Criterion-Referenced Tests

CRTs can be developed by teachers. The advantage to developing your own CRT is that the test items are directly linked to the curriculum. The following steps can be used when developing a CRT (Rivera, Taylor, and Bryant, 1994–1995; Taylor, 1993):

Step 1: Identify the Knowledge, Processes, or Skills to Be Measured

Pinpoint the knowledge, processes, skills, and subskills that the student has been taught. These can be taken from the curriculum and from the student's individual educational program (IEP).

Step 2: Develop Instructional Objectives or Subobjectives for the Skills

Each of the skills and subskills is broken down into smaller steps, and these become the instructional objectives and subobjectives.

Step 3: Develop Test Items for Each Objective or Subobjective

In order to measure each skill, test items must be developed for each one.

Step 4: Determine the Performance Standards or Criteria for Performance

Each of the objectives and subobjectives is given at least one criterion that indicates acceptable levels of performance.

Step 5: Administer the Test Items

Once you have developed the CRT, the items can be administered. An advantage to using criterion-referenced tests is that, unlike norm-referenced tests, the items on a CRT can be administered frequently in order to document the progress that the student has made.

Step 6: Score the Test Items and Present the Results in a Graph or Chart

The performance of the student on the CRT should be recorded. Graphing or charting the results can help both students and teachers in monitoring progress.

Step 7: Analyze and Interpret the Results

Knowledge about the student's level of performance facilitates the development of new instructional objectives and modifications.

PUBLISHED CRITERION-REFERENCED TESTS

BRIGANCE® Inventories. The *BRIGANCE® Diagnostic Inventories* are criterion-referenced tests that are similar in purpose, scoring, administration, and interpretation. They are useful in program planning and in monitoring programs. Table 6.5 summarizes the achievement sections of each of the inventories.

The administration and scoring for the BRIGANCE® inventories is similar for all of the inventories. Not all items or all subtests must be administered to a student. The examiner uses professional judgment to determine the items and subtests that are to be administered. A record booklet is used for each student, and it follows the student through several years of school.

Because these inventories are criterion-referenced, they can be administered frequently to monitor progress. The student's responses to each item are color-coded so that the teacher can see which skills have been mastered. There are no summary scores. Instructional objectives accompany the items, facilitating program planning.

CONNECTING INSTRUCTION WITH ASSESSMENT: ALTERNATIVE ASSESSMENT

The term *informal tests* is an older term that describes approaches to assessment other than standardized tests. The terms *alternative assessment* and *informal assessment* are some-

TABLE 6.5   BRIGANCE® Inventories

Name	Ages/grades	Achievement domains
BRIGANCE® Diagnostic Inventory of Basic Skills (Brigance, 1977)	grades K through 6	1. Reading 2. Grammar 3. Mechanics 4. Reference Skills 5. Mathematics 6. Measurement
BRIGANCE® Diagnostic Inventory of Essential Skills (Brigance, 1980)	grades 4 through 12	1. Mathematics 2. Reading 3. Writing 4. Spelling 5. Reference Skills 6. Schedules and Graphs 7. Measurement 8. Money and Finance
BRIGANCE® Diagnostic Comprehensive Inventory of Basic Skills (Brigance, 1983)	pre-K through 9	1. Mathematics 2. Reading 3. Writing 4. Spelling 5. Reference Skills 6. Graphs and Maps 7. Measurement
BRIGANCE® Assessment of Basic Skills–Spanish Edition (Brigance, 1984)	grades K through 6	1. Reading 2. Mathematics 3. Writing 4. Measurement
BRIGANCE® Inventory of Early Development–Revised (Brigance, 1991)	ages birth to 7 years	1. Reading 2. Writing 3. Mathematics
BRIGANCE® Employability Skills Inventory (Brigance, 1995)	vocational secondary adult education job training	1. Reading 2. Writing 3. Mathematics

times used interchangeably to refer to these approaches. Examples of alternative assessment—which are each discussed later—are probes, error analysis, checklists, questionnaires, student journals, open-ended essay questions, performance-based assessment, portfolios, and exhibitions.

A fundamental principle of alternative approaches is that assessment of achievement should be linked to the curriculum that has been taught. Linking instruction to the assessment of achievement means that:

- Assessment occurs as a normal part of the student's work. Assessment activities should emerge from the curriculum and the teaching situation. The student does not stop work to do an assessment; the work and the assessment are linked. Examples of this type of assessment include the use of journals, notebooks, essays, oral reports, homework, classroom discussions, group work, and interviews. These assessment activities can occur individually or in small groups and can take place during one session or over multiple sessions (Marolda and Davidson, 1994).

- The conditions for assessment need to be similar to the conditions for doing meaningful tasks. Students should have sufficient time, have access to peers, be able to use appropriate tools (books, calculators, manipulatives, etc.), and have the chance to revise their work.
- Assessment tasks should be meaningful and multidimensional. For example, they should provide students with the opportunity to demonstrate problem solving, drawing conclusions, understanding relationships, making inferences, and generating new questions.
- Feedback to students should be specific, meaningful, prompt, and inform the students' thinking.
- Students participate in the assessment process. They help to generate and apply standards or rubrics. A rubric is an assessment scale that defines criterion that will be used in evaluating students. Self-assessment and peer assessment are included as part of the assessment process.

Assessment Approaches

Assessment activities and feedback from peers and teachers help to promote student achievement. Ways in which the teacher can gather information and provide feedback to parents and students include (National Council of the Teachers of Mathematics, 1991):

- probes
- error analysis
- oral descriptions
- written descriptions
- checklists
- questionnaires
- interviews
- conferences
- student journals and notebooks
- performance-based assessment
- portfolios
- exhibitions
- discussions between students, parents, and teachers

Probes

A **probe** is a diagnostic technique in which instruction is modified in order to determine whether an instructional strategy is effective. Probes can be used to diagnose student problems and assist in planning instruction. For example, suppose a teacher wants to determine whether a fourth grade student who is engaged in science investigations is ready to proceed to the next investigation. The teacher can present a science problem to the student and observe the strategies that the student uses to solve it. The teacher probes with questions such as, "What will happen if the temperature is increased?" The student in this case is able to successfully solve the problem, but has difficulty understanding that an experiment may work under certain conditions but not under other conditions. The teacher then helps the student by further probing and guiding the student through the steps of the experiment.

Instructional probes are implemented during the process of instruction. When designing an instructional probe, the following steps can be used:

1. The teacher identifies the area of achievement that is to be observed and measures whether the student can perform the task.

For example, in science the student is studying how moving objects are affected when pushed or pulled.

2. The teacher probes by modifying the task. For example, the teacher adds weight to one of the objects. (Examples of other instructional modifications can be found in the next section.)

3. The teacher measures whether the student can perform the task.

When conducting a diagnostic probe the teacher should document the student's performance during step 1 (baseline), step 2 (instruction), and step 3 (baseline).

Types of Modifications for Use with Probes

Types of modifications that can be made to instruction include:

Instructional modifications
- change from written presentation to oral presentation
- combine verbal instruction with written explanation
- require fewer problems to be completed
- provide additional practice
- slow the pace of instruction
- provide additional time to complete problems

Materials modifications
- use manipulatives
- place fewer questions, problems, or items on a page
- use color, word, or symbolic cues
- simplify the problem or the wording
- combine tactile mode with visual, oral, or kinesthetic modes

Environmental modifications
- change location of instruction or probe
- change time of day for instruction or probe

- provide a work area that is quiet and free of distractions
- change lighting of work area
- change seating arrangements.

Error Analysis

The purposes of **error analysis** are to: (1) identify the patterns of errors or mistakes that students make in their work, (2) understand why students make the errors, and (3) provide targeted instruction to correct the errors. When conducting an error analysis, the student's work is checked and the errors are categorized.

After conducting an error analysis, the error patterns are summarized. However, many errors that students make may not fall into a pattern. Alternatively, if a pattern emerges it does not mean that the problem is serious. Error analysis should be viewed as a preliminary form of assessment, and further evaluation of the student's work should always be conducted.

This approach to analyzing student work is frequently used in assessing students' reading abilities. Error analysis, when it is applied to reading, is commonly referred to as *miscue analysis.* When conducting a miscue analysis, teachers look for patterns of errors. According to Goodman (1984; 1989) these are "natural" errors rather than mistakes. Chapter 8 and Chapter 11 describe the application of error analysis to the assessment of reading and mathematics, respectively.

Oral Descriptions

Verbal descriptions of a student's work are used to provide immediate feedback to a student by a teacher or peer. Oral descriptions are especially useful because they are quick, efficient, direct, and can be easily integrated into instruction. They can be used for program planning and program evaluation.

Oral descriptions do have several drawbacks, however. They can be subjective and, since the descriptions are given verbally, there is no permanent record. In addition, specific disabilities may limit the ability of the student to understand, remember, or reply to what has been said.

Written Descriptions

A written description is a brief narrative that records feedback about the student's work. It can be shared with students, teachers, or parents. A written description, like an oral description, conveys an impression of important aspects of the student's work. Written descriptions can be used for program planning and program evaluation.

Before writing the narrative, the teacher should carefully review the student's work. The teacher writes the description, noting areas of strength as well as problem areas. A written description provides feedback to the student about the quality of the work. Because it is recorded, the student can refer to it as she or he continues to work. For example, a student who is engaged in environmental science is asked to work on the following project: Investigate the migration patterns of killer bees. After developing graphs that depict migration patterns and studying the habitats of killer bees, develop conclusions and make predictions about future migrations to new geographic areas.

After examining the student's results, a teacher can comment on: labeling, graphing, spelling, and use of language. In addition, the teacher can discuss the use of graphing and knowledge of geography to solve real-world problems, completeness of the results, the student's disposition toward science, the ability to plan ahead, work habits, and attention to detail (Kulm, 1994). Two disadvantages of using written descriptions are that the parents may have difficulty reading or they may not have knowledge of written English.

Checklists and Questionnaires

Checklists and questionnaires are convenient ways to provide feedback about a student's work or attitudes. A checklist is an assessment approach that can be completed quickly. Figure 6.2 is an example of a checklist that provides feedback about student confidence, willingness, perseverance, and interest. Checklists can be used for screening, diagnosis, program planning, and program evaluation.

MY BELIEFS ABOUT SCHOOL			
1. I like to go to school	most of the time	sometimes	never
2. My favorite subjects are	language arts social studies	mathematics health	science physical education
3. When I am at school I like to	read use the computer	write use the library	do projects use the playground
4. I like to work	by myself	with one other person	with several peers
5. I do homework	most of the time	sometimes	never
6. If I need help doing homework, I usually ask	my parent no one	my brother or sister	a friend
7. Some things I like about my teacher are:			

FIGURE 6.2

Assessing Attitudes, Interests, and Habits

Questionnaires provide an opportunity for teachers and students to collect information in more detail than checklists. Questionnaires can be open-ended, allowing respondents to express their attitudes, opinions, and knowledge in depth or they can be structured so that the respondents just need to fill in one or two words, circle responses, or indicate the appropriate picture or icon.

Interviews

The topic of conducting interviews was discussed in Chapter 5. Interviews are used to guide discussions, to encourage students, to determine motivation and enthusiasm, and to identify work and study habits. One basic approach is to interview students individually about their likes and dislikes. Asking questions such as the following can be informative: "What do you like about social studies?" "What are your interests?" "What don't you like?" Interviews can be used for screening, diagnosis, program planning, and program evaluation.

Structured interviews provide a more systematic way to assess achievement. A structured interview offers the opportunity to observe, question, and discuss areas of achievement.

An example of using a structured interview in science is to ask students to observe the sky several times during one evening and the next day to answer the following questions:

1. What is the pattern of the stars as they move across the sky?
2. What is the pattern of the planets?
3. Do the planets follow the same pattern as the stars?
4. After showing students several pictures of the planets and stars, ask students to develop several hypotheses about their size, appearance, and motion.

Conferences

A conference is a conversation about the student's work that can include the student, educators, and parents. In a conference, partici-pants share their views of the student's work with the goal of providing feedback and recommendations. Teacher-student conferences are helpful when assessing one piece of work or when summarizing the student's work over a period of time. The discussion in a conference can be strictly verbal or it can be audiotaped, videotaped, or summarized in written form. Conferences can be used for diagnosis, program planning, and program evaluation.

Student Journals

Students can keep a notebook or journal that allows them to record their work as well as their attitudes and feelings. A journal provides students the opportunity to record the steps to plan for an assignment, reflect on their own work, communicate about their learning, and document their progress (Kulm, 1994). In a journal, students can indicate what they like and don't like and areas in which they have difficulty. Journals can be used for program planning and program evaluation. The following is a sample mathematics journal outline (Kulm, 1994, p. 48):

Today's topic:

Two important ideas:

What I understood best:

What I need more work on:

How this topic can be used in real life:

Performance-Based Assessment

When used to assess achievement, **performance-based assessment** is the demonstration of knowledge, skills, or behavior. Performance assessment requires students to develop a product or to demonstrate an ability or skill based on an understanding of concepts and relationships. Chapter 7 describes performance-based assessment in detail.

Portfolios

A **portfolio** is a systematic collection of a student's work, assembled over a period of time.

Student's Name		Date				
AFTER COMPLETING MY SOCIAL STUDIES ASSIGNMENT, I CAN	*1* *Great!*	*2*	*3*	*4*	*5* *Need more work*	
1. make comparisons among different points of view.						
2. distinguish between fact and opinion.						
3. apply new skills in using information.						
4. understand new vocabulary.						
5. make inferences about events.						
6. integrate new information.						
7. discuss new concepts and theories.						

FIGURE 6.3

Self-Assessment Checklist—Social Studies

When used to document and assess achievement, portfolios can provide information about conceptual understanding, problem solving, reasoning, communication abilities, habits, motivation, enthusiasm, creativity, work habits, and attitudes. Portfolios help students to see that knowledge is interconnected. They can be used for program planning and program evaluation. A more extensive discussion of the use of portfolios can be found in Chapter 7.

SELF-ASSESSMENT

Self-assessment provides students with an opportunity to review concepts and identify processes. It is an occasion for students to reflect on their learning. Figure 6.3 is an example of a checklist that students use when assessing their own learning.

PEER ASSESSMENT

Peer assessment allows students insight into the thinking and reasoning abilities of their peers. When conducting peer assessments, stu-

dents have an opportunity to reflect on the learning processes of their peers as well as their own. Figure 6.4 is an example of a checklist that students use when conducting a peer assessment.

REPORT CARD GRADES AS MEASURES OF ACHIEVEMENT

Report card grades can be helpful in understanding a student's achievement levels, strengths, and weaknesses. When report cards from the current and previous years are reviewed, they can provide information about whether the student's problems are new or long-standing. They can indicate trends in student achievement. Is the problem recent? Has the student had difficulty during previous years? Is the problem in one area or in several areas? In what areas does the student do well?

Report Card Grading

There are two major viewpoints regarding the assignment of report card grades to students

	Yes	No	Somewhat
Student's Name	**Date**		
Peer's Name			
1. My peer used new information to solve a problem.			
2. My peer used new vocabulary.			
3. My peer demonstrated the ability to think analytically.			
4. My peer integrated and synthesized information.			
5. My peer made several generalizations.			

FIGURE 6.4

Peer Assessment—Science

with disabilities (Gersten, Vaughn, and Brengelman, 1996). The first position considers grading standards to be absolute. Report card grades for all students should be based on the same standards; that is, an A, B, C, or failing grade means the same for a student with a disability or a student without a disability. The second perspective is that grading should be based on individual effort. However, this second option has several drawbacks: 1) it is difficult to measure effort; 2) basing grades on effort can prevent students from making progress because the grade creates the illusion that the student *is* making progress; 3) it is difficult to use just one grade to communicate multiple meanings such as progress, effort, and peer comparisons (Bursuck, Polloway, Plante, Epstein, Jayanthi, and McConeghy, 1996).

Grading Students with Disabilities

Alternatives to traditional report cards for students with disabilities are:

Supplementary progress reports. This is a written narrative that accompanies the traditional report card and that describes the student's academic and behavioral performance during a specific ranking period (Mehring, 1995).

Contracts. This is a written agreement between the student and the teacher that specifies the level of performance that the student must sustain to obtain a particular grade (Mehring, 1995).

Progress checklist. This is a list of skills or competencies that are taught. Evaluation of the skills or competencies is made by checking a box under the column "mastered" or "needs improvement" (Mehring, 1995).

Developing modifications. A list of options for the teacher when grading a student with a disability can be used. These modifications can be jointly developed by the teacher, student, and parents. Figure 6.5 presents suggested modifications.

OBSERVING THE STUDENT WITHIN THE ENVIRONMENT

In Chapter 5 you learned about the importance of considering the student within the physical, learning, and social environments. The interactions between the student and the environment are important assessment considerations.

The following procedures could be jointly developed by the school, student, and parent when specifying grading options.

Tests

- Administer test orally, with questions and answers.
- Teacher, other student, or resource teacher reads regular test to student. (Please give resource teacher at least one day's notice.)
- Administer regular test using open book, class notes, or both.
- Modify modality of test, written or oral, such as multiple choice instead of essay questions.
- Redo test if not passed.
- Lower criterion for passing.

In-Class Assignments

- Give regular assignments with lower criteria for passing.
- Shorten the regular assignment (e.g., half the questions).
- Grade assignments as "complete" rather than with a letter grade.
- Modify the set of questions students will answer.

- Pair the student with another student for help.
- Require the student to give oral answers to teacher.
- Redo assignments if incorrect.
- Give credit for appropriate behaviors not normally graded, such as taking notes.

Homework

Same options as "In-Class Assignments."

Class Participation, Behavior, and Effort

- Same expectations as for other class members, but student may need extra encouragement and frequent feedback from teacher.
- Focus on a specific study skill or behavior deficit by giving a Pass/No Pass each day for that behavior. (Examples: coming prepared to class with correct materials, or volunteering answers during class discussions.)

Other Considerations

- Give extra credit for projects that student or teacher suggests.
- Have student aide tape reading assignments or read aloud to student.
- Set expectations for attendance.

FIGURE 6.5

Sample of Criteria for Grading a Student who Receives Special Education Services

Source: Guskey, T. R. (1996). *Communicating Student Learning: 1996 ASCD Yearbook.* Alexandria, Va.: Association for Supervision and Curriculum Development. Copyright © 1996. ASCD. Used by permission.

Physical Environment

The physical environment can influence the student's performance. The temperature, lighting, and seating arrangements of the spaces used for teaching and learning can affect how well the student performs. Figure 6.6 is a checklist that can be used to study the physical environment.

Learning Environment

A comfortable learning environment facilitates the acquisition of a positive disposition and contributes to achievement. The curriculum, instructional methods, materials, and the assessment approaches are all areas of concern. Developing a positive disposition is influenced

◀ POINT STREET SCHOOL ▶
Physical Environment

Student's Name __Karen S.__   Date __3/13__   Time __10:35__

Observer __T.S.__   Location __English__

Characteristic	Always	Sometimes	Never
1. Seating Is the student seated properly?			X
▶ Suggestions for improvement: Karen's feet do not reach the floor when she is sitting at her desk. She needs to have a foot rest.			
2. Lighting Is the lighting appropriate?	X		
▶ Suggestions for improvement:			
3. Noise Is the noise level appropriate?		X	
▶ Suggestions for improvement: There are times when the noise level seems high. This may make it difficult for Karen and other students to concentrate. Suggest that the teacher and students monitor the noise level.			
4. Distractions Is the student distracted by activities in the room?		X	
▶ Suggestions for improvement: While Karen is distracted at times, she is able to refocus on the tasks at hand.			
5. Temperature Is the temperature of the room appropriate?		X	
▶ Suggestions for improvement: There are times when the room is too hot. This does not seem to affect Karen's performance. However, this should be monitored.			
6. General Atmosphere Does the student appear to be comfortable in the environment?	X		
▶ Suggestions for improvement:			

FIGURE 6.6

Observing the Physical Environment

by the learning environment. Figure 6.7 is a checklist that can help to determine the appropriateness of the learning environment.

Social Environment

Relationships with students and teachers can affect achievement. The social environment is important to the development of self-concept and self-esteem. These, in turn, contribute to a positive disposition toward achievement. By observing the social environment, teachers can study the relationships students have with peers and adults. Figure 6.8 is a checklist that can help to determine the appropriateness of the social environment.

PREFERRED PRACTICES

Achievement tests, when carefully chosen, can be important sources of information. The achievement approaches discussed in this chapter include multiple sources of information that should be used when assessing achievement. School records and past and current classroom performance are important sources of information. Other sources include criterion-referenced assessment, curriculum-based assessment, journals, notebooks, essays, oral reports, homework, discussions, group work, interviews, alternative assessment, performance testing, self-assessment, peer assessment, systematic observations, anecdotal records, interviews with teachers and students, and samples of student's work.

Assessment and instruction are closely linked and intertwined. When assessing achievement, the teacher must be knowledgeable about the curriculum that has been *taught* to students in contrast to the *written* curriculum. Achievement tests should mea-

sure what has been *taught*. Teachers should carefully examine the test content in order to determine that there is a very close match between the test items and the curriculum that has been taught. The information that has been gathered through the assessment process should inform and support learning and instruction.

EXTENDING LEARNING

6.1 Identify one topic for instruction. Develop two assessment tasks that link the instruction directly to assessment.

6.2 Obtain a copy of a standardized achievement test. Review the test items in one curriculum area. What items represent the curriculum that is being taught in the local schools? What items differ? What conclusions and recommendations can you offer?

6.3 Mr. Lincoln, a new teacher, suspected that Simon, an 8-year-old in second grade, was having difficulty keeping up with his classroom peers. Ms. Sloan, who taught high school students, was puzzled when Katy, a 15-year-old, was falling behind her classmates. Choose one of these teachers. What suggestions could you give the teacher for assessing the achievement of these students?

6.4 Compare the test items of a group achievement test with an individual achievement test. What are the similarities? Differences? When would it be appropriate to use each of these tests?

6.5 Choose a curriculum area with which you are familiar. Working with a partner, identify a unit of instruction. Using the steps suggested in this chapter, develop a criterion-referenced test. Share your

◀ POINT STREET SCHOOL ▶
Learning Environment

Student's Name **Karen S.** Date **3/13** Time **10:35**

Observer **T.S.** Location **English**

Characteristic	Always	Sometimes	Never
1. Materials Are a variety of materials available?	X		
▶ Suggestions for improvement:			
2. Manipulatives Are appropriate manipulatives available?			
▶ Suggestions for improvement: *N/A*			
3. Curriculum Does the curriculum reflect recent reform standards?	X		
▶ Suggestions for improvement:			
4. Activities Is instruction oriented toward the use of various materials rather than paper and pencil tasks?		X	
▶ Suggestions for improvement: *Karen performs best when actively involved in projects. Suggest that options for assignments be developed for Karen and other students.*			
5. Instructional Demands Are the instructional demands appropriate for the student?		X	
▶ Suggestions for improvement: *Karen needs to have directions for assignments clarified. She should be asked to repeat the directions to make sure that she understands what is expected.*			
6. Modifications Have modifications been made to instruction to accommodate the learning needs of the student?	X		
▶ Suggestions for improvement:			

FIGURE 6.7

Observing the Learning Environment

◄ POINT STREET SCHOOL ►
Social Environment

Student's Name ___Karen S.___   Date ___3/13___ Time ___10:35___
Observer ___T.S.___   Location ___English___

Characteristic	Always	Sometimes	Never
1. Teacher-Student Interactions Are interactions warm and friendly?	X		
▶ Suggestions for improvement:			
2. Disruptions Are disruptions kept to a minimum?		X	
▶ Suggestions for improvement: Announcements and the public address system interruptions can distract Karen and other students in the class. An effort should be made to reduce these interruptions.			
3. Behavioral interventions Are behavioral interventions effective and appropriate?	X		
▶ Suggestions for improvement:			
4. Peer interactions Are peer interactions appropriate?	X		
▶ Suggestions for improvement:			
5. General Atmosphere Does the student appear to be comfortable in the social environment?	X		
▶ Suggestions for improvement:			

FIGURE 6.8

Observing the Social Environment

CRT with other groups and provide feedback.

REFERENCES

American Educational Research Association, American Psychological Association, and National Council on Measurement in Education (1985). *Standards for educational and psychological testing.* Washington, D.C.: Author.

Anastasi, A. (1988). *Psychological testing.* New York: Macmillan.

Balow, I. H., R. C. Farr, and T. P. Hogan (1992). *Metropolitan achievement test 7* San Antonio, Tex.: The Psychological Corporation.

Berk, R. A. (1988). Criterion-referenced tests. In *Educational research, methodology, and measurement: An international handbook,* ed. J. P. Keeves, 365–370. Oxford: Pergamon.

Brigance, A. (1977). *BRIGANCE® diagnostic inventory of basic skills.* No. Billerica, Mass.: Curriculum Associates.

Brigance, A. H. (1980). *BRIGANCE® diagnostic inventory of essential skills.* No. Billerica, Mass.: Curriculum Associates.

Brigance, A. H. (1983). *BRIGANCE® diagnostic comprehensive inventory of basic skills.* No. Billerica, Mass.: Curriculum Associates.

Brigance, A. H. (1984). *BRIGANCE® assessment of basic skills–Spanish edition.* No. Billerica, Mass.: Curriculum Associates.

Brigance, A. H. (1991). *BRIGANCE® diagnostic inventory of early development–revised.* No. Billerica, Mass.: Curriculum Associates.

Brigance, A. H. (1995). *BRIGANCE® diagnostic employability skills inventory.* No. Billerica, Mass.: Curriculum Associates.

Bursuck, W., E. A. Polloway, L. Plante, M. J. Epstein, J. Jayanthi, and J. McConeghy (1996). Report card grading and adaptations: A national survey of classroom practices. *Exceptional Children* 62: 301–318.

Choate, J. S., B. E. Enright, L. J. Miller, J. A. Poteet, and T. A. Rakes (1995). *Curriculum-based assessment and programming.* Boston: Allyn & Bacon.

CTB/Macmillan/McGraw-Hill (1993). *California achievement tests/5.* Monterey, Calif.: Author.

Engel, B. (1990). An approach to assessement in early literacy. In *Achievement testing in the early grades,* ed. C. Kamii, 119–134. Washington, D.C.: National Association for the Education of Young Children.

Feldt, L. S., R. A. Forsyth, T. N. Ansley, and S. D. Alnot (1993). *Iowa tests of educational development.* Chicago: The Riverside Publishing Company.

Gersten, R., S. Vaughn, and S. U. Brengelman (1996). Grading and academic feedback for special education students and students with learning difficulties. In *ASCD yearbook,* ed. T. R. Guskey, 47–57. Alexandria, Va.: Association for Supervision and Curriculum Development.

Goodman, K. (1984). Unity in reading. In *Becoming readers in a complex society:* The 83rd yearbook of the national society of the study of education, Part I, eds. A. Purves and O. Niles, 79–114. Chicago, Ill.: University of Chicago Press.

Goodman, K. (1989). Roots of the whole-language movement. *Elementary School Journal* 90: 207–222.

Harcourt Brace Educational Measurement (1996). *Stanford achievement test* (9th ed.). San Antonio, Tex.: Author.

Harcourt Brace Educational Measurement (1992). *Wechsler individual achievement test.* San Antonio, Tex.: Author.

Hoover, H. D., A. N. Hieronymous, D. A. Frisbie, & S. B. Dunbar (1993). *Iowa tests of basic skills.* Chicago: The Riverside Publishing Company.

Howell, K. W., and R. Rueda (1996). Achievement testing with culturally and linguistically diverse students. In Handbook of multicultural assessment, L. S. Suzuki, P. J. Meller, and J. G. Ponterotto (Eds.). San Francisco: Jossey-Bass Publishers.

Kaufman, A. S., and N. L. Kaufman (1985). *Kaufman test of educational achievement.* Circle Pines, MN: American Guidance Service.

Kulm, G. (1994). Mathematics assessment. San Francisco: Jossey-Bass Publishers.

Markwardt, Jr., F. C. (1989). *Peabody individual achievement test–revised.* Circle Pines, MN: American Guidance Service.

Marolda, M. R., and P. S. Davidson (1994). *Assessing mathematical abilities and learning approaches. Windows of opportunity* (pp. 83–113). Reston, VA: National Council of the Teachers of Mathematics.

Mehrens, W. A., and I. J. Lehmann (1990). *Measurement and evaluation in education and psychology.* Fort Worth, Tex.: Holt, Rinehart and Winston.

Mehring, T. A. (1995). Report card options for students with disabilities in general education. In *Report card on report cards*. T. Azwell and E. Schmar (Eds.). Portsmouth, NH: Heinemann.

Naslund, R. A., L. P. Thorpe, and D. W. Lefever (1985). *SRA achievement series*. Chicago: Science Research Associates.

National Council of the Teachers of Mathematics. (1991). *Mathematics assessment*. Reston, Va.: Author.

Newcomer, P. (1990). *Diagnostic achievement battery-2*. Austin, Tex.: PRO-ED.

Nitko, A. J. (1996). *Educational assessment of students*. Englewood Cliffs, N.J.: Prentice Hall.

Prescott, G. A., I. H. Balow, T. R. Hogan, and R. C. Farr. (1984). *Metropolitan achievement tests 6: Survey battery*. San Antonio, Tex.: Harcourt Brace Educational Measurement.

Rivera, D. P., R. L. Taylor, and B. R. Bryant (1994–1995). Review of current trends in mathematics assessment for students with mild disabilities. *Diagnostique* 20: 143–174.

Salvia J., and J. A. Ysseldyke (1995). *Assessment*. Boston: Houghton Mifflin.

Sattler, J. (1988). *Assessment of children*. San Diego: Jerome M. Sattler.

Scannell, D. P., O. M. Hough, B. H. Lloyd, and C. F. Risinger (1993). *Tests of achievement and proficiency*. Chicago: The Riverside Publishing Company.

Sonnenschein, J. L. (1983). *Basic achievement skills individual screener*. San Antonio, Tex.: Harcourt Brace Educational Measurement.

Taylor, R. L. (1993). *Assessment of exceptional students*. 3d ed. Boston, Mass.: Allyn & Bacon.

Wilkinson, G. (1993). *Wide range achievement test 3*. Wilmington, Del.: Jastak Assoicates.

Woodcock, R. W., and M. B. Johnson (1989). *Woodcock-Johnson psychoeducational battery–revised*. Allen, Tex.: DLM.

Performance-Based Assessment

OVERVIEW

In this chapter alternatives to traditional assessment approaches are examined. Each of the alternative methods, performance-based assessment and authentic assessment, is evolving as we search for improved practices and tools for linking instruction with assessment. Portfolios, performance tasks, exhibitions, or other documentation of students' achievement are used to measure student accomplishments. While norm-referenced tests have their place in the assessment process, alternatives to norm-referenced tests provide a rich variety of approaches that can be used to collect many types of information. This is an exciting area and we encourage you to develop your own variations on the topics that are discussed.

CHAPTER OBJECTIVES

After completing this chapter, you should be able to:

Provide a rationale for the use of performance-based assessment methods.

Describe performance-based assessment, authentic assessment, and portfolio assessment.

Develop and implement performance-based assessment methods.

Develop scoring rubrics.

WHAT SHAPES OUR VIEWS

Contemporary views of learning have influenced the development of alternative assessment approaches. From cognitive learning theory we know the following (Herman, Aschbacher, and Winters, 1992):

1. Knowledge is constructed from new information and prior learning.

   Implications for assessment:
   - Divergent thinking, rather than the search for one right answer, and multiple solutions should be fostered.
   - Multiple forms of expression are encouraged.
   - Critical thinking skills must be fostered.
   - New information needs to be related to prior knowledge.
2. Students of all ages and abilities can solve problems. All learning is not developed in a linear progression of separate skills.

   Implications for assessment:
   - All students need to be involved in problem solving.
   - Problem solving and critical thinking do not have to be contingent on mastery of basic skills.
3. Students approach learning with a multiplicity of learning styles, attention spans, and developmental and cognitive differences.

   Implications for assessment:
   - Choices in how to demonstrate what has been learned need to be available.
   - Allot time to complete assessment tasks generously.
   - Concrete types of tasks (manipulatives) and other opportunities for demonstration of what has been learned should be provided.

4. Students do better when they know the goals and understand how their performance will be evaluated.

   Implications for assessment:
   - Students need to be involved in establishing goals.
   - Criteria for performance are discussed and described.
   - Examples of acceptable levels of performance are routinely furnished.
5. Students should know when to use knowledge and how to direct their own learning.

   Implications for assessment:
   - Provide opportunities for students to monitor and evaluate their own learning.
   - Utilize authentic (real-world) opportunities for assessment.
6. Students' learning is affected by motivation, effort, and self-esteem.

   Implications for assessment:
   - The design of assessment tasks, as a standard, consider motivation, self-esteem, and the promotion of best efforts.

ASSESSING PERFORMANCE

Performance-based assessment describes one or more approaches for measuring student progress, skills, and achievements. Performance-based assessment consists of portfolios performance tasks, exhibitions, or other documentation of student accomplishments. One way of looking at performance assessment is to think of it as the ultimate form of linking instruction with assessment. Grant Wiggins has been a strong proponent of performance assessment. He has urged educators to construct "tests worth taking" (Brandt, 1992, p. 35).

Gardner (1991) has written that performance-based assessments can be described according to developmental levels. Gardner views students as learners who are at various points in their learning. For example, some students might be required to exhibit the performance of beginning learners while others would be asked to demonstrate the performance of experts. Evaluations do not just have to focus on what students demonstrate about their academic or cognitive abilities but can determine the extent to which students work cooperatively, are sensitive to others, or use computers, manipulatives, or other resources.

Performance-based assessment is particularly useful when students are working on long-term projects. In this way, they are able to bring into play a variety of resources and to demonstrate mastery of various concepts and principles. Performance-based assessments are most closely related to the types of assessments that students will most likely be involved in after they leave school (Gardner, 1991). The following is a list of characteristics of performance tasks (National Council of Teachers of Mathematics, 1991; Cohen, 1995):

- use processes appropriate to the discipline
- are valued by students
- lead to other problems, questions, and possibilities
- are thought provoking and deepen understanding
- are frequently interdisciplinary
- support persistence
- assist the student in constructing meaning
- are appropriate and safe
- accommodate and support various thinking and learning styles
- are accessible to a variety of students
- have more than one correct answer
- contribute to positive attitudes toward learning

Developing Performance-Based Assessments

There are four questions that can guide us as we think about performance assessment (Diez and Moon, 1992):

1. What is important for students to know and to be able to do? This question requires us to rethink curricula, standards, and approaches to teaching.
2. What is acceptable performance? In establishing criteria for performance, we must think about mastery. What does mastery of a specific skill or behavior look like? The criteria must be general enough so that students can practice those skills on which they will be evaluated.
3. How can expert judgments be made? In developing the criteria for acceptable performance, we must be able to specify them in advance. For example, suppose we want to know how well a student can retell a story or demonstrate knowledge about the community in which the student lives. Criteria that could be specified in advance include the use of details, accuracy, vocabulary, and expression.
4. How can feedback be provided? Performance assessment always requires more than one solution or one type of performance. Is the student using the skills under consideration in school and at home? How can the family, educators, and peers provide feedback to the student? The criteria for making judgments become the goals for instruction and progress.

Figure 7.1 is a checklist that can be used when developing performance-based assessments.

Performance Tasks "Worth Doing"			
Criteria	Never	Sometimes	Definitely
1. Essential—The task is a "big idea" that fits the core of the curriculum.			
2. Authentic—The task relates to real-world problems.			
3. Rich—The task leads to new problems and raises questions.			
4. Engaging—The task is absorbing and thought provoking.			
5. Active—The student is involved in developing solutions and creating new problems.			
6. Feasible—The task can be done within a reasonable time frame, is appropriate, and is safe.			
7. Equitable—The completion of the task requires a variety of learning styles.			
8. Open—The task has more than one solution.			

FIGURE 7.1

Checklist for Developing Performance-Based Assessments

Source: Adapted from NCTM (1991).

AUTHENTIC ASSESSMENT

Authentic assessment is similar to performance assessment except that the student completes or demonstrates knowledge, skills, or behavior in a real-life context (Meyer, 1992) and real-world standards are used to measure the student's knowledge, skills, or behavior. The conditions for the authentic assessment may be quite different from those of the performance assessment. In performance assessment, the conditions are often contrived or artificial, while in authentic assessment the task complexity, motivation, standards, and stimuli are quite different. Just as with performance-based assessment, the criteria for authentic assessment must be developed.

Authentic performance has a number of characteristics, which include that they (Cushman, 1990):

Structure

Are public

Involve an audience or panel

Require some collaboration

Are worth practicing

Involve the modification of school policies and schedules to support them

Design

Are essential

Are enabling

Are contextualized

Involve complex processes, not isolated tasks or outcomes

Assess habits, attitudes, behaviors, motivation, and creativity

Are representative

Are engaging

Are open-ended

Scoring

Involve criteria that are essential

Are graded according to performance standards

Involve self-assessment

Use multifaceted scoring, not one grade

Equity

Are fair

Involve multiple areas of learning

Are responsive to culture, gender, learning style, and language

Table 7.-1 presents a list of examples of authentic assessment.

TABLE 7.1   Examples of Authentic Assessment

Literacy	*Oral expression*
audiotape of reading	debate
videotape of peer conferencing	book talk
book review	play reading
book poster	phone call to obtain information
article for school newspaper	speech
job application	
resumé	
The Arts	*Mathematics*
scenery design for a play	solving real-life problems
play performance	using a checking account
musical performance	designing and building a structure
design for a public space	development of a budget
sculpture	teaching a lesson
dance performance	
Science	*Social studies*
experiment	map of a nature trail
original investigation	development of a museum exhibit
journal of observations	development of a political campaign
investigation of local pollution problems	design of a children's playground
designing and building a bridge	
developing a solar car	

Adapted from Poteet, Choate, and Stewart (1993).

PORTFOLIO ASSESSMENT

A portfolio is a systematic collection of a student's work that has been assembled over a period of time. Portfolios can include works in progress, a student's best work, or work of which the student is most proud. Materials in the portfolio can be linked directly to a student's individualized education program to show growth toward the objectives (Swicegood, 1994; Wesson and King, 1996).

Purposes of Portfolios

Special education teachers find portfolios helpful in answering questions regarding what a student knows and can do. First, portfolios demonstrate a student's growth and progress over time. They can be developed over the course of a school year and shared during parent-teacher conferences and during annual reviews of the student's individualized educational program. Portfolios may become part of the student's records and are retained as a student moves from one grade or level to the next.

Second, portfolios present examples of the student's best work(s). Portfolios may be developed over one or more years and be part of graduation requirements, be used for evaluations of individualized programs, or be shared with potential employers to illustrate what the student has learned.

Benefits

Portfolio assessment provides benefits to students, teachers, and family members (Airasian, 1996; Gillespie, Ford, Gillespie, and Leavell, 1996). Some examples include:

- For students:

  selecting items to include in their portfolios

  engaging in a noncompetitive activity

  experiencing a collaborative climate among students through peer collaboration activities

having ownership and tangible evidence of learning

building self-esteem

clarifying expectations

reflecting and judging their own works

having ongoing feedback regarding their works

- For teachers:

  connecting assessment and instruction

  providing diagnostic information about a student's strengths and instructional needs

  generating meaningful examples of student growth

  constructing knowledge of what constitutes high-quality work

  having concrete examples of student performance to discuss with family members

- For family members:

  viewing student progress over time

  having easy-to-understand examples

In one study (Shepard and Bliem, 1995) parents reported that talking about their child's progress and seeing samples of their child's work were very useful (77 percent and 60 percent, respectively), whereas, only 43 percent of parents reported report cards useful and 14 percent reported standardized tests useful.

Contents of a Portfolio

The contents of a portfolio consist of products as well as process items. Product items are works, such as papers, drawings, photographs, models, language samples, creative art, and other artifacts. Process items include successive drafts of a paper, works in progress, works in which students have cooperated with others, and self-reflections about a particular unit of study. Reflective statements developed by students are critical components of a portfolio (Cole, Ryan, and Kick, 1995). Finally, a portfolio may include teacher and parent comments, scores of standardized tests, school attendance records, and school activities.

Organizing the Portfolio

Materials in the portfolio can be organized according to curriculum areas, skill areas, or chronological order. In this section, we will examine ways to organize portfolios at various grade levels.

1. *Early Education:* The two models in Figure 7.2 are designed for young children and illustrate ways that a teacher can conceptualize portfolios. Model A is organized to reflect curriculum areas, and Model B is designed to focus on skill and knowledge areas. Some of the contents of the portfolio in Model A has been modified for a student with disabilities in the classroom and relate to the student's IEP.

2. *Middle School.* Portfolios can focus on documenting academic progress and on assisting students in understanding themselves. Figure 7.3 illustrates this approach.

Model A: Curriculum Areas

Language and Literacy
  *1. Audiotapes of child retelling a story
  2. Drawing of favorite part of the story
  *3. Writing samples using word prediction software
  4. List of favorite books written or dictated by child
Science and Mathematics
  1. Paper and pencil drawings and written descriptions of mathematics problems
  2. Written log/drawings of child's observations of science experiments
  3. Chart with a series of predictions
  4. Photographs of child engaged in measuring, sorting, classifying, or seriation activities
  5. Child's graph of group data from the class
Art and Music
  1. Paintings and drawings
  2. Audiotape of song/music created by child
  3. Photographs of art projects
  4. Copies of projects drawn using software
Community and Culture
  1. Student maps of the classroom, school, or community
  2. Copies of student e-mail sent to pen pal in another city or state
  3. Photographs and teacher-transcribed descriptions of field trips
  4. Copies of student thank-you letters to community speakers
Physical Education
  1. Photographs of child on climbing structure
  *2. Checklist of child's skills completed by the teacher

*3. Videotapes of child participating in an activity
  4. List of favorite activities written or dictated by child
Social Skills
  *1. Child's evaluation of cooperative learning activities
  2. Copies of peer evaluations of cooperative learning activities
  *3. Videotapes of student working with others
  *4. Checklists of skills or observations completed by the teacher

Model B: Knowledge and Skills

Academic
  1. Writing log and videotape of integrated unit activity
  2. Student notes from learning a search process on the Internet
Self-esteem
  1. A series of drawings about feelings
  2. Comments from teachers and peers on accomplishments
Cooperative group
  1. Teacher feedback notes regarding a cooperative learning activity
  2. Student products, reflections on group activities
Citizenship
  1. Summary of a community project and self-reflection
  2. List of activities regarding "How I Helped My School"

* Some of the contents in this portfolio have been modified for a student with disabilities. The items that are asterisked (*) show how the teacher modified the contents for this portfolio.

FIGURE 7.2

Portfolio Models in Early Education

I. Who I am
   A. Interests
   B. Friends
   C. Family
   D. Other
II. Skills that I am developing
   A. Working independently
   B. Working cooperatively with others
   C. Problem solving
   D. Conflict resolution
   E. Other
III. My academic progress
   A. Language Arts (reading, writing, listening, speaking)
   B. Mathematics
   C. Science
   D. Social Studies
   E. Music
   F. Art
   G. Other
IV. Service to my community
   A. Volunteer work
   B. Special projects
   C. Other

FIGURE 7.3

Portfolio Model for Middle School Students

Source: Adapted from portfolio models developed by Milton Union School faculty, June 1993, and Joan Schindler (Incarnation); Alvine Wilson, Mary Galdeen, Deborah Carey, Rae Ann Herman (West Carrollton Junior High School); and Cindy Hill (Weisenborn Institute), June 1993, as cited in Cole, Ryan, and Kick, 1995, pp. 40–42.

3. *Secondary School.* Portfolios may be designed to help students synthesize information about career plans (Figure 7.4) or may be a graduation requirement.

Portfolios, because of their breadth and integrative format, can be used as part of graduation requirements. Central Park East Secondary School requires students to complete a portfolio across fourteen categories and to display their portfolios to a graduation committee (Darling-Hammond, Ancess, and Falk, 1995). The portfolio is based on the individual student's work; however, some of the requirements can be based on group work. Students present seven of the fourteen categories orally to a graduation committee comprised of the student's faculty advisor, another faculty member, an adult chosen by the student, and another student. The student candidates may be asked about the other seven categories during the Graduation Committee Hearing. Students also complete a final project that is in an area of particular interest to the student, such as one of the portfolio items explored in greater depth. The portfolio can be created and presented in any number of ways—there is no one "right" way.

I. Introduction
   A. Title page
   B. Table of contents
   C. Preface (student's reflection on the portfolio)
II. Student Profile
   A. Autobiography
   B. School service projects
   C. Community service
III. Educational Achievement
   A. My beliefs about my education (a personal philosophy)
   B. My education goals
   C. Copies of exceptional work
   D. Evaluations of education progress
   E. Other
IV. Preparing for the Future
   A. Interest surveys
   B. Career exploration
   C. Home and family
   D. Recreation
   E. Other

FIGURE 7.4

Portfolio Model for Students in an Alternative High School

Source: Adapted from portfolio models developed by LIMA OWE faculty, November 1991, as cited in Cole, Ryan, and Kick, 1995, p. 44.

Helping Students Construct Portfolios

Students learn a great deal from making selections, assembling and reviewing their materials, and refining their portfolios. Teachers help students during each step in the construction process:

1. Deciding what they want to demonstrate in their portfolios.

For portfolios to be valid, students must understand the performance that is expected. Teachers should discuss with students at the beginning of the year what should be included in the portfolio and how it will be evaluated.

2. Incorporating self-reflections, which are important components of a portfolio.

A self-reflection is a writing activity in which the student analyzes learning and accomplishments. In the written reflection students describe their views of the learning process and the importance of the task. To help students become more familiar with the process of reflection, a teacher can use class discussions to encourage students to think about an activity or event. For example, a teacher could pose questions about a popular movie or television show: "What did you like best about the movie?" or "What do you think makes a movie good?"

Cole, Ryan, and Kick (1995) suggest that the teacher develop several questions to assist students in reflecting on their works in progress or their completed works:

a. Why is this your best work?
b. How did you go about accomplishing this task?
c. What would you do differently if you did a task like this again?
d. Where do you go from here? (p. 16)

3. Understanding how portfolios will be evaluated.

It is important that students understand how their portfolio will be evaluated. Teachers need to spend time discussing with the class the many ways of evaluating a work. Consider the following example of two elementary students who responded to an interviewer's question:

First Classroom:

Interviewer: "What kind of reader are you?"

Tara: "Pretty good."

Interviewer: "What makes you say that?"

Tara: "I'm in the Red Group."

Second Classroom:

Interviewer: "What kind of reader are you?"

Sheila: "I like funny stories and books about animals, but often I just kind of get stuck on the same author for months at a time." (Adapted from Johnston, as cited in Hewitt, 1995, p. 188)

4. Choosing the pieces to include.

Students learn a great deal in choosing and selecting the materials to include in the portfolio. Teachers help students by choosing assignments that require a diversity of skills and with individual student ability and areas of interest in mind.

5. Determining how to present the pieces.

Some content areas more readily lend themselves to one format than another. For example, the complexity or creativity of a model of a city or construction of a sailboat may be better represented in a photograph than in written text. A videotape captures areas in which movements or interactions are important.

Using Technology

Teachers can organize and preserve student information, including text, sound (talking, singing, music, reading), scanned images (pictures, drawings, and photographs), and video (individual and group performances), on computer disk, compact disc (CD), and student home pages on the World Wide Web. Student- or teacher-developed Web sites can be used to display the students' portfolios.

Incorporating the use of technology offers the capabilities of computer searching and combining information in meaningful ways.

When the contents of a portfolio are preserved on disk, the disk can follow students from one grade to the next. After graduation, students can provide a disk to prospective employers or to college or university admissions officers to illustrate what they know and are able to do.

Several software programs, such as the Electronic Portfolio (1996) and The Portfolio Assessment Kit (1996) allow teachers and students to organize portfolio items. Figure 7.5 illustrates a student's work and the set of goals established by the school that delineates the school's expectations for student performance. The program allows each element of the student's portfolio to be linked to any number of goals. Over time, students collect work that

represents their abilities and accomplishments as they relate to these sets of goals.

Another software program, The Grady Profile™ (1995), includes suggestions for scoring rubrics. In The Grady Profile™, the mathematics area includes standards of the National Council of Teachers of Mathematics (NCTM), the cognitive area includes descriptors based on Howard Gardner's theory of multiple intelligences, and the behavior area includes a lengthy list of behavioral descriptors. The Grady Profile™ allows teachers to define their own rubrics and the levels of achievement. This program also includes components for student self-evaluation and evaluation by family members (Figure 7.6).

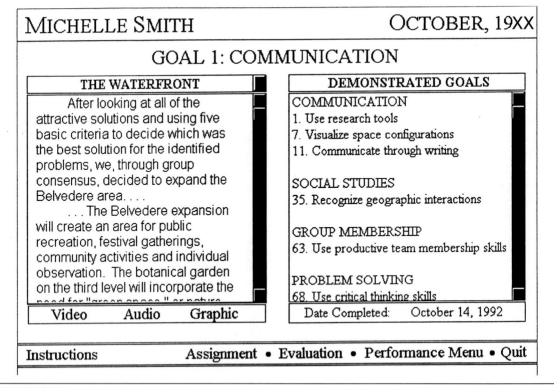

FIGURE 7.5

Sample Screen from Michelle's Digital Portfolio

Source: Niguidula, D. (1994). *The Digital Portfolio: A Richer Picture of Student Performance.* (Studies on Exhibitions No. 13). Providence, R.I.: Brown University, Coalition of Essential Schools. Reprinted by permission.

SNAPSHOT

Linking Daryl's IEP with Portfolio Assessment

Last year, when Daryl was in third grade, he was identified as having a learning disability. He had difficulties in reading, written language, and getting along with other students, and he was often argumentative. One of Daryl's IEP goals is that he will improve in reading.

His fourth grade teacher is using portfolios to document student progress. His teacher believes that Daryl can demonstrate progress in language and literacy by documenting activities in the portfolio. Daryl will keep a reading log that lists the books that he has read and a brief summary of each. Periodically, Daryl will complete a more extensive book report. Daryl will use a word processing program with a word prediction feature that will allow him to record his thoughts more efficiently. Copies of his writing drafts will be added to the portfolio

periodically. Daryl's teacher will share these materials with the IEP team during the annual review of Daryl's individualized education program.

Daryl's portfolio will also include a section on Working with Others. This area relates directly to another IEP goal for building social skills. Daryl and his teacher discussed ways in which Daryl can make and keep friends and decided how they should document his progress. One of the ideas that they discussed was for Daryl to complete a daily self-assessment checklist. The teacher talked about her observations of Daryl on the playground this week and some examples of cooperating with others. They agreed that she will continue to share her observations with Daryl at the end of the day and together they will record positive examples on a graph.

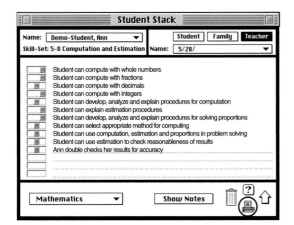

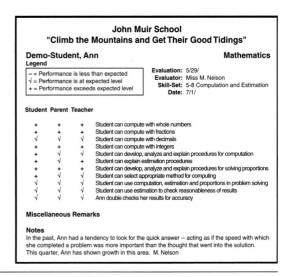

FIGURE 7.6

Grady Profile

Source: The Grady Profile™ (1995). St. Louis, Mo.: Aurbach & Associates. Reprinted by permission.

EXHIBITIONS

An **exhibition** is a display of a student's work that demonstrates knowledge, abilities, skills, and attitudes concerning one project or a unit of work. An exhibition provides a student the opportunity to summarize and to synthesize what has been accomplished. Exhibitions are useful in a variety of academic content areas and in interdisciplinary studies because students can realize by their own efforts that learning is more than just a series of worksheets or exercises and that it involves conceptual understanding, problem solving, and reasoning. Exhibitions are useful for program planning and program evaluation.

RESPONDING TO DIVERSITY

Using portfolio assessment with students with disabilities requires teachers to be sensitive to the unique needs of students. Gordon and Bonilla-Bowman (1996) report that portfolio assessment serves as a concrete reminder of work and progress. Fuchs (1994) identifies several examples that present challenges in using portfolio assessment with students with disabilities. First, students who are experiencing difficulties in writing are at a disadvantage when constructing a writing portfolio because it may be difficult to determine whether an inadequate response results from poor writing skills, poor mastery of the content, poor problem-solving skills, lack of creativity, or a combination of these factors. Second, teachers should carefully consider the consequences of allowing students to respond in a different format. For example, students with disabilities in language who are allowed to tape a response rather than complete a written response miss the authentic task of writing. Writing is a task required in the real world.

Portfolios may not be useful for students with chaotic lives or who have chronic health problems. Portfolios are not effective for students who come infrequently to school (Wolf, 1996). Understanding portfolio expectations requires regular school attendance and ongoing discussions with the teacher regarding one's work.

Gordon and Bonilla-Bowman (1996) discuss concerns voiced by teachers and parents regarding the use of portfolios with students from diverse cultural, ethnic, and linguistic groups. There are two potential difficulties with portfolio assessment for these students. First, students rely on their own use of language, more so than on standardized tests; and, second, the teacher may introduce bias in assessing the portfolio, a bias that is mitigated by standardized tests. Portfolios have the potential of providing students with ways of demonstrating conceptual understandings beyond the ability to understand English. Yet, in a review of portfolios, Gordon and Bonilla-Bowman (1996) found little evidence or representation of students' home cultures and few portfolios that included students' home languages.

Limited research has been conducted on bias in portfolio assessment. Some research raises questions about bias in alternative assessment in general. For example, Nuttall and Goldstein (as cited in Madaus, Haney, and Kreitzer, 1992) found that the achievement gap between various groups of students was greater on alternative assessment instruments than on traditional tests. Identifying activities that are authentic, especially for students whose lives will be very different from the teacher's, is difficult (Fuchs, 1994).

Much research is needed on the use of portfolios and the effects of this method on student learning. Questions to keep in mind include: Does the use of portfolios in the classroom increase student achievement? Are portfolios effective measures for meeting the goals of the individualized education program for students with disabilities? What types of evidence show learning?

DEVELOPING SCORING SYSTEMS

Rubric

A **rubric** is an assessment scale that identifies the area(s) of performance and defines various levels of achievement. The rubric also includes a description of the various levels of achievement. Rubrics that are designed to provide rich information about the level of achievement on the assessment scale use **descriptors**. Descriptors are written descriptions that detail each level of achievement. Scoring systems generally fall into two main types: analytic and holistic.

Analytic Scoring

An **analytic scoring** system reports an independent score for each of the criteria of the assessment scale. For a rubric developed for a writing portfolio there might be four criteria: organization, details, voice, and grammar. An analytic scoring system reports separate scores for each of these criteria. Within each of these criteria, the various levels of achievement can be described either numerically or categorically. In an example of a writing portfolio, we might identify the following achievement levels of organization:

> Criterion: Organization
> > 4 = Extensive
> >
> > 3 = Moderate
> >
> > 2 = Slight
> >
> > 1 = Lacking

Notice that we have used both numerical and corresponding categorical descriptions of achievement in this rubric.

In our example, the rubric does not include descriptors of the levels of achievement. Thus, without further descriptions of the terms "moderate" and "slight," one teacher might rank the organization of a student's paper a "3" while another teacher would rank organization a "2." Detailed descriptors are helpful to teachers and others during evaluation procedures and serve to increase interrater reliability.

One example of a rubric that provides detailed descriptors is the Vermont Writing Assessment Guide (Figure 7.7). Compare the detailed descriptors given in the Vermont Analytic Assessment Guide with the numeric and category listing in the example above. We see that to receive a top score ("extensively") on the organization of a paper in Figure 7.7, detailed information is provided regarding that level of achievement: the paper is organized from beginning to end; there must be a logical progression of ideas; the paper has a clear focus; and the writing must be fluent and cohesive.

Descriptors are helpful to students and parents. Detailed information regarding levels of achievement assist students in understanding not only how their work will be evaluated but how they can evaluate the work themselves. Descriptors are helpful to parents in understanding what their child can do.

Depending on the richness and detail of the descriptors, analytic scoring can provide diagnostic information about the student's achievement. Scores on the individual criteria can be examined to indicate areas of strengths and areas of improvement. Because this type of scoring system is an effective diagnostic tool, student scores should be reported as categorical rather than numerical. Analytic scores that are reported as numerical can be totaled and averaged, but these calculations result in the loss of rich analytic information (Hewitt, 1995).

Holistic Scoring

Holistic scoring is a type of scoring in which the teacher assigns a single score to the student's work (Figure 7.8). For example, the writing portfolio receives a single overall score. The writing is not analyzed by separate criteria such as organization, details, voice, and gram-

Vermont Writing Assessment
Analytic Assessment Guide

	Purpose	Organization	Details	Voice or Tone	Grammar/Usage/Mechanics
In assessing, consider...	...how adequately intent and focus are established and maintained (success in this criterion should not depend on the reader's knowledge of the writing assignment: the writing should stand on its own)	...coherence: ...whether ideas or information are in logical sequence or move the piece forward ...whether sentences and images are clearly related to each other (Indenting paragraphs is a matter of Grammar/Usage/Mechanics)	...whether details develop ideas or information ...whether details elaborate or clarify the content of the writing with images, careful explanation, effective dialogue, parenthetical expressions, stage directions, etc.	...whether the writing displays a natural style, appropriate to the narrator ...or whether the tone of the writing is appropriate to its content	...the conventions of writing, including: *Grammar (e.g., sentence structure, syntax) *Usage (e.g., agreement and word choice) *Mechanics (e.g., spelling, capitalization, punctuation)
Ask how consistently, relative to length and complexity...	intent is established and maintained within a given piece of writing	the writing demonstrates coherence	details contribute to development of ideas and information, evoke images or otherwise elaborate or clarify the content of the writing	an appropriate voice or tone is established and maintained	as appropriate to grade level, command of conventions is evident, through correct English or intentional, effective departure from conventions
Extensively	Establishes and maintains a clear purpose and focus.	Organized from beginning to end, logical progression of ideas, fluent and coherent.	Details are pertinent, vivid or explicit and provide ideas/information in depth.	Distinctive personal expression or distinctive tone enhances the writing.	Few or no errors present; or departures from convention appear intentional and are effective.
Frequently	Establishes a purpose and focus.	Organization moves writing forward with few lapses in unity or coherence.	Details develop ideas information; or details are elaborated.	Establishes personal expression or effective tone.	Some errors or patterns of errors are present.
	⌐Yes┐ _Is author's focus clear within the writing?_ └No⌐	⌐Yes┐ _Does the organization move the writing forward?_ └No⌐	⌐Yes┐ _Do details enhance and/ or clarify the writing?_ └No⌐	⌐Yes┐ _Can you hear the writer? Or, is the tone effective?_ └No⌐	⌐Yes┐ _Does the writing show grade-appropriate command of G/U/M?_ └No⌐
Sometimes	Attempts to establish a purpose; focus of writing is not fully clear.	Lapse(s) in organization affect unity or coherence.	Details lack elaboration, merely listed or unnecessarily repetitious.	Attempts personal expression or appropriate tone.	Numerous errors are apparent and may distract the reader.
Rarely	Purpose and focus not apparent.	Serious errors in organization make writing difficult to follow.	Details are minimal, inappropriate, or random.	Personal expression or appropriate tone not evident.	Errors interfere with understanding.
NON-SCORABLE	*is illegible: i.e., includes so many indecipherable words that no sense can be made of the writing, or *is incoherent: i.e., words are legible but syntax is so garbled that response makes no sense, or *is a blank piece of paper *For Portfolio: Does not have required minimum contents				

©1994 Vermont Department of Education

FIGURE 7.7

Analytic Assessment Guide

Source: Vermont Analytic Assessment Guide, Vermont Department of Education, 120 State Street, Montpelier, Vt. 05620. Reprinted by permission.

Description	Numerical Score
The paper is well organized, provides a sufficient number of explicit details in supporting statements, and contains no major grammatical errors.	4
The paper shows organization but may lack coherence, details are appropriate, and/or it contains some grammatical errors.	3
The paper lacks consistency in organization, details are not elaborate, and/or it contains many grammatical errors.	2
The paper has serious problems in organization, lack of details, and/or it contains frequent grammatical errors.	1

FIGURE 7.8

Holistic Rubric for Scoring Student Writing

Figure 7-9 Benchmarks for Evaluating Student Use of Persuasive Writing

Benchmark Examples	Scoring Guide	Score
"The sports drink advertizement uses comparison and customer appeal to sell its product. The ad shows the advantages of this drink over similar drinks on the market. The ad appeals to the customer cost-wise because it is cheaper than other drinks. It appeals to health-conscious customers because it is not only nutritious but healthy and contains no preservatives. The drink is marketed in an attractive container that is easy to hold and is eye catching."	Student response describes at least three ways in which the advertisement is designed to be persuasive. The response provides ample support from the writing prompt and demonstrates prior knowledge of persuasive techniques.	4
"The advertisement is persuasive because it uses facts to back up its product. The ad uses bright colors to help the sports drink stand out. Having additional information about the nutrients and ingredients in the sport drink helps persuade the consumer because these things are important and if the advertisement states that you can get the nutrients from their product it is a selling point."	Student response describes at least two ways in which the advertisement is designed to be persuasive. Response provides valid arguments for example chosen.	3
"The cost of sports drinks is important to people. The ad appeals to the customer because the drink is a good value. The drink is less expensive than other sports drinks that you can buy in the store."	Student response describes one way in which the advertisement is designed to be persuasive. The response provides valid explanation and support.	2
"This advertisement is persuasive. It shows a picture of the sports drink. I really like the choice of colors in this ad and I have tried this sports drink. It is really good."	Student response discusses advertising or sports drinks but does not contain a valid argument.	1
"I don't like these kinds of drinks. They taste very strange. Besides they are just as expensive as soda."	Student response is irrelevant or wrong.	0

FIGURE 7.9

Scoring Guide and Benchmark Examples

mar. Like analytic scoring, holistic scoring should include descriptors of each of the achievement levels.

This type of scoring lacks the depth of information contained in analytic scoring; however, it tends to be easier to design and score than analytic scoring.

Benchmarks

Benchmarks are examples of student work that illustrate each scoring level on the assessment scale. Teachers evaluate student work by using scoring standards and benchmarks. Benchmarks can be in the form of papers, such as example essays, or a small sample of student work, such as possible answers to a question. Figure 7.9 illustrates the scoring guide and benchmarks to an open-response question in writing for grade 12 students. Students were asked to write a response to a writing prompt that touted a new sports drink.

Hewitt (1995) cautions teachers to select benchmark examples that demonstrate the midrange of each of the achievement levels. When a teacher scores a student's portfolio, benchmarks provide the teacher with a framework and serve to increase reliability.

Benchmarks can be helpful to students in understanding how their performance or portfolio will be assessed. However, benchmarks should be shared carefully with students so that they will not think they must replicate the example, thus loosing the individual nature of their work. Providing students with several different examples of benchmarks at various achievement levels can reduce this potential problem.

ENSURING TECHNICAL ADEQUACY

Reliability

The purpose of the assessment affects how crucial the issue of reliability is. Some assessments are low-stakes assessments; that is, the consequences of the assessment do not have a major impact on the student's future. For example, an assessment designed to answer questions regarding student progress is a low-stakes assessment.

Assessments that are part of graduation requirements have much higher stakes. High-stakes assessments refer to situations in which the information being collected will have a direct and potentially adverse impact on the student. In high-stakes assessment, issues of reliability are critical.

Consistency and Stability

Reliability of performance-based assessments focuses on the consistency and the stability of the assessment. When using performance-based assessment, students frequently have multiple opportunities to perform individually. For example, a teacher is able to create a number of opportunities in which students are required to work together cooperatively; however, individual oral presentations on a unit of study are arranged infrequently because of the amount of class time these presentations require. Thus, consistency of student response is unknown due to low frequency of performance.

Multiple categories or points on the assessment scale affect the degree of interrater agreement. The more categories or points, the more difficult it may be to obtain interrater agreement, especially if the categories are vague. We have discussed one method of increasing consistency by including descriptors in each of the achievement levels. We have examined how descriptors assist evaluators in making determinations regarding students' scores and help students evaluate their own work.

Another approach to addressing consistency actually adjusts for differences between evaluators by accepting adjacent scores recorded by two readers (Hewitt, 1995). For example, two teachers reviewed a student's writing using the holistic scoring system in Figure 7.8. The first reader rated the paper a 1; the second reader rated the paper a 2. Since the evaluators have adjacent scores, the difference is adjusted by averaging the two, and the student receives a score of the average, 1.5.

Teachers also want to be assured of the stability of the performance. Stability is a function of the scoring system and environmental factors. Stability is affected when error occurs in the scoring systems; for example, when the teacher assigns an incorrect score or when a calculation error is made. Environmental factors also affect stability. A student's performance can be altered by the learning and social environments of the classroom that impact the student's motivation, attitude, self-esteem, confidence, and anxiety.

Consequential Validity

Consequential validity is the extent to which an assessment instrument promotes the intended consequences (Linn and Baker, 1996). This type of validity has been used to describe performance-based assessments. One of the primary reasons for using this type of assessment is to improve student learning, and the extent to which performance-based assessment improves student learning defines consequential validity. Factors that can affect student learning, and thus impact consequential validity, include school reform activities, instructional improvements, staff development activities, levels of student achievement, and accountability systems (Linn and Baker, 1996).

Validity can be addressed from both the student and teacher perspectives.

For students: For the assessment to be valid, students must know what is expected. Students must know what skills and knowledge are included in the assessment, what types of performance demonstrates these skills and knowledge, and how their performance will be evaluated.

For teachers: For the assessment to be valid, teachers must take care in designing tasks that accurately reflect achievement for students from nondominant cultures. For example, oral presentations may be difficult

for students whose first language is not English. An oral presentation in science, for example, might be supplemented by information presented in another format, such as a detailed drawing to illustrate the concepts presented.

Fairness

Fairness of the assessment instrument is an important aspect of consequential validity. One of the driving forces behind the evolution of performance-based assessment has been the impetus to develop assessment instruments that are fair to students. Tests are opportunities for students to demonstrate learning regardless of culture, gender, race, socioeconomic status, or disability. Fairness means that bias has been minimized, that the assessment is equitable, and that the measures are sensitive to diverse populations.

Improving Reliability and Validity

Airasian (1996) suggests several guidelines to improve reliability and validity of performance-based and portfolio assessments:

1. Know the purpose of the assessment.
2. Teach and give students practice on the criteria that will be used in the assessment.
3. State the criteria in observable behaviors.
4. Select criteria that are at an appropriate level of difficulty for the students.
5. Limit the number of criteria to a manageable number.
6. Maintain a written record (pp. 174–175).

Cautions When Using Performance-Based, Authentic, and Portfolio Assessment

Careful design of performance, authentic, and portfolio assessments is important to ensure that appropriate conclusions can be drawn. If we are unclear about our expectations, then the usefulness of the assessment is diminished. There are several questions that can guide us in using these assessment techniques.

Is the assessment representative of the student's work? For example, a performance task could demonstrate how a student develops a first draft of a book review, but not a finished one. Videotapes might contain images of play rehearsals, but not the opening-night production.

Are the criteria for assessment clear to all evaluators and students? Ambiguity, inconsistency in judging performance and authentic assessments, and subjectivity can be major problems. The student and the evaluators must know what is to be done, the conditions under which the assessment tasks are to be performed, and the criteria for evaluation.

Have the criteria for evaluation changed over time? When designing an assessment the educator may have specified that all of the creative writings of a student be evaluated. Later, it may be unclear whether this meant all the finished writing or all the stories whether they were finished or not.

Who evaluates the contents? Depending on who evaluates the performance or authentic assessment tasks, interpretations can vary; and depending on the training of the educator, different conclusions can be reached (Arter and Spandel, 1991).

Are performance and authentic assessments fair? The use of performance and authentic assessments does not automatically mean that they are unbiased toward students with disabilities, certain cultural groups, minorities, economic groups, and those to whom English is a second language.

PREFERRED PRACTICES

The development and implementation of performance-based assessment present challenges to educators. Although they are not without problems, these assessment procedures have the potential of helping us to develop valid and fair approaches to assessing students. However, as this area continues to develop, we must proceed carefully. Figure 7.10 summarizes the advantages and limitations of alternative assessment procedures.

Before assessment procedures are developed, standards that specify what students should know and be able to do need to be developed through discussion with educators and parents. Unless there is consensus among the stakeholders, it is unlikely that valid assessment will result.

Assessment procedures should assist educators and policymakers in improving instruction and learning. If assessment is to be beneficial, the procedures must provide useful information about the capabilities of students. If the purposes of assessment are not beneficial, then the assessment procedures should not be used.

All assessment procedures have to be fair to all students. Assessment procedures should be unbiased; and they should be attentive to differences in development and disabilities and to differences in culture, race, socio-economic, and gender. Students must be given multiple opportunities to demonstrate what they know. Educational decisions cannot be based on a single test score.

The assessment tasks must be reliable and valid and represent the standards that children are expected to achieve. Multiple-choice tests give children inadequate opportunities to demonstrate what they know. Alternatives to traditional assessment, such as performance-based assessment, portfolios, and exhibitions are rich sources of information.

Educators should be involved in the development and implementation of assessment procedures. Because assessment is closely linked to instruction, educators must participate in the development, administration, scoring, and interpretation of assessment procedures. We need to continue to revise and improve upon assessment procedures (Hymes, Chafin, and Gonder, 1991).

FIGURE 7.10

Assessment Alternatives	Advantages for Teachers	Disadvantages for Teachers	Suggestions for Improved Use
	Formative Assessment Techniques		
1. Conversations and comments from other teachers	(a) Fast way to obtain certain types of background information about a student. (b) Permit colleagues to share experiences with specific students in other learning contexts, thereby broadening the perspective about the learners. (c) Permit attainment of information about a student's family, siblings, or peer problems that may be affecting the student's learning.	(a) Tend to reinforce stereotype and biases toward a family or a social class. (b) Students' learning under another teacher or in another context may be quite unlike their learning in the current context. (c) Others' opinions are not objective, often based on incomplete information, personal life view, or personal theory of personality.	(a) Do not believe hearsay, rumors, biases of others. (b) Do not gossip or reveal private and confidential information about students. (c) Keep the conversation on a professional level, focused on facts rather than speculation and confidential so it is not overheard by others.
2. Casual conversations with students	(a) Provide relaxed, informal setting for obtaining information. (b) Students may reveal their attitudes and motivations toward learning that are not exhibited in class.	(a) A student's mind may not be focused on the learning target being assessed. (b) Inadequate sampling of students' knowledge; too few students assessed. (c) Inefficient: students' conversation may be irrelevant to assessing their achievement.	(a) Do not appear as in inquisitor, always probing students. (b) Be careful so as not to misperceive a student's attitude or a student's degree of understanding.
3. Questioning students during instruction	(a) Permits judgments about students' thinking and learning progress during the course of teaching, gives teachers immediate feedback. (b) Permits teachers to ask questions requiring higher-order thinking and elaborated responses. (c) Permits student-to-student interaction to be assessed. (d) Permits assessment of students' ability to discuss issues with others orally and in some depth.	(a) Some students cannot express themselves well in front of other students. (b) Requires education in how to ask proper questions and to plan for asking specific types of questions during the lesson. (c) Information obtained tends to be only a small sample of the learning outcomes and of the students in the class. (d) Some learning targets cannot be assessed by spontaneous and short oral responses; they require longer time frames in which students are free to think, create, and respond. (e) Records of students' responses are kept only in the teacher's mind, which may be unreliable.	(a) Be sure to ask questions of students who are reticent or slow to respond. Avoid focusing on verbally aggressive and pleasant "stars." (b) Wait 5–10 seconds for a student to respond before moving on to another. (c) Avoid limiting questions to those requiring facts or a definite correct answer, thereby narrowing the focus of the assessment inappropriately. (d) Do not punish students for failing to participate in class question sessions or inappropriately reward those verbally aggressive students who participate fully. (e) Remember the students' verbal and nonverbal behavior in class may not indicate their true attitudes/values.

(Continued)

FIGURE 7.10 (Continued)

Assessment Alternatives	Advantages for Teachers	Disadvantages for Teachers	Suggestions for Improved Use
	Formative Assessment Techniques		
4. Daily homework and seatwork	(a) Provide formative information about how learning is progressing. (b) Allow errors to be diagnosed and corrected. (c) Combine practice, reinforcements, and assessment.	(a) Tend to focus on narrow segments of learning rather than integrating large complexes of skills and knowledge. (b) Sample only a small variety of content and skills on any one assignment. (c) Assignment may not be complete or may be copied from others.	(a) Remember that this method assesses learning that is only in the formative stages. It may be inappropriate to assign summative letter grades from the results. (b) Failure to complete homework or completing it late is no reason to punish students by embarrassing them in front of others or by lowering their overall grade. Learning may be subsequently demonstrated through other assessments. (c) Do not inappropriately attribute poor test performance to the student not doing the homework. (d) Do not overemphasize the homework grade and overuse homework as a teaching strategy (e.g., using it as a primary teaching method).
5. Teacher-made quizzes and tests	(a) Although primarily useful for summative evaluation, they may permit diagnosis or errors and faulty thinking. (b) Provide for students' written expression of knowledge.	(a) Require time to craft good tasks useful for diagnosis. (b) Focus exclusively on cognitive learning targets.	(a) Do not overemphasize lower level thinking skills. (b) Use open-ended or constructed response tasks to gain insight into a student's thinking processes and errors. (c) For better diagnosis of a student's thinking, use tasks that require students to apply and use their knowledge to "real-life" situations.
6. In-depth interviews of individual students	(a) Permit in-depth probing of students' understandings, thinking patterns, and problem-solving strategies. (b) Permit follow-up questions tailored to a student's responses and allow a student to elaborate answers. (c) Permit diagnosis of faulty thinking and errors in performances.	(a) Require a lot of time to complete. (b) Require keeping the rest of the class occupied while one student is being interviewed. (c) Require learning skills in effective educational achievement interviewing and diagnosis.	(a) If assessing students' thinking patterns, problem-solving strategies, etc., avoid prompting student toward a prescribed way of problem solving. (b) Some students need their self-confidence bolstered before they feel comfortable revealing their mistakes.

7. Growth and learning progress portfolios	(a) Allow large segments of a student's learning experiences to be reviewed. (b) Allow monitoring a student's growth and progress. (c) Communicates to students that growth and progress are more important than test results. (d) Allow student to participate in selecting and evaluating material to include in the portfolio. (e) Can become a focus of teaching and learning.	(a) Be very clear about the learning targets toward which you are monitoring progress. (b) Use a conceptual framework or learning progress model to guide your diagnosis and monitoring. (c) Coordinate portfolio development and assessment with other teachers. (d) Develop scoring rubrics to define standards and maintain consistency.
	(a) Require a long time to accumulate evidence of growth and progress. (b) Requires special effort to teach students how to use appropriate and realistic self-assessment techniques. (c) Require high-level knowledge of the subject matter to diagnose and guide students. (d) Require the ability to recognize complex and subtle patterns of growth and progress in the subject. (e) Results tend to be inconsistent from teacher to teacher.	
8. Attitude and values questionnaires	(a) Assess effective characteristics of students. (b) Knowing student's attitudes and values in relation to a specific topic or subject-matter may be useful in planning teaching. (c) May provide insights into students' motivations.	(a) Remember that the way questions are worded significantly affects how students respond. (b) Remember that attitude questionnaire responses may change drastically from one occasion or context to another. (c) Remember that your personal theory of personality or personal value system may lead to incorrect interpretations of students' responses.
	(a) The results are sensitive to the way questions are worded. Students may misinterpret, not understand, or react differently than the assessor intended. (b) Can be easily "faked" by older and testwise students.	

Summative Assessment Techniques

1. Teacher-made tests and quizzes	(a) Can assess a wide range of content and cognitive skills. (b) Can be aligned with what was actually taught. (c) Use a variety of task formats. (d) Allow for assessment or written expression.	(a) Do not overemphasize lower level thinking skills. (b) Do not overuse short-answer and response-choice items.
	(a) Difficult to assess complex skills or ability to use combinations of skills. (b) Require time to create, edit, and produce good items. (c) Craft task requiring students to apply knowledge to "real life." Class period is often too short for a complete assessment. (d) Focus exclusively on cognitive outcomes.	
2. Tasks focusing on procedures and processes	(a) Allow assessments of nonverbal as well as verbal responses. (b) Allow students to integrate several simple skills and knowledge to perform a complex, realistic task.	(a) Investigate carefully the reason for student's failure to complete the task successfully. (b) Use a scoring rubric to increase the reliability and validity of results.
	(a) Focus on a narrow range of content knowledge and cognitive skills. (b) Require great deal of time to properly formulate, administer, and rate.	

(Continued)

FIGURE 7.10 (Continued)

Assessment Alternatives	Advantages for Teachers	Disadvantages for Teachers	Suggestions for Improved Use
	Summative Assessment Techniques		
	(c) Allow for group and cooperative performance and assessment. (d) Allow assessment of steps used to complete an assignment.	(c) May have low interrater reliability unless scoring rubrics are used. (d) Results are often specific to the combination of student and task. Students' performance quality is not easily generalized across different content and tasks. (e) Tasks that students perceive as uninteresting, boring, or irrelevant do not elicit the students' best efforts.	(c) Do not confuse the evaluation of the process a student uses with the need to evaluate the correctness of the answers. (d) Allow sufficient time for students to adequately demonstrate the performance.
3. Tasks focusing on products and projects	(a) Same as 2(a), (b), and (c). (b) Permit several equally valid processes to be used to produce the product or complete the project. (c) Allow assessment of the quality of the product. (d) Allow longer time than class period to complete the tasks.	(a) Same as 2(a), (b), (c), (d), and (e). (b) Students may have unauthorized help outside of class to complete the product or project. (c) All students in the class must have the same opportunity to use all appropriate materials and tools in order for the assessment to be fair.	(a) Same as 2(a), (b), (c), and (d). (b) Give adequate instruction to students on the criteria that will be used to evaluate their work, the standards that will be applied, and how students can use these criteria and standards to monitor their own progress in completing the work. (c) Do not mistake the aesthetic appearance of the product for substance and thoughtfulness. (d) Do not punish tardiness in completing the project or product by lowering the student's grade.
4. Best work portfolios	(a) Allow large segments of a student's learning experience to be assessed. (b) May allow students to participate in the selection of the material to be included in the portfolio. (c) Allow either quantitative or qualitative assessment of the works in the portfolio. (d) Permit a much broader assessment of learning targets than tests.	(a) Require waiting a long time before reporting assessment results. (b) Students must be taught how to select work to include as well as how to present it effectively. (c) Teachers must learn to use a scoring rubric that assesses a wide variety of pieces of work. (d) Interrater reliability is low from teacher to teacher. (e) Require high levels of subject matter knowledge to evaluate students' work properly.	(a) Be very clear about the learning targets to be assessed to avoid confusion and invalid portfolio assessment results. (b) Teach a student to use appropriate criteria to choose the work to include. (c) Do not collect too much material to evaluate. (d) Coordinate portfolio development with other teachers. (e) Develop and use scoring rubrics to define standards and maintain consistency.
5. Textbook-supplied tests and quizzes	(a) Allow for assessment of written expression.	(a) Often do not assess complex skills or ability to use combinations of skills.	(a) Be skeptical that the items were made by professionals and are of high quality.

	Advantages	Limitations	Implications for the Teacher
	(b) Already prepared, save teachers time. (c) Match the content and seqence of the textbook or curricular materials.	(b) Often do not match the emphases and presentations in class. (c) Focus on cognitive skills. (d) Class period is often too short for a complete assessments.	(b) Carefully edit or rewrite the item to match what you have taught. (c) Remember that you are personally responsible for using a poor quality test. You must not appeal to the authority of the textbook.
6. Standardized achievement tests	(a) Assess a wide range of cognitive abilities and skills that cover a year's learning. (b) Assess content and skills common to many schools across the country. (c) Items development and screened by professionals, resulting in only the best items being included. (d) Corroborate what teachers know about pupils; sometimes indicate unexpected results for specific students. (e) Provide norm-referenced information that permits evaluation of students' progress in relation to students nationwide. (f) Provide legitimate comparisons of a student's achievement in two and more curricular areas. (g) Provide growth scales so students' long-term educational development can be monitored. (h) Useful for curriculum evaluation.	(a) Focus exclusively on cognitive outcomes. (b) Often the emphasis on a particular test is different from the emphasis of a particular teacher. (c) Do not provide diagnostic information. (d) Results usually take too long to get back to teachers, so are not directly useful for instructional planning.	(a) Avoid narrowing your instruction to prepare students for these tests when administrators put pressure on teachers. (b) Do not use these tests to evaluate teachers. (c) Do not confuse the quality of the learning that did occur in the classroom with the results on standardized tests when interpreting them. (d) Educate parents about the tests' limited validity for assessing a student's learning potentials.

FIGURE 7.10

Advantages and Limitations of Alternate Types of Assessment Techniques

Source: Educational Assessment of Students, 2d ed., by Nitko, Anthony J. © 1996. Reprinted by permission of Prentice-Hall, Inc., Upper Saddle River, N.J.

Portfolios should be used with caution in high-stakes testing. High-stakes testing is the use of tests to make classification, retention, or promotion decisions about students. Student work can be compromised by the pressure of such a situation. The lack of a research base in this relatively new type of assessment and concerns regarding validity and reliability are additional reasons why practitioners should not use portfolios in high-stakes testing.

In constructing a portfolio, students take responsibility for planning and illustrating their learning. Portfolios provide a vehicle for students to slip into the driver's seat and acquire ownership of their learning. However, this road remains untested; until there is a stronger research base, portfolios should be used with caution. Perhaps there will always be a place for different types of assessment practices. Consider the following parable:

> There is a big difference between naming hammers and pounding nails in a wall. However, lest anyone believe that naming hammers is not important, just ask someone to get a particular type of hammer and see what happens if the person fetching it doesn't know the types of hammers. On the other hand, and more importantly, standing with a hammer in one's hand and knowing its name doesn't make one a builder or tell one how to use it. Could there be a place for both knowledge and application? (Farr and Tone, 1994, cited in Gillespie et al., 1996, p. 490)

EXTENDING LEARNING

7.1 Working with a small group of students, develop a set of questions for two or more chapters in this textbook. Your question sets should include multiple-choice, short-answer, and essay questions. Next, review the same chapters and identify how knowledge of the information could be demonstrated by either performance or portfolio assessment. What method of assessment do you prefer? Why?

7.2 Compare the various methods of scoring performance-based assessments. What are the advantages and disadvantages of each?

7.3 Use one of the search engines on the Internet to locate a user group of individuals interested in portfolio assessment. What types of information are available? Is there help for teachers who would like to implement portfolios in their classroom? Are there examples of scoring rubrics?

7.4 Why are concerns relating to reliability and validity so important when using performance-based assessments?

7.5 Review one or two portfolio software programs. Compare and contrast the features. Do the programs include scoring systems? Which program would you recommend? Why?

REFERENCES

Airasian, P. W. (1996). *Assessment in the classroom.* New York: McGraw-Hill.

Airasian, P. W., and G. F. Madaus (1983). Linking testing and instruction: Policy issues. *Journal of Educational Measurement* 20: 103–108.

Arter, J. A., and V. Spandel (1991). *Using portfolios of student work in instruction and assessment.* Portland, Ore.: Northwest Regional Education Laboratory.

Aurbach, E. (1995). *The Grady Profile*™ [Computer software]. St. Louis, Mo.: Aurbach and Associates, Inc.

Bagnato, S. J., and J. T. Neisworth (1990). *System to plan early childhood services.* Circle Pines, Minn.: American Guidance Service.

Brandt, R. (1992). On performance assessment: A conversation with Grant Wiggins. *Educational Leadership* 49: 35–37.

Cohen, P. (1995). Designing performance assessment tasks. *Education update* 37(1): 4–5, 8.

Cole, D. J., C. W. Ryan, & F. Kick (1995). *Portfolios across the curriculum and beyond.* Thousand Oaks, Calif.: Corwin Press, Inc.

Cushman, P. (1990). Performances and exhibitions: The demonstration of mastery. *Horace* 6: 17–24.

Darling-Hammond, L., J. Ancess, and B. Falk (1995). *Authentic assessment in action.* New York: Teachers College Press.

Diez, M. E., and C. J. Moon (1992). What do we want students to know? . . . and other important questions. *Educational Leadership* 49: 38–41.

Digital Portfolio [Computer software prototype]. (1993). Providence, R.I.: Coalition of Essential Schools, Brown University.

Electronic Portfolio CD [Computer software]. (1996). New York: Scholastic.

Fuchs, L. (1994). *Connecting performance assessment to instruction.* Reston, Va.: Council for Exceptional Children.

Fuchs, L., and S. Deno (1981). The relationship between curriculum-based mastery measures and standardized achievement tests in reading. Research Report No. 57. Minneapolis: University of Minnesota, Institute for Research on Learning Disabilities. (ERIC Document Reproduction Service No. ED 212 662)

Fuchs, L. S., D. Fuchs, and S. L. Deno (1982). Reliability and validity of curriculum-based informal reading inventories. *Reading Research Quarterly* 18: 6–26.

Galagan, J. E. (1985). Psychoeducational testing: Turn out the lights, the party's over. *Exceptional Children* 52: 288–299.

Gardner, H. (1991). *The unschooled mind.* New York: Basic Books.

Gillespie, C. S., K. L. Ford, R. D. Gillespie, and A. G. Leavell (1996). Portfolio assessment: Some questions, some answers, some recommendation. *Journal of Adolescent and Adult Literacy* 39(6): 480-491.

Gordon, E.W., and C. Bonilla-Bowman (1996). Can performance-based assessments contribute to the achievement of educational equity? In *Per-formance-based student assessment: Challenges and possibilities,* J. B. Baron and D. P. Wolf, eds. 32–51. Chicago, Ill.: University of Chicago Press.

The Grady Profile™ [Computer Software]. (1995). St. Louis, Mo.: Aurbach and Associates.

Herman, J. L., P. R. Aschbacher, and L. Winters (1992). *A practical guide to alternative assessment.* Alexandria, Va.: Association for Supervision and Curriculum Development.

Hewitt, G. (1995). *A portfolio primer: Teaching, collecting, and assessing student writing.* Portsmouth, N.H.: Heinemann.

Hymes, D. L., A. E. Chafin, and P. Gonder (1991). The changing face of testing and assessment, problems and solutions. Arlington, Va.: American Association of School Adminstrators.

Jervis, K. (1996). *Eyes of the child: Three portfolio stories.* New York: Teachers College Press.

Linn, R. L., and E. L. Baker (1996). Can performance-based student assessments be psychometrically sound? In *Performance-based student assessment: Challenges and possibilities,* eds. J. B. Baron and D. P. Wolf, 84–103. Chicago, Ill.: The University of Chicago Press.

Madaus, G., W. Haney, and A. Kreitzer (1992). Testing and evaluation. New York: Council for Aid to Education.

Meyer, C. A. (1992). What's the difference between *authentic* and *performance* assessment? *Educational Leadership* 49: 39–40.

Meyers, J., J. Pfeffer, and V. Erlbaum (1985). Process assessment: A model for broadening assessment. *Journal of Special Education* 18: 1–84.

National Council of the Teachers of Mathematics (1991). *Mathematics assessment.* Alexandria, Va.: Author.

Niguidula, D. (1994). *The digital portfolio: A richer picture of student performance.* Studies on Exhibitions No. 13. Providence, R.I.: Coalition of Essential Schools, Brown University.

Nitko, A. J. (1996). *Educational assessment of students.* Englewood Cliffs, N.J.: Prentice Hall.

The Portfolio Assessment Kit. [Computer software]. (1996). New York: Super School.

Poteet, J. A., J. S. Choate, and S. C. Stewart (1993). Performance assessment and special education: Practices and prospects. *Focus on Exceptional Children* 26: 1–20.

Shepard, L., and C. L. Bliem (1995). Parents' thinking about standardized tests and performance assessment. *Educational Researcher* 24(8): 25–32.

Smith, C. R. (1980). Assessment alternatives: Non-standardized procedures. *School Psychology Review* 1: 46–56.

Swicegood, P. (1994). Portfolio-based assessment practices. *Intervention in School and Clinic* 30(1): 6–15.

Tindal, G., and D. Marston (1986). *Approaches to assessment: Psychoeducational perspectives on learning disabilities.* New York: Academic Press.

Webster, R., E. McInnis, and L. Carver (1986). Curriculum biasing effects in standardized and criterion-referenced reading achievement tests. *Psychology in the Schools* 23: 205–213.

Wesson, C. L., and R. P. King (1996). Portfolio assessment and special education students. *Teaching Exceptional Children* 28(2): 44–48.

Wolf, D. (1996). Performance-based student assessment: Challenges and possibilities. Paper presented at the annual meeting of the American Educational Research Association, April. New York, N.Y.

Reading

OVERVIEW

Literacy involves being able to read, write, think, and communicate. Probably no other subject receives as much emphasis in the early grades. As students progress through the grades, the ability to be literate is expected of all students. In school, literacy is linked to achievement. Once students leave school, being able to read and write is required in everyday life and is tied to career success, socioeconomic status, and personal satisfaction. Yet, students continue to experience difficulties in learning to be literate.

Attempts to improve literacy have received renewed attention. Efforts have focused on improving classroom practices and generating attitudes and skills that foster the development of lifelong readers. One of the priorities of school reform efforts is an emphasis on connecting and integrating assessment with improvements in classroom practices (Langer et al., 1995).

Current instructional practices stress the integral link between reading and writing. This chapter focuses on the assessment of reading. Chapter 9 is devoted to a discussion of the assessment of written language.

CHAPTER OBJECTIVES

After completing this chapter you should be able to:

Contrast several theoretical perspectives regarding the development of literacy.

Explain the appropriate use of standardized achievement tests in the assessment of literacy.

Describe specific tests of literacy.

Describe the use of alternative assessment instruments that are directly linked to instruction, program planning, and program evaluation.

Describe how the physical, learning, and social environments influence literacy performance.

WHAT SHAPES OUR VIEWS

The assessment of reading abilities and skills should involve a variety of approaches in order to reflect an understanding of what students know and are able to do. Assessment of reading and writing should reflect integrated activities that evaluate students' ability to think, rethink, construct, and interpret knowledge. This means that as students read they should know when to read, how to read, how to think about what they have read, and how to communicate their knowledge and understanding (Langer et al., 1995). The assessment purposes and approaches used in reading assessment are described in Table 8.1.

READING THEORISTS

Many theorists have studied the development of reading and have influenced current thinking about the link between reading and writing instruction and assessment (Rhodes and Shanklin, 1993).

TABLE 8.1 Assessment Questions, Purposes, and Approaches

Assessment questions	Steps and purposes	Approaches
	Screening	
Is there a possibility of a disability in reading?	To determine whether students *may* have a disability in reading and should be referred for further assessment	Norm-referenced instruments Curriculum-based assessment Criterion-referenced assessment Observations Checklists Norm-referenced instruments
	Eligibility	
Does the student have a disability? What disability does the student have? Does the student meet the criteria for services? What are the strengths and weaknesses? Why is the student having difficulty reading?	To determine if there is a disability To compare the student's performance in reading with the performance of the peer group To determine specific strengths and weaknesses in reading To understand why the student is having difficulty	Curriculum-based assessment Criterion-referenced assessment Observations Probes Error analysis Interviews Checklists Student, parent, and/or teacher conferences Performance assessment
CONNECTING INSTRUCTION WITH ASSESSMENT		
	Program Planning	
What does the student not understand about reading? Where should instruction in reading begin?	To understand what the student knows and does not know To plan the student's program To determine instructional approaches	Norm-referenced instruments Curriculum-based assessment Criterion-referenced assessment Observations Probes Error analysis Interviews Checklists Student, parent, and/or teacher conferences Performance assessment

Psycholinguistic Theory

Kenneth Goodman (Goodman, 1984; Goodman, 1989; Rhodes and Shanklin, 1993) considers reading and its development to be a process in which the reader constructs meaning. The construction of meaning involves using background knowledge to make predictions, confirm predictions, integrate information, and interpret information.

Goodman terms errors that occur in reading **miscues,** or "natural" errors rather than mistakes. As we assess reading, these miscues help us to view the cognitive processes that the student uses while reading. These errors may be omissions, substitutions, additions, repetitions, self-corrections, and pauses.

Schema Theory

Cognitive psychologists have theorized that individuals use **schemas** to help make sense of new information. A schema is an "interlocking knowledge network" (Rhodes and Shanklin, 1993, p. 151). Schemas assist in the organization, remembering, and integration of knowl-

TABLE 8.1 (Continued)

Assessment questions	Steps and purposes	Approaches
Program Monitoring		
Once instruction begins, is the student making progress in reading? Should reading instruction be modified?	To understand the strategies and concepts the student uses To monitor the student's program	Curriculum-based assessment Criterion-referenced assessment Observations Probes Error analysis Interviews Checklists Student, parent, and/or teacher conferences Portfolios Exhibitions Journals Written descriptions Oral descriptions
Program Evaluation		
Has the student met the goals of the IEP in reading? Has the instructional program been successful for the student? Has the student made progress? Has the instructional program achieved its goals?	To determine whether the IEP goals have been met To determine whether the goals of the program have been met To evaluate program effectiveness	Curriculum-based assessment Criterion-referenced assessment Observations Probes Error analysis Interviews Checklists Student, parent, and/or teacher conferences Portfolios Exhibitions Journals Written descriptions Oral descriptions Surveys

edge. As we learn, schemas develop and are refined. Some readers may lack schemas, may not use schemas, or may be unable to maintain the schemas they have. Schemas relate to the individual's knowledge of graphophonics, semantics, syntax, and pragmatics.

Graphophonics refers to the knowledge of letters and their associated sounds. **Semantics** reflects an understanding of the meaning of language. For example, the ability to understand the meaning of the word *time* is reflected in distinguishing "What time is it?" from "He came on time." **Syntax** is the system of rules that dictate how words are combined into meaningful phrases and sentences. Knowledge of syntax governs the arrangement of word sequences. For example, in the English language the most frequently used word order is subject, verb, direct object. In other languages, the verb may come first in the sentence, and the subject last. Finally, **pragmatics** refers to how individuals use language in a specific context. For example, knowledge of what to say upon first being introduced to someone reflects pragmatic ability.

Transactional Theory

Rosenblatt (1995), a leading proponent of this theory, believes that readers use different strategies depending on the purpose of reading. Reading is a unique event that engages the reader and the text at a particular time and under particular circumstances. During the transaction, the reader responds to the text in a variety of ways that are specific to the text and the individual's personal and cultural experiences. Gender, ethnicity, culture, and socioeconomic context are important factors that influence reading.

Socio-Psycholinguistic Theory

Frank Smith's theory of reading is complex and includes several aspects of the theories previously discussed (Rhodes and Shanklin, 1993; Smith, 1988). Smith emphasizes the im-

portance of short-term and long-term memory in the reading process. Long-term memory guides the reading process while short-term memory assists in the recognition of information. Smith is credited for recognizing that the nonvisual information individuals bring to reading helps to facilitate the reading process.

Synthesis of the Theories

These theories emphasize the contributions of cognitive psychology to our understanding of the reading process and reading development. Together, they construct contemporary beliefs about reading:

- Background knowledge influences reading performance.
- Schemas are related to the creation of meaning.
- Social and cultural factors affect reading.
- Knowledge of graphophonics, semantics, syntax, and pragmatics influences the reading process.
- Skilled readers are fluent.
- Reading involves the restructuring, application, and flexible use of knowledge in new situations.

INSTRUCTIONAL APPROACHES

Theories of reading are applied in various ways by teachers in the teaching and learning process (Stahl and Kuhn, 1995). Depending on the background and orientation of the teacher, one or more of the approaches in Table 8.2 may be used.

ASSESSMENT PRINCIPLES

In 1991 the International Reading Association (IRA) (Rhodes and Shanklin, 1993) issued "Resolutions on Literacy Assessment." These reso-

TABLE 8.2   **Instructional Approaches in Reading**

Instructor variables	Direct instruction	Explicit instruction	Cognitive approach	Whole language
Orientation to reading	Emphasis is on the teaching of subskills (e.g., phonics, sight words, etc.)	Strategies are explicitly taught	Meaning is constructed from the text	Immersion in a print environment
Instruction	Directed by teacher	Directed by teacher	Teacher and student collaborate	Student, with teacher guidance
Instructional materials	Workbooks, worksheets, basal readers	Worksheets, basals, literature-based program	Literature-based program, small discussion groups	Literature-based program, integrated writing, individual and small discussion groups

Source: Adapted from Stahl and Kuhn (1995).

lutions are comprehensive and state that the two major purposes of literacy assessment are: 1) to inform learning and instruction and 2) to demonstrate that literacy programs are effective. Among the resolutions are several that are pertinent to the assessment of students with special needs:

• Assessments should include a variety of observations that consider the complexity of the processes involved in reading, writing, and in using language. The assessment tasks must include high-quality texts, various genres, and authentic tasks.
• Assessment tasks should be age-appropriate.
• Assessment tools should be unbiased.
• Assessment of reading, writing, and language must include a variety of approaches.
• Assessment approaches should consider the purposes for which the assessment tools were developed and the settings in which the assessment is conducted.
• Assessment activities should reflect instruction.

Eleven Principles of Literacy Assessment

According to Rhodes and Shanklin (1993), there are eleven principles of literacy assessment:

1. Assess authentic reading and writing.

When students read and write they must know the letters and their associated sounds (graphophonics), understand the meaning of language (semantics), and grasp the flow of the language (syntax).

2. Assess reading and writing in various contexts.

An understanding of students' reading and writing abilities must consider the contexts in which reading and writing occur. Contexts are related to the types of reading materials, the purpose of the reading, and strategies that are used.

3. Assess the literacy environment, instruction, and students.

Reading and writing assessment must consider environments in which reading occurs, types of instruction provided, and the characteristics of students.

4. Assess processes and products of reading.

The assessment of reading processes and students' products can provide a comprehensive understanding of students' abilities.

5. Analyze error patterns.

The understanding of patterns of errors in reading and writing can help improve student performance. Errors in reading include miscues, omissions, substitutions, additions, repetitions, self-corrections, and pauses.

6. Include the assessment of background knowledge.

Experience, prior learning, and background knowledge influence reading and writing performance.

7. Consider developmental patterns in reading and writing.

Knowledge of typical developmental patterns in reading and writing can contribute to our understanding of reading and writing abilities.

8. Use sound principles of assessment.

Use sound principles or standards when assessing students. These standards apply to reliability, validity, observation, and scoring. Many of these principles were discussed in Chapters 3 and 4.

9. Use triangulation.

Triangulation means that conclusions about student performance are based on multiple (here, at least three) sources of information. Caution is warranted in drawing conclusions about students when using only one source of information.

10. Include students, parents, teachers, and other school personnel in the assessment process.

The involvement of students, parents, and other educators in the assessment process provides for the inclusion of multiple perspectives.

11. Assessment activities should be ongoing.

Assessment activities should occur frequently and routinely. In this way, assessment activities can be integrated into and inform instruction.

12. Record, analyze, and use assessment information.

Assessment information is useful only when it is used. Record assessment data frequently, analyze it, and use it on a routine basis to guide instruction.

STANDARDIZED INSTRUMENTS

There are many standardized tests of reading (Table 8.3). In addition, Table 8.4 lists achievement batteries that contain reading subtests.

Gray Oral Reading Tests-3

The *Gray Oral Reading Tests-3 (GORT-3)* (Wiederholt and Bryant, 1992) is an individually administered norm-referenced test of reading comprehension and oral reading for students ages 6.6 through 18.11. Each of the two forms of the *GORT-3* contains 13 reading passages arranged in order of difficulty. Although the title of the test indicates that the *GORT-3* is a revision of the previous edition, this test is almost identical to its predecessor, *Gray Oral Reading Test, Revised (GORT-R)*.

Administration

For each passage, the examiner reads one or two sentences that provide motivation. After reading each passage orally, the student responds to five multiple-choice questions that the examiner reads aloud. The examiner records the student's responses.

Scoring

Scores are reported as grade equivalents; percentiles; standard scores for the total scores for rate, accuracy, passage, and comprehension; and Oral Reading Quotient.

Standardization

The GORT-3 was standardized on 1,485 students, ages 7 through 18.11, who resided in 18 states. The selection of the sample was based on U.S. Census reports and was stratified ac-

TABLE 8.3 Standardized Tests of Reading

Test	Ages/grades	Abilities
Diagnostic Reading Scales (Spache, 1981)	grades 1 through 7	phonics, word analysis skills, auditory discrimination
Durrell Analysis of Reading Difficulty (Durrell and Catterson, 1980)	prereading through grade 6	oral reading, silent reading, listening comprehension, reading skills, phonics, vocabulary
Formal Reading Inventory (Wiederholt, 1986)	grades 1 through 12	reading comprehension (literal, inferential, critical, affective), oral miscues
Gates-MacGinitie Reading Tests, 3d Ed (MacGinitie and MacGinitie, 1989)	grades K through 12	literacy concepts, oral language, phonics, vocabulary, reading comprehension
Gates-McKillop-Horowitz Reading Diagnostic Tests (Gates, McKillop, and Horowitz, 1981)	grades 1 through 6	oral reading skills, phonics, word attack, auditory discrimination, written expression
Gray Oral Reading Tests-3 (Wiederholt and Bryant, 1992)	ages 6.6 through 18.11	comprehension, oral reading skills
Nelson-Denny Reading Test (Brown, Fishco, and Hanna, 1993)	grades 9 through adult, including college	vocabulary, comprehension, reading rate
Prescriptive Reading Inventory (CTB/McGraw-Hill, 1980)	grades K through 9	oral reading skills, word attack, word analysis, vocabulary, study skills, reading in the content areas
Standardized Reading Inventory (Newcomer, 1986)	preprimer through grade 8	oral reading, word recognition, comprehension
Stanford Diagnostic Reading Test (4th ed.) (Harcourt Brace Educational Measurement, 1995)	grades 1.5 through 13	phonetic ability, vocabulary, comprehension
Test of Early Reading Ability, Second Edition (Reid, Hresko, and Hammill, 1989)	ages 3 through 9.11	contextual meaning, alphabet, conventions
Test of Phonological Awareness (Torgeson and Bryant, 1994)	K through grade 2	awareness of individual sounds in words
Test of Reading Comprehension-3 (Brown, Hammill, and Wiederholt, 1995)	ages 7.0 through 17.11	vocabulary, syntactic similarities, comprehension, sentence sequencing
Woodcock Reading Mastery Tests–Revised (Woodcock, 1987)	K through adult	visual-auditory learning, letter identification, word identification, word attack, word comprehension

TABLE 8.4 Test Batteries That Contain Reading Subtests

Test	Ages/grades
BRIGANCE® Diagnostic Inventory of Basic Skills (Brigance, 1977)	grades K through 6
BRIGANCE® Diagnostic Inventory of Essential Skills (Brigance, 1981)	grades 4 through 12
BRIGANCE® Diagnostic Comprehensive Inventory of Basic Skills (Brigance, 1983)	grades K through 9
BRIGANCE® Assessment of Basic Skills–Spanish Edition (Brigance, 1984)	grades K through 8
Basic Achievement Skills Individual Screener (BASIS) (Sonnenschein, 1983)	grades 1 through 12 and post–high school
Diagnostic Achievement Battery-2 (DAB-2) (Newcomer, 1990)	ages 6.0 through 14.0
Diagnostic Achievement Test for Adolescents-2 (DATA-2) (Newcomer and Bryant, 1993)	grades 7 through 12
Hudson Education Skills Inventory (Hudson, Colson, Welch, Banikowski, and Mehring (1989)	grade K through 12
Kaufman Assessment Battery for Children (K-ABC) (Kaufman and Kaufman, 1983)	ages 2.6 through 12.6
Kaufman Test of Educational Achievement (K-TEA) (Kaufman and Kaufman, 1985)	grades 1 through 12 ages 6.0 to 18.11
Peabody Individual Achievement Test–R (PIAT-R) (Markwardt, 1989)	grades K through 12, ages 5.0 to 18.11
Wide Range Achievement Test 3 (WRAT-3) (Wilkinson, 1994)	ages 5 to 75
Wechsler Individual Achievement Test (WIAT) (Harcourt Brace Educational Measurement, 1992)	grades K through 12, ages 5.0 to 19.11
Woodcock-Johnson Psychoeducational Battery–Revised (WJ-R) (Woodcock and Johnson, 1989)	grades K through 12 ages 2 to 90

cording to geographic region, place of residence (urban, rural), grade, gender, and ethnicity.

Reliability

Internal consistency reliability coefficients range from .79 to .96. Test-retest reliability of the alternate forms range from .62 to .90. In general, the reliability coefficients are adequate.

Validity

For the most part, concurrent validity of the *GORT-3* is based on the *GORT-R*. The major criticism of the validity of this test is that the manual does not report whether the *GORT-3*

actually measures the purposes of the test as stated by the authors.

Summary

The *Gray Oral Reading Tests-3* is an individually administered norm-referenced test of reading comprehension and oral reading. The standardization is adequate. However, information is lacking as to the socioeconomic status of the sample, and whether students with disabilities and students whose first language is not English were systemically included. While the reliability is acceptable, additional evidence of validity is needed.

Stanford Diagnostic Reading Test

The *Stanford Diagnostic Reading Test (4th ed.) (SDRT4)* (Harcourt Brace Educational Measurement, 1995) is a norm-referenced test for students in grades 1.5 through 13. The test has six overlapping levels:

Grade	Level
1.5 through 2.5	red
2.5 through 3.5	orange
3.5 through 4.5	green
4.5 through 6.5	purple
6.5 through 8.9	brown
9.0 through 13.0	blue

The purposes of the *SDRT4* are to assist in making eligibility decisions, diagnose difficulties in reading, evaluate programs, and provide information about program effectiveness. The test assesses phonetic ability, vocabulary, reading comprehension, and the ability to scan for information.

Administration

The *SDRT4* is a group-administered test. All subtests do not have to be administered. The examiner can decide to administer only one or two of the subtests. The items are a combination of multiple choice and free response. This test can be administered individually following standardized procedures for test administration.

Scoring

Raw scores are converted to percentiles, stanines, normal curve equivalents, grade equivalents, and scaled scores. The *SDRT4* can be hand scored (using a stencil provided by the publisher) or machine scored.

Standardization

The standardization sample is stratified according to socioeconomic status, size of school district, and geographic region.

Reliability

Both alternate form and internal consistency reliabilities are reported. The reliability coefficients are adequate.

Validity

Content and criterion-related validity are reported. Teachers are encouraged to examine the test items to determine the extent to which the *SDRT4* matches reading as it has been taught.

Summary

The *Stanford Diagnostic Reading Test 4* is a norm-referenced test for students in grades 1.5 through 13. The test has six overlapping levels and is intended to be administered to groups of students. However, it can be useful when administered to individual students. The items consist of both multiple-choice and free-response items.

Test of Reading Comprehension-3

The *Test of Reading Comprehension (TORC-3)* (Brown, Hammill, and Wiederholt, 1995) is an individually administered norm-referenced test of vocabulary and silent reading comprehension for students ages 7.0 through 17.11. The *TORC-3* contains eight subtests:

General Vocabulary. The student reads three words and then selects two words that are related to the three words.

Syntactic Similarities. The student reads five sentences and then chooses two of the sentences that are the most closely related.

Paragraph Reading. After reading brief paragraphs, the student answers multiple-choice questions for each paragraph.

Sentence Sequencing. After reading five sentences, the student must arrange them in a logical sequence.

Mathematics Vocabulary. This subtest is similar to the General Vocabulary subtest, except that the vocabulary consists of words related to mathematics.

Social Studies Vocabulary. This subtest is similar to the General Vocabulary subtest except that the vocabulary consists of words related to social studies.

Science Vocabulary. This subtest is similar to the General Vocabulary subtest except that the vocabulary consists of words related to science.

Reading the Directions of Schoolwork. The student reads directions and responds on the answer sheet.

Administration

The *TORC-3* is individually administered. However, it can be administered to small groups of students.

Scoring

Raw scores are converted to age and grade equivalents, percentiles, and standard scores.

Standardization

TORC-3 is the third edition of the *TORC,* originally published in 1968. It was revised in 1986. This third edition was renormed. Information about the proportion of students by age, geographic region, gender, residence, race, ethnicity, and disabilities included in the standardization sample is reported.

Reliability

Test-retest and internal consistency reliability coefficients are reported. Reliabilty for the *TORC-3* is adequate.

Validity

Content and criterion-related validity are reported. Teachers are encouraged to examine the test items to determine the extent to which the *TORC-3* matches reading as it has been taught.

Summary

The *Test of Reading Comprehension-3* is a norm-referenced test of vocabulary and reading comprehension. Evidence of reliabilty and validity is adequate. However, the teacher should exam-

---

> **BOX 8.1**
>
> ## THE TEST OF READING COMPREHENSION-3 (TORC-3)
>
> *Publication Date:* 1995
>
> *Purpose:* Measures vocabulary and reading comprehension.
>
> *Age/Grade Levels:* Ages 7 years through 17 years 11 months.
>
> *Time to Administer:* one to three hours, depending on the age of the student.
>
> *Technical Adequacy:* Evidence of reliabilty and validity is adequate. Test items should be examined by the evaluator in order to determine congruence with reading instruction.
>
> *Suggested Uses:* Measure of vocabulary; indicates strengths and weaknesses in silent reading comprehension.

ine the test items in order to determine congruence with the school curriculum.

Woodcock Reading Mastery Test—Revised

The *Woodcock Reading Mastery Test–Revised (WRMT-R)* (Woodcock, 1987) is an individually administered test of reading skills and reading comprehension for individuals from kindergarten through age 75. The *WRMT-R* consists of six tests arranged in clusters. The Visual-Auditory Learning and Letter Identification tests compose the Readiness Cluster. The Word Identification and Word Attack tests form the Basic Skills Cluster and the Word Comprehension and Passage Comprehension tests consitute the Reading Comprehension Cluster. The following section describes each of the tests.

Visual-Auditory Learning. Rebuses that are associated with words are presented to the student. The student must "read" the rebuses.

Letter Identification. Upper- and lowercase letters of the alphabet are shown to the student. The student must name each of the letters.

Word Identification. The student must read single words that are presented.

Word Attack. The student is asked to demonstrate a knowledge of phonics and word attack skills by pronouncing nonsense syllables.

Word Comprehension. This subtest is composed of three parts: Antonyms, Synonyms, and Analogies.

Passage Comprehension. The student reads a brief passage and supplies the missing words.

Administration

The *WRMT-R* is administered individually.

Scoring

Raw scores can be converted to standard scores, percentiles, and age and grade equivalents. In addition, there is a relative performance index (RPI) that provides an estimate of expected performance. The *WRMT-R* scoring forms include visual profiles for describing performance.

Standardization

The *WRMT-R* was renormed between October 1995 and November 1996. Stratification of the standardization sample was done according to age, gender, region, race, ethnicity, and economic status as estimated by parental education. The standardization sample of the *WRMT-R* was linked to the standardization samples for the *Kaufman Test of Achievement (K-TEA), Peabody Individual Achievement Test–Revised (PIAT-R),* and the *KeyMath-R.* The renorming sample for the *WRMT-R* consisted of students in kindergarten through age 22. The sample of individuals over the age of 22 was not updated. The linking sample was developed by having the test examinees in the norm sample take one of the complete test batteries and one or more subtests from another battery. This linking approach permits the making of comparisons of test performance across batteries.

Reliability

Internal consistency reliability coefficients are only reported for grades 1, 3, 5, 8, 11, and adult. The coefficients are in the .80s and .90s. Test-retest reliability coefficients are not provided.

Validity

The manual provides evidence of content validity. Concurrent validity is reported with the *Woodcock-Johnson Psychoeducational Battery–Revised.* The *WRMT-R* is based on a traditional, somewhat outdated approach to reading. Evidence is needed to support the validity of the clusters. Examiners should carefully review the test in order to determine the correspondence between test items and the literacy curriculum.

Summary

The *WRMT-R* is an individually administered test of reading skills and reading comprehension for individuals from kindergarten through age 75, consisting of six tests arranged in three clusters. There is some question about validity of the test in view of current approaches to teaching literacy.

CONCERNS ABOUT STANDARDIZED READING TESTS

Norm-referenced tests of reading can be useful in identifying students with reading difficulties, pinpointing strengths and weaknesses, and evaluating programs. In 1991 the International Reading Association directly addressed concerns about the use of standardized reading tests when it "resolved that literacy assessments must be based in current research and theory, not limited by traditional psychometric concepts, and must reflect the complex and dynamic interrelationship of reading, writing, and language abilities" (Rhodes and Shanklin, 1993, p. 47). Most experts in reading believe that standardarized norm-referenced tests of reading have a number of shortcomings.

Norm-Referenced Tests of Reading	Contemporary Theories of Reading Assessment
Contain brief, incomplete passages	Longer, complete passages
Fail to tap background knowledge	Encourage the reader to use background knowledge while reading
Questions are literal	Encourage the use of higher-order thinking; involves the restructuring, application, and flexible use of knowledge in new situations
Questions may be biased	Equitable assessment strategies
Multiple-choice questions	Open-ended questions
Only one correct answer to each question	More than one answer is encouraged
Fail to assess the use of a variety of reading strategies	Assess a variety of reading strategies
Do not assess reading attitudes and habits	Assess reading attitudes and habits
Few or no direct links to instruction	Assessment tools are directly linked to instruction

CONNECTING INSTRUCTION WITH ASSESSMENT

Curriculum-based assessment (CBA), introduced in Chapter 6, is a broad approach to linking assessment to instruction. CBA has three purposes: 1) to determine eligibility, 2) to develop the goals for instruction, and 3) to evaluate the student's progress in the curriculum. There are a number of approaches to develop-

---

BOX 8.2

WOODCOCK READING MASTERY TEST–REVISED (WRMT-R)

Publication Date: 1987

Purposes: Measures reading readiness, reading skills, and reading comprehension.

Age/Grades Levels: Kindergarten through age 75.

Time to Administer: 30 minutes to 50 minutes.

Technical Adequacy: Reforming was completed in 1996; reliability is adequate. Validity is acceptable; however, the test items should be examined to determine the extent to which they assess reading as it has been taught. Many of the test items reflect a skills approach to learning to read.

Suggested Uses: Can be cautiously used as a measure of overall reading achievement. Examiners should evaluate the test items because the test does not reflect contemporary approaches to the teaching of literacy.

---

ing and using curriculum-based assessment instruments in the assessment of literacy. We will examine two approaches: One approach is referred to as curriculum-based assessment, and the other is known as curriculum-based measurement.

Curriculum-Based Assessment: Idol, Nevin, Paolucci-Whitcomb Model

Rate of reading, reading errors, accuracy, and reading comprehension can be measured with this assessment model. Although the developers (Idol, Nevin, and Paolucci-Whitcomb, 1996) assume that a basal reading series is used by students, this model can be adapted to a literature-based reading program. Materials that are used for instruction are also employed in the construction of the CBA. Levels of mastery are established by the teacher. The following steps are used in developing and administering the CBA:

1. The teacher photocopies three 100-word passages from the first quarter of each of the basal readers for grades 1 through 6. For preprimers and primers, passages of 25 or 50 words are selected. The passages are labeled and arranged in order of difficulty.

2. On three successive days, beginning with the easiest passage and proceeding to the more difficult ones, the student reads orally one of the passages. The teacher records the total number of seconds it took for the student to read the passage. From this, the teacher can determine the number of correct words the student reads per minute.

3. The teacher records errors made while the student is reading. Types of errors include omissions, substitutions, additions, repetitions, self-corrections, and pauses. To determine the percentage of reading accuracy, the number of words read correctly is divided by the total number of words in the passage. For example, Peter read a 100-word passage and made five errors. To calculate reading accuracy, his teacher followed these steps:

   - Subtract total number of errors from number of words in the passage

     $100 - 5 = 95$ words read correctly

   - Divide the number of words read correctly by the total number of words in the passage

     $$\frac{95}{100} = 95\% \text{ level of accuracy}$$

4. After each passage is read, the teacher asks the student six comprehension questions that the teacher has constructed. The acceptable level of performance is answering 5 of the 6 questions correctly. The questions should be constructed as follows:

   - two text-explicit (TE) questions
     These are questions with answers that can be found precisely in the passage.

     Example: What is the name of the main character?

   - two text-implicit (TI) questions
     These are questions with answers that are implied by the passage.

     Example: What is a solar system?

   - two script-implicit (SI) questions
     These are questions that require the reader to combine prior knowledge with details found in the passage.

     Example: What is the moral of the story?

Curriculum-Based Measurement

Curriculum-based measurement (CBM) (Marston, 1989) is a type of curriculum-based assessment that emphasizes repeated direct measurement of student performance. CBM is based on the belief that reading fluency depends on speed and accuracy of reading. Like the previous model, CBM emphasizes: 1) the direct link between the assessment and the student's curriculum, 2) brief, frequent assessments, 3) multiple forms of the assessment instrument, 4) low cost of the development of assessment materials, and 5) sensitivity to measuring the improvement of student performance.

To construct a CBM, the teacher selects a brief passage or word list and asks the student to read it orally. When the student finishes reading, the teacher counts the number of words that were read correctly and incorrectly. The teacher and the student use a graph to plot the number of words that were read correctly. This can be repeated many times in order to document the progress that the student makes.

Criterion-Referenced Assessment

Instead of comparing a student's performance to a norm group, criterion-referenced tests measure a student's performance with respect to a well-defined content domain (Anastasi, 1988), as discussed in Chapter 6. Criterion-referenced tests can be used in each of the assessment approaches described in Table 8.1. While norm-referenced tests in reading are designed to discriminate between the performance of individual students on specific test items, criterion-referenced tests provide a description of a student's curriculum-referenced knowledge, skills, or processes.

The BRIGANCE® Diagnostic Inventories are criterion-referenced tests that are similar in purpose, scoring, administration, and interpretation. The tests are described in detail in Chapter 6, and Table 8.5 summarizes the reading sections of each of the inventories.

Principles

It is a fundamental principle that instruction in reading be directly linked to assessment. Connecting instruction to assessment in reading means that:

TABLE 8.5   BRIGANCE® Inventories

Name	Ages/grades	Reading abilities
BRIGANCE® Diagnostic Inventory of Basic Skills (Brigance, 1977)	grades K through 6	1. Word Recognition 2. Reading Comprehension 3. Word Analysis 4. Vocabulary
BRIGANCE® Diagnostic Inventory of Essential Skills (Brigance, 1981)	grades 4 through 12	1. Word Recognition 2. Oral Reading 3. Reading Comprehension 4. Word Analysis 5. Functional Word Recognition
BRIGANCE® Diagnostic Comprehensive Inventory of Basic Skills (Brigance, 1983)	Pre-K through 9	1. Word Recognition 2. Oral Reading 3. Reading Comprehension 4. Word Analysis 5. Functional Word Recognition
BRIGANCE® Assessment of Basic Skills–Spanish Edition (Brigance, 1984)	grades K through 6	1. Functional Word Recognition 2. Oral Reading 3. Reading Comprehension 4. Word Analysis 5. Listening
BRIGANCE® Inventory of Early Development–Revised (Brigance, 1991)	ages birth to 7 years	1. Letter Recognition 2. Word Recognition 3. Oral Reading 4. Letter-Sound Recognition
BRIGANCE® Life Skills Inventory (Brigance, 1994)	vocational secondary adult education	1. Words on Common Signs 2. Words on Common Labels
BRIGANCE® Employability Skills Inventory (Brigance, 1995)	vocational secondary adult education job training	1. Reading Grade-Placement 2. Direction Words 3. Words Related to Employment 4. Abbreviations

- Assessment occurs as a normal part of the student's work. Assessment activities emerge from the teaching situation. The student does not stop work to do an assessment; the work and the assessment are linked. Examples of this type of assessment include the use of journals, notebooks, essays, oral reports, homework, classroom discussions, group work, and interviews. These assessment activities can occur individually or in small groups and can take place during one session or over multiple sessions.
- The conditions for assessment should be similar to the conditions for doing meaningful tasks. Students must have sufficient time, have access to peers, be able to use appropriate literacy materials, and have the chance to revise their work.
- Assessment tasks need to be meaningful and multidimensional. They should provide students with the opportunity to demonstrate a variety of reading abilities and skills.
- Feedback to students is frequent, specific, meaningful, prompt, and assists students' acquisition of reading.
- Students participate in the assessment process. They help to generate and apply standards or rubrics. Self-assessment and peer assessment are included as part of the assessment process.

Assessment Approaches

Formal assessment and feedback from peers and teachers encourages the development of reading abilities. Ways in which the teacher can gather information and provide feedback to parents and students include:

- probes
- miscue, or error, analysis
- cloze procedure
- think-alouds
- retelling
- oral descriptions
- written descriptions

- checklists
- questionnaires
- interviews
- conferences
- student journals and notebooks
- sharing portfolios
- exhibitions
- discussions between students, parents, and teachers

Probes

A probe is a diagnostic technique in which instruction is varied in order to examine whether an instructional schema is working. As discussed in Chapter 6, probes can be used to diagnose student problems and assist in planning instruction. For example, suppose a teacher wants to determine whether a student is ready to proceed to a more difficult reading book. The teacher can present the student with a selection from the book and observe the strategies that the student uses when reading. The student may be able to read the words on the page but needs some help learning new vocabulary. The teacher can then help the student by introducing the new vocabulary and providing background knowledge.

Instructional probes are implemented during the process of instruction. When designing an instructional probe, the following steps are suggested:

1. The teacher identifies the area of reading that is to be observed and determines whether the student is able to do the tasks or use certain reading strategies. Examples include locating the title page, retelling a story, and recognizing common warning signs such as Danger and Keep Out.
2. The teacher modifies the assignment. For example, to facilitate the recognition of warning signs the teacher can have the student say, trace, recognize, and write the words. To assist in retelling, a teacher can ask: What happened after? Tell me more about where the story takes place.

brothers / bothers	Longhand superscriptions denote substitution miscues—oral observed responses that differ from expected responses to printed text.
∧	Insertion miscue (word not printed in text, added by oral reader). Example: Gwen ∧ poured him a big glass. *(proudly)*
(word)	Circled word or words; circled period or other punctuation indicates omission miscue—word in printed text, omitted in oral reading.
st-	In substitution miscues, partial word plus hyphen stands for partial word substituted in oral reading for text word.
Billy⌐cried,	Reversal miscue of words in text by oral reader.
ℝ Then he	In passages recording miscues, underlines denote repetitions—portions the reader repeats in oral reading.
© ⌐	Miscue corrected through regression. Example: © the / Then he …
ⓤ© ⌐	Miscue with unsuccessful attempt at correction through regression. Example: ⓤ© All / Tell me what you see …
Ⓐ© ⌐	Reader abandons correct form. Reader replaces an initially correct response with an incorrect one.
ⓓ with	Circled letter d preceding a miscue superscription denotes a variation in sound, vocabulary, or grammar resulting from a dialect difference between the author and the reader.
$	Nonword miscue. The reader either produces a nonword orally in place of text word or supplies a phonemic dialect variation. Examples: $ larther / I sat in a large leather chair. $ cawed / What his mother called him depended on what he did last.
✦	Oral reader sounds out the word in segments. Example: $ sooth + thing / I guess they do have a soothing sound.

FIGURE 8.1

Miscue Symbols

Source: Reprinted by permission of Lynn K. Rhodes and Nancy L. Shanklin from *Windows into Literacy: Assessing Learners K–8.* Portsmouth, N.H.: Heinemann, A division of Reed Elsevier, Inc., 1993, p. 163.

3. The teacher determines whether the student can read the words or can retell the passage.

When conducting a diagnostic probe, the teacher should document the student's performance during step 1 (baseline), step 2 (instruction), and step 3 (baseline).

Miscue (or Error) Analysis

As defined in Chapter 6, the purposes of error analysis are: (1) to identify the patterns of errors or miscues that students make in their work, (2) to understand why students make the errors, and (3) to provide instruction to help correct the errors. In a miscue or error analysis of reading skills, the student reads aloud and the errors are categorized. Figure 8.1 shows common symbols and how they are used when marking miscues.

After conducting a miscue analysis, the error patterns should be summarized. However, many errors will not have a pattern, and a pattern of errors does not mean that there is a serious problem. Miscue analysis is always a preliminary form of assessment and further evaluation of the student's work should be conducted.

Students will frequently correct their own miscues. Calling attention to the student's miscues can interrupt the student's understanding of the passage. Teachers should allow students to proceed to the end of the sentence or paragraph before providing feedback. Useful assessment information can be gathered when teachers observe whether the student makes self-corrections when rereading a passage.

The *Classroom Reading Miscue Assessment (CRMA)* (Rhodes and Shanklin, 1993) (Figure 8.2) was developed to assist teachers in using miscue analysis. As the student reads a passage, the teacher uses the *CRMA* to determine the types of miscues that the student makes. To begin, the teacher selects a complete passage or story, from 300 to 500 words in length with which the student is unfamiliar. The passage should be at an acceptable level of difficulty,

which is estimated at between 1 and 9 semantically unacceptable miscues in the first 100 words that the student reads. As the student reads the passage, the teacher marks the miscues.

Once the teacher identifies the miscues, the student is asked to retell the story. The teacher can use open-ended probes to assist in the retelling. Figure 8.3 provides examples of probes to use in the retelling.

Cloze Procedure

The cloze procedure is generally used to determine whether reading material is within a student's ability. The teacher selects a passage to be read and reproduces it, leaving out every fifth word. The assumption of the technique is that if the student can fill in the blanks, the reading is within the student's ability. Some alternatives to using the fifth-word rule are (Rhodes and Shanklin, 1993):

- The teacher decides which words to omit.
- The teacher can read orally and ask the student to fill in the missing word.
- Blanks can be left so that various parts of speech are omitted.

Think-Alouds

A think-aloud is the verbalization of a student's thoughts about a text before, during, or after reading. Think-alouds provide insight into the student's comprehension abilities and thinking processes. For example, before beginning to read a story about immigrants in the United States, the teacher could ask, "What do you think that this story will be about?" or "What do you already know about immigrants?" During the reading, the student might verbalize, "I don't know that word" or "My mother told me about that." After reading, the student might say "I didn't understand that" or "That was hard."

When eliciting think-alouds, teachers can use the following procedures (Rhodes and Shanklin, 1993):

Reader's Name __Richard_____   Date _____

Grade level __Gr 4-Chapter 1__   Teacher _____

Selection read __Wolf_____

CLASSROOM READING MISCUE ASSESSMENT

I. What percent of the sentences read make sense?

Sentence by sentence tally | Total

Number of semantically acceptable sentences   ~~THL THL THL THL THL~~ ~~THL THL THL THL THL~~ /   __51__

Number of semantically unacceptable sentences   ~~THL~~ ///   __8__

% Comprehending score:

$$\frac{\text{Number of semantically acceptable sentences}}{\text{Total number of sentences read}} \times 100 = \underline{\quad 86 \quad}\%$$

II. In what ways is the reader constructing meaning?

	Seldom	Sometimes	Often	Usually	Never
A. Recognizes when miscues have disrupted meaning	①	2	3	4	5
B. Logically substitutes	①	2	3	4	5
C. Self-corrects errors that disrupt meaning	①	2	3	4	5
D. Uses picture and/or other visual clues	1	2	3	④	5

In what ways is the reader disrupting meaning?

	Seldom	Sometimes	Often	Usually	Never
A. Substitutes words that don't make sense	1	②	3	4	5
B. Makes omissions that disrupt meaning	①	2	3	4	5
C. Relies too heavily on graphophonic cues	1	②	3	4	5

III. If narrative text is used:

	No		Partial		Yes
A. Character recall	1	2	3	4	⑤
B. Character development	1	2	3	4	⑤
C. Setting	1	2	3	4	⑤
D. Relationship of events	1	2	3	4	⑤
E. Plot	1	2	3	④	⑤
F. Theme	1	2	3	4	5
G. Overall retelling	1	2	3	4	⑤

If expository text is used:

	No		Partial		Yes
A. Major concepts	1	2	3	4	5
B. Generalizations	1	2	3	4	5
C. Specific information	1	2	3	4	5
D. Logical structuring	1	2	3	4	5
E. Overall retelling	1	2	3	4	5

FIGURE 8.2

Classroom Reading Miscue Assessment

Source: Reprinted by permission of Lynn K. Rhodes and Nancy L. Shanklin from *Windows into Literacy: Assessing Learners K–8.* Portsmouth, N.H.: Heinemann, A division of Reed Elsevier, Inc., 1993, p. 177.

Character Recall:	Who else was in the story?
Character Development:	What else can you tell me about _____ ?
Setting:	Where did _____ happen?
	When did _____ happen?
	Tell me more about _____ place.
Events:	What else happened in the story?
	How did _____ happen?
Event Sequence:	What happened before _____ ?
	What happened after _____ ?
Plot:	What was _____'s main problem?
Theme:	What did you think (*the major character*) learned in the story?
	What do you think the author might have been trying to tell us in this story?
Good probes to use with expository text are:	
Major Concept(s):	What was the main thing the author wanted you to learn?
Generalizations:	What other important information about _____ did the author tell you?
Specific Information:	Is there any other information you remember the author told about?
	What specific facts do you remember?
Logical Structuring:	How did the author go about presenting the information? (comparison, examples, steps in a process, etc.)

FIGURE 8.3

Probes

Source: Reprinted by permission of Lynn K. Rhodes and Nancy L. Shanklin from *Windows into Literacy: Assessing Learners K–8.* Portsmouth, N.H.: Heinemann, A division of Reed Elsevier, Inc., 1993, p. 181.

1. Ask students to think aloud while they are reading. Explain that thinking aloud will help students to understand the text.
2. Indicate where the student should stop reading in order to think aloud.
3. Model how a think-aloud is done.
4. While the student is thinking aloud, record the student's comments.
5. Analyze the think-aloud for patterns, such as the use of context clues, substitutions, misunderstandings, inferences, use of information, and the addition of information to the text.

Retelling

Retelling is a comprehension exercise in which the student retells as much of a text as can be remembered after reading it. Retelling provides considerable information about comprehension. The following procedures can be used in retelling (Rhodes and Shanklin, 1993):

1. Tell the student that a retelling will be requested at the end of the reading.
2. Once the student has finished reading, request the retelling.

My Beliefs About Reading			
1. I like to read at school	most of the time	sometimes	never
2. I like to read	books	magazines	newspapers
3. I like to read the following types of stories	fiction	biography/ autobiography	science
	history/ politics	science fiction	adventure
4. I like to read at home	most of the time	sometimes	never
5. I talk with my friends about what I read	most of the time	sometimes	never
6. I think I am a good reader	most of the time	sometimes	never
7. Some books that I like are:			

FIGURE 8.4

Assessing Attitudes, Interests, and Habits

Student's Name   **Date**
Teacher's Name

Directions: Show a book that is unfamiliar to the student. Ask the student to tell you about the book.

Concept	Demonstrates	Does not demonstrate	Observations
1. front			
2. back			
3. title			
4. author			
5. letters			
6. words			
7. pictures			
8. page numbers			
9. punctuation			
10. story elements			

FIGURE 8.5

Assessing Knowledge of Books

3. Audiotape the retelling.
4. Once the student has finished the retelling, ask if there is anything else that the student would like to add.
5. At this point, the teacher can choose to ask questions or use prompts to elicit additional information.
6. Use a checklist or record form to analyze the retelling for patterns and trends in knowledge of story structure, story elements, use of details, and use of language.

Oral Descriptions

Verbal descriptions of a student's work can be used to provide immediate feedback to a student by a teacher or peer. Oral descriptions are useful because they are quick, efficient, direct, and can be easily integrated into instruction. They are adaptable for program planning and program evaluation. An example of providing oral feedback to a student who has just completed reading a passage is: "You did a nice job recognizing when words didn't make sense. You understood the events that occurred in the passage and retold the story with only two prompts."

Oral descriptions do have several drawbacks, however. They are subjective and, since the descriptions are given verbally, there is no permanent record. In addition, specific disabilities may limit the ability of the student to understand, remember, or reply to what has been said.

Written Descriptions

A written description is a brief narrative that records feedback about the student's work. It can be shared with the student, other teachers, or parents. A written description, like an oral description, conveys an impression of important aspects of the student's work. Written descriptions can also be used for program planning and program evaluation.

Before writing the narrative, the teacher should carefully review what the student has accomplished. The teacher then writes the description, noting areas of strength as well as problem areas. Such written description provides feedback to the student about the quality of the student's reading. Because it is recorded, the student can refer to it and can also share it with other teachers or family. The disadvantage of using written descriptions arises when parents have difficulty reading or do not have knowledge of written English.

Checklists and Questionnaires

Checklists and questionnaires are convenient ways to provide information about a student's work. A checklist is a procedure that can be completed quickly. Figure 8.4 is an example of a checklist for students that provides feedback to parents and teachers about students' reading habits and attitudes. Figure 8.5 is a checklist used to gather information about students' knowledge of books. Checklists can be used for screening, diagnosis, program planning, and program evaluation.

Questionnaires provide an opportunity for teachers and students to collect information in more detail than checklists permit. Questionnaires can be open-ended, allowing respondents to express their attitudes, opinions, and knowledge in depth, or they can be structured so that the student just needs to fill in one or two words or circle a response.

Interviews

There are special considerations when using this technique in reading assessment. Interviews can be used to guide discussions, to encourage students, and to determine reading attitudes and habits. One basic approach is to interview students individually about their likes and dislikes. Asking questions such as "What do you like about reading?" "What are your interests?" or "What don't you like?" can be informative. Interviews are utilized for screening, diagnosis, program planning, and program evaluation. Figure 8.6 is an example of an interview that can be used with a parent to gather information about how they view their child's development as a reader.

Name _____ Date _____

Child's name _____ Grade _____

PARENT INTERVIEW

1. How do you think your child is doing as a reader/writer? Why? (If a young child: What signs have you seen that your child is ready to learn to read/write?)
_____
_____
_____
_____

2. What would you like your child to do as a reader/writer that he or she isn't doing now?
_____
_____
_____
_____

3. Do you ever notice your child reading/writing at home? Tell me about it.
_____
_____
_____
_____

4. What do you think your child's attitude is toward reading/writing? What do you think has helped to create this attitude?
_____
_____
_____
_____

5. What sorts of questions about your role in helping your child become a better reader/writer might you like to ask me?
_____
_____
_____
_____

6. Since I like to help the children read and write about things they are interested in, it helps me to know each individual child's interests. What kinds of things does your child like to do in his or her free time?
_____
_____
_____
_____

7. Is there anything about the child's medical history that might affect his or her reading/writing? Is there anything else that might affect his or her reading/writing?
_____
_____
_____
_____

8. Is there anything else that you think would be helpful for me to know in teaching your child?
_____
_____
_____
_____

FIGURE 8.6

Parent Interview

Source: "Parent Interview" by Lynn K. Rhodes. Reprinted by permission from *Literary Assessment: A Handbook of Instruments,* edited by Lynn K. Rhodes, Portsmouth, N.H.: Heinemann, A division of Reed Elsevier Inc., 1993, pp. 152–153.

Conferences

A conference is a conversation about the student's work that can include the student, educators, and parents. In a conference, participants share their views of the student's work with the goal of providing feedback and recommendations. Teacher-student conferences are helpful when assessing the student's reading ability. The discussion in a conference can be strictly verbal, or it can be audiotaped, videotaped, or summarized in written form. Conferences are used for diagnosis, program planning, and program evaluation. Figure 8.7 is an example of a progress report that a teacher can use as a guide when having a conference with a parent.

Student Journals

Students can keep a notebook or journal that allows them to record their work as well as their attitudes and feelings about reading and what they have read. In a journal, students can indicate what they like and don't like about reading and list areas in which they have difficulty. A journal provides students the opportunity to reflect on their reading, to communicate about their learning, and to document their progress. Journals can be used for program planning and program evaluation. The following is a sample reading journal outline:

What I read today:

Two important ideas:

What I liked best about the passage or story:

What I didn't like about the passage or story:

What the author was telling us:

Performance-Based Assessment

When used in the measurement of reading ability, performance-based assessment refers to the demonstration of reading and writing abilities,

skills, and behavior. Performance-based assessment requires students to demonstrate that they can read a passage or story for a purpose, use one or more cognitive skills as they construct meaning from the text, and write about what they read, usually in response to a prompt or task (Farr and Tone, 1994). This assessment approach can be used in program planning and program evaluation. The following are examples of performance tasks students can be asked to undertake after reading a book or story:

write a poem

draw pictures with captions

build a model

develop a story map

write a review for the newspaper

interview the author or a character in the story

have a discussion with a peer, teacher, or other adult

write a letter to the author

write a letter to the editor of a newspaper or magazine

write a report about a subject related to the story

adapt a nonfiction article or book to fiction

write lyrics to a song

write a play

Portfolios

A portfolio is a deliberate collection of a student's work that demonstrates the student's efforts, progress, and achievement. When used to document and assess reading ability, portfolios provide information about reading, skills, comprehension, attitudes toward reading, work habits, and written communication abilities. Portfolios in literacy assessment are used for program planning and program evaluation. A more extensive discussion of the applications of portfolios can be found in Chapter 7.

	1st	2nd	3rd	4th
READING				
Level at which child is working				
Phonics and word attack skills				
Word recognition				
Comprehension				
Reference skills				
Oral reading				
Independent reading				
Completes assignments				
Demonstrates effort				
SPELLING				
Mastery of spelling words				
Application of spelling skills in written work				
Completes assignments				
Demonstrates effort				
LANGUAGE				
Correctly uses language mechanics				
(punctuation, capitalization, etc.)				
Grammar (word usage/sentence structure)				
Demonstrates creative written expression				
Oral expression				
Completes assignments				
Demonstrates effort				
HANDWRITING				
Conforms to letter form, size, spacing, and slant				
Writes legibly and neatly in daily work				
Demonstrates effort				

FIGURE 8.7

Progress Report

Source: Reprinted by permission of Lynn K. Rhodes and Nancy L. Shanklin from *Windows into Literacy: Assessing Learners K–8.* Portsmouth N.H.: Heinemann, A division of Reed Elsevier, Inc., 1993, p. 385.

A portfolio is not just a folder of worksheets or of all the work that the student has completed. The selection of the contents of a portfolio needs to be carefully considered. The following are suggestions for inclusion in student portfolios:

writing samples collected over time

photographs of student projects

student logs

projects that involve students in portraying characters or plot

journals in which students record their thoughts about what they have read

written dialogues between student and teacher

audiotapes of students reading

Student's Name	Date				
	1	2	3	4	5
After reading the story I:	Great!				Darn!
1. understand the assignment.					
2. believe that I can restate the assignment.					
3. feel that I can complete the assignment in a timely manner.					
4. feel that I am a usually successful reader.					

FIGURE 8.8

Self-Assessment Checklist

videotapes of students conferencing with each other

teacher-developed tests

anecdotal records

student think-alouds

Exhibitions

An exhibition is a display of a student's work that demonstrates knowledge, abilities, skills, and attitudes concerning one project or a unit of work. An exhibition offers a student the opportunity to summarize and to synthesize what has been accomplished. In reading and writing assessment, exhibitions are valuable because students can realize that reading and writing involves integration, understanding, problem solving, and reasoning. This tool is useful for program planning and program evaluation. Examples of exhibitions in reading and writing include:

- story boards
- series of letters to editors
- diary of one of the characters in the story
- reviews of related books
- dialogues among the characters
- maps depicting the travels of the characters

SELF-ASSESSMENT

Self-assessment provides students with an opportunity to analyze their own reading and writing. It is an occasion for students to reflect on their learning. Figure 8.8 is an example of a checklist that students use when assessing their own learning.

PEER ASSESSMENT

Peer assessment allows students insight into reading and writing abilities of their peers. Students have an opportunity to reflect on the learning processes and strategies of others as well as on their own. Figure 8.9 is an example of a checklist that students use when conducting a peer assessment.

OBSERVING THE STUDENT WITHIN THE ENVIRONMENT

In Chapter 5 you learned about the importance of considering the student within the physical, learning, and social environments. The interac-

	:(	:|	:)
Student's Name _____ Date _____ Peer's Name _____			
1. My peer understood the story.			
2. My peer understood the assignment.			
3. My peer completed the assignment.			
4. My peer conferenced with me.			
5. My peer's work is neat.			

FIGURE 8.9

Peer Assessment Checklist

tions between the student and the environment are important assessment considerations.

Physical Environment

The physical environment influences the student's reading performance. The temperature, lighting, and seating arrangements of the spaces used for teaching and learning can affect how well the student performs. Figure 8.10 is a checklist that serves as an example study of the physical environment.

Learning Environment

A comfortable learning environment facilitates the development of reading and writing abilities, positive attitudes, and habits. The curriculum, instructional methods, books, materials, and the assessment procedures are all areas of concern. Students will be willing to engage in reading and writing activities when: (1) the activities are challenging; (2) students realize that the assignments and the assessment activities are worth doing; (3) reading and writing assignments and assessment activities are accessible to a wide range of students; (4) a variety of instructional approaches, books, and materials are used; and (5) multiple assessment procedures are used. Figure 8.11 is a checklist that can help to determine the appropriateness of the learning environment.

Social Environment

Relationships with students and teachers can affect performance in reading and writing. The social environment is important to the development of self-concept and self-esteem. These, in turn, contribute to positive attitudes toward literacy development. By observing the social environment, teachers can study the relationships students have with peers and adults. Figure 8.12 is a checklist designed to determine the appropriateness of the social environment.

◀ POINT STREET SCHOOL ▶
Physical Environment ▶ Literacy

Student's Name ___Chris___   Date __10/19__ Time __9:15__

Observer ___Mr. T.___   Location ___Classroom___

Characteristic	Always	Sometimes	Never
1. Seating Is the student seated properly?	X		
▶ Suggestions for improvement:			
2. Lighting Is the lighting appropriate?		X	
▶ Suggestions for improvement: Due to Chris' vision problems, the lighting should be adjusted. The curtains should be adjusted so that the glare is eliminated.			
3. Noise Is the noise level appropriate?		X	
▶ Suggestions for improvement: When group activities are underway, the noise level of the classroom tends to rise. Both teacher and students should monitor this.			
4. Distractions Is the student distracted by activities in the room?	X		
▶ Suggestions for improvement:			
5. Temperature Is the temperature of the room appropriate?	X		
▶ Suggestions for improvement:			
6. General Atmosphere Does the student appear to be comfortable in the environment?		X	
▶ Suggestions for improvement: The physical layout of the room should be arranged so that Chris does not trip or bump into the tables. An emergency exit should be planned in case of fire.			

FIGURE 8.10

Observing the Physical Environment

◀ POINT STREET SCHOOL ▶
Learning Environment ▶ Literacy

Student's Name ___Chris___   Date ___10/19___ Time ___9:15___

Observer ___Mr. T.___   Location ___Classroom___

Characteristic	Always	Sometimes	Never
1. Materials Are a variety of reading materials available?	X		
▶ Suggestions for improvement:			
2. Curriculum Does the reading/writing curriculum reflect contemporary views of reading and writing?	X		
▶ Suggestions for improvement:			
3. Activities Is instruction oriented toward the use of various reading and writing materials?	X		
▶ Suggestions for improvement:			
4. Instructional Demands Are the instructional demands appropriate for the student?		X	
▶ Suggestions for improvement: Although Chris is severely myopic (nearsighted), he is capable of keeping up with his peers. Instructional demands should be appropriate in keeping with his abilities.			
5. Modifications Have modifications been made to instruction in order to accommodate the learning needs of the student?		X	
▶ Suggestions for improvement: Chris needs software which enlarges print on the computer screen.			
6. Assessment Are a variety of assessment tools used to provide feedback to the student? Is information collected on the student's progress and performance?	X		

FIGURE 8.11

Observing the Learning Environment

▶ Suggestions for improvement:			
7. **Grouping** If grouping is used, is it appropriate?		X	
▶ Suggestions for improvement: Chris should be grouped with students who can actively engage Chris in group discussions in projects.			
8. **Expectations** Are teacher expectations appropriate?		X	
▶ Suggestions for improvement: Teacher expectations should be high. Although it may take Chris longer to complete assignments, he is able to achieve at a high level.			
9. **Student Involvement** Is the student actively involved in reading and writing activities?	X		
▶ Suggestions for improvement:			
10. **Instruction** Is instruction matched to the assessed needs of the student? Are a variety of instructional methods used?	X		
▶ Suggestions for improvement:			
11. **Pace of Instruction** Is the pace of instruction appropriate?	X		
▶ Suggestions for improvement:			
12. **Schedule** Is the student's schedule appropriate?		X	
▶ Suggestions for improvement: Chris needs a longer time than his peers to change classrooms.			
13. **Transitions** Are transitions made smoothly?		X	
▶ Suggestions for improvement: Planning for transitions should occur. Chris needs extra time to take out and put away materials.			

◄ POINT STREET SCHOOL ►
Social Environment ► Literacy

Student's Name _____Chris_____   Date __10/19__ Time __9:15__

Observer _____Mr. T._____   Location _____Classroom_____

Characteristic	Always	Sometimes	Never
1. Teacher-Student Interactions Are interactions warm and friendly?	X		
► Suggestions for improvement:			
2. Disruptions Are disruptions kept to a minimum?	X		
► Suggestions for improvement:			
3. Behavioral Interventions Are behavioral interventions effective and appropriate?	X		
► Suggestions for improvement:			
4. Peer Interactions Are peer interactions appropriate?		X	
► Suggestions for improvement: Due to Chris' vision problems, he is reluctant to initiate peer interactions. A circle of friends should be convened.			
5. General Atmosphere Does the student appear to be comfortable in the social environment?		X	
► Suggestions for improvement: Some students seem to be uncomfortable with Chris' disabilities. With Chris' permission, the special education teacher could be asked to explain Chris' disabilities to the students. Chris can also be asked to share his feelings with the students.			

FIGURE 8.12

Observing the Social Environment

PREFERRED PRACTICES

The assessment of literacy must reflect the integral link between reading and written language, be conducted frequently, and produce results useful in planning instruction.

Individual standardized tests of reading should be used cautiously. Many norm-referenced tests do not reflect contemporary views of reading and writing. Because reading and writing instruction varies considerably throughout the United States, assessment instruments must be carefully screened in order to select the instrument that best matches the curriculum.

Most standardized achievement tests are biased toward students from various cultural, linguistic, ethnic, and socioeconomic groups. Cultural patterns of teaching and learning may not be reflected in the construction of tests. Low socioeconomic status limits access and participation in educational activities.

Mulitiple approaches should be used in the assessment of reading, including standardized tests, curriculum-based assessment, criterion-referenced assessment, and alternative forms of assessment. Assessment needs to be conducted routinely. The slogan for the assessment of literacy is "multiple, multiple, and frequent"—use multiple approaches, multiple instruments, and assess frequently!

EXTENDING LEARNING

8.1 Develop two assessment tasks that link instruction in reading directly to assessment of reading.

8.2 Develop a checklist or rating scale that assesses students' attitudes and habits in reading.

8.3 Examine a norm-referenced standardized reading test. Compare the development of this test with the contemporary views of reading assessment discussed in this chapter.

8.4 Develop an interview guide that can be used with parents to assess students' reading attitudes and habits at home.

8.5 Identify three assessment approaches discussed in the chapter. Compare the purposes, advantages, and disadvantages of each approach.

REFERENCES

Anastasi, A. (1988). *Psychological testing.* New York: Macmillan.

Brigance, A. H. (1977). *BRIGANCE® diagnostic inventory of basic skills.* No. Billerica, Mass.: Curriculum Associates.

Brigance, A. H. (1981). *BRIGANCE® diagnostic inventory of essential skills.* No. Billerica, Mass.: Curriculum Associates.

Brigance, A. H. (1983). *BRIGANCE® diagnostic comprehensive inventory of basic skills.* No. Billerica, Mass.: Curriculum Associates.

Brigance, A. H. (1984). *BRIGANCE® assessment of basic skills–Spanish edition.* No. Billerica, Mass.: Curriculum Associates.

Brigance, A. H. (1991). *BRIGANCE® diagnostic inventory of early development–revised.* No. Billerica, Mass.: Curriculum Associates.

Brown, J. I., V. V., Fishco, and G. S. Hanna (1993). *Nelson-Denny reading test.* Chicago, Ill.: The Riverside Publishing Company.

Brown, V. L., D. D., Hammill, and J. L. Wiederholt (1995). *Test of reading comprehension-3.* Austin, Tex.: PRO-ED.

CTB/McGraw-Hill (1980). *Prescriptive reading inventory/reading system.* Monterey, Calif.: Author.

Durrell, D., and J. Catterson (1980). *Durrell analysis of reading difficulty.* San Antonio, Tex.: The Psychological Corporation.

Farr, R., and B. Tone (1994). *Portfolio and performance assessment.* Fort Worth, Tex.: Harcourt Brace College Publishers.

Gates, A. I., A. S., McKillop, and E. C. Horowitz (1981). *Gates-McKillop-Horowitz reading diagnostic tests.* (2d ed.) New York: Teachers College Press.

Goodman, K. (1984). Unity in reading. In *Becoming readers in a complex society: The 83rd yearbook of the national society of the study of education, Part*

I, eds. A. Purves and O. Niles, 79–114. Chicago, Ill.: University of Chicago Press.

Goodman, K. (1989). Roots of the whole-language movement. *Elementary School Journal,* 90: 207–222.

Harcourt Brace Educational Measurement (1995). *Stanford diagnostic reading test 4.* 4th ed. San Antonio, Tex.: Author.

Harcourt Brace Educational Measurement (1992). *Wechsler individual achievement test.* San Antonio, Tex.: Author.

Hudson, F. G., S. E., Colson, D. L., Welch, A. K., Banikowski, and T. A. Mehring (1989). *Hudson education skills inventory.* Austin, Tex.: PRO-ED.

Idol, L., A., Nevin, and P. Paolucci-Whitcomb (1996). *Models of curriculum-based assessment.* Austin, Tex.: PRO-ED.

Kaufman, A. S., and N. L. Kaufman (1983). *Kaufman assessment battery for children.* Circle Pines, Minn.: American Guidance Service.

Kaufman, A. S., and N. L. Kaufman (1985). *Kaufman test of educational achievement.* Circle Pines, Minn.: American Guidance Service.

Langer, J. A., J. R., Campbell, S. B., Neumann, I. V. S., Mullis, H. R., Persky, and P. L. Donahue (1995). *Reading assessment redesigned.* Washington, D.C.: U.S. Department of Education.

MacGinitie, W. H., and R. K. MacGinitie (1989). *Gates-MacGinitie reading tests.* Chicago, Ill.: The Riverside Publishing Company.

Markwardt, F. C. (1989). *Peabody individual achievement test–Revised.* Circle Pines, Minn.: American Guidance Service.

Marston, D. (1989). A curriculum-based measurement approach to assessing academic performance: What it is and why do it. In *Curriculum-based measurement,* ed. M. R. Shinn, 18–78. New York: The Guilford Press.

Newcomer, P. L. (1990). *Diagnostic achievement battery.* 2d ed. Austin, Tex.: PRO-ED.

Newcomer, P. (1986). *Standardized reading inventory.* Austin, Tex.: PRO-ED.

Newcomer, P. L., and B. R. Bryant (1993). *Diagnostic achievement test for adolescents.* 2d. ed. Austin, Tex.: PRO-ED.

Reid, D. K., W. P. Hresko, and D. D. Hammill (1989). *Test of early reading ability.* 2d ed. Austin, Tex.: PRO-ED.

Rhodes, L. K., and N. L. Shanklin (1993). *Windows into literacy.* Portsmouth, N.H.: Heinemann.

Rosenblatt, L. (1995). *The reader, the text, the poem.* Carbondale, Ill: Southern Illinois University Press.

Slosson, R. L. (1990). *Slosson oral reading test.* East Aurora, N.Y.: Slosson Educational Publications.

Smith, F. (1988). *Understanding reading.* 4th ed. New York: Holt, Rinehart & Winston.

Sonnenschein, J. L. (1983). *Basic achievement individual skills screener.* San Antonio, Tex.: Author.

Spache, G. D. (1981). *Diagnostic reading scales.* Monterey, Calif.: CTB Macmillan/McGraw-Hill.

Stahl, S. A., and M. R. Kuhn (1995). Does whole language or instruction matched to learning styles help children learn to read? *School Psychology Review* 24: 393–404.

Torgeson, J. K., and B. R. Byrant (1994). *Test of phonological awareness.* Austin, Tex.: PRO-ED.

Wiederholt, L. (1986). *Formal reading inventory.* Austin, Tex.: PRO-ED.

Wiederholt, L., and B. Bryant (1992). *Gray oral reading tests-3.* Austin, Tex.: PRO-ED.

Wilkinson, G. (1994). *Wide range achievement test 3* Austin, Tex.: PRO-ED.

Woodcock, R. (1987). *Woodcock Reading Mastery Tests–Revised.* Circle Pines, Minn.: American Guidance Service.

Woodcock, R. W., and M. B. Johnson (1989). *Woodcock-Johnson psychoeducational battery–Revised.* Chicago: Riverside.

Written Language

OVERVIEW

Contemporary instructional practices stress the integral link between reading and writing for both instruction and assessment. In the previous chapter we discussed approaches used in the assessment of literacy, emphasizing the assessment of reading. This chapter continues this discussion and highlights the assessment of written language.

CHAPTER OBJECTIVES

After completing this chapter you should be able to:

Understand contemporary views of written language instruction.

Explain the integral link between reading instruction, written language instruction, and assessment.

Describe approaches to written language assessment, including norm-referenced standardized tests, writing samples, journals, notebooks, essays, homework, discussions, group work, interviews, alternative assessment, performance testing, self-assessment, and peer assessment.

Describe how physical, learning, and social environments influence written language performance.

WHAT SHAPES OUR VIEWS

Contemporary views of the assessment of written language are based on the essential link between reading and written language. Theories of the development of written language are applied in various ways by teachers in the teaching and learning process. Some teachers emphasize the link between the development of reading and writing and view the development of written language as a process. Other teachers emphasize the development of specific skills, such as correct spelling, punctuation, capitalization, and grammar. Some teachers use a combination of these approaches. Depending on the background and orientation of the teacher, one or more of the assessment approaches in Table 9.1 may be used.

The assessment of written language reflects the direct connection between reading and writing and is based on the following principles (Rhodes and Shanklin, 1993):

1. Assess reading and writing in various contexts.

Reading and writing varies with the context. Contexts are related to the types of reading materials, the purpose of the writing, and strategies that are used. An understanding of students' reading and writing abilities must consider the contexts in which reading and writing occur.

2. Assess the literacy environment, instruction, and students.

Reading and writing assessment must consider environments in which reading and writing occurs, types of instruction, and student factors.

3. Assess processes and products of writing.

The assessment of writing processes as well as the products can provide a comprehensive understanding of students' abilities.

4. Analyze error patterns.

Understanding the patterns of errors in writing improves student performance.

5. Include the assessment of background knowledge.

TABLE 9.1 Instructional Approaches in the Development of Written Language

Instructor variables	Direct instruction	Explicit instruction	Cognitive approach	Whole language
Orientation to reading and writing	Emphasis is on the teaching of sub-skills (e.g., punctuation, capitalization, grammar, spelling etc.)	Skills are explicitly taught	Meaning is constructed from the text	Immersion in a print environment; close link between reading and writing activities
Instruction	Directed by teacher	Directed by teacher	Teacher and student collaborate	Student, with teacher guidance
Instructional materials	Workbooks, worksheets, spelling lists	Worksheets, literature-based program	Literature-based program, small discussion groups, writing projects	Literature-based program, integrated writing, individual and small discussion groups

Adapted from Stahl and Kuhn (1995).

Experience, prior learning, and background knowledge influence reading and writing performance.

6. Consider developmental patterns in reading and writing.

Knowledge of typical developmental patterns in reading and writing contributes to our understanding of reading and writing abilities.

7. Use sound principles of assessment.

Employ sound principles or standards when assessing students. These standards apply to reliability, validity, observation, and scoring, discussed in previous chapters.

8. Use **triangulation.**

Triangulation signifies that conclusions about student performance are based on multiple (here, at least three) sources of information. In turn, information about students should be corroborated by using several sources of data. Considerable caution is required when drawing conclusions about students using only one source of information.

9. Include students, parents, teachers, and other school personnel in the assessment process.

The involvement of students, parents, and other educators in the assessment process ensures the inclusion of multiple perspectives.

10. Assessment activities should be ongoing.

Assessment activities can inform instruction best when they are conducted frequently and routinely.

11. Record, analyze, and use assessment information.

Assessment information is useful only when it is used. Record assessment data frequently, analyze it, and use it on a routine basis to guide instruction. Linking instruction with assessment means that:

- Assessments include a variety of observations that consider the complexity of the processes involved in reading, writing, and language.
- Assessment tasks are age-appropriate.
- Assessment tools are unbiased.

- Assessment of reading, writing, and language must incorporate a variety of approaches.
- Assessment approaches should consider the purposes for which the assessment tools were developed and the settings in which the assessment is conducted.
- Assessment should reflect classroom instruction.

PURPOSES AND APPROACHES

The assessment of written language abilities and skills requires a variety of approaches in order to reflect an understanding of students' abilities, developmental levels, maturity, gender, and ethnic and racial background. Assessment techniques must include standardized testing as well as a variety of other approaches. The assessment questions, purposes, and approaches used in written language assessment are described in Table 9.2.

STANDARDIZED TESTS OF WRITTEN LANGUAGE

Standardized norm-referenced tests of written language can be useful in identifying students with writing difficulties, pinpointing strengths and weaknesses, and evaluating programs.

Content Validity

Content validity is a primary concern of any achievement test, including tests of written language. This type of validity measure relates the extent to which the test items reflect the instructional objectives of a test. An estimate of the content validity of a test is obtained by thoroughly and systematically examining the test items to determine the extent to which

TABLE 9.2 Assessment Questions, Purposes, and Approaches

Assessment questions	Steps and purposes	Approaches
Screening		
Is there a possibility of a disability in writing?	To determine whether students *may* have a disability in writing and should be referred for further assessment	Norm-referenced instruments Curriculum-based assessment Criterion-referenced assessment Observations Checklists
Eligibility		
Does the student have a disability? What disability does the student have? Does the student meet the criteria for services? What are the strengths and weaknesses? Why is the student having difficulty writing?	To determine if there is a disability To compare the student's performance in writing with the performance of the peer group To determine specific strengths and weaknesses in writing To understand why the student is having difficulty	Norm-referenced instruments Curriculum-based assessment Criterion-referenced assessment Observations Probes Error analysis Interviews Checklists Student, parent, and/or teacher conferences Performance assessment
CONNECTING INSTRUCTION WITH ASSESSMENT		
Program Planning		
What does the student not understand about writing? Where should instruction in writing begin?	To understand what the student knows and does not know To plan the student's program To determine instructional approaches	Norm-referenced instruments Curriculum-based assessment Criterion-referenced assessment Observations Probes Error analysis Interviews Checklists Student, parent, and/or teacher conferences Performance assessment

they reflect the instructional objectives and the content that was intended to be tested.

While the test developer must describe the process used to establish content validity of a test, the test examiner must make an independent determination. This is especially important when deciding on the content validity of written language tests. The test examiner has to compare the test objectives, format, number of responses or prompts, and types of responses or prompts with the curriculum that the student has been taught.

Scoring

Scoring tests of written language can be problematic for the test examiner. Students vary in their writing abilities and many test manuals

TABLE 9.2 (Continued)

Assessment questions	Steps and purposes	Approaches
	Program Monitoring	
Once instruction begins, is the student making progress in written language? Should writing instruction be modified?	To understand the strategies and concepts the student uses To monitor the student's program	Curriculum-based assessment Criterion-referenced assessment Observations Probes Error analysis Interviews Checklists Student, parent, and/or teacher conferences Portfolios Exhibitions Journals Written descriptions Oral descriptions
	Program Evaluation	
Has the student met the goals of the IEP in written language? Has the instructional program been successful for the student? Has the student made progress? Has the instructional program achieved its goals?	To determine whether the IEP goals have been met To determine whether the goals of the program have been met To evaluate program effectiveness	Curriculum-based assessment Criterion-referenced assessment Observations Probes Error analysis Interviews Checklists Student, parent, and/or teacher conferences Portfolios Exhibitions Journals Written descriptions Oral descriptions Surveys

contain general directions, which are sometimes ambiguous, for scoring writing samples. Because the test examiners must use judgment in scoring, there may be variations and inconsistencies between test scores.

There are a number of standardized tests of written language. Table 9.3 lists tests of written language and tests that have subtests in the areas of handwriting, spelling, mechanics,

grammar, or written language. Some of the commonly used individual, standardized tests of written language are described in this section. All of the tests in this section are norm-referenced and are administered and scored according to standardized procedures. The tests yield a variety of scores, including standard scores, percentiles, age equivalents, grade equivalents, and normal curve equivalents.

TABLE 9.3 Instruments That Contain Subtests of Spelling and Written Language

Name	Ages/grades	Group/individual	Areas
Basic Achievement Skills Individual Screener (BASIS) (Sonnenschein, 1983)	Grades 1 through 12 & post–high school	Individual	Spelling Written language
BRIGANCE® Diagnostic Inventory of Basic Skills (Brigance, 1977)	Grades K through 6	Individual	Spelling Grammar Mechanics Handwriting
BRIGANCE® Diagnostic Inventory of Essential Skills (Brigance, 1981)	Grades 4 through 12	Individual	Spelling Handwriting Mechanics
BRIGANCE® Diagnostic Comprehensive Inventory of Basic Skills (Brigance, 1983)	Grades K through 9	Individual	Spelling Handwriting Mechanics
BRIGANCE® Assessment of Basic Skills–Spanish Edition (Brigance, 1984)	Grades K through 8	Individual	Handwriting
Diagnostic Achievement Battery-2 (DAB-2) (Newcomer, 1990)	Ages 6.0 through 14.0	Individual	Spelling Grammar Mechanics Written language
Diagnostic Achievement Test for Adolescents-2 (DATA-2) (Newcomer and Bryant, 1993)	Grades 7 through 12	Individual	Spelling Grammar Written language
Hudson Education Skills Inventory (Hudson, Colson, Welch, Banikowski, and Mehring, 1989)	Grade K through 12	Individual	Spelling Handwriting Written language
Kaufman Test of Educational Achievement (K-TEA) (Kaufman and Kaufman, 1985)	Grades 1 through 12; ages 6.0 to 18.11	Individual	Spelling
Oral and Written Language Scales (Carrow-Woolfolk, 1996)	Ages 5 through 21	Individual or small group	Use of conventions Use of linguistic forms Content

Oral and Written Language Scales

The *Oral and Written Language Scales (OWLS)* (Carrow-Woolfolk, 1996) is an individualized test of oral and written language. The *OWLS* has three scales: Listening Comprehension,

Oral Expression, and Written Expression. The description of the *OWLS* in this chapter will focus on the Written Expression Scale. The Listening Comprehension and Oral Expression scales are described in Chapter 10. The Written Expression Scale is intended to be used with

TABLE 9.3 (Continued)

Name	Ages/grades	Group/individual	Areas
Peabody Individual Achievement Test–Revised (PIAT-R) (Markwardt, 1989)	Grades K through 12; ages 5.0 to 18.11	Individual	Spelling Written language
Test of Adolescent and Adult Language (TOAL-3) (Hammill, Brown, Larsen, and Wiederholt, 1994)	Ages 12.0 through 24.11	Individual or group	Grammar Written language
Test of Early Written Language-2 (TEWL-2) (Hresko, Herron, and Peak, 1996)	Ages 3.0 through 10.11	Individual	Spelling Mechanics Written language
Test of Written Expression (TOWE) (McGhee, Bryant, Larsen, and Rivera, 1995)	Ages 6.6 through 14.11	Individual or group	Spelling Mechanics Grammar Written language
Test of Written Language-3 (TOWL-3) (Hammill and Larsen, 1996)	Ages 7.6 through 17.11	Individual or group	Spelling Mechanics Grammar Written language
Test of Written Spelling (TWS-3) (Larsen and Hammill, 1994)	Grades 1 through 12	Individual or group	Spelling
Wide Range Achievement Test-3 (WRAT-3) (Wilkinson, 1994)	Ages 5 through 75	Individual	Spelling
Wechsler Individual Achievement Test (WIAT) (Harcourt Brace Educational Measurement, 1992)	Grades K through 12; ages 5.0 to 19.11	Individual	Spelling Written language
Woodcock-Johnson Psychoeducational Battery–Revised (WJ-R) (Woodcock and Johnson, 1989)	Ages 2 to 90; grades K through 12	Individual	Spelling Mechanics Written language

individuals ages 5 through 21. The Written Expression Scale consists of four overlapping sets of items in the following areas:

Use of conventions—The skills measured include letter formation, correct spelling, punctuation, capitalization, and conventions.

Use of linguistic forms—The abilities measured include the use of language forms such as modifiers, verb forms, and complex sentences.

Content—The ability to communicate subject matter in a meaningful way.

Administration

The *OWLS* can be administered individually or to a small group.

Scoring

Depending on the item, the examiner follows from 1 to 11 scoring rules. Raw scores are converted to standard scores, percentiles, normal curve equivalents, stanines, and age and grade equivalents.

Standardization

The *OWLS* was standardized between April 1992 and August 1993. The standardization sample of 1,985 individuals who were stratified by age, gender, race, ethnic group, geographic region, and economic status, based on the mother's level of education, was based on 1991 U.S. Census data from the 1991 *Current Population Survey*. The three scales of the *OWLS* were co-normed.

Reliability

Reliability information is presented for split-half reliability, test-retest reliability, and interrater reliability. For the Written Expression Scale the coefficients range from .77 (ages 19 through 21) to .89 (age 6). For test-retest reliability the coefficient for ages 8 through 10.11 years was .88; for ages 16 through 18.11 years, the coefficient was .87. Interrater reliability ranged from .91 (ages 12 through 14) to .98 (ages 5 through 7).

Validity

Adequate evidence of content, criterion-related, and construct validity is presented. The *OWLS* was administered concurrently with the *Kaufman Test of Educational Achievement, Comprehensive Form, Peabody Individual Achievement Test–Revised, Woodcock Reading Mastery Test–Revised, Peabody Picture Vocabulary Test–Revised, Clinical Evaluation of Language Fundamentals–Revised, Wechsler Intelligence Scale for Children-III, and Kaufman Brief Intelligence Test.*

Small studies were conducted with students who were identified as language impaired, mentally handicapped, learning disabled, hearing impaired, or as receiving Chapter One assistance in reading. Students from these studies were not included in the standardization sample. The results of these studies are limited because only one study was conducted with each group and because the samples were so small.

Summary

The *Oral and Written Language Scales* is an individualized test of oral and written language. The test is based on contemporary views of written language. Reliability and validity are adequate.

Test of Early Written Language-2

The *Test of Early Written Language-2 (TEWL-2)* (Hresko, Herron, and Peak, 1996) is a revision

---

BOX 9.1

ORAL AND WRITTEN LANGUAGE SCALES, WRITTEN EXPRESSION SCALE

Publication Date: 1996

Purposes: Measures use of conventions, use of linguistic forms, and the ability to communicate subject matter in a meaningful way.

Age/Grade Levels: 5 through 21 years

Time to Administer: Approximately 30 to 45 minutes

Technical Adequacy: The standardization sample is appropriate. Reliability and validity are adequate.

Suggested Uses: The test is based on contemporary views of written language and is effective for assessing overall ability to use written language and areas of strength and weakness.

of the first edition. Designed to be used with students ages 4.0 through 10.11, the *TEWL-2* is a downward extension of the *Test of Written Language (TOWL-3),* which is described below. The *TEWL-2* contains two subtests:

Basic Writing. This subtest contains 57 items and assesses spelling, capitalization, punctuation, sentence construction, and metacognitive knowledge.

Contextual Writing. This subtest contains 14 items and assesses the student's ability to write a story when presented with a picture prompt.

Test of Written Expression

The *Test of Written Expression (TOWE)* (McGhee, Bryant, Larsen, and Rivera, 1995) is intended for students ages 6.6 through 14.11. This test can be administered to individuals or groups. The *TOWE* assesses skills associated with written language production, such as ideation, grammar, vocabulary, capitalization, punctuation, spelling, and general ability to produce written language.

Test of Written Language-3

The *Test of Written Language (TOWL-3)* (Hammill and Larsen, 1996) is the third edition of this test. The *TOWL-3* is intended to be used with students ages 7.6 through 17.11. It contains eight subtests organized into two formats: spontaneous and contrived. The spontaneous format is assessed through the analysis of a student written essay, and the contrived format directly assesses specific skills associated with writing.

Subtest	Abilities/Skills Assessed
SPONTANEOUS FORMAT	
Contextual Conventions	capitalization, punctuation, spelling
Contextual Language	vocabulary, syntax, grammar
Story Construction	plot, character development, general composition
CONTRIVED FORMAT	
Vocabulary	word usage
Spelling	correct spelling
Style	capitalization, punctuation
Logical Sentences	rewriting of sentence so that they make sense
Sentence Combining	rewrite one sentence from two sentences

Administration

The *TOWL-3* is individually administered. However, it can be administered to small groups of students.

Scoring

Raw scores are converted to percentiles and standard scores.

Standardization

The *TOWL-3* is the third edition of the *TOWL,* originally published in 1978. It was revised in 1988. This third edition, published in 1994, was renormed. Information about the age, geographic region, gender, residence, race, ethnicity, income of parents, education of parents, and disabilities factors represented in the standardization sample is reported.

Reliability

Test-retest and internal consistency reliability coefficients are reported. The reliabilty for the *TOWL-3* is adequate.

Validity

Content, criterion-related, and construct validity are reported. Teachers are encouraged to examine the test items to determine the extent to which the *TOWL-3* matches writing as it has been taught in the curriculum.

Summary

The *Test of Written Language-3* is a norm-referenced test of skills and abilities associated with written language and the writing process. Evidence of reliabilty and validity is adequate. However, the teacher should examine the test items in order to determine congruence with the school curriculum.

Test of Written Spelling

The *Test of Written Spelling (TWS-3)* (Larsen and Hammill, 1994) is the third edition of this test and is intended to be administered to students in grades 1 through 12. The *TWS-3* assesses predictable words (words with spellings that are predictable using letter-sound patterns) and unpredictable words (words with spellings that are unpredictable, or are "word

---

B O X 9 . 2

TEST OF WRITTEN LANGUAGE-3

Publication Date: 1996

Purposes: Assesses writing conventions, grammar, syntax, vocabulary, spelling, sentence construction, and story construction.

Age/Grade Levels: Ages 7 years, 6 months through 17 years, 11 months

Time to Administer: 1½ hours

Technical Adequacy: The standardization sample is adequate. Reliability is good; further evidence of validity is required.

Suggested Uses: Provides evidence of strengths and weaknesses in written language, spelling, and vocabulary. Examiners should evaluate the test items to determine the extent to which they reflect writing as it has been taught to the student.

---

demons"). It is administered by having the test examiner say a word, say a sentence that contains the word, and say the word again. The student writes the word only; words are not written in a sentence.

CONCERNS ABOUT STANDARDIZED TESTS OF WRITTEN LANGUAGE

The International Reading Association (1991) directly addressed concerns about the use of standardized reading tests when it "resolved that literacy assessments must be based in current research and theory, not limited by traditional psychometric concepts, and must reflect the complex and dynamic interrelationship of reading, writing, and language abilities" (Rhodes and Shanklin, 1993, p. 47). Most experts in literacy believe that standardarized, norm-referenced tests of writing have a number of shortcomings.

Norm-referenced Tests of Written Language	*Contemporary Theories of Written Language Assessment*
Writing abilities are assessed separately from reading abilities	Link the assessment of writing with the assessment of reading
Fail to tap background knowledge	Encourage the writer to use background knowledge while writing
Questions emphasize skills (spelling, punctuation, capitalization, grammar, etc.)	Assess a variety of writing processes
Questions may be biased	Equitable assessment strategies
Multiple-choice questions	Open-ended questions
Do not assess writing attitudes and habits	Assess writing attitudes and habits
Few or no direct links to instruction	Assessment tools are directly linked to instruction

CONNECTING ASSESSMENT WITH INSTRUCTION

It is a fundamental principle that assessment of written language abilities and skills must be directly linked to reading instruction. Linking instruction to assessment in reading and written language means that:

- Assessment occurs as a normal part of the student's work. Assessment activities should emerge from the teaching and learning situation. Examples of this type of assessment include the use of journals, notebooks, essays, oral reports, homework, classroom discussions, group work, and interviews. These assessment activities can occur individually or in small groups and can take place during one session or over multiple sessions.
- The conditions for assessment are similar to the conditions for doing meaningful tasks. Students should have sufficient time, have access to peers, be able to use appropriate literacy materials, and have the chance to revise their work.
- Assessment tasks are meaningful and multidimensional. They should provide students with the opportunity to demonstrate a variety of writing abilities and skills.
- Feedback to students is specific, meaningful, prompt, and informs the students' work.
- Students participate in the assessment process. They help to generate and apply standards or rubrics. Self-assessment and peer assessment are included as part of the assessment process.

Ways in which the teacher can gather information and provide feedback to parents and students include:

- curriculum-based measurement
- criterion-referenced assessment
- probes
- error analysis

- oral descriptions
- written descriptions
- checklists
- questionnaires
- interviews
- conferences
- student work samples and products
- student journals and notebooks
- performance-based assessment
- portfolios
- exhibitions
- discussions between students, parents, and teachers

Curriculum-Based Measurement

Curriculum-based measurement (CBM) was introduced in Chapter 6. To construct a CBM in writing , the teacher selects a brief story starter or topic sentence and asks the student to write it out in three minutes. When the student finishes writing, the teacher has four choices for scoring: 1) count the number of words written correctly; 2) count the number of words spelled correctly; 3) count the number of letters written correctly; or 4) count the number of correct word sequences. Word sequences are two words together that are both correctly spelled and grammatically correct. The teacher and the student can then use a graph to plot the results. This can be repeated many times in order to document the progress that the student makes.

Criterion-Referenced Assessment

Teachers can create criterion-referenced tests in written language. Such teacher-developed criterion-referenced tests can be used for screening, determining eligibility, diagnosis of strengths and needs, program planning, progress monitoring, and program evaluation. For example, a teacher can enumerate spelling words that must be spelled correctly, can identify punctuation that must be used accurately, or can list words that require correct capitalization in order to develop a criterion-referenced test.

BRIGANCE® Diagnostic Inventories

The BRIGANCE® Diagnostic Inventories are criterion-referenced tests that contain subtests in written language. The inventories are similar in purpose, scoring, administration, and interpretation. The tests are described in detail in Chapter 6, but Table 9.3 summarizes those sections of the BRIGANCE® inventories that assess aspects of written language.

Probes

A probe is a diagnostic technique that we have already discussed. Probes can be especially useful in diagnosing student problems and in planning instruction in written language. For example, suppose a teacher wants to determine whether a student has considered feedback from peers when revising a writing sample. The teacher can review the student's written draft, inquire about the use of peer feedback, and assist the student in incorporating peer feedback into a revision of the draft.

Error Analysis

The purposes of error analysis are to: (1) identify the patterns of errors or mistakes that students make in their work; (2) understand why students make the errors; and (3) provide instruction so as to correct the errors. A systematic approach to error analysis helps both the student and the teacher identify errors and correct them.

A checklist, developed by the teacher, the student, or through collaboration, can be helpful in identifying errors. Figure 9.1 is an example of a checklist that Toni, a sixth grader, developed with her teacher to help Toni with editing.

Spelling

Error analysis is important in the development of spelling. Spelling should be evaluated as part of the process of the development of written language rather than as a finished product.

Have I checked and corrected:

Editing	Checked		Corrected	
	yes	no	yes	no
1. Grammar				
2. Periods				
3. Question marks				
4. Exclamation points				
5. Quotation marks				
6. Paragraphing				
7. Spelling				

FIGURE 9.1

Toni's Editing Checklist

Four principles can be used in the evaluation of spelling (Wilde, 1989a):

- Evaluate spelling on the basis of natural writing rather than by tests of words in isolation.
- Evaluate spelling analytically rather than as correct or incorrect.
- Analyze spelling by discovering the strategies that were used in the context of writing.
- The teacher is informed about language development and about language disabilities and how they can affect the development of written language as a matter of good professional practice in this area.

Questions to ask about a student's spelling include (Rhodes and Shanklin, 1993; Wilde, 1989a; Wilde, 1989b):

1. Is the word spelled as it sounds?
2. Is the spelling unusual?
3. Is the word a sight word?
4. Is the word a real word?
5. Is the word a "placeholder"?
6. Is a homophone used?
7. What strategies does a student use when the spelling is unknown?
   a. writes down what it sounds like
   b. writes down what student thinks the word looks like
   c. looks around the classroom to find the word

d. thinks about parts of the word
e. uses spelling rules
 f. uses a dictionary or spell checker
g. asks someone for the correct spelling
h. uses a personal spelling list

Oral Descriptions

Verbal descriptions of a student's work provide immediate feedback to the student by a teacher or peer. Oral descriptions are quick, efficient, direct, and can be integrated easily into instruction. However, they should not be off-the-cuff expressions, but as well thought out as written descriptions. Oral descriptions can be used for program planning and program evaluation. An example of providing oral feedback to a student who has just completed writing a first draft is, "You did a nice job getting your ideas down. While developing your ideas you consulted several sources and asked a peer for help with spelling."

Notwithstanding, oral descriptions do have several drawbacks. They can be subjective, and there is no permanent record. In addition, specific disabilities may limit the ability of the student to understand, remember, or reply to what has been said.

Written Descriptions

A written description is a brief narrative that records feedback about the student's work. It can be shared with the student, teachers, or parents. A written description, like an oral description, conveys an impression of important aspects of the student's work. Written descriptions are effective for program planning and program evaluation.

Before writing the narrative, the teacher carefully reviews what the student has accomplished. The teacher should write the description noting areas of strength as well as problem areas. A written description provides feedback to the student about the quality of the student's writing, and because it is recorded, the student can refer to it and share it with the student's family.

Two potential problems of written descriptions are that parents who have difficulty reading or who do not have knowledge of written English are at a disadvantage.

Checklists and Questionnaires

Checklists and questionnaires are convenient ways to provide feedback about a student's work. A checklist is a procedure that can be completed quickly.

Questionnaires enable teachers and students to collect information in more detail than checklists. Questionnaires can be open-ended, allowing respondents to express their attitudes, opinions, and knowledge in depth, or they can be structured so that the student just needs to fill in one or two words or to circle a response. Figure 9.2 is an example of an open-ended questionnaire.

Interviews

The topic of conducting interviews was discussed in Chapter 5. There are special considerations when using this technique in the assessment of written language. Interviews can be used to develop ideas for writing, to encourage students, to learn more about a student's written piece, and to determine writing attitudes and habits. Asking questions such as the following can be informative: "What do you like about writing?" "Describe the process you use in developing a new piece of writing." "What are your interests?" "What don't you like?" Interviews are used for screening, diagnosis, program planning, and program evaluation.

Conferences

A conference is a conversation about the student's work that can include the student, educators, and/or parents. In a conference participants share their views of the student's work

---

What Kind of Writer I am

1. Things I like to write at home (examples: notes, letters, poems, stories, etc.)
2. What other people think of my writing:
3. What I think of myself as a writer:
4. Things I like to write at school:
5. What I like about my writing:
5. What I don't like about my writing:

FIGURE 9.2

Open-Ended Writing Questionnaire

---

with the goal of offering feedback and recommendations. Teacher-student conferences can be helpful when assessing the student's written language. The discussion can be strictly verbal or it can be audiotaped, videotaped, or summarized in written form. Conferences can be utilized for diagnosis, program planning, and program evaluation.

Student Work Samples and Products

Examining students' written work provides an opportunity to identify the skills, abilities, and processes that the student uses while developing the written piece. The writing process can be divided into overlapping steps (Rhodes and Shanklin, 1993):

1. Writing authentic work.

Students should have opportunities to engage in authentic writing. This means that when students write in school they must write for the same reasons that writing is done outside of school. Students need to have control over their writing. They should have the necessary materials available, know how to use them, know the purposes for writing, and know how much time is available to them.

2. Rehearsing writing.

Rehearsing means that students know what is expected and are able to choose the type of writing that is appropriate for the purpose. Rehearsing can involve drawing pictures, developing semantic webs, taking notes, and brainstorming.

3. Developing the first draft.

Writing the first draft entails fluency, spelling, and rereading. Fluency is being able to put ideas into writing and having the thoughts flow. Spelling is a consideration in this step as well, because like writing, spelling is a process. Reading and rereading the draft are important because this allows the student to identify and correct errors and to elaborate ideas.

4. Conferencing with peers and/or teachers.

Feedback from peers or teachers can yield important suggestions and ideas as the student develops the written piece.

5. Revising the written piece.

Revising a piece of writing gives the student an opportunity to reflect on his or her own reading of it and on the feedback from peers and teachers. The student can choose to elaborate, clarify, take away information, make corrections, and change the sentence or paragraph structure.

6. Editing.

Editing allows the student to make surface corrections to the written piece. This means making the piece conform to writing conventions and it also involves organization and ideas (Rhodes and Shanklin, 1993).

7. Producing and sharing the finished piece.

The final piece can take various forms, depending on the purpose for writing. For example, the written piece may be a newspaper article, review of a story, poem, play, story, or report. Figure 9.3 is a checklist that can be

Writing Process

Student's Name _____ Date _____

Authentic Writing	Always	Sometimes	Never
1. Does the writer have an authentic, meaningful reason to write?			
2. If the written piece is to be shared, does the writer know the audience?			
3. Is the writer able to take risks in order to express ideas?			
4. Is the writer able to critique the written text?			

☐ **Suggestion for improvement:**

Rehearsal of Writing	Always	Sometimes	Never
5. To what extent does the writer think or plan before writing?			
6. To what extent does the writer consult with others before writing?			
7. To what extent does the writer use readings as a source of ideas?			
8. To what extent does the writer help others develop ideas?			

☐ **Suggestion for improvement:**

Developing the Draft	Always	Sometimes	Never
9. To what extent is the writer able to put thoughts on paper?			
10. Do the ideas flow?			
11. Is the writer able to physically write? Is an alternative input device or communication device used?			
12. Is the writer hindered due to spelling difficulties?			
13. Does the writer's attitude support writing?			
14. Does the writer read and reread the written text?			
15. Does the writer need to be prompted to read and reread the written text?			
16. Does the writer make changes based on the reading and rereading of the written text?			*Continued*

FIGURE 9.3

Assessing the Writing Process

Source: Adapted from Rhodes, Lynn K., and Nancy Shanklin (1993).

Revising	Always	Sometimes	Never
17. Does the writer elaborate or add information?			
18. To what extent does the writer incorporate feedback?			
19. Does the writer use transition?			
20. Does the writer develop one or more introductions or endings to determine which is suitable?			
☐ **Suggestion for improvement:**			

Editing	Always	Sometimes	Never

21. To what extent is the writer able to edit:
  a. spelling
  b. capitalization
  c. punctuation
  d. grammar
  e. paragraphing			

22. Is the writer willing to edit the draft?			
☐ **Suggestion for improvement:**			

FIGURE 9.3 (continued)

Assessing the Writing Process

used when assessing writing samples to provide feedback to students.

Student Journals

Keeping a notebook or journal allows students to record their work as well as their attitudes and feelings about reading and writing. A journal can contain sample pieces the student has written as well as spontaneous types of entries. Journals are useful in program planning and program evaluation. The following samples of written language can be included in a journal:

  poems

  short stories

  fragments of writing

  student's comments about writing

  log entries on specific topics

  interdisciplinary writing

  quotations from the student's readings

  comments by peers or teachers

Performance-based Assessment

Performance assessment of reading and writing abilities measures the integration of reading and writing and evaluates demonstrations of reading and writing abilities. Performance assessment requires students to read a passage or story for a purpose, use one or more cognitive skills as they construct meaning from the text, and write about what they read, usually in

SNAPSHOT

Seth is a curious and energetic sixth grader. One of his most favorite things to do is spend time with his cat. Seth's teacher recently asked him to write a creative story. After reading Seth's story about his cat, use one or more of the checklists that we have described in this section to analyze Seth's written language.

A Day in the Life of My Cat
by Seth

For those of you who don't now me, you probably don't now my cat. Since this story is going to be about him, you may find it helpful for me to give you a discription him. His name sounds like a good place start. It is Kelev which in Hebrew means dog. This sounds crazy but since my dad wanted a dog we named the cat Kelev. He is huge 20 pound black and white tabby with large green eyes. By the way, this story will be written from the cat's point of view. Most of the dialog in the story is what the cat thnking.

Buzzzzzzzzzzzz, meoooooooooooooow. I hate that kid's didgatal alarm. It startles me every morning. How come I'm the only one awake? It is supposed to wake him up, too, but he just sleeps through it like a dead mouse. I think it is about time to bther his parants.

Soon the boy and his mothr and fathr leave the house. O boy! I hve the hous to myself.

Soon, the son comes home and the family eats dinner. I keep them compeny and wander around the boy's chair hoping to get a scrap of food. After suppar, everyone, including me, retreat into the TV room and relax. I crawl up on top of the boy and down. He pats me. I then get up for some more food. When I finish, I journey to the bathroom and open the cabinet to reveal my little house. I go to sleep in it. I wake to find the house silent. Everyone is sleeping. Again, I make a trips to the boy's bed, where he is now sleeping and I sit down. I now wait for that scary buzz I hear every morning.

---

response to a prompt or task (Farr and Tone, 1994). Performance assessment can be used in program planning and program evaluation.

Portfolios

A portfolio, as we have discussed, is a deliberate collection of a student's work that demonstrates the student's efforts, progress, and achievement. When used to document and assess written language ability, portfolios provide information about reading, writing, spelling skills, comprehension, attitudes, and work habits. Portfolios in literacy assessment are used for program planning and program evaluation. A more extensive discussion of the use of portfolios can be found in Chapter 7.

The following are suggestions for materials that could be included in student writing portfolios:

newsletter articles

student logs

plays

poems

lyrics to a song

creative writing

nonfiction writing

projects that involve students in portraying characters or plot

journals in which students record their thoughts about what they have read

written dialogues between student and teacher

videotapes of students conferencing with each other

photographs of student writing projects

Exhibitions

An exhibition displays a student's work and demonstrates how the student combines knowledge, abilities, skills, and attitudes. This tool gives a student the opportunity to summarize and synthesize what has been accomplished. In reading and writing assessment, exhibitions are useful because students realize that reading and writing involves integration, understanding, problem solving, and reasoning. In this way, teachers have concrete information for program planning and program evaluation.

The parts of an exhibition that involve writing can be divided into elements. These elements do not necessarily occur in a sequential order but they are useful when thinking about the development of exhibitions (Willis, 1996):

- Prompt
  A prompt is what students are asked to do. This can be as basic as "write a research report about the city in which you live," "write a description of a new tool that would make a task easier," or as comprehensive as "develop an exhibition of your vision for the city of the future."
- Vision
  A vision is what the exhibition will be like. For example, the exhibition on cities will in-

clude oral, written, and multimedia components that demonstrate students' skills and abilities to reflect on their learning, to analyze, to conduct research, and to synthesize. Students may be asked to integrate one or more disciplines, to write reports, create multimedia presentations, and incorporate the arts.

- Agreement on Standards
  Educators and students must agree on what makes an exhibition good. Various scoring systems or rubrics can be developed to assist in the evaluation of exhibitions.
- Audience
  Students' work is exhibited to other students, educators, parents, or community members.
- Coaching
  Peers and teachers should be engaged in coaching students toward the development of their exhibitions. Coaching, rather than evaluating, is important in the development phase of the exhibition.
- Reflection
  All participants should reflect on their exhibitions. This allows all of the participants to develop an appreciation for what has been learned and accomplished. Reflection also provides an opportunity to think about how to do it better the next time.

Examples of exhibitions in reading and writing include:

- storyboards
- series of letters to editors
- diary of one of the characters in the story
- reviews of related books
- dialogues among the characters
- maps depicting the travels of the characters

SCORING

Two types of scoring, holistic and analytic, are used when evaluating writing samples, written

Score	Criteria
	Holistic Scoring Guide—Writing
5	The paper is superb. The ideas are very well developed. If there are any errors in mechanics, grammar, or spelling, they are very minor. Sentence structure is very clear and varied. There is a clear sense of purpose and audience. Ideas are explained and very well supported.
4	The paper is very good. The ideas are very well developed. There are few errors in mechanics, grammar, or spelling. Sentence structure is clear and varied. There is a clear sense of purpose and audience. Ideas are explained and supported.
3	The paper is good. The ideas are well developed. There are some errors in mechanics, grammar, or spelling. Sentences follow a similar pattern. There is some sense of purpose or audience. Ideas are not always explained or supported.
2	The paper is moderate. Some ideas are developed. There are frequent errors in mechanics, grammar, or spelling. Sentences follow a similar pattern. There may be sentence fragments. There is little sense of purpose or audience. Ideas are infrequently explained or supported.
1	The paper is poor. Ideas are rarely developed. There are many errors in mechanics, grammar, or spelling. Sentences follow a similar pattern. There are sentence fragments. There is no sense of purpose or audience. Ideas are rarely explained or supported.

FIGURE 9.4

Holistic Scoring

products, portfolios, performance assessments, and exhibitions.

Holistic Scoring

Holistic scoring (Figure 9.4) is a type of scoring that is quick and efficient. One score is produced that provides an impression of writing ability. Holistic scoring rests on the assumption that all of the elements of writing, such as organization, mechanics, fluency, and so forth, work together in the whole text. This type of scoring can be useful when the teacher is looking for one or two previously identified characteristics in a student's work. One important disadvantage of holistic scoring is that it does not provide detailed information about the success of the student in specific areas of writing (Spandel and Stiggins, 1990).

Analytic Scoring

Analytic scoring (Figure 9.5) is a type of scoring that produces a detailed analysis of the written text. The teacher uses a scale or rubric to assign points to different levels of performance in the areas that are assessed. For example, a teacher wants to describe the writing performance of students to organize, use mechanics, and use paragraphing. The teacher rates the students' writing samples on a scale, from 1 to 5 or 1 to 6, in each of these three areas and the student receives three separate scores. Care should be taken when scoring each of these areas so that the teacher's impression in one area—for example, organization—does not influence the impression in another area—such as mechanics in this example (Spandel and Stiggins, 1990).

Analytic scoring is frequently done by two or more raters, working independently, who rate the same written text. When they have finished, comparisons are made between their ratings to determine their similarity. If the ratings are dissimilar, the two teachers can discuss why they gave certain ratings or a third teacher may be asked to rate the text.

Analytic Scoring—Writing				
1	*2*	*3*	*4*	*5*
Development of Ideas Little understanding of audience; little elaboration of ideas	Some understanding of audience; some elaboration of ideas	Good understanding of audience; good elaboration of ideas	Very good understanding of audience; very good elaboration of ideas	Excellent understanding of audience; superb elaboration of ideas
Organization No evidence of an organized plan for writing; ideas and paragraphs run together	Some evidence of an organized plan for writing; ideas and paragraphs are loosely organized	Good evidence of an organized plan for writing; ideas and paragraphs are organized	Very good evidence of an organized plan for writing; ideas and paragraphs are well organized	Excellent evidence of organized plan for writing; ideas are original and paragraphs are well organized
Fluency Language is very limited and repetitive; written text is very brief	Language is somewhat limited and repetitive; written text is brief	Language is good and there are few repetitions; written text has adequate elaboration	Language is very good and varied; there are no repetitions; written text has very good elaboration	Language is excellent and varied; and there are no repetitions; written text has excellent elaboration
Spelling Few words are spelled correctly	Most words are spelled phonetically; most sight words are spelled correctly	Most words are spelled correctly; some errors with homophones and endings	Words are spelled correctly; there are few errors	Words are spelled correctly; errors are minor
Capitalization & Punctuation No capitalization or punctuation	Some evidence of correct capitalization and punctuation	Good evidence of capitalization and punctuation	Very good evidence of capitalization and punctuation; few errors	Excellent evidence of capitalization and punctuation; errors are rare

FIGURE 9.5

Analytic Scoring

Anchor Papers

Anchor papers are students' papers that represent writing at different levels of performance. They can be useful in the development of rubrics. For example, after a group of students completes a writing assignment, the teacher reviews all of the papers to determine which three represent by degrees high-quality performance, typical or average performance, and low performance. These are the anchor papers. Next, the teacher evaluates all of the student papers, using the anchor papers as a guide to determine high, typical, or low performance.

Name	Date
Authentic Writing	*My Comments*

Authentic Writing

1. I know my audence.
2. I take risks when I write.

Rehearsal of Writing

3. I think or plan ahead when I write.
4. I consult with my peers.
5. I use print and nonprint media as sources.
6. I help others to write.

Developing the Draft

7. I feel that I can put my thoughts down on paper.
8. I have a good attitude toward writing.
9. I am able to spell most words.
10. I know which words to capitalize.
11. I know how to use punctuation.
12. I make changes to my text based on rereading.

Revising

13. I incorporate feedback.
14. I make changes, such as beginnings, transitions, and endings.

Editing

15. I am willing to edit my draft.
16. I am able to edit and correct spelling.
17. I am able to edit and correct punctuation.
18. I am able to edit and correct capitalization.
19. I am able to edit and correct grammar.
20. I am able to edit and correct paragraphing.

FIGURE 9.6

Self-Assessment Checklist

SELF-ASSESSMENT

Self-assessment provides students with an opportunity to analyze their own writing and to reflect on their own learning. Figure 9.6 is an example of a questionnaire that students can use when assessing their own writing.

PEER ASSESSMENT

When conducting peer assessments, students have an opportunity to reflect on the writing processes, skills, and strategies of their peers as well as on their own writing processes, skills, and strategies. Figure 9.7 is an example

	☹	😐	😊
1. My peer writes for a purpose.			
2. My peer consulted me before writing.			
3. My peer made changes based on my feedback.			
4. My peer conferenced with me.			
5. My peer uses transitions.			
6. My peer is able to edit the written text.			

Student's Name _____   Date _____

Peer's Name _____

FIGURE 9.7

Peer Assessment Checklist

of a checklist that students use when conducting a peer assessment.

OBSERVING THE STUDENT WITHIN THE ENVIRONMENT

In previous chapters we have discussed the influence of the physical, learning, and social environments on teaching and learning. Temperature, lighting, and seating arrangements affect how well the student reads and writes. A comfortable learning environment facilitates the development of writing abilities and positive attitudes and habits. Finally, the relationships that students have with peers and teachers affect performance.

PREFERRED PRACTICES

The assessment of literacy must reflect the close link between the development of reading and written language. Best practice requires that the assessment of literacy be conducted frequently and that the results are used to guide instruction.

Reliance on individual standardized tests is a decision to be taken cautiously. Many norm-referenced tests do not reflect contemporary views of reading and writing. When selecting an instrument, careful consideration is required to match the curriculum and the test content. Reading and writing instruction varies considerably throughout the United States. Therefore, selection of an instrument that best matches the curriculum is essential.

Most standardized achievement tests are biased toward students from various cultural, ethnic, and socioeconomic groups. Cultural patterns of teaching and learning may not be reflected in the construction of tests. Low socioeconomic status often limits access and participation in educational activities.

Scoring of tests can be problematic. Students vary in their abilities and most test manuals contain general directions for scoring. The test examiner must use judgment in scoring. This can be a problem because the judgment of test examiners differs, and this leads to inconsistencies in scoring and interpretation.

Performance-based assessment, portfolios, and exhibitions can be problematic as well. Questions remain about reliability and validity of these approaches.

Assessment of literacy requires that multiple approaches be used, including standardized tests, curriculum-based assessment, criterion-referenced assessment, and alternative forms of assessment. The rule for the assessment of literacy is, "Multiple, multiple, and frequent"— use multiple approaches, multiple instruments, and assess frequently!

by moving south west detaching itself from Saudi Arabia and Europe. Now it was Australia's turn to slide out the Bengal bay and float south east. Aisa and Europe which was the main link for Pangea stayed where they were. This explains how continents moved with the continental drift.

9.4 Examine a norm-referenced, standardized writing test. Compare the development of this test with the contemporary views of assessment discussed in this chapter.

9.5 Identify three assessment approaches discussed in the chapter. Compare the purposes, advantages, and disadvantages of each approach.

EXTENDING LEARNING

9.1 Develop two assessment tasks that link the instruction in writing directly to assessment of writing.

9.2 Develop a checklist or rating scale that assesses students' attitudes and habits in writing.

9.3 After reading the following writing sample that Yizhong, a fourth grader, wrote, develop a checklist and use it to analyze Yizhong's writing.

Pangea

Pangea was the supercontenient that was made up of the seven other continents linked together. This explains how I think the continents dissembled themselves and how they got where they are today. South America which was nestled in the curve of Africa rotated 90° to the right and moved westward. North America above South America was connected to Europe with the middle part of Canada. This medium size continent made another 90° right turn and again moved to the west. After these continents unhooked themselves Africa followed

REFERENCES

Brigance, A. H. (1977). *BRIGANCE® diagnostic inventory of basic skills.* No. Billerica, Mass.: Curriculum Associates.

Brigance, A. H. (1981). *BRIGANCE® diagnostic inventory of essential skills.* No. Billerica, Mass.: Curriculum Associates.

Brigance, A. H. (1983). *BRIGANCE® diagnostic comprehensive inventory of basic skills.* No. Billerica, Mass.: Curriculum Associates.

Brigance, A. H. (1984). *BRIGANCE® assessment of basic skills–Spanish edition.* No. Billerica, Mass.: Curriculum Associates.

Carrow-Woolfolk, E. (1996). *Oral and Written Language Scales.* Minneapolis, Minn.: American Guidance Service.

Farr, R., and B. Tone (1994). *Portfolio and performance assessment.* Fort Worth, Tex.: Harcourt Brace College Publishers.

Hammill, D. D., V. L. Brown, S. C. Larsen, and J. L. Wiederholt (1994). *Test of adolescent and adult language.* 3d ed. Austin, Tex.: PRO-ED.

Hammill, D. D., and S. C. Larsen (1996). *Test of written language.* 3d ed. Austin, Tex.: PRO-ED.

Harcourt Brace Educational Measurement (1992). *Wechsler individual achievement test.* San Antonio, Tex.: Author.

Hresko, W. P., S. R. Herron, and P. K. Peak (1996). *Test of early written language.* 2d ed. Austin, Tex.: PRO-ED.

Hudson, F. G., S. E. Colson, D. L. Welch, A. K. Banikowski, and T. A. Mehring (1989). *Hudson education skills inventory.* Austin, Tex.: PRO-ED.

Kaufman, A. S., and N. L. Kaufman (1985). *Kaufman test of educational achievement.* Circle Pines, Minn.: American Guidance Service.

Larsen, S. C., and D. D. Hammill (1994). *Test of written spelling.* 3d ed. Austin, Tex.: PRO-ED.

Markwardt, F. C. (1989). *Peabody individual achievement test–Revised.* Circle Pines, Minn.: American Guidance Service.

McGhee, R., B. R. Bryant, S. C. Larsen, and D. M. Rivera (1995). *Test of written expression.* Austin, Tex.: PRO-ED.

Newcomer, P. L. (1990). *Diagnostic achievement battery.* 2d ed. Austin, Tex.: PRO-ED.

Newcomer, P. L., and B. R. Bryant (1993). *Diagnostic achievement test for adolescents.* 2d ed. Austin, Tex.: PRO-ED.

Rhodes, L. K., and N. L. Shanklin (1993). *Windows into literacy.* Portsmouth, N.H.: Heinemann.

Sonnenschein, J. L. (1983). *Basic achievement skills individual screener.* San Antonio, Tex.: Author.

Spandel, V., and R. J. Stiggins (1990). *Creating writers.* New York: Longman.

Stahl, S. A., and M. R. Kuhn (1995). Does whole language or instruction matched to learning styles help children learn to read? *School Psychology Review* 24: 393–404.

Wilde, S. (1989a). Looking at invented spelling: A kidwatcher's guide to spelling, Part I. In *The whole language evaluation book,* eds. K. S. Goodman, Y. M. Goodman, and W. J. Hood, 213–226. Portsmouth, N.H.: Heinemann.

Wilde, S. (1989b). Understanding spelling strategies: A kidwatcher's guide to spelling, Part II. In *The whole language evaluation book,* eds. K. S. Goodman, Y. M. Goodman, and W. J. Hood, 227–236. Portsmouth, N.H.: Heinemann.

Wilkinson, G. (1994). *Wide range achievement test.* 3d ed. Austin, Tex.: PRO-ED.

Willis, S. (1996). Student exhibitions put higher-order skills to the test. *Education Update* 38 (March): 1, 3.

Woodcock, R. W., and M. B. Johnson (1989). *Woodcock-Johnson psychoeducational battery–Revised.* Chicago: Riverside.

Oral Language

OVERVIEW

Language involves the use of symbols to communicate thoughts, feelings, ideas, and information. To communicate meaning, these symbols are spoken or produced through synthesized speech, written by using the visual symbols of the language, or expressed manually through signing or gestures. Each of us uses these symbols of language every day.

Oral language is closely related to assessment areas described in other chapters in this book. The assessment of oral language skills is important when assessing achievement, development, ability, and behavior. As you read this chapter, keep in mind how assessment of children and youth in one domain might be related to assessment in another area.

CHAPTER OBJECTIVES

After completing this chapter, you should be able to:

Contrast several theoretical perspectives regarding the development of oral language.

Describe the use of standardized tests for assessing oral language.

Compare assessment approaches that are directly linked to instruction, program planning, and program evaluation.

Describe how the physical, learning, and social environments influence oral language.

WHAT SHAPES OUR VIEWS

Contemporary perspectives on the development of speech and language skills and abilities provide a basis for the various approaches to assessment. We will examine three different perspectives: the behavioral approach, the social learning theory approach, and the psycholinguistic approach.

Behavioral Approach

This approach emphasizes the importance of external factors (outside of the individual) in influencing and promoting language development. Verbal ability develops as a result of the contingent relationship among the antecedent, the behavior, and the consequence. Speech and language are learned as a result of adult interaction with the child (stimulus, or antecedent), the child's vocalization (verbal response behavior), and the reinforcement (the consequence of vocalization). Language abilities are refined through the process of **shaping,** or reinforcing, the sounds or word as the vocalization more closely approximates the sound or word in the language.

For example, the first step will be for the child to make any sound(s) when requesting a glass of juice. The next step in the progression will be for the child to vocalize "juu," a sound that is close to the target word. Gradually, the child's response becomes more like the target word.

Shaping is a behavioral term that refers to reinforcing the behavior (each progressive step) as it becomes more and more like the target behavior. Thus, as children become older, gradual reinforcement for making sounds common to the language occurs. Eventually, strings of sounds are shaped to approximate words.

Child: "Orrr"

Adult: "More? Do you want more juice?"

Child: "Orrr"

Adult: "More juice?"

Child: "Ma jus."

Adult: "That's right! More juice!"

Effect on Assessment Practices

Assessment focuses on the stimulus or antecedent (A), the verbal response or behavior (B), and the reinforcements or consequences (C) offered in the environment. This type of assessment is often referred to as the ABC approach. The behavior (B) may be divided into smaller steps, depending on the needs and abilities of the individual. Breaking the behavior into small, discrete, sequential steps is called **task analysis.** Chapter 15 contains a detailed explanation of the ABC approach and of task analysis procedures in assessment practices.

Social Learning Theory

According to this perspective, individuals learn a set of rules about the syntax of language through the modeling of language (Bandura, 1977). As defined earlier, syntax is the system of rules that dictate how words are combined into meaningful phrases and sentences; syntax governs the arrangement of word sequences. This set of rules allows people to produce new and novel combinations of words, such as phrases or sentences, that they have never heard or produced before. When a child develops competence in syntax, the child can speak and understand an infinite number of sentences.

Adults frequently use a technique, called **expansion,** to increase language development. Expansion involves restating the individual's (the learner's) language and adding words and more complex phrases.

Child: "Wan dawg."

Adult: "You want to pat the dog?"

Child: "Wan pa dawg."

Effect on Assessment Practices

This approach emphasizes the importance of adults and peers in the student's environment and their effect on the development of language. The modeling of language, the use of syntax, and the expansion of language are areas of assessment focus.

Psycholinguistic Approach

The psycholinguistic approach, developed by Noam Chomsky (1967), is based on the belief that children are born ready to develop language skills and that they have an inborn language-developing ability that helps them understand and learn language. This is called the "language acquisition device," and it enables the child to interpret language, construct grammatical rules, and generate an infinite variety of phrases and sentences.

Effect on Assessment Practices

This perspective presents difficulties to educators who work with students with language disabilities. The view that children and youth are innately predisposed and have an inborn ability implies that individuals with language impairments are not born with this ability and will never have this ability. This approach provides little encouragement for intervention and instruction for students who are experiencing delays in language development.

UNDERSTANDING SPEECH AND LANGUAGE DISORDERS

Students with suspected **speech** and **language disorders** are screened first for possible hearing loss. The hearing screening consists of listening to several tones within the speech range. If a student has difficulty hearing one or more of these tones, the examiner refers the student for a complete hearing assessment. Chapter 16 describes a hearing assessment.

Language Disorders

Assessment questions focus on the student's **expressive language, receptive language,** or **inner language.** Expressive language refers to the student's ability to use language to communicate with others. Assessing expressive language involves examining the actual production of sound, speech, and language. Speech is the production of oral language for the purpose of expression.

Receptive language refers to the student's understanding of the language of others. Assessment of receptive language usually involves having the student listen to words or phrases and then demonstrating understanding. For example, a student might be asked to put the book on top of or under the table or to point to the picture that shows the boy putting on a jacket. Many standardized instruments are designed to measure expressive and receptive language.

Inner language involves the use of language during thinking, planning, and other mental processes. The assessment of inner language skills and abilities is a complex process and continues to evolve as more and more research addresses this area. Some standardized instruments like the *Oral and Written Language Scales* (Carrow-Woolfolk, 1995) assess higher-order thinking.

Speech Disorders

Assessment questions are raised when a parent or teacher has difficulty in understanding a student's speech. A speech and language pathologist (SLP) usually conducts the assessment. In fact, the speech and language pathologist is the primary practitioner to plan assessment in this area.

Students who have difficulty in producing the correct sounds of speech generally have problems in one or more of four areas of speech production.

1. Respiration: To produce sounds, an individual must be able to control the inhaling and exhaling of breath. This must occur while the air is forced through the larynx.
2. Phonation: An individual must contract specific muscles to allow the vocal folds of

SNAPSHOT

Bethany

The teacher's words fell on Bethany's ears at an overwhelming rate. Bethany knew that the teacher was explaining the assignment for tomorrow. Although Bethany has average intelligence, she is not able to comprehend all that the teacher says. Before the class was dismissed, Bethany's teacher handed her a written copy of the assignment, and Bethany smiled quickly as she gathered her books.

Bethany's teacher returned the smile as she remembered the problems that Bethany had experienced earlier in the year. Through the referral and assessment process, the teacher was able to discover Bethany's difficulty in comprehending oral directions and in following class discussions.

Bethany's teacher had observed that even though Bethany seemed to be attentive, she had difficulty in following daily class discussions. She had talked to Bethany to see if she was having difficulty in hearing her or the other students. A week later the school nurse had conducted a hearing screening on all the students in her classroom. Bethany passed the screening with no problems.

During the first three weeks in September, Bethany frequently submitted incomplete homework assignments and, when questioned, would apologetically add that she didn't ". . . know we had to do that." As the difficulty seemed to persist, the teacher decided to confer with Bethany's former teachers. Both teachers vaguely remembered that Bethany was not consistent in her work. Some of the assignments were done well, they remembered. One teacher felt that she did not seem to be motivated.

The following week, the teacher called Bethany's parents and asked them to come in for a conference. Both parents were surprised to hear about the teacher's concerns. When asked if Bethany needed to have the volume high on the television, her mother replied that Bethany seldom seemed to be interested in watching television or in going to the movies. Bethany's parents were concerned about her missing assignments. They tried to pinpoint some of their concerns: Why doesn't Bethany turn in complete assignments? Why doesn't she participate in class discussions? Is there a reason why Bethany does not like to watch television or go to the movies? They agreed that the teacher should make a referral to the assessment team. Perhaps the team might be able to provide some answers to these puzzling questions.

Through the assessment process, the team identified Bethany's problem. She had difficulty processing oral language. Her teacher used several accommodations, such as written assignment slips and outlines of lecture material, to help Bethany be more successful in the classroom.

the larynx to be drawn together. Forcing the air through the larynx causes the air to vibrate and produce sound.

3. Resonation: The vibrating air is passed through the throat, mouth, and sometimes the nasal cavities. The quality of the sound is shaped during this process.

4. Articulation: The formation of the specific sounds of speech are produced by the position of the tongue, lips, teeth, and mouth.

RESPONDING TO DIVERSITY

Today, many children learn a language at home that is not European American English. European American English is the term used to describe the type of English that is spoken by the dominant group as opposed to dialectical, cultural, or regional variations of English. In addition, many children come from homes in

SNAPSHOT

Eugene

In the following Snapshot, we meet Eugene's teacher, Ms. Wong, who has questions regarding her observations of Eugene's speech and his stuttering problem.

"Cccan I sh-sh-sharpen my pencil?"

Ms. Wong looked up to see Eugene waving his hand in the air. She nodded and motioned toward the pencil sharpener. As Eugene left his work group of three other students, Ms. Wong thought again about Eugene's stuttering problem.

He was a new student in her class this year. When she had first observed his stuttering problem, she had checked the records that were forwarded by Eugene's former school. They contained no mention of a stuttering problem. She thought that Eugene might overcome the stuttering with time; but it did not seem to disappear. In fact, today marked the beginning of the third week of school and he seemed to be having more difficulty getting his ideas across as time went on.

Will the stuttering become worse or will he outgrow it in time? Should she try to correct him? She wrote herself a reminder to fill out a referral form concerning Eugene's speech problems before the end of the week. The referral form would be sent to the school's coordinator of the assessment team.

By the end of the school year, Eugene was very grateful to his teacher for recognizing his speech problem and referring him for assessment. Through the IEP process, Eugene received services from the speech and language pathologist, who taught him specific strategies to counter his stuttering. By learning ways to control his breathing and plan what he wanted to say in class, Eugene was able to learn life skills in decreasing his stuttering problem.

Questions and concerns about a student's oral language always need to be referred as soon as possible to the assessment team. In Eugene's case, after filling out the referral form his teacher should consult with members of the team, such as the speech and language pathologist, about ways to work with Eugene in the classroom. Her questions regarding how to handle classroom stuttering need to be addressed as soon as the difficulty is observed.

which the family's native language is the home language. These children are considered to be culturally and linguistically diverse.

In order to benefit from their education program, many children who are culturally and linguistically diverse need bilingual education or English as a second language instruction. Some children need additional tutoring due to limited linguistic experiences. Most children who are culturally and linguistically diverse do not have a special need that requires a referral to special services.

Some students whose first language is not European American English should receive special education or related services. How can teachers distinguish language differences from speech and language disorders in linguistically and culturally diverse students? First, a teacher can observe speech production. A student needs to be referred if the student's speech contains mispronunciations, dysfluencies, unusual pitch, rate, hoarseness, omitted words or word endings, words used in unusual ways, or atypical sequences when compared to dialect peers (Moran, 1996).

Second, a teacher can tell when a linguistically and culturally diverse student should be referred to the assessment team when some of the following behaviors are observed in comparison to similar peers (Roseberry-McKibbin, 1995):

1. Nonverbal aspects of language are culturally inappropriate.
2. Student does not express basic needs adequately.
3. Student rarely initiates verbal interaction with peers.
4. When peers initiate interaction, student responds sporadically/inappropriately.
5. Student replaces speech with gestures, communicates nonverbally when talking would be appropriate and expected.
6. Peers give indications that they have difficulty understanding the student.
7. Student often gives inappropriate responses.

8. Student has difficulty conveying thoughts in an organized, sequential manner that is understandable to listeners.
9. Student shows poor topic maintenance ("skips around").
10. Student has word-finding difficulties that go beyond normal second language acquisition patterns.
11. Student fails to provide significant information to the listener, leaving the listener confused.
12. Student has difficulty with conversational turn-taking skills (may be too passive, or may interrupt inappropriately).
13. Student perseverates (remains too long) on a topic even after the topic has changed.
14. Student fails to ask and answer questions appropriately.
15. Student needs to hear things repeated, even when they are stated simply and comprehensibly.
16. Student often echoes what she or he hears.

The focus of the assessment question, "How does the student communicate within the first-language setting?" and the standard that teachers can apply is whether the student's language reflects characteristics that are different from the student's first-language community (Moran, 1996). Students should not be identified as having a speech and language disability simply based on the comparison of the student's language with the dominant language—such as European American English—of the school community.

SPEECH AND LANGUAGE ASSESSMENT

An assessment of speech and language is influenced by the perspectives of the examiner who is gathering the information as well as the choice of the assessment approach. Many standardized instruments focus on expressive and receptive language, whereas authorities in the field (Bloom and Lahey, 1978, cited by Kaiser, Alpert, and Warren, 1988; Semel, Wiig, and Secord, 1995b) describe oral language as consisting of three areas or components: form, content, and use.

Form

Form relates to the structural properties of language. Students with articulation disorders often have difficulty in producing sounds. The term **phonology** refers to the system of speech sounds of a language. The smallest units of sound are **phonemes.** The English language makes use of only about 44 different phonemes.

The word *truck* consists of four phonemes (/T/R/U/K/). Substituting one phoneme for another and omitting phonemes are common mistakes that students make. Speech and language pathologists may describe this as a problem in articulation. For example:

- substituting letter(s): wabbit for rabbit
- omitting letter(s): car for cars

Some students have difficulty in associating phonemes with their written equivalents, called **graphemes.** One of the reasons that English is such a difficult language is that: 1) a single grapheme can represent more than one phoneme and 2) different graphemes can represent the same phoneme (Polloway and Smith, 1992, p. 10). In teaching that a single grapheme can represent more than one phoneme, we say that a letter has different sounds. For example, how many sounds does the letter *a* have?

Morphology

Morphology is the study of the units of letters that form a single unit of meaning. The basic unit of meaning is a **morpheme.** Morphemes can be a word such as *house,* or *car,* or a meaningful part of a word such as *re* in *renew.* Prefixes and suffixes, such as *re-, in-, -s,*

-er are morphemes. Because morphemes are units of meaning, they are frequently used to measure expressive language development by obtaining a sample of the student's language and counting the individual morphemes per speech utterance. A speech utterance is the single phrase or sentence that the student expresses. The number of morphemes is totaled and divided by the number of speech utterances to obtain the average mean length of utterance (MLU).

The following conversation was recorded during a five-minute observation of Andre during free play in the kindergarten classroom.

Diane: "My block . . ." (2 morphemes)

Andre: "No, I want this." (4 morphemes)

Andre: "You can be the driver." (6 morphemes [-er is a suffix])

Adding up Andre's use of morphemes, the total comes to 10 and is divided by the number of Andre's speech utterances (2). Although the MLU may be an oversimplification of the concept of spoken language, the MLU is useful in comparing levels of linguistic development and increases in individual mastery of expressive language (Polloway and Smith, 1992). Other considerations that will affect the MLU are: (1) the length of the recording needed to obtain an adequate language sample of speech utterances, and (2) the environment(s) that will be observed.

Content

Content relates to the meaning of language. Content includes semantics and syntax.

Semantics

Semantics is the study of word meanings. Development of semantics begins with association of single concrete morphemes, for example, the association of *mama* with a particular person. Development typically progresses to understanding complex utterances; for example,

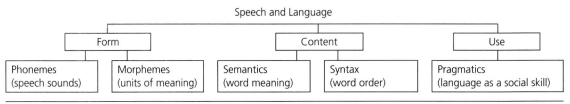

FIGURE 10.1

Linguistic Aspects of Speech and Language

"Please, get me the book" and more complex language such as, "It's raining cats and dogs."

Syntax

Syntax refers to the rules for arranging words into a sentence or phrase. In English, for example, adjectives are commonly placed before nouns. The combination of syntax and morphology is known as grammar.

Use

This aspect of language, introduced earlier by the term pragmatics, refers to the ability to use language in functional ways: for example, the ability to use language in taking turns, to enter into a conversation or discussion with other children (or adults), to continue the conversation, to interpret the meaning of the speaker, or to "read" the listener's nonverbal cues.

Figure 10.1 illustrates the relationship between the aspects of speech and language we have discussed.

ASSESSMENT QUESTIONS, PURPOSES, AND APPROACHES

Questions regarding a student's oral language abilities and skills require the practitioner to conduct a variety of assessment approaches in order to obtain an understanding of the student's ability, developmental level, maturity, gender, and cultural, ethnic, and racial background. These approaches should include standardized testing as well as probes, language samples, interviews, checklists, and so on. The assessment purposes and approaches used in oral language assessment are described in Table 10.1.

STANDARDIZED TESTS OF ORAL LANGUAGE

There are a number of standardized tests of oral language (Table 10.2). Some of the commonly used individual, standardized tests of oral language are described in this section. All the tests in this section are norm-referenced and are administered and scored according to standardized procedures. The tests yield a variety of scores, including standard scores, percentiles, stanines, age equivalents, and normal curve equivalents (NCEs).

Clinical Evaluation of Language Fundamentals-3

The *Clinical Evaluation of Language Fundamentals-3 (CELF-3)* (Semel, Wiig, and Secord, 1995a) is designed to identify, diagnose, and follow up the evaluation of language skills deficits in students ages 6 through 21. The *CELF-3* contains 11 subtests that measure selected receptive and expressive skills in morphology, syntax, semantics, and memory (Figure 10.2). The Examiner's Manual includes a chapter on extension testing and instructional objectives with many excellent examples of follow-up probes that can be used to assess and monitor students in the classroom.

Also included in the Examiner's Manual is a timely chapter devoted to dialectal variations and cultural sensitivity. The authors have addressed issues of bias in assessment of oral language by submitting the *CELF-3* test materials

TABLE 10.1 Assessment Questions, Purposes, and Approaches

Assessment questions	Steps and purposes	Approaches
Screening		
Is the student's speech and language typical for the student's age?	To determine whether students *may* have speech and language delays or disabilities and should be referred for further assessment	Norm-referenced instruments Curriculum-based assessment Criterion-referenced assessment Observations Questionnaires Checklists
Eligibility		
Does the student have a severe language disability? Does the student meet the criteria for services? What are the strengths and weaknesses? Why does the student have a speech and language disorder? How extensive is the disability?	To determine if there is a disability and the extent of the speech and language problems To determine the need for special education and related services To compare the student's performance with the performance of the peer group To determine specific strengths and weaknesses To understand why the student is having difficulty	Norm-referenced instruments Curriculum-based assessment Criterion-referenced assessment Observations Probes Error analysis Interviews Checklists Student, parent, and/or teacher conferences Performance assessment

CONNECTING INSTRUCTION WITH ASSESSMENT

Program Planning		
What types of services should be provided? What classroom modifications and adaptations should be implemented? What skills does the student have? What should be taught?	To determine the locations and type of services(s) to be received To assess the physical, learning, and social classroom environments To understand what the student knows and does not know To plan the student's program To determine where instruction should begin To determine instructional approaches	Norm-referenced instruments Curriculum-based assessment Criterion-referenced assessment Observations Probes Error analysis Interviews Checklists Questionnaires Student, parent, and/or teacher conferences Performance assessment
Program Monitoring		
Once instruction begins, is the student making progress? Should the instruction be modified?	To understand the pace of instruction To understand what the student knows prior to and after instruction	Curriculum-based assessment Criterion-referenced assessment Observations Probes Error analysis Interviews

Continued

TABLE 10-1   (Continued)

Assessment questions	Steps and purposes	Approaches
	To understand the strategies and concepts the student uses To monitor the student's program	Checklists Questionnaires Student, parent, and/or teacher conferences Portfolios Exhibitions Journals Written descriptions Oral descriptions
	Program Evaluation	
Has the student made progress? Has the student met the goals of the IEP? Has the instructional program been successful for the student? Has the instructional program achieved its goals?	To determine whether the IEP goals have been met To determine whether the goals of the program have been met To evaluate program effectiveness	Curriculum-based assessment Criterion-referenced assessment Observations Probes Error analysis Interviews Checklists Questionnaires Student, parent, and/or teacher conferences Portfolios Exhibitions Journals Written descriptions Oral descriptions Surveys

to a panel of experts who reviewed the test specifically for gender, racial/ethnic, and regional biases. For Spanish-speaking individuals, the *CELF-3* Spanish Edition is a parallel, not translated, version of the instrument.

Administration

The *CELF-3* is administered individually and takes 30–45 minutes.

Scoring

Raw scores are converted to standard scores, percentile ranks, stanines, or normal curve equivalents. Confidence intervals of 68 percent and 90 percent may be reported.

Standardization

The *CELF-3* was standardized between 1994 and 1995. The standardization sample consisted of 2,450 individuals who were stratified by age, gender, race/ethnicity, geographic region, and parent education level. None of the individuals in the standardization sample received language therapy or had a diagnosed or identified language disorder.

Only individuals who could understand and speak English and were English-language dominant participated in the standardization. Approximately 30 percent of the standardization sample included individuals with regional or di-

C E L F® 3

Clinical Evaluation of Language Fundamentals
THIRD EDITION

Record Form

Name _Alicia Fuller_

Age _9-5_ Gender _f_ Grade _4th_

School _Cable Elementary_

Teacher _Mrs. Perez_

Examiner _N. Townsend_

Address _3115 West Ave._

_78062_

	Year	Month	Day
Test Date	19xx	10	15
Birth Date	19xx	5	8
Chronological Age	9	5	7

Ages 6-8 Scoring Summary	Raw Score	Standard Score	Confidence Interval (__% Level)	PR	Confidence Interval
Sentence Structure			to		to
Concepts and Directions			to		to
World Classes			to		to
Sum of 3 Standard Scores					
RECEPTIVE LANGUAGE SCORE			to		to
Word Structure			to		to
Formulated Sentences			to		to
Recalling Sentences			to		to
Sum of 3 Standard Scores					
EXPRESSIVE LANGUAGE SCORE			to		to
Sum of RL and EL Scores					
TOTAL LANGUAGE SCORE			to		to
Sum of 6 Raw Scores		Age Equivalent ____			

Ages 9 and Above Scoring Summary	Raw Score	Standard Score	Confidence Interval (90% Level)	PR	Confidence Interval
Concepts and Directions	18	7	5 to 9	16	5 to 37
World Classes	20	9	7 to 11	37	16 to 63
Semantic Relationships	10	8	6 to 10	25	9 to 50
Sum of 3 Standard Scores		24			
RECEPTIVE LANGUAGE SCORE		88	81 to 95	21	10 to 37
Formulated Sentences	23	6	4 to 8	9	2 to 25
Recalling Sentences	29	7	5 to 9	16	5 to 37
Sentence Assembly	6	7	5 to 9	16	5 to 37
Sum of 3 Standard Scores		20			
EXPRESSIVE LANGUAGE SCORE		80	73 to 87	9	4 to 9
Sum of RL and EL Scores		168			
TOTAL LANGUAGE SCORE		83	78 to 88	13	7 to 21
Sum of 6 Raw Scores	106	Age Equivalent _5-2_			

Supplementary Subtests	Raw Score	Standard Score	Confidence Interval (__% Level)	PR	Confidence Interval
Listening to Paragraphs			to		to
Word Associations			to		to

Supplementary Subtests	Raw Score	Standard Score	Confidence Interval (90% Level)	PR	Confidence Interval
Listening to Paragraphs	5	8	5 to 11	25	5 to 63
Word Associations	27	7	4 to 10	16	2 to 50

Receptive/Expressive Differences

Higher Score (Receptive or Expressive)	88	
Lower Score (Receptive or Expressive) minus	-80	
Difference	8	

Prevalence

Percentage of Sample	Obtained Difference
1%	≥30
5%	≥23
10%	≥19
15%	≥16
25%	≥14

Ⓨ THE PSYCHOLOGICAL CORPORATION®
Harcourt Brace & Company
SAN ANTONIO

0154035041

Score Graphs for Plotting Confidence Intervals

Core

Subtest Standard Scores	CD	WC	SR	FS	RS	SA
	7	9	8	6	7	7

Receptive: CD WC SR
Expressive: FS RS SA

Composite Standard Scores	Receptive Language Score	Expressive Language Score
150		
145		
140		
135		
130		
125		
120		
115		
110		
105		
100		
95	X	
90		
85		X
80	X	
75		
70		X
65		
60		
55		
50		

FIGURE 10.2

CELF-3 Completed Scoring Summary

Source: From the _Clinical Evaluation of Language Fundmentals_—Third Edition. Copyright © 1995, 1987, 1980 by The Psychological Corporation. Standardization Edition copyright © 1994 by The Psychological Corporation. Reproduced by permission. All rights reserved.

TABLE 10.2   Standardized Instruments of Oral Language

Instrument	Age range	Type	Areas assessed	Comments regarding technical adequacy
Bankson Language Test (2d ed.) (Bankson, 1990)	3 through 6 years	Norm-referenced	Syntax, semantics and pragmatics	Norming sample limited.
BRIGANCE® Diagnostic Inventory of Early Development–Revised (Brigance, 1991)	Birth through 7 years	Criterion-referenced	Speech and language, including receptive language, gestures, vocalizations, expressive language, sentence length, and auditory memory	Skill sequences and associated age levels were developed by a review of the literature.
BRIGANCE® Diagnostic Comprehensive Inventory of Basic Skills (Brigance, 1983)	5 through 15 years	Criterion-referenced	Speech, including syntax and fluency, expressive language, articulation, and speech quality. Listening skills, including auditory discrimination, auditory memory, and receptive language.	Skill sequences and associated grade levels were developed by a review of the literature.
*Clinical Evaluation of Language Fundamentals-3 (CELF-3) (Semel, Wiig, and Secord, 1996)	6 through 21 years	Norm-referenced	Receptive and expressive language, morphology, syntax, semantics, and memory	During test development, items were reviewed for bias and cultural sensitivity. Test addresses dialectical variations. Additional studies concerning test-retest reliability and concurrent validity needed.
Comprehensive Receptive and Expressive Vocabulary Test (CREVT) (Wallace and Hammill, 1994)	4 through 17 years	Norm-referenced	Expressive and receptive language	Adequate
Expressive Vocabulary Test (EVT) (Williams, 1997)	2.5 through 85+ years	Norm-referenced	Expressive vocabulary and language retrieval	Pictures contain a good balance of gender and ethnic representations. Adequate reliability and validity.

Test	Age Range	Type	Areas Assessed	Comments
Expressive One-Word Picture Vocabulary–Revised (EOWPVT-R) (Gardner, 1990) English and Spanish Forms	2 through 12 years	Norm-referenced	Expressive language	Limited information regarding norming sample
Oral and Written Language Scales (OWLS) (Carrow-Woolfolk, 1995)	3 through 21 years	Norm-referenced	Vocabulary, syntax, pragmatics, and higher-order thinking	Internal and test-retest reliability is weak for some age groups.
Peabody Picture Vocabulary Test-Third Edition (PPVT-III) (Dunn and Dunn, 1997)	2.5 through 90 years	Norm-referenced	Receptive language	During test development, items were reviewed for bias and cultural sensitivity. Adequate reliability and validity.
*Prueba del Desarrollo Inicial del Lenguaje (Hresko, Reid, and Hammill, 1982)	3 to 7 years	Norm-referenced; norming sample consisted of 549 Spanish-speaking children from Mexico, Puerto Rico, and the U.S.	Receptive and expressive language for Spanish-speaking children	This test is a direct translation of the Test of Early Language Development.
*Test de Vocabulario en Imágenes Peabody (TVIP) (Dunn, Lugo, Padilla, and Dunn, 1986)	2.5 through 18 years	Norm-referenced; norms are available for Mexican and Puerto Rican standardization samples	Receptive language for Spanish-speaking children and adolescents	This test is a direct translation of the Peabody Picture Vocabulary Test-R (Dunn and Dunn, 1981).
*Preschool Language Scale-3 (PLS-3) (Zimmerman, Steiner, and Pond, 1992)	Birth through 6 years	Norm-referenced	Auditory comprehension, expressive language	Adequate
Test of Adolescent and Adult Language (3d ed.) (TOAL:3) (Hammill, Brown, Larsen, and Wiederholt, 1996)	12 through 24 years	Norm-referenced	Expressive and receptive language, syntax semantics, and phonology, reading and writing	Adequate for measuring components of oral language
Test of Early Language Development (2d ed.) (TELD-2) (Hresko, Reid, and Hammill, 1991)	2 through 7 years	Norm-referenced	Expressive and receptive language, syntax and semantics	Adequate
Test of Language Development–Primary (2d ed.) (TOLD-P:2) (Newcomer and Hammill, 1988)	4 through 8 years	Norm-referenced	Expressive and receptive language, syntax, semantics, and phonology	Adequate
Test of Language Development–Intermediate (2d ed.) (TOLD-I:2) (Hammill and Newcomer, 1988)	8.6 through 12 years	Norm-referenced	Expressive and receptive language, syntax, semantics, and phonology	Adequate

Continued

TABLE 10.2 (Continued)

Instrument	Age range	Type	Areas assessed	Comments regarding technical adequacy
Test of Pragmatic Language (Phelps-Terasaki and Phelps-Gunn, 1992)	5 through 13 years	Norm-referenced	Pragmatic language	Additional information concerning reliability and validity would be helpful.
Utah Test of Language Development (3d ed.) (Mecham, 1989)	3 through 9 years	Norm-referenced	Expressive and receptive language	Additional information concerning reliability and validity would be helpful.
Woodcock Language Proficiency Battery–Revised English Form (Woodcock, 1991)	2 years through adult	Norm-referenced	Auditory memory, expressive and receptive language, verbal analogies, reading and written language	Adequate
*Woodcock Language Proficiency Battery–Spanish Form (Woodcock and Muñoz-Sandoval, 1995)	2 years through adult	Norm-referenced; norming sample of Spanish version included individuals from Argentina, Costa Rica, Mexico, Peru, Puerto Rico, Spain, and several locations within the United States	Auditory memory, expressive and receptive language, verbal analogies, reading and written language	Spanish version is an adaptation, not a direct translation of, the English Form.
*Woodcock-Muñoz Language Survey, English and Spanish Forms (Woodcock and Muñoz-Sandoval, 1993)	4 years through adult	Norm-referenced; norming sample of Spanish version included individuals from Argentina, Costa Rica, Mexico, Peru, Puerto Rico, Spain, and several locations within the United States	Oral language including picture vocabulary and verbal analogies, reading (letter-word identification) and writing (spelling, punctuation, capitalization, and word usage)	A screening test. Spanish version is an adaptation, not a direct translation of, the English Form.

*Spanish form available

alectal differences, including Black English, Southern English, General American, Appalachian English, Western Pennsylvania, Middle Atlantic, among others.

Reliability

Reliability information is presented for internal consistency, test-retest reliability, and inter-rater reliability. Internal consistency coefficients for composite scores ranged from .83 (receptive language for age 15 and ages 17–21) to .95 (total language for ages 7–11). Test-retest coefficients for composite scores ranged from .77 (receptive and expressive language for age 13) to .94 (total language for age 10). One small interrater reliability study was conducted and showed adequate results.

Validity

Adequate evidence of content, construct, and concurrent validity is presented. The *CELF-3* was administered concurrently with the *Clinical Evaluation of Language Fundamentals–Revised, the Clinical Evaluation of Language Fundamentals–Preschool,* and the *Wechsler Intelligence Scale for Children-III.*

Summary

The *Clinical Evaluation of Language Fundamentals-3* is designed to identify, diagnose, and follow up the evaluation of language skills deficits in students ages 6 through 21. The *CELF-3* contains 11 subtests that measure selected receptive and expressive skills in morphology, syntax, semantics, and memory. The authors have addressed cultural sensitivity and test bias; and the examiner's manual addresses dialectal variations. Technical characteristics are adequate with the exception that additional studies should be conducted regarding concurrent validity with instruments other than the *CELF* series. Additional studies concerning interrater reliability would be helpful.

BOX 10.1

CLINICAL EVALUATION OF LANGUAGE FUNDAMENTALS-3 (CELF-3)

Publication Date: 1995
Purposes: Measures selected receptive and expressive skills in morphology, syntax, semantics, and memory.
Age/Grade Levels: Ages 6 through 21
Time to Administer: 30–45 minutes
Technical Adequacy: The standardization sample, reliability, and validity are very good.
Suggested Use: Identify, diagnose, and follow up the evaluation of language skills deficits. For Spanish-speaking individuals, the CELF-3 Spanish Edition is a parallel, not translated, version of the instrument.

Expressive Vocabulary Test

The *Expressive Vocabulary Test (EVT)* (Williams, 1997) is designed to measure expressive vocabulary and word retrieval for Standard American English in individuals ages 2 years 5 months (2.5) through 90+ years. The *EVT* is administered using a stimulus book with pictures that contain a good balance of gender and ethnic representations.

The individual is asked to respond to two types of items, labeling and synonyms. For labeling items, the examiner points to a picture or a part of the body and asks a question. For the synonyms, the examiner presents a picture and a stimulus word.

Administration

The *EVT* is administered individually and takes 10–25 minutes.

Scoring

Raw scores are converted to standard scores, percentile ranks, stanines, NCEs, or age equivalents, and confidence intervals at the 90 and 95 percent level can be calculated. The *EVT* standard score has a mean of 100 and a standard deviation of 15.

Standardization

The *EVT* was standardized on 2,725 individuals, the same population used in the *Peabody Picture Vocabulary Test-III* standardization. Based on the 1990 census data, the sample was controlled for age, gender, race/ethnicity, region, and SES (based on parent or self education level).

Reliability

Test-retest reliability ranged from .77 to .90; split half reliability ranged from .83 to .97. Internal reliability was high.

Validity

Evidence is presented for content and construct validity. Criterion-related validity studies were conducted with the *EVT* and the *Oral and Written Language Scales (OWLS)* with correlations in the moderate to high range. The reason for this range is that the *EVT* only measures one area of language, expressive vocabulary, while the *OWLS* measures language in a broad context. Additional criterion-related validity studies would be helpful.

Several small studies examined the performance of different clinical groups matched to control groups. Children in clinical groups represented specific diagnostic or special education categories including: speech impairment, language delay, language impairment, mental retardation, learning disability (reading), hearing impairment, and gifted students as well as adults with mild mental retardation. Individuals from these studies were not included in the standardization sample.

Summary

The *Expressive Vocabulary Test* is designed to measure expressive vocabulary and word re-

---

BOX 10.2

EXPRESSIVE VOCABULARY TEST (EVT)

Publication Date: 1997

Purposes: Measures expressive vocabulary and word retrieval.

Age/Grade Levels: Ages 2.5 through 90+

Time to Administer: 10–25 minutes

Technical Adequacy: The standardization sample and reliability studies are very good. Validity is adequate.

Suggested Use: Identify, diagnose, and follow-up the evaluation of expressive language and word retrieval skill deficits.

---

trieval for Standard American English in individuals representing a wide age range (ages 2.5 through 90+ years). The test has adequate technical characteristics, although additional criterion-related validity studies would be helpful.

Oral and Written Language Scales

The *Oral and Written Language Scales (OWLS)* (Carrow-Woolfolk, 1996) is an individualized test of oral and written language. The *OWLS* has three scales: Listening Comprehension, Oral Expression, and Written Expression. The Written Expression Scale is described in Chapter 9. The Listening Comprehension and Oral Expression Scales are intended to be used with children and young adults ages 3 through 21. The *OWLS* measures vocabulary, syntax, pragmatics, and higher-order thinking, including interpretation of figurative language, inference, synthesizing information, and so on.

Administration

The Listening Comprehension and Oral Expression Scales are individually administered.

Scoring

Raw scores are converted to standard scores, including percentile ranks, normal curve equivalents, and stanines. Confidence intervals of 68 percent, 90 percent, or 95 percent may be selected.

Standardization

The *OWLS* was standardized between April 1992 and August 1993. The standardization sample was based on 1991 U.S. Census Bureau data and included 1,985 individuals who were stratified by age, gender, race, ethnic group, geographic region, and economic status, based on the mother's level of education. The three scales of the *OWLS* were co-normed.

Reliability

Reliability information is presented for split-half reliability, test-retest reliability, and interrater reliability. For the Listening Comprehension Scale, the split-half reliability coefficients range from .75 (age 8) to .89 (age 4); for the Oral Expression Scale, the coefficients range from .76 (ages 19–21) to .91 (age 4). For test-retest reliability, the coefficients for the Listening Comprehension Scale range from .73 to .80; for the Oral Expression Scale the coefficients range from .77 to .86. Interrater reliability for the Oral Expression Scale ranged from .90 to .93.

Validity

Adequate evidence of content, criterion-related, and construct validity is presented. The *OWLS* was administered concurrently with the *Test for Auditory Comprehension of Language–Revised, Peabody Picture Vocabulary Test–Revised, Clinical Evaluation of Language Fundamentals–Revised, Kaufman Assessment Battery for Children, Wechsler Intelligence Scale for Children–Third Edition, Kaufman Brief Intelligence Test, Kaufman Test of Educational Achievement, Comprehensive Form,* and the *Woodcock Reading Mastery Tests–Revised.*

Small studies were conducted with students who were identified as speech impaired, language delayed, language impaired, mentally handicapped, learning disabled, hearing impaired, or as receiving Chapter One assistance in reading. Students from these studies were not included in the standardization sample. The results are limited because only one study was conducted with each group and because the samples were so small.

Summary

The *OWLS* is an individualized test of oral and written language. The instrument is designed to provide in-depth information regarding the use of oral language, including vocabulary, syntax, pragmatics, and higher-order thinking, and the use of written language. Internal and test-retest reliability is weak for some age groups. Interrater reliability is good for the Oral Expression Scale. Adequate evidence of validity is presented.

BOX 10.3

ORAL AND WRITTEN LANGUAGE SCALES (OWLS)

Publication Date: 1996
Purposes: Measures written and oral language including vocabulary, syntax, pragmatics, and higher-order thinking including interpretations of figurative language, inference, and so on.
Age/Grade Levels: Ages 3 through 21
Time to Administer: 15–25 minutes
Technical Adequacy: Standardization sample is adequate, reliability is weak for some age groups. Validity is adequate.
Suggested Use: Assesses listening comprehension, oral expression, and written expression.

Peabody Picture Vocabulary Test–Third Edition

The *Peabody Picture Vocabulary Test–Third Edition (PPVT-III)* (Dunn and Dunn, 1997) is designed to measure receptive language (vocabulary) for individuals 2 years 5 months through 90+ years of age. In the development of this revised instrument, a bias review panel reviewed test items, and an analysis for item bias by race/ethnicity, gender, and region was completed.

The test consists of a series of pictures or test plates that include depictions of individuals from various ethnic backgrounds and individuals with disabilities. Each plate has four pictures and the individual is asked to point to the one that best tells the meaning of the word (Figure 10.3). This instrument has two parallel forms, Form IIIA and Form IIIB. This test is also available in Spanish *(TVIP: Test de Vocabulario en Imágenes Peabody).* The *TVIP* (Dunn, Lugo, Padilla, and Dunn, 1986) measures the recep-

FIGURE 10.3

Peabody Picture Vocabulary Test–Third Edition.

Source: From the Peabody Picture Vocabulary Test–Third Edition © 1997 by Lloyd M. Dunn and Leota M. Dunn. America Guidance Service, Inc., 4201 Woodland Road, Circle Pines, MN 55014. Reprinted with permission of the Authors/Publisher. All rights reserved.

tive vocabulary of Spanish-speaking students, ages 2 years, 5 months to 18 years.

Administration

The *PPVT-III* is an individually administered test.

Scoring

The individual's response to each test item is recorded and the item is marked pass/fail. Raw scores are converted to standard scores, percentiles, stanines, NCEs, or age equivalents and confidence intervals at the 68, 90, and 95 percent level can be calculated. The *PPVT-III* standard score has a mean of 100 and a standard deviation of 15.

Standardization

The norming sample consisted of 2,725 individuals ages 2 years, 5 months through 90 years. Based on the 1994 population survey, the sample was controlled for age, gender, race/ethnicity, region, and SES (based on parent or self education level). In the Spanish version, norms are available for both combined and separate Mexican and Puerto Rican standardization samples.

Reliability

Internal consistency reliabilities indicated a high degree of item uniformity within each of the form: correlations ranged from .83 to .97 with a median reliability of .94 for Form IIIA and .91 for Form IIIB. Test-retest and alternate form reliabilities were high.

Validity

The test manual reports rationale to support content and construct validity. Criterion-related validity studies were completed with instruments of intelligence and oral language. Two small studies were completed with the *PPVT-III* and the *OWLS*. Correlations are in the moderate to high range (.63 to 83). The reason for this range is that the *PPVT-III* only measures

one area of language, receptive vocabulary, while the *OWLS* measures language in a broad context. Additional criterion-related validity studies would be helpful.

Several small studies examined the performance of different clinical groups matched to control groups. The clinical groups represented specific diagnostic or special education categories including: speech impairment, language delay, language impairment, mental retardation, learning disability (reading), hearing impairment, and gifted students as well as adults with mild mental retardation.

Summary

The *Peabody Picture Vocabulary Test-III* is a standardized instrument for assessing receptive language skills in children, youth, and adults from 2 years, 5 months through 90 years of age. The drawings used to illustrate the stimulus words consist of gender and ethnic balance. The instrument is well normed and technically adequate, although additional criterion-related validity studies would be helpful.

This instrument is available in Spanish, *TVIP: Test de Vocabulario en Imágenes Peabody,* and is designed to assess receptive vocabulary of Spanish-speaking students. The *TVIP* is a direct translation of an earlier version of the *PPVT-III*, the *Peabody Picture Vocabulary Test-R* (Dunn and Dunn, 1981).

Preschool Language Scale-3

The *Preschool Language Scale-3 (PLS-3)* (Zimmerman, Steiner, and Pond, 1992) is designed to measure language acquisition and prelanguage skills in children birth through 6 years, 11 months (6.11). The test has two subscales: an auditory comprehension and an expressive communication that includes preverbal communication skills. This revision is the first time that the *PLS* has been standardized. The test also has a Spanish-language version, the

---

BOX 10.4

PEABODY PICTURE VOCABULARY TEST–THIRD EDITION (PPVT-III)

Publication Date: 1997
Purposes: Measures receptive language skills in children, youth, and adults.
Age/Grade Levels: Ages 2 years 5 months through 90+ years
Time to Administer: 5–10 minutes
Technical Adequacy: Standardization sample, validity, and reliability adequate.
Suggested Use: Assesses receptive language skills for Standard American English. A Spanish edition, the *Test de Vocabulario en Imágenes Peabody* (TVIP), is based on items translated from the PPVT-R.

Preschool Language Scale-3, Spanish Edition, that is designed to test receptive and expressive language in Spanish. According to the manual, common dialectal variations are listed for testing children who live in different Spanish-speaking regions, including Cuba, Mexico, Guatemala, and Puerto Rico.

Administration

This instrument takes approximately 20 to 30 minutes to administer. Both English and Spanish versions use the same materials.

Scoring

Scores are reported as standard scores and percentile ranks by age. Language age equivalents may also be obtained.

Standardization

Approximately 1,200 children from ages 2 weeks through 6 years, 11 months participated in the standardization sample. The sample was stratified by race, parent education level, and geographic region. The sample approximated the 1980 U.S. Census. Spanish-speaking children from regions in the United States participated in the standardization sample for the Spanish version.

Reliability

Three types of reliability are reported: internal consistency, test-retest, and interrater reliability. Internal consistency coefficients for the total language scores ranged from .74 (children birth through 2 months) to .94 (children 3 years 6 months through 3 years 11 months). The two subscales generally fall within this range also, with the exception of the Auditory Comprehension scale in children birth through two months (.47).

Test-retest reliability coefficients ranged from .91 to .94 for children ages 3 to 5. No reliability studies were reported for younger children. Interrater reliability was .98.

Validity

Three types of validity are reported: content, construct, and concurrent. The authors state that content validity is demonstrated by the fact that the language skills tested by the *PLS-3* are documented in the literature.

Construct validity was assessed by examining whether or not the instrument differentiated between children, ages 3 to 5 years, with no language needs and those children with language disorders. The *PLS-3* correctly identified 3-year-old children as language disordered or non–language disordered 66 percent of the time; 4-year-old children 80 percent of the time; and 5-year-old children 70 percent of the time.

Concurrent validity studies compared the *PLS-3* with several standardized instruments (*Denver Developmental Screening Test II, Preschool Language Scale–Revised,* and the *Clinical Evaluation of Language Fundamentals–Revised*). Correlations ranged from .66 to .88.

Summary

The *Preschool Language Scale-3* is a standardized instrument for measuring preverbal and language skills in young children ages birth through 6 years, 11 months. The norming sample is representative of the 1980 U.S. Census according to race, parent education level, and geographic region of the country. Reliability studies report good internal consistency and high test-retest and interrater reliability coefficients. Construct validity studies found the instrument to be somewhat successful in identifying children who had previously been identified as having a language disorder but the *PLS-3* erred in not identifying some children who may be language disordered. The *Preschool Language Scale-3, Spanish Edition,* assesses Spanish expressive and receptive language skills. The instrument is designed to address the common Spanish dialects and can be used with children who come from different geographic regions.

BOX 10.5

PRESCHOOL LANGUAGE SCALE-3 (PLS-3)

Publication Date: 1992

Purposes: Measures auditory comprehension and expressive communication that includes preverbal communication skills.

Age/Grade Levels: Ages 2 weeks through 6 years, 11 months.

Time to Administer: 20–30 minutes

Technical Adequacy: Norming sample is based on 1980 U.S. Census and will need to be renormed and restandardized.

Suggested Use: Assesses language acquisition and prelanguage skills in children. A Spanish edition is designed to test receptive and expressive language in Spanish.

Test of Adolescent and Adult Language—3

The *Test of Adolescent and Adult Language–3 (TOAL-3)* (Hammill, Brown, Larsen, and Wiederholt, 1994) assesses language skills in individuals from 12 through 24 years, 11 months. The test consists of ten areas, including listening, speaking, reading, writing, spoken language, written language, vocabulary, grammar, receptive language, and expressive language.

Administration

The *TOAL-3* can be administered individually or to a small group. Administration time is one to three hours.

Scoring

Raw scores are transformed to composite quotients, with a mean of 100 and a standard deviation of 15 for each of the ten areas assessed. Additionally, an Overall Language Ability quotient can be obtained.

Standardization

The standardization sample was based on the 1990 U.S. Census. The *TOAL-3* was standardized on approximately 3,000 individuals who were stratified by region, gender, age, race, and residence.

Reliability

Reliability information is presented for internal consistency and test-retest reliability, and all coefficients exceeded .80.

Validity

Adequate evidence of content, criterion-related, and construct validity is presented. The *TOAL-3* was administered concurrently with the *Test of Language Development-I:2, Peabody Picture Vocabulary Test, Detroit Test of Learning Abilities-3,* and *Test of Written Language-2.*

Summary

The *TOAL-3* assesses language skills in individuals from 12 through 24 years, 11 months. The test consists of ten areas, including listening, speaking, reading, writing, spoken language, written language, vocabulary, grammar, receptive language, and expressive language. Evidence of reliability and validity appears to be adequate.

Test of Language Development—Primary

The *Test of Language Development–Primary (TOLD-P:2)* (Newcomer and Hammill, 1988) is designed for children ages 4 through 8. According to the manual, the purposes of the *TOLD-P:2* are: 1) to identify children who are significantly below their peers in language proficiency, 2) to determine specific strengths and weaknesses in language skills, 3) to document progress in language as a result of an intervention program, and 4) to measure language in research studies. The test consists of the following seven subtests: Picture Vocabulary, Oral Vocabulary, Grammatic Understanding, Sentence Imitation, Grammatic Completion, Word Discrimination, and Word Articulation.

Administration

There are no time limits on the *TOLD-P:2* and the time to administer the test may vary from 30 minutes to one hour. The seven subtests must be administered in sequential order.

Scoring

Raw scores may be transformed into percentiles, standard scores for the subtests, and quotients for the composites. Composites include Spoken language, Listening, Speaking, Semantics, Syntax, and Phonology.

Standardization

The *TOLD-P:2* was standardized on 2,436 children and the sample was stratified according to the 1985 *Statistical Abstract of the United States.*

Reliability

Five studies of internal consistency reported coefficients that exceed .80. High (over .80) test-retest reliability was reported in two studies.

Validity

Content validity was addressed by asking professionals (50 out of 100 asked) to rate the pool of test items. Criterion-related validity was examined by comparing subtests of the *TOLD-P:2* with well-known instruments. Coefficients were computed at ages 4, 6, and 8 years. In general, the correlation coefficients ranged from .54 to .86. The *TOLD-P:2* manual describes evidence of construct validity by correlating *TOLD-P:2* scores with age, intelligence, achievement, and school readiness.

Summary

The *Test of Language Development–Primary (TOLD-P:2)* is a norm-referenced instrument. The test is designed for children ages 4 through 8 and is individually administered. Reliability and validity are adequate. The test may be use-

---

BOX 10.6

TEST OF ADOLESCENT AND ADULT LANGUAGE-3 (TOAL-3)

Publication Date: 1994
Purposes: Assesses listening, speaking, reading, writing, spoken language, written language, vocabulary, grammar, receptive language, and expressive language.
Age/Grade Levels: Ages 12 through 24 years, 11 months.
Time to Administer: One to three hours.
Technical Adequacy: The standardization sample, reliability, and validity are adequate.
Suggested Use: Assesses language skills in youth.

test item that measures the student's understanding of common objects in the environment might include the task, "Point to the ball." Test developers vary in how they represent the object "ball," that is, some materials may be more concrete than others. In the following list of test materials, how could the items be ordered from most concrete to most abstract?

black and white line drawing of a ball

cartoon of a ball

photograph of a ball

The test items should be represented in an appropriate way for the student who is being assessed. For example, items that are represented in abstract terms or items that are culture-bound, may not be a true measure of the student's receptive language. The type of symbols used, the inclusion of regional or cultural items familiar to the individual, and the response mode that the student is given to indicate a choice are all factors that are particularly salient in the assessment of receptive language skills.

ful in identifying children with speech and language impairments.

CONCERNS ABOUT STANDARDIZED TESTS

Receptive Language

The assessment of receptive language requires a determination of the student's understanding of language. Many standardized tests use symbol recognition as a key measure of receptive language, therefore the symbols used in the test items to represent word meanings have to be examined for appropriateness and clarity. We know that during an individual's cognitive development, understanding of symbols moves from concrete to abstract levels. A

Expressive Language

An individual must have a reason for using language as well as one for wanting to respond. Young children may not be motivated to perform or a student may not want to comply with the examiner's request. Assessment results from standardized instruments will be affected by the student's need or desire to communicate.

CONNECTING ASSESSMENT WITH INSTRUCTION

Some assessment approaches can be more effective in connecting assessment with instruction than the use of standardized instruments.

In the following section, we will examine some of these assessment approaches.

Language Probes

A **language probe** is a sampling of words or sounds that elicit specific information on a receptive or expressive skill (Polloway and Smith, 1992, p. 133). Probes are helpful diagnostic techniques and assist in planning instruction because they take advantage of the natural environment. For example, probes can be used in labeling activities. The high school special education teacher in a life skills class selects six objects from a job setting. Each object is presented to the student twice and the teacher asks, "What is this? What is this used for?" The teacher sets the criteria of correct responses for each item.

Language Samples

Language samples are examples of a student's use of language, such as explaining a topic of interest, telling a story, or stating and supporting an opinion. Language samples yield information about the student's vocabulary, use of syntax, morphemes, phonemes, pragmatics, understanding of semantics, and proficiency in articulation. Samples should include examples of conversations with peers.

Samples of the student's language can be tape-recorded or written on a chart. Teachers and parents collect samples of the student's language during various daily routines, activities, and assignments. Information may be supplemented by the use of commercial instruments for assessing speech and language skills.

Other Approaches

In previous chapters, we have described and examined other helpful approaches in linking assessment questions to instruction. In assess-

ing oral language, these approaches are used by the teacher to gather information and provide feedback to students and parents regarding skill-level and progress. These approaches include:

- oral descriptions
- written descriptions
- checklists
- questionnaires
- interviews
- conferences
- audio- and videotapes
- discussions with students, parents, and teachers

OBSERVING THE CLASSROOM ENVIRONMENT

In previous chapters we have discussed the importance of considering the student within the physical, learning, and social environments. The interactions between the student and the environment are important assessment considerations when assessing oral language.

Physical Environment

The physical setting can influence the student's development and use of language. Observations outside the regular classroom, such as in the hallways, cafeteria, and playground, provide a better understanding of the student's language than in the more structured classroom (Moran, 1996).

Learning Environment

The learning environment influences and promotes the development of a student's language. For example, the types of questions a teacher asks directly influence the level of response that a student gives. Some questions require a yes or no; these are minimal-response

SNAPSHOT

Nina

Nina is in the ninth grade and enjoys all her classes in school. She has mental retardation and receives special education and related services. Her IEP states that the speech and language pathologist will work with Nina and will consult with her special education teacher. Her special education teacher has been working with the speech and language pathologist to provide a rich language environment not only for Nina but for all the students in her classroom. Her teacher encourages Nina to expand her vocabulary and to articulate clearly so that others can understand her. Assessment focuses on planning for instruction and evaluating progress.

Each week the teacher invites the students to share a story or discuss current community and national events. Each student has an individual audiotape and is encouraged to make a recording of his or her individual participation. The following segment reflects Nina's latest recording.

"The School Boar (Board) is going to meet tonight. My father is going. They are going to vo (vote). Many people want low (lower) tax (taxes). I don't want them to cut the swim (swimming program). Everyone should vo (vote)."

Nina's teacher will replay the sample for Nina, and they will discuss whether it should be added to Nina's portfolio.

---

questions. Some questions require students to think about the materials that they are using; these questions, called thought-provoking, may require a phrase or a few sentences to answer. Other questions require students to think and weigh possible responses; they are open-ended questions.

In addition to questioning techniques, there are other teaching strategies to promote the development of oral language. Expansion and modeling are two strategies that may be observed in the classroom.

Expansion

Expansion is a strategy that helps students learn syntax by supplying omitted structures. Billy, who is in kindergarten, told his teacher, "I want to use that thing." His teacher answered, "You want to use the scale at the science table?"

Modeling

Teachers can assist students in learning semantic features by expanding and modeling. Conversation one:

Agata: "My brother got shot at the doctor's yesterday."

Teacher: "Your brother had a shot at the doctor's yesterday?" "And did you get a shot at the doctor's too?"

Conversation two:

Agata: "My brother got shot at the doctor's yesterday."

Teacher: "Don't say 'got' say 'had a shot.'"

If you were Agata, which conversation would encourage you to continue telling about your experience? Teachers are more effective when

Observation setting:

Physical Environment

1. How does the physical setting encourage conversations among students?

Learning Environment

2. Does the teacher provide materials and activities that encourage discussion?
3. Does the teacher create student groups during some learning activities?
4. Does the teacher use appropriate modeling of language?
5. Does the teacher provide opportunities for students to use language for different purposes?

   For example:
   _____ recalling a story or event
   _____ dictating directions
   _____ presenting facts or an opinion

6. Does the teacher provide opportunities for using language with different audiences?

   For example:
   _____ telling a fable to younger children
   _____ making a presentation to the PTA
   _____ describing an exhibit to community members
   _____ taking a position on an issue and defending it to peers

7. Does the teacher employ techniques to enhance language opportunities?

   _____ uses expansion techniques
   _____ asks questions that are thought-provoking or open-ended

Social Environment

8. Does the school day provide for "free" socialization among students?
9. Is lunchtime scheduled in such a way as to support socialization?

   _____ sufficient time to eat and socialize
   _____ students have choices where they may sit
   _____ students are allowed to talk

FIGURE 10.4

Checklist for Observing a Language-rich Environment

they use correction sparingly. A checklist of strategies for supporting language can be found in Figure 10.4.

Social Environment

Relationships with students and teachers can influence language performance. The social environment is important to the development of self-concept and self-esteem. These, in turn, contribute to skills in communicating effectively with others, in communicating with a variety of audiences, and in listening to others.

By observing the social environment, teachers can study the relationships students have with peers and adults.

STUDENTS WITH SEVERE COMMUNICATION DISORDERS

Some students have severe communication disorders as a result of or in combination with other disabilities, including motor impairments, developmental disabilities, inappropriate and bizarre behaviors, or inappropriate repetitions. These disabilities affect the ability to communicate.

Augmentative or Alternative Communication Systems

Some students with severe physical disabilities are not able to use oral language efficiently. For example, ten-year-old Felix is an honor-roll student who loves basketball games. He has cerebral palsy and uses a motorized wheelchair. The cerebral palsy has affected Felix's ability to use oral language. Although he can produce some sounds, his oral speech is not an effective way to communicate.

Felix, like many other students with severe physical disabilities, uses an **augmentative or alternative communication** (AAC) system or a **voice output communication aid** (VOCA) for oral language assistance. An AAC is any method or device that assists communication. The Individuals with Disabilities Act Amendments of 1997 provide for the "functional evaluation" of a child with a disability and assistance in selecting, acquiring, and using an assistive technology (AT) device. An AAC is an assistive technology device for oral language such as a picture book or a communication board comprised of symbols. These materials require the student to point to a picture, symbol, or letter by using a finger, toe, or headstick.

Synthesized speech in voice output communication aids (VOCA) is on the high end of the assistive technology scale. This type of ACC enables students with severe communication disabilities to participate more fully with peers without disabilities. Students using VOCA access the device in any number of ways: by pointing to pictures, by using a single switch, or by activating the device through eye gaze. These methods of access provide a wider range of input options than traditional communication books and boards. Frequently used messages can be stored in the communication device, which allows the user to access a prestored message with only one keystroke. Some systems have a word prediction feature for older children who are using written language. However, it is important to remember that the VOCA is only a part of a student's communication system. VOCA users, as well as other people, use a variety of communication forms including gestures or eye gaze, eye blinks, and winks!

Assessment for ACC and VOCA

The assessment and selection of a specific communication device should be made by the team that includes the individual (when possible), family members, a speech and language pathologist, an occupational therapist, and an educator, as well as other interested team members. The assessment of an individual for an augmentative/alternative communication device depends on a number of factors, including chronological age, imitative ability, motor control, cognitive ability, and visual needs. As members of the team, educators contribute information on classroom and academic performance. Educators assist other team members by defining communications skills needed to complete academic and vocational courses and to interact with classmates (Tanchak and Sawyer, 1995). Some of the key questions for teachers, students, and family members to consider during an assessment are listed in Figure 10.5.

Concerns about Assessing Students with Severe Speech and Language Disabilities

Before beginning the assessment, the examiner will need to ensure that the student not only understands how to respond but is physically able to make the response. The teacher who wishes to assess the student's knowledge in academic areas can use a similar approach.

Caution should be used in assessing communication development, in identifying prerequisite skills, as well as in drawing assumptions. Students with some types of disabilities,

1. What are the environments where the student spends a portion of the day?
   _____ home
   _____ school
   _____ after-school care
   _____ other (please specify)

2. What types of communication does the student presently use?

   How well do others understand?

_____points	poor	good	excellent
_____gestures	poor	good	excellent
_____eye gazes	poor	good	excellent
_____other (please specify)	poor	good	excellent

3. During a typical day:
   a) with whom might the student interact?

   _____   _____   _____

   _____   _____   _____

   _____   _____   _____

   b) what are some messages that the student might use?

   To state a feeling:

   To make a request:

   To ask a question:

   To greet someone or say good-bye

4. How could additional opportunities to communicate be provided:
   a) by modifying the present system?
   b) by using another device?

FIGURE 10.5

Questionnaire for Assessment of an Augmentative/Alternative Communication Device for a Student

such as autism or pervasive developmental disorder (PDD), conventionally experience great difficulty with expressive language. Students with severe communication disorders can have poor—or excellent—receptive language skills but show little indication of them.

PREFERRED PRACTICES

Teachers must identify young students as soon as possible or early problems in oral language will develop into difficulties with written language and reading. Once students have been identified, best practice recommends ongoing assessment activities for the purpose of planning instruction. Teachers need opportunities to conduct observations of classrooms that have been identified as language-rich environments. Classroom observations should focus on aspects that support language development and build language skills. Teachers need opportunities to plan and discuss helpful strategies with other teachers and the speech and language pathologist. Coordinating classroom activities with speech and language therapy will enhance student skills.

EXTENDING LEARNING

10.1 Create a checklist for observing the physical, learning, or social environment. Visit two different classrooms and use your checklist to identify aspects in the environment that support the students' oral language.

10.2 Ask a friend to tape a conversation of you working with a student. Conduct an analysis of the tape. How did you support the student's use of language. What might you do differently next time?

10.3 Interview a speech and language pathologist regarding assessment tools. What tools does this individual use in gathering information about content, form, and use?

10.4 Reread the Snapshot about Nina. What would you say about Nina's language sample on a simple analysis form?

Form:

Content:

Use:

How might the teacher use this information in planning instruction? Check your ideas with the suggestions described in the section of this chapter on the learning environment.

10.5 Obtain two or more standardized tests for assessing oral language. Compare and contrast the content of the two instruments. Would one of these instruments be helpful in answering assessment questions identified in one of the Snapshots in this chapter?

10.6 Evaluate the technical aspects of one of the commercial instruments. Develop your own format for evaluating or use the format suggested in Chapter 4.

REFERENCES

Bandura, A. (1977). *Social learning theory.* Englewood Cliffs, N.J.: Prentice Hall.

Bankson, N. W. (1990). *Bankson language test.* 2d ed. Austin, Tex.: Pro-Ed.

Brigance, A. H. (1983). *BRIGANCE® comprehensive inventory of basic skills.* No. Billerica, Mass.: Curriculum Associates.

Brigance, A. H. (1991). *BRIGANCE® diagnostic inventory of early development–Revised.* No. Billerica, Mass.: Curriculum Associates.

Carrow-Woolfolk, E. (1996). *Oral and written language scales.* Minneapolis, Minn.: American Guidance Service.

Chomsky, N. (1967). The formal nature of language. In *Biological foundations of language,* ed. E. Lenneberg. New York: John Wiley.

Dunn, L. M. and L. M. Dunn (1981). *Peabody picture vocabulary test–Revised.* Circle Pines, Minn.: American Guidance Service.

Dunn, L. M., and L. M. Dunn (1997). *Peabody picture vocabulary test–Third edition.* Circle Pines, Minn.: American Guidance Service.

Dunn, L. M., D. E. Lugo, E. R. Padilla, and L. M. Dunn (1986). *Test de vocabulario en imagenes Peabody.* Circle Pines, Minn.: American Guidance Service.

Gardner, M. F. (1990). *Expressive one-word picture vocabulary test–Revised.* Novato, Calif.: Academic Therapy.

Hammill, D. D., and P. L. Newcomer (1988). *Test of language development–Intermediate.* 2d ed. Austin, Tex.: Pro-Ed.

Hammill, D. D., V. L. Brown, S. C. Larsen, and J. L. Wiederholt (1996). *Test of adolescent and adult language.* 3d ed. Austin, Tex.: Pro-Ed.

Hresko, W. P., D. K. Reid, and D. D. Hammill (1991). *Test of early language development.* 2d ed. Austin, Tex.: Pro-Ed.

Hresko, W. P., D. K. Reid, and D. D. Hammill (1982). *Prueba del desarrollo inicial del lenguaje.* Austin, Tex.: Pro-Ed.

Kaiser, A. P., C. L. Alpert, and S. F. Warren (1988). Language and communication disorders. In *Handbook of developmental and physical disabilities,* eds. V. B. VanHasselt, P. S. Strain, and M. Hersen. New York: Pergamon Press.

Mecham, M. J. (1989). *Utah test of language development.* 3d ed. Austin, Tex.: Pro-Ed.

Moran, M. R. (1996). Educating children with communication disorders. In *Exceptional children in today's schools,* 3d ed., ed. E. L. Meyen (281–314). Denver: Love.

Newcomer, P. L., and D. D. Hammill (1988). *Test of language development–primary.* 2d ed. Austin, Tex.: Pro-Ed.

Phelps-Terasaki, D., and T. Phelps-Gunn (1992). *Test of pragmatic language.* Austin, Tex.: Pro-Ed.

Polloway, E. A., and T. E. C. Smith (1992). *Language instruction for students with disabilities.* Denver, Col.: Love.

Roseberry-McKibbin, C. (1995, Summer). Distinguishing language differences from language disorders in linguistically and culturally diverse students. *Multicultural Education,* 12–16.

Semel, E., E. H. Wiig, and W. Secord (1996a). *Clinical evaluation of language fundamentals.* 3d ed. San Antonio, Tex.: The Psychological Corporation, Harcourt Brace Javanovich.

Semel, E., E. H. Wiig, and W. Secord (1996b). *Technical manual.* San Antonio, Tex.: The Psychological Corporation, Harcourt Brace Javanovich.

Tanchak, T. L., and C. Sawyer (1995). Augmentative communication. In *Assistive technology: A resource for school, work, and community,* eds. K. F. Flippo, K. J. Inge, and J. M. Barcus. Baltimore: Paul H. Brookes.

Wallace, G., and D. D. Hammill (1994). *Comprehensive receptive and expressive vocabulary test.* Austin, Tex.: Pro-Ed.

Williams, K. T. (1997). *Expressive vocabulary test.* Circle Pines, Minn.: American Guidance Service.

Woodcock, R. E. (1991). *Woodcock language proficiency battery–Revised English form.* Chicago: Riverside.

Woodcock, R. E., and A. F. Munoz-Sandoval (1995). *Woodcock language proficiency battery–Spanish form.* Chicago: Riverside.

Zimmerman, I. L., V. G. Steiner, and R. E. Pond (1992). *Preschool language scale-3.* San Antonio, Tex.: The Psychological Corporation.

Mathematics

OVERVIEW

A vision of mathematics instruction was introduced by the National Council of Teachers of Mathematics (NCTM) that has changed the direction of teaching and assessment of mathematics (National Council of the Teachers of Mathematics, 1989, 1991a). This comprehensive approach to mathematics instruction means that students are engaged in the study of mathematics that

> includes the ability to explore, conjecture, and reason logically; to solve nonroutine problems; to communicate about and through mathematics; and to connect ideas within mathematics and between mathematics and other intellectual activity. Mathematical power also involves the development of personal self-confidence and a disposition to seek, evaluate, and use quantitative and spatial information in solving problems and in making decisions. Students' flexibility, perseverance, interest, curiosity, and inventiveness also affect the realization of mathematical power (NCTM, 1991b, p. 1).

The thrust of this initiative is the precept that *all* students regardless of their ability, culture, ethnicity, race, language, geographic region of origin, gender, disability, or economic status will be provided with high quality mathematics instruction and assessment. The study of mathematics builds on students' knowledge or prior experiences and actively involves them as doers of mathematics.

CHAPTER OBJECTIVES

After completing this chapter you should be able to:

Understand contemporary views of mathematics instruction.

Explain the integral link between mathematics instruction and assessment.

Describe approaches to mathematics assessment.

Describe how the physical, learning, and social environments influence mathematics performance.

WHAT SHAPES OUR VIEWS

The contemporary view of mathematics instruction is based on the following beliefs (Trafton and Claus, 1994):

- All students need to learn mathematics in order to function successfully in the world today.
- All students must develop skills and confidence that will enable them to be capable problem solvers.
- All students should be able to communicate and reason mathematically.
- All students need to value mathematics as important and useful.

Today's mathematics programs should be designed around rich mathematics problems that build on students' knowledge or prior experiences and that actively engage students in accomplishing mathematics. Table 11.1 summarizes these National Council for Teachers of Mathematics Curriculum Standards on which instruction should be based. According to the NCTM, knowing mathematics means doing mathematics. The doing of mathematics necessarily involves students in problems and tasks that:

- are mathematically meaningful
- require students to think rather than to memorize
- require students to hypothesize and to generalize
- generate further mathematics questions or problems
- require that students learn while solving a task
- allow for more than one acceptable answer (Speer and Brahier, 1994).

TABLE 11.1   Summary of Curriculum Standards of the National Council of Teachers of Mathematics

Grades K through 4	Grades 5 through 8	Grades 9 through 12
Mathematics as Problem Solving	Mathematics as Problem Solving	Mathematics as Problem Solving
Mathematics as Communication	Mathematics as Communication	Mathematics as Communication
Mathematics as Reasoning	Mathematics as Reasoning	Mathematics as Reasoning
Mathematical Connections	Mathematical Connections	Mathematical Connections
Estimation	Number and Number Relationships	Algebra
Number Sense and Numeration	Number Systems and Number Theory	Functions
Concepts of Whole Number	Computation and Estimation	Geometry from a Synthetic Perspective
Operations	Patterns and Functions	Trigonometry
Whole Number Computation	Algebra	Statistics
Geometry and Spatial Sense	Statistics	Probability
Measurement	Probability	Discrete Mathematics
Statistics and Probability	Geometry	Conceptual Underpinnings of Calculus
Fractions and Decimals	Measurement	Mathematics Structure
Patterns and Relationships		

Synopsis of curriculum standards from *Curriculum and Evaluation Standards for School Mathematics* (NCTM, 1989).

TABLE 11.2 Assessment Questions, Purposes, and Approaches

Assessment questions	Steps and purposes	Approaches
Screening		
Is there a possibility of a disability in mathematics?	To determine whether students *may* have a disability in mathematics and should be referred for further assessment	Norm-referenced instruments Curriculum-based assessment Criterion-referenced assessment Observations Checklists
Eligibility		
Does the student have a disability in mathematics? What disability does the student have? Does the student meet the criteria for services? What are the strengths and weaknesses in mathematics? Why is the student having trouble doing mathematics? What does the student understand?	To determine if there is a disability in mathematics To compare the student's performance in mathematics with the performance of the peer group To determine specific strengths and weaknesses To understand why the student is having difficulty	Norm-referenced instruments Curriculum-based assessment Criterion-referenced assessment Observations Probes Error analysis Interviews Checklists Student, parent, and/or teacher conferences Performance assessment

CONNECTING INSTRUCTION WITH ASSESSMENT

Program Planning		
What does the student not understand? Where should instruction in mathematics begin?	To understand what the student knows and does not know in mathematics To plan the student's program in mathematics To determine instructional approaches	Norm-referenced instruments Curriculum-based assessment Criterion-referenced assessment Observations Probes Error analysis Interviews Checklists Student, parent, and/or teacher conferences Performance assessment
Program Monitoring		
Once instruction begins, is the student making progress in mathematics? Should the instruction be modified?	To understand the pace of instruction To understand what the student knows prior to and after instruction To understand the strategies and concepts the student uses To monitor the student's program	Curriculum-based assessment Criterion-referenced assessment Observations Probes Error analysis Interviews Checklists Student, parent, and/or teacher conferences Portfolios Exhibitions Journals Written descriptions Oral descriptions

Continued

TABLE 11.2 (Continued)

Assessment questions	Steps and purposes	Approaches
Program Evaluation		
Has the student met the goals of the IEP in mathematics?	To determine whether the IEP goals in mathematics have been met	Curriculum-based assessment
		Criterion-referenced assessment
Has the instructional program in mathematics been successful for the student?		Observations
	To determine whether the goals of the program have been met	Probes
		Error analysis
		Interviews
Has the student made progress in mathematics?	To evaluate program effectiveness	Checklists
		Student, parent, and/or teacher conferences
Has the instructional program achieved its goals?		Portfolios
		Exhibitions
		Journals
		Written descriptions
		Oral descriptions
		Surveys

EVALUATING MATHEMATICAL POWER

According to the *Statement of Principles on Assessment in Mathematics and Science Education* (U.S. Department of Education and the National Science Foundation (NSF), n.d.), all assessment programs should be based on the equity principle. This means that, "Assessment should support every student's opportunity to learn important mathematics and science" (p. 9). In designing the *Statement of Principles,* the U.S. Department of Education and the NSF emphasize that *all* students are to be included in instruction and assessment activities and that assessment instruments by design and intent are to be equitable. While not specifically mentioning students with disabilities, these major government organizations indicate that *all* assessment tools must consider or be applicable to *all* students and that they must yield information that will improve student learning. Accordingly, all assessment programs should:

- assess knowledge and understanding in complex ways and include the assessment of higher-order thinking and problem solving
- be fair, valid, and reliable

- be based on the knowledge of how students develop and learn
- be executed so that the assessments can be interpreted only for the purposes for which they were designed
- be used to improve instruction and develop curriculum
- promote equity by providing optimal opportunities for students to demonstrate their knowledge.

Equitable evaluation of mathematical abilities and skills presupposes a variety of approaches in order to reflect an understanding of students' abilities, culture, ethnicity, race, language, geographic region of origin, gender, disability, and economic status in assessments. Emphasis must be placed on students solving real-world problems that involve making conclusions, understanding relationships, and generating new questions (Marolda and Davidson, 1994). Assessment methods include standardized testing as well as other kinds of approaches. The assessment purposes and approaches used in mathematics assessment are described in Table 11.2. Table 11.3 describes the standards for the evaluation of mathematics that were developed by the NCTM.

TABLE 11.3 **Summary of the Evaluation Standards of the National Council of Teachers of Mathematics**

1. Methods and tasks for assessing students' learning should be aligned with the curriculum's

   • goals, objectives, and mathematical content

   • relative emphases given to various topics and processes and their relationships

   • instructional approaches and activities, including the use of calculators, computers, and manipulatives.

2. Decisions concerning students' learning should be made on the basis of a convergence of information obtained from a variety of sources. These sources should encompass tasks that

   • demand different kinds of mathematical thinking

   • present the same mathematical concept or procedure in different contexts, formats, and problem situations.

3. Assessment methods and instruments should be selected on the basis of

   • the type of information sought

   • the use to which the information will be put

   • the developmental level and maturity of the student.

4. The assessment of students' mathematical knowledge should yield information about their

   • ability to apply their knowledge to solve problems within mathematics and in other disciplines

   • ability to use mathematical language to communicate ideas

   • ability to reason and to analyze

   • knowledge and understanding of concepts and procedures

   • disposition toward mathematics

   • understanding of the nature of mathematics

   • integration of these aspects of mathematical knowledge.

5. The assessment of students' ability to use mathematics in solving problems should provide evidence that they can

   • formulate problems

   • apply a variety of strategies to solve problems

   • solve problems

   • verify and interpret results

   • generalize solutions.

6. The assessment of students' ability to communicate mathematics should provide evidence that they can

   • express mathematical ideas by speaking, writing, demonstrating, and depicting them visually

   • understand, interpret, and evaluate mathematical ideas that are presented in written, oral, or visual forms

   • use mathematical vocabulary, notation, and structure to represent ideas, describe relationships, and model situations.

Continued

TABLE 11.3   (Continued)

7. The assessment of students' ability to reason mathematically should provide evidence that they can

   • use inductive reasoning to recognize patterns and form conjectures

   • use reasoning to develop plausible arguments for mathematical statements

   • use proportional and spatial reasoning to solve problems

   • use deductive reasoning to verify conclusions, judge the validity of arguments, and construct valid arguments

   • analyze situations to determine common properties and structures

   • appreciate the axiomatic natures of mathematics.

8. The assessment of students' knowledge and understanding of mathematical concepts should provide evidence that they can

   • label, verbalize, and define concepts

   • identify and generate general examples and nonexamples

   • use models, diagrams, and symbols to represent concepts

   • translate from one mode of representation to another

   • recognize the various meanings and interpretations of concepts

   • identify properties of a given concept and recognize conditions that determine a particular concept

   • compare and contrast concepts.

Students should provide evidence of the extent to which they have integrated their knowledge of various concepts.

9. The assessment of students' knowledge procedures should provide evidence that they can

   • recognize when a procedure is appropriate

   • give reasons for the steps in a procedure

   • reliably and efficiently execute procedures

   • verify the results of procedures empirically (e.g., using models) or analytically

   • recognize correct and incorrect procedures

   • generate new procedures and extend or modify familiar ones

   • appreciate the nature and role of procedures in mathematics.

10. The assessment of students' mathematical disposition should seek information about their

    • confidence in using mathematics to solve problems, to communicate ideas, and to reason

    • flexibility in exploring mathematical ideas and trying alternative methods in solving problems

    • willingness to persevere in mathematical tasks

    • interest, curiosity, and inventiveness in doing mathematics

TABLE 11.3 (Continued)

- inclination to monitor and reflect on their own thinking and performance

- valuing of the application of mathematics to situations arising in other disciplines and everyday experiences.

- appreciation of the role of mathematics in our culture and its value as a tool and as a language.

11. Indicators of a mathematics program's consistency with the Standards should include

- student outcomes

- program expectations and support

- equity for all students

- curriculum review and change.

Indicators of the program's match to the Standards should be collected in the areas of curriculum, instructional resources, and forms of instruction.

12. In an evaluation of a mathematics program's consistency with the Curriculum Standards, the examination of curriculum and instructional resources should focus on

- goals, objectives, and mathematical content

- relative emphases of various topics and processes and their relationships

- instructional approaches and activities

- articulation across grades

- assessment methods and instruments

- availability of technological tools and support materials.

13. In an evaluation of a mathematics program's consistency with the Curriculum Standards, instruction and the environment in which it takes place should be examined, with special attention to

- mathematical content and its treatment

- relative emphases assigned to various topics and processes and the relationships among them

- opportunities to learn

- instructional resources and classroom climate

- assessment methods and instruments

- the articulation of instruction across grades.

14. Program evaluations should be planned and conducted by

- individuals with expertise and training in mathematics education

- individuals with expertise and training in program evaluation

- individuals who make decisions about the mathematics program

- users of the information from the evaluation.

Synopsis of the Evaluation Standards (NCTM, 1989).

RESPONDING TO DIVERSITY

Multicultural mathematics is the study of the way persons all over the world use mathematics in a variety of activities, including counting, measuring, performing calculations, using calendars, building homes, and playing games. Attention to the ways persons of various cultures use mathematics is important to our understanding of equity in the teaching and the assessment of mathematics (Zaslovsky, 1996). Consider the following:

- The Mende people of Sierra Leone and the Yup'ik (Innuit, or Eskimo) count by twenties. They count fingers, and toes are counted symbolically.
- The Chinese, Islamic, and Hebrew calendars are lunar. For the Islamic calendar time is reckoned from 622 C.E.
- Measures of length are often based on body parts. In fact, the "foot" is still part of our system. Other cultures use the palm, hand span, and the cubit. (The cubit is an old measure based on the length of a person's forearm.) The Yup'ik people use the width of the fingers to measure the openings for fish traps.

These few examples point out the importance of using assessments that are sensitive to specific customs and practices. A student's culture, ethnicity, race, language, geographic region of origin, gender, disability, and economic status has to be considered when assessing mathematics performance.

STANDARDIZED INSTRUMENTS

This section describes the use of standardized, norm-referenced tests of mathematical abilities. Referring to the instruments listed in Table 11.4, standardized, norm-referenced tests can be used for screening, determining eligibility, and conducting a program evalua-

TABLE 11.4   Standardardized Tests of Mathematics

Name	Ages/grades	Group/individual
Diagnostic Screening Tests Math (DSTM)(Gnagey, 1980)	Grades 1 through 10	Individual or group
ENRIGHT™ Diagnostic Inventory of Basic Arithmetic Skills (Enright, 1983)	Grades K through 12 (students functioning level less than grade 7)	Individual or group
KeyMath-R (Connolly, 1988)	Grades K through 9	Individual
Sequential Assessment of Mathematics Inventories–Standardized Inventory (Reisman, 1985)	Grades K through 8	Individual
Slosson-Diagnostic Math Screener (S-DMS) (Erford & Boykin, 1996)	Ages 6 through 13	Individual or group
Stanford Diagnostic Mathematics Test (4th ed.) (Harcourt Brace Educational Measurement, 1995)	Grades 1 through 8	Individual or group
Test of Early Mathematics Ability (TEMA-2) (Ginsburg & Baroody, 1990)	Ages 3.0 to 8.11	Individual
Test of Mathematical Abilites-2 (TOMA-2) (Brown, Cronin, & McEntire, 1994)	Grades 3 through 12	Individual

tion. Scores obtained on these tests can be compared with the performance of students of similar age or grade who usually are selected as part of a national standardization sample. In addition, to individual tests of mathematical abilities (Table 11.4), Table 11.5 contains a list of tests that have mathematics subtests.

KeyMath–Revised: A Diagnostic Inventory of Essential Mathematics

KeyMath–Revised: A Diagnostic Inventory of Essential Mathematics (KeyMath-R) (Connolly, 1988) is an individually administered test of mathematics skills, concepts, and operations.

TABLE 11.5 Test Batteries That Contain Mathematics Subtests or Mathematics-Related Subtests

Name	*Ages/grades*
BRIGANCE® Diagnostic Inventory of Basic Skills (Brigance, 1977)	Grades K through 6
BRIGANCE® Diagnostic Inventory of Essential Skills (Brigance, 1980)	Grades 4 through 12
BRIGANCE® Diagnostic Comprehensive Inventory of Basic Skills (Brigance, 1983)	Grades K through 9
BRIGANCE® Assessment of Basic Skills–Spanish Edition (Brigance, 1984)	Grades K through 8
BRIGANCE® Diagnostic Life Skills Inventory (Brigance, 1994)	Vocational Secondary Adult education
BRIGANCE® Diagnostic Employability Skills Inventory (Brigance, 1995)	Vocational Secondary Adult education Job training
BRIGANCE® Diagnostic Inventory of Early Development–Revised (Brigance, 1991)	Ages birth to 7 years
Basic Achievement Skills Individual Screener (BASIS) (Sonnenschein, 1983)	Grades 1 through 12 & post–high school
Diagnostic Achievement Battery (DAB-2) (Newcomer, 1990)	Ages 6.0 through 14.0
Diagnostic Achievement Test for Adolescents-2 (Newcomer & Bryant, 1993)	Grades 7 through 12
Hudson Education Skills Inventory (Hudson, Colson, Welch, Banikowski, & Mehring, 1989)	Grade K through 12
Kaufman Assessment Battery for Children (K-ABC) (Kaufman & Kaufman, 1983)	Ages 2.6 through 12.6
Kaufman Test of Educational Achievement (K-TEA) (Kaufman & Kaufman, 1985)	Grades 1 through 12 Ages 6.0 to 18.11
Peabody Individual Achievement Test–Revised (Markwardt, 1989)	Grades K through 12 Ages 5.0 to 18.11
Wide Range Achievement Test-3 (WRAT-3) (Wilkinson, 1994)	Ages 5 to 75
Wechsler Individual Achievement Test (Harcourt Brace Educational Measurement, 1992)	Grades K through 12; ages 5.0 to 19.11
Woodcock-Johnson Psychoeducational Battery–Revised (Woodcock & Johnson, 1989)	Ages 2 to 90; grades K through 12

TABLE 11.6 Content Specification of KeyMath-R: Areas, Strands, and Domains

AREAS:	*Basic concepts*	*Operations*	*Applications*
STRANDS AND DOMAINS:	**Numeration** 1. Numbers 0–9 2. Numbers 0–99 3. Numbers 0–999 4. Multidigit numbers and advanced numeration topics	**Addition** 1. Models and basic facts 2. Algorithms to add whole numbers 3. Adding rational numbers	**Measurement** 1. Comparisons 2. Using nonstandard units 3. Using standard units—length, area 4. Using standard units—weight, capacity
	Rational Numbers 1. Fractions 2. Decimals 3. Percents	**Subtraction** 1. Models and basic facts 2. Algorithms to subtract whole numbers 3. Subtracting rational numbers	**Time and Money** 1. Identifying passage of time 2. Using clocks and clock units 3. Monetary amounts to one dollar 4. Monetary amounts to one hundred dollars and business transactions
	Geometry 1. Spatial and attribute relations 2. Two-dimensional shapes and their relations 3. Coordinate and transformational geometry 4. Three-dimensional shapes and their relations	**Multiplication** 1. Models and basic facts 2. Algorithms to multiply whole numbers 3. Multiplying rational numbers	**Estimation** 1. Whole and rational numbers 2. Measurement 3. Computation
		Division 1. Models and basic facts 2. Algorithms to divide whole numbers 3. Dividing rational numbers	**Interpreting Data** 1. Charts and tables 2. Graphs 3. Probability and statistics
		Mental Computation 1. Computation chains 2. Whole numbers 3. Rational numbers	**Problem Solving** 1. Solving routine problems 2. Understanding nonroutine problems 3. Solving nonroutine problems

Source: Connolly, A. J. (1988). KeyMath–Revised. Circle Pines, Minn.: American Guidance Service, p. 6. Reprinted with permission of the publisher.

The *KeyMath-R* is intended for use with children in grades kindergarten through grade 9. There are two forms and, according to the author, the *KeyMath-R* has the following five uses:

1. To guide general instructional planning
2. To develop remedial instruction
3. To assist in global assessment by making comparisons with the results of other instruments
4. To use as a pretest and posttest instrument when conducting research and program evaluation
5. To assist in assessing the usefulness of mathematics curriculum.

When developing the scope and sequence of the test content, the author surveyed the basal mathematics textbooks of many publishers as well as materials published by the National Council of Teachers of Mathematics. The resulting scope and sequence was organized into three areas: Basic Concepts, Operations, and Applications. These are divided into thirteen strands, and the strands are subdivided into four domains (Table 11.6).

Administration

The KeyMath-R can be administered by regular and special education teachers, aides, paraprofessionals, counselors, and school psychologists. Depending on the age of the student, it takes approximately 35 to 50 minutes to administer this test.

Scoring

Raw scores can be converted to standard scores, percentile ranks, grade and age equivalents, stanines, and normal curve equivalents. Using an optional scoring procedure for domain scores, a student's scores can be rated as weak, average, or strong. Figure 11.1 shows the front cover of the test record form.

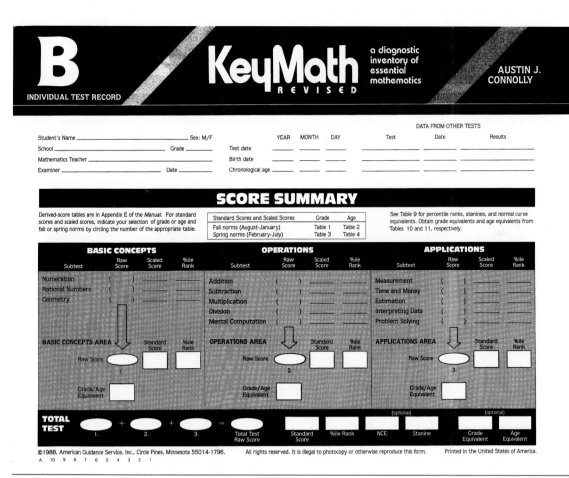

FIGURE 11.1

KeyMath–Revised Record Form

Source: KeyMath–Revised by Austin J. Connolly. © 1988. American Guidance Service, 4201 Woodland Road, Circle Pines, Minn. 55014-1796, p. 33. Reprinted with permission of the Publisher. All rights reserved.

Standardization

The *KeyMath-R* was renormed between October 1995 and November 1996. Stratification of the standardization sample was done according to age, gender, region, race, ethnicity, and economic status as estimated by parental education. The standardization sample of the *KeyMath-R* was linked to the standardization samples for the *Kaufman Test of Individual Achievement (K-TEA), Peabody Individiual Achievement Test–Revised (PIAT-R),* and the *Woodcock Reading Mastery Tests–Revised (WRMT-R).* For the *KeyMath-R* the renorming sample consisted of students who were in kindergarten through age 22. The linking sample was developed by having the test examinees in the norm sample take one of the complete test batteries and one or more subtests from another battery. This linking approach permits the making of comparisons of test performance across batteries.

Reliability

Alternate-form reliability was determined by retesting approximately 70 percent of the children in grades kindergarten, 2, 4, 6, and 8 who took part in the fall standardization. A time interval of between two and four weeks was used to administer the tests. The reliability coefficients that are reported are for the subtests, areas, and the total test score. Alternate-form reliability is not reported for each grade. For the subtests, the reliability coefficients ranged from .50s to .70s; for the areas, the correlations were in the low .80s. The average alternate-form correlation for the total test was .90.

Split-half reliabilities are reported by grade and were calculated by correlating the odd and even test items. For the subtests, most of the correlations were in the .70s and .80s; for the areas, the split-half reliability coefficients were in the .90s. The total test reliability coefficients were in the middle to high .90s.

Validity

When developing the *KeyMath-R,* the author developed a test blueprint, which detailed the content of the test for the areas, strands, and domains. Next, items were developed according to the blueprint that was intended to assess mathematics achievement. When using achievement tests, educators must determine the content validity themselves. Test examiners should review the curriculum as it has been taught and determine the extent to which the test items measure the curriculum.

According to the manual, construct validity was determined in several ways. Evidence is presented that demonstrates that knowledge about mathematics increases with age, that the subtests intercorrelate with the areas and the total test score, and that scores on the KeyMath-R correlate with scores on other tests of mathematical achievement.

Summary

The KeyMath–Revised: A Diagnostic Inventory of Essential Mathematics is an individually administered test of mathematics achievement. The reliabilities for the subtests and the areas are too low to make instructional decisions. Content validity should be determined by the educator by comparing the test items with the curriculum that has been taught.

Stanford Diagnostic Mathematics Test

The *Stanford Diagnostic Mathematics Test (SDMT4)* (Harcourt Brace Educational Measurement, 1995) is a norm-referenced test for students in grades 1.5 through 13. It has been developed using the standards developed by the NCTM. The test has six overlapping levels:

Grade	Level
1.5 through 2.5	red
2.5 through 3.5	orange
3.5 through 4.5	green
4.5 through 6.5	purple
6.5 through 8.9	brown
9.0 through 13.0	blue

> ### BOX 11.1
>
> ### KEYMATH–REVISED: A DIAGNOSTIC INVENTORY OF ESSENTIAL MATHEMATICS
>
> *Publication Date:* 1988
> *Purposes:* Measures mathematics concepts, skills, operations, and applications.
> *Age/Grade Levels:* Kindergarten through grade 9
> *Time to Administer:* 30 to 50 minutes
> *Technical Adequacy:* Standardization sample is acceptable. The reliabilities for the subtests and the areas are too low to make instructional decisions. Content validity should be determined by comparing the test items with the curriculum that has been taught.

The purposes of the *SDMT4* are to assist in making eligibility decisions, diagnose difficulties in mathematics, and evaluate programs and provide information about program effectiveness. The *SDMT4* has been devised using the standards developed by the National Council of Teachers of Mathematics (NCTM). The test assesses basic skills and concepts in mathematics, problem solving, and problem-solving strategies.

Administration

The *SDMT4* is a group-administered test. All subtests do not have to be administered; the examiner can decide to administer only one or two of the subtests. The items are a combination of multiple choice and free response. This test can be administered individually following standardized procedures for test administration.

Scoring

Raw scores are converted to percentiles, stanines, normal curve equivalents, grade equivalents, and scaled scores. The *SDMT4* can be hand scored using a stencil provided by the publisher or machine scored.

Standardization

The standardization sample is stratified according to socioeconomic status, size of school district, and geographic region.

Reliability

Both alternate-form and internal consistency reliabilities are reported. The reliability coefficients are adequate.

Validity

Content and criterion-related validity are reported. Teachers are encouraged to examine the test items to determine the extent to which the *SDMT4* matches reading as it has been taught.

Summary

The *Stanford Diagnostic Mathematics Test 4* is a norm-referenced test for students in grades 1.5 through 13. The test has six overlapping levels. The test is intended to be administered to groups of students. However, it can be useful when administered to individual students.

Test of Early Mathematics Ability-2

The *Test of Early Mathematics Ability (2d ed.) (TEMA-2)* (Ginsburg and Baroody, 1990) is a norm-referenced test that assesses several aspects of mathematical abilities in children ages 3 years through 8 years, 11 months. The *TEMA-2* has 35 informal problems and 30 formal problems. The informal problems measure concepts of relative magnitude, counting skills, and calculation. The formal problems measure reading and writing numerals, number facts, calculated algorithms, and base-ten concepts.

Administration

The *TEMA-2* is administered individually to students in approximately 20 minutes. The test requires children to read calculations, listen, respond verbally and nonverbally, and to write numerals.

SNAPSHOT

Kara

Kara is a 12-year-old in sixth grade. Her interests include drawing and soccer. Kara has an exuberant sense of humor and loves to play jokes on her friends and family. She has just finished making a book of her drawings that she intends to give to her grandmother who lives with Kara, her 5-year-old brother, John, and her mother and father. Kara was diagnosed as having a learning disability in mathematics when she was in third grade.

Observation

Kara was observed in her sixth grade classroom. The 25 other students in the classroom were involved in small groups solving problems that the teacher had assigned. The class was lively and the students were engaged in their work—all except Kara. Kara sat with a small group of three other students. Kara appeared to be unsure of how she could contribute to the problem-solving activity. She was quiet, had a puzzled look on her face, and was listening to the students in the group.

Teacher's Comments

Kara's teacher described Kara as a student who lagged considerably behind her peers in mathematics. The rest of the class was working on graphing, geometry, and probability. An examination of her recent homework showed that Kara had trouble with basic number facts and that she reversed numbers when writing them.

Summary of Test Performance

At the end of the last school year, the IEP team met to review Kara's program. The special education consultant reported that Kara's full scale intelligence as measured by the Wechsler Intelligence Scale-III (WISC-III) was 118, above average. On the Kaufman Test of Educational Achievement (K-TEA), Kara scored above average on the reading and spelling subtests but considerably below average on the Mathematical Applications and Mathematical Computation subtests. On the KeyMath-Revised her scores in the areas of Basic Concepts, Operations, and Applications were all well below average.

Standardization

The standardization sample is a combination of the sample from the previous edition and additional students selected to approximate the 1980 U.S. Census.

Scoring

Raw scores are converted to standard scores, percentiles, and age equivalents.

Reliability

Internal consistency reliability coefficients range from .92 to .96. Test-retest reliability is reported only for the previous edition.

Validity

While there is some evidence of validity, much of it is based on the previous edition. Examiners should carefully compare the mathematics curriculum with the test items in order to determine content validity.

Summary

The *Test of Early Mathematics Ability* (2d edition) *(TEMA-2)* is a norm-referenced test for use with children ages 3 years to 8 years, 11 months. The *TEMA-2* lacks adequate reliability and validity. It may be useful as a screening device and may be helpful in identifying

---

BOX 11.2

TEST OF EARLY MATHEMATICS ABILITY (2D ED.)

Publication Date: 1990
Purposes: Measures concepts of relative magnitude, counting skills, calculation, reading and writing numerals, number facts, calculated algorithms, and base-ten concepts.
Age/Grade Levels: 3 years through 8 years, 11 months
Time to Administer: 20 minutes
Technical Adequacy: Lacks adequate reliability and validity. The TEMA-2 is useful as a screening device and may be helpful in identifying strengths and weaknesses. Caution should be used when administering this test to young children because the TEMA-2 requires listening, reading, writing, and speaking.

---

strengths and weaknesses. Caution should be used when administering this test to young children because the *TEMA-2* requires listening, reading, writing, and speaking.

Test of Mathematical Abilities-2

The *Test of Mathematical Abilities (TOMA-2)* (Brown, Cronin, and McEntire, 1994) is a norm-referenced test of attitudes toward mathematics, mathematics vocabulary, computation, general information relating to mathematics, and mathematical story problems. The *TOMA-2* can be individually administered or group-administered to students in grades 3 through 12, and contains five subtests:

Attitude Toward Math. Students respond to questions on a 3-point scale on their opinions about mathematics. This scale is an adaptation of the Estes Attitude Scales (Estes, Estes, Richards, and Roettger, 1981).

Vocabulary. Students read 20 mathematical terms and define them in writing in English. This subtest is administered to students who are at least 11 years old.

Computation. Students solve 25 arithmetic problems in writing in an answer booklet.

General Information. Students respond orally when presented with 30 problems relating to general applications about mathematics.

Story Problems. After reading a word problem, students respond in writing in an answer booklet. This subtest is not administered to students who are nonreaders.

Administration

The *TOMA-2* can be individually administered or group-administered.

Scoring

Raw scores are converted to standard scores and percentile ranks. Subtest scores have a mean of 10 and a standard deviation of 3. The total test scores are called Math Quotients; they have a mean of 100 and a standard deviation of 15. An error analysis can be performed by the test examiner on individual responses to items that have been written in the student answer booklet.

Standardization

The *TOMA-2* was standardized on approximately 1,500 students residing in five states. The sample approximated U.S. Census information according to gender, residence, geographic region, and race.

Reliability

Reliability coefficients are in the .80s and .90s. Reliability is acceptable.

Validity

While there is some evidence of validity, much of it is based on the previous edition. Examiners should carefully compare the mathematics

---

BOX 11.3

**TEST OF MATHEMATICAL
ABILITIES (2D ED.)**

Publication Date: 1994
Purposes: Measures attitudes toward mathematics, mathematics vocabulary, computation, general information relating to mathematics, and mathematical story problems.
   Age/Grade Levels: Grades 3 through 12
   Time to Adminster: 45 to 90 minutes
   Technical Adequacy: Information of reliability and validity is sparse. Test examiners are encouraged to evaluate the content validity of the test. The TOMA-2 is best used as a screening measure.

---

curriculum with the test items in order to determine content validity.

Summary

The *Test of Mathematical Abilities* (2d ed.) *(TOMA-2)* is an individually administered and a group-administered test of various aspects of mathematical abilities. Information of reliability and validity is sketchy. Test examiners are encouraged to evaluate the content validity of the test. The *TOMA-2* is best used as a screening test.

CONNECTING INSTRUCTION WITH ASSESSMENT

A fundamental principle is that assessment of mathematical abilities and skills should be linked to mathematics instruction. Linking instruction to assessment in mathematics means that:

- Assessment occurs as a normal part of the student's work. Assessment activities should emerge from the teaching situation. The student does not stop work to do an assessment; the work and the assessment are linked. Examples of this type of assessment include the use of journals, notebooks, essays, oral reports, homework, classroom discussions, group work, and interviews. These assessment activities can occur individually or in small groups and can take place during one session or over multiple sessions (Marolda and Davidson, 1994).

- The conditions for assessment are similar to the conditions for doing meaningful tasks. Students should have sufficient time, have access to peers, be able to use appropriate tools (books, calculators, manipulatives, etc.), and have the chance to revise their work.

- Assessment tasks are meaningful and multidimensional. They should provide students with the opportunity to demonstrate mathematical abilities, including problem solving, drawing conclusions, understanding relationships, and generating new questions.

- Feedback to students is specific, meaningful, prompt, and informs the students' thinking about mathematics.

- Students participate in the assessment process. They help to generate and apply standards or rubrics. Self-assessment and peer assessment are included as part of the assessment process.

One of the most important aspects of assessment is feedback. Standardized, norm-referenced assessment coupled with feedback from peers and teachers encourages the development of mathematical and scientific thinking. Ways in which the teacher can gather information and provide feedback to parents and students include (NCTM, 1991a):

- criterion-referenced assessment
- probes
- error analysis
- oral descriptions
- written descriptions
- checklists
- questionnaires
- interviews
- conferencess
- student journals and notebooks
- performance-based assessment
- portfolios
- exhibitions
- discussions between students, parents, and teachers.

Criterion-Referenced Assessment

Instead of comparing a student's performance to a norm group, criterion-referenced tests measure a student's performance with respect to a well-defined content domain (Anastasi, 1988; Berk, 1988). Criterion-referenced tests can be used in each of the assessment steps described in Table 11.2. While norm-referenced tests in mathematics are constructed so as to discriminate between the performance of individual students on specific test items, criterion-referenced tests provide a description of knowledge, skills, or behaviors in a specific range, or domain, of test items.

BRIGANCE® Diagnostic Inventories

The BRIGANCE® Diagnostic Inventories are criterion-referenced tests that are similar in purpose, scoring, administration, and interpretation. These inventories assess mastery of mathematics skills and concepts (Table 11.7), and they are useful in program planning and in monitoring programs. The tests are described in detail in Chapter 6.

ENRIGHT® Diagnostic Inventory of Basic Arithmetic Skills

ENRIGHT® Diagnostic Inventory of Basic Arithmetic Skills (Enright, 1983) is an individually

administered criterion-referenced test for students beginning in grade 4 through adults. The test measures mastery of subtraction, multiplication, division, fractions, and decimals. The ENRIGHT® is useful in identifying specific areas of weakness, in developing instructional programs, and in monitoring progress.

The ENRIGHT® has three levels:

Wide Range Placement Test—A broad test that determines areas needing further assessment.

Skill Placement Test—A test that identifies specific weaknesses.

Skill Test—A test that identifies specific problem areas in subskills. The items are arranged in order of difficulty from easy to hard.

Administration

The examiner begins with the Wide Range Placement Test and then proceeds through each of the tests in order to pinpoint specific areas of weakness. In all, 144 arithmetic problems are arranged in 13 sections: Addition of Whole Numbers, Subtraction of Whole Numbers, Multiplication of Whole Numbers, Division of Whole Numbers, Conversion of Fractions, Addition of Fractions, Subtraction of Fractions, Multiplication of Fractions, Division of Fractions, Addition of Decimals, Subtraction of Decimals, Multiplication of Decimals, and Division of Decimals.

Scoring

The student's responses to each item are recorded in a record book. Caution should be used when interpreting grade levels at which skills are taught because the ENRIGHT® was based on several textbooks that are now obsolete.

Reliability

Split-half reliability coefficients were determined for each of the 13 sections. Coefficients

TABLE 11.7 BRIGANCE® Inventories

Name	Ages/grades	Mathematics skills
BRIGANCE® Diagnostic Inventory of Basic Skills (Brigance, 1977)	Grades K through 6	1. Number Sequences 2. Operations 3. Measurement 4. Geometry
BRIGANCE® Diagnostic Inventory of Essential Skills (Brigance, 1980)	Grades 4 through 12	1. Numbers 2. Number Facts 3. Computation of Whole Numbers 4. Fractions and Mixed Numbers 5. Decimals 6. Percents 7. Measurement 8. Metrics 9. Math Vocabulary 10. Money and Finance
BRIGANCE® Diagnostic Comprehensive Inventory of Basic Skills (Brigance, 1983)	Pre-K through 9	1. Numbers 2. Number Facts 3. Computation of Whole Numbers 4. Fractions and Mixed Numbers 5. Decimals 6. Percents 7. Measurement 8. Metrics 9. Math Vocabulary

are in the .90s. Test-retest reliability coefficients are not reported.

Validity

The inventory does not reflect current views of activity-based problem solving in mathematics. As with all achievement tests, the teacher should determine the content validity.

Summary

The ENRIGHT® Diagnostic Inventory of Basic Arithmetic Skills is an individually administered criterion-referenced test that measures mastery of subtraction, multiplication, division, fractions, and decimals. The ENRIGHT is intended for students beginning in grade 4 through adults. The test is useful in identifying specific areas of weakness, in developing instructional programs, and in monitoring progress. However, it should be used cautiously because it is based on a dated view of mathematics instruction.

Probes

As we have discussed in previous chapters, a probe is a diagnostic technique in which instruction is modified. Probes can be used to diagnose and assist with student problems and assist in planning instruction. For example, suppose a teacher wants to determine whether a third grade student is ready to proceed to a two-step word problem after mastering one-step word problems.

TABLE 11.7 (Continued)

Name	Ages/grades	Mathematics skills
BRIGANCE® Assessment of Basic Skills–Spanish Edition (Brigance, 1984)	Grades K through 6	1. Number Sequences 2. Operations 3. Measurement
BRIGANCE® Diagnostic Inventory of Early Development–Revised (Brigance, 1991)	Ages birth to 7 years	1. Number Concepts 2. Rote Counting 3. Reads Numerals 4. Numeral Comprehension 5. Ordinal Position 6. Numerals in Sequence 7. Writes Following and Preceding Numerals 8. Writes Numerals Dictated 9. Addition Combinations 10. Subtraction Combinations 11. Recognition of Money 12. Time
BRIGANCE® Diagnostic Life Skills Inventory (Brigance, 1994)	Vocational Secondary Adult education	1. Money 2. Operations 3. Finance 4. Money Management
BRIGANCE® Diagnostic Employability Skills Inventory (Brigance, 1995)	Vocational Secondary Adult education Job training	1. Operations 2. Fractions 3. Measurement 4. Geometry 5. Math Vocabulary

The teacher presents a basic two-step word problem to the student and observes the strategies that the student uses to solve the problem. The student may be able to successfully solve the problem, but has difficulty organizing her work. The teacher then can help the student by showing her how to draw a grid on her paper and put each step of the problem in a cell of the grid. Eventually, using another probe, the teacher is able to use fading to gradually lighten the lines of the grid until the student does not need the grid to successfully complete the problem.

Instructional probes are implemented during the process of instruction. When conducting an instructional probe the teacher should document the student's performance during step 1 (baseline), step 2 (instruction), and step 3 (baseline). When designing an instructional probe, the following steps can be used:

Step 1. (Baseline) The teacher identifies the area of mathematical performance that is to be observed and measures whether the student can perform the task. Examples include number recognition, counting, addition, subtraction, and so on.

Step 2. (Instruction) The teacher probes the task. For example, to facilitate number recognition the teacher asks the student to say, trace, recognize, and write a numeral.

Step 3. (Baseline) The teacher measures whether the student can perform the task.

Types of modifications for use in probes in mathematics instruction include:

Instructional modifications for use with probes
- change from written presentation to oral presentation
- combine verbal instruction with written explanation
- require fewer problems to be completed
- provide additional practice
- slow the pace of instruction
- provide additional time to complete problems
- take tests orally

Materials modifications
- use manipulatives
- place fewer problems on a page
- use color cues or other cues for mathematical operations
- simplify the problems
- combine tactile mode with visual, oral, or kinesthetic modes

Environmental modifications
- change location of instruction or test
- change time of day for instruction or test
- provide a work area that is quiet and free of distractions
- change lighting of work area
- change seating arrangements

Error Analysis

The purposes of error analysis are to: (1) identify the patterns of errors or mistakes that students make in their work; (2) understand why students make the errors; and (3) provide targeted instruction so as to correct the errors. When conducting an error analysis, the student's mathematics problems are checked and the errors categorized. The following is a list of errors that students commonly make (Ashlock, 1986; Berman and Friederwitzer, 1981; Kilian, Cahill, Ryan, Sutherland, and Taccetta, 1980; Tindal and Marston, 1990).

Addition and Subtraction
- lack of understanding of regrouping
- confusion of 1s and 10s in carrying and writing
- forgetting to carry 10s and 100s
- forgetting to regroup when subtracting 10s and 100s
- regrouping when it is not required
- incorrect operation (the student subtracts instead of adding)
- lack of knowledge of basic number facts

Multiplication and Division
- forgetting to carry in multiplication
- carrying before multiplying
- ignoring place value in division
- recording the answer from left to right
- lack of alignment of work in columns
- lack of knowledge of basic number facts

Fractions
- incorrect cancellation
- failure to reduce to lowest common denominator
- ignoring the remainder
- incorrect conversion of mixed numbers to fractions

Word Problems
- difficulty in reading
- inability to relate to context of problem
- inability to understand the language and vocabulary of the problem
- difficulty in identifying the relevant and the irrelevant information
- difficulty in identifying the number of steps required to solve the problem
- trouble in doing mathematical operations (addition, subtraction, multiplication, division)

After conducting an error analysis, summarize the error patterns. Notice, however, that many errors that students make do not fall into a pattern and some patterns that emerge do not indicate a serious problem. Error analysis must be viewed as a preliminary form of assessment and further evaluation of the student's work should be conducted.

Oral Descriptions

Verbal descriptions of a student's work provide immediate feedback to a student by a teacher or peer. Oral descriptions are quick, efficient, direct, and can be easily integrated into instruction. They must not be off the cuff; oral descriptions should be as well thought out as written descriptions. Oral descriptions can be used for program planning and program evaluation.

Oral descriptions do have several drawbacks, however. They can be subjective and, since the descriptions are given verbally, there is no permanent record. In addition, specific disabilities limit the ability of the student to understand, remember, or reply to what has been said.

Written Descriptions

A written description is a brief narrative that records feedback about the student's work that can be shared with the student, teachers, or parents. A written description, like an oral description, conveys an impression of important aspects of the student's work. Written descriptions can be used for program planning and program evaluation.

Before writing the narrative, the teacher carefully reviews the student's work. The teacher then writes the description, noting areas of strength as well as any problems. A written description provides information to the student about the quality of the work. Because it is recorded, the student can refer to it as the student continues to work.

For example, a student is asked to solve the following problem:

Luke wants to paint one wall of his room. The wall is 20 feet wide and 8 feet high. It takes one can of paint to cover 80 square feet, and the paint is sold at $4.99 a can. What else does Luke need to think of? Make a plan for Luke's trip to the store for supplies for this painting job (Kulm, 1994, p. 12).

After examining the student's solution, a teacher can comment on the organization, labeling, processes used in solving the problem, computations, spelling, and use of language. Moreover, the teacher can discuss the use of mathematics to solve real-world problems, completeness of the solution, the student's disposition toward mathematics, the ability to plan ahead, work habits, and attention to detail (Kulm, 1994). Two disadvantages to using written descriptions are that the parents may have difficulty reading or they may not have knowledge of written English.

Checklists and Questionnaires

Checklists and questionnaires are convenient ways to provide feedback about a student's work. A checklist is quickly completed. Figure 11.2 is an example of a checklist for teachers to provide feedback about the mathematical disposition or student confidence, willingness, perseverance, and interest in doing mathematics. Checklists are useful for screening, diagnosis, program planning, and program evaluation.

Questionnaires allow teachers and students to collect information in more detail than checklists. Questionnaires can be open-ended, allowing respondents to express their attitudes, opinions, and knowledge in depth, or they can be structured so that the respondents just need to fill in one or two words or circle a response.

Interviews

The topic of conducting interviews was discussed in Chapter 5. There are special considerations when using this technique in mathematics assessment. Interviews can be used to guide discussions, to encourage students, and to determine disposition toward mathematics. One basic approach is to interview students individually about their likes and dislikes. Asking questions such as the following can be informative: "What do you like about mathematics?" "What are your interests?" "What don't you like?" Interviews can be used for screen-

What students have experienced:	Date and Activity	
1. Confidence in using mathematics	10/29 Correctly solved all problems assigned.	1/19 Actively worked as part of small group that solved a problem.
2. Flexibility in doing mathematics	11/2 Generated several ways of solving an addition problem.	4/8 Students challenged each other on solution methods.
3. Persevering at mathematical tasks	9/29 Worked all day on collecting and displaying data — "favorite ice cream".	2/5 Kept working on different ways of making change for 50¢ — all ways found.
4. Curiosity in doing mathematics	11/10 Solved a "what if" question, expressing answer in own words.	4/7 In small group generated own units for measuring room.
5. Reflecting on their own thinking	Every day students explain working on a problem.	their thinking after
6. Valuing applications of mathematics	2/23 All students brought in pictures for math applications bulletin board.	5/24 field trip to science museum to see how mathematics is used.
7. Appreciating role of mathematics	10/15 Brought in newspaper articles that used mathematical terms.	1/29 Appreciated place-value system by finding sums using Roman numerals.

FIGURE 11.2

Inventory of Mathematical Disposition Experiences

Source: Curriculum and Evaluation Standards for School Mathematics, p. 236, copyright 1989 by the National Council of Teachers of Mathematics.

ing, diagnosis, program planning, and program evaluation.

Structured interviews are a more systematic way to assess mathematics performance. A structured interview is an opportunity to observe, question, and discuss mathematics. In addition, unexpected information about the student may be elicited. Kulm (1994) described three ways of using structured interviews in mathematics:

- The teacher can question a student about the performance of a physical activity, such as measuring the length of a table.
- Students who lack reading skills, oral language skills, or whose native language is not English can communicate nonverbally, through pantomime, or can use manipulatives to demonstrate answers and solutions.
- Gifted students may find it easier to communicate about mathematics at high

cognitive levels, such as making judgments, justifying, and evaluating.

One example of using a structured interview is to give students a piece of paper and record the students' answers to the following questions (Kulm, 1994):

1. What is a perimeter of a rectangle?
2. What is a perimeter used for?
3. Show me the perimeter of the rectangle.
4. How could you measure the perimeter?
5. How would you estimate the perimeter?
6. What do you estimate the perimeter to be?
7. After giving a ruler to the student, ask the student to check the estimate by measuring the perimeter.
8. How could we use this information?
9. Are there other ways to find the perimeter without measuring all four sides?

Conferences

A conference is a conversation about the student's work that can include the student, educators, and/or parents. Each participant in a conference shares his or her views of the student's work with the goal of providing feedback and recommendations. Teacher-student conferences can be helpful when assessing one piece of work or when summarizing the student's work over a period of time. The discussion in a conference can be strictly verbal or it can be audiotaped, videotaped, or summarized in written form. Conferences are used for diagnosis, program planning, and program evaluation.

Student Journals

Journals induce students to reflect on their own work, communicate about their learning, and document their progress (Kulm, 1994). Students can keep a notebook or journal that allows them to record their work, attitudes, and feelings about mathematics. In a journal students can indicate what they like and don't like

about doing mathematics and areas in which they have difficulty. Journals are effective for program planning and program evaluation. The following is a sample mathematics journal outline (Kulm, 1994):

Mathematics topic:

Two examples of problems that I solved:

Two important ideas:

What I understand best:

What I need more work on:

How I can use this topic in real life:

Performance-Based Assessment

When used to assess mathematics instruction, performance-based assessment is the demonstration of mathematical abilities, skills, and disposition. Performance-based assessment requires students to demonstrate that they can develop a product or to demonstrate an ability or skill based on an understanding of concepts and relationships. This type of assessment is used in program planning and program evaluation. The following are examples of performance tasks:

- Pretend we own a children's shoe store. We need to know whether to have more cloth or more leather shoes for sale in our store. What could we decide to do? (NCTM, 1989, p. 55).
- Here is a rectangle. About how many centimeters long would you estimate its perimeter to be? Use the ruler to measure the perimeter. How close was your estimate? (Kulm, 1994, p. 44).
- Use a spreadsheet program to make a table of multiples of the first five whole numbers (Kulm, 1994, p. 45).

Portfolios

As we have defined in Chapter 7, a portfolio is a deliberate collection of a student's work that

FIGURE 9.2

BELLINGHAM PUBLIC SCHOOLS MATH DESCRIPTORS

Descriptors for Grades K–2

EXPLORATION: Becoming aware of math concepts; interacts with materials.

EMERGENT: Benefits from monitoring and help in problem solving; is beginning to understand math concepts; needs assistance to produce work.

BEGINNING: Solves problems with assistance; needs assistance learning math concepts; needs support to complete math tasks successfully; beginning to learn and use math facts.

DEVELOPING: Solves problems with occasional assistance; understands math concepts; usually completes math tasks accurately; can recall and use some math facts.

CAPABLE: Solves problems independently; applies previously learned math concepts; shows accuracy on math tasks; recalls and uses math facts.

EXPERIENCED: Uses a variety of strategies to solve problems independently; independently applies previously learned math concepts; demonstrates high accuracy on math tasks; confidently recalls and uses all math facts.

Descriptors for Grades 3–5

EMERGENT: Descriptors supplied by the teacher.

BEGINNING: Can solve problems and complete assignments with support; some understanding of math concepts; requires support to produce accurate work, is learning to use math facts.

DEVELOPING: Completes required assignments; solves problems with assistance; needs assistance learning math concepts; needs support to produce accurate assignments; beginning to use math facts.

CAPABLE: Completes required assignments; solves problems with occasional assistance; understands math concepts; usually accurate on assignments; recalls and uses math facts.

STRONG: Does some enrichment/extra credit math work; solves problems independently; applies previously learned math concepts; shows accuracy on assignments; confidently recalls and uses math facts.

EXCEPTIONAL: Extends self with math enrichment/extra credit work; uses thinking strategies to solve problems independently; independently applies previously learned math concepts; demonstrates high accuracy on assignments; confidently recalls and uses all math facts.

FIGURE 11.3

Math Descriptors

Source: Guiskey, T. R. (1996). *Communicating Student Learning: 1996 ASCD Yearbook,* p. 94. Alexandria, Va.: Association for Supervision and Curriculum Development. Copyright © 1996. ASCD. Used by permission.

demonstrates the student's efforts, progress, and achievement. When used to document and assess mathematical abilities, portfolios provide information about conceptual understanding, problem solving, reasoning, communication abilities, disposition toward mathematics, creativity, work habits, and attitudes. Mathematics portfolios help students see that the study of mathematics is more than discrete rules and procedures (Kulm, 1994). Portfolios in mathematics assessment aid in program planning and program evaluation. A more extensive discussion of the use of portfolios can be found in Chapter 7.

A portfolio is not just a folder of practice worksheets or of all the work that the student has completed. The selection of the contents of a portfolio is always carefully considered, and the following are suggestions for inclusion in student mathematics portfolios (National Research Council, 1993; Kulm, 1994):

- photographs of student projects of bridge building, using rods of different lengths
- worksheets that involve students in creating new shapes
- projects that involve students in using software to design quilts from squares
- performance tasks that require students to demonstrate knowledge of geometry
- journals in which students record the processes used in problem solving
- experiments with probability
- audiotapes of students collaborating on projects
- videotapes of students constructing designed structures or demonstrating what they have learned after analyzing data on rainfall.

Exhibitions

An exhibition is a display of a student's work in which the student summarizes and synthesizes what has been accomplished. Customarily, it demonstrates knowledge, abilities, skills, and attitudes concerning one project or a unit of work. In mathematics assessment, exhibitions are useful because students realize that doing mathematics is more than just a series of worksheets or exercises and that it involves conceptual understanding, problem solving, and reasoning, and teachers find them effective in program planning and program evaluation.

RUBRICS

The development and use of rubrics to describe student performance is discussed in Chapter 7. Rubrics provide a detailed description of student performance. The teacher uses a scale or rubric to assign points or a grade to levels of performance. Figure 11.3 is an example of a rubric that was developed to describe mathematics performance.

SELF-ASSESSMENT

Self-assessment provides students with an opportunity to review concepts and identify mathematical processes. It is an occasion for students to reflect on their learning. Figure 11.4 is an example of a checklist that students use when assessing their own learning.

PEER ASSESSMENT

Peer assessment allows students insight into the thinking and reasoning abilities of their peers. By engaging in collaborative learning and problem solving, students have an opportunity to reflect on the learning processes of their peers as well as on their own. Figure 11.5

Student's Name _____ Date _____					
	1	2	3	4	5
After reading the mathematical word problem, I can:	Great!				Darn!
1. draw a picture to help solve the problem.					
2. identify the operations to solve the problem.					
3. list the steps to solve the problem and explain why each step is necessary.					
4. use correct labeling.					
5. use numbers and symbols to write equation(s) to solve the problem.					
6. verify the results.					
7. interpret the results.					

FIGURE 11.4

Self-Assessment Checklist

Student's Name _____   Date _____

Peer's Name _____

	☹	😐	☺
1. My peer used the data in the tables to solve the mathematical story problem.			
2. My peer used correct mathematical notation.			
3. My peer used pictures to illustrate the story problem.			
4. My peer used labeling.			
5. My peer's work is neat.			

FIGURE 11.5

Peer Assessment

is an example of a checklist that students use when conducting a peer assessment.

OBSERVING THE STUDENT WITHIN THE ENVIRONMENT

In Chapter 5 you learned about the importance of considering the student within the physical, learning, and social environments. The interactions between the student and the environment are crucial assessment considerations.

Physical Environment

The physical environment can influence the student's mathematics performance. The temperature, lighting, and seating arrangements of the spaces used for teaching and learning affect how well the student performs. Figure 11.6 is a checklist that can be employed to study the physical environment.

Learning Environment

A comfortable learning environment facilitates the acquisition of a positive disposition toward mathematics and can contribute to mathematics achievement. The curriculum, instructional methods, materials, and the assessment procedures are all areas of concern. Developing a positive disposition toward mathematics is influenced by the learning environment. Students will be willing to do mathematics when: (1) mathematics problems are challenging; (2) students realize that mathematics problems are worth doing; (3) mathematics problems are accessible to a wide range of students; (4) a variety of instructional approaches are used; and (5) multiple assessment procedures are used. Figure 11.7 is a checklist that can help to determine the appropriateness of the learning environment.

Social Environment

Relationships with students and teachers affect mathematics achievement. The social environment is pivotal in the development of self-concept and self-esteem. These, in turn, contribute to a positive disposition toward mathematics. By observing the social environment, teachers can study the relationships students have with peers and adults. Figure 11.8 is a checklist for examining the appropriateness of the social environment.

PREFERRED PRACTICES

Recent reform initiatives in mathematics have a major impact on curriculum, instruction, and assessment in mathematics. While students with disabilities are not specifically identified as being included in the reform efforts, the new initiatives do emphasize that *all* students are to be included. As special educators, we must monitor and be responsive to these reforms.

The reform efforts in mathematics provide a welcome opportunity for educators to involve students with special needs in mathematics and to link instruction directly to assessment activities. Specifically, instruction and assessment approaches can be oriented (National Council of Teachers of Mathematics, 1991a, p. 3):

- toward classrooms as mathematical communities—away from classrooms as simply collections of individuals
- toward logic and mathematical evidence as verification—away from the teacher as the sole authority for right answers
- toward conjecturing, inventing, and problem solving—away from an emphasis on mechanistic answer-finding
- toward connecting the learning of mathematics to its fundamental ideas and its applications—away from treating mathematics as a body of isolated concepts and procedures.

◄ POINT STREET SCHOOL ►
Physical Environment ► Mathematics

Student's Name _____S.C._____   Date __5/21__ Time __10:15__

Observer _____Ms. P._____   Location _____classroom_____

Characteristic	Always	Sometimes	Never
1. Seating Is the student seated properly?	X		
► Suggestions for improvement:			
2. Lighting Is the lighting appropriate?	X		
► Suggestions for improvement:			
3. Noise Is the noise level appropriate?		X	
► Suggestions for improvement: When group activities are underway, the noise level of the classroom tends to rise. Both teacher and students should moniter this.			
4. Distractions Is the student distracted by activities in the room?	X		
► Suggestions for improvement:			
5. Temperature Is the temperature of the room appropriate?	X		
► Suggestions for improvement:			
6. General Atmosphere Does the student appear to be comfortable in the environment?		X	
► Suggestions for improvement: Group activities take up much of the class time. At times S.C. has difficulty moving from one group to the next.			

FIGURE 11.6

Observing the Physical Environment

◀ POINT STREET SCHOOL ▶
Learning Environment ▶ Mathematics

Student's Name ___S.C.___   Date ___5/21___ Time ___10:15___

Observer ___Ms. P.___   Location ___Classroom___

Characteristic	Always	Sometimes	Never
1. Materials Are a variety of mathematics materials available?	X		
▶ Suggestions for improvement:			
2. Manipulatives Are appropriate manipulatives available? Are a variety of manipulatives available?	X		
▶ Suggestions for improvement:			
3. Curriculum Does the curriculum reflect recent reform efforts and standards?	X		
▶ Suggestions for improvement:			
4. Activities Is instruction oriented toward the use of various materials rather than paper and pencil tasks?	X		
▶ Suggestions for improvement:			
5. Modifications Have modifications been made to instruction in order to accommodate the learning needs of the student?		X	
▶ Suggestions for improvement: *S.C. needs to use a talking calculator.*			
6. Instructional Demands Are the instructional demands appropriate for the student?	X		

FIGURE 11.7

Observing the Learning Environment

◀ POINT STREET SCHOOL ▶
Social Environment ▶ Mathematics

Student's Name _____S.C._____   Date __5/21__ Time __10:15__

Observer _____Ms. P._____   Location _____Classroom_____

Characteristic	Always	Sometimes	Never
1. **Teacher-Student Interactions** Are interactions warm and friendly?	X		
▶ Suggestions for improvement:			
2. **Disruptions** Are disruptions kept to a minimum?	X		
▶ Suggestions for improvement:			
3. **Behavioral Interventions** Are behavioral interventions effective and appropriate?		X	
▶ Suggestions for improvement: *Consultation with the behavioral specialist should be undertaken in order to revise the behavioral plan for S.C.*			
4. **Peer Interactions** Are peer interactions appropriate?		X	
▶ Suggestions for improvement: *Due to S.C.'s behavioral problems, peers are reluctant to interact with S.C. The behavioral plan should be revised.*			
5. **General Atmosphere** Does the student appear to be comfortable in the social environment?		X	
▶ Suggestions for improvement: *Some students seem to be uncomfortable with S.C.'s behavior. Strategies for successful interactions should be developed.*			
6. **Schedule** Is the student's schedule appropriate?		X	
▶ Suggestions for improvement: *S.C. may need additional one-to-one instruction in mathematics.*			
7. **Transitions** Are transitions made smoothly?	X		
▶ Suggestions for improvement:			

FIGURE 11.8

Observing the Social Environment

EXTENDING LEARNING

11.1 Identify one topic for instruction in mathematics. Develop two assessment tasks that link the instruction directly to assessment.

11.2 Develop a checklist or rating scale that assesses students' dispositions in mathematics.

11.3 A teacher suspects that Frances, a 10-year-old in fourth grade, is having difficulty doing mathematics. What suggestions can you give the teacher for determining whether these suspicions are correct?

11.4 Examine a norm-referenced standardized mathematics test. Compare the development of this test with the vision of mathematics assessment discussed in this chapter.

11.5 Identify three assessment approaches discussed in the chapter. Develop a table that shows the purposes, advantages, and disadvantages of each approach.

11.6 Visit a school and observe a mathematics class in session. How does the environment affect student learning? Use the Point Street School form in this chapter or develop your own checklist to collect information about the learning environment.

11.7 Obtain two or more standardized tests. Compare the test items. Read the instructor's manual of one of the tests and evaluate the technical characteristics.

11.8 Working with one or two other students, identify a unit of study in mathematics. Develop a criterion-referenced test to assess this unit.

REFERENCES

American Association for the Advancement of Science (AAAS) (1993). *Benchmarks for science literacy.* New York: Oxford University Press.

Anastasi, A. (1988). *Psychological testing.* New York: Macmillan.

Ashlock, R. B. (1986). *Error patterns in computation: A semi-programmed approach.* 5th ed. Columbus, Ohio: Merrill.

Berk, R. A. (1988). Criterion-referenced tests. In *Educational research, methodology, and measurement: An international handbook,* ed. J. P. Keeves, pp. 365–370. Oxford: Pergamon Press.

Berman, B., and F. J. Friederwitzer (1981). A diagnostic-prescriptive approach to remediation of regrouping errors. *Elementary School Journal* 82: 109–115.

Brigance, A. H. (1977). *BRIGANCE® diagnostic inventory of basic skills.* No. Billerica, Mass.: Curriculum Associates.

Brigance, A. H. (1980). *BRIGANCE® diagnostic inventory of essential skills.* No. Billerica, Mass.: Curriculum Associates.

Brigance, A. H. (1983). *BRIGANCE® diagnostic comprehensive inventory of basic skills.* No. Billerica, Mass.: Curriculum Associates.

Brigance, A. H. (1984). *BRIGANCE® assessment of basic skills–Spanish edition.* No. Billerica, Mass.: Curriculum Associates.

Brigance, A. H. (1991). *BRIGANCE® diagnostic inventory of early development–revised.* No. Billerica, Mass.: Curriculum Associates.

Brigance, A. H. (1994). *BRIGANCE® diagnostic life skills inventory.* No. Billerica, Mass.: Curriculum Associates.

Brigance, A. H. (1995). *BRIGANCE® diagnostic employability skills inventory.* No. Billerica, Mass.: Curriculum Associates.

Brown, V. L., M. E. Cronin, and E. McEntire (1994). *Test of mathematical abilities.* 2d. ed. Austin, Tex.: PRO-ED.

Connolly, A. J. (1988). *KeyMath–Revised: A diagnostic inventory of essential mathematics.* Circle Pines, Minn.: American Guidance Service.

Enright, B. E. (1983). ENRIGHT® Diagnostic Inventory of Basic Arithmetic Skills. No. Billerica, Mass.: Curriculum Associates.

Erford, B. T., and R. R. Boykin (1996). *Slosson-diagnostic math screener.* East Aurora, N.Y.: Slosson Educational Publications, Inc.

Estes, T. H., J. J. Estes, H. C. Richards, and D. Roettger (1981). *Estes attitude scales.* Austin, Tex.: PRO-ED.

Ginsburg, H. P., and A. J. Baroody (1990). *Test of*

early mathematics ability. 2d. ed. Austin, Tex.: PRO-ED.

Gnagey, T. D. (1980). *Diagnostic screening tests math.* East Aurora, N.Y.: SLOSSON Educational Publications, Inc.

Harcourt Brace Educational Measurement. (1995). *Stanford diagnostic mathematics test 4.* 4th ed. San Antonio, Tex.: Author.

Harcourt Brace Educational Measurement. (1992). *Wechsler individual achievement test.* San Antonio, Tex: Author.

Hudson, F. G., S. E. Colson, D. L. Welch, A. K. Banikowski, and T. A. Mehring (1989). *Hudson education skills inventory.* Austin, Tex.: PRO-ED.

Kaufman, A. S., and N. L. Kaufman (1983). *Kaufman assessment battery for children.* Circle Pines, Minn.: American Guidance Service.

Kaufman, A. S., and N. L. Kaufman (1985). *Kaufman test of educational achievement.* Circle Pines, Minn.: American Guidance Service.

Kilian, L., E. Cahill, C. Ryan, D. Sutherland, and D. Tacetta (1980). Errors that are common in multiplication. *Arithmetic Teacher* 27: 22–25.

Kulm, G. (1994). *Mathematics assessment.* San Francisco: Jossey-Bass.

Lake, K., and K. Kafka (1996). Reporting methods in grade K-8. In *Communicating student learning,* ed. T. R. Guskey, 90–118. Alexandria: Va.: Association for Supervision and Curriculum Development.

Markwardt, F. C. (1989). *Peabody individual achievement test–Revised.* Circle Pines, Minn.: American Guidance Service.

Marolda, M. R., and P. S. Davidson (1994). Assessing mathematical abilities and learning approaches. In *Windows of opportunity,* eds. C. A. Thornton and N. S. Bley, 83–113. Reston, Va.: National Council of the Teachers of Mathematics.

Mathematics Curriculum Framework and Criteria Committee (1992). *Mathematics framework for California public schools.* Sacramento, Calif.: California Department of Education.

National Council of the Teachers of Mathematics (1989). *Curriculum and evaluation standards for school mathematics.* Reston, Va.: Author.

——— (1991a). *Mathematics assessment.* Reston, Va.: Author.

——— (1991b). *Professional standards for the teaching of mathematics.* Reston, Va.: Author.

National Research Council (1993). *Measuring up.* Washington, D.C.: National Academy Press.

Newcomer, P. L. (1990). *Diagnostic achievement battery.* 2d. ed. Austin, Tex.: PRO-ED.

Newcomer, P. L., and B. R. Bryant (1993). *Diagnostic achievement test for adolescents.* 2d. ed. Austin, Tex.: PRO-ED.

Reisman, F. K. (1985). *Sequential assessment of mathematics inventories–Standardized inventory.* San Antonio, Tex.: Harcourt Brace Educational Measurement.

Sonnenschein, J. L. (1983). *Basic achievement skills individual screener.* San Antonio, Tex.: Harcourt Brace Educational Measurement.

Speer, W. R., and D. J. Brahier (1994). Rethinking the teaching and learning of mathematics. In *Windows of opportunity,* eds. C. A. Thornton and N. S. Bley, 41–59. Reston, Va.: National Council of the Teachers of Mathematics.

Tindal, G. A., and D. B. Marston (1990). *Classroom-based assessment.* Columbus, Ohio: Merrill.

Trafton, P. R., and A. S. Claus (1994). A changing curriculum for a changing age. In *Windows of opportunity,* eds. C. A. Thornton and N. S. Bley, 19–39. Reston, Va.: National Council of the Teachers of Mathematics.

U.S. Department of Education, and National Science Foundation (n.d.). *Statement of principles on assessment in mathematics and science education.* Washington, D.C.: Author.

Wilkinson, G. (1994). *Wide range achievement test.* 3d ed. Austin, Tex.: PRO-ED.

Woodcock, R. W., and M. B. Johnson (1989). *Woodcock-Johnson psychoeducational battery–Revised.* Chicago: Riverside.

Zaslavsky, C. (1996). *The multicultural math classroom.* Portsmouth, N.H.: Heinemann.

Development of Young Children

OVERVIEW

Gathering information about the development of young children before they are enrolled in school is very different from the assessment of school-age children. Working with young children and their families can involve locating a mother and her preschool child in a homeless shelter, receiving a referral form from a community clinic, or working with a family recently arrived from another country where services for young children and families are not available. Assessment questions focus on the young child's general development in one or more areas. These areas, or **developmental domains,** concern physical, cognitive, communication, social-emotional, and adaptive development. The focus on development differs in significant ways from the focus on academic and achievement difficulties of school-age children and youth we have been discussing.

In this chapter we will examine the federal requirements for the assessment of young children, birth through age 8. We will identify and describe assessment approaches and explore some of the issues when children make the transition to school.

CHAPTER OBJECTIVES

After completing this chapter, you should be able to:

Describe the general requirements for the assessment of young children as mandated by federal legislation.

Explain the considerations involved in assessing young children.

Identify and describe how to evaluate screening and developmental assessment instruments.

Discuss transition assessment of young children.

Discuss issues in the assessment of school readiness.

WHAT SHAPES OUR VIEWS: THE CHILDREN

Teachers and administrators in public school programs usually define **young children** as students in grades kindergarten through 3; early intervention specialists define young children as ages birth through 5 years. Thus, the definition of the term "young children" may imply different age ranges, depending on the professional's frame of reference. Two national organizations of professionals, the Division of Early Childhood (DEC) of the Council for Exceptional Children (CEC) and the National Association for the Education of Young Children (NAEYC), define *young* as children ages birth through age 8. We will use this latter definition in our discussion of young children.

Professionals feel that development, which is influenced by the child's interests, abilities, and opportunities in the natural environment, proceeds at individual variations during the early years. For example, 4-year-old Arron is interested in dinosaurs and can identify which are carnivores and which are herbivores! Will, who is also 4 years old, spends much of his time playing with his dump trucks. He speaks in two- to three-word phrases. The variations between Arron and Will may be due to genetic or biological factors such as the child's temperament or to prenatal factors such as consumption of alcohol or use of tobacco during pregnancy. Moreover, they can be influenced by social expectations and ways of caring for Arron and Will or be a result of opportunity or its absence. Most probably, according to many developmental theorists, two or more factors interact.

Today, young children with special needs who can benefit from special services are identified early in life. Medical professionals identify many newborns with or at-risk for disability before leaving the hospital; visiting nurses and early intervention specialists screen infants in their homes; and early childhood special educators work with toddlers and preschoolers in their homes, child care centers, or early education programs. Professionals working with young children and their families represent a variety of disciplines, including audiology, family counseling, medicine, occupational therapy, physical therapy, psychology, social work, speech and language pathology, as well as education. These professionals work on assessment teams to identify needs and to develop and implement appropriate programs. How did early identification and services develop?

FEDERAL LEGISLATION AFFECTING THE ASSESSMENT OF YOUNG CHILDREN

In 1986, the passage of P.L. 99–457, the Education of the Handicapped Act Amendments, focused on the identification and provision of services for young children ages 3 to 5. This federal legislation mandated the same provision of services to preschool-age children as the original special education law, P.L. 94–142, the Education for All Handicapped Children Act, had mandated services for school-age children and youth in 1975. In addition to focusing on young children ages 3 to 5, P.L. 99–457 was written to encourage states to develop regulations for serving infants and toddlers with special needs and their families.

P.L. 102–119, the Amendments to the IDEA of 1992 and P.L. 105-17, the Individuals with Disabilities Act Amendments of 1997, served to further refine services to young children. This legislation provided an opportunity for states to use a noncategorical term of eligibility known as **developmental delay** for young children through age 9 rather than the same categories of eligibility defined under IDEA for school-age children (see Chapter 1). Although young children vary greatly in their rate of development, this term was designed to reflect a significant delay in development.

During the 1990s personnel in many states developed definitions for developmental delay as well as the eligibility criteria for providing special education services to young children.

For example, some states developed eligibility criteria that include a combination of the use of standardized instruments and observations. Typical practice is that a child's developmental delay is documented by (1) performance on a comprehensive standardized developmental assessment and reported in standard deviations below the mean, and by (2) a specific assessment or observations of one of the developmental domains (McLean, Smith, McCormick, Schakel, and McEvoy, 1991).

In many states, regulations identify young children under a broad eligibility term such as developmental delay; a few states determine eligibility under the traditional Part B (school-age) categories and criteria of IDEA (Table 12.1).

There is great variability among states in the categories of disability and in the criteria that are used to determine eligibility for services. The system that your state has developed directly affects the assessment process and the assessment approaches that you will choose to use. Teachers and other professionals who conduct developmental assessments will need to obtain a copy of their state laws or check with

state-level personnel to learn the process used for determining eligibility of young children for free, appropriate public education (FAPE).

SCREENING

Screening is a process used to identify children who may have a disability and who will be referred for a comprehensive assessment. Some of the common questions raised by parents, caregivers, and early childhood teachers are illustrated in Table 12.2.

Screening typically involves testing large numbers of young children, usually in a short amount of time. Screening does not identify children for services but rather pinpoints children who need to be further assessed. Based on a comprehensive assessment, some children are identified as needing early intervention or special education and related services.

In many cases, families are unaware of early childhood screenings and need to be alerted to the benefits of early intervention and purposes

TABLE 12.1   The Eligibility System for Young Children State by State

States	Type of eligibility	Description
AL, DC, FL, IA, IL, IN, MD, NC, ND, NE, NY, OK, TX, WI	Categorical	These states may use the same eligibility categories and the criteria for preschool-age and school-age children for FAPE or they may use the same categories but modify some or all criteria for FAPE.
AK, AR, AZ, CO, DE, GA, HI, ID, KY, LA, ME, MI, MN, MS, MT, NH, NM, NV, OR, PA, RI, SC, TN, UT, VA, WA, WV, WY	Combination	These states use a combination of both school-age and some kind of preschool-specific category. In some of these states the preschool-specific category replaces certain school-age categories, such as mental retardation or learning disabilities.
CT, KS, MA, MO, NJ, OH, SD, VT	Noncategorical	Some of these states use a preschool specific category only; some of these states use a noncategorical system for all eligible school-age children, preschool-age as well as school-age children.

Source: Adapted from Snyder, P., D. B. Bailey, and C. Auger (1994). Preschool eligibility determination for children with known or suspected learning disabilities under IDEA. *Journal of Early Intervention* 18(4): 380–390.

TABLE 12.2   Assessment Questions, Purposes, and Approaches

Assessment questions	Steps and purposes	Approaches
	Screening	
Is the child developing typically? Is there a *possibility* that the child has a delay in development or a disability?	To determine whether the child *may* have a disability and should be referred for further assessment	Norm-referenced instruments Curriculum-based assessment Criterion-referenced assessment Observations Checklists Questionnaires Interviews Parent reports Review of developmental history
	Eligibility	
Does the child have a delay in development or a disability? What disability does the child have? How extensive is the disability or delay? Does the child meet the criteria for services? What are the child's strengths and weaknesses in development? What is the child having trouble doing? What does the child understand?	To determine if there is a disability or a developmental delay To compare the child's performance with the performance of the peer group To determine the need for early intervention or special education and related services To determine specific strengths and weaknesses To understand why the child is having difficulty	Norm-referenced instruments Curriculum-based assessment Criterion-referenced assessment Observations Probes Error analysis Interviews Checklists Questionnaires Parent-teacher conferences Performance assessment Parent reports Review of developmental history
	CONNECTING INSTRUCTION WITH ASSESSMENT	
	Program Planning	
What types of early intervention or special education and/or related services should be provided? At what location(s) should the child and family receive services? What environmental modifications and adaptations should be implemented?	To plan the child's program To determine family resources, priorities, and concerns To determine the locations and type of services(s) to be received To assess the physical, learning and social environments	Family-directed assessment Norm-referenced instruments Curriculum-based assessment Criterion-referenced assessment Observations Probes Error analysis Interviews Checklists

of screening. These awareness activities are known as Child Find. Through Child Find, parents and caregivers become aware of screening activities, the first step in the process of identifying young children who fit the eligibility criteria for special services.

Community screenings can be sponsored by the public school, by the state early intervention agency, or by community agencies. Customarily, a screening has several components, such as a physical examination by a doctor or nurse, a developmental history obtained by interviewing the parent, vision and hearing tests, and an assessment of the child's general devel-

TABLE 12.2   (Continued)

Assessment questions	Steps and purposes	Approaches
What is the child's knowledge or level of skill development?	To understand the child's level of skill or development	Parent-teacher conferences Performance assessment
Where should intervention begin?	To determine where intervention or instruction should begin	Parent reports Review of developmental history
Program Monitoring		
Once intervention or instruction begins, is the child making progress?	To monitor the child's program To understand the pace of intervention	Curriculum-based assessment Criterion-referenced assessment Observations Probes
Should the intervention or instruction be modified?	To understand what the child can do prior to and after intervention or instruction	Error analysis Interviews Checklists Parent-teacher conferences Portfolios Exhibitions Journals Written descriptions Oral descriptions
Program Evaluation		
Has the child met the goals of the IFSP or IEP?	To determine whether the program was successful in meeting the child and family goals (IFSP)	Curriculum-based assessment Criterion-referenced assessment Observations Probes
Has the child made progress?		
Has the program been successful for the child and family?	To determine if the program was successful in meeting the child's goals (IEP)	Error analysis Interviews Checklists Questionnaires
Does the child continue to need services?	To determine if the child continues to need services	Parent-teacher conferences Portfolios Exhibitions
Has the program achieved its goals?	To evaluate program effectiveness	Journals Written descriptions Oral descriptions Surveys

opment, including the physical, cognitive, communication, social-emotional, and adaptive domains. Professionals typically use a screening instrument to assist in making decisions regarding the screening outcome.

Choosing Appropriate Screening Instruments

According to Meisels and Wasik (1990) developmental screening tests "should be brief, norm-referenced, inexpensive, standardized in administration, objectively scored, broadly focused across all areas of development, reliable, and valid" (p. 613). Screening tests are generally used to evaluate large numbers of children to determine if further assessment is necessary, and accordingly they paint a broad picture and provide general information. Too narrow a focus can mean that important aspects about the child are missed. Additional time and

SNAPSHOT

Luiz and His Mother Visit the Community Screening Clinic

Recently Luiz's mother, Maria Hermetz, heard about a community screening clinic from a friend at the local convenience store. The clinic is held on the first Tuesday of each month at the community center and is free for all children in the community. Health and education professionals are available to answer questions about children's development.

Although Ms. Hermetz does not have any specific questions about 4-year-old Luiz, she decided that she would like to know if he is doing "what he should be doing" at this age. The following month she brought Luiz to the screening.

When Ms. Hermetz arrived at the community center, she observed that the large room had been separated into various areas (Figure 12.1).

The central area had a variety of toys and books for the children and chairs for the parents. "¡Buenos dias!" Ms. Hermetz was greeted by one of the clinic volunteers and asked to complete a brief form with questions regarding her son's development. Ms. Hermetz was relieved to see that the form was written in English on one side and Spanish on the other. Although she speaks English, she prefers to use her native Spanish. Another volunteer invited Luiz to join two other children who were playing with blocks nearby.

The practitioner who makes observations in this informal setting must identify the types of information to be gathered and will need to choose a method for recording observation data as discussed in Chapter 5. Observing children, a teacher watches and notes important information. How does the child approach the toys and other children? How does the child interact with the materials? How does the child communicate with adults? With other children?

FIGURE 12.1

A Community Screening Program with Five Separate Stations

Source: Cohen, Libby G. and Loraine J. Spenciner (1994). *Assessment of Young Children.* White Plains, N.Y.: Longman Publishers. Reprinted with permission.

B O X   1 2 . 1

FIRSTSTEP: SCREENING TEST FOR EVALUATING PRESCHOOLERS

Publication Date: 1992

Purposes: Screening test which addresses the following areas: cognition, communication, motor, social-emotional, and adaptive behavior. Additional checklists may be completed by the child's parent or teacher.

Age/Grade Levels: Ages 2 years, 9 months through 6 years, 2 months.

Time to Administer: 15 minutes.

Technical Adequacy: The standardization sample, reliability, and validity are very good.

Suggested Use: May be used as part of an overall screening procedure.

| **4. _Put Together Game_** | CREDIT
Child places stick(s) | 60 seconds for each item |
| ITEM | | |

 1. Place sticks A and B to the right of the pole (2 shortest sticks).
**Here is a fire fighter. He wants to slide down to get his hat.
Find the stick that makes the right size pole for him.**

B

2. Place sticks B, C, and D parallel to the trunk (3 longest sticks).
**Here is a baby kitty. Here is a mommy cat. Fix the tree
so that the baby can slide down to his mommy. Use only
two sticks.**

B and D

3. Place sticks A, B, C, and D below the road.
**Here is a baby elephant and here is a mommy elephant. Let's
make a road for the baby to get to his mommy. Use _some_ of
these sticks to make a road to his mommy.**

A, B, and D

FIGURE 12.2A

Selected Items in the Cognitive Domain from the _FirstSTEP: Screening Test for Evaluating Preschoolers_

An early childhood special educator gave Luiz a colorful name tag and invited him to come with her to one of the five screening stations. This teacher, along with other members of the screening team, was using the _FirstSTEP: Screening Test for Evaluating Preschoolers_ (Miller, 1992). They presented Luiz with a number of activities in the areas of cognitive (Figures 12.2a and b), communication, motor, social-emotional, and adaptive development.

Luiz liked pointing to various pictures in the examiner's book. After completing this station, Luiz moved to the next station to work with the speech and language pathologist. Later, he worked with the physical therapist at the motor development station. At the last station, a volunteer checked his hearing and vision. At each station he received another colored sticker on his name tag. This procedure allowed the examiners to quickly determine which stations the child had completed.

After the screening, the nurse met with Ms. Hermetz to talk about the results of the screening and to answer any questions. Depending on the family's needs, the nurse may discuss various community resources.

Today, she and Ms. Hermetz chatted about Luiz's development. About a week later, Ms. Hermetz received a letter in the mail that stated that the screening results had been completed and that no further assessment was indicated.

FIGURE 12.2B

Stimulus Booklet for Cognitive Item 1, Put Together Game from the _FirstSTEP: Screening Test for Evaluating Preschoolers_

money can be devoted to conducting comprehensive assessments on children who are identified by the screening.

Screening calls for norm-referenced tests, which compare a child's performance with the performance of other children who have taken the test. The norm sample must include children who have similar backgrounds and characteristics to the child or children being screened. For example, if the children to be evaluated come from an inner-city area, then the screening instrument that is used must have been developed with children from urban areas included in the norming sample.

Many different professionals and paraprofessionals administer and score screening tests. The administration of screening tests is standardized as is their scoring. This means that the directions, calculation of scores, and determination of outcomes is clearly explained and must be the same for all children who are screened. Because many different test examiners are involved, the outcomes of screening should not be subject to the judgment and biases of individual test examiners. Table 12.3 illustrates common screening instruments and their technical characteristics.

Planning the Screening Procedure

In planning the screening procedure, the screening team must address several key areas.

Environment

The screening should always be conducted in a setting that is quiet and free from distractions. The child should be assessed in the company of a familiar caregiver. Young children should never be challenged during assessment activities by separation from their parent or caregiver (Greenspan and Meisels, 1993, p. 14).

Rapport

Each examiner must allow time for the child to become familiar with the situation. Many chil-

dren take time to "warm up" to strangers. If the child does not feel comfortable, the responses given may not reflect the child's ability.

Physical Status

As routine practice, an examiner observes the child's current health status. Young children frequently have colds, leading to middle ear infections (a result of which is a temporary decrease in hearing). Can the child hear the directions? Does the child appear to be tired? If so, consider screening at another time. Don't forget that young children have a limited attention span. A child's attention will wander or be lost if the screening test has too many test items.

Development

Although separate areas of development have been defined (physical, cognitive, communication, social-emotional, and adaptive), these areas are not independent, but interact in complex ways. Screening procedures must be comprehensive in coverage, not focused on one or two developmental areas.

Parent Concerns

Some parents are very anxious about their child's screening test. "When will my child start talking?" or "Will this person find something wrong with my child?" parents may ask—or may not ask, although it is a matter of primary concern. Be sure that parents fully understand the reason for screening their child. An important component of any screening procedure is a period for answering parents' questions, either before or after the testing.

LIMITATIONS OF SCREENING

The screening process has several significant limitations. Members of assessment teams must be knowledgeable about these limits because screening results determine whether or

TABLE 12.3 Selected Screening Instruments for Young Children

Instrument	Areas Assessed	Age Range	Reliability	Validity	Norms	Time to Administer
AGS Early Screening Profiles (Harrison et al., 1990)	Cognitive/language, self-help/social, articulation survey, behavior survey, motor survey, home profile, and health history survey	2 to 6.11 years	Internal consistency mean .85; test-retest range .78–.89; interrater mean .92	Numerous studies support concurrent, predictive, and construct validity	1,149 children from 26 states and the District of Columbia stratified by geographic region, race, age, gender, socioeconomic status, and enrollment of school district	15–30 minutes for children; 10–15 minutes for teacher and parent questionnaires
Battelle Developmental Screening Test (1984; norm recalibration, Newborg, Stock, Wnek, Guidubaldi, & Sviniski, 1988)	Personal-social, adaptive, motor, communication, and cognitive	Birth to 8.6 years	None reported	Limited information reported	800 children stratified by age, race, and gender	10–30 minutes
BRIGANCE® Preschool Screen (Brigance, 1985)	11 skill areas	2.9 to 5 years	None reported	None reported	Criterion-referenced test	12–15 minutes
Denver Developmental Screening Test II (DDST II) (Frankenburg & Dodds, 1990)	Gross motor, language, fine motor–adaptive, and personal-social	Birth to 6 years	Limited information reported	Limited information reported	2,096 children stratified by maternal education, residence, and ethnicity	20–30 minutes

Continued

Table 12.3 (Continued)

Instrument	Areas Assessed	Age Range	Reliability	Validity	Norms	Time to Administer
Developmental Indicators for the Assessment of Learning–Revised (DIAL-R) (Mardell-Czudnowski & Goldenberg, 1990)	Motor skills, conceptual abilities, and language skills	2 to 5.11 years	Test-retest reliability is based on 1983 edition; median internal consistency coefficients range from .70 to .87	Validity data reported on 1983 edition; limited validity data reported for 1990 edition	Reanalysis of 1983 standardization; sample was stratified by age and gender; minority sample is overrepresented	20–30 minutes
Early Screening Inventory (ESI) (Meisels & Wiske, 1988)	Visual-motor/adaptive, language and cognition, gross motor/body awareness	4 to 6 years	Interscorer reliability .91; test-retest .82	Evidence of validity is adequate	465 Caucasian children from low-to lower-middle-class urban communities	15–20 minutes
FirstSTEP (Miller, 1992)	Cognitive, communication, motor, socio-emotional, and adaptive	2.9 to 6.2 years	Test-retest reliability coefficients range from .85 to .92; interrater reliability .77 to .96	Adequate concurrent validity	1,433 stratified by gender, geographic regions and race/ethnicity based on 1988 U.S. Census	15 minutes

not the child is referred for a comprehensive assessment.

Snapshots

The results obtained from a screening instrument, like some other assessment approaches, are only a snapshot of a child's development at one point in time. There are many variables that can affect screening results. These include the child's physical, emotional, or motivational states, the examiner's familiarity with the screening tools, the examiner's understanding of child development and ability to establish rapport, and the screening environment.

Since the results of screening represent only a brief picture, best practices in screening suggest that a child be given periodic screening tests. The advantages of using the same standardized instrument each time the child is screened are the ease and usefulness of comparing the child's development on subsequent administrations. However, the effectiveness of the instrument is reduced by the cumulative effect of repeating items on periodic screenings and by the tendency of some caregivers to "practice" the items with the child.

Screening Tasks

Most standardized screening instruments include toys that the child is asked to use or to play with in specific ways. For example, a common test item on several screening instruments requires the examiner to tell the child to build a tower with a small pile of 1-inch cubes. Using toys in very specific ways is a new experience for many young children. In most early education programs, children are encouraged to choose a toy, to explore its properties, and to use it in a way that they choose. Thus, when given several small cubes, a child may decide to make a train rather than a tower. To pass this item on a screening test, the child must make a tower; however, a young child may

have no motivation or interest to comply with the examiner's request because the child has a more interesting idea (the train or road).

False Negatives

A child who, in fact, does have a disability may pass through the screening without being identified for further assessment. The causes of **false negative** results are lack of sensitivity of the screening instrument, lack of training, limited clinical knowledge of the examiner(s), or other factors.

False Positives

A child who does not have a disability may be identified for further assessment. These **false positive** results increase parental anxiety and place an extra burden on the family until a comprehensive assessment is completed. The causes of false positives are lack of specificity of the screening instrument, lack of training, lack of clinical knowledge of the examiner(s), or other factors.

COMPREHENSIVE DEVELOPMENTAL ASSESSMENT

As a result of screening procedures, a young child may be referred to an assessment team. The team addresses concerns about the child's development and individual team members participate in planning and conducting a comprehensive assessment. Team members include the child's parents and professionals representing various disciplines, encompassing education, medicine, occupational therapy or physical therapy, psychology, speech and language pathology, and social work.

Educators play a major role on the assessment team. They often conduct observations

SNAPSHOTS

Special Challenges

Some families face special challenges that impact on Child Find activities and the screening and referral processes. We meet several families in the following snapshots:

- Fourteen year old Cheryl and her baby Samantha live on the streets of a large urban city. They occasionally sleep at a downtown shelter or in one of the vacant buildings on the waterfront.
- Mindy and her 3-year-old son are illegal immigrants living with her cousin in a small apartment house. Mindy worries that city officials will locate her and re-

turn her and her child to their native country.
- Christy graduated from college a few years ago and finds herself torn between the responsibilities of her job and her toddler. She often resents the demands that her child makes.
- Rita and Alexander and their three preschoolers live in a trailer at the end of a dirt road several miles from town. They have exhausted their meager savings since the mill closed and both parents lost their jobs. This rural family cannot readily access community resources and services.

of the child in an early education setting or they complete a developmental assessment on the child. Typically, developmental assessments cover a variety of developmental areas, including physical (gross and fine motor), cognitive, communication, social or emotional, and adaptive development.

WHAT SHAPES OUR VIEWS: DEVELOPMENTAL ASSESSMENT

Many of the instruments that assess development are based on various theories of child growth and development.

Piaget

Jean Piaget developed a theory of cognitive development that emphasizes the interaction of early motor abilities with developing cognitive

abilities. During cognitive development, according to Piaget, a child passes through specific developmental stages; however, one child may pass through a stage at a different time than another. Assessment instruments and practices that are built on Piagetian theory include test items that address these cognitive stages: sensorimotor intelligence, preoperational thought, concrete operations, and formal operations. Preoperational thought typically develops between the ages of 2 and 7 years and is the stage when the child becomes capable of symbolic representations.

Effect on Assessment Practices

An examiner who comes from a Piagetian perspective may choose to gather information about the child's development by observing the child at play. Let's sit in on the observation of two children, both of whom have been referred for a developmental assessment. Jamie, who is 3 years old, picks up the blocks and randomly throws or tosses them away. Occasionally, he puts a block in his mouth. Sarah, who is also 3 years old, lines the blocks up in a double row. She then takes a long rectangular block and starts to push it down the middle of the row. She explains to the observer that she is going shopping at the grocery store for her birthday party.

Functional Approach

In contrast, the functional (behavioral) approach emphasizes the importance of factors external to the child in skill development. The functional approach emphasizes the skills a child will need to live and play in their natural environment. Many of the instruments are criterion-referenced.

Effect on Assessment Practices

Let's join another examiner who is conducting an assessment of the two 3-year-old children whom we met earlier, Jamie and Sarah. The examiner is using a criterion-referenced instrument, the HELP for Preschoolers (VORT, 1995). According to this instrument, cognitive skills address reasoning, problem solving, and knowledge. At 3 years of age children should be able to sort objects according to big and little, point to the same item in two different settings, and identify objects based on category. How will this examiner's orientation to gathering information differ in the use of blocks with Jamie and Sarah?

Biological Approach

A third approach to developmental assessment focuses on the physical state of the child and originates within the fields of neurology and pediatrics. The biological approach emphasizes the importance of the reciprocity between the child's temperament and behavior and the caregiver's response. There appears to be some evidence that assessment within this

---

BOX 12.2

HELP FOR PRESCHOOLERS

Publication Date: 1995

Purposes: A criterion-referenced test that includes the following development areas: cognitive, language, gross motor, fine motor, social-emotional, and adaptive.

Age/Grade Levels: 3 to 6 years.

Time to Administer: Varies since only areas of interest need to be assessed.

Technical Adequacy: Since this is a criterion-referenced instrument, norms were not developed through administering the test but, rather, they were drawn from the literature. The manual does not cite literature references. There is no information concerning reliability and validity.

Suggested Use: Assesses a wide area of development in young children. Several strands are particularly helpful to the unique needs of some children, and these areas include sign language, speechreading, and wheelchair skills.

---

framework can be used across cultures with infants (Barr, 1989).

CHOOSING APPROPRIATE DEVELOPMENTAL ASSESSMENT INSTRUMENTS

One of the purposes of a developmental assessment is to answer questions about the child's development based on the referral and screening information. The team will need to determine if the child is eligible for early intervention or special education services. For children who have a diagnosed disability, the developmental assessment is helpful in an-

TABLE 12.4 Selected Developmental Assessment Instruments

Instrument	Areas	Age range	Type	Reliability	Validity
Arizona Basic Assessment and Curriculum Utilization System (ABACUS) (McCarthy, Lund, & Bos, 1986)	Adaptive, communication, socioemotional, and preacademic	2 to 5.5 years	System for planning, monitoring, and evaluating a child's progress	Not reported	Teachers should examine materials to make decisions for their program.
Battelle Developmental Inventory (Newborg, Stock, Wnek, Guidubaldi, & Sviniski, 1988)	Personal-social, adaptive, motor, communication, and cognitive	Birth through 8 years	Norm-referenced: 800 children participated; data reanalyzed in 1987	Test-retest adequate	Adequate
Bayley Scales of Infant Development II (Bayley, 1993)	Mental scale and motor scale	1 through 3.6 years	Norm-referenced: 1,700 children participated; stratification based on 1988 U.S. census	Adequate	Adequate
BRIGANCE® Diagnostic Inventory of Early Development–Revised (Brigance, 1991)	Preambulatory, gross motor, fine motor, adaptive, speech and language, general knowledge and comprehension, social-emotional, reading readiness, basic reading, writing, and math	Birth to 7 years	Criterion-referenced; norms developed from a literature review	Not reported	Not reported
Carolina Curriculum for Preschoolers with Special Needs (Johnson-Martin, Attermeier, & Hacker, 1990)	Cognition, communication, social, adaptive, fine motor, and gross motor	3 to 5 years	Criterion-referenced	Not reported	Not reported. Teachers should review materials to make decisions for their program.

Instrument	Areas assessed	Age range	Standardization	Reliability	Validity/Comments
Child Development Inventory (Ireton, 1992)	Social, self-help, gross motor, fine motor, expressive language, language comprehension, letters, and numbers	1.3 to 6 years	Norm-referenced: 568 children living in St. Paul, MN participated	.70 to .89 for children ages 1 to 4.5 years	Adequate
HELP for Preschoolers (Vort, 1995)	Cognitive, language, gross motor, fine motor, social, and self-help	3 through 6 years	Curriculum-based	Descriptions and guidelines in the manual are designed to promote consistency.	Teachers should review materials to make decisions for their program.
Infant-Preschool Play Assessment Scale (Flagler, 1996)	Cognitive, communication, sensory motor, fine motor, gross motor, and social-emotional skills	Birth through 5 years	Criterion-referenced	Not reported	Teachers should review materials to make decisions for their program.
Kaufman Survey of Early Academic and Language Skills (K-SEALS) (Kaufman & Kaufman, 1993)	Expressive language, receptive language, number, letter, and word skills	3 through 6 years	Norm-referenced: 1,000 children from 28 states stratified by geographic region, race, age, gender, socioeconomic status, and enrollment of school district	Adequate	Evidence of concurrent and predictive validity is presented.
Mullen Scales of Early Learning (Mullen, 1995)	Gross motor, visual reception, fine motor, receptive language, and expressive language	Birth through 5.9 years	Norm-referenced: 1,849 children from 4 geographic regions stratified by age, gender, race/ethnicity, father's occupations, and urban/rural	Adequate for younger age groups; interscorer reliability excellent	Evidence of construct validity is presented.
System to Plan Early Childhood Services (SPECS) (Bagnato & Neisworth, 1990)	Communication, sensorimotor, physical, self-regulation, congition, and self/social	2 to 6 years	System that links assessment of the child to program planning, development of the individualized plan, and evaluation	test-retest (most items greater than .70)	Teachers should examine materials and make decisions regarding their program.

swering questions about program planning. For children who are already receiving services, a developmental assessment provides a method of monitoring progress. Good practice dictates that developmental assessment instruments be used in conjunction with observations of the child and a parent report.

A number of commonly used instruments are designed for a broad age range of young children, ages birth through 2 years and older. For example, the *Bayley Scales of Infant Development II* can be used with children ages 1 to 42 months; the *Battelle Developmental Inventory* is designed for children birth to 8 years.

Other instruments, including criterion-referenced tests and checklists, provide age range expectations and can be helpful in monitoring progress. Table 12.4 lists these selected instruments and summarizes key areas of information.

CONCERNS REGARDING THE ASSESSMENT OF YOUNG CHILDREN

Practitioners should be aware of a number of issues regarding developmental assessment. First, instruments that focus on assessment of infants, toddlers, and preschoolers typically include the following developmental domains: cognitive, expressive and receptive language, fine and gross motor, and adaptive. Notice that these are not exactly the same as the domains included under the term *developmental delay* that was described earlier in this chapter. Many commonly used instruments do not include the social-emotional domain. Yet this area is perhaps one of the most critical in increasing opportunities for young children of differing abilities to play and work together.

In discussing appropriate practices for primary grades serving 5- through 8-year-olds, the National Association for the Education of Young Children (NAEYC) describes the importance of viewing domains of development as integrated.

> Development in one dimension influences and is influenced by development in other dimensions. This premise is violated when schools place a great emphasis on the cognitive domain while minimizing other aspects of children's development. Because development cannot be neatly separated into parts, failure to attend to all aspects of an individual child's development is often the root cause of a child's failure in school. For example, when a child lacks social skills and is neglected or rejected by peers, her or his ability to work cooperatively in a school setting is impaired (Bredekamp, 1987, p. 63).

BOX 12.3

BATTELLE DEVELOPMENTAL INVENTORY

Publication Date: 1988

Purposes: Assesses development in the following areas: personal-social, adaptive, motor, communication, and cognitive.

Age/Grade Levels: Birth through 8 years of age.

Time to Administer: Approximately 60 minutes for infants and toddlers; 90 minutes to 2 hours for children 3 and up.

Technical Adequacy: The instrument was standardized in the mid- to late 1980s and needs to be restandardized to reflect changes in the diversity of the U.S. population. Reliability and validity are adequate.

Suggested Use: This full assessment battery can be used as part of a multidisciplinary assessment of young children.

SNAPSHOT

Bennie Knight

Bennie Knight is a shy, 36-month-old child who has frequent colds, earaches, and fevers. When he isn't sick, he likes to ride on the family tractor. At the urging of Grandmother, Bennie's father brought him to a well-baby and screening clinic in their rural community. Grandmother was concerned about Bennie's health and his slow development. Just recently he had begun to talk in complete sentences.

As part of the screening process, the *Denver Developmental Screening Test II* (*DDST II*) was given to Bennie, as it was to each child who came to the screening clinic. Based on observations conducted during the screening, the parent's report, and the *DDST II*, Bennie was referred to the Developmental Evaluation Clinic for a comprehensive assessment.

At the Developmental Evaluation Clinic, the assessment team included a physician, a physical therapist, a speech and language pathologist, a psychologist, an educator, and a social worker. Bennie's appointment lasted all morning and part of the afternoon. During this time, each member of the team observed or assessed Bennie and spoke with his dad.

For Bennie and his family, the developmental assessment will be helpful in answering questions about his development: Is there a developmental delay? Does he qualify for special services? What are the child's needs? What skills are developing?

BOX 12.4

DENVER DEVELOPMENTAL SCREENING TEST II

Publication Date: 1990

Purposes: A screening tool which assesses the following areas: personal-social, fine motor-adaptive, language, and gross motor.

Age/Grade Levels: Birth through 5 years, 11 months.

Time to Administer: Approximately 5 to 10 minutes.

Technical Adequacy: The standardization sample is not representative; additional information is needed concerning reliability and validity.

Suggested Use: Screening children for possible problems and monitoring children at risk for developmental problems.

In conducting assessment, examiners use various tools to collect information about the child in various developmental areas. Team members work together in interpreting results and in planning special services for the child based on these needs. In the process, the team must keep in mind that development in any one area is not separate and distinct from development in other areas.

Another concern is the fact that criterion-referenced tests group items by the age at which children who are developing typically ac-

SNAPSHOT

The Hodgkin Family

The Hodgkin family consists of Danny, age 4, Joe, age 7, and their parents. Shortly after birth, Danny was identified as having Trisomy 21 (Down syndrome). Danny and his family have been involved in early intervention services since he was a baby. For the past two years, an early intervention specialist has conducted weekly home visits, helping Danny in his development. Recently, his parents have become increasing concerned with Danny's lack of progress in talking. An evaluation completed by a speech and language pathologist includes a suggestion that the family begin to explore teaching Danny sign language. Both of Danny's parents hope that he will be able to go to a neighborhood preschool in the fall. Figure 12.3 illustrates a portion of Danny's IFSP which provides an opportunity for parents to indicate the areas that are important to them.

Figure 12.3 also illustrates a way of completing family-directed assessment. (In Chapter 2 we discussed several other methods.) Based on family concerns, priorities, and resources as they relate to Danny's development, the team will identify one or more outcome statements that describe what they would like to work on in the next six months. The outcome statements will guide the choice of services to be delivered. In Danny's IFSP, the outcome statements reflect both child and family outcomes:

Major Outcomes: Child
Danny will learn to communicate in order to make his needs known.
Major Outcomes: Family
Mr. and Mrs. Hodgkin will receive information about parent groups in the community in order to meet other parents and receive peer parent support regarding issues of mutual interest including learning more about using sign language.

Individualized Family Service Plan: Family Considerations

Child's name: _Danny Hodgkin_ Person providing information _Mrs. Hodgkin_

1. Please describe your child (likes, dislikes, and strengths)

Danny is a happy, outgoing child. He has not been sick over the last 6 months. He seems to understand a lot that is said to him.

2. What are your concerns or how would you describe your child's needs?

We are worried about his lack of talking-and his slow progress in speech therapy.

3. What do you believe the strengths of your family are in meeting the child's needs?

My husband spends time playing with Danny and takes him shopping.

4. What would be helpful for your child and family?

To understand how to help Danny more. We want to understand what he wants and what he is trying to tell us.

5. Which of the following are concerns or areas about which you would like more information?

About the child

____ feeding
_X_ communicating
_X_ learning
____ vision or hearing
____ problem behaviors
____ equipment or supplies

About the family

_X_ meeting other families whose child has similar needs
_X_ finding out more about different services
____ child care
_X_ transportation
____ information about my child's disability
____ information about SSI or Medicaid

6. Are there other concerns which you would like to discuss at the IFSP meeting?

We would like to meet families who use sign language with their children.

FIGURE 12.3

From Danny's IFSP

quire that skill. However, development may not occur this way, particularly for children with special needs. For example, children who are blind can lag behind their peers in gross-motor development. In addition, acquisition of certain skills may not follow the same sequence as children with normal vision. In planning and monitoring progress of children, team members will want to supplement criterion-referenced assessment information with observations, videos and audiotapes, and other assessment approaches.

WORKING WITH FAMILIES

For some parents, learning that their child has a disability comes as a surprise; but for other parents, the finding comes as a relief. These parents may have had questions and concerns

---

- Provide family members with an opportunity to receive the assessment report in a one-to-one setting rather than during a large IFSP or IEP team meeting. This meeting allows the family time to ask questions with an empathetic practitioner and to reflect on the information prior to the larger, full-staff meeting.
- Share information with both parents (or major caregivers) at the same time.
- Be honest and straightforward regarding the disability.
- Be willing to say when you don't know.
- Allow time for families to express their feelings.
- Be sensitive to families if they are not ready to hear details.
- Offer to provide additional information.
- Suggest additional resources.
- Be available to the family for further discussions.
- Arrange to have a native language interpreter available if families need assistance.

FIGURE 12.4

Tips for Sharing Eligibility Information with Families

for some time regarding their child's development. Figure 12.4 presents a number of general tips for sharing assessment information with family members.

In sharing knowledge and information, respect the point where the family is at any one period of time. One strategy is to offer choices. For example, in discussing the results of a diagnostic assessment which were inconclusive, the practitioner might ask, "Do you want to know the range of options or just the more likely?"

Be honest. Say "I don't know" when you don't, but also always follow up with "I'll find out" or "The field just doesn't know at this point."

TRANSITION AND ASSESSMENT

Children with special needs and their families are usually involved in transitions during three time periods: first, when the child turns 3 years old and moves from infant and toddler early intervention to preschool services; second, when the child turns 5 years old and moves from preschool to school-age services; and, third, when the young adult leaves the education system and moves to the community, work, or further education. Transition is often a difficult time for children and families, perhaps because of a new school program, new teachers and therapists, or new procedures. Rosenkoetter, Hains, and Fowler (1994) describe **transition** as times during which children and families begin working with a new set of professionals, start attending new programs, adjust to new schedules and customs, accept altered expectations and meet new challenges and opportunities. Figure 12.5 identifies areas of change experienced during the transition process.

Transitions involve careful planning by the early childhood team so that the movement between programs can be successful. Assessment questions that the team addresses involve aspects of the new program and needs of

Seamless Transition Practices by Component and Age Group

Component	Age Group		
	(0–3 years)	*(4–15 years)*	*(16–21 years)*
Curriculum	• Neurobehavioral • Developmentally appropriate • Activity-based • Play-based • Social interaction • Child-directed	• Academics applied to work, community, and daily living • Prevocational skills • Life-based approach • Socialization and independence • Self-determination • Advocacy skills	• Academic • Functional life skills • Vocational evaluation • Employment skills • Inclusive adult world • Independent living • Life-long learners
Location	• Hospital • Home • Day care • Communities	• Preschool • Elementary schools • Middle schools • Communities	• Schools • Communities • Employment settings • Residential settings
Futures planning	• IFSP document with transition plans • ICC transition plans • Family-centered	• IEP document with transition plans • Family/student-centered	• Transition IEP document • Family/school-centered • Postschool outcome orientation
Multiagency collaboration	• Interagency Collaborative Councils (ICCs) • Public/private day care personnel • Agency personnel (school, work, medical, community)	• ICCs • School advisory councils • Agency personnel (school, work, medical, community)	• ICCs • School advisory councils • Agency personnel (school, work, medical community) • Adult service provides
Family and student focus	• Family-centered • Family as service coordinator • Family needs and outcomes • Family service centers • Family empowerment	• Family/student centered • Family as service coordinator • Support groups • Family service centers • Family and student advocacy	• Family/student centered • Family/student as service coordinator • Family service centers • Self-advocacy

FIGURE 12.5

Transition Practices by Component and Age Group

Source: Repetto, J. B., and V. I. Correa (1996). Expanding views on transition. *Exceptional Children* 62(6): 551–563. Reprinted with the permission of the publisher.

the child. Let's examine some of the transition questions regarding the new program.

• What is the physical layout of the room, and what types of adaptations to the environment will be needed?

• What materials are available, and are they accessible to children?

• What are the classroom routines and expectations of children?

For example: Do children have a designated place for their clothing and materials?

TABLE 12.5 Characteristics Identified as Important for Entering Kindergarten

Child characteristics	Kindergarten teachers	Parents
Communicates wants and needs verbally	84%	92%
Shares and takes turns	56%	92%
Approaches new activities with enthusiasm and curiosity	76%	84%
Sits still and pays attention	42%	80%
Uses pencil or paintbrushes	21%	65%
Counts to 20 or more	7%	59%
Knows the letters of the alphabet	10%	58%

Adapted from National Center for Education Statistics (1993). Readiness for kindergarten: Parent and teacher beliefs. NCES Publication No. NCES 93-257. Washington, D.C.: U.S. Department of Education, Office of Educational Research and Improvement.

Are the children permitted to carry materials from one center to other centers?

• What are the classroom procedures?

For example: Do children clean up after themselves?

Do children obtain and return materials independently?

Are some centers limited in the number of children at any one time?

A teacher can collect information about the new program by means of a checklist or rating scale. By identifying this information early, adaptations to the environment can be completed and children can be taught some of the routines or exposed to new procedures before entering the new program.

Transition assessment also includes identifying the skills that will be helpful to the child in the new program. Transition activities provide opportunities for parents and teachers to work together, to exchange information, and to build common understandings before a child enters a new program. Sometimes parents and teachers have different expectations. In one study,

kindergarten teachers identified social skills as being important to beginning kindergarten; whereas parents identified more academic skills (Table 12.5).

During transition activities, parents and early childhood teachers and caregivers have increased opportunities to facilitate skills before the child enters kindergarten. A checklist (Figure 12.6) for teachers and parents is helpful in collecting this information.

Transition assessment should never be used to exclude children from programs. Transition assessment does not mean assessing school readiness. Rather, it is designed to identify the needs and supports that will make entry into the new program as successful as possible.

ASSESSING SCHOOL READINESS

Teachers and other educators working with young children are often asked questions about a child's "readiness" for school. The concept that children must obtain certain skills before

Communication	Yes	No
1. Communicates wants and needs		
2. Follows adult requests		
3. Follows two-step directions		
4. Initiates and maintains peer interaction		
Communication supports needed:		

Social-emotional		
1. Shares toys and materials with others		
2. Respects others' property		
3. Expresses emotions appropriately		
4. Takes turns		
Social-emotional supports needed:		

Adaptive		
1. Puts on and takes off outer clothing		
2. Cleans up after oneself		
3. Cares for toileting needs		
4. Eats independently		
Adaptive supports needed:		

FIGURE 12.6

Checklist for Transitioning into Kindergarten

Adapted from Chandler, L. (1993). Steps in preparing for transition: Preschool to kindergarten. *Teaching Exceptional Children* 25(4): 52–55.

entering school is troublesome for many educators. Tests of school readiness are usually administered before children enter school. Typically, readiness tests are derived from the behaviorists tradition, which holds that learning can be separated into constituent parts or subskills (Shepard, 1990).

Academic readiness tests are a form of high-stakes testing because they are frequently used to make decisions about children's entrance into school. High-stakes testing, as we have discussed before, is the use of readiness or achievements tests to make classification, retention, or promotion decisions about children (Meisels, 1989). A child's performance on a school readiness test can be used to determine whether the child will be (1) asked to delay entrance into school; (2) allowed to enter school with the child's age-mates; (3) identified as at-risk and asked to participate in additional testing; or (4) asked to participate in a special class before entering kindergarten. The latter decision is viewed by many experts as a form of retention. Thus, a child can be retained before actually entering school!

Shepard (1990) believes that the research on readiness, especially on reading readiness, is "outmoded and seriously flawed" (p. 169) and inadequate. The tests rely on outdated theories in which learning is fragmented into skills and subskills. The child is supposed to somehow integrate these skills at a later time. Another criticism of school readiness tests is that they lack predictive validity. That is, for the most part, there are limited data on how accurately school readiness tests predict performance in school.

In addition, these tests are inadequate as technical bases for such decisions about school placements as those involving special education placements, two-year kindergarten placements, and delays in school entry (Shepard, 1990).

In contrast to the notion that "children must be ready for school" is the idea that "schools must be ready for children." The Division for Early Childhood of the Council for Exceptional Children (1992) published a position paper that stated that schools should be ready to accept and effectively educate all children. Children should not be screened into or out of early education programs; rather, all children must have an opportunity to learn. Teachers must receive training in a wide variety of developmentally appropriate curricula, materials, and procedures to maximize each child's growth and development. Schooling will succeed or fail, not children.

PREFERRED PRACTICES

Teachers and other professionals need to become familiar with the characteristics of good screening and developmental assessments. The use of observations and the careful recording of data must be integral aspects of assessing young children. Sensitivity to parent concerns and involvement of parents and caregivers throughout the assessment process are key components in working with young children.

Teachers and therapists have to guard against planning the child's program based solely on test performance. Items that the child fails should not be identified by the team as discrete items that need to be taught. For example, from the test item "Child stacks 3 blocks," an inappropriate objective would be, "Randy will stack 3 blocks." A more appropriate programming activity would be to provide the child opportunities to manipulate a variety of materials in different ways, one of which might involve stacking.

Finally, assessment should not be used to determine if children are "ready" for school or to delay children's entrance into school until they reach a certain level. Rather, children who are entering school for the first time can be helped by a transition assessment that identifies needs and supports to make entry into the new program successful.

EXTENDING LEARNING

12.1 Research the position statements of two or more professional organizations such as Division of Early Childhood (DEC), a subdivision of the Council for Exceptional Children (CEC); the National Association for the Education of Young Children (NAEYC); or The Association of Persons with Severe Handicaps (TASH). What are their positions regarding the assessment of young children? How do these positions compare? Develop your own position statement.

12.2 Contact your state department of education regarding the eligibility system used for young children. How is eligibility determined? What criteria are used? Does your state use "developmental delay" or other terms in determining eligibility for special services for young children? If so, how is a developmental delay determined?

12.3 Conduct a comprehensive review of several screening instruments. Compare how they are administered, standardized, and scored. What do the manuals state about reliability and validity?

12.4 A young child was referred for a comprehensive assessment based on his screening results. After examining the results of the comprehensive assessment, team members decided that the child was developing typically and there was no indication of delay. Explain several possible reasons that the child was referred based on the screening test.

12.5 Review two or three developmental assessment instruments. Compare the test items for a particular age group. What are the similarities? How are the items different? If you are assessing for the purpose of planning the child's program, which test items would provide the most helpful information?

12.6 Refer to the Snapshot that describes "special challenges." Choose one family and discuss how their situation will affect the assessment process.

12.7 Make arrangements to visit a kindergarten or community screening program. What are the components of the screening program? Compare your visit and observations with the Snapshot of Luiz. Present your observations to the class.

12.8 Kindergarten screening tests are a form of high-stakes testing. What other tests that students take are also a form of high-stakes testing?

REFERENCES

Bagnato, S. J., and J. T. Neisworth (1990). *System to plan early childhood services (SPECS).* Circle Pines, Minn.: American Guidance Service.

Barr, R. G. (1989). Recasting a clinical enigma: The case of infant crying. In *Challenges to developmental paradigms: Implications for theory, assessment, and treatment,* eds. P. R. Zelazo and R. G. Barr, 43–64. Hillsdale, N.J.: Lawrence Erlbaum Associates.

Bayley, N. (1993). *Bayley scales of infant development.* 2d ed. San Antonio, Tex.: The Psychological Corp.

Bredekamp, S. (Ed.). (1987). *Developmentally appropriate practice in early childhood programs serving children from birth through age 8.* Washington, D.C.: National Association for the Education of Young Children.

Brigance, A. H. (1985). *BRIGANCE® preschool screen for three- and four-year-old children.* No. Billerica, Mass.: Curriculum Associates, Inc.

Brigance, A. H. (1991). *BRIGANCE® diagnostic inventory of early development–Revised.* No. Billerica, Mass.: Curriculum Associates, Inc.

Chandler, L. (1993). Steps in preparing for transition: Preschool to kindergarten. *Teaching Exceptional Children* 25(4): 52–55.

Division for Early Childhood of the Council for Exceptional Children (1992). DEC position statement on goal one of America 2000: All children should begin school ready to learn. *DEC Communicator* 19(3): 4.

Flagler, S. (1996). *Infant-preschool play assessment scale.* Lewisville, N.C.: Kaplan.

Frankenburg, W. K., and J. B. Dodds (1990). *Denver II screening manual.* Denver, Colo.: Denver Developmental Materials, Inc.

Greenspan, S. I., and S. Meisels (1993). Toward a new vision for the developmental assessment of infants and young children. Paper presented at the Zero to Three/National Center for Clinical Infant Programs' Eighth Biennial National Training Institute, December, Washington, D.C.

Harrison, P. L., A. S. Kaufman, N. L. Kaufman, R. H. Bruininks, J. Rynders, S. Ilmer, S. S. Sparrow, and D. V. Cicchetti (1990). *AGS early screening profiles.* Circle Pines, Minn.: American Guidance Service.

Ireton, H. R. (1992). *Child development inventory.* Minneapolis, Minn.: Behavior Science Systems, Inc.

Johnson-Martin, N. M., S. M. Attermeier, and B. J. Hacker (1990). *The Carolina curriculum for preschoolers with special needs.* Baltimore: Paul Brookes.

Kaufman, A. S., and N. L. Kaufman (1993). *Kaufman survey of early academic and language skills.* Circle Pines, Minn.: American Guidance Service.

Mardell-Czudnowski, C., and D. S. Goldenberg (1990). *Developmental indicators for the assessment of learning–Revised (DIAL-R).* Circle Pines, Minn.: American Guidance Service.

McCarthy, J. M., K. A. Lund, and C. S. Bos (1986). *ABACUS system manual.* Book One. Denver: Love.

McLean, M., B. J. Smith, K. McCormick, J. Schakel, and M. McEvoy (1991). *Developmental delay: Establishing parameters for a preschool category of exceptionality.* DEC Position Paper. Reston, Va.: Council for Exceptional Children.

Meisels, S. J. (1989). High-stakes testing in kindergarten. *Educational Leadership* 46(7): 16–22.

Meisels, S. J., and M. S. Wiske (1988). *Early screening inventory.* New York: Teachers College Press.

Meisels, S. J., and B. A. Wasik (1990). Who should be served? Identifying children in need of early intervention. In *Handbook of early childhood intervention,* eds. S. J. Meisels and J. P. Shonkoff, 605–632. Cambridge: Cambridge University Press.

Miller, L. J. (1992). *FirstSTEP: Screening test for evaluating preschoolers.* San Antonio, Tex.: The Psychological Corporation, Harcourt Brace.

Mullen, E. M. (1995). *Mullen scales of early learning.* Circle Pines, Minn.: American Guidance Service.

National Center for Education Statistics. (1993). *Readiness for kindergarten: Parent and teacher beliefs.* NCES Publication No. NCES 93-257. Washington, D.C.: U.S. Department of Education, Office of Educational Research and Improvement.

Newborg, J., J. R. Stock, and L. Wnek (1988). *Battelle developmental inventory.* Allen, Tex.: DLM.

Newborg, J., J. R. Stock, L. Wnek, J. Guidubaldi, and J. Sviniski (1988). *Battelle developmental inventory screening test.* Allen, Tex.: DLM.

Repetto, J. B., and V. I. Correa (1996). Expanding views on transition. *Exceptional Children* 62(6): 551–563.

Rosenkoetter, S. E., A. H. Hains, and S. A. Fowler (1994). *Bridging early services for children with special needs and their families.* Baltimore: Paul H. Brookes.

Shepard, L. (1990). Readiness testing in local school districts: An analysis of backdoor policies. *Journal of Education Policy* 5(5): 159–179.

Snyder, P., D. B. Bailey, and C. Auger (1994). Preschool eligibility determination for children wtih known or suspected learning disabilities under IDEA. *Journal of Early Intervention* 18(4): 380–390.

VORT Corporation. (1995). *HELP for preschoolers.* Palo Alto, CA: Author.

Cognitive Development

OVERVIEW

What is intelligence? What makes us intelligent? The nature of intelligence has received a great deal of attention over the years. One view of intelligence is that it is an arbitrary concept, impossible to define or quantify. Other views are that intelligence consists of multifaceted, complex, highly organized abilities that can be identified and measured. One common conception of intelligence is that it is the ability to apply prior knowledge to new situations. As specific intelligence tests are described in this chapter, you will see that they are not based on one common view of the construct of intelligence.

CHAPTER OBJECTIVES

After completing this chapter, you should be able to:

Explain the concept of intelligence tests as samples of behavior.

Discuss the stability of test performance.

Describe specific tests of intelligence.

WHAT SHAPES OUR VIEWS

Although there is still a great deal that we do not know about intelligence, Sternberg (1996) has described nine "truths" about intelligence:

1. Intelligence is multidimensional. There is still a great deal that we have to learn about the dimensions of intelligence.
2. The social order in our society has been partially created by tests. Tests are used to sort and categorize people according to the abilities measured by the tests.
3. Intelligence can be taught to some extent, but extreme changes are unlikely at this time.
4. Intelligence tests measure skills that are of average importance in school and of moderate importance in success on the job.
5. Intelligence tests can be useful when measuring abilities. However, in order to be useful, tests must be used and interpreted properly.
6. Intelligence test scores have been rising since the 1930s in the United States and in other countries.
7. Intelligence is the result of the influences of heredity and environment.
8. We still have much to learn about the relationships between race, intelligence, and environment.
9. While tests of intelligence provide an indication of cognitive skills, they are not measures of the worth of individuals.

INTELLIGENCE TESTS AS SAMPLES OF BEHAVIOR

If we were able to measure intelligence directly, we would have to monitor the electrical activities, neurochemical changes, and neurobiological changes that occur during cognition. As educators, we rely on indirect measures or tests to estimate intelligence. Intelligence tests only sample behaviors that are associated with intelligence. Like a knife cutting through a cake, the knife reveals a sample of the cake. We assume that the texture and flavor of the cake is the same in the uncut or unsampled portion. This same analogy can be applied to intelligence tests. While the tests sample behaviors, our assumption is that the sample provides information about the intellectual abilities of the individual.

Although there are many intelligence tests, an analysis of them shows that they sample similar behaviors. Salvia and Ysseldyke (1995) have described these behaviors:

1. Discrimination—Intelligence tests sample skills that relate to figural, symbolic, or semantic discrimination usually by asking the student to find the item that is different from the other items.
2. Generalization—Skills relating to figural, symbolic, or semantic understanding are sampled. The student is asked to recognize the response that goes with the stimulus item.
3. Motor Behavior—Young children are asked to demonstrate a motor response. For instance, they are asked to throw objects, construct block towers, and place objects in certain places on a board. Older students are asked to draw geometric forms, solve mazes, or reproduce designs from memory. In addition to these items, many other test items evaluate motor abilities because students are asked to point, imitate, or perform other motor activities in order to complete certain test items.
4. General Information—These items are similar to items that are found on many achievement tests; they evaluate what the individual has learned. Examples of these items include, "What is the opposite of uncle?" and "How many eggs are in a dozen?"
5. Vocabulary—Intelligence tests assess knowledge of vocabulary in different ways. The

individual may be asked to point to a picture that has been named, to define words that are presented orally, or to identify a word that matches a definition.

6. Induction—Students are asked to induce or to infer a general principle after being presented with several stimuli. For example, after being shown a rock, block of wood, metal object, and a toothpick, the individual is asked to describe the general rule about why certain objects float.

7. Comprehension—The student is asked to demonstrate understanding of or the nature of meaning of certain stimuli. The student may be asked to show that directions, certain materials, or societal customs are understood. Some tests ask the student to respond to certain situations such as, "What should you do if you see a young child playing with an electrical cord?"

8. Sequencing—The student is required to identify the correct sequences for a series of items. The items can, for example, consist of numbers, geometric figures, or abstract geometric designs.

9. Detail Recognition—A few tests evaluate detail recognition. The individual is asked to identify details that are missing from a picture or is asked to draw a picture that will be evaluated on the basis of how many details the individual included in the drawing.

10. Analogies—Items consist of a statement to which the student must give the appropriate response. The stimuli may consist of a series of words, geometric designs, or numbers. An example of an item is: parent : child :: goose : .

11. Abstract Reasoning—Various types of items assess abstract reasoning. Students can be asked to identify the absurdity in a statement or picture, to state the meaning of a proverb, or to solve problems of arithmetic reasoning.

12. Memory—A variety of test items evaluate both long-term and short-term memory. Students are asked to repeat sentences, a series of digits, to retell what they have read, or to reproduce a design from memory.

13. Pattern Completion—Students are asked to complete a pattern or matrix that has a missing piece.

There are many behaviors that intelligence tests do not sample. These behaviors include mechanical, musical, artistic, motivational, emotional, and attitudinal behaviors (Anastasi, 1988). Recent research on the nature of intelligence has begun to explore the contribution of these behaviors to our understanding of intelligence.

RESPONDING TO DIVERSITY

The value of intelligence testing has been debated over the years. Arguments against the use of intelligence testing include that testing limits opportunities, can be harmful to individuals from various cultural and ethnic groups, and facilitates the placement of students into categories. Advocates of intelligence testing have argued that intelligence testing assists in diagnosis, helps to identify individuals who need specialized instruction or therapy, and promotes educational opportunities (Sattler, 1988).

The score on an intelligence test can be affected by membership in a cultural or ethnic group, socioeconomic status, educational attainment, language, and acculturation. Bias in the assessment of intelligence is reduced or prevented by being: 1) aware of individual characteristics; 2) knowledgeable in test use and test selection; and 3) sensitive when adminstering, scoring, and interpreting performance (Suzuki, Vraniak, and Kugler, 1996).

Intelligence tests provide us with only a part of what we want to know about an individual. The assessment of individuals should never be dependent on the results of one test; rather, good practice requires that the results of additional standardized tests as well as observations, interviews, checklists, rating scales, samples of work, and other types of assessment be used in appropriate combination to gather information.

In summary, it is important to remember that:

- intelligence tests do not measure innate ability

- intelligence test scores change as individuals become older
- intelligence test scores are estimates, or approximations, of abilities
- intelligence is one of many abilities that individuals have

TABLE 13.1   Tests of Intelligence

Test	Abilities measured
Arthur Adaptation: Leiter International Performance Scale (Arthur, 1990)	Measures nonverbal intelligences; ages 2 through 12
*Batería-R Tests of Cognitive Ability (Woodcock & Muñoz-Sandoval, 1996)	Spanish version of the Woodcock-Johnson Psychoeducational Battery–Revised; measures cognitive ability, scholastic aptitude, and Spanish oral language
Blind Learning Aptitude Test (Newland, 1969)	Uses a bas-relief format; assesses discrimination, generalization, sequencing, analogies, and matrix completion; ages 6 through 12
Cognitive Abilities Test, Form 5 (Thorndike & Hagan, 1993)	Group intelligence test; grades kindergarten through 12
Columbia Mental Maturity Scale (Burgenmeister, Blum, & Lorge, 1972)	Nonverbal tests; ages 3.6 through 9.11
Comprehensive Test of Nonverbal Intelligence (CTONI) (Hammill, Pearson, & Wiederholt, 1996)	Measures nonverbal problems solving and reasoning; ages 6 through 18.11
Detroit Tests of Learning Aptitude-Primary (Second Edition) (Hammill & Bryant, 1991)	Assesses abilities in three domains: linguistic, attentional, motoric; ages 3 years through 9 years, 11 months
Detroit Tests of Learning Aptitude-3 (Hammill, 1991)	Measures intelligence, aptitude, and achievement; ages 6 through 17
Differential Ability Scales (Elliott, 1990a)	Measures cognitive ability and achievement; ages 2 years, 6 months through 17 years, 11 months
*Escala de inteligencia Wechsler para niños–Revisada de Puerto Rico (EIWN-R PR) (1993)	Spanish adaptation of the WISC-R. Normed on 2,200 Puerto Rican children, ages 6 years through 16 years, 11 months
*Escala de inteligencia Wechsler para Niños–Revisada (EIWN-R) (1983)	Spanish adaptation of the WISC-R. Published without norms, it is intended for use with Chicano, Puerto Rican, and Cuban children
Griffiths Mental Development Scales (Griffiths, 1979)	Useful with nonverbal children; ages birth through 8 years

*Spanish form

- intelligence scores from various intelligence tests may not have the same meaning
- multiple methods and types of assessment need to be used when assessing an individual (NAEYC Position Statement, 1988, cited in Sattler, 1988).

STANDARDIZED INSTRUMENTS

Many of the commonly available tests of intelligence and some of their application characteristics are presented in Table 13.1.

TABLE 13.1 (Continued)

Test	Abilities measured
Kaufman Adolescent & Adult Intelligence Test (Kaufman & Kaufman, 1993)	Measures general intelligence; ages 11 years through 85+
Kaufman Assessment Battery for Children (Kaufman & Kaufman, 1983)	Measures mental ability and achievement; ages 2.6 through 12.6
Kaufman Brief Intelligence Test (Kaufman & Kaufman, 1990)	Measures verbal and nonverbal intelligence; ages 4 through 90
McCarthy Scales of Children's Abilities (McCarthy, 1972)	Assesses general intellectual ability; ages 2.6 through 8.6
Nebraska Test of Learning Aptitude (Hiskey, 1966)	Assesses learning aptitude of children who are deaf or hearing impaired; ages 3 through 16 years
Perkins-Binet Tests of Intelligence for the Blind (Davis, 1980)	Assesses cognitive ability of children who are blind; ages 4 to 8 years
Pictorial Test of Intelligence (French, 1964)	Children respond either by pointing to the correct response or by movement of the eyes; ages 3 to 8 years
Slosson Full-Range Intelligence Test (SFRIT-R) (Slosson, 1991)	Assesses verbal intelligence; ages 4 through 65
Slosson Intelligence Test Revised (SIT-R) (Algozzine, Eaves, Mann, & Vance, 1993)	Assesses verbal skills, quantitative abilities, memory, abstract reasoning; ages 5 through adult
Stanford-Binet Intelligence Scale: Fourth Edition (Thorndike, Hagan, & Sattler, 1986a)	Assesses cognitive abilities; ages 2 through 23
Test of Nonverbal Intelligence-2 (Brown, Sherbenou, & Johnsen, 1990)	Measures abstract figural problem solving; ages 5 through 85 years, 11 months
Wechsler Intelligence Scale for Children–III (Wechsler, 1991)	Assesses global intellectual ability; ages 6 through 16 years, 11 months
Wechsler Preschool and Primary Scale of Intelligence–Revised (Wechsler, 1989)	Measures general intellectual ability; ages 3 through 7
Woodcock-Johnson Psychoeducational Battery–Revised (Woodcock & Johnson, 1989)	Assesses cognitive and academic abilities; ages 2 through adult

Batería-R

The *Batería-R COG* and the *Batería-R ACH* (Woodcock and Muñoz-Sandoval, 1996) form a parallel Spanish version of the *Woodcock-Johnson Psychoeducational Battery–Revised*. The *Batería-R COG* and *ACH* is an individually administered battery that assesses cognitive, academic, and language abilities in Spanish-speaking individuals ages 2 years through adulthood. The battery consists of two parts, Tests of Cognitive Ability (*Batería-R COG*) and the Tests of Achievement (*Batería-R ACH*).

Like the *Woodcock-Johnson Psychoeducational Battery–Revised,* the *Batería-R COG* is based on the Horn-Cattell theory of cognitive processing. A discussion of this theory can be found in the description of the *Woodcock-Johnson Psychoeducational Battery–Revised* later in this chapter.

Administration

The time to administer the *Batería-R* varies from 20 minutes to more than one hour, depending on whether both parts are administered. Raw scores are converted to age and grade equivalents, percentile ranks, and standard scores. The scoring can be cumbersome and it is advisable to use a computer scoring program.

Technical Adequacy

Technical adequacy of the *Batería-R* is based on the *Woodcock-Johnson Psychoeducational Battery–Revised (WJ-R)*. The standardization sample of the *WJ-R* was used to develop the scoring procedures and other technical information for the *Batería-R*. The *Batería-R* was calibrated on 3,911 native Spanish-speaking individuals from Costa Rica, Mexico, Peru, Puerto Rico, Spain, Arizona, California, Florida, New York, and Texas. The purpose of this calibration was to develop a parallel form of the *WJ-R*.

The authors argue that because the *Batería-R* has been calibrated with the *WJ-R,* reliability and validity information from the *Woodcock-Johnson Psychoeducational Battery-R* can be used with this test.

Summary

The *Batería-R COG* and the *Batería-R ACH* (Woodcock and Muñoz-Sandoval, 1996) form a parallel Spanish version of the *Woodcock-Johnson Psychoeducational Battery–Revised*. This a norm-referenced, individually administered battery that assesses cognitive, academic, and language abilities in Spanish-speaking individuals ages 24 months through adulthood. Reliability information is lacking. Additional investigation of validity is warranted.

BOX 13.1

BATERÍA-R

Publication Date: 1996

Purposes: The Batería-R is a parallel Spanish version of the Woodcock-Johnson Psychoeducational Battery–Revised. The Batería-R assesses cognitive, academic, and language abilities in Spanish-speaking individuals.

Age/Grade Levels: 2 years through adulthood; grades kindergarten through college

Time to Administer: one hour to more than two hours, depending on whether both the Tests of Cognitive Ability and the Tests of Achievement are administered.

Technical Adequacy: Reliability information is lacking. Additional investigation of validity is warranted.

Suggested Uses: Measures general cognitive abilities, aptitude, and achievement in Spanish-speaking students. Results should be cautiously used.

Cognitive Abilities Test

The *Cognitive Abilities Test, Form 5 (CogAT)* (Thorndike and Hagen, 1993) was developed from the Lorge-Thorndike Intelligence Tests and consists of a series of group-administered intelligence tests for students in grades kindergarten through 12. The *CogAT* assesses: 1) ability to follow directions; 2) ability to hold material in short-term memory; 3) strategies for scanning pictorial and figural stimuli to obtain either specific or general information; 4) general information and verbal concepts; 5) ability to compare stimuli and detect similarities and differences in relative size, position, quantity, shape, and time; 6) ability to classify, categorize, or order familiar objects; and 7) ability to use quantitative and spatial relationships and concepts. Table 13.2 shows the batteries and subtests of the *CogAT*.

Administration

The teacher reads aloud all of the directions for Levels 1 and 2. Students are not required to read but must be able to follow the directions of the teacher. The student's responses are limited to identifying the one correct response by filling in an oval. Levels A-H are administered to groups of students, rather than to individual students.

Scoring

Separate scores are obtained for the Verbal, Quantitative, and Nonverbal batteries. There is a Composite score. Scores are not reported for the individual subtests. Scores that are reported include percentiles, stanines, and standard scores.

Standardization

The *CogAT* was normed at the same time as the *Iowa Tests of Basic Skills* and the *Tests of Achievement and Proficiency*. Public schools across the United States were stratified according to geographic region, enrollment, and socioeconomic status. In addition, private non-Catholic schools and Catholic schools were also sampled.

Reliability

Internal consistency reliability is acceptable. No other types of reliability are reported.

Validity

Evidence of validity is absent from the manual.

Summary

The *Cognitive Abilities Test, Form 5* is a group intelligence test that is intended for students in kindergarten through grade 12. While the standardization of this test is commendable, evidence of reliability and validity is lacking.

Comprehensive Test of Nonverbal Intelligence

The *Comprehensive Test of Nonverbal Intelligence (CTONI)* (Hammill, Pearson, and Wieder-

---

TABLE 13.2 CogAT Subtests

Level	Verbal battery	Quantitative battery	Nonverbal battery
The CogAT consists of Levels 1 and 2 for students in grades kindergarten through grade 3, and Levels A-H for students in grades 3 through 12.	Verbal Reasoning Oral Vocabulary	Relational Concepts Quantitative Concepts	Figure Classification Matrices
Levels A-H contain three separate batteries: Verbal Battery, Quantitative Battery, and the Nonverbal Battery.	Verbal Classification Sentence Completion Verbal Analogies	Quantitative Relations Number Series Equation Building	Figure Classification Figure Analogies Figure Analysis

holt, 1996) is a nonverbal measure of abstract/figural problem solving and reasoning for use with individuals ages 6 years through 18 years, 11 months. It can be used when assessing the performance of individuals who have language or motor problems that in some cases make it difficult for them to respond to more traditional tests. The test is arranged into six subtests: Pictorial Analogies, Geometric Analogies, Pictorial Categories, Geometric Categories, Pictorial Sequences, and Geometric Sequences. For each of these subtests, the examinee must solve a visual problem that either consists of pictures (e.g., shoe, ball, cube) or geometric shapes (e.g., triangle, circle, diamond).

Administration

The test items are contained in an easel and the examiner can pantomime the instructions or give them orally. If the examiner chooses to pantomime the instructions, the examiner uses facial gestures, hand movements, and head movements. The student shows the correct response by pointing or by some other motor response. This nonverbal method of test administration does have several advantages. The examinee is not required to listen to directions, speak, read, or write. The test is untimed.

Scoring

Items are scored as either correct or incorrect. Raw scores are converted to standard scores, percentile ranks, and age equivalents.

Standardization

The *CTONI* standardization sample consisted of 2,129 individuals, ranging in age from 6 years to 18 years. It is unclear whether the sample was stratified according to major demographic variables. Characteristics of the sample are reported for age, gender, race (white, black, other), ethnic group (Native American, Hispanic, Asian, African American, other) geographic region, residence (rural, urban), family income, disability status, and educational background of the parents.

Reliability

Internal consistency reliability and test-retest reliability are reported. The average coefficient for internal consistency was .97. Test-retest reliability coefficients are only reported for students enrolled in third grade, eleventh grade, and the total sample. These coefficients ranged from .79 to .94.

Validity

Validity is concerned with determining whether a test measures what it purports to measure. While the manual reports the results of several validity studies, more extensive research must be conducted in order to determine whether this instrument measures the construct of intelligence and to determine its usefulness in measuring intellectural abilities of persons with disabilities.

Summary

The *CTONI* is a nonverbal measure that assesses visual problem solving and reasoning. Reliability is adequate. It should be used cautiously until additional information relating to validity can be gathered.

Detroit Tests of Learning Aptitude—Primary (Second Edition)

The *Detroit Tests of Learning Aptitude–Primary (Second Edition) (DTLA-P:2)* (Hammill and Bryant, 1991) is designed to measure the intellectual aptitudes or abilities of individuals ages 3 years, 0 months to 9 years, 11 months. This is the second edition of the *DTLA-P*. According to the authors, the *DTLA-P:2* has four uses: 1) to discover strengths and weaknesses among mental abilities, 2) to identify children who perform significantly below their peers, 3) to predict future performance, and 4) to aid as a research tool when investigating children's aptitude, intelligence, and cognitive ability. Depending on the child's age and abilities, the *DTLA-P* takes between 15 and 45 minutes to administer.

COMPREHENSIVE TEST OF NONVERBAL INTELLIGENCE

Publication Date: 1996
Purposes: Measures nonverbal abstract/figural problem solving and reasoning in individuals who have language or motor problems that may make it difficult for them to respond to more traditional tests.
Age/Grade Levels: Ages 6 years through 18 years, 11 months
Time to Administer: 20 to 45 minutes
Technical Adequacy: Information about the standardization sample is sparse. Reliability is adequate but additional information concerning validity is needed.
Suggested Use: The CTONI may be useful as a screening instrument. It should be used cautiously until additional information relating to validity can be gathered.

The *DTLA-P: 2* consists of 100 items arranged in order from the easiest to the most difficult. The items yield six subtest scores and a general, overall mental ability score. The six subtests and the domains in which they are grouped are as follows:

LINGUISTIC DOMAIN

1. Verbal Quotient—Assesses the understanding, integration, and use of spoken language.
2. Nonverbal Quotient—Assesses abilities involved in spatial relationships and nonverbal symbolic reasoning.

ATTENTIONAL DOMAIN

3. Attention-Enhanced Quotient—Evaluates immediate recall, memory, and ability to concentrate.
4. Attention-Reduced Quotient—Measures long-term memory, understanding, reasoning ability, and comprehension of abstract relationships.

MOTORIC DOMAIN

5. Motor-Enhanced Quotient—Assesses complex motor abilities, especially fine-motor abilities.
6. Motor-Reduced Quotient—Evaluates aptitude with reduced demands for motor activities. The child is asked to indicate the correct response by either pointing or speaking.

Administration

Examiners are expected to have some background in assessment. Directions for administration are on the test protocol. For some items, directions for administration are in the examiner's manual. The test is designed to be administered individually. Since the items are arranged from least to most difficult, the examiner begins testing at certain entry points. These entry points are determined by the student's chronological age. Testing continues until a ceiling is reached.

Scoring

The responses are scored either correct or incorrect. The scores for each item are used in the computation of the total score and the subtest scores. Raw scores can be converted to age equivalents, percentiles, and quotients, which are standard scores that have a mean of 100 and a standard deviation of 15.

Standardization

The standardization sample of the *DTLA-P:2* consisted of 2,095 children in 36 states. In developing this instrument, the authors used data from the standardization sample (March–June 1985) of the *DTLA-P* and tested an additional 619 children between September 1989 and June 1990. These two samples were then combined to form the standardization sample for the *DTLA-P:2*. Information on the percentage of children for each of the following variables is reported: gender, residence (urban, rural), race, geographic area (Northeast, North Central, South, West), ethnicity (American Indian, Hispanic, Asian, other), and age.

Reliability

Internal consistency reliability was estimated using a random sample of 350 protocols from the standardization sample. The average reliabilities for the total score and the six subtests ranged from .88 to .94. Test-retest reliability was also estimated. However, little information about the characteristics of the sample, qualifications of the examiners, or the test-retest interval is provided.

Validity

The authors maintain that the *DTLA-P:2* has content validity because it measures behaviors that are found in a list of behaviors that Salvia and Ysseldyke (1995) have developed. To demonstrate concurrent validity, the authors used evidence from four concurrent validity studies that were conducted with the *DTLA-P*. The size of the samples used in each of these correlations ranged from 28 to 68 children. The reliability coefficients that are reported ranged from .31 to .87.

No evidence of predictive validity is contained in the *DTLA-P:2* manual. While the authors present evidence of construct validity, additional validity studies need to be conducted.

Summary

The *Detroit Tests of Learning Aptitude–Primary* (Second Edition) is an individually administered test for children ages 3 years, 0 months to 9 years, 11 months. It is designed to measure intellectual ability using six subtests and a general, overall score. Questions remain as to the appropriateness of the standardization sample, reliability, and validity. Until additional evidence is presented, the *DTLA-P:2* should be used cautiously.

Detroit Tests of Learning Aptitude-3

The *Detroit Tests of Learning Aptitude-3* (Third Edition) *(DTLA-3)* (Hammill, 1991) is designed to measure the intellectual aptitudes or abilities

---

BOX 13.3

DETROIT TESTS OF LEARNING APTITUDE–PRIMARY (SECOND EDITION)

Publication Date: 1991
Purposes: Measures general intellectual aptitudes or abilities
Age/Grade Levels: Ages 3 years to 9 years, 11 months
Time to Administer: 15 to 45 minutes
Technical Adequacy: Questions remain as to the appropriateness of the standardization sample, reliability, and validity.
Suggested Use: The DTLA-2 can be used as a screening instrument. Caution should be exercised when using test scores to make decisions regarding the identification of students and eligibility for special services.

---

of students ages 6 through 17. According to the authors, the *DTLA-3* is designed to measure intelligence, aptitude, and achievement. The *DTLA-3* consists of 11 subtests:

Word Opposites—The student must verbalize the opposite of a word that the examiner says.

Design Sequences—The student must arrange cubes in a pattern from memory after being shown a picture of the pattern for five seconds.

Sentence Imitation—The student repeats a sentence after listening to the examiner say the sentence.

Reversed Letters—The examiner recites a series of letters. The student must record the letters, reversing their order of presentation.

Story Construction—After viewing three pictures, the student makes up three stories.

Design Reproduction—The student must draw a design from memory after being shown a design for five seconds.

Basic Information—The student responds to factual questions.

Symbolic Relations—The student views a design and must choose from among six designs the one that completes the pattern.

Word Sequences—The student repeats a series of unrelated words after listening to the examiner recite the words.

Story Sequences—The student arranges a series of cartoonlike pictures to make a story.

Picture Fragments—The student is asked to say the names of common objects after viewing pictures of the objects that have parts missing.

Administration

Examiners are expected to have some background in assessment.

Directions for administration are on the test protocol. For some items, directions for administration are in the examiner's manual. Administration takes between 50 minutes and 2 hours.

Scoring

The responses are scored either correct or incorrect. The scores for each item are used in the computation of the total score and the subtest scores. Raw scores can be converted to age equivalents, percentiles, and quotients, which are standard scores that have a mean of 100 and a standard deviation of 15.

Standardization

The standardization sample of the *DTLA-3* consisted of 2,587 students in 36 states. In developing this instrument, the authors used data from the standardization sample of the *DTLA-2* and selected additional samples. The standardization of the *DTLA-3* is confusing and ambiguous.

Reliability

Internal consistency reliability was estimated using a random sample of 600 protocols from the standardization sample. The average relia-bilities for the total score and the six subtests ranged from .70 to .95. Test-retest reliability was calculated based on a sample of 34 students living in Austin, Texas. The coefficients ranged from .77 to .96.

Validity

The authors maintain that the *DTLA-3* has content validity because it measures behaviors that are found in a list of behaviors that Salvia and Ysseldyke (1995) have developed and by relating the subtests to the theories of intelligence developed by John Horn, Raymond Cattell, David Wechsler, and Jagannath Das. While the authors present evidence of construct validity, additional validity studies need to be conducted.

Summary

The *Detroit Tests of Learning Aptitude-3* is an individually administered test for students ages 6 through 17. Questions remain as to the appropriateness of the standardization sample, reliability, and validity.

Differential Ability Scales

The *Differential Ability Scales (DAS)* (Elliott, 1990a) is a revision of the *British Ability Scales*. The *DAS* is designed to measure cognitive ability and achievement in individuals ages 2 years, 6 months to 17 years, 11 months. The test is not based on any one theory of mental ability. According to the manual, the test

> is built on a collection of subtests that sample a range of human abilities thought to be useful in assessing individuals, particularly students with learning difficulties. The selection of the abilities sampled was influenced by a variety of theoretical approaches (1990b, p. 14).

The *DAS* is organized into a hierarchical structure. The first level consists of the subtest scores, at the next level are the cluster scores, and at the general level the *DAS* yields a general cognitive ability score (GCA). The test contains 17 cognitive subtests and 3 school achievement subtests. Not all of the subtests are given to every individual. Depending on the age of the student, selected subtests are administered. The subtests and clusters are described in Table 13.3.

Administration

The administration of the *DAS* should be done by an examiner who has a background in the principles of assessment. The total time to administer the *DAS* is approximately 35 minutes for children ages 2 years, 6 months to 3 years, 5 months; administration to children ages 3 years, 6 months to 5 years, 11 months takes approximately 65 minutes; and it takes between 65 and 85 minutes for students older than 6 years of age. Separate directions for administering each of the subtests are provided in the manual.

The administration of the *DAS* does have several unique features. These include decision points, alternative stopping points, teaching a failed item, extended selection of subtests, and out-of-level testing. While the starting points for each subtest are based on the individual's age, the administration of items continues until the individual reaches a *decision point.* When a decision point is reached, the examiner decides whether to stop, to continue to administer the difficult items, or to drop back and administer easier items. Alternative stopping points are provided so that the examiner can halt the test administration if the items are too difficult or if rapport has not been obtained. In addition to these features, some subtests allow the examiner to teach the individual an item if the item is failed. *Extended selection* of subtests refers to the option of allowing the examiner to administer additional subtests that measure similar abilities. This may occur with young children when further assessment is considered necessary. *Out-of-level testing* refers to the administration of additional subtests to individuals who have unusually low or high abilities. These subtests may not be appropriate for individuals who have average ability.

For individuals with hearing impairments, speech, or language problems, nonverbal subtests can be administered. These include Block Building and Picture Similarities. The scores from these subtests form a Special Nonverbal Composite, which, according to the manual, can be used in place of the GCA. However, separate norms for special populations are not included.

Scoring

Raw scores are compared to Ability Scores. These are scores that are unique to the *DAS* and provide an estimate of the individual's performance on specific subtests. However, ability scores of different subtests have an important limitation. They cannot be compared. Another transformation is required to convert Ability Scores to T-scores (T-scores have a mean of 50 and a standard deviation of 10), percentiles, and standard scores (mean of 100, standard deviation of 15). Age and grade equivalents are provided for the achievement tests. Separate guidelines are provided for scoring each of the subtests.

TABLE 13.3   Differential Ability Scales: Subtests and Clusters

Preschool Core Subtests

Block Building (2 years, 6 months–4 years, 11 months). Measures motor and perceptual abilities. The individual is required to copy wooden block designs.

Verbal Comprehension (2 years, 6 months–6 years, 11 months). Measures receptive language ability. The child is asked to point to pictures that are named or to place objects and chips according to the examiner's instructions (e.g., under the bridge).

Picture Similarities (2 years, 6 months–7 years, 11 months). Measures nonverbal reasoning ability. After being shown a row of four pictures or designs, the child must choose the best picture or design that goes with the ones that are shown.

Naming Vocabulary (2 years, 6 months–8 years, 11 months). Measures expressive vocabulary. The child is asked to name several objects and pictures that are shown.

Pattern Construction (3 years–17 years, 11 months). Measures visual-spatial problem solving. The individual is asked to construct patterns using foam squares and plastic blocks.

Early Number Concepts (2 years, 6 months–7 years, 11 months). Measures prenumerical and number concepts and skills. The child is asked to count chips and to answer questions about pictures. Many, but not all of the subtests, are nonverbal.

Copying (3 years, 6 months–7 years, 11 months). Measures ability to copy, motor ability, and the ability to perceive similarities. After being shown a line drawing, the child is required to reproduce it.

School-Age Core Subtests

Recall of Designs (5 years through 17 years, 11 months). Assesses short-term recall, motor ability, and visual-spatial ability. After being shown a nonpictorial line drawing for five seconds, the individual must draw it from memory.

Word Definitions (5 years through 17 years, 11 months). Measures verbal knowledge. The examiner says a word and the individual must provide the meaning.

Pattern Construction (3 years through 17 years, 11 months). This subtest has already been discussed in the *Preschool Core Subtests* section.

Matrices (5 years through 17 years, 11 months). Measures nonverbal reasoning ability. The student is shown a series of matrices. For each one, the student is asked to choose the design that best completes the matrix.

Similarities (5 years through 17 years, 11 months). Measures verbal reasoning. The individual must respond orally to a series of questions.

Sequential and Quantitative Reasoning (5 years through 17 years, 11 months). Assesses the ability to perceive sequential patterns or rules in numerical relationships. The items consist of abstract figures or numbers to which the student must respond.

Diagnostic Subtests

Matching Letterlike Forms (4 years through 7 years, 11 months). Measures the ability to visually discriminate among similar letterlike figures. The student is asked to match similar figures that look like letters and are rotated on a page.

Recall of Digits (2 years, 6 months through 17 years, 11 months). Assesses short-term auditory-sequential recall of digits. The individual must repeat a series of 2 to 9 digits.

continued

TABLE 13.3   (Continued)

Recall of Objects–Immediate and Delayed (4 years through 17 years, 11 months). Assesses short-term and delayed verbal memory. The individual recalls as many objects as possible after being shown a card with a number of objects on it.

Recognition of Pictures (2 years, 6 months through 17 years, 11 months). Assesses short-term visual memory. After being shown a card with one or more pictures for a few seconds, the individal is shown another set of pictures and must point to the pictures that were displayed in the first picture.

Speed of Information Processing (5 years, 0 months through 17 years,11 months). Assesses speed of simple mental operations. After being shown a page consisting of figures or numbers, the individual must mark, as quickly as possible, the circle containing the largest number of boxes or the highest number.

School Achievement Tests

Basic Number Skills (6 years, 0 months through 17 years, 11 months). Assesses basic computational skills. The individual is asked to solve problems on a worksheet.

Spelling (6 years, 0 months through 17 years, 11 months). Assesses ability to spell based on phonetically regular and irregular words. Children ages 6 years, 0 months to 8 years, 11 months are also asked to write their names. The examiner says the word, uses the word in a sentence, and repeats the word.

Word Reading (5 years, 0 months through 17 years, 11 months). Assesses ability to decode words in isolation. The student is asked to read a series of words that are shown on a card.

Clusters of the Preschool Level of the Cognitive Battery (3 years, 6 months–5 years, 11 months). Verbal Ability. Assesses learned verbal concepts and knowledge. The subtests that form this cluster are Verbal Comprehension and Naming Vocabulary.

Nonverbal Ability. Assesses complex, nonverbal mental processing. The subtests that form this cluster include Picture Similarities, Pattern Construction, and Copying.

Clusters of the School-Age Level of the Cognitive Battery (6 years, 0 months–17 years, 11 months). Verbal Ability. Assesses verbal mental processing and acquired knowledge. The subtests that form this cluster are Word Definitions and Similarities.

Nonverbal Reasoning Ability. Assesses nonverbal inductive reasoning and mental processing. The subtests that form this cluster include Matrices, Sequential, and Quantitative Reasoning.

Spatial Ability. Assesses complex visual-spatial processing. The subtests that form this cluster are Recall of Designs and Pattern Construction.

Standardization

The standardization sample consisted of 3,475 individuals evenly divided by gender, with 175 individuals for each six-month interval for ages 2 years, 6 months to 4 years, 11 months and 200 individuals at one-year intervals for ages 5 years, 0 months to 17 years, 11 months. Other stratification variables were race/ethnicity (black, Hispanic, white, other including Asian, Pacific Islander, American Indian, Eskimo, Aleut), parent education, geographic region, and educational preschool enrollment.

Individuals who were identified as learning disabled, speech impaired, emotionally disturbed, physically impaired, mentally retarded, and gifted were included in the standardization sample in approximate proportion to U.S. population data. Individuals with severe disabilities were excluded. Separate norms are not provided. According to the manual:

The mere inclusion of individuals with exceptional needs in a norm sample does not make the instrument appropriate for use with such children, nor does their exclusion make the test inappropriate. During item and subtest development, the DAS team sought to create tasks that would be suitable in content, format, and difficulty for many exceptional children. The success of these efforts, like those of any other test development project, can be determined only through research that focuses on how the test works with such children (Elliot, 1990b, p. 116).

Reliability

Internal reliabilities for each of the subtests and for out-of-level testing were determined. For the most part, the reliabilities were within the moderate range.

Test-retest reliability was estimated by selecting 100 individuals from the standardization sample for each of the following age ranges: 3 years, 6 months to 4 years, 5 months; 5 years, 0 months to 6 years, 11 months; and 12 years, 0 months to 13 years, 11 months. The testing interval ranged from two to seven weeks. While the reliabilities were in the moderate range for the subtests, the reliabilities of the clusters and the general cognitive ability score were higher than the reliabilities for the subtests.

Validity

The manual does provide evidence of the separate factor structure for the subtests and the clusters. Concurrent validity with other ability tests and achievement tests is reported. In addition, studies of small samples of students labeled educably mentally retarded, learning disabled, reading disabled, and gifted are described. However, since this is a relatively new test, additional studies need to be conducted by independent researchers in order to confirm and extend our understanding of the validity of this instrument. Caution should be used when interpreting the performance of individuals with special needs.

BOX 13.5

DIFFERENTIAL ABILITY SCALES

Publication Date: 1990
Purposes: Measures cognitive ability and achievement
Age/Grade Levels: 2 years, 6 months to 17 years, 11 months
Time to Administer: 35 to 85 minutes
Technical Adequacy: The standardization sample is acceptable. Reliability is adequate. Additional evidence of validity is needed.
Suggested Use: Can be helpful in determining areas of strength and weakness. Exercise caution when using test scores in making decisions regarding identification of students with special needs and determining eligibility for special services.

Summary

The *DAS* is an individually administered ability test for use with individuals ages 2 years, 6 months to 17 years, 11 months. The subtests are designed to measure cognitive ability and selected areas of achievement. Reliability is adequate. However, additional evidence of validity is needed before it can be confidently used with individuals with exceptional needs.

Kaufman Adolescent & Adult Intelligence Test

The *Kaufman Adolescent & Adult Intelligence Test (KAIT)* (Kaufman and Kaufman, 1993) is a test of general intelligence for individuals ages 11 to over 85 years. The test is based on three theories of intellectual functioning: Golden's modification of the Luria-Nebraska system of neuropsychological assessment, Piaget's formal operations stage, and the Horn-Cattell theories of fluid and crystallized intelligence.

The *KAIT* is composed of two scales: crystallized intelligence and fluid intelligence. Crystallized intelligence "measures acquired concepts and depends on schooling and acculturation for success" (Kaufman and Kaufman, 1993, p. 1) while fluid intelligence measures "the ability to solve new problems" (Kaufman and Kaufman, 1993, p. 1). The test has a Core Battery and an Expanded Battery. The Core Battery contains six subtests, and the Expanded Battery has ten subtests. In addition, a supplementary subtest assesses the respondent's attention and orientation. A description of the subtests and the abilities they measure can be found in Table 13.4.

Administration

The *KAIT* is an individually administered test that should be overseen by persons who have had graduate training in individual assessment

of intelligence. The average time to administer the Core Battery is 65 minutes; the Expanded Battery takes approximately 90 minutes.

Scoring

Each of the three intelligence scales, Crystallized, Fluid, and Composite, yields an IQ score with a mean of 100 and a standard deviation of 15. In addition, percentile ranks can be obtained. Each of the ten subtests yields standard scores with a mean of 10 and a standard deviation of 3. Figure 13.1 shows the front page from the KAIT Individual Test Record Form.

TABLE 13.4   Kaufman Adolescent & Adult Intelligence Test

Core Battery Subtests

Definitions	Respondents identify a word after being shown the word with several letters missing and after being given a definition of the word. (*crystallized intelligence*)
Rebus Learning	Respondents associate a word or concept with a rebus and then "read" phrases and sentences that are comprised of several rebuses. (*fluid intelligence*)
Logical Steps	Respondents are presented with logical premises in both visual and aural form. They answer a question that relates to these premises. (*fluid intelligence*)
Auditory Comprehension	After listening to a recording of a news story, respondents answer literal and inferential questions. (*crystallized intelligence*)
Mystery Codes	After looking at the codes associated with several pictures, the respondents solve the code for a pictorial stimulus. (*fluid intelligence*)
Double Meanings	After examining two groups of words, respondents recall a word that is associated with the two groups of words. (*crystallized intelligence*)

Expanded Battery

Rebus Delayed Recall	Respondents "read" phrases and concepts that are formed from rebuses that they learned earlier in the test. (*delay recall*)
Auditory Delayed Recall	Respondents answer questions about news stories that they listened to earlier in the test. (*delayed recall*)
Memory for Block Designs	Respondents construct a block design from memory after briefly looking at a printed copy. (*fluid intelligence*)
Famous Faces	After looking at a picture of a famous person and hearing a clue about the person, respondents name the person. (*crystallized intelligence*)

Supplementary Subtest

Mental Status	Respondents answer ten questions relating to their attention and orientation to the world.

**Kaufman
Adolescent & Adult
Intelligence Test**

**Individual
Test Record**

by Alan S. Kaufman and Nadeen L. Kaufman

Name _____   ☐ Male   ☐ Female

Home address _____   Phone _____

_____

	Year	Month	Day
Test date	____	____	____
Birth date	____	____	____
Chronological age	____	____	____

Parent or Guardian _____
(if applicable)
School _____   Grade _____
(if applicable)
Current or previous occupation _____
(if applicable)
Highest school grade completed _____

Examiner _____

Mental Status

Raw Score | Descriptive Category

SUBTESTS	Raw Score	Subtest Scaled Score (Table D.1) M = 10, SD= 3			Percentile Rank	Other Data Specify:
		Crystallized Scale	Fluid Scale	Delayed Recall		
CORE BATTERY						
1. Definitions						
2. Rebus Learning						
3. Logical Steps						
4. Auditory Comprehension						
5. Mystery Codes						
6. Double Meanings						
EXPANDED BATTERY						
7. Rebus Delayed Recall						
8. Auditory Delayed Recall		*Add only if substituting for subtest 1, 4, or 6.*	**Add only if substituting for subtest 2, 3, or 5.			
9. Memory for Block Designs			** ( )			
10. Famous Faces		* ( )				

	Crystallized Scale	Fluid Scale	Composite Intelligence Scale	Crystallized and Fluid IQ Comparison
Sum of Three Core Subtest Scaled Scores		+	=	Crystallized IQ ⬭
IQ	(Table D.2)	(Table D.3)	(Table D.4)	Fluid IQ ⬭
Confidence Interval ☐ 90% ☐ 95%	—	—	—	IQ Difference ⬭
Percentile Rank				
Mean Scaled Score				
Descriptive Category				

Statistical Significance (check one)	Difference Required for Significance at .05 and .01 Levels		
		Significance Level	
	Age	.05	.01
☐ NS	14 or younger	11	14
☐ .05	15 - 34	9	12
☐ .01	35 or older	8	11

FIGURE 13.1

Kaufman Adult Individual Intelligence Test, Individual Test Record

Source: Kaufman Adolescent & Adult Intelligence Test (KAIT) by Alan S. Kaufman and Nadeen L. Kaufman. © 1992. American Guidance Service, Inc., 4201 Woodland Road, Circle Pines, Minn. 55014-1796. Reprinted with permission of the Publisher. All rights reserved.

Standardization

The *KAIT* was standardized between 1988 and 1991. Census information from 1988 was used to select the sample. Over 2,600 individuals, ages 11 to 94 years, at 60 sites participated. The final standardization sample of 2,000 individuals composed of 14 age groups was selected from the initial group.

The proportion of males and females closely approximated census data. The Northeast geographic region was somewhat underrepresented, and the West was slightly overrepresented. The North Central and Central regions approximated census data. Socioeconomic status and racial and ethnic groups closely match census information. Data was collected for persons designated as white, black, Hispanic, and other (other includes Native Americans, Asian, Alaskan Natives, Pacific Islanders, and other groups not categorized as white, black, or Hispanic).

Reliability

Split-half and test-retest reliability were calculated: for split-half reliability of the subtests, average coefficients ranged from .79 (Memory for Block Designs) to .93 (Rebus Learning); for the scales, the average split-half reliability coefficients were .95 (Crystallized, Fluid) and .97 Composite Intelligence.

Test-retest reliability was calculated for two test administrations of the *KAIT* to 153 individuals. The interval between the administrations ranged from 6 to 99 days with an average interval of 31 days. Average test-retest coefficients for the scales are .94 (Crystallized), .87 (Fluid), and .94 (Composite). One study is reported of a sample of 60 individuals who were retested after an interval of one year. Average test-retest coefficients for the scales are .85 (Crystallized), .79 (Fluid), and .92 (Composite).

Validity

Construct validity is based on studies of age changes on the subtests and the IQ scales, correlations between the subtests and the IQ scales, factor analyses of the *KAIT*, and correlations between the *KAIT* and other tests.

The studies of age changes on the *KAIT* demonstrate that as individuals grow older, *KAIT* scores change. According to the test manual, this pattern of age changes is consistent with the Horn-Cattell theory, one of the theories of intelligence on which the *KAIT* is based.

Correlations between the *KAIT* subtests and the Composite IQ score were computed. For the six Core subtests, coefficients ranged from .64 (Mystery Codes) to .75 (Definition), with an average coefficient of .70. These coefficients indicate that there is some support that indicates that the *KAIT* subtests measure a unifying ability.

Factor analyses were computed in order to support the authors' assertion that the *KAIT* measures theory-based intelligence. Results of the factor analyses demonstrated that the *KAIT* was composed of two factors consistent with the crystallized and fluid scales. Additional factor analyses were conducted between the *KAIT* and the *Wechsler Intelligence Scale for Children-Revised (WISC-R)* and the *Wechsler Adult Intelligence Scale–Revised (WAIS-R)*. These studies indicate that the *KAIT* Fluid Scale and the Wechsler Performance scales measure different constructs. However, the *KAIT* Crystallized Scale and the Wechsler Verbal scales are almost the same.

Concurrent validity was calculated by computing correlations between the *KAIT* and the *Kaufman Brief Intelligence Test (K-BIT)* and the *Peabody Picture Vocabulary Test–Revised (PPVT-R)*. The correlations between the *KAIT* Composite IQ and the *K-BIT* Composite IQ were .81 at ages 11 to 19 years and .87 at ages 20 to 88 years. The correlations between the *KAIT* Composite IQ and the *PPVT-R* standard scores were .83 for ages 15 to 40 years and .66 for ages 41 to 92 years. Note that the norm tables for the *PPVT-R* only reach 40 years, so that when concurrent validity calculations were made, the norm tables for ages 35 to 40 were used. Additional concurrent validity studies need to be conducted using additional instruments.

The manual reports several studies regarding the diagnostic validity of the *KAIT* using various samples such as Alzheimer's patients, persons with neurological impairments, clinical depression, or reading disabilities. The studies support the diagnostic utility of the *KAIT* in these areas. The authors are to be commended for their initial investigations of the diagnostic validity of this test. Further studies in this area should be conducted.

Summary

The Kaufman Adolescent and Adult Intelligence Test is an individually administered test of general intelligence for persons ages 11 to over 85 years. It is based on three theoretical models of intelligence. The test is well standardized. There is good evidence for reliability and validity.

Kaufman Assessment Battery for Children

The *Kaufman Assessment Battery for Children (K-ABC)* (Kaufman and Kaufman, 1983) as-

---

BOX 13.6

KAUFMAN ADOLESCENT & ADULT INTELLIGENCE TEST

Publication Date: 1993
Purposes: Measures general intelligence, crystallized and fluid intellectual abilities
Age/Grade Levels: 11 years to over 85 years
Time to Administer: 65 to 90 minutes
Technical Adequacy: The test is well standardized. There is good evidence for reliability and validity.
Suggested Uses: Determine general intellectual ability, areas of strength and weakness

---

sesses the intelligence and achievement of individuals ages 2.6 through 12.6. The test consists of 16 subtests that take from 35 minutes for young children to 75 minutes for elementary school–age children. A maximum of 13 subtests are administered to each individual. The subtests are arranged into three scales: Sequential Processing Scale, Simultaneous Processing Scale, and the Achievement Scale.

Intelligence is "defined in terms of an individual's style of solving problems and processing information" (Kaufman and Kaufman, 1983, p. 2). The intelligence scales are based on a theoretical model of mental processing developed by J. P. Das, A. R. Luria, and others that holds that information is primarily processed sequentially or simultaneously. The Sequential Processing Scale requires that problems be solved in a sequential, or serial, order. The Simultaneous Processing Scale requires that information be integrated or synthesized to obtain a solution.

The Mental Processing Scale is a combination of the Sequential and the Simultaneous Processing scales. It is a measure of total intelligence. The Mental Processing Composite score has a mean of 100 and a standard deviation of 15.

The Achievement Scale assesses knowledge and skills gained through formal and informal experiences. The manual states that the Achievement Scale does not yield a diagnostic assessment of achievement skills; it does provide a global estimate of achievement in the areas of reading, arithmetic, general information, early language development, and language concepts. A description of the subtests can be found in Table 13.5.

Depending on the age of the individual, various subtests can be combined to form the Nonverbal Scale. The Nonverbal Scale provides an estimate of intelligence for individuals who demonstrate communication problems, and can be used with children who are deaf, hearing-impaired, speech or language disabled, autistic, or who do not speak English.

TABLE 13.5   Kaufman Assessment Battery for Children

Sequential Processing Scale

Hand Movements (ages 2.6 to 12.5). A series of hand movements is performed in the same sequence as the examiner.

Number Recall (ages 2.6 to 12.5). A series of digits is repeated in the same order as the examiner says them.

Word Order (ages 4.0 to 12.5). A series of silhouettes of common objects is touched in the same order as the examiner identifies them.

Simultaneous Processing Scale

Magic Window (ages 2.6 to 4.11). A picture is slowly revealed as the examiner rotates it behind a narrow window.

Face Recognition (ages 2.6 to 12.5). Faces in a group photograph are identified that were exposed on the preceding page.

Gestalt Closure (ages 2.6 to 12.5). An object or scene that is depicted in an "inkblot" drawing is named.

Triangles (ages 4.0 to 12.5). Triangles are formed into a pattern that matches a design.

Matrix Analogies (ages 5.0 to 12.5). A picture or abstract design is identified that best completes a visual analogy.

Spatial Memory (ages 5.0 to 12.5). The position of pictures on a page that is briefly exposed are recalled.

Photo Series (ages 6.0 to 12.5). Photographs of an event are placed in chronological order.

Achievement Scale

Expressive Vocabulary (ages 2.6 to 4.11). An object that is pictured in a photograph is identified.

Faces & Places (ages 2.6 to 12.5). A famous person, fictional character, or geographic location is identified.

Arithmetic (ages 3.0 to 12.5). Knowledge of mathematical concepts is demonstrated.

Riddles (ages 3.0 to 12.5). When presented with a list of characteristics the concept is named.

Reading/Decoding (ages 5.0 to 12.5). Letters and words are read.

Reading/Understanding (ages 7.0 to 12.5). Reading comprehension is shown by following written commands.

Administration

The manual provides comprehensive directions for the administration of the *K-ABC*. In addition, instructions for administering the battery in Spanish are provided in a supplement. The starting point for each subtest is determined by the student's chronological age, and each subtest has a designated stopping point in order to avoid administering too many items to any child. In addition, a discontinue rule can be invoked if a student misses a number of items in a row. The first item of each subtest is designated as the sample item and the next two items are labeled teaching items. For the sample and teaching items, it is permissible for the examiner to teach the child how to respond to the items in the subtest. Each item on the *K-ABC* is scored as correct or incorrect.

The *K-ABC* provides for out-of-level testing for students who are 4 or 5 years old. This helps to provide flexibility in testing young children. At age 5, the number and difficulty of the subtests that should be administered changes. The subtests of Matrix Analogies, Spatial Memory, and Reading/Decoding are introduced. Magic Window, Face Recognition, and Expressive vocabulary are intended for children younger than 5 years. For children who are between the ages of 5 years, 0 months to 5 years, 11 months and who may be suspected of being mentally retarded or developmentally delayed, portions of the *K-ABC* that would normally be intended for 4-year-olds may be administered. Similarly, if children ages 4 years, 6 months to 4 years, 11 months are thought to be advanced or gifted, subtests for children age 5 and older may be administered.

Separate norms are provided for students who have been tested out-of-level. The scores obtained from out-of-level testing, while helpful, must be used cautiously. The norms were extended upward and downward by estimating the performance of students. A nationally representative sample was not tested to obtain these extended norms.

For the Nonverbal Scale, the examiner can pantomime the instructions (although this is not required) and the child responds by gesturing, pointing, or demonstrating. The subtests for the Nonverbal Scale are:

Age 4
Face Recognition
Hand Movements
Triangles

Age 5
Hand Movements
Triangles
Matrix Analogies
Spatial Memory

Ages 6–12
Hand Movements
Triangles
Matrix Analogies
Spatial Memory
Photo Series

Standardization

The standardization sample of the *K-ABC* consisted of 2,000 children between the ages of 2 years, 6 months and 12 years, 5 months. Based on the 1980 U.S. Census, the children were stratified within each age group according to gender, geographic region, socioeconomic status, race or ethnicity (African American, Caucasian, Hispanic, other), community size, and educational placement of the child (regular or special classes).

In order to make the *K-ABC* sensitive to the needs of the diverse population in the United States, an additional 469 African American and 119 Caucasian children were tested with the goal of developing sociocultural norms. However, African Americans were overrepresented in the higher education group and underrepresented in the lower education group.

Subtest scores for the mental processing scales are reported as scaled scores (mean of 10, standard deviation of 3) and percentiles. These subtest scores can be combined to yield standard scores (mean of 100, standard deviation of 15) for the Sequential Processing, Simultaneous Processing, Mental Processing Composite, and Nonverbal scales. Achievement subtests are reported as percentiles and standard scores. Age equivalents are provided for the Mental Processing Scales and grade equivalents are reported for the Achievement Scale.

Reliability

Split-half, internal consistency, and test-retest reliabilities are reported in the manual. For the most part, the reliability coefficients are acceptable. Many coefficients exceed .90 and, in general, the composite scores are more reliable than the individual subtest scores. Mean split-half reliability coefficients ranged from .71 (Gestalt Closure) to .91 (Reading/Understanding). Mean internal consistency coefficients for the global scales ranged from .89 (Sequential Processing) to .97 (Achievement). Test-retest reliability coefficients extended from .77 (Sequential Processing) to .97 (Achievement).

Standard errors of measurement (SEM) vary by age. For school-age students on the subtests, the SEM for the Mental Processing Subtests ranged from 1.1 (Matrix Analogies) to 1.6 (Gestalt Closure); on the Achievement Scale SEM varied from 4.0 (Reading/Decoding) to 5.9 (Faces and Places). For the global scales, the SEM ranged from 2.7 (Achievement) to 5.0 (Sequential Processing).

Validity

The manual reports the results of many studies relating to the validity of the *K-ABC*. The test authors as well as numerous independent researchers have conducted studies investigating its validity. Reviewers of the *K-ABC* have been mixed in their evaluation of the validity of this instrument (Anastasi, 1985; Coffman, 1985; Merz, 1984; Page, 1985).

In an independent study of 100 Mexican American and 100 Caucasian fifth and sixth grade girls and boys (Valencia, Rankin, and Livingston, 1995) concluded that the Mental Processing Scales showed little evidence of bias. However, numerous items on the Achievement Scale were biased against Mexican-American children.

Summary

The *Kaufman Assessment Battery for Children (K-ABC)* (Kaufman and Kaufman, 1983) is designed to assess the intelligence and achievement of individuals ages 2.6 through 12.6. According to the manual, the test measures sequential processing, simultaneous processing, mental processing composite, and achieve-

ment. The *K-ABC* was designed to be sensitive to the preschool population and to the U.S. society, which is becoming increasingly pluralistic. The manual presents extensive evidence for the reliability and validity of the test. Additional research needs to be conducted to confirm that the test does measure sequential and simultaneous processing. There is some concern that the African-American sample is biased toward the upper education levels. The Achievement Scale is biased toward Mexican Americans.

Kaufman Brief Intelligence Test

The *Kaufman Brief Intelligence Test (K-BIT)* (Kaufman and Kaufman, 1990) measures ver-

---

B O X   1 3 . 7

KAUFMAN ASSESSMENT BATTERY FOR CHILDREN

Publication Date: 1983

Purposes: Assesses intelligence (sequential and simultaneous processing) and achievement in vocabulary, arithmetic, and reading

Age/Grade Levels: 2.6 through 12.6 years

Time to Administer: 35 to 75 minutes

Technical Adequacy: The standardization sample is dated. Reliability is very good; validity is acceptable. However, additional evidence of validity is needed to support the theoretical basis of this test.

Suggested Uses: The K-ABC should be used cautiously with students who have diverse backgrounds because some test items may be biased. The K-ABC can be helpful in determining general intellectual ability and overall achievement in vocabulary, arithmetic, and reading.

bal and nonverbal intelligence in individuals ages 4 through 90 years old. Because it is a brief test, the authors explain that it should not be used as a substitute for a more comprehensive measure. The test is for screening only; it is not to be used for diagnostic, placement, or neurological assessment purposes. In addition to its use as a screening instrument, the *K-BIT* was developed to provide an estimate of intelligence for persons who may have psychiatric disorders, job applicants, people awaiting court hearings, and individuals whose intellectual status needs to be monitored periodically.

The *K-BIT* consists of two subtests, Vocabulary and Matrices. The Vocabulary subtest contains 82 items to which individuals are asked to respond verbally. The Vocabulary subtest contains two parts, A and B. Part A, Expressive Vocabulary, contains 45 items that are administered to all persons who take this test. The individual is asked to name an object that is pictured (e.g., lamp, calendar). Part B, Definitions, contains 37 items and is administered only to persons who are older than 8 years of age.

The second subtest, Matrices, consists of 48 items to which each individual is asked to respond by pointing to the correct response or by saying the corresponding letter. The items on this subtest contain people, objects, abstract designs, and symbols and are arranged so that an individual must understand the relationship among these items. This subtest is designed to measure nonverbal reasoning ability.

Administration

A wide variety of professionals can administer the test, including psychologists, special education teachers, educational diagnosticians, remedial reading teachers, counselors, social workers, nurses, and speech and language therapists. In addition, under certain circumstances, technicians and paraprofessionals can administer the *K-BIT*. According to the manual, test administrators require little training to administer the test but the interpretation of the results should be done by a trained professional.

The administration of the *K-BIT* takes from 15 to 20 minutes for children who are between 4 and 7 years of age; for persons older than 7 years, test administration can take up to 30 minutes.

Scoring

Items are scored either correct or incorrect. Raw scores are converted to standard scores and percentile ranks. Scores are obtained for each of the subtests, Vocabulary and Matrices, and a composite intellectual ability score can be computed. The standard score is similar to intellectual ability scores for other tests. It has a mean of 100 and a standard deviation of 15.

Some guidance is provided for interpreting test scores. There is evidence that discrepancies between specific subtests can provide helpful diagnostic information. Using the results of the *K-BIT,* discrepancies between the standard scores on the Vocabulary and Matrices subtests can be determined. Since this instrument contains only two subtests, the interpretation of discrepancies should be made cautiously and only after further extensive testing.

The authors reported that the mean *K-BIT* scores were 6 points lower than full scale scores from the *Wechsler Intelligence Scale for Children–Revised (WISC-R)*. This may be of little concern since the *WISC-R* has been revised; however, information is not available on how the *K-BIT* scores compare with scores from the *Wechsler Intelligence Scale for Children-III (WISC-III)*.

Standardization

The *K-BIT* was standardized on 2,022 individuals between the ages of 4 and 90 years at 60 locations. Most of the standardization sample was between the ages of 4 and 19. The sample was stratified according to gender, geographic region, socioeconomic status, and race or ethnic group. The minority groups included black, Hispanic, and other (Native Americans, Alaskan natives, Asians, Pacific Islanders).

The test examiners were teachers, counselors, psychologists, and graduate students who had received training by watching a videotape and practice in administering the test.

Reliability

Split-half reliabilities were computed for the two subtests and for the composite score. For Vocabulary, the split-half reliability coefficients ranged from .89 to .97; for Matrices the split-half reliability coefficients ranged from .74 to .95. The composite split-half reliability varied from .88 to .98. Lower reliabilities occurred at young ages.

To obtain test-retest reliability, the authors administered the *K-BIT* twice to 232 individuals between the ages of 5 and 89. The interval between the two tests ranged from 12 to 145 days, with an average of 21 days. There were 53 children in the age range between 5 and 12 years. For this group, test-retest reliabilities ranged from .83 to .92.

Validity

Concurrent validity studies of the *K-BIT* with the *Test of Nonverbal Intelligence (TONI)* and with the *Slosson Intelligence Test (SIT)* are reported. For the *TONI,* the validity coefficients ranged from −0.04 (Vocabulary subtest) to .36 (Matrices subtest). When the *K-BIT* composite score was correlated with the *SIT* scores of typical children, correlation coefficients ranged from .50 to .76; and when the *K-BIT* composite score was correlated with *SIT* scores from a gifted sample the validity coefficient was .44.

Concurrent validity is also reported for the *Kaufman Test of Educational Achievement (K-TEA)* (Comprehensive Form) for normal samples. Using *K-BIT* composite scores, validity coefficients ranged from .33 to .78; and when *K-BIT* scores were correlated with scores from the *K-TEA* Comprehensive Form for two samples of students with learning disabilities, validity coefficients ranged from .32 to .65.

Evidence of construct validity is based on five normal samples. *K-BIT* composite scores were correlated with scores from the *Kaufman Assessment Battery for Children (K-ABC), Wechsler Intelligence Scale for Children–Revised (WISC-R)* (1974), and the *Wechsler Adult Intelligence Scale–Revised (WAIS-R).* Validity coefficients ranged from .41 to .80. Thus, while there is some evidence that the *K-BIT* is assessing similar abilities to the *K-ABC, WISC-R,* and the *WAIS-R,* it is apparent that it is also assessing some abilities that the other instruments are not. Based on this, it would be difficult to justify the use of the *K-BIT* as a substitute for the administration of these other instruments. With regard to testing young children, there is limited evidence as to the usefulness of the *K-BIT* with this population.

Summary

The *K-BIT* is a brief intelligence test. It can be used when a quick screening is required, but it should not be substituted for a more comprehensive intelligence test. Reliability appears to be adequate, and there is some evidence of validity. However, evidence of validity with samples of young children is limited. Utilize the *K-BIT* cautiously when testing young children.

Stanford-Binet Intelligence Scale: Fourth Edition

The *Stanford-Binet Intelligence Scale:* Fourth Edition (Thorndike, Hagen, and Sattler, 1986a) is a revised edition of the *Stanford-Binet Intelligence Scale: Form L-M.* The test was originally developed by Alfred Binet and Theodore Simon in France in 1905. Lewis M. Terman, a professor at Stanford University, revised the Binet-Simon test and introduced it to the United States in 1916. In 1937, Terman, along with Maud A. Merrill, standardized it again and created two revised forms, Form L and Form M. In 1960, Form L-M was created from the two forms but the test was not restandardized until 1972. The Fourth Edition has some similarities to previous editions: 1) it spans the same age range; 2) many of the item types are the same; and 3) basal and ceiling levels are established.

The fourth edition of the Stanford-Binet assesses cognitive abilities in individuals ages 2 through 23 years. The test contains 15 subtests that evaluate four broad areas titled Verbal Reasoning, Abstract/Visual Reasoning, Quantitative Reasoning, and Short-Term Memory. In addition, there is a composite score which estimates g, general intellectual ability. Administration of specific subtests depends on the age of the individual to be assessed; however, not all subtests are administered to each examinee.

The test is based on a three-level hierarchical model of intelligence. At the first, or top, level, there is *g,* general reasoning ability. General ability consists "of the cognitive assembly and control processes that an individual uses to organize adaptive strategies for solving novel problems. In other words, *g* is what an individual uses when faced with a problem that he or she has not been taught to solve" (Thorndike, Hagen, and Sattler, 1986b, p. 3).

The second level consists of three broad factors: crystallized abilities, fluid-analytic abilities, and short-term memory. Crystallized abilities are defined as "the cognitive skills necessary for acquiring and using information about verbal and quantitative concepts to solve problems" (Thorndike, Hagen, and Sattler, 1986b, p. 4). It is thought that crystallized abilities are affected by experiences in school and outside of school. Fluid-analytic abilities are "the cognitive skills necessary for solving new problems that involve figural or other nonverbal stimuli" (Thorndike, Hagen, and Sattler, 1986c, p. 4). This factor is influenced by general experiences and is related to flexibility and the ability to deal with novel situations.

The third level is based on three factors: verbal reasoning, quantitative reasoning, and abstract/visual reasoning. The rationale for including these factors is that "they have special meaning to clinicians and educators" (1986b,

p. 5). Performance on the subtests bears on these three factors; and these factors contribute to the abilities in the second level.

It is hypothesized that the Fourth Edition measures inferred abilities and influences. The 15 subtests and the abilities that they measure can be found in Table 13.6 (Delaney and Hopkins, 1987; Sattler, 1988).

Administration

Although the test contains 15 subtests, no one individual is administered all of the subtests. All of the examinees are administered the Vocabulary Test first. This is referred to as the routing test. The performance on this subtest, along with the individual's chronological age, determines the remaining subtests to be administered. Depending on the age of the individual, 8 to 13 subtests are administered. This can take between one and two hours. For each subtest, specific instructions for administration are provided.

The routing test is sometimes inappropriate for individuals who are mentally retarded or who have other disabilities because the entry items are too difficult. Because of this, the entry level may have to be adjusted by test examiners in order to make it appropriate for these individuals (Sattler, 1988).

There are several short or abbreviated forms of the test that can be administered for screening purposes. A quick screening battery consists of four subtests: Vocabulary, Bead Memory, Quantitative, and Pattern Analysis. Another abbreviated form consists of six subtests: Vocabulary, Bead Memory, Quantitative, Memory for Sentences, Pattern Analysis, and Comprehension. In addition, there is a recommended brief battery for individuals who may be gifted.

The *Examiner's Handbook: An Expanded Guide for Fourth Edition Users* (Delaney and Hopkins, 1987) provides guidelines for modifying the test administration for persons who may be mentally retarded, deaf, visually impaired, blind, or who have limited English proficiency or who are non–language proficient. When making modifications in the test admin-

---

TABLE 13.6   Stanford-Binet Intelligence Scale: Fourth Edition

---

Verbal Reasoning

Vocabulary—Measures recall of expressive word knowledge and verbal comprehension.

Comprehension—Reflects verbal comprehension, vocabulary development, verbal expression, social knowledge, and factual information.

Absurdities—Assesses visual perception, factual knowledge, discrimination, verbal expression, attention, and social knowledge.

Verbal Relations—Assesses vocabulary development, concept formation, discrimination, inductive reasoning, verbal expression, and discrimination of essential details.

Quantitative Reasoning

Quantitative—Reflects knowledge of number facts, computation skills, and knowledge of mathematics concepts and procedures.

Number Series—Assesses logical reasoning, concentration, mathematics concepts and computation, and inductive reasoning.

Equation Building—Reflects knowledge of mathematics concepts and procedures, inductive reasoning, logic, flexibility, and trial and error.

Abstract/Visual Reasoning

Pattern Analysis—Measures visual-motor ability, spatial visualization, pattern analysis, and visual-motor coordination.

Copying—Measures visual imagery, visual perception, visual-motor ability, and eye-hand coordination.

Matrices—Evaluates attention, concentration, visual perception, visual analysis, spatial visualization, and inductive reasoning.

Paper Folding and Cutting—Reflects spatial ability, visual perception, visual analysis, and inductive reasoning.

Short-Term Memory

Bead Memory—Assesses short-term memory of visual stimuli. Also measures form perception, visual imagery, visual memory, discrimination, and alertness to detail.

Memory for Sentences—Measures short-term auditory memory, verbal comprehension, concentration, and attention.

Memory for Digits—Evaluates short-term auditory memory and attention.

Memory for Objects—Reflects visual comprehension, attention, concentration, and visual memory.

---

istration, examiners are urged to keep in mind that all individuals possess unique abilities.

Scoring

The manual provides clearly written directions for scoring. The scoring of the subtests varies from one subtest to another. Fourth Edition raw scores are converted to a Standard Age Score (SAS), which is a normalized standard score with a mean of 50 and a standard deviation of 8. The Standard Age Scores are converted to Area Scores and to a Composite SAS. These scores have a mean of 100 and a standard deviation of 16.

There is some evidence that scores on the Fourth Edition will be somewhat lower than scores on the Form L-M. In one study, 139 children, with an average age of 6 years, 11 months, were administered the Fourth Edition with the Form L-M edition. The average Composite score on the Fourth Edition was 105.8 with a standard deviation of 13.8; the mean Total score on the Form L-M was 108.1 with a standard deviation of 16.7.

Standardization

The standardization sample was based on the 1980 census and five variables were used to select participants: geographic region, community size, ethnic group (white, African American, Hispanic, Asian/Pacific Islander), age, and gender. A total of 5,013 individuals participated in the standardization. Because the sample consisted of too many persons in the upper socioeconomic categories, weighting procedures were used to adjust the final sample to the 1980 data on the U.S. population.

Reliability

Internal consistency coefficients for the individual subtests ranged from .73 (Memory for Objects) to .94 (Paper Folding and Cutting). In general, the reliabilities for subtests administered to older individuals were higher than the reliabilities for the subtests that were administered to younger children.

For all age groups, the internal consistency of the Composite Score ranged from .95 to .99. The internal consistency reliability of the Area Scores ranged from .82 (Quantitative Reasoning Area for 2-year-olds) to .97 (Abstract/Visual Reasoning for 18- to 23-year-olds), with many of the reliability coefficients in the .90s.

In order to examine test-retest reliability, two groups of persons were tested. One group consisted of 57 children who were 5 years old; the second group was composed of 55 persons who were 8 years old. Both groups were retested between two and eight months apart. For the 5-year-old group, the subtest reliabilities ranged from .56 (Bead Memory) to .77 (Memory for Sentences). Area Score reliabilities ranged from .71 (Quantitative Reasoning) to .88 (Verbal Reasoning). The Composite Score reliability was .91. For the 8-year-old group, subtest reliabilities varied from .28 (Quantitative) to .86 (Comprehension). Area Scores extended from .51 (Quantitative Reasoning) to .87 (Verbal Reasoning); and Composite Score reliability was .90.

Validity

Construct validity was investigated by conducting a factor analysis of the subtest scores across all ages in the standardization sample. The Stanford-Binet: Fourth Edition is based on the theory that the test measures g, general ability. Evidence of g was found across all ages although the factor loadings on g were greater in the 18- to 23-year-olds than in the younger ages.

Several studies examined concurrent validity. In the study of 139 children with an average age of 6.11 years who were administered the Fourth and the Form L-M editions, the correlation between the Composite score (Fourth Edition) and the Total score (Form L-M) was .81. Another study, with a sample of 205 children with an average age of 9 years, 5 months, investigated the correlations between Area scores and Composite scores on the Fourth Edition and Verbal IQs, Performance IQs, and Full Scale IQs on the *Wechsler Intelligence Scale for Children–Revised (WISC-R)* (1974). Correlations of the four Area scores with Verbal IQ and Performance IQ ranged from .60 to .72 and the correlation between the Composite score on the Fourth Edition with Full Scale IQ on the *WISC-R* was .83. While evidence of validity is presented by the authors, additional research must be conducted over time with varied populations.

Summary

The *Stanford-Binet Intelligence Scale: Fourth Edition* is a well-normed, reliable instrument. Evidence of validity is adequate. However, additional studies must be undertaken that investigate construct validity. While one important strength of the instrument is that it can be administered to individuals over a broad age range, not all subtests are administered to all examinees. Thus, comparisons between the performance of examinees over time is difficult. Another disadvantage is that the administration of the Fourth Edition can be more time-consuming compared with other intelligence tests.

Test of Nonverbal Intelligence, Second Edition

The *Test of Nonverbal Intelligence,* Second Edition *(TONI-2)* (Brown, Sherbenou, and Johnsen, 1990) is a nonverbal measure of abstract/figural problem solving for use with individuals ages 5 years to 85 years, 11 months. It can be used when assessing the performance of individuals who have language or motor problems that make it difficult for them to respond to more traditional tests. The authors state that it can be useful when assessing persons who have "aphasia, hearing impairments, lack of proficiency with spoken or written English, cerebral palsy, stroke, head trauma, and lack of familiarity with the culture of the United States" (Brown, Sherbenou, and Johnsen, 1990, p. 5). The test has two forms, each containing 55 items. The items consist of a series of abstract figures that require individuals to select the correct response by problem solving.

Administration

The test items are contained in an easel and the examiner pantomimes the instructions. The examiner begins the testing by pointing to a blank square in a pattern of figures, making a broad gesture to indicate the possible responses, pointing to the blank square again, and then looking questioningly at the individual. The student shows the correct response by pointing or by some other motor response. Throughout the administration of this instrument, neither the examiner nor the examinee speaks. This test is untimed, and the examiner is encouraged to allow examinees sufficient time to respond to each test item. The total time to administer the *TONI-2* is approximately 15 minutes. The advantages of this nonverbal method of test administration are that the examinee is not required to listen to directions, speak, read, or write.

The test is designed to be administered individually, however, the manual does contain directions for administering the *TONI-2* to groups of up to five individuals. Nonverbal administration is utilized, just as it is for an individual. With a small group the examiner goes from one examinee to the next, giving each one a turn to respond to the same item, making sure to use a separate answer booklet for each child.

BOX 13.8

STANFORD-BINET INTELLIGENCE SCALE: FOURTH EDITION

Publication Date: 1986

Purposes: Assesses general intellectual abilities (*g*) and cognitive abilities in four broad areas: Verbal Reasoning, Abstract/Visual Reasoning, Quantitative Reasoning, and Short-Term Memory.

Age/Grade Levels: 2 through 23 years

Time to Administer: one to two hours

Technical Adequacy: Well-normed, reliable instrument. Evidence of validity is adequate.

Suggested Uses: Assess intellectual ability, strengths and weaknesses. Can be used, in combination with other tests and forms of assessment, to identify students with special needs and determine eligibility for services; can be used when conducting a psychoeducational assessment and for clinical and neuropsychological assessment.

According to the authors, the TONI-2 can be administered by teachers, psychologists, psychological associates, and educational diagnosticians. It is expected that examiners have sufficient training and knowledge in the area of assessment.

Scoring

Items are scored as either correct or incorrect. Raw scores are converted to deviation quotients (standard scores with a mean of 100 and a standard deviation of 15) and percentile ranks. Since there are no subtests on the TONI-2, only the total score is reported.

Standardization

The *TONI-2* standardization sample consisted of 2,764 individuals, ranging in age from 5 years to 85 years, 11 months stratified by age. The characteristics of the sample are reported according to gender, race, ethnic group, geographic region, residence (rural, urban, suburban), and educational background. These demographic characteristics approximated the U.S. population, but some variables were either over- or underrepresented. For example, individuals who were classified as Caucasian were underrepresented while those from rural areas were overrepresented.

Reliability

Reliability for the *TONI-2* was calculated in several ways. Internal consistency reliability has a mean reliability coefficient of .95 for Form A and .96 for Form B.

Alternate-form reliability was calculated. This was done by correlating the scores from Forms A and B after they administered to the same individuals back-to-back. The mean reliability coefficient was .86. Alternate form reliability coefficients were reported for the various age groups in the sample. Reliability coefficients were computed for children age 5 (.80), age 6 (.86), age 7 (.84), and age 8 (.85).

The alternate forms were also administered in a delayed retest design. Both forms of the *TONI-2* were administered seven days apart to 39 individuals, ranging in age from 7 years, 9 months to 15 years, 9 months. The estimated reliability coefficient was .85.

Reliability coefficients were also reported for special populations, such as individuals who were mentally retarded, learning disabled, deaf, gifted, and Spanish-speaking. The coefficients that were reported were in the moderate range. However, for the most part, the number of persons included in the special population samples is small and additional research must be undertaken in this area.

Validity

Validity is concerned with determining whether a test measures what it purports to measure. The manual reports the results of studies conducted by the authors of the TONI-2 and by independent researchers. A number of validity studies were conducted and validity coefficients range from low to moderate when the *TONI-2* was correlated with measures of achievement and measures of intelligence.

Summary

The *TONI-2* is a nonverbal measure that assesses one aspect of intelligence, namely, problem solving. Reliability and validity coefficients are low to moderate. It must be used cautiously when assessing young children.

Wechsler Intelligence Scale for Children— Third Edition

The *Wechsler Intelligence Scale for Children– Third Edition (WISC-III)* (Wechsler, 1991) is a revision of the *Wechsler Intelligence Scale for Children–Revised* and is the third edition of the *Wechsler Intelligence Scale for Children,* which was originally published in 1949. It is an individually administered test designed to assess the intellectual ability of children ages 6 years through 16 years, 11 months. Wechsler conceptualizes intelligence as a global ability,

BOX 13.9

TEST OF NONVERBAL INTELLIGENCE, SECOND EDITION

Publication Date: 1990

Purposes: Nonverbal measure of abstract/figural problem solving that can be used when assessing the performance of individuals who have language or motor problems that may make it difficult for them to respond to more traditional tests.

Age/Grade Levels: 5 years to 85 years, 11 months

Time to Administer: 15 to 20 minutes

Technical Adequacy: The standardization sample is just acceptable. Reliability and validity coefficients are low to moderate.

Suggested Uses: The TONI-2 assesses one aspect of intelligence—problem solving. It is to be used with caution.

which is defined as the "capacity of the individual to act purposefully, to think rationally, and to deal effectively with his or her environment" (Wechsler, 1944, p. 3, cited in Wechsler, 1991). According to the manual, the *WISC-III* can be used for a number of purposes, including psychoeducational assessment, diagnosis of exceptional needs, and clinical and neuropsychological assessment.

The *WISC-III* consists of ten subtests and three optional subtests grouped into two scales, the Verbal Scale and the Performance Scale. The sum of the scores on the Verbal subtests result in a Verbal IQ score; the total of the scores on the Performance subtests result in a Performance IQ score. The scores on both the Verbal and Performance subtests result in a Full Scale IQ score. A completed *WISC-III* Record Form can be found in Figure 13.2 A description of each of the subtests can be found in Table 13.7.

The *WISC-III* also contains four factor-based index scores: Verbal Comprehension, Perceptual Organization, Freedom from Distractibility, and Processing Speed. Twelve of the 13 subtests yield the four factors. The arrangement of the four factors and their subtests is as follows:

Factor	Subtests
I Verbal Comprehension	Information, Similarities, Vocabulary, Comprehension
II Perceptual Organization	Picture Completion, Picture Arrangement, Block Design, Object Assembly
III Freedom from Distractibility	Arithmetic, Digit Span
IV Processing Speed	Coding, Symbol Search

Administration

The *WISC-III* is administered individually. The manual clearly explains the directions for administration and scoring for each of the 13 subtests. Each subtest has separate starting points, and the rules for stopping vary among the subtests. Administration time is approximately 60 to 90 minutes.

The *WISC-III* overlaps with the *Wechsler Preschool and Primary Scale of Intelligence–Revised (WPPSI-R)* for children who are 6 years to 7 years, 3 months. The manual recommends that for children who fall within this age range and who are of low ability that the *WPPSI-R* be used; for children who have high ability or are gifted, the *WISC-III* is recommended.

Scoring

The manual provides clearly written directions for scoring. The scoring of the subtests varies from one subtest to another. Raw scores are

WISC-III™
Wechsler Intelligence Scale for Children – Third Edition

Name _Loretta M. Flanagan_ Sex _f_

School _Cicero Elementary_ Grade _6_

Examiner _Sarah Draper_ Handedness _R_

Subtests	Raw Scores	Scaled Scores					
Picture Completion	22		11		11		
Information	20	13		13			
Coding	53		12				12
Similarities	19	11		11			
Picture Arrangement	30		9		9		
Arithmetic	22	15				15	
Block Design	46		12		12		
Vocabulary	42	14		14			
Object Assembly	33		12		12		
Comprehension	25	12		12			
(Symbol Search)	29		((13))				13
(Digit Span)	18	((14))				14	
(Mazes)	19		(19)				
Sum of Scaled Scores		65	56	50	44	29	25
		Verbal	Perfor.	VC	PO	FD	PS

Full Scale Score **121** OPTIONAL

	Year	Month	Day
Date Tested	91	8	20
Date of Birth	80	3	10
Age	11	5	10

	Score	IQ/Index	%ile	90% Confidence Interval
Verbal	65	118	88	112 – 122
Performance	56	108	70	101 – 114
Full Scale	121	114	82	109 – 118
VC	50	114	82	107 – 119
PO	44	107	68	99 – 113
FD	29	126	96	115 – 130
PS	25	114	82	104 – 120

Subtest Scores

Verbal						Performance					
Inf	Sim	Ari	Voc	Com	DS	PC	Cd	PA	BD	OA	SS	Mz
13	11	15	14	12	14	11	12	9	12	12	13	9

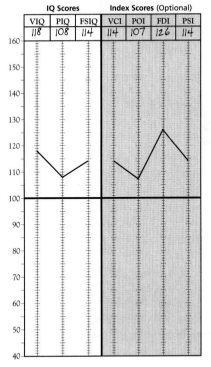

IQ Scores / Index Scores (Optional)

VIQ	PIQ	FSIQ	VCI	POI	FDI	PSI
118	108	114	114	107	126	114

THE PSYCHOLOGICAL CORPORATION®
HARCOURT BRACE JOVANOVICH, INC.

Copyright © 1991, 1986, 1974, 1971 by The Psychological Corporation
Standardization edition copyright © 1989 by The Psychological Corporation
Copyright 1949 by The Psychological Corporation
Copyright renewed 1976 by The Psychological Corporation
All rights reserved. Printed in the United States of America.

09–980004

FIGURE 13.2

Wechsler Intelligence Scale for Children-III, Record Form

TABLE 13.7 Wechsler Intelligence Scale for Children-III

Verbal Scale

Information. Questions that ask about common knowledge about events, objects, places, and people are presented orally by the examiner.

Similarities. The examinee explains the correspondence between pairs of words.

Arithmetic. Mathematical problems that the student solves mentally and responds to verbally.

Vocabulary. Words are presented orally and examinee defines them orally.

Comprehension. Questions that assess understanding of familiar problems and social concepts are presented orally by the examiner.

Digit Span. The individual repeats a series of numbers forward in the Digits Forward section and a series of numbers in reverse order in the Digits Backward section.

Performance Scale

Picture Completion. A picture with a missing part is shown to the examinee who must identify the missing piece.

Picture Arrangement. The individual must correctly sequence a series of pictures.

Block Design. The examinee reproduces a pattern using blocks.

Object Assembly. The individual assembles five jigsaw puzzles.

Coding. The examinee copies geometric symbols that are paired with either numbers or shapes.

Mazes. The individual completes a series of mazes using a pencil.

Symbol Search. The individual searches two groups of paired shapes to locate the target shape.

---

converted to scaled scores, which are a form of standard score with a mean of 100 and a standard deviation of 15. The scaled scores are used to determine the Verbal, Performance, and Full Scale IQ scores. The factor-based scores are optional and can be calculated from the scaled scores.

When children are retested using a revised instrument, there is usually some fluctuation in scores. When the *WISC-III* Verbal, Performance, and Full Scale scores were compared with the scores from the *WISC-R*, it was found that the *WISC-III* scores were lower than *WISC-R* scores. In general, *WISC-III* Full Scale scores were from 5 to 9 points lower than

WISC-R scores. Verbal and Performance Scale scores on the *WISC-III* ranged from 2 to 7 points lower than *WISC-R* scores. The average difference between *WISC-III* scores and *WPPSI-R* scores was about 4 points, with *WPPSI-R* scores generally being lower than *WISC-III* scores. However, this difference can be larger with children who fall at the upper or lower ends of the IQ range.

Standardization

The *WISC-III* was standardized based on 1988 data obtained from the U.S. Bureau of the Census. The standardization sample consisted of 2,200 children in each of 11 age groups extending from 6 to 16 years. The sample was stratified according to age, gender, race, ethnicity, geographic region, and parental education.

Students with exceptional needs were not systematically included in the *WISC-III* standardization sample and separate norms are not provided for these children. However, the manual provides summaries of several studies conducted by independent researchers with special populations, including gifted, mentally retarded, learning disabled, and those with attention-deficit hyperactivity disorder, behavior disorder, epilepsy, speech and language delays, and hearing impairment. For the most part, these studies are few in number and contain small samples. However, they are encouraging. Additional research is needed in this area.

Reliability

Reliability refers to the consistency or stability of test performance. Split-half reliability coefficients are reported for each of the subtests, for the three IQ scales, and for the four factor-based scales. Because reliability is affected by the length of a test, the highest reliability coefficient reported was for Full Scale IQ (.96). For the subtests, reliability coefficients ranged from .69 (Object Assembly) to .87 (Vocabulary and Block Design). Reliability coefficients for the factor-based scales ranged from .85 (Processing Speed) to .94 (Verbal Comprehension).

Test-retest reliability is an estimate of the stability of test scores over time. Test-retest reliability was assessed using a separate group of 353 children who were tested with the instrument twice. The median interval between testings was 23 days. Separate reliability coefficients were calculated for various age groups; for ages 6 and 7, reliability coefficients for the subtests ranged from .60 (Mazes) to .82 (Vocabulary, Picture Completion). Because the reliabilities for the subtests are low, the results of individual subtests should be interpreted with caution. For the IQ scores, test-retest reliabilities ranged from .86 (Performance IQ) to .92 (Full

Scale IQ); for the factor-based scores test-retest reliabilities ranged from .74 (Freedom from Distractibility) to .89 (Verbal Comprehension).

Like many tests, *WISC-III* scores show a slight increase when the testing interval is short. For example, for children ages 6 and 7, when the median test-retest interval was 23 days, Verbal IQ scores increased 1.7 points, Performance IQ scores increased 11.5 points, and Full Scale IQ scores increased 7 points.

Interscorer reliabilities were calculated for those subtests that require more judgment in scoring. For the subtests Similarities, Vocabulary, Comprehension, and Mazes, the interscorer reliability coefficients exceeded .90. The manual concludes that subtests that require some judgment in scoring can be reliably scored.

Validity

According to the manual, because the *WISC-R* is valid, the *WISC-III* is also valid. While it is true that there is considerable evidence for the validity of the *WISC-R,* the *WISC-III* is a substantial revision of the earlier version. Therefore, the evidence for the validity of the *WISC-III* based on the *WISC-R* must be relied on with this caveat in mind.

The manual does provide evidence for the separate factor structure of the subtests. In general, Verbal subtests correlate more strongly with each other than with Performance subtests; Performance subtests correlate more strongly with each other than with Verbal subtests. Factor analyses of the *WISC-III* scores confirm the likelihood of the four factors, Verbal Comprehension, Perceptual Organization, Freedom from Distractibility, and Processing Speed. However, Sattler (1992) has indicated that the Freedom from Distractibility factor may be weak and that interpretations based on this factor be made cautiously.

WISC-III scores were also correlated with scores from several other tests. This evidence supports the validity of the *WISC-III*. However,

SNAPSHOT

Andres

Andres is 11 years old and is in the fifth grade. He grew up in his neighborhood, and he has many friends there. Routinely, when Andres arrives home after school, he has a snack and then races outdoors. Andres has disliked school ever since he can remember. He always had a hard time with reading, writing, and spelling but he achieved somewhat better grades in mathematics.

Last week, there was a meeting at the school to discuss Andres' continuing academic difficulties. Andres attended the meeting along with his parents. His teachers, while praising him for working hard, reported that Andres lags considerably behind his peers in academic areas. His teachers agreed that Andres is a delight to have in class. The participants in the meeting agreed that an assessment of Andres' cognitive abilities should be conducted in order to gain a better understanding of his learning needs.

After permission was obtained from Andres's family, the psychologist administered the WISC-III to Andres. Keeping in mind that a standard score of 10 ± 3 falls within the average range, the following is a summary of the results:

	Standard Score
Verbal Scale	
Information	6
Similarities	11
Arithmetic	8
Vocabulary	9
Comprehension	7
Digit Span	7

Verbal Scale IQ	90
Average range is 85 to 115	
Performance Scale	
Picture Completion	10
Coding	8
Picture Arrangement	15
Block Design	15
Object Assembly	8
Symbol Search	14
Performance IQ	108
Average range is 85 to 115	
Full Scale IQ	98
Average range is 85 to 115	
Verbal Comprehension Index	91
Perceptual Organization Index	113
Freedom from Distractibility Index	87
Processing Speed Index	106

The psychologist summarized Andres' performance on the WISC-III. She wrote that Andres had significant strengths in both verbal and nonverbal concept formation, abstract reasoning, and visual sequencing; and relative weaknesses, although still within the average range, in using short-term memory and in visualizing the whole from the sum of its parts.

The psychologist recommended that new concepts should be presented globally first and then broken down into their components and that instruction in academic areas should take into consideration the weaknesses in short-term memory. Andres will need repetition in content areas when new concepts are presented and help in organizing his thoughts to make connections with prior knowledge in order to retrieve information at a later time.

additional research studies must be conducted in order to add to our knowledge about the validity of the *WISC-III.*

Summary

The *WISC-III* is an individually administered test of intelligence. Reliabilities of the individual subtests, for 6 and 7 year old children, is lower than for the Full Scale IQ score. Validity appears to be adequate. While additional research needs to be conducted to contribute to our understanding of it, this instrument is useful in the assessment of students.

Wechsler Preschool and Primary Scale of Intelligence—Revised

The *Wechsler Preschool and Primary Scale of Intelligence–Revised (WPPSI-R)* (Wechsler, 1989) is a revision of the *Wechsler Preschool and Pri-*

mary *Scale (WPPSI)* (Wechsler, 1967). It is an individually administered test of intelligence for children ages 3 to 7 years. The *WPPSI-R* is similar in format and content to the *WISC-III*. The *WPPSI-R* contains 12 subtests, two of which are optional, that are arranged in two scales: Verbal and Performance. Individual scores can be obtained for each of the subtests. Verbal, Performance, and Full Scale IQ scores are calculated from the subtest scores. Each of the subtests is described in Table 13.8.

Administration

Like the *WISC-III,* the *WPPSI-R* is administered individually. The directions for administering and scoring the 12 subtests are clearly presented in the manual. The subtests are administered in a specified order, and each subtest has separate starting and stopping points. The *WPPSI-R* overlaps with the *WISC-III* for children who are 6 years to 7 years, 3 months. The *WPPSI-R* manual recommends that if a child is suspected of having either average or below average ability, the *WPPSI-R* be used; for children who may be gifted, the *WISC-III* is recommended.

Scoring

Directions for scoring are clearly explained in the manual. Raw scores are converted to scaled scores, which have a mean of 100 and a standard deviation of 15. These scaled scores are used to calculate the Verbal, Performance, and Full Scale IQ scores.

Comparisons of *WPPSI-R* scores with other tests are reported in the manual. *WPPSI* Full Scale IQ scores are approximately 8 points higher than Full Scale IQ scores of the *WPPSI-R*. *WPPSI* Performance Scale IQ scores are approximately 9 points higher and Verbal Scale IQ scores were 5 points higher than WPPSI-R scores. The Stanford-Binet Composite scores and McCarthy Scales of Children's Abilities General Cognitive Index scores are approximately 2 points higher than *WPPSI-R* Full

---

BOX 13.10

WECHSLER INTELLIGENCE SCALE FOR CHILDREN–THIRD EDITION

Publication Date: 1991

Purposes: Assesses intellectual ability, areas of strength and weakness.

Age/Grade Levels: 6 years through 16 years, 11 months

Time to Administer: 60 to 90 minutes

Technical Adequacy: The standardization sample is excellent. Reliability is very good. Validity is adequate. Rely on evidence for the validity of the WISC-III based on the WISC-R with caution.

Suggested Uses: Can be used when conducting a psychoeducational assessment, diagnosis of exceptional needs, determining eligibility for services, and clinical and neuropsychological assessment.

TABLE 13.8 Wechsler Preschool and Primary Scale of Intelligence–Revised

Object Assembly. Pieces of a puzzle are arranged in front of the examinee in a standardized configuration. The individual must put the pieces together within a certain time limit.

Information. The examinee is asked to respond to items that demonstrate knowledge about events or objects in the environment. Depending on the level of difficulty of the item, responses are expressed either verbally or by pointing to a picture of an item.

Geometric Design. This subtest includes two types of items. The first asks the examinee to match a visual stimulus with one of the four choices that are presented. For the second type of item, the individual is asked to copy a geometric figure.

Comprehension. The individual is asked to express an understanding of the reasons for certain actions and consequences.

Block Design. The examinee must reproduce patterns of two-colored flat blocks that the examiner constructs.

Arithmetic. This subtest assesses the individual's understanding of basic quantitative concepts. Pictures, counting tasks, and word problems are presented.

Mazes. Using paper and pencil the examinee must solve, within specified time limits, printed mazes that increase in difficulty.

Vocabulary. Depending on the age of the examinee, the individual is asked to name objects that are pictured or to give oral definitions of words that the examiner presents verbally.

Picture Completion. The examinee must identify what is missing from objects or events that are pictured.

Similarities. The individual's understanding of the concept of similarities is assessed in three ways:
1) the examinee points to one of several objects that are pictured that have a common attribute; 2) the examinee completes a sentence that the examiner presents verbally and that contains an analogy or similarity; and 3) the individual explains orally how two objects or events are similar.

Animal Pegs. The examinee must associate a colored peg with each animal according to a key that is at the top of the board. This optional subtest assesses speed and accuracy.

Sentences. The examinee repeats a sentence that the examiner says. Like the Animal Pegs subtest, this subtest is optional.

Scale IQ scores. Similarly, the Mental Processing Composite of the *Kaufman Assessment Battery for Children (K-ABC)* was 6 points higher than the *WPPSI-R* Full Scale IQ score.

Standardization

The standardization sample was selected based on 1986 data obtained from the Bureau of the Census. The sample consisted of 1,700 children, ages 3 to 7 years, 3 months. The sample was stratified according to age, gender, geographic region, ethnicity, parental education, and parental occupation. Four hundred minority group children were oversampled in order to investigate item bias.

Children with exceptional needs were not systematically included in the standardization sample. However, several small studies were conducted with groups of children with exceptional needs. A sample of 16 gifted children who had been tested with the Stanford-Binet showed that some of these children would not be classified gifted based on their performance on the *WPPSI-R*. Studies of children who are mentally retarded, learning disabled, and who have speech/language impairments showed that the *WPPSI-R* could be useful with these groups. However, the studies were limited and additional research is needed in this area.

Reliability

Interscorer and test-retest reliabilities were determined. Interscorer reliability of the Comprehension, Vocabulary, Similarities, and Mazes subtests were calculated using a sample of 151 scorers; and for the Geometric Design subtest, 188 scorers were used. The interscorer reliabilities were: Comprehension .96, Vocabulary .94, Similarities .96, Mazes .94, and Geometric Design .88.

Test-retest reliability was determined from a sample of 175 children who were randomly selected from the standardization sample. The test-retest interval ranged from three to seven weeks. Corrected coefficients for the subtests ranged from .52 (Mazes) to .82 (Picture Completion). The correlation coefficients for the three scales were: Verbal Scale .90, Performance Scale .88, and Full Scale IQ .91. Because the coefficients on the subtests are relatively weak, less emphasis should be placed on their interpretation.

Validity

Part of the discussion in the manual on the validity of the *WPPSI-R* is based on previous research conducted on the earlier WPPSI. However, the *WPPSI-R* is a comprehensive revision and much of the evidence presented for validity of the WPPSI is not applicable to the *WPPSI-R*.

Descriptions of concurrent validity studies with the *WPPSI-R* and other instruments are presented. In general, the *WPPSI-R* correlated higher with the *WPPSI* and the *Wechsler Intelligence Scale for Children–Revised (WISC-R)*.

Moderate correlations were obtained with the Stanford-Binet and the McCarthy Scales. Relatively low coefficients resulted when *WPPSI-R* scores were correlated with *K-ABC* scores.

Summary

The *WPPSI-R* is an individually administered test of intelligence for children ages 3 to 7 years. The standardization is adequate. Information about reliability and validity is limited.

Woodcock-Johnson Psychoeducational Battery—Revised, Tests of Cognitive Ability

The *Woodcock-Johnson Psychoeducational Battery–Revised (WJ-R)* (Woodcock and Johnson, 1989) is an individually administered battery that assesses cognitive and academic abilities in individuals ages 2 years through adulthood. The battery consists of two tests, *Woodcock-Johnson Tests of Cognitive Ability (WJ-R COG)* and the *Woodcock-Johnson Tests of Achievement (WJ-R ACH)*. Each part contains a Standard Battery and a Supplemental Battery. Each standard battery can be administered alone or with the supplemental batteries. The *WJ-R* has the following purposes: 1) diagnosis, 2) determination of psychoeducational discrepancies, 3) program placement, 4) individual program planning, 5) guidance, 6) assessing growth, 7) program evaluation, and 8) research.

The *WJ-COG* is based on the Horn-Cattell theory of cognitive processing. The abilities measured by the *WJ-COG* are fluid reasoning, comprehension knowledge, visual processing, auditory processing, processing speed, long-term retrieval, and short-term memory. The subtests, which include at least two measures of each factor, form clusters for each of these abilities. These are described in Table 13.9.

Administration

The time to administer the *WJ-R* varies from 20 minutes to several hours depending on whether both the *WJ-R COG* and the *WJ-R ACH* are administered and whether the Standard Batteries

---

TABLE 13.9   Woodcock-Johnson Psychoeducational Battery–Revised, Tests of Cognitive Ability

---

The Standard Battery of the WJ-RCOG consists of seven subtests, one for each hypothesized ability. For children who are younger than kindergarten age, five subtests can be combined to form the Early Development Scale. These subtests are Memory for Names, Memory for Sentences, Incomplete Words, Visual Closure, and Picture Vocabulary.

Memory for Names. Assesses the ability to learn the names of nine drawings of space creatures after the examiner has said the name. This subtest is intended to measure long-term retrieval.

Memory for Sentences. Assesses the ability to repeat phrases and sentences that are presented either by the examiner or by listening to an audiotape. This subtest is intended to measure short-term memory and attention.

Visual Matching. Assesses the ability to match numbers within a three-minute time interval. This subtest is intended to measure processing speed.

Incomplete Words. Assesses the ability to repeat a word that has several phonemes missing. This subtest is intended to measure auditory processing.

Visual Closure. Assesses the ability to name a picture or drawing that has been distorted, has lines missing, or has a superimposed pattern. This subtest is intended to measure visual processing.

Picture Vocabulary. Assesses the ability to identify pictures of familiar and unfamiliar objects. This subtest measures comprehension intelligence or crystallized knowledge.

Analysis-Synthesis. Assesses the ability to identify the missing pieces in a logic puzzle. This subtest measures reasoning or fluid intelligence.

There are an additional 14 subtests in the Supplemental Battery.

Visual-Auditory Learning. Measures the ability to associate abstract visual symbols with familiar words. This subtest measures long-term retrieval.

Memory for Words. Assesses the ability to repeat lists of unrelated words. This subtest measures short-term memory and attention.

Cross Out. Measures the ability to match five drawings in a row of 20 drawings within a three-minute time interval. This subtest measures visual-processing speed.

---

and the Supplemental Batteries are used. Raw scores can be converted to age and grade equivalents, percentile ranks, and standard scores. The scoring can be cumbersome, and it is advisable to use a computer scoring program.

Norms

The *WJ-R* was standardized on 6,359 individuals in over 100 communities. The preschool sample consisted of 705 children who were 2 to 5 years of age and not enrolled in kindergarten. There were 3,245 individuals in the kindergarten through grade 12 sample. The rest of the standardization sample consisted of individuals who were in college or not in school. The sample was stratified according to region, community size, sex, race (Caucasian, African American, Native American, Asian Pacific, Hispanic (non-Hispanic), funding of col-

TABLE 13.9   (Continued)

Sound Blending. Assesses the ability to say whole words after hearing the syllables. This subtest measures auditory processing.

Picture Recognition. Requires the ability to recognize a group of pictures that have previously been presented with a group of distracting pictures. This subtest measures visual processing.

Oral Vocabulary. Measures the ability to provide synonyms or antonyms in response to words read by the examiner. This subtest measures comprehension knowledge or crystallized intelligence.

Concept Formation. Assesses the ability to provide a concept when various stimuli are presented. This subtest measures reasoning or fluid intelligence.

Delayed Recall–Memory for Names. Measures the ability to recall the names of the space creatures that were presented in the previous subtest Memory for Names after an interval of one to eight days. This subtest measures long-term retrieval.

Delayed Recall–Visual-Auditory Learning. Assesses the ability to recall the symbols that were presented in the subtest Visual-Auditory Learning after an interval of one to eight days. This subtest measures long-term retrieval.

Numbers Reversed. Assesses the ability to say a series of numbers backward. This subtest measures short-term memory and attention.

Sound Patterns. Measures the abilities to identify whether certain sound patterns that are presented on an audiotape are the same or different. This subtest measures reasoning and auditory processing.

Spatial Relations. Assesses the ability to match shapes. This subtest measures fluid intelligence and visual processing.

Listening Comprehension. Measures the ability to provide the missing word after listening to a brief audiotaped passage. This subtest measures comprehension knowledge or crystallized intelligence.

Verbal Analogies. Assesses the ability to complete phrases that contain analogies. This subtest measures comprehension knowledge or crystallized intelligence.

lege/university, type of college/university, occupational status of adults, and occupation of adults. The norms are continuous-year norms, that is, they were collected throughout the year.

Reliability

For both *WJ-R COG* and the *WJ-R ACH,* only one type of reliability, internal consistency, is reported, and these reliabilities are reported only for certain ages. Of special interest is that for young children, reliabilities are only reported for ages 2, 4, and 6. No reliability information is provided for ages 3, 5, 7, or 8. Users of this battery must be cautious in interpreting the reliability information.

For the *WJ-R COG* the internal consistency reliabilities for the subtests for ages 2, 4, and 6 range from .73 to .92. For the Early Development Scale the reliabilities range from .91 (age

6) to .95 (age 2). For the *WJ-R ACH* Standard Battery, the internal consistency reliabilities for the subtests are reported by age and not by grade. The reliabilities for ages 2, 4, and 6 range from .74 to .93. For the clusters, the reliabilities ranged from .91 to .97.

Validity

The manual reports a number of validity studies for both the cognitive and achievement batteries. In general, there is evidence to support content, concurrent, and construct validity. It should be remembered that the achievement portion of the battery reflects a skills-oriented approach to assessment, and that the cognitive portion represents a single theoretical perspective, the Horn-Cattell theory. The extent to which various subtests reflect students' abilities depends on the orientation of the team to assessment.

Summary

The *Woodcock-Johnson Psychoeducational Battery–Revised (WJ-R)* (Woodcock and Johnson, 1989) is a norm-referenced, individually administered battery that assesses cognitive and academic abilities in individuals ages 24 months through adulthood. The battery consists of two parts, cognitive and achievement. Reliability information is lacking. Additional investigation of validity is warranted, especially regarding the use of the battery with young children.

PREFERRED PRACTICES

Our understanding of intelligence has developed and changed over the years. Theorists have written about the nature of intelligence and how it should be measured. Although there are differing perspectives, we do know that intelligence is not a unitary construct. Various theorists have conceptualized intelligence as

---

BOX 13.11

WOODCOCK-JOHNSON PSYCHO-EDUCATIONAL BATTERY–REVISED, TESTS OF COGNITIVE ABILITY

Publication Date: 1989

Purposes: Assesses cognitive abilities, including fluid reasoning, comprehension knowledge, visual processing, auditory processing, processing speed, long-term retrieval, and short-term memory

Age/Grade Levels: 2 years through adulthood

Time to Administer: Approximately one hour

Technical Adequacy: The standardization sample is appropriate. Reliability information is lacking. Validity is adequate.

Suggested Uses: Diagnosis, determining eligibility for services, program placement, individual program planning, program evaluation

---

being composed of various abilities. However, they have disagreed about the exact nature of these constituent abilities.

New conceptualizations of the construct of intelligence are emerging. Howard Gardner (1991) has developed the theory of multiple intelligences (MI). According to Gardner, individuals

> are capable of at least seven different ways of knowing the world—ways that I have elsewhere labeled the *seven human intelligences.* According to this analysis, we are able to know the world through language, logical-mathematical analysis, spatial representation, musical thinking, the use of the body to solve problems or to make things, an understanding of other individuals, and an understanding of ourselves (Gardner, 1991, p. 12).

According to MI theory, individuals have different profiles of strengths of the seven intelligences, and individuals differ in the ways they invoke and combine the various intelligences to carry out tasks and to solve problems. Gardner believes that school environments need to be developed based on these seven ways of knowing. According to Gardner, curriculum that is founded on these ways of knowing is worth assessing; if the curriculum is not appropriately structured, then the assessment is useless.

MI theory may be used as an approach to assessment. Although there are no formal assessment tools that are based on MI theory, Gardner advocates the use of this approach to develop alternative and authentic forms of assessment.

Robert Sternberg (1985) has described a theory of intelligence, called the Triarchic Theory, which has three components: metacomponents, performance components, and knowledge-acquisition components. Metacomponents are similar to metacognitive processes in that they help to plan, monitor, and evaluate an individual's performance of a task.

Sternberg (1985) listed ten metacomponents as important to intelligent functioning:

1. recognition that a problem of some kind exists,
2. recognition of just what the nature of the problem is,
3. selection of a set of lower-order, nonexecutive components for the performance on a task,
4. selection of a strategy for task performance, combining the lower-order components,
5. selection of one or more mental representations for information,
6. decision on how to allocate attentional resources,
7. monitoring or keeping track of one's place in task performance and of what has been done and needs to be done,

8. understanding of internal and external feedback concerning the quality of task performance,
9. knowing how to act on the feedback that is received, and
10. implementation of action as a result of the feedback (p. 62).

Performance components are employed to execute a variety of strategies for task performance. These are lower-order processes, and they include:

1. encoding the nature of a stimulus,
2. inferring the relations between two stimulus terms that are similar in some ways and different in others, and
3. applying a previously inferred relation to a new situation (Sternberg, 1985, p. 62).

Knowledge-acquisition components are processes that are used to learn new information and to store this new information in memory. There are three knowledge-acquisition components:

1. selective encoding, which involves selecting between relevant and irrelevant information;
2. selective combination, which involves combining what has been selectively encoded in order to maximize its coherence and connectedness; and,
3. selective comparison, which consists of relating the information that has been selectively encoded and combining it with information already stored in memory in order to optimize the connectedness of the new knowledge (Sternberg, 1985, p. 62).

When interpreting an individual's performance on an intelligence test, the following cautions should be kept in mind:

1. The examinee's background, environment, motivation, health, and emotional state can affect performance. Other factors include examiner bias, cultural and linguistic differences between the examinee and the

examiner, rapport, the skill of the examiner, the test environment, and the demands of the test (Taylor, 1990).

2. Intelligence tests sample behaviors. Performance on a test helps us in our understanding of the examinee's approach to the demands of the tasks that are presented. There are many behaviors that intelligence tests do not sample and our understanding of these is emerging.

3. Performance on an intelligence test should be regarded as helping to describe rather than to explain behavior. Scores on an IQ test represent the examinee's performance at a given moment in time. We know that, especially with young children, tested intelligence can change over time (Anastasi, 1988; Sattler, 1988).

EXTENDING LEARNING

13.1 Explain how our conceptualization of intelligence has evolved over time.

13.2 When measuring intelligence, what special considerations need to be made when testing a student from another culture?

13.3 What is meant by the following statement: The results of intelligence tests should be used to describe rather than explain behavior?

13.4 Examine several different intelligence tests. How do they differ in form and content?

13.5 What do you think intelligence tests will be like 20 years from now?

REFERENCES

Algozzine, B., R. C. Eaves, L. Mann, and H. R. Vance (1993). *Slosson full-range intelligence test.* East Aurora, N.Y.: Slosson Educational Publications.

Anastasi, A. (1985). Review of the Kaufman assessment battery for children. In *Mental measurements yearbook: Vol. 1,* ed. G. Mitchell, 769–771. Lincoln: University of Nebraska.

Anastasi, A. (1988). *Psychological testing.* New York: Macmillan.

Brown, L., R. J. Sherbenou, and S. K. Johnsen (1990). *Test of nonverbal intelligence-2.* Austin, Tex.: PRO-ED.

Burgenmeister, B., L. Blum, and I. Lorge (1972). *Columbia mental maturity scale.* San Antonio, Tex.: The Psychological Corporation.

Cattell, P. (1960). *Cattell infant intelligence scale.* San Antonio, TX: The Psychological Corporation.

Cattell, P. (1980). *The measurement of intelligence of infants and young children.* (1940. Fifth reprinting.) San Antonio, Tex.: The Psychological Corporation.

Coffman, W. E. (1985). Review of the Kaufman assessment battery for children. In *Mental health measurements yearbook: Vol. 1,* ed. G. Mitchell, 771–773. Lincoln: University of Nebraska.

Das, J. P., J. R. Kirby, and R. F. Jarman (1975). Simultaneous and successive syntheses: An alternative model for cognitive abilities. *Psychological Bulletin* 82: 87–103.

Das, J. P., J. R. Kirby, and R. F. Jarman (1979). *Simultaneous and successive cognitive processes.* New York: Academic Press.

Das, J. P., and G. N. Molloy (1975). Varieties of simultaneous and successive processing in children. *Journal of Educational Psychology* 67: 213–220.

Davis, C. (1980). *Perkins-Binet test of intelligence for the blind.* Watertown, Mass.: Perkins School for the Blind.

Delaney, E. A., and T. F. Hopkins (1987). *The Stanford-Binet intelligence scale: Fourth Edition, Examiner's Handbook.* Chicago: Riverside.

Elliot, C. D. (1990a). *Differential ability scales—Administration and scoring manual.* San Antonio, Tex.: The Psychological Corporation.

Elliot, C. D. (1990b). *Differential ability scales—Introduction and technical handbook.* San Antonio, Tex.: Psychological Corporation.

Fancher, R. E. (1985). *The intelligence men.* New York: W. W. Norton.

French, J. L. (1964). *Pictorial test of intelligence.* Boston, Mass.: Houghton-Mifflin.

French, J. L., and R. L. Hale (1990). A history of the development of psychological and educational testing. In *Handbook of psychological and educa-*

tional assessment of children, eds. C. R. Reynolds and R. W. Kamphaus, 3–28. New York: Guilford Press.

Gardner, H. (1991). *The unschooled mind.* New York: Basic Books.

Griffiths, R. (1979). *The abilities of young children.* London: Child Development Research Center.

Guilford, J. P. (1967). *The nature of human intelligence.* New York: McGraw-Hill.

Hammill, D. D. (1991). *Detroit tests of learning aptitude-3.* Austin, Tex.: PRO-ED.

Hammill, D. D., and B. R. Bryant (1991). *Detroit tests of learning aptitude–primary.* 2d ed. Austin, Tex.: PRO-ED.

Hammill, D. D., N. A. Pearson, and J. L. Wiederholt (1996). *Comprehensive test of nonverbal intelligence.* Austin, Tex.: PRO-ED.

Hiskey, M. S. (1966). *Hiskey-Nebraska test of learning aptitude.* Lincoln, Nebr.: Author.

Horn, J. L. (1985). Remodeling old models of intelligence. In *Handbook of intelligence,* ed. B. B. Wolman, 267–300. New York: John Wiley & Sons.

Kaufman, A. S., and N. L. Kaufman (1983). *Kaufman assessment battery for children.* Circle Pines, Minn.: American Guidance Service.

Kaufman, A. S., and N. L. Kaufman (1990) *Kaufman brief intelligence test.* Circle Pines, Minn.: American Guidance Service.

Kaufman, A. S., and N. L. Kaufman (1993). *Kaufman adolescent & adult intelligence test.* Circle Pines, Minn.: American Guidance Service.

Kelves, D. J. (1985). *In the name of eugenics.* New York: Knopf.

Leiter, R. G. (1979). *Leiter international performance scale* (rev. ed.). Wood Dale, Il.: Stoelting.

McCarthy, D. (1972). *McCarthy scales of children's abilities.* New York: The Psychological Corporation.

Merz, W. R. (1984). Review of the Kaufman assessment battery for children. In *Test Critiques: Vol. 1,* ed. K. Sweetland, 393–404. Kansas City, Mo.: Test Corporation of America.

Neisworth, J. T., and S. J. Bagnato (1992). The case against intelligence testing in early intervention. *Topics in Early Childhood Special Education* 12: 1–20.

Page, E. B. (1985). Review of the Kaufman assessment battery for children. In *Mental health measurements yearbook: Vol. 1,* ed. G. Mitchell, 773–777. Lincoln: University of Nebraska.

Reynolds, C. R., and A. S. Kaufman (1985). Clinical assessment of children's intelligence with the Wechsler scales. In *Handbook of Intelligence,* ed. B. B. Wolman, 601–661. New York: John Wiley & Sons.

Salvia, J., and J. Ysseldyke (1988). *Assessment in special and remedial education.* Boston, Mass.: Houghton-Mifflin.

Salvia, J., and J. Ysseldyke (1995). *Assessment.* Boston, Mass.: Houghton-Mifflin.

Sattler, J. (1988). *Assessment of children.* San Diego, Calif.: Jerome M. Sattler.

Sattler, J. (1992). *WISC-III and WPPSI-R supplement to assessment of children.* San Diego, Calif.: Jerome M. Sattler.

Slosson, R. (1991). *Slosson intelligence test.* East Aurora, N.Y.: Slosson Educational Publications.

Sternberg, R. (1985). Cognitive approaches to intelligence. In *Handbook of intelligence,* ed. B. B. Wolman, 59–118. New York: John Wiley & Sons.

Sternberg, R. (1996). Myths, countermyths, and truths about intelligence. *Educational Researcher,* 25: 11–16.

Suzuki, L. A., D. A. Vraniak, and J. F. Kugler (1996). Intellectual assessment across cultures. In *Handbook of multicultural assessment,* eds. L. A., Suzuki P. J. Meller, and J. G. Ponterotto, 141–177. San Francisco: Jossey-Bass.

Taylor, R. (1990). Intellectual assessment tips. *Diagnostique* 16: 52–54.

Thorndike, R. L., and E. Hagen (1993). *Cognitive abilities test, Form 5.* Chicago: Riverside.

Thorndike, R. L., E. P. Hagen, and J. M. Sattler (1986a). *Technical manual Stanford-Binet intelligence scale: Fourth edition.* Chicago: Riverside.

Thorndike, R. L., E. P. Hagen, and J. M. Sattler (1986b). *Guide for administering and scoring the fourth edition.* Chicago: Riverside.

Thorndike, R. L., E. P. Hagen, and J. M. Sattler (1986c). *Stanford-Binet intelligence scale: Fourth edition.* Chicago: Riverside.

Thorndike, R. M., and D. F. Lohman (1990). *A century of ability testing.* Chicago: Riverside.

Valencia, R. R., R. J. Rankin, and R. Livingston (1995). K-ABC content bias: Comparisons between Mexican-American and White children. *Psychology in the schools* 32: 153–169.

Wechsler, D. (1944). *The measurement of adult intelligence.* 3rd ed. Baltimore: Williams & Wilkins.

Wechsler, D. (1967). *Manual of the Wechsler preschool and primary scale of intelligence.* San Antonio, Tex.: The Psychological Corporation.

Wechsler, D. (1989). *WPPSI-R manual.* San Antonio, Tex.: The Psychological Corporation.

Wechsler, D. (1991). *Wechsler intelligence scale for children-III.* San Antonio, Tex.: The Psychological Corporation.

Woodcock, R. W., and M. B. Johnson (1989). *Woodcock-Johnson psychoeducational battery–Revised.* Allen, Tex.: DLM.

Woodcock, R. W., and A. F. Muñoz-Sandoval (1996). *Batería-R tests of cognitive ability.* Itasca, Ill.: Riverside.

Adaptive Skills

OVERVIEW

Adaptive skills are competencies that an individual has in the following areas: communication, self-care, home living, social skills, community use, self-direction, health and safety, functional academics, leisure, and work (American Association on Mental Retardation, 1992). The concept of adaptive skills is an outgrowth of the term adaptive behavior, which is defined as "the quality of everyday performance in coping with environmental demands" (Grossman, 1983, p. 42). The concept of adaptive behavior has been influenced by theory, professional practice, politics, and litigation. However, because the concept of adaptive skills reflects a more contemporary approach to this area, we will use the term *adaptive skills* in this book rather than adaptive behavior.

According to the American Association on Mental Retardation, the designation *adaptive skills*

implies an array of competencies and, thus, provides a firmer foundation in several of the definition's key statements; that is, adaptive skill limitations often coexist with strengths in other adaptive skills or other areas of personal competence, and the existence of these limitations and strengths in adaptive skills must be both documented within the context of community environments typical of the individual's age peers and tied to the person's individualized needs for support (American Association on Mental Retardation, 1992, p. 4).

CHAPTER OBJECTIVES

After completing this chapter, you should be able to:

Define and describe the concept of adaptive skills.

Explain the changing nature of the concepts of adaptive behavior and adaptive skills.

Describe maladaptive behavior and problem behavior.

Describe specific tests of adaptive skills, adaptive behavior, and maladaptive behavior.

WHAT SHAPES OUR VIEWS

For students who are in school, the measurement of adaptive skills plays a large part in determining whether a student is labeled mentally retarded. According to the American Association on Mental Retardation

> mental retardation refers to substantial limitations in present functioning. It is characterized by significantly subaverage intellectual functioning, existing concurrently with related limitations in two or more of the following adaptive skill areas: communication, self-care, home living, social skills, community use, self-direction, health and safety, functional academics, leisure, and work. Mental retardation manifests before age 18 (American Association on Mental Retardation, 1992, p. 5).

The identification of a student as mentally retarded is related to the identification of at least two limitations in **adaptive skills.** An individual's adaptive skills reflect the competencies that the person has for functioning at home, work, and in the community. The ten adaptive skill areas are described in Table 14.1.

Identification of strengths and weaknesses in adaptive skill areas document the need for supports. **Supports** are

> resources and strategies that promote the interests and causes of individuals with or without disabilities; that enable them to access resources, information, and relationships inherent within integrated work and living environments; and that result in their enhanced interdependence/interdependence, productivity, community integration, and satisfaction (American Association on Mental Retardation, 1992, p. 101).

The assessment of adaptive skills should result in the identification of supports that an individual needs. The desired outcomes of using supports include contributions to personal, social, and emotional development; strengthening of the individual's self-esteem and self-worth; and providing opportunities to make contributions. Supports have a number of functions, can come from many resources, and can vary in intensity (American Association on Mental Retardation, 1992). Figure 14.1 illustrates the interrelationships between desired outcomes, support resources, support functions, and intensities of support.

Cautions

Because our views of adaptive skills and **adaptive behavior** have changed and will continue to change over time, there is considerable disagreement over how current assessment instruments measure these skills. In general, instruments that assess adaptive skills are useful when determining eligibility, engaging in program planning, and monitoring progress. There is considerable overlap between instruments that assess adaptive skills, adaptive behavior, problem behavior, functional skills, and development. In addition, almost all of the commerically published instruments refer to adaptive behavior rather than to adaptive skills. Finally, adaptive behavior instruments are based on different views of adaptive behavior, and the assessment of adaptive behavior and adaptive skills depends on the orientations of the developers of the instruments.

RESPONDING TO DIVERSITY

Adaptive skills are influenced by gender, racial, ethnic, or cultural groups, community expectations, and the life cycle. What is considered an adaptive skill in one environment is not considered an adaptive skill in another environment. The quality of adaptive skills that are demonstrated are different at various ages. In addition, the presence of a disability can compound the identification of adaptive skills. Limitations in motor ability, expressive and receptive abili-

TABLE 14.1 Adaptive Behavior Skills

1. *Communication:* Skills include the ability to comprehend and express information through symbolic behaviors (e.g., spoken word, written word/orthography, graphic symbols, sign language, manually coded English) or non-symbolic behaviors (e.g., facial expression, body movement, touch, gesture). Specific examples include the ability to comprehend and/or receive a request, an emotion, a greeting, a comment, a protest, or rejection. Higher level skills of communication (e.g., writing a letter) would also relate to functional academics.

2. *Self-Care:* skills involved in toileting, eating, dressing, hygiene, and grooming.

3. *Home-Living:* skills related to functioning within a home, which include clothing care, housekeeping, property maintenance, food preparation and cooking, planning and budgeting for shopping, home safety, and daily scheduling. Related skills include orientation and behavior in the home and nearby neighborhood, communication of choices and needs, social interaction, and application of functional academics in the home.

4. *Social:* skills related to social exchanges with other individuals, including initiating, interacting, and terminating interaction with others; receiving and responding to pertinent situational cues; recognizing feelings; providing positive and negative feedback; regulating one's own behavior; being aware of peers and peer acceptance; gauging the amount and type of interaction with others; assisting others; forming and fostering of friendships and love; coping with demands from others; making choices; sharing; understanding honesty and fairness; controlling impulses; conforming conduct to laws; violating rules and laws; and displaying appropriate socio-sexual behavior.

5. *Community Use:* skills related to the appropriate use of community resources, including traveling in the community; grocery and general shopping at stores and markets; purchasing or obtaining services from other community businesses (e.g., gas stations, repair shops, doctor and dentist's offices); attending church or synagogue; using public transportation and public facilities, such as schools, libraries, parks and recreational areas, and streets and sidewalks; attending theaters; and visiting other cultural places and events. Related skills include behavior in the community, communication of choices and needs, social interaction, and the application of functional academics.

6. *Self-Direction:* skills related to making choices; learning and following a schedule; initiating activities appropriate to the setting, conditions, schedule, and personal interests; completing necessary or required tasks; seeking assistance when needed; resolving problems confronted in familiar and novel situations; and demonstrating appropriate assertiveness and self-advocacy skills.

7. *Health and Safety:* skills related to maintenance of one's health in terms of eating; illness identification, treatment, and prevention; basic first aid; sexuality; physical fitness; basic safety considerations (e.g., following rules and laws, using seat belts, crossing streets, interacting with strangers, seeking assistance); regular physical and dental check-ups; and personal habits. Related skills include protecting oneself from criminal behavior, using appropriate behavior in the community, communicating choices and needs, participating in social interactions, and applying functional academics.

Source: American Association on Mental Retardation (1992). Washington, D.C.: American Association on Mental Retardation, pp. 40–41. Reprinted with permission of the publisher.

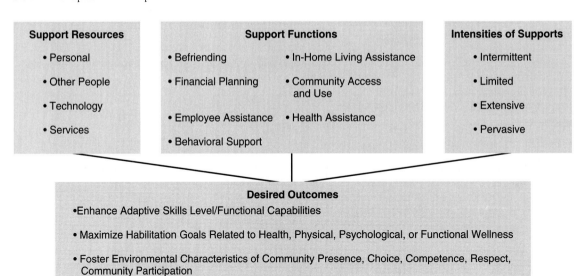

FIGURE 14.1

Support Resources, Functions, Intensities, and Desired Outcomes

Source: American Association on Mental Retardation (1992). Washington, D.C.: American Association on Mental Retardation, p. 102. Reprinted with permission of the publisher.

ties, or in other areas can make the assessment of adaptive skills difficult or impossible.

INFORMANTS

Instruments that assess adaptive skills, adaptive behavior, and maladaptive behavior usually rely on an informant. An **informant** is an individual who knows the student well and provides information about the student. The informant responds to questions about the individual either through an interview with the examiner or by completing a checklist or scale. Because the assessment of adaptive skills and adaptive behavior relies on ratings provided by informants, the instruments can be administered frequently.

The informant can be a parent, teacher, counselor, aide, nurse, or social worker. Informants provide different information about students, although there may be considerable overlap. For instance, the teacher, social

worker, or counselor provides information about peer relationships while the parent offers information about sibling relationships and activities around the home.

The information that the informants provide is considered to be judgmental, and can vary from one informant to the next. Informants bring their own perspectives, experiences, attitudes, response styles, and biases; and the student is likely to behave differently, depending on the environment or the situation. Because of these variables, it is important to evaluate the reliability and validity of the information that is supplied. It is helpful to ask more than one informant to complete an instrument or scale (Sattler, 1988).

MALADAPTIVE BEHAVIOR

Maladaptive behaviors are those behaviors that are considered to be problem behaviors. Examples of maladaptive behaviors include bed wetting, unusual physical aggressiveness, poor attention, impulsivity, self-injurious behaviors, rocking back and forth repetitively, and poor eye contact. In general, a student's actions are considered a problem when they adversely affect the student, another student, or the environment (Bruininks, Thurlow, and Gilman, 1987). Problem behaviors affect the extent to which individuals can be integrated into social and community settings. With older students, the presence of problem behaviors can have a negative impact on vocational and community placements (Bruininks, Thurlow, and Gilman, 1987).

The concept of maladaptive behavior, like the concept of adaptive behavior, is not without controversy. The assessment of maladaptive behavior is related to expectations tied to the student's age, family, culture, gender, and community. For example, thumb sucking is not considered a maladaptive behavior for a 2-year-old, but may be considered maladaptive for an 8-year-old.

STANDARDIZED INSTRUMENTS

The instruments that are described in this chapter have been specifically developed to evaluate adaptive behavior. Many assess adaptive skills and some assess maladaptive behavior. There are many other tests that assess adaptive skills in addition to the tests described in this chapter. These tests are listed in Tables 14.2, 14.3, and 14.4.

Adaptive Behavior Inventory

The *Adaptive Behavior Inventory (ABI)* (Brown and Leigh, 1986) is a norm-referenced measure of adaptive development intended for use with students ages 6 years through 18 years old who have disabilities and for students ages 5 through 18 years who are not disabled. The *ABI* has five subscales: Self-Care Skills, Communication Skills, Social Skills, Academic Skills,

TABLE 14.2 Tests That Assess Self-Help Skills

AGS Early Screening Profiles

Battelle Developmental Inventory

BRIGANCE® Diagnostic Inventory of Early Development–Revised

The Carolina Curriculum for Infants and Toddlers with Special Needs

The Carolina Curriculum for Preschoolers with Special Needs

FirstSTEP

Hawaii Early Learning Profile (HELP) for Preschoolers

HELP for Special Preschoolers

Learning Accomplishment Profile (LAP)

and Occupational Skills. Each subscale contains 30 items. A short form of the *ABI, ABI-Short,* has 50 items.

Administration

The *ABI* and the *ABI-Short* can be completed by the teacher or another professional in about 25 minutes.

Scoring

Standard scores and percentile ranks can be obtained for each of the subscales and the full scale.

Standardization

The *ABI* was standardized on 1,296 children with normal intelligence and 1,076 children who were mentally retarded. Although the characteristics of the sample are described, information about the selection of the sample is lacking.

Reliability

Information about internal consistency and test-retest reliability is provided. For the most part, the reliability coefficients are in the .80s and .90s.

TABLE 14.3   Tests of Adaptive Behavior

Test	Ages	Behaviors measured
AAMR Adaptive Behavior Scale–School Edition: 2 (ABS-S:2) (Lambert, Nihira, & Leland, 1993)	3 through 18.11	Independent functioning, physical development, economic activity, language development, numbers and time, prevocational/vocational activity, self-direction, responsibility, socialization, social behavior, conformity, trustworthiness, stereotypes and hyperactive behavior, self-abusive behavior, social engagement, disturbing interpersonal behavior
Adaptive Behavior Inventory (ABI) (Brown & Leigh, 1986)	5 through 18.11	Self-care, communication, social skills, academic skills, occupational skills
Adaptive Behavior Inventory for Children (ABIC) (Mercer & Lewis, 1977) The manual has been translated into Spanish. The same record form is used for administration in English or Spanish.	5 through 11	Student role performance in the family, community, peer group, nonacademic settings; earner/consumer activities; self-maintenance
Checklist of Adaptive Living Skills (CALS) (Morreau & Bruininks, 1991)	Infants through adult	Personal-living skills, home-living skills, community-living skills, employment skills
Escalas de conducta independiente Spanish version of the Scales of Independent Behavior (SIB) (1984)	Infants through adult	Home, social, and community skills
Scales of Independent Behavior–Revised (SIB-R) (Bruininks, Woodcock, Weatherman, & Hill, 1996)	Infants through adult	Home, social, and community skills
Vineland Adaptive Behavior Scales (Sparrow, Balla, & Cicchetti, 1984)	Birth through 18.11	Communication, daily living skills, socialization, and motor skills

Validity

Limited information about validity is described. The manual provides information about concurrent validity. Additional information about the validity of the *ABI* needs to be provided.

Summary

The *ABI* and the *ABI-Short* are norm-referenced instruments that evaluate the adaptive development of students in five areas: Self-Care Skills, Communication Skills, Social Skills, Academic Skills, and Occupational Skills. Addi-tional information about the technical adequacy of this test is needed.

Adaptive Behavior Scales

Originally developed by the American Association on Mental Retardation, the *Adaptive Behavior Scales (ABS)* consists of two scales and both have been revised. One, the *Adaptive Behavior Scales–Residential and Community: 2* (ABS-RC:2) (Lambert, Leland, and Nihira, 1993a), is intended for individuals who may be living either in institutional or community settings. It has

TABLE 14.4   Tests That Include Measures of Adaptive Behavior

Test	Ages	Behaviors measured
AGS Early Screening Profiles (Harrison, et al., 1990)	2 through 6 years, 11 months	Cognitive language, motor, and self-help abilities; home survey, health survey, and behavior survey
Assessment, Evaluation, and Programming System (AEPS), Vols. 1 & 2 (Bricker, 1992; Bricker, 1993)	Birth through 3 years	Feeding, personal hygiene, undressing
Battelle Developmental Inventory (BDI) (Newborg, Stock, & Wnek, 1988)	Birth through 8 years	Attention, eating, dressing, personal responsibility, toileting
BRIGANCE® Diagnostic Inventory of Early Development–Revised (Brigance, 1991)	Birth through 7 years	Self-help
Carolina Curriculum for Infants and Toddlers with Special Needs (CCITSN) (Johnson-Martin, Jens, Attermeier, & Hacker, 1991)	Birth through 24 months	Eating, dressing, grooming
Carolina Curriculum for Preschoolers with Special Needs (CCPSN) (Johnson-Martin, Attermeier, & Hacker, 1990)	2 through 5 years	Eating, dressing, grooming, toileting, responsibility
Developmental Profile II (DP-II) (Alpern, Boll, & Shearer, 1986)	Birth through 12 years	Self-help
FirstSTEP (Miller, 1993)	2 years 9 months through 6 years 2 months	Daily living, self management, social interaction, functioning within the community
Hawaii Early Learning Profile (HELP) (Furuno et al., 1988)	Birth through 36 months	Self-help
HELP for Special Preschoolers (Santa Cruz County Office of Education, 1987)	3 through 6 years	Self-help
Learning Accomplishment Profile (LAP) (Sanford & Zelman, 1981)	3 years through 6 years	Self-help

*Spanish form

two parts: Part One assesses personal independence, coping skills, and daily living skills. The other scale, the *Adaptive Behavior Scales–School Edition: 2 (ABS-S:2)* (Lambert, Leland, and Nihira, 1993b), is intended for use with individuals who are from 3 through 21 years and who will be attending school or are in school. Only the *ABS-S:2* will be described here.

The *ABS-S:2* is divided into two parts; Part One is divided into the nine domains listed below.

Independent Functioning. Assesses eating, toileting, maintaining a clean and neat appearance, dressing, and using transportation and other public facilities.

Physical Development. Evaluates physical and motor abilities.

Economic Activity. Assesses ability to manage money and to be a consumer.

Language Development. Evaluates receptive and expressive language and behavior in social situations.

Numbers and Time. Examines basic mathematical skills.

Prevocational/Vocational Activity. Assesses skills related to school and job performance.

Responsibility. Assesses the extent that an individual can be held accountable for his or her actions, belongings, and duties.

Self-Direction. Examines whether individuals choose to maintain an active or passive lifestyle.

Socialization. Assesses the ability to interact with others.

Part Two of the *ABS-S:2* focuses on social maladaptation. The behaviors that are examined are divided into the seven domains listed below.

Violent and Antisocial Behavior. Examines behaviors that are physically or emotionally abusive.

Rebellious Behavior. Assesses aspects of rebelliousness.

Untrustworthy Behaviors. Examines behaviors that are related to stealing, lying, cheating, and showing disrespect for public and private property.

Stereotyped and Hyperactive Behavior. Assesses behaviors such as making inappropriate physical contact, behaving in stereotypical ways, and being over active.

Eccentric Behavior. Examines behaviors considered to be very unusual.

Withdrawal. Assesses the degree to which an individual withdraws or fails to respond to others.

Disturbed Behavior. Examines bothersome types of behaviors.

Administration

The *ABS-S:2* is administered by an interviewer.

Scoring

Raw scores are converted to standard scores and percentiles. Scores are also converted to quotients that have a mean of 100 and a standard deviation of 15.

Standardization

The *ABS-S:2* was standardized in 31 states. The sample included both persons with disabilities and those who were not disabled.

Reliability and Validity

According to the authors, the *ABS-S:2* is a reliable and valid instrument, and there is considerable research that documents the usefulness of this instrument.

Summary

The *Adaptive Behavior Scales–School Edition: 2* is an instrument that assesses the adaptive and maladaptive behavior of school-age children. This should be a useful tool.

Checklist of Adaptive Living Skills

The *Checklist of Adaptive Living Skills (CALS)* (Moreau and Bruininks, 1991) is a criterion-referenced checklist of approximately 800 items in the areas of self-care, personal independence, and adaptive functioning. It was developed to measure the adaptive behaviors of infants through adults and is individually administered, using an interview format, to a respondent who knows the individual well.

The *CALS* is related, conceptually and statistically, to the *Scales of Independent Behavior (SIB)* (Bruininks, Woodcock, Weatherman, and Hill, 1984). The reason for this, according to the manual, was to allow users to predict scores on the SIB. The *Adaptive Living Skills Curriculum (ALSC)* (Bruininks, Moreau, Gilman, and Anderson, 1991), which is linked to the *CALS,* contains

BOX 14.1

ADAPTIVE BEHAVIOR SCALES–SCHOOL EDITION: 2

Publication Date: 1993

Purposes: To assess personal independence, coping skills, daily living skills, and maladaptive or problem behaviors

Age/Grade Levels: Ages 3 through 21

Time to Administer: Approximately 30 minutes in an interview format

Technical Adequacy: The standardization sample is representative. Reliabilty and validity are very good.

Suggested Uses: Can be used to determine adaptive and maladaptive (problem) behaviors in individuals who are mentally retarded, developmentally delayed, or who exhibit problem behaviors. Useful in identification, program planning, and program monitoring.

Scoring

Items are checked if the student performs the skill independently.

Standardization

This measure is criterion-referenced and was not standardized. The manual states that the *CALS* was tried out with 627 individuals who ranged in age from infancy to over 40 years old. The respondents were from 8 states. Approximately one-half of the sample were individuals who were disabled and approximately equal numbers of females and males were selected. Little demographic information about the sample is provided.

Reliability

Internal consistency and split-half reliabilities were calculated. The information on reliability is limited.

Validity

Evidence of criterion-related validity is based on two studies and is very limited.

Summary

The *CALS* is a criterion-referenced instrument. Evidence of reliability as well as content and construct validity is limited. Additional information about the sample is needed. This instrument is used with caution. It may be most appropriate for program planning.

training objectives, strategies, and activities to facilitate program planning and intervention.

The *CALS* is divided into four domains: Personal Living Skills, Home Living Skills, Community Living Skills, and Employment Skills. Each of these domains are organized into 24 specific skills modules. Each item covers a range of behaviors and are arranged in order of difficulty.

Administration

The respondent must know the student well. Persons with varied backgrounds, including parents, rehabilitation counselors, teachers, aides, and others can serve as respondents. Depending on the needs of the student, not all items must be administered. Because the *CALS* is a criterion-referenced checklist, the items can be readministered periodically. It takes approximately 60 minutes to complete.

Pyramid Scales

The *Pyramid Scales* (Cone, 1984) is a criterion-referenced, rather than a norm-referenced, measure of adaptive development. The scales are intended to be used with persons from birth through adulthood, consisting of 20 subtests organized into three skills clusters (Table 14.5). Because this is a criterion-referenced test, comparisons to a norm group are not made. Rather, the student is rated on how well certain behaviors are demonstrated.

TABLE 14.5   Pyramid Scales

Sensory skill cluster

tactile

auditory

visual responsiveness

Primary skill cluster

gross motor

eating

fine motor

toileting

dressing

social interaction

washing and grooming

receptive language

expressive language

Secondary skill cluster

recreation and leisure

writing

domestic behavior

reading

vocational

time

money

numbers

Administration

The *Pyramid Scales* can be administered in three different ways: 1) an interview can be conducted with an informant who is familiar with the student; 2) an informant can complete the items without an interviewer; and 3) an evaluator can observe the student and complete the scales. It takes approximately 30 to 45 minutes to complete all of the scales, but not all of the scales must be completed. The evaluator can select the scales that would be most appropriate for the student.

Scoring

Each item is scored on a four-point system. Raw scores are converted to percentage correct, and then the percentage correct is plotted on a graph for each of the subscales.

Technical Characteristics

This test is unlike the other tests in this chapter in that it is criterion-referenced, not norm-referenced. Therefore, there is no standardization or norm sample. Several reports of reliability and validity are detailed in the manual. For the most part, this test is technically adequate.

Summary

The *Pyramid Scales* are a criterion-referenced measure of adaptive behavior from birth through adulthood. This test is useful for program planning.

Responsibility and Independence Scale for Adolescents

The *Responsibility and Independence Scale for Adolescents (RISA)* (Salvia, Neisworth, and Schmidt, 1990) is a measure of adaptive behavior of individuals who are between the ages of 12 and 19 years 11 months. The scale is intended to measure responsibility and independence in adolescents. Responsibility is defined as "a broad class of adaptive behaviors that meet social expectations and standards of reciprocity, accountability, and fairness and that enable personal development through self- and social management, age appropriate behavior and social communication" (p. 2). Individuals who are responsible are "dependable, trustworthy, and able to shape, as well as comply with, social rules" (p. 2). Independence is defined as "a broad class of adaptive behaviors that allow individuals to live separately and free from the control or determination of others and to conduct themselves effectively in matters such as domestic and financial management, citizenship, personal organization, transportation, and career development" (p. 2). Independence means that an individual can make good decisions, makes plans, and deals effectively with situations that might affect self-reliance.

The 136 items are arranged in two subtests: Responsibility and Independence. The Responsibility subtest has 52 items that are clustered in three areas: Self-Management, Social Maturity, and Social Communication.

Administration

The *RISA* is administered in an interview format to an individual who is familiar with the student. Informants can be a parent, guardian, surrogate parent, or spouse. The 136 questions take between 30 to 45 minutes to administer.

Scores

The scoring is dichotomous with a score of 1 given when the informant responds yes, or a variation such as the phrase "I'm pretty sure" (p. 3). A score of 0 given when the informant answers no, or a variation such as the phrase "I don't think so" (p. 3). Scores can be converted to percentiles and standard scores. Standard score differences can be obtained but the manual cautions that these differences should be used carefully. Figure 14.2 shows the front of the test form.

Standardization

The sample consisted of ratings of 1,900 adolescents who were from nine age groups. Gender, community size, educational level of the parents or guardians, and geographical region were weighted so that the sample approximated the 1980 census. Race and ethnic group were not weighted because the sample closely represented the proportions in the United States population.

Reliability

Split-half and test-retest reliability are reported. The coefficients are at least .90 or higher.

Validity

Three types of validity are reported: content, criterion-related (concurrent), and construct. Content validity appears to be adequate. To demonstrate concurrent validity, the RISA is correlated with the *Vineland Adaptive Behavior Scales* and the *Scales of Independent Behavior*. The sample consisted of only 93 individuals, thus evidence of concurrent validity is weak. The coefficient for the *Vineland Adaptive Behavior Scales* total scale is .55, and the coefficient for the Scales of Independent Behavior total .55. Several studies are reported in the manual that discuss construct validity. Additional research needs to be conducted to confirm construct validity.

Summary

The *Responsibility and Independence Scale for Adolescents (RISA)* is an individually administered measure of adaptive behavior of adolescents. The scale is intended to measure responsibility and independence. Evidence of reliability is adequate. Additional studies should be conducted to confirm construct validity.

Scales of Independent Behavior–Revised

The *Scales of Independent Behavior–Revised (SIB-R)* (Bruininks, Woodcock, Weatherman, and Hill, 1996) is an individually administered, norm-referenced measure of adaptive behavior intended to measure the adaptive and problem behavior of individuals ages infant through adult. According to the authors, the SIB-R can be used for identification, placement, program planning, and monitoring progress. The instrument is composed of 14 subscales that form four adaptive behavior clusters: Motor Skills, Social Interaction and Communication Skills, Personal Living Skills, and Community Living Skills. There are four clusters of maladaptive or problem behavior also: General Maladaptive

RESPONSIBILITY AND INDEPENDENCE SCALE FOR ADOLESCENTS

RECORD FORM

RISA

John Salvia   John T. Neisworth   Mary W. Schmidt

Name of Adolescent _____   Sex ☐ Male ☐ Female

Testing Date _____   School/Agency _____

Birth Date _____   Teacher/Counselor _____

Age _____ Rounded Age* _____

* Age at last birthday unless 15 or fewer days from the next birthday, then round up to the next age.   Examiner _____

Grade or Placement _____   Referred by _____

Diploma or GED Earned ☐ Yes ☐ No   Reason for Referral _____

Respondent _____   Place of Interview _____

Relationship to Adolescent _____   Primary Language of Respondent _____

Is there any reason to question the validity of the interview (seven or more "DK" and/or "NA" responses, defensiveness on the part of the respondent, language barriers or other communication problems, or inconsistent responses?)

_____

_____

CALCULATION OF SCORES

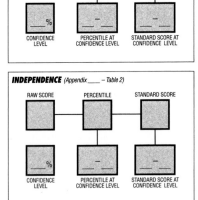

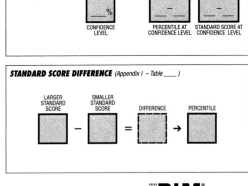

DLM®

One DLM Park • Allen, Texas 75002   1

FIGURE 14.2

Responsibility and Independence Scale for Adolescents Record Form

Source: Copyright © 1990. From the *Responsibility and Independence Scale for Adolescents,* by John Salvia, John T. Neisworth, and Mary W. Schmidt, p. 47. Reprinted with permission of The Riverside Publishing Company.

Behavior, Internalized Maladaptive Behavior, Asocial Maladaptive Behavior, and Externalized Maladaptive Behavior. In addition, there are two short forms: *SIB-R* Short Form and the Early Development Form.

Administration

The Full Scale takes from 45 to 60 minutes to administer, and it takes 15 to 20 minutes for the Short Form or the Early Development Form.

Standardization

The *SIB-R* was standardized on 2,182 individuals to represent the 1990 U.S. Census. It is linked to the *Woodcock-Johnson Psychoeducational Battery–Revised*. (This test is described in Chapter 13.) The sample included persons who were disabled and who were not disabled.

Scoring

Various types of scores can be obtained, including age scores, percentile ranks, standard scores, stanines, normal curve equivalents, and expected scores.

Reliability

Median reliability coefficients for the clusters are in the .80s and .90s.

Validity

Content validity for the *SIB-R* is adequate. Criterion-related validity was established by correlating the *SIB-R* with other adaptive behavior scales and with the *Woodcock-Johnson Psychoeducational Battery–Revised*. Information relating to content validity and criterion-related validity also support the claims of construct validity.

Summary

The *Scales of Independent Behavior–Revised* is an individually administered, norm-referenced measure of adaptive behavior intended to measure the adaptive and problem behavior of individuals ages infant through adult. Evidence of reliability and validity is acceptable.

BOX 14.2

SCALES OF INDEPENDENT BEHAVIOR–REVISED

Publication Date: 1996
Purposes: Measures adaptive and problem behaviors
Age/Grade Levels: Ages infant through adult
Time to Administer: Approximately 30 to 45 minutes in an interview format
Technical Adequacy: The standardization sample is representative. Reliability and validity are acceptable.
Suggested Uses: Can be used for identification, placement, program planning, and monitoring progress of individuals who are mentally retarded, developmentally delayed, or who exhibit problem behaviors.

Vineland Adaptive Behavior Scales

The *Vineland Adaptive Behavior Scales (VABS)* has three forms.

Expanded Form. The Expanded Form (Sparrow, Balla, and Cicchetti, 1984a) contains 577 items, 297 of which can be found on the Survey Form. It provides a comprehensive assessment of adaptive behavior and, according to the manual, is useful for developing educational, habilitative, or treatment programs.

Survey Form. The Survey Form (Sparrow, Balla, and Cicchetti, 1984b) consists of 297 items and it is intended to be used to identify strengths and weaknesses.

Classroom Edition. The Classroom Edition (Harrison, 1985) contains 244 items and yields an evaluation of adaptive behavior in the classroom. In addition to items from the Survey Form and the Expanded Form, the Classroom Edition contains items relating to school performance.

All three forms measure communication, daily living skills, socialization, and motor skills. The Expanded Form and the Survey Form assess maladaptive behavior. The domains are divided into subdomains: receptive, expressive, written communication, personal, domestic, community daily living skills, interpersonal relationships, play and leisure time, coping skills for socialization, gross and fine motor skills.

Administration

Both the Expanded Form and the Survey Form can be administered in a semistructured interview with a parent, caregiver, or an adult who is disabled. The Expanded Form takes approximately 60 to 90 minutes to administer; it takes approximately 20 to 60 minutes to administer the Survey Form. The Classroom Edition is administered as a questionnaire to be completed by a teacher of a child who is between the ages of 3 years through 12 years, 11 months. It takes approximately 20 minutes to complete the questionnaire.

Scores

Standard scores are obtained for the domains and the Adaptive Behavior Composite. Other scores included are percentile ranks, stanines, age equivalents, and adaptive levels. Adaptive levels are based on ranges of standard scores and provide a qualitative label for performance, for example, high, moderately high, adequate, moderately low, and low. Tables are given for determining significant and unusual differences. Figure 14.3 shows the scoring on the front of the Vineland test form.

Standardization

The Expanded Form was not administered during the standardization, which was done by equating the Expanded Form to the Survey Form using the common items of each. The Survey Form was standardized on 3,000 individuals, with about 100 individuals in each of 30 age groups between birth and 18 years, 11 months. The standardization sample was based on the 1980 U.S. Census and was stratified according to sex, race/ethnic group, community size, region, and parents' level of education. Supplementary norms for both the Survey Form and the Expanded Form were also developed. These included approximately 1,800 ambulatory and nonambulatory adults who were either mentally retarded, 18 years of age or older, and who were clients in residential and nonresidential facilities or emotionally disturbed, hearing impaired, and visually impaired individuals, 6 through 15 years old, who were clients of residential facilities.

The standardization sample for the Classroom edition consisted of 2,984 children ages 3 years to 12 years, 11 months. The children selected for the sample were randomly chosen by teachers, and this resulted in a sample that is largely unrepresentative of the U.S. population as of 1980.

Reliability

For the Survey Form, split-half, test-retest, and interrater reliability are reported. Median split-half reliabilities, based on odd-even correlations, ranged from .83 (Motor Skills) to .90 (Daily Living Skills). The coefficient for the Adaptive Behavior Composite was .94; Maladaptive Behavior, Part 1, coefficients ranged from .77 to .88.

Test-retest reliability for the Survey Form was determined by administering the Survey Form twice to parents and caregivers of 484 children and youth from the age of 6 months to 18 years, 11 months. The time interval between the two administrations was from two to four weeks. Most of the coefficients were in the .80s and .90s. The average difference between the first administration and the second was very small.

FIGURE 14.3

Vineland Adaptive Behavior Scales: Classroom Edition

Source: Vineland Adaptive Behavior Scales (VABS) by Sara S. Sparrow, David A. Balla, and Domenic V. Cicchetti. © 1984, 1985. American Guidance Service, Inc., 4201 Woodland Road, Circle Pines, Minn. 55014-1796. Reprinted with permission of the Publisher. All rights reserved.

Interrater reliability for the Survey Form was estimated by interviewing the parents or caregivers of 160 persons in the standardization sample who were from 6 months to 18 years, 11 months of age. The average time between the two interviews was eight days. Coefficients were in the .90s.

Reliability information for the Expanded Form was estimated based on data obtained during the standardization of the Survey Form. For the Expanded Form, estimated median split-half reliability coefficients ranged from .91 (Motor Skills) to .95 (Daily Living Skills). The coefficient for the Adaptive Behavior Composite

SNAPSHOT

Jean[1]

"I'm concerned about Jean," remarked Mr. Chen, referring to Jean, a 14-year-old student who is in Mr. Chen's homeroom. She is currently identified as having a language disability, mental retardation, and a behavior disorder. According to her school records, Jean was administered the Wechsler Individual Intelligence Scale-III (WISC-III) last year and obtained a Verbal IQ score of 63 (1st percentile) and a Performance IQ score of 74 (4th percentile), giving her a Full Scale IQ of 66 (1st percentile). The Vineland Adaptive Behavior Scales (VABS) were administered in order to evaluate Jean's functional life skills and to review areas of behavioral concern. Jean's mother was the respondent. Jean's scores on the VABS revealed her to be functioning well below the average range when compared to other 14-year-old students. The Adaptive Behavior Composite was 23 (+ 1–6) which constitutes functioning at less than the first percentile. Skill domain scores are as follows:

Communications Domain	23 SS	< 0.1 percentile
Daily Living Skills Domain	< 20 SS	< 0.1 percentile
Socialization Domain	34 SS	< 0.1 percentile

Jean's score in the Maladaptive Behavior Domain was judged to be significant with a score of 19. Areas of noted concern were the student's tendency to be withdrawn and having poor concentration and attention.

In a conference with Jean's teachers, Jean's mother expressed great concern regarding Jean's future. She noted that Jean has "no friends in the neighborhood" and prefers to play with her 6-year-old sister. In thinking about Jean's future, her mother believes that Jean would be able to get a job at a local motel as a chambermaid. She does admit, however, that Jean has generally low levels of skill in this area.

In her conversation with Jean's mother, Jean's special education teacher described Jean as generally withdrawn. She noted that Jean had no friends in the school and that she tended to gravitate toward the youngest and smallest students during recess. The special education teacher commented that Jean had not expressed any interest in a particular vocational activity.

---

[1]Brandt, J. E. (1994). *Assessment and transition planning: A curriculum for school psychologists and special educators.* Biddeford, Maine: University of New England. Adapted with permission.

was .97; Maladaptive Behavior, Part 1, coefficients ranged from .77 to .88.

Test-retest reliability and interrater reliability were not estimated for the Expanded Form.

For the Classroom Edition, only internal consistency reliability was estimated. Median reliability coefficients ranged from .80 (Motor Skills) to .95 (Daily Living Skills). The median coefficient for the Adaptive Behavior Composite was .98.

Validity

According to the authors, content validity for the Survey Form and Classroom Edition was established through a review of the literature, an analysis of the test items, item tryout, and

---

B O X   1 4 . 3

VINELAND ADAPTIVE BEHAVIOR SCALES, CLASSROOM EDITION

Publication Date: 1984
Purposes: Identifies adaptive and maladaptive behaviors
Age/Grade Levels: Ages 3 years through 12 years 11 months.
Time to Administer: 20 minutes
Technical Adequacy: The standardization sample is appropriate but should be updated. Reliability and validity are good.
Suggested Uses: Can be used to identify adaptive and problem behaviors in students. Useful for determining eligibility, program planning, and program monitoring.

---

standardization. No independent evaluation of content validity is provided.

Criterion-related validity for the Survey Form and the Classroom Edition was established by correlating the VABS with other adaptive behavior scales and intelligence scales.

Evidence of construct validity for the Survey Form and the Classroom Edition is demonstrated by a developmental progression of scores over the age span, by factor analysis, and by profiles of scores for supplementary norm groups. Information relating to content validity and criterion-related validity also support the claims of construct validity.

For the Expanded Form, independent validity studies were not conducted. According to the authors, the validity of the Expanded Form is based on the Survey Form.

Summary

The Vineland Adaptive Behavior Scales consist of three forms: the Expanded Form, the Survey Form, and the Classroom Edition. The VABS is a norm-referenced, individually administered measure of adaptive and maladaptive behavior. Reliability and validity are adequate. However, the reliability and validity of the Expanded Form is based on the reliability and validity of the Survey Form.

PREFERRED PRACTICES

The identification of limitations in adaptive skills along with significantly below-average intellectual functioning plays a large part in determining whether a student will be identified as mentally retarded. Frequently, the term *adaptive behavior* is used instead of the newer term *adaptive skills*.

The assessment of adaptive skills and adaptive behavior is not without controversy. The assessment of adaptive skills and adaptive behavior is related to age, gender, race, cultural and ethnic norms, and disability. As individuals develop, cultural expectations change.

The concepts of adaptive skills and adaptive behavior are dynamic and our views of these constructs change over time. However, the assessment of adaptive skills and adaptive behavior will continue to be important for identification, determining eligibility, program planning, and program evaluation.

EXTENDING LEARNING

14.1 Keeping in mind that the concept of adaptive skills is related to cultural norms, give an example of a behavior that might be considered adaptive in one context and not adaptive in another.

14.2 In what ways are instruments that assess development similar to ones that assess adaptive skills?

14.3 In what ways are instruments that assess functional skills similar to adaptive behavior scales?

14.4 How do the concepts of adaptive skills, adaptive behavior, and intelligence overlap?

14.5 Examine two or more of the instruments described in this chapter. Compare the test items. Which instrument would you recommend? Why?

REFERENCES

Alpern, G., T. Boll, and M. Shearer (1986). *Developmental profile II.* Los Angeles: Western Psychological Services.

American Association on Mental Retardation (1992). *Mental retardation.* 9th ed. Washington, DC: Author.

Brandt, J. E. (1994). *Assessment and transition planning: A curriculum for school psychologists and special educators.* Biddeford, Maine: University of New England.

Bricker, D. (1992a). *Assessment, evaluation, and programming system for infants and children: Vol. 1.* Baltimore, Md.: Paul H. Brookes.

Bricker, D. (1992b). *Assessment, evaluation, and programming system for infants and children: Vol. 2.* Baltimore, Md.: Paul H. Brookes.

Brigance, A. H. (1991). *BRIGANCE® diagnostic inventory of early development–Revised.* No. Billerica, Mass: Curriculum Associates.

Brown, L., and J. E. Leigh (1986). *Adaptive behavior inventory.* Austin, Tex.: PRO-ED.

Bruininks, R. H., M. Thurlow, and C. J. Gilman (1987). Adaptive behavior and mental retardation. *Journal of Special Education* 21(1): 69–88.

Bruininks, R. H., L. E. Moreau, C. J. Gilman, and J. L. Anderson (1991). *Manual for the adaptive living skills curriculum.* Allen, Tex.: DLM.

Bruininks, R. H., R. W. Woodcock, R. F. Weatherman, and B. K. Hill (1996). *Scales of independent behavior–revised.* Chicago: Riverside.

Cone, J. D. (1984). *Pyramid scales.* Austin, Tex.: PRO-ED.

Coulter, W. A., and H. W. Morrow (1978). *Adaptive behavior: Concepts and measurements.* New York: Grune & Stratton.

Furano, S., K. A. O'Reilly, C. M. Hosaka, T. T. Inatsuka, B. Zeisloft-Falbey, and T. Allman (1988). *Hawaii early learning profile.* Palo Alto, Calif.: VORT.

Grossman, H. (1983). *Classification in mental retardation.* Washington, D.C.: American Association on Mental Retardation.

Harrison, P. L. (1985). *Classroom edition manual, Vineland adaptive behavior scales.* Circle Pines, Minn.: American Guidance Service.

Harrison, P. L., A. S. Kaufman, N. L. Kaufman, R. H. Bruininks, J. Rynders, S. Ilmer, S. S. Sparrow, and D. V. Cicchetti (1990). *AGS early screening profiles.* Circle Pines, Minn.: American Guidance Service.

Johnson-Martin, N. M., K. G. Jens, S. M. Attermeier, and B. J. Hacker (1991). *The Carolina curriculum for infants and toddlers with special needs.* 2d ed. Baltimore, Md.: Paul H. Brookes.

Johnson-Martin, N. M., S. M. Attermeier, and B. J. Hacker (1990). *The Carolina curriculum for infants and toddlers with special needs.* Baltimore, Md.: Paul H. Brookes.

Lambert, N., H. Leland, and K. Nihira (1993a). *Adaptive behavior scales–Residential and community edition: 2.* Austin, Tex.: PRO-ED.

Lambert, N., H. Leland, and K. Nihira (1993b). *Adaptive behavior scales–School edition: 2.* Austin, Tex.: PRO-ED.

Mercer, J. R., and J. F. Lewis (1977). *Adaptive behavior inventory for children.* San Antonio, Tex.: Harcourt Brace Educational Measurement.

Miller, L. J. (1993). *FirstSTEP Screening Test for Evaluating Preschoolers.* San Antonio, TX: The Psychological Corp.

Moreau, L. E., and R. H. Bruininks (1991). *Checklist of adaptive living skills.* Allen, Tex.: DLM.

Newborg, J., J. R. Stock, and L. Wnek (1988). *Battelle developmental inventory.* Allen, Tex.: DLM.

Sanford, A. R., and J. G. Zelman (1981). *Learning accomplishment profile.* Lewisville, N.C.: Kaplan Press.

Salvia, J., J. Neisworth, and M. Schmidt (1990). *Responsibility and independence scale for adolescents.* Allen, Tex.: DLM.

Sattler, J. (1988). *Assessment of children.* San Diego, Calif.: Jerome M. Sattler.

Sparrow, S. S., D. A. Balla, and D. V. Cicchetti (1984a). *Inteview edition, expanded form manual, Vineland adaptive behavior scales.* Circle Pines, Minn.: American Guidance Service.

Sparrow, S. S., D. A. Balla, and D. V. Cicchetti (1984b). *Inteview edition, survey form manual, Vineland adaptive behavior scales.* Circle Pines, Minn.: American Guidance Service.

Woodcock, R. W., and M. B. Johnson (1977). *Woodcock-Johnson psychoeducational battery–Revised.* Allen, Tex.: DLM Teaching Resources.

Behavior in the Classroom

OVERVIEW

In this chapter, we view student behaviors as occurring within the context of various environments. This conceptual framework influences the way we gather assessment information. Assessing behavior in the classroom involves examining classroom management strategies and other aspects of the learning environment as well as observing strategies that classroom teachers employ to help students build skills in working with others. The assessment process also examines the behavior to determine the function that it serves the student. By organizing and interpreting this information, teachers and other team members are able to develop one or more recommendations.

CHAPTER OBJECTIVES

After completing this chapter, you should be able to:

Differentiate among various perspectives on emotional and problem behaviors and their effects on assessment practices.

Describe considerations in assessing the physical, learning, and social environments.

Compare standardized instruments.

Discuss the process for planning observations, collecting, and interpreting observation data on behavior in the classroom.

TYPES OF PROBLEM BEHAVIORS OBSERVED IN THE CLASSROOM

Problem behaviors in the classroom include antisocial behavior, aggression, withdrawal behavior, delayed social skills, and difficulties with interpersonal relationships. The term **externalizing behaviors** is used to refer to a broad array of disruptive and antisocial behavior; whereas the term **internalizing behaviors** includes social withdrawal, anxious or inhibited behaviors, or somatic problems. Behaviors in the classroom can be measured and changed on a number of dimensions (White and Haring, as cited in Alberto and Troutman, 1995). A behavior can occur many times or only occasionally (frequency); a behavior can last a long or a short time (duration); upon request, a behavior can occur immediately or after a period of time (latency); a behavior can be described (topography); a behavior can be performed strongly or weakly (intensity); and a behavior can occur in one or more locations (locus).

Along each of these dimensions, cultural expectations dictate a range of behavior. "Typical" behaviors differ, depending on the expectations of the group members. Atypical behavior can be identified by observing the individual's behavior and that of members of the comparison group.

In the classroom, students exhibit a range of behavioral dimensions. Students with problem behaviors of high frequency or behaviors that have a strong intensity are easily identified. Students who exhibit low frequency or low levels of intensity of behavior are often equally needy. However, these students are not as easily identified because students who are quiet, withdrawn, or depressed may not be recognized as having problem behaviors.

SNAPSHOT

Mr. Norford's Seventh Grade Class

Andy has difficulty sitting still; he plays with his pencil, shuffles his feet, and jingles the coins in his pocket. Mr. Norford describes his activity level, or frequency of behavior, as high. When Andy becomes upset, he reacts strongly. He becomes angry, shouts, and quickly resorts to pushing and shoving. The intensity of his behavior is also high.

Shelly is an average student. When she becomes upset, she becomes sullen and uncooperative. She refuses to talk with the teacher or to other students. Mr. Norford describes Shelly's level of activity as low; but her intensity is high. Her behavior may be overlooked more readily than Andy's behavior. Shelly's problem behavior may not be as disruptive to the classroom as Andy's

problem behavior, but it is disruptive to her learning.

Kenichi enrolled in the middle school last spring, soon after his family moved to this country from Japan. Kenichi had no difficulty understanding English, as he had studied the language for several years. Over the past few months, Mr. Norford has observed that he has become very quiet and rarely speaks in class. Walking between classes and in the cafeteria, Kenichi is usually seen alone. His teacher believes that he is experiencing periods of sadness and depression for many days at a time. Kenichi's behavior frequency often is low and the intensity of his behavior is weak. Mr. Norford has observed these behaviors in several locations (locus).

WHAT SHAPES OUR VIEWS

Examiners may use different perspectives when assessing problem behaviors, based on their backgrounds and theoretical approaches. These are described in Table 15.1. In the fol-

lowing section, we will examine some of these perspectives in more detail.

Behavioral Perspective

The **behavioral perspective** emphasizes the importance of factors external to or outside of

---

TABLE 15.1   Current Perspectives on Assessing Behavior

Perspective	Associated keywords	Focus
Behavioral	Applied behavior analysis antecedents (A) behavior (B) consequences (C) Learning theory task analysis chaining	Behavior is learned and can be modified. Learning a complex behavior can be accomplished by identifying the components of the behavior.
Biological	Neuroanatomical and/or neurochemical components Biochemical inhibitors	Behaviors are the result of neuroanatomical features or chemical imbalances in the brain. Biologically based brain disorders affect individuals' behavior.
Developmental	Critical periods Bonding	A student's early experiences and nurturing are critical in social-emotional development.
Ecological	Environment	Behaviors can be improved by altering the environment.
Emotional	Emotional intelligence	The individual's emotional intelligence is important for success.
Humanistic	Self-direction Self-motivation	The social environment is critical in supporting student behavior.
Psychoanalytical	Id Ego Superego Life crises	Assessment is conducted by a licensed psychologist or psychiatrist for the purpose of uncovering the illness or pathology.
Psychoeducational	Motivation	The interaction of pathology and the individual's motivation or underlying conflicts result in problem behaviors.
Temperament	Rhythmicity Mood Activity Adaptability Distractibility Persistence Threshold Intensity Approach	The relationship between an individual's disposition, behavior, and the environment is critical.

the student as catalysts for the development of problem behaviors. Events in the environment provide stimuli for the behaviors to occur and reinforcement for the behaviors to occur more frequently. Applied behavior analysis and task analysis are used to identify and describe the behaviors.

Applied Behavior Analysis

A basic principle in **applied behavior analysis** holds that behaviors are learned as a result of the individual's interactions with the environment. Behaviors may be manipulated by a *stimulus,* such as environmental conditions, or by events, teachers, or other individuals. A stimulus which is presented, contingent upon a response, and which increases the future probability of the response, is called a *positive reinforcer.* A positive reinforcer may or may not be pleasant; howsoever, it has the effect of increasing the probability of the behavior if it is satisfying to the individual. For example, a teacher's angry look can operate as a positive reinforcer if behavior increases in the future after the teacher's look is delivered, contingent upon behavior. To whatever degree, the teacher's attention itself is satisfying to the student.

A *negative reinforcer* involves the removal of a stimulus, contingent upon a response, which increases the future probability of the response. The stimulus could be, for example, a loud noise, a bright light, or extreme cold or heat. Behaviors that are followed by consequences that are satisfying to the individual tend to be repeated, whereas behaviors that result in consequences that are not, tend not to be repeated. Behaviors that are repeated are learned.

The events that occur before the behavior is performed are called *antecedents.* The antecedents are the stimuli for the behavior and act as cues for the behavior to reoccur. When the antecedent is changed or eliminated, the behavior may be reduced or eliminated.

Thus, the two basic principles in this approach are:

Behaviors can be learned, taught, and modified;

Behaviors (B) can be controlled by antecedents (A) and consequences (C)

Applied behavior analysis uses an Antecedent-Behavior-Consequence approach (ABC approach): the behavior is cued by antecedent events and the behavior is followed by a consequence.

Effect on Assessment Practices

Observations are conducted within a specified time period and the behavior is defined in observable terms. The consequence(s) that follow the behavior and the antecedent event(s) are carefully recorded. The assessment focus is on the events that cause or sustain specific problem behaviors.

Task Analysis

Task analysis is a procedure for identifying the subskills that comprise a specific skill or behavior in order to assist a student in acquiring that skill or behavior. The behavior that will be acquired or eliminated is referred to as the **target behavior.** Target behaviors are acquired (or eliminated!) by manipulating the antecedents and consequences. During a task analysis, the examiner follows a series of steps in assessing the target behavior and in planning for instruction (Figure 15.1).

Effect on Assessment Practices

Assessment includes a task analysis, data collection, and monitoring procedures. The target behavior is analyzed into subskills using task analysis. Students are assessed while attempting the skills, and data are recorded on a checklist or rating scale. Assessment is usually conducted with the student actively engaged in or carrying out an activity.

Biological Perspective

The **biological perspective** focuses on the effects of the biological, chemical, neurological,

The examiner:

1. Describes the target behavior in observable terms so that the behaviors can be measured and the student's progress can be evaluated.
2. Examines the behavior and divides it into small, discrete, sequential steps.
3. Assesses the student's skill levels in one or more of these sequential steps.
4. Plans instruction that focuses on the sequential steps of the target behavior.
5. Links the sequential steps, or subskills, from the task analysis to achieve the more complex target behavior.
6. Carefully determines the reinforcement by observing the student's behavior.
7. Carefully arranges antecedent events to elicit behaviors and plan consequences to reinforce behavior. This step serves to increase the frequency and/or intensity of behavior.
8. Examines the student's everyday routines to determine the behaviors that need to be taught.

FIGURE 15.1

Steps in Conducting a Task Analysis

and physical status of the individual and the individual's behavior. A biological approach often is used in assessing students with severe emotional behaviors.

Neurobiological Disorders

The **neurobiological perspective** centers on the neuroanatomical and/or neurochemical components of the individual. This kind of analysis is helpful in assessing students who have emotional issues related to an organic disorder. Research focuses on regional neural activity, brain structure, and neuropathological characteristics (Mesulam, 1990), as well as on how excesses or deficiencies of various chemicals found in the body impact on the individual's functioning and behavior. Assessment involves the use of medical biochemical tests and diagnosis.

Temperament

An individual's disposition or tendencies affect the individual's behavior. **Temperament** includes a number of general features such as

the student's overall demeanor, the ability to adapt to new situations, and the ability to attend to or persist in an activity. A visit to a school classroom reveals individual differences in students. Some students work quietly by themselves; others talk with others or signal frequently for the teacher's attention. There is a reciprocal nature between an individual's temperament and the physical, learning, and social environments. Figure 15.2 illustrates the general features of temperament.

Effect on Assessment Practices

Standardized instruments, including behavior rating scales, interviews, and checklists, assess various aspects of temperament. For example, the *Child Behavior Checklist/4–18* (Achenbach, 1988, 1991a, 1991b), the *Conners' Rating Scales–Revised* (1997), the *Revised Behavior*

The general features of temperament (Thomas, Chess, and Birch, 1970; Thomas and Chess 1977) include:

- *rhythmicity:* the regularity of the student's activity patterns, such as eating, playing, studying, bladder, and bowel functions.
- *mood:* the student's overall demeanor, such as happy or sad, friendly or unfriendly
- *activity:* the frequency of movement
- *adaptability:* the ability of the student to adapt to new situations
- *distractibility:* the ease with which the student is interrupted from an activity
- *persistence:* the student's ability to attend to or persist in an activity
- *threshold:* the student's sensitivity to stimuli and changes in the environment, such as noise or temperature
- *intensity:* the student's magnitude of response to a specific stimulus, such as the tendency to smile or laugh when amused or to scream or whimper when hurt
- *approach:* the student's attraction or withdrawal to novel stimuli and situations

FIGURE 15.2

General Features of Temperament

Problem Checklist (Quay and Peterson, 1987), and the *Systematic Screening for Behavioral Disorders* (Walker and Severson, 1992) contain items that assess aspects of temperament.

Developmental Approach

The **developmental perspective** focuses on the social emotional development of the student. In Chapter 12 you learned that social-emotional development is one of the five areas or domains of development that is assessed when working with young children (the others are physical, cognitive, communication, and adaptive).

Theories that focus on a developmental approach to understanding social-emotional development (Brazelton, 1992; Erikson, 1950; Greenspan, 1992; Kopp, 1994; White, 1975; Zero to Three, 1995) emphasize that all children progress through regular stages or periods. Individual variations affect the amount of time a given individual remains at a certain stage. Thus, qualitative differences within stages are commonly observed, depending on individual differences.

The foundation for social and emotional skills begins during a child's early years. These early years are critical in providing the basis for social-emotional development in later childhood, adolescence, and adulthood. These time are often referred to as **critical periods.**

Critical Periods of Development

The theory of critical periods states that there is an interval of time in which the child is most responsive. If the individual has little or no opportunity to develop the skill or behavior during this period, the individual may have difficulty in doing so later on. Skills and behaviors that are fundamental to success in school begin to develop in the first three years of life (Zero to Three, 1992, p. 3). Children who do not have opportunities to develop these skills (Figure 15.3) can exhibit problem behaviors in the classroom. These behaviors continue to escalate as they become older, unless the problem

1. *Confidence:* the child has a sense of being successful and that adults will be helpful.
2. *Curiosity:* the child has a sense that learning is positive and pleasurable.
3. *Intentionality:* the child has a desire to and the capacity to have an impact and to act upon that with persistence.
4. *Self-control:* the child can control personal actions in age-appropriate ways.
5. *Relatedness:* the child can engage with others, can understand, and can be understood.
6. *Capacity to communicate:* the child wants to and has the ability to communicate.
7. *Cooperativeness:* the child has the ability to balance own needs with those of others in a group activity.

FIGURE 15.3

Skills and Behaviors Important to School Success
Adapted from *Zero to Three,* 1992.

behaviors are identified and intervention is implemented.

Effect on Assessment Practices

Interviews with parents, caregivers, and teachers provide information about the student during critical periods of development.

Humanistic Perspective

The **humanistic perspective** is built on the belief that teaching and learning should be meaningful to the student (Rogers, 1983). Humanists believe that students learn best and most efficiently when the learning is personally significant and that choosing the direction of one's learning is highly motivating. Equally important in this view is designing the learning environment so that students may have responsibility for their learning, thereby decreasing problem behaviors. The social environment is thus responsive to the student's feelings, and learning is enhanced when the environment is free from threat.

Effect on Assessment Practices

Assessment practices focus on understanding problem behavior from the student's perspective. Student interviews provide information about the problem behaviors from the student's perspective. During assessment activities, aspects of the learning and social environments are examined. Ways in which the learning environment is responsive to the student are recorded.

WHAT CONTRIBUTES TO PROBLEM CLASSROOM BEHAVIORS?

Expectations of society, the school, and the teacher contribute to or compound problem behaviors in the classroom. Some behaviors may be tolerated or accepted as the norm in the community; yet these behaviors may not be tolerated by the school or be accepted by the classroom teacher. School and teacher expectations differ widely. The teacher's tolerance for activity level and intensity level affects whether the teacher refers the student for special education services or whether behavior concerns are handled in the classroom.

RESPONDING TO DIVERSITY

Characteristics and expectations of some cultural and ethnic groups influence student behaviors. For example, some Asian and Muslim groups have strict rules about interactions between the sexes. Certain activities that involve body contact between males and females are taboo. Students who are asked to participate in these activities may exhibit problem behaviors (Dresser, 1996).

A student's disability can hasten the development of problem behaviors. For example, a student with Tourette's syndrome develops multiple motor and one or more vocal tics dur-

ing the illness. These symptoms occur many times throughout the day, although not necessarily simultaneously. Sometimes the student develops patterns of verbal outbursts, such as words and phrases that are inappropriate. The student is not able to repress these outbursts, and medication may not control the problem satisfactorily. The problem behaviors contribute to decreases in the student's self-concept and self-esteem and affect the development of social skills and interpersonal relationships.

Disabilities in communication can foster problem behaviors. Students with disabilities who have difficulty communicating quickly learn to use behaviors that attract another's attention. Some attention behaviors are appropriate while others are antisocial, aggressive, or inappropriate.

Medication can affect student behavior. Medications may be prescribed for students who have inattention or hyperactivity. Methylphenidate, sold under the trade name Ritalin, is one of the most frequently prescribed medications. Methylphenidate temporarily controls overactivity, inattention, and impulsivity; however, its side effects (insomnia, irritability, and reduced emotional affect) can influence problem behaviors.

CLASSROOM BEHAVIORS WITHIN AN INTERVENTION CONTEXT

Classroom Management Methods

Assessing behavior problems in the classroom occurs within the context of an intervention sequence. When a behavior problem first occurs, the classroom teacher assesses the use of classroom management methods. The teacher customarily confers with the school assistance team, behavioral specialist, or special education consultant in order to develop and implement a management method for the specific problem behavior. This process can involve implementing one or more different strategies over a period of weeks.

Successful teachers use several key principles in managing student behaviors.

1. Clear guidelines of the behavior expected in the classroom are established for students. Ideally, these guidelines are dis-

played in the classroom as a reminder to students.

2. Rules, or guidelines, are stated in terms of what the student should do so that the behavioral expectations are clear. ("We listen when another student is talking.")

3. Teachers must provide positive reinforcement to students engaged in appropriate classroom behavior.

◀ **POINT STREET SCHOOL** ▶
Behavior Management

Student's Name _____   Date _____ Time _____
Observer _____
Teacher _____
Location _____

Characteristic

1. Classroom Guidelines
Are behavior guidelines posted in the classroom?
Are guidelines written in positive terms describing the behavior expected of students?
√ Suggestions for improvement:

2. Student Understanding
Does the student understand the classroom guidelines for behavior?
√ Suggestions for improvement:

3. Teacher Reinforcement
How does the teacher react when the student behaves appropriately?

Does the teacher use:
_____ social reinforcers
_____ activity reinforcers
_____ tangible reinforcers
_____ edible reinforcers
√ Suggestions for improvement:

4. Teacher Interventions
How does the teacher react when the student behaves inappropriately?

Does the teacher:

_____ ignore some behaviors
Explain:

_____ use directives
Explain:

_____ use contingency contracts

_____ teach pro-social skills
Explain:

✔ Suggestions for improvement:

5. Classroom Consequences
What consequences does the teacher use when the student behaves inappropriately?

✔ Suggestions for improvement:

6. Classroom Consistency
Is the teacher consistent in managing the student's behavior?
Is the management of the student's behavior consistent with that of all students in the classroom?
✔ Suggestions for improvement:

FIGURE 15.4

Point Street School Classroom Observation Form

SNAPSHOT

Mr. Wing's Classroom

Mr. Wing is beginning his first year of teaching. His class consists of 23 students; three students have been identified as having disabilities. Mr. Wing is concerned about one of these students, Mark D., and how to help him. Mr. Wing worries if he is meeting Mark's needs, and decides to ask the special education consultant, Mr. Sanford, for help.

Mr. Wing describes his concerns: "During class time, Mark never seems to pay attention. When I call on him, he is usually on the wrong page of our book. He rarely knows the answer to my questions. I don't think he has ever participated in class discussions, and he is very disruptive when others are talking. Academically, his grades are very low this first quarter."

Mr. Sanford listened carefully as Mr. Wing talked about Mark. He thought about how he could lead the conversation away from focusing on the student to a more general discussion of classroom management strategies. When there was a pause in the conversation, he asked, "When Mark or some other student disrupts class, what strategies have you found that work well in dealing with this behavior?" The two teachers spent some time talking about strategies and Mr. Wing's apparent frustrations. As the discussion proceeded, Mr. Wing expressed an interest in reviewing his classroom management plan and translating his expectations into procedures and rules. If Mr. Wing continues to be concerned about Mark's classroom behavior, what would you suggest, based on your knowledge of the classroom environment?

4. Teachers need to use directive statements to tell students how to act correctly and responsibly. ("Holly, if you don't want Sheri to do that, you need to use words to tell her to stop.")
5. Teachers should teach pro-social skills such as:
   a. how to ask for help,
   b. how to join a group of students engaged in an activity,
   c. how to join a group discussion,
   d. how to make friends.
6. For students who disregard behavior guidelines, teachers will provide consequences.
7. Teachers must be consistent with all students in their management of classroom behavior.

Figure 15.4 illustrates a behavior management observation form that was developed by a special education teacher for conferring with classroom teachers.

OBSERVING THE STUDENT IN THE ENVIRONMENT

If the problem behavior continues after several changes have been implemented, the teacher, usually with the school assistance team, examines the physical, learning, and social environment. They complete an environmental analysis that addresses the physical, learning, and social settings of the classroom and make any changes that seem necessary. Several modifications in the classroom may be implemented over a period of several weeks in order to find ones that are successful.

Physical Environment

The physical environment impacts on school-functioning skills by creating a structure and a set of expectations for student behavior. The physical environment must consist of predictable classroom routines and schedules and have a posted list or notice of classroom behavioral expectations.

Learning Environment

Behaviors in the classroom can be associated with events in the classroom. Frequent interruptions, unclear directions, activities that are too difficult, and a variety of other circumstances are apt to foster problem behaviors.

Teacher movement throughout the classroom and the position of the teacher in relation to the student can help in preventing behavior problems. One study (Gunter, Shores, Jack, Rasmussen, and Flowers, 1995) found that paraprofessionals responsible for monitoring the student area were observed to remain seated 91.7 percent of the time. When the time that they were seated decreased, the time that students remained on-task increased.

The design of the student observation is based on the format for recording data, which is often in the form of ABC recordings (Bijou, Peterson, and Ault, 1968) where the antecedent (A), student behavior (B), and the consequence (C) are observed (Figure 15.5).

Social Environment

Classroom teachers employ strategies that affect students' behavior and help them to build skills in working with others. These strategies

Antecedent	Behavior	Consequences
Anecdotal observation: Sidney was wandering around the room for a number of minutes. He glanced occasionally in the teacher's direction. He observed different groups of children at a distance but made no attempt to join them. No teacher or child interacted with him. →	Sidney threw the book into the fish tank. →	Children playing nearby laughed. ↘ → Two teachers came over to the fish tank area. One teacher placed her hand on Sidney's shoulder and said, "We don't throw books in the fish tank." The other, the teacher assistant, retrieved the book. Sidney was told, "Now go choose something to do. You have five more minutes before it's time to get ready for lunch."
	→ Sidney sat down in the middle of the floor. →	→ One of the teachers asked, "Do you want to listen to a story?"
	→ Sidney nodded his head "yes." →	→ Another child came over and said, "I want to hear a story."
		→ Teacher gets book.

FIGURE 15.5

The ABC Format for Recording Behavior

allow students to build relationships with their peers by creating an environment that promotes skills in communication, conflict resolution, and respect for others. During a visit to the classroom, the observer may note one or more of these strategies that teachers employ. Some of these strategies used by classroom teachers that are effective in promoting social relations among students with and without disabilities include:

1. Teachers are involved in active facilitation of social interactions. Teachers plan and work to facilitate social exchanges between students. Students are placed in cooperative groupings and teachers encourage collaborative problem solving. Teachers create opportunities for peer tutoring and assign students to various classroom roles of assisting and helping others. Teachers structure the classroom schedule so that students have opportunities to develop social relationships.
2. Teachers involve students in the responsibility for social inclusion of all students.
3. Teachers build a feeling of community in the classroom. Teachers work to create a climate of concern for others among students.
4. Teachers model acceptance.

QUESTIONS, PURPOSES, AND APPROACHES

If the problem behavior in the classroom continues after a series of teaching and classroom interventions, the student's parents are notified and the teacher completes a referral to the IEP team. The questions, purposes, and approaches in assessing behavior problems are described in Table 15.2. The Individuals with Disabilities Education Act amendments of 1997 state that the IEP team must consider strategies, including positive behavioral intervention, and supports for students whose behavior impedes learning or that of others.

WORKING WITH OTHER PROFESSIONALS IN ASSESSING PROBLEM BEHAVIORS

Collecting information about more serious problem behaviors must be done by multiple examiners using various methods of gathering information that include observations, interviews, and standardized instruments. During the assessment process, teachers collaborate with school psychologists, mental health professionals, social workers, and other individuals. In the following section we will examine how professionals collaborate in answering questions about attention-deficit hyperactivity disorder (ADHD).

Attention-Deficit Hyperactivity Disorder

Questions regarding ADHD can best be answered by collecting information from a variety of sources. Observations from teachers and family members provide details about activity and attention level across environments and over a period of time. Direct observation is a valuable method for collecting information about a student's attention, activity, negative interpersonal behaviors, and vocalizations. Research has demonstrated (Platzman, Stoy, Brown, Coles, Smith, and Falek, 1992) the validity of classroom observations and the importance of classroom teachers in the determination of ADHD.

A clinician or psychiatrist uses the diagnostic criteria for ADHD in the *Diagnostic and Statistical Manual of Mental Disorders IV* (DSM-IV) (American Psychiatric Association, 1994). According to DSM-IV, symptoms of inattention are maladaptive and have persisted for at least six months. A portion of the criteria in the area of inattention is listed below:

Inattention
a. often fails to give close attention to details or makes careless mistakes in schoolwork, work, or other activities;
b. often has difficulty sustaining attention in tasks or play activities;

TABLE 15.2   Assessment Questions, Purposes, and Approaches

Assessment questions	Steps and purposes	Approaches
Screening		
Is the student's behavior typical for the student's age?	To determine whether the student may have emotional or problem behaviors and should be referred for further assessment	Norm-referenced instruments Curriculum-based assessment Criterion-referenced assessment Observations Checklists Questionnaires Rating scales
Eligibility		
Does the student have a severe emotional or behavior problem? What problem does the student have? Is the problem associated with a disability (ADHD, autism, severe emotional disturbance, traumatic brain injury)? Does the student meet the criteria for special education services?	To determine the extent of emotional or problem behaviors To determine if the behaviors are associated with a specific disability To determine the need for special education and related services To understand why the student is having difficulty	Norm-referenced instruments Curriculum-based assessment Criterion-referenced assessment Observations Probes Error analysis Interviews Checklists Questionnaires Rating scales Student, parent, and/or teacher conferences Performance assessment

CONNECTING INSTRUCTION WITH ASSESSMENT

Program Planning		
What types of special education and/or related services should be provided? What classroom modifications and adaptations should be implemented? What skills does the student have? What should be taught? What type of behavior management plan should be developed?	To determine the locations and type of services(s) to be received To assess the physical, learning, and social classroom environments To determine where instruction should begin and how the behavior may be managed	Norm-referenced instruments Curriculum-based assessment Criterion-referenced assessment Observations Probes Error analysis Interviews Checklists Student, parent, and/or teacher conferences Performance assessment

c. often does not seem to listen when spoken to directly;

d. often does not follow through on instructions and fails to finish schoolwork, chores, or duties in the workplace;

e. often has difficulty organizing tasks and activities;

f. often avoids, dislikes, or is reluctant to engage in tasks that require sustained mental effort;

TABLE 15.2 (Continued)

Assessment questions	Steps and purposes	Approaches
	Program Monitoring	
Once instruction begins, is the student making progress? Should the instruction be modified?	To understand the pace of instruction To understand what the student knows prior to and after instruction To understand the strategies and concepts the student uses To monitor the student's program	Curriculum-based assessment Criterion-referenced assessment Observations Probes Error analysis Interviews Checklists Questionnaires Rating scales Student, parent, and/or teacher conferences Portfolios Exhibitions Journals Written descriptions Oral descriptions
	Program Evaluation	
Has the student made progress? Has the student met the goals of the IEP? Has the instructional program been successful for the student? Has the instructional program achieved its goals?	To determine whether the IEP goals have been met To determine whether the student continues to need special education services To determine whether the goals of the program have been met To evaluate program effectiveness	Curriculum-based assessment Criterion-referenced assessment Observations Probes Error analysis Interviews Checklists Questionnaires Rating scales Student, parent, and/or teacher conferences Portfolios Exhibitions Journals Written descriptions Oral descriptions Surveys

g. often loses things necessary for tasks or activities;

h. is often easily distracted by extraneous stimuli; and

i. is often forgetful in daily activities. (American Psychiatric Association, 1994, pp. 83–84)

An assessment of ADHD must incorporate consideration of associated disabilities, including mental retardation, autism, or other health problems (Shelton and Barkley, 1993).

School psychologists and teachers often use standardized instruments designed to assess aspects of attention and hyperactivity. Selected standardized instruments are described in Table 15.3. Utilization of multiple sources of information is critical because reliance on behavior rating scales alone is problematic. Generally, behavior rating scales use cutoff scores to identify whether or not ADHD is present, yet few instruments have cutoff scores that have been validated (Spenciner and Cohen, 1994–1995).

STANDARDIZED INSTRUMENTS FOR ASSESSING PROBLEM BEHAVIORS

Standardized instruments usually are in the form of rating scales or checklists designed to be completed by school psychologists, teachers, parents, or students themselves. Instruments that assess problem behaviors focus on one or more specific areas. The choice of an instrument is based on the presenting questions and concerns. Table 15.3 illustrates the areas of assessment questions and concerns, standardized instruments which address these areas, and their technical characteristics. Several of these instruments are described in more detail in the following section.

Attention-Deficit Disorders Evaluation Scale—School Version

The *Attention-Deficit Disorders Evaluation Scale–School Version (ADDES-SV)* (McCarney, 1989a) consists of a rating scale that divides behavior into three subscales: Inattention, Impulsivity, and Hyperactivity. According to the manual, the instrument can be used to screen students suspected of having attention deficits, to contribute information to the diagnosis of ADHD, and to plan an individualized program. There is a companion instrument available to assess the student in the home environment, the *Attention-Deficit Distorders Evaluation Scale–Home Version (ADDES-HV)* (McCarney, 1989b).

Administration
This rating scale is completed by the teacher and takes about 20 minutes.

Standardization
The instrument was normed on 4,876 students between the ages of 4 to 21 years and included both students with and without attention deficit problems. Over 75 percent of the sample was comprised of younger students (grades K–6).

Scoring
Raw scores are converted to standard scores.

Reliability
Adequate coefficients are reported for test-retest, internal consistency, and interrater reliability.

Validity
Evidence is reported for content and construct validity.

Summary
The *Attention-Deficit Disorders Evaluation Scale–School Version* is a rating scale used by classroom teachers or other educators familiar with the student. The instrument is helpful in screening students suspected of having attention-deficit problems.

BOX 15.1

ATTENTION-DEFICIT DISORDERS EVALUATION SCALE–SCHOOL VERSION

Publication Date: 1989
Purposes: Assesses inattentive, impulsive, and hyperactive behaviors
Age/Grade Levels: Ages 4 to 21
Time to Administer: 20 minutes
Technical Adequacy: Standardization sample, reliability, and validity are good
Suggested Use: This rating scale is useful in screening students with problems of attention and hyperactivity.

TABLE 15.3 Behavior Rating Scales and Checklists

Assessment concerns	Name of instrument	Grade or age range	Technical characteristics	Comments
Autism	Autism Screening Instrument for Educational Planning Second Edition (ADIEP-2) (Krug, Arick, & Almond, 1993)	Individuals with language and social skill functioning between 3 and 49 months	Concerns regarding the norming sample, reliability, and validity	Useful qualitative information, may be used in conjunction with other assessment approaches
	Childhood Autism Rating Scale (CARS) (Schopler, Reichler, & Renner, 1986)	Ages 2 and up	Developed over a 15-year period with more than 1,500 individuals	Uses a 7-pt. scale to indicate degree of behavior
	Gilliam Autism Rating Scale (Gilliam, 1995)	Ages 3–22	Norming sample adequate; adequate internal consistency, test-retest reliability, and interscorer reliability (.80–.90)	Uses standard scores and percentiles
Attention Hyperactivity Social skills Oppositional behavior	ADD-H: Comprehensive Teacher's Rating Scale (ACTeRS)-Second Edition (Ullmann, Sleator, & Sprague, 1991)	Grades K through 8	Internal consistency adequate; test-retest reliability ranges from .78-.82	Scores are converted to percentiles and can be plotted on a summary profile sheet.
Hyperactivity Impulsivity Inattention	Attention-Deficit Disorders Evaluation Scales (School and Home Versions) (McCarney, 1989a and 1989b)	Ages 4 to 21	Norming sample consisted of students both with and without attention-deficit disorders; more children in the lower grades were included than in the higher. Reliability and validity adequate for screening purposes	Can be completed by teachers. Raw scores yield a standard score and a total score percentile rank.
	Attention-Deficit/ Hyperactivity Disorder Test (Gilliam, 1995)	Ages 3 to 23	High internal consistency and test-retest reliability; evidence for content, construct, and criterion-related validity; concurrent validity established with the Conners' Rating Scales and ADD-H Comprehensive Teacher's Rating Scale	Based on the diagnostic criteria of DSM IV. Can be completed by teachers and parents

continued

TABLE 15.3 (Continued)

Assessment concerns	Name of instrument	Grade or age range	Technical characteristics	Comments
Problem behaviors Adaptive skills Externalizing problems Internalizing problems	*BASC: Behavior Assessment System for Children (Reynolds & Kamphaus, 1992)	Ages 4 through 18	Adequate reliability and validity	Scores are converted to T-scores and percentiles. BASC is available in software that administers and analyzes results.
	Behavior Evaluation Scale-2 (McCarney & Leigh, 1990)	Grades K through 12	Adequate reliability and validity	This checklist consists of five subscales: learning problems, interpersonal difficulties, inappropriate behavior, unhappiness/depression, and physical symptoms/fears.
Problem behaviors Interpersonal relationships	Behavior Rating Profile-2 (Brown & Hammill, 1990)	Grades 1 through 12	Internal consistency adequate; concurrent validity established with Walker Problem Behavior Identification Checklist, Vineland, and others	Includes six norm-referenced rating scales that are completed by the student, parent, teachers, and student's peers
Withdrawal, anxious and depressed Somatic complaints Delinquent behavior Aggressive behavior Social problems Attention and hyperactivity	Child Behavior Checklists (CBCL/4–18) (Achenbach 1988, 1991a) and Teacher Report Form (Achenbach, 1991b)	Ages 4 through 18	Interrater, test-retest, and internal consistency is adequate. Construct validity and criterion-related validity is adequate	Uses direct observation
Inattention Impulsivity Hyperactivity Conduct problems/aggressiveness	Children's Attention & Adjustment Survey (CAAS) (Lambert, Hartsough, & Sandoval, 1990)	Ages 5 through 13	Adequate reliability and validity	Consists of two forms: Home Form, which is completed by the parent or primary caregiver, and School Form, which is completed by the teacher. Uses DSM IV criteria

Attention Hyperactivity	Conner's Rating Scales-Revised (Conners, 1997)	Ages 3 to 17 (Parent) and Grades 4 to 12 (Teacher)	Internal and test-retest reliability adequate; construct validity adequate; continued research on predictive validity needed	Conners' Rating Scales-Revised include parent, teacher, and adolescent self-report and ADHD/DSM IV Scales
Emotional problems Problem behaviors	Devereux Behavior Rating Scales (Naglieri, LeBuffe, & Pfeiffer, 1995)	Ages 5 through 18	Extensive reliability and validity data are provided.	The Devereux Behavior Rating Scales consist of the Devereux Scales of Mental Disorders and the Devereux Behavior Rating Scale–School Form.
	*TEMAS (in English, TEMAS is an acronym for Tell-Me-A-Story; in Spanish, the word means "themes") (Costantino, Malgady, & Rogler, 1986)	Ages 5 to 18	Norm group included over 600 children (5 to 13 years) from diverse ethnic and cultural backgrounds; the manual reports psychometric studies that include African American, Hispanic, and Caucasian children.	This multicultural test screens children for emotional and behavior problems.
Conduct disorder Socialized aggression Attention problems Anxiety/withdrawal Psychotic behavior Motor excess	Revised Behavior Problem Checklist (Quay & Peterson, 1987)	Grades K through 12	Internal consistency, interrater, and test-retest reliability adequate; concurrent and construct validity adequate	Classifies behavior across six dimensions
Internalizing behaviors Externalizing behaviors	Systematic Screening for Behavior Disorders (Walker & Severson, 1990)	Grades 1 to 6	Test-retest adequate for Steps 1 and 2; interrater reliability adequate for Steps 1 and 3. Concurrent and construct validity adequate; predictive validity low to moderate	Designed to be used as a screening instrument
Problem behavior Social skills	Social Skills Rating System (Gresham & Elliott, 1990)	Grades Pre-K through 12	Good technical characteristics	Separate questionnaires for preschool, elementary, and secondary level students. Separate forms designed for teachers and parents; self-report form for students

continued

TABLE 15.3 (Continued)

Assessment concerns	Name of instrument	Grade or age range	Technical characteristics	Comments
Inattention Impulsivity	T.O.V.A.: Test of Variables of Attention (visual version) (Greenberg, 1989) T.O.V.A.–A Test of Variables of Attention–Auditory version (Greenberg, 1996)	Ages 4 through 80	Norm groups for both versions of the T.O.V.A. included individuals who lived in Minnesota and who were primarily Caucasian.	The T.O.V.A. series are computer software programs designed to screen for ADHD.
Social skills Peer relations	Walker-McConnell Scale of Social Competence (Walker & McConnell, 1988; Walker, Steiber, & Eisert, 1991)	Grades K through 6; 7 through 12	Good technical characteristics	Contains positively worded items. Not designed to measure problem behaviors. Designed for use by teachers and other school personnel

*Spanish form available

Behavior Evaluation Scale-2

The *Behavior Evaluation Scale-2 (BES-2)* (McCarney and Leigh, 1990) is a rating scale designed to assess emotional and behavioral disorders. According to the manual, the purpose of this instrument is to screen for behavior problems, to assist in the diagnosis of behavior disorders or emotional disturbance, and to assist in developing and monitoring the individualized education program. It consists of five scale scores: learning problems, interpersonal difficulties, inappropriate behavior, unhappiness/depression, and physical symptoms/fears. The authors attempt to link the behavioral descriptions to the eligibility terminology described in IDEA for students with serious emotional disturbance.

Administration

Teachers and other educators familiar with the student complete the *Behavior Evaluation Scale-2,* which consists of 76 items. Time to complete this rating scale is approximately 15 to 20 minutes.

Scoring

Items are scored on a seven-point scale. Subscale scores can be reported in standard scores or percentiles; the total scale is reported in a total quotient or in a percentile.

Standardization

The norming sample included 2,272 students in grades K–12 and approximated the 1980 census data for gender, race, ethnicity, geographic area, and educational status of parents.

Reliability

Adequate internal consistency and test-retest reliability are reported. Unfortunately, there is no report regarding interrater reliability.

Validity

Evidence is presented to support content, criterion-related, and construct validity.

Summary

The *Behavior Evaluation Scale-2* is a rating scale designed to assess school-age children and youth. The instrument is useful for the purposes of screening students for behavior and emotional problems.

Child Behavior Checklist System

The *Child Behavior Checklist System (CBCL)* (Achenbach, 1988, 1991a, 1991b) consists of two different rating scales, the *CBCL/2–3* designed for children ages 2 through 3 and the *CBCL/4–18* designed for students ages 4 through 18. The *CBCL System* conceptualizes emotional or behavioral problems as external and internal behavioral clusters. Although the *CBCL* is entitled a "checklist," the instruments are really rating scales in that they require the observer to rate items on a numerical scale. The *CBCL* consists of several forms; each has its own technical manual and scoring system. These include:

BOX 15.2

BEHAVIOR EVALUATION SCALE-2

Publication Date: 1990

Purposes: Assesses learning problems, interpersonal difficulties, inappropriate behavior, unhappiness/depression, and physical symptoms/fears

Age/Grade Levels: K through 12

Time to Administer: 15 to 20 minutes

Technical Adequacy: Norming sample, reliability (internal consistency and test-retest), and validity adequate. Additional information regarding interrater reliability is needed.

Suggested Use: Screening students suspected of having behavioral and emotional problems

1. *Child Behavior Checklist and 1991 Profile for ages 4–18 (CBCL/4–18).* This scale is designed to be completed by the parent and consists of two sections: competence items and problem items. A student's score is converted to percentile ranks and T-scores. This checklist has adequate technical characteristics.

2. *Child Behavior Checklist and 1992 Profile for ages 2 to 3.* This scale consists of 99 items and is designed to be completed by the parent or other caregiver. Similar to the checklist for older children, scores on this instrument can be converted to percentile ranks and T-scores. Additional studies should be undertaken to establish adequate technical characteristics.

3. *Teacher's Report Form and 1991 Profile for ages 5 through 18 (TRF).* This scale is modeled after the *CBCL/4–18* and is designed to be completed by the teacher. The *Teacher's Report Form* consists of three main areas: academic performance, adaptive characteristics, and problem behaviors. Percentiles and T-scores can be calculated. The standardization sample underrepresents the U.S. population by race and some geographic regions; reliability is adequate.

4. Youth Self-Report. This rating scale is designed for youth ages 11 through 18 years of age. Students must have at least fifth-grade reading ability. Test items are similar to those in the *CBCL/4–18*. Scores can be converted into percentile ranks and T-scores. Additional reliability and validity studies are needed; however, the instrument may be helpful when used with other information.

5. *Direct Observation Form.* This form is used to collect observation data on the student during a ten-minute observation period. A list of problem behaviors is provided to assist in organizing observation of the student. Many of the items correspond to the *CBCL/4–18* and the *TRF*. Percentile and T-scores can be calculated to determine whether the student's behavior falls within clinical or normal range. The manual contains no information about reliability or validity. The instrument should be used in conjunction with other forms of the *CBCL*.

Administration

The various forms take 10 to 45 minutes to complete, depending on the amount of information to be recorded.

Standardization

For the *CBCL/4–18,* the norming sample consisted of 2,368 children, ages 4 through 18 years. The sample was stratified by age, gender, geographic region, urban/rural, socioeconomic status, and ethnicity. For the *CBCL/2–3,* 386 children participated, with over half the children coming from Massachusetts.

Scoring

Scoring may be completed by hand or by the *CBCL* software program that can be purchased separately.

Reliability

For the *CBCL/4–18,* adequate reliability coefficients are reported for interrater, test-retest, and internal consistency. For the *CBCL/2–3,* small studies were completed that suggest moderate to adequate reliability. Additional studies are needed.

Validity

Evidence is reported to support construct validity for the *CBCL/4–18.* Criterion-related validity is reported between the *CBCL* and the *Conners' Rating Scales* and the *Revised Behavior Problem Checklist* as .82 and .81, respectively. Evidence of content validity, criterion-related validity, and construct validity is presented for the *CBCL/2–3.*

Summary

The *CBCL* is a comprehensive assessment system designed for use with children and youth from 2 through 18 years of age. The system consists of various instruments that are completed by the examiner, parent, teacher, and student. These multiple sources of information provide a variety of perspectives on the problem behaviors.

Conners' Rating Scales-Revised

The *Conners' Rating Scales–Revised (CRS-R)* (Conners, 1997) are designed to assess behaviors in children and youth ages 3 to 17 years. The *CRS-R* consist of a set of main scales and a set of auxiliary scales.

Main Scales

The three main scales include: two parent, two teacher, and two adolescent self-report scales for assessing problem behaviors, each consisting of two versions, a long form and a shorter form.

1. *Long Forms.* The long form is typically used when comprehensive information is needed or a diagnosis according to DSM-IV is being considered. The *Conners' Parent Rating Scale–Revised: Long Form (CPRS-R:L)* consists of 80 statements to which parents (or guardians) indicate agreement or disagreement regarding their child's behavior over the past month. The statements include a broad range of behaviors, for example, "Does not get invited to friends' houses." and "Clings to parents and other adults." The statements of the *Conners' Parent Rating Scale–Revised: Long Form* are divided among the following 12 subscales:
   - Oppositional-Defiant*
   - Cognitive Problems*
   - Hyperactivity-Impulsivity*
   - Anxious-Shy
   - Perfectionism
   - Social Problems
   - Psychosomatic
   - Conners' Global Index
   - ADHD Index*
   - DSM-IV Symptom Scale
   - DSM-IV Inattention
   - DSM-IV Impulsivity

   The "*" indicates the subscales that are also on the short form.

   The *Conners' Teacher Rating Scale–Revised: Long Form (CTRS-R:L)* contains the same subscales as the parent long form with the exception of the Psychosomatic subscale. Teachers are asked to consider the student's behavior and actions during the past month. The scales contains 59 items such as "Appears to be unaccepted by group" or "Poor in spelling."

2. *Short Forms.* The short version is typically used when multiple administrations over time are desired. The parent version, *Conners' Parent Rating Scale–Revised: Short Form (CPRS-R:S)*, contains 27 items divided among the four subscales indicated above by the "*."

For teachers, *Conners' Teacher Rating Scale–Revised: Short Form (CTRS-R:S)* contains 29 items and the same subscales as in the short form for parents. The similarities between the forms help to facilitate comparisons between parent and teacher responses. Test scores are plotted to create a profile of the problem behaviors (Figure 15.6).

3. *Adolescent Self-Report Scales.* The *Conners-Wells' Adolescent Self-Report Scales: Long Form (CASS:L)* and the *Conners-Wells' Adolescent Self-Report Scales: Short Form (CASS:S)* can be used with adolescents who have at least a fifth grade reading level. The scales are designed to obtain information that is available from no one else but the individual student. The long form is used when extensive information and DSM-IV compliance is required. Sample items include "My parents' discipline is too harsh" and "My parents do not reward or notice my good behavior."

Auxiliary Scales

The auxiliary scales include a global index (the hyperactivity index in the original Conners' Rating Scales) for parents and teachers and a set of ADHD/DSM-IV scales for the parent, teacher, and student.

1. *Conners' Global Index.* Both the parent and teacher scales, *Conners' Global Index-Parent (CGI-P)* and *Conners' Global Index-Teacher (CGI-T)* consist of 10 items each. The items on this scale, formerly known as the hyperactivity index, are divided between two separate factors: emotional lability and hyperactivity

2. *Conners' ADHD/DSM-IV Scales.* These scales include a scale for parents, *Conners' ADHD/DSM-IV Scales-Parent (CADS-P),* for teachers, *Conners' ADHD/DSM-IV Scales-Teacher (CADS-T),* and for the student, *Conners' ADHD/DSM-IV Scales-Self Report (CADS-S).*

Each scale contains 30 items that are divided between the following areas:
- ADHD Index
- DSM-IV Symptom Scale
- Inattention
- Hyperactivity

For screening purposes, the examiner can choose to administer just the ADHD Index; to confirm DSM-IV diagnoses, the DSM-IV Symptom Scale can be used.

Administration

All of the short scales take 5 to 10 minutes to administer; the long scales take between 15 and 20 minutes.

Scoring

T-scores may be calculated for each of the scales.

Standardization

The rating scales were originally developed on a clinical population at Johns Hopkins University Hospital in Baltimore. The manual states that 8,000 individuals participated in the norms for the new scales. The manual states that the norm sample included individuals from over 95% of the states and provinces in North America and that there were large samples obtained for all of the age groups and for both genders. The manual further states that minority group samples were represented.

Reliability

Internal reliability is adequate for both the short and long forms of the parent and teacher rating scales and the adolescent self-report scales. Test-retest reliability was examined following a 6–8 week interval. In general, test-retest reliabilities for the *CRS-R* were adequate across the various forms.

Validity

Adequate construct validity is reported for the teacher, parent, and self-report forms. Small

Profile for Males: Conners' Teacher Rating Scale - Revised (S)

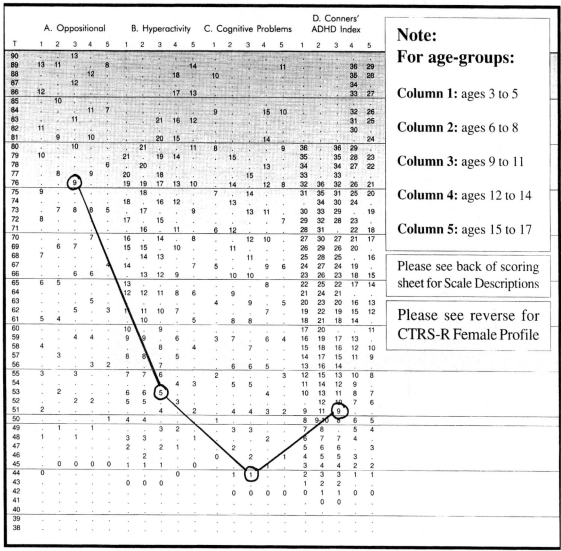

FIGURE 15.6

Conners' Teacher Rating Scale Profile

studies report the correlation between the *CRS-R* and the *Children's Depression Inventory* and performance measures. Continued research will be helpful.

Summary

The *Conners' Rating Scales–Revised (CRS-R)* consist of a set of scales for parents, teachers, and students to assist in gathering information about problem behaviors. The revised scales add several important dimensions to the original *Conners' Rating Scales.* The self-report forms provide information from the student's perspective. The auxiliary ADHD forms provide information from parent, teacher, and student perspectives and link the information to DSM-IV. Usefulness of the instrument would be enhanced if more information were provided about the sample of individuals who participated in the development of this revised edition. The *CRS-R* can be administered by computer or scored using computer software.

Revised Behavior Problem Checklist

The *Revised Behavior Problem Checklist (RBPC)* (Quay and Peterson, 1987) is designed for school-age children and youth. Similar to the *CBCL,* this instrument has a rating scale format and includes 89 problem-behavior items that are clustered into six areas.

Administration

The instrument can be completed by parents or teachers.

Scoring

Raw scores are converted to T-scores.

Standardization

The test norms were developed from different populations including: gifted fourth grade students, middle school students from a university laboratory school, children in a public

---

BOX 15.4

CONNERS' RATING SCALES– REVISED

Publication Date: 1997

Purposes: Assesses behavior in terms of oppositional-defiant, cognitive problems, hyperactivity-impulsivity, anxious-shy, perfectionism, social problems, psychosomatic (parent scale), a global index (emotional lability and hyperactivity) and ADHD.

Age/Grade Levels: The CRS-R are designed for children and youth ages 3 to 17 years.

Time to Administer: Short scales take 5 to 10 minutes to administer; the long scales take between 15 and 20 minutes.

Technical Adequacy: Adequate reliability and validity. Additional information regarding the standardization sample would be helpful.

Suggested Use: Measures student behavior from the perspectives of the parents, teachers and the individual.

---

school classroom for seriously emotionally disturbed students, and so on. Caution must be used in interpretation because these groups are not representative of the general population. Conversions from raw score to T-scores are based on a small sample of public school children in three states.

Reliability

Information about internal consistency, inter-rater, and test-retest reliability is adequate.

Validity

Information about concurrent and construct validity is adequate.

Summary

The *Revised Behavior Problem Checklist* is designed for assessing problem behaviors in school-age children and youth. The instrument is more useful for assessing externalizing behavior clusters than internalizing behaviors. However, T-scores and interpretations of them should be used with extreme caution because of the select nature of the groups comprising the norm sample.

Systematic Screening for Behavioral Disorders

The *Systematic Screening for Behavioral Disorders (SSBD)* (2d edition) (Walker and Severson, 1992) is designed to be used as a screening tool for emotional and behavioral problems for children in grades 1 to 6. This tool conceptualizes problem behaviors as occurring in clusters of externalizing and internalizing behaviors.

Administration

The SSBD uses a **gating** administration procedure, which consists of a series of three steps in which the assessment becomes more precise and specific:

1. Step 1. The classroom teacher rank-orders all students in the class according to items that correspond to externalizing and internalizing profiles. Three students with the highest score on the externalizing profile and the three students with the highest score on the internalizing profile pass on to the second step.
2. Step 2. The classroom teacher completes rating scales on the six students identified in Step 1. Student scores are compared to normative criteria, and students who exceed the cutoff score are referred to the third step.
3. Step 3. Repeated observations of the student(s) are conducted by another professional (another teacher, school psychologist, or counselor). Students who exceed normal criteria are referred to the assessment team for further evaluation. The instrument includes videotapes and quizzes to assist in training the observer in this step.

Scoring

Step 1 produces a rank ordering of students. Step 2 produces two indexes of behavior: the Critical Events Index, which includes adaptive and maladaptive behavior, and the Combined Frequency Index. Step 3 produces the Academic Engage Time score, which consists of the time that the student is engaged in instructional tasks. A Peer Social Behavior score reports behavior in five categories: social engagement, participation, parallel play, alone, and other. In Steps 2 and 3, scores can be converted to T-scores and percentile ranks.

Standardization

The *SSBD* was normed on students attending regular education programs in eight states.

BOX 15.5

REVISED BEHAVIOR PROBLEM CHECKLIST

Publication Date: 1987

Purposes: Assesses 89 different problem behaviors

Age/Grade Levels: School-age children and youth

Time to Administer: 15–30 minutes

Technical Adequacy: Norming sample is not representative; reliability and validity adequate

Suggested Use: The instrument is more useful for assessing externalizing behavior clusters than internalizing behaviors.

Specific demographic data concerning the norming sample are not available.

Reliability

Test-retest reliability coefficients are adequate for Steps 1 and 2. No test-retest reliability information is reported for Step 3. Interrater reliabilities for Steps 1 and 3 are generally good.

Validity

Information about concurrent and construct validity is generally adequate; predictive validity is in the low to moderate range.

Summary

The *SSBD* is an instrument for screening students with problem behaviors. The instrument consists of three steps, the first of which is designed to screen a large group of students. Reliability and validity are generally adequate. Additional information about the normative sample would be helpful.

OBSERVING THE STUDENT

Observation is a powerful tool in assessing problem behaviors. Observations allow the educator to collect information about the student in a variety of areas associated with the problem behaviors. These areas alone may not be significant; however, in conjunction with other information, they help to provide important information from the observer's perspective (Figure 15.7).

OTHER ASSESSMENT APPROACHES

In addition to standardized instruments and student observations, other assessment approaches are used in gathering information

- Behavorial characteristics descriptions:
  Is the student's activity level appropriate to the situation?
  Does the student maintain attention (attention span)?
  Does the student appear implusive and distractible?
- Social-emotional descriptions:
  How does the student react to praise and frustration?
  Does the student display appropriate affect?
  What is the student's overall mood state?
  What is the student's overall level of social skills?
  Does the student seem overly anxious or nervous?
- Cognitive descriptions:
  What is the level of communication skills?
  What is the student's level of insight into the current problem?
  What is the student's organizational level?
  How well does the student plan?
- Academic functioning descriptions:
  What is the student's general academic functioning?
  Is academic functioning consistent?

FIGURE 15.7

Areas Included in a Behavioral Observation

Adapted from Merrill, K. W. (1994).

about problem behaviors and the effectiveness of intervention plans. For example, work samples, portfolios, exhibits, journals, and notebooks can illustrate the student's progress in the development of social skills. Students and teachers work together in using these approaches to identify ways to illustrate growth and progress.

Interviews

Interviews are helpful in identifying variables that activate problem behaviors or that main-

BOX 15.6

SYSTEMATIC SCREENING FOR BEHAVIORAL DISORDERS (2D EDITION)

Publication Date: 1992
Purposes: A screening tool that conceptualizes problem behaviors as occurring in clusters of externalizing and internalizing behaviors
  Age/Grade Levels: Grades 1 to 6
  Time to Administer: Uses a gating administrative procedure
  Technical Adequacy: The norming sample consisted of students in regular education programs; however, limited demographic information is available. Reliability and validity are generally adequate.
  Suggested Use: Screening problem behaviors in the regular classroom

tain them. Student interviews provide information about the student's self-concept and self-esteem. Interviews with parents can provide a wealth of information about the way that the student functions at home and in the community. Parents can share their own expectations regarding their child's behavior and the approaches that they have found to be helpful in addressing problem behaviors. Parents can also provide information about their child's behavior difficulties in the past and the types of interventions that were attempted and successful. They can describe complications or changes in the family structure that the child is currently experiencing at home, including unemployment of parents, death, birth, and divorce, all of which create additional stresses on family members. More information about the interview process is described in earlier chapters: Special considerations when conducting interviews with family members are addressed in Chapter 2, and Chapter 5 provides detailed information in planning and conducting student interviews and conferring with other teachers.

Past Performance

Information about the student's past performance is often helpful in assessing the current situation. A student's cumulative record should be reviewed for information concerning any previous problem behaviors and the types of interventions that were tried. Interviews with former teachers, coaches, and others who have worked with the student provide information about previous concerns and whether interventions were successful. The types of interventions and special education services that have been provided should be examined.

School Records

School records also contain information about student attendance. Irregular attendance over one or more years signals a possible pattern of lack of motivation, lack of family support, or lack of connection with the school community. Alternatively, irregular attendance is a signal for other problems such as health issues, problems in the home environment, or attitude and adjustment difficulties.

PREFERRED PRACTICES

Teachers who have students with emotional or problem behaviors in the classroom must work closely with other professionals. Answering assessment questions and planning, implementing, monitoring, and evaluating an individualized education program for a student with emotional or problem behaviors involves working closely with the school psychologist, social workers, and mental health practitioners. Merrell (1994) writes that classifying behavior is easier than changing behavior.

Because of the wide degree of individuality and variation in the biology, behavior, and temperament that human beings exhibit, developing effective interventions for our behavioral, social, and emotional problems requires a tremendous understanding of the conditions under which those problems occur, as well as a great deal of clinical sensitivity on the part of the therapist. It will be an extraordinary challenge to the emerging generation of mental health professionals and educators to develop classification systems that not only reliably codify a wide array of problems but also provide information that will directly translate into valid treatment planning. (p. 41)

EXTENDING LEARNING

15.1 Obtain one or two commercial instruments for assessing behavior problems. Compare and contrast the types of information gathered. Which tool would be more useful to you? Why?

15.2 Make arrangements to visit a classroom and observe student behavior. Create an ABC form and fill in the information that you observe. What classroom behaviors did you witness? What were the consequences that followed each behavior that occurred? Could you identify the antecedent conditions?

15.3 Visit two or more classrooms and observe one student in each. Compare their classroom behaviors.

15.4 Wayne is a student in Mrs. Frank's classroom. His teacher reports that he seems to argue constantly with other students.

The arguments escalate quickly and often end with the students shoving and pushing each other. Wayne seems to have few friends and often spends his time at recess alone. You have observed that he likes to shoot baskets at the hoop on the playground. Develop a set of questions that you might use in interviewing Wayne.

15.5 Develop a scale that collects information about student attitudes and interests. What are some of the technical considerations to consider before using your scale?

15.6 What WWW sites focus on issues in assessing behaviors in the classroom? Share your findings with the class.

REFERENCES

Achenbach, T. M. (1988). *Child behavior checklist/2–3*. Burlington, Vt.: Center for Children, Youth, and Families.

Achenbach, T. M. (1991a). *Child behavior checklist/4–18*. Burlington, Vt.: Center for Children, Youth, and Families.

Achenbach, T. M. (1991b). *Teacher's report form.* Burlington, Vt.: Center for Children, Youth, and Families.

Alberto, P. A., and A. C. Troutman (1995). *Applied behavior analysis for teachers.* 4th ed. Englewood Cliffs, N.J.: Merrill, an imprint of Prentice Hall.

American Psychiatric Association. (1994). *Diagnostic and statistical manual of mental disorders.* 4th ed. Washington, D.C.: Author.

Bijou, S. W., R. F. Peterson, and M. H. Ault (1968). A method to integrate descriptive and experimental field studies at the level of data and empirical concepts. *Journal of Applied Behavior Analysis* 1(2):175–191.

Brazelton, T. B. (1992). *Touchpoints: Your child's emotional and behavioral development.* Reading, Mass.: Addison Wesley.

Brown, L., and D. D. Hammill (1990). *Behavior rating profile-2.* Austin, Tex.: Pro-Ed.

Campbell, S. B. (1990). *Behavior problems in preschool children.* New York: Guilford Press.

Cohen, L., and L. Spenciner (1996). Assessment of social-emotional development in young children. In eds., M. Breen and C. Fiedler: 503–580 *Behavioral approach to assessment of youth with emotional/behavioral disorders: A handbook for school-based practitioners,* Austin, Tex.: Pro-Ed.

Conners, C. K. (1997). *Conners' rating scales-revised.* North Tonawanda, N.Y.: Multi-Health Systems.

Costantino, G., R. G. Malgady, and L. H. Rogler (1986). *TEMAS (Tell-Me-A-Story).* Los Angeles: Western Psychological Services.

Dresser, N. (1996). *Multicultural manners: New rules of etiquette for a changing society.* New York: John Wiley & Sons.

Erikson, E. (1950). *Childhood and society.* New York: Norton.

Gilliam, J. E. (1995a). *Attention-deficit/hyperactivity disorder test.* Austin, Tex.: Pro-Ed.

Gilliam, J. E. (1995b). *Gilliam autism rating scale.* Austin, Tex.: Pro-Ed.

Greenberg, L. (1989). *Test of variables of attention.* Los Alamitos, Calif.: Universal Attention Disorders.

Greenberg, L. (1996). *Test of variables of attention-Auditory.* Los Alamitos, Calif.: Universal Attention Disorders.

Greenspan, S. I. (1992). *Infancy and early childhood: The practice of clinical assessment and intervention with emotional and developmental challenges.* Madison, Conn.: International Universities Press.

Gresham, F. M., and S. N. Elliott (1990). *Social skills rating system.* Circle Pines, Minn.: American Guidance Service.

Gunter, P. L., R. E. Shores, S. L. Jack, S. K. Rasmussen, and J. Flowers (1995). On the move. *Teaching Exceptional Children* 28(1): 12–14.

Gunter, P. L., R. E. Shores, S. L. Jack, S. K. Rasmussen, and J. Flowers (1995). On the move. *Teaching Exceptional Children* 28(1): 12–14.

Krug, D. A., J. R. Arick, and P.J. Almond (1993). *Autism screening instrument for educational planning second edition.* Austin, Tex.: PRO-ED.

Kopp, C. (1994). *Baby Steps: The "whys" of your child's behavior in the first two years.* New York: W. H. Freeman.

Lambert, N., C. Hartsough, and J. Sandoval (1990). *Children's attention & adjustment survey (CAAS).* Circle Pines, Minn.: American Guidance Service.

McCarney, S. B. (1989a). *Attention deficit disorder evaluation scale–School version.* Columbia, Mo.: Hawthorne Educational Services.

McCarney, S. B. (1989b). *Attention deficit disorder evaluation scale–Home version.* Columbia, Mo.: Hawthorne Educational Services.

McCarney, S. B., and J. E. Leigh (1990). *Behavior evaluation scale-2.* Columbia, Mo.: Hawthorne Educational Services.

Merrell, K. W. (1994). *Assessment of behavioral, social, and emotional problems.* New York: Longman.

Mesulam, M. (1990). Schizophrenia and the brain. *New England Journal of Medicine* 322(12): 842–844.

Naglieri, J. A., P. A LeBuffe, and S. I. Pfeiffer (1995). *Devereux behavior rating scales.* San Antonio: Tex.: The Psychological Corporation, Harcourt Brace.

Platzman, K. A., M. R. Stoy, R. T. Brown, C. D. Coles, I. E. Smith, and A. Falek (1992). Review of observational methods in attention deficit hyperactivity disorder (ADHD): Implications for diagnosis. *School Psychology Quarterly* 7(3): 155–177.

Quay, H. C., and D. R. Peterson (1987a). *Revised behavior problem checklist.* Odessa, Fla.: Psychological Assessment Resources.

Quay, H. C., and D. R. Peterson (1987b). *Manual for the revised behavior problem checklist.* Odessa, Fla.: Psychological Assessment Resources.

Reynolds, C. R., and R. W. Kamphaus (1992). *BASC: Behavior assessment system for children.* Circle Pines, Minn.: American Guidance Service.

Rogers, C. R. (1983). *Freedom to learn for the 80's.* Columbus, Ohio: Merrill.

Salisbury, C. L., C. Gallucci, M. M. Palombaro, and C. A. Peck (1995). Strategies that promote social relations among elementary students with and without severe disabilities in inclusive schools. *Exceptional Children* 62(2): 125–137.

Schopler, E., R. J. Reichler, and B. R. Renner (1986). *Childhood autism rating scale.* Los Angeles: Western Psychological Services.

Shelton, T. L., and R. A. Barkley (1993). Assessment of attention-deficit hyperactivity disorder in young children. In eds. J. L. Culbertson and D. J. Willis, *Testing young children,* 290–318. Austin, Tex.: Pro-Ed.

Spenciner, L. J., and L. G. Cohen (1994–1995). Recognizing attention deficit/hyperactivity disorder

(ADHD): Defining and assessing the disability. *Diagnostique* 20(1–4): 211–224.

Thomas, A. and S. Chess (1977). *Temperament and development*. New York: Bruner/Mazel.

Thomas, A., S. Chess, and H. G. Birch (1970). The origin of personality. *Scientific American* 223: 102–109.

Ullmann, R. K., E. K. Sleator, and R. L. Sprague (1991). *ADD-H: Comprehensive teacher's rating scale (ACTeRS)–2nd edition*. Chicago: Riverside.

Walker, H. M., and M. Bullis (1991). Behavior disorders and the social context of regular class integration: A conceptual dilemma? In *The regular education initiative: Alternative perspectives on concepts, issues, and models,* eds. J. W. Lloyd, N. Singh, and A. C. Repps, Pacific Grove, Calif.: Brookes Cole.

Walker, H. M., and H. H. Severson (1992). *Systematic screening for behavior disorders*. 2d ed. Longmont, Calif: Sopris West.

White, B. (1975). *The first three years of life*. Englewood Cliffs, N.J.: Prentice Hall.

Zero to Three (1992). *Heart start: The emotional foundations of school readiness*. Arlington, Va.: Author.

Zero to Three/National Center for Clinical Infant Programs. (1995). *Diagnostic classification: 0–3: Diagnostic classification of mental health and developmental disorders of infancy and early childhood*. Arlington, Va.: Author.

Sensory and Motor Abilities

OVERVIEW

Sometimes teachers have questions regarding a student's hearing or vision, or teachers observe that a student is clumsy or has difficulty in balancing activities. Learning the signs of possible vision, hearing, or motor difficulties helps teachers know when to refer students for further assessments. Correspondingly, a grasp of the common terminology and assessment procedures that therapists and specialized teachers utilize helps classroom teachers in comprehending assessment reports completed by professionals in other disciplines.

Educators who teach students with sensory or physical disabilities work closely with other professionals, such as itinerant teachers with expertise in blindness and visual impairments, teachers of the deaf, audiologists, physical and occupational therapists. To plan an appropriate educational program for the student, to monitor it, and evaluate its progress, the educator must be able to understand and interpret assessments completed by professionals skilled in areas of sensory and motor functioning. This chapter is an introduction to the specialized assessment of students with disabilities in the areas of vision, hearing, and mobility. Through case studies of specific students, we will meet professionals from other disciplines and examine some of the common assessment procedures and instruments that they use.

Identifying and Assessing Students Who Are Blind or Who Have Visual Impairments

SECTION OBJECTIVES

After completing this section, you should be able to:

Describe warning signs that indicate the need for referring a student for an eye examination.

Discuss key aspects in interpreting a vision report.

Describe the terms and procedures for assessing distance, near, and functional vision.

Discuss the components of an orientation and mobility assessment.

UNDERSTANDING BLINDNESS AND OTHER VISUAL IMPAIRMENTS

A **visual impairment** is a loss in one or more of the areas of visual functioning, including near and distance acuity, visual field, or color vision. The amount and usefulness of the vision is affected in three ways:

- age of onset
- type of impairment or condition
- extent or degree of the impairment

Age of Onset

Congenital visual impairments (including congenital blindness) are conditions affecting sight that develop during the prenatal period or result from events during the birth process. Other conditions develop during childhood as the result of heredity, accident, or disease and

are referred to as **adventitious visual impairments.** Individuals who are adventitiously blind may have some visual memory. Visual memory of objects is helpful in concept development; similarly, visual memory of environments can aide learning of new travel skills.

Types of Visual Impairments

Visual impairments can affect the entire eye or only a portion of the eye, or result from the absence of all or part of the structures of the eye. Infectious diseases such as toxoplasmosis and trachoma can cause damage to the eye, either before or during birth. Infants who are born prematurely are at a high risk for visual impairments, including retinopathy of prematurity (ROP) (blindness caused by too high a concentration of oxygen given a newborn), amblyopia, strabismus (a muscle imbalance that causes one eye to be turned inward, outward, up, or down), cortical blindness, or extreme nearsightedness (an inability to see objects at a distance), cataracts, glaucoma, and albinism (an inherited disorder that results in lack of pigmentation and low vision). Table 16.1 lists and describes some of the common types of visual impairments.

Some types of visual impairments cause fluctuations in visual acuity, and these fluctuations may be seen periodically or on a regular basis. Thus, a student may have difficulty with a visual task at times while on other days experience no difficulty.

Extent of Visual Impairments

Almost all students with visual impairments have some vision, albeit limited. In fact, most students who are blind have some usable vision; few students who are "blind" have no sight at all. Often times, students who are blind have enough vision to see hand or finger movement at a close distance. Students unable to see hand movement may have light perception that will enable them to see the shape of large forms and to identify the direction of a light source.

TABLE 16.1   Common Effects of Visual Impairments

Condition	Effect	Prognosis
Amblyopia	The image is seen as a double image. Onset is by age 6 and is sometimes referred to as "lazy eye."	Correctable
Astigmatism	The image is seen out of focus.	Correctable
Cataracts	The image is clouded.	Correctable
Glaucoma	The image is hazy and the field of vision is constricted.	Controllable with medication
Myopia	The image is blurred.	Correctable
Achromatopsia	An inability to identify one or more primary colors. This condition is sometimes referred to as "colorblindness."	Noncorrectable
Cortex damage	A loss of vision due to a lesion in the cortex area.	Noncorrectable
Optic nerve damage	A loss of vision due to incomplete development or damage to the optic nerve.	Noncorrectable
Nystagmus	The image is blurred due to the involuntary movement of the eye.	Noncorrectable

SIGNALS OF VISUAL PROBLEMS

Some visual impairments have no warning signs; other visual impairments have early warning signals. Table 16.2 enumerates some of the more common signals. If a teacher has any doubt, the student should be referred to the school nurse for screening. The teacher or school nurse can then discuss any concerns they have with the student's parents who should be encouraged to take their child to an ophthalmologist, a medical doctor who specializes in treating vision and eye problems, or to an optometrist, an individual who examines the eye and prescribes glasses to correct visual acuity.

TABLE 16.2   Signals of Visual Problems

1. Student does not track a moving object with both eyes in proper alignment.
2. Student is extremely light sensitive.
3. Student rubs eyes frequently.
4. Student's eyes are frequently red or watery.
5. Student's eyes do not focus properly.
6. Student examines objects at very close range.
7. Student squints when attempting close work.
8. Student experiences difficulty in judging distances.
9. Student avoids close visual work.

Discovering Amblyopia

One of the most common signs is that the student's eyes appear to be out of alignment. This condition, called amblyopia or "lazy eye," results from a muscle imbalance in one of the eyes that causes the individual to receive a double image. This dissonance prompts the brain to suppress the image from the problem eye. Left untreated, the suppressed eye will gradually lose the ability to function. However, if the condition is identified and treated by age 6, there is no permanent loss of vision. Students suspected of having amblyopia should be referred to a specialist for an eye examination.

Treatment for amblyopia includes corrective surgery and/or a temporary patch over the dominant eye.

SCREENING INSTRUMENTS

Screening instruments to assess visual functioning require an individual to identify a symbol of an object or a letter in the alphabet. One

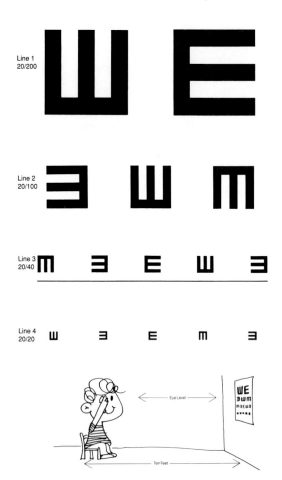

FIGURE 16.1

The Pointing Game

Source: From *Home Eye Test for Preschoolers* by the National Society to Prevent Blindness, 1991. Copyrighted by the National Society to Prevent Blindness.

common tool, the New York Lighthouse Symbol Flash Card Vision Test (Lighthouse Low Vision Services, 1970), assesses distance acuity using three symbols: an apple, a house, and an umbrella. The symbols are pictured in varying sizes from 20/20 to 20/200 per card and may be used with young children or students with multiple disabilities who are not able to identify letters.

When conducting the screening, the adult checks to make sure that the individual can identify each of the symbols. The student is given the cards and asked to name a card while both eyes are open. If the student answers correctly, then the cards are shown at varying distances of 5, 10, and 20 feet. The student is tested at each distance, testing each eye separately, then both eyes together.

Another common screening device is the Pointing Game using the letter *E* (National Society to Prevent Blindness, 1991). First, the adult shows the *E* in various positions and the student is asked to point like *E* points. During the actual screening test, the student is seated 10 feet from the eye chart and the adult begins with the largest *E* on line one (Figure 16.1).

Students who do not pass the screening test or students who are suspected of having a visual impairment are referred to an ophthalmologist.

INTERPRETING A VISION REPORT

An ophthalmological examination furnishes much information about the individual's eye condition. This information is summarized in a vision report that is helpful to team members in planning the student's educational program, in adapting materials, and in modifying curriculum. The prognosis of the eye condition is helpful in outlining the skills the student will need to acquire and the services that should be provided.

The ophthalmological vision report (Figure 16.2) contains information about the history of the eye condition, distance and near visual acu-

EYE REPORT FOR CHILDREN WITH VISUAL PROBLEMS

Name of Pupil ___*Reza*___ _____ ___*J.*___ Sex __*M*__ Race _____
   (Type or Print)   (First)   (Middle)   (Last)

Address ___*2 Newberry St.*___ _____ Date of Birth __*2*__ __*21*__ __*XX*__
    (No. and street)   (City or town)   (Country)   (State)   (Month) (Day) (Year)

Grade ___*6*___ School _____ Address _____

I. HISTORY

A. Probable age at onset of vision impairment. Right eye (O.D.) _____ Left eye (O.S.) *early childhood – exact age unknown*

B. Severe ocular infections, injuries, operations, if any, with age at time of occurance _____
_____

C. Has pupil's ocular condition occured in any blood relative(s)? __*yes*__ If so, what relationship(s)? __*parent*__

II. MEASUREMENTS (see back of form for preferred notation for recording visual acuity and table of approximate equivalents)

A. VISUAL ACUITY

	DISTANT VISION			NEAR VISION			PRESCRIPTION		
	Without correction	With best correction*	With low vision aid	Without correction	With best correction*	With low vision aid	Sph.	Cyl.	Axis
Right eye (O.D.)	5/200	5/200							
Left eye (O.S.)	HM	HM							
Both eyes (O.U.)							Date _____		

B. If glasses are to be worn, were safety lenses prescribed in: Plastic _____ Tempered glass _____   *with ordinary lenses

C. If low vision aid is prescribed, specify type and recommendations for use. _____

D. FIELD OF VISION: Is there a limitation? __*yes*__ If so, record results of test on chart on back of form.

What is the widest diameter (in degrees) of remaining visual field? O.D. _____ O.S. _____

E. Is there impaired color perception? _____ If so, for what color(s) _____

III. CAUSE OF BLINDNESS OR VISION IMPAIRMENT

A. Present ocular condition(s) responsible for vision impairment. (If more than one, specify all but underline the one which probably first caused severe vision impairment.)

O.D. *Congenital optic atrophy*
O.S.

B. Preceding ocular condition, if any, which led to present condition, or the underlined condition, specified in A.

O.D. _____
O.S. _____

C. Etiology (underlying cause) of ocular condition primarily responsible for vision impairment. (e.g., specific disease, injury, poisoning, heredity or other prenatal influence.)

O.D. *Hereditary– autosomal dominant*
O.S.

D. If etiology is injury or poisoning, indicate circumstances and kind of object or poison involved. _____
_____

IV. PROGNOSIS AND RECOMMENDATIONS

A. Is pupil's vision impairment considered to be: Stable __*X*__ Deteriorating _____ Capable of improvement _____ Uncertain _____

B. What treatment is recommended, if any? _____

C. When is reexamination recommended? ___*1 year*___ ___*–recommend low vision work-up*___

D. Glasses: Not needed _____ To be worn constantly _____ For close work only _____ Other (specify) _____

E. Lighting requirements: Average _____ Better than average __*X*__ Less than average _____

F. Use of the eyes: Unlimited _____ Limited, as follows: _____

G. Physical activity: Unrestricted _____ Restricted, as follows: _____

TO BE FORWARDED BY EXAMINER TO:

Date of examination __*August 3, 19XX*__
Signature of examiner _____ Degree _____

continued

FIGURE 16.2

Reza's Eye Report

Source: Prevent Blindness America, Schaumburg, Ill. Reprinted with permission from the publisher.

PREFERRED VISUAL ACUITY NOTATIONS

DISTANT VISION. Use Snellen notation with test distance of 20 feet. (Examples: 20/100, 20/60). For acuities less than 20/200 record distance at which 200 foot letter can be recognized as numerator of fraction and 200 as denominator. (Examples: 10/200, 3/200). If the 200 foot letter is not recognized at 1 foot record abbreviation for best distant vision as follows:

HM	HAND MOVEMENTS
PLL	PERCEIVES AND LOCALIZES LIGHT IN ONE OR MORE QUADRANTS
LP	PERCEIVES BUT DOES NOT LOCALIZE LIGHT
No LP	NO LIGHT PERCEPTION

NEAR VISION. Use standard A.M.A. notation and specify best distance at which pupil can read. (Example: 14/70 at 5 in.)

TABLE OF APPROXIMATE EQUIVALENT VISUAL ACUITY NOTATIONS

These notations serve only as an indication of the approximate relationship between recordings of distant and near vision and point type sizes. The teacher will find in practice that the pupil's reading performance may vary considerably from the equivalents shown.

Distant Snellen	Near A.M.A.	Near Jaeger	Near Metric	% Central Visual Efficiency for Near	Point	Usual Type Text Size
20/20 (ft.)	14/14 (in.)	1	0.37 (M.)	100	3	Mail order catalogue
20/30	14/21	2	0.50	95	5	Want ads
20/40	14/28	4	0.75	90	6	Telephone directory
20/50	14/35	6	0.87	50	8	Newspaper text
20/60	14/42	8	1.00	40	9	Adult text books
20/80	14/56	10	1.50	20	12	Children's books 9-12 yrs
20/100	14/70	11	1.75	15	14	Children's books 8-9 yrs.
20/120	14/84	12	2.00	10	18 ⎫	Large type text
20/200	14/140	17	3.50	2	24 ⎬	
12.5/200	14/224	19	6.00	1.5		
8/200	14/336	20	8.00	1		
5/200	14/560					
3/200	14/900					

FIELD OF VISION. Record results on chart below.

Type of text used: _____   Illumination in ft. candles: _____

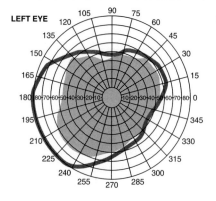
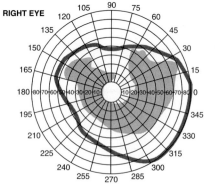

Text object: Color(s) _____ Size(s) _____   Text object: Color(s) _____ Size(s) _____

Distance(s): _____   Distance(s): _____

FIGURE 16.2 *Continued*

ity, visual field, color vision, causes of the present eye condition, and prognosis. Let's examine the types of information that are included in the report.

History

Age of onset of the visual impairment and occurrences of infections, injuries, and operations affect an individual's visual memory of the environment.

Measurements

Measurement of the individual's vision includes both distant and near vision, field of vision, and color perception.

Distance Acuity

Distance visual acuity is usually measured by twenty feet. Individuals with normal vision are described as having 20/20 vision; a person with a visual impairment may have 20/200. In other words, this person can see at 20 feet what a person with normal vision can see at 200 feet. However, sometimes a person cannot see the letters or picture symbols at the target distance of 20 feet and needs to have the letters or symbols at a closer range. The eye specialist may then report the distance acuity at 10/200, which means that the individual recognized at 10 feet what a person with normal vision could identify at 200 feet. The following abbreviations are used in reporting acuity in the left, right, and both eyes:

O.D. Right eye
O.S. Left eye
O.U. Both eyes

Persons who have low distance visual acuity may not be able to see figures on the eye chart at any distance; however, they may be able to count fingers, identify hand movement, or recognize a light source. The following abbreviations are typically used to note these acuities:

C.F. Counts fingers (farthest distance)
H.M. Hand movement (farthest distance)
L.P. Light perception (ability to tell whether it is light or dark)
N.L.P. No light perception

Near Vision Acuity

The use of near vision enables the individual to explore their immediate environment and to learn by watching others. Measurements of **near visual acuity** are usually given in inches, meters, or Jaeger chart numbers, a set of numbers that refer to type size.

Visual Field

The term "field of vision" refers to central and peripheral vision. Some students may have very good central visual acuity but limited peripheral vision; others may have "islands" of vision in an otherwise restricted field (for example, Reza's right eye in Figure 16.2). For these students, tilting the head or gazing indirectly at the object is the only way to stimulate the usable field. The vision report provides an illustration to indicate field loss. It confirms areas of visual functioning allowing trained teachers to suggest intervention strategies such as positioning and direction of gaze. This information about field loss helps in developing strategies to use in scanning the environment and for using what's called **functional vision.**

Color Vision

Some individuals experience difficulty in distinguishing colors because their retinal cone receptors lack the necessary pigments or are less sensitive in general to certain light waves. These individuals are unable to discriminate some (or all) colors and may exhibit photophobia. Students often compensate for color blindness by detecting brightness or differences in the grayness of colors.

SNAPSHOT

Working with Other Professionals at Millbrook Middle School

Melinda Teraz eased her compact car into the parking lot of Millbrook Middle School. Today, a new student would be joining her class. She thought back to the meeting yesterday afternoon. During their team planning time, Melinda and the other sixth grade teachers met with the assistant principal, Dr. Wentzel, and two visitors to the school. Dr. Wentzel explained that a new student, Reza J., would be enrolling in the school soon and then introduced the visitors: an itinerant teacher for students with visual impairments, Dan Jenkins, and an orientation and mobility instructor, Sara Walden.

Dan and Sara explained that they would be visiting the school on a regular basis to assist Melinda and the rest of the staff in planning for Reza's needs. Dan discussed the fact that Reza has low vision and showed the staff a vision report from the ophthalmologist (Figure 16.2). He talked about functional vision and explained that he hoped to complete a functional vision assessment within the next few weeks. Dan continued that this assessment would give the teachers information about the way that Reza uses his remaining vision. Since Reza is a braille reader, Dan will be working with Reza on a regular basis to increase braille literacy skills. Dan explained to the team that he would be a resource to the teachers and that he hoped to participate in their regularly scheduled planning meetings.

Sara gave the staff a brief overview of the areas covered in orientation and mobility instruction. She explained that *orientation* refers to the process that an individual with a visual impairment uses to establish one's position in the environment by using the other senses, and that *mobility* refers to the ability to move safely and efficiently from one place to another. She discussed safety issues after pointing out the door that was partially open. For Reza or any student with low vision, Sara noted, a door that was shut at times and partially opened at other times represents a hazard. Sara said that she would be working with Reza after school for the first few weeks, to orient him to the new surroundings and to help him navigate the building and bus stop. Later, she will be available for consultation on an as-needed basis.

Causes of Vision Impairment

This section of the vision report describes the type of condition that affects the eye. Sometimes the cause of the visual impairment is unknown.

Prognosis and Recommendations

Information about the prognosis of the condition is important in program planning. Is the condition stable or will the condition deteriorate? If the condition is not stable, what are some signs that indicate a change in vision? What recommendations should be included in the individualized education program?

ASSESSMENTS SPECIFIC FOR STUDENTS WITH VISUAL IMPAIRMENTS

Students with visual impairments have unique needs that require specific instruction in curriculum areas beyond that of their sighted peers. Assessing students with visual impairments for the purpose of planning an appropriate education program should involve gathering information about functional vision, braille reading and writing, listening skills, orientation and mobility, and social and recreational skills (Silberman, 1996). Table 16.3 lists some of the assessment questions in these various areas.

Most norm-referenced instruments that have been developed to assess these areas are outdated. The *Oregon Project for Visually Im-*

TABLE 16.3 Assessment Questions for Planning an Education Program for a Student with a Visual Impairment

Functional vision assessment

>How does the student use residual vision?

>How does the student use other senses?

Language and listening

>Does the student understand important concepts: temporal, quantatative, positional, directional, and sequential?

Braille Literacy Plan

>What is the student's present literacy performance?

Orientation and mobility skills

>How does the student move from place to place?

>Does the student move independently?

>How does the student travel within the home? school? neighborhood and community?

Academic skills

>What is the student's achievement level in braille reading and writing?

>Does the student use auditing skills?

Adapted from Hall, Scholl, and Swallow (1986). Position statement from the Council for Exceptional Children, Division on Visual Handicaps, 1991.

paired and Blind Preschoolers, 5th Edition (Anderson, Davis, and Boigion, 1991), a helpful criterion-referenced instrument, is designed for students up to 7 years of age. This inventory assesses: cognitive, language, self-help, socialization, fine motor, and gross motor abilities. Some items indicate skills that are particularly important for a child with a visual impairment ("Locates dropped object up to 8 feet away with sound clue") or are appropriate for the child who will need orientation and mobility training ("Runs trailing a wall or rope").

For older students, regular, ongoing assessments using a variety of approaches need to be conducted to make modifications to the student's education program. Teachers and therapists can construct curriculum-based assessments, develop performance-based assessments, and use other approaches discussed in earlier chapters.

Functional Vision

Functional vision is measured in terms of visual efficiency; in other words, how well does the individual use residual vision? A functional vision assessment must be completed by a teacher trained to work with students with visual impairments. This assessment, conducted informally using materials in the classroom, provides specific information about how the student is using vision during daily routines and under what conditions in the environment the student's vision is optimal. Although some instruments have been developed to measure visual efficiency, they are outdated and of minimal use. Increasingly, teachers with backgrounds in blindness and low vision have been very successful in designing their own functional vision assessments based on the individual student's natural environment (Pawelski, 1992).

Braille Literacy

Assessing skills in reading and writing braille is another area completed by the teacher who is trained to work with students with visual impairments. The Individuals with Disabilities Education Act Amendments of 1997 state that the IEP team must consider (for students who are blind or visually impaired) instruction in braille and the use of braille unless the team determines that instruction or use of braille is not appropriate.

Orientation and Mobility (O & M) Skills

Orientation refers to the ability to determine one's position in the environment. Different cues such as sounds, light, or pavement surface assist an individual in orientation. Mobility refers to the ability to move from place to place and to travel safely. Learning to use aids such as a seeing eye dog or a cane increase a person's mobility.

The O & M instructor takes the lead role in assessing formal orientation and mobility skills in conjunction with parents and other team members. Particular skill areas that may be assessed include (Hill, 1992):

- ability to align the body to objects and sounds
- use of search patterns to explore the environment
- use of search patterns to recover a dropped object
- knowledge of how and when to ask for assistance

Assessment of Academic and Adaptive Skills

A comprehensive assessment helps in planning the specialized instruction relating to visual needs as well as instruction within the general academic program. A comprehensive assessment includes academic achievement; intelligence; motor skills; and, beginning at age 14, transition service needs that focus on the student's courses of study. A variety of assessment approaches, including performance-based assessment, curriculum-based assessment, inter-

views, and other approaches discussed in earlier chapters should be used.

Standardized Instruments

Developing norm-referenced tests for students with visual impairments is problematic. Few reliable and valid instruments exist because of the difficulty in standardizing an instrument (Barraga and Erin, 1992; Silberman, 1996). Since a visual impairment is a low incidence disability and the variation in types of visual loss and visual functioning among individuals are great, the development of a standardized instrument is extremely difficult.

Three widely used tests of achievement, the *Stanford Achievement Test* (Harcourt Brace Educational Measurement, 1996), the *Iowa Tests of Basic Skills* (Hoover, Hieronymous, Frisbie, and Dunbar, 1993), and the *BRIGANCE® Comprehensive Inventory of Basic Skills* (Brigance, 1983) are available in braille from the American Printing House for the Blind but they should be used with caution because norm-referenced tests that have been developed for sighted students are not always appropriate for students with visual impairments. First, many of the most common instruments do not include students with visual impairments in the norming sample; and second, some of the subtests or individual test items are dependent on vision.

PREFERRED PRACTICES

Today, many students have multiple disabilities; vision may be only one area of need. Assessment teams should ensure that at least one team member has training and expertise in the field of visual impairment. Information about visual functioning provides the team with critical information regarding the student's use of functional vision in the classroom, at home, and in the community.

Knowledge of the student's visual efficiency will assist team members in assessing areas of achievement, cognitive ability, and transition planning. During the assessment process, the team will need to consider the types of accommodations that the student may need. The educator with specific training in working with students with visual impairments should provide consultation and interpretation.

Teachers will need to consider a variety of assessment approaches described in earlier chapters. Assessment items and tasks must be carefully examined to ensure that they are fair to the student who will be assessed. By examining information collected over a period of time, the educator can obtain an accurate account of the student's abilities and needs, especially if the student experiences a fluctuation in vision.

Identifying and Assessing Students Who Are Deaf or Who Have Hearing Impairments

SECTION OBJECTIVES

After completing this section, you should be able to:

Define the terms that describe hearing impairment.

Identify early signs of hearing impairments.

Compare methods used in the evaluation of hearing impairments.

UNDERSTANDING HEARING IMPAIRMENTS

A **hearing impairment** is an umbrella term that covers all types of hearing losses. As with visual impairments, the amount and usefulness of residual hearing is affected by several factors:

- Age of onset
- Type of impairment or condition
- Extent or degree of the impairment

Age of Onset

The age of onset directly affects the ability to use speech. A hearing loss that occurs before the child develops language (prelingual) has a greater impact than a loss that occurs after developing language (postlingual). Some conditions that result in deafness or a hearing loss develop during the prenatal period or result from events during the birth process; these situations are referred to as congenital deafness. Other conditions develop during childhood as the result of heredity, an accident, or disease and are referred to as adventitious conditions.

Types of Hearing Impairments

A hearing loss occurs when one or more of the parts of the ear or auditory nerve do not function properly. Thus, hearing loss is classified according to the physiological basis for the hearing loss.

Conductive Hearing Loss

A **conductive hearing loss** is due to some barrier to the sound waves that travel from the outer ear to the inner ear. Causes of conductive hearing loss include otitis media (inflammation in the middle ear), severe accumulation of wax, or poorly developed physiological structures in the ear (Bradley-Johnson and Evans, 1991; Ross, Brackett, and Maxon, 1991). Most hearing impairments from conductive losses can be corrected through surgery or other medical treatments. A student with a conductive hearing loss may hear speech but certain sounds or discussions can be difficult if they are not loud enough. Amplification of sounds often helps; however, a hearing aid amplifies all sounds. A student wearing a hearing aid will hear all sounds in the environment with equal amplification; this includes extraneous noise in the classroom as well as the teacher talking.

Sensorineural Hearing Loss

Problems with the inner ear or auditory nerve can result in **sensorineural hearing loss.** Sensorineural hearing loss may be due to extended exposure to very loud noise, extended high fevers, tumors in the ear, brain damage, developmental problems, genetic factors, prenatal and/or post-natal infections, anoxia (deficient amounts of oxygen), and trauma (Bradley-Johnson and Evans, 1991; Ross, Brackett, and Maxon, 1991). A student with a sensorineural hearing loss hears distorted sounds even with amplification.

Mixed Hearing Loss

A **mixed hearing loss** is a combination of conductive and sensorineural hearing loss. A student with a mixed hearing loss hears distorted sounds due to the damage to the inner ear and auditory nerve (sensorineural loss) and is unable to hear sounds below a certain decibel level (conductive loss).

Extent of Hearing Impairments

Hearing impairments range from mild to profound hearing losses, from hearing sound reductions or interruptions to total **deafness.** In general, the term *deaf* is used to describe individuals whose hearing is inadequate for the comprehension of speech without visual cues, such as speechreading or signing. Students who are deaf have an absence of hearing in both ears. The term *hard of hearing* is generally used to describe persons who can understand speech through listening if other conditions (e.g., lighting, background noise, a properly functioning hearing aid) are adequate. Students who have a hearing impairment have significant hearing loss in one or both ears.

SIGNALS OF HEARING IMPAIRMENTS

Early identification of hearing loss is critical so that intervention can begin as soon as possible. Table 16.4 contains a checklist of symptoms for early detection of hearing loss.

Students suspected of having difficulty hearing must be referred for a hearing test. Referrals can be made to a physician, school nurse, speech-language pathologist, audiologist, or to an **otologist** or **otolaryngologist.** An audiologist is a specialist in testing hearing, an otologist or otolaryngolist is a physician who specializes in disorders of the ear.

MEASURING HEARING LOSS

Early identification of hearing loss maximizes the student's opportunities to benefit from intervention. Early identification has a tremendous impact on a child's speech, social, and academic skills. In this section, we will examine four procedures used to determine hearing loss: pure-tone audiometry, bone conduction audiometry, speech audiometry, and immitance audiometry.

TABLE 16.4 Checklist of Symptoms for Early Detection of Hearing Loss

1. Does the student respond when her/his name is called?

2. Does the student startle when there is a loud noise or bang?

3. Does the student follow directions?

4. Does the student ask to have directions repeated?

5. Does the student speak clearly or demonstrate language difficulties?

6. Does the student have a history of earaches, colds, or allergies?

Pure-Tone Audiometry

One of the most common procedures is pure-tone, or air conduction, audiometry. This assessment establishes the type, configuration, laterality, and degree of hearing loss. The type of hearing loss is sensorineural, conductive, or mixed, and the configuration is the pattern of hearing acuity depicted in an **audiogram.** An audiogram is a graph that traces the intensity of sounds detected at five different frequencies. Laterality refers to each ear; that is, the configuration can be different for each ear.

Audiometers present tones at different levels of loudness (intensity) and pitch. Typically, headphones are placed on the individual's head and the individual is asked to respond to a series of tones by pointing or turning the head. There are many different types of audiometers; some are more specialized than others. An audiometer produces a graph that describes the hearing loss (Figure 16.3).

Loudness

On the vertical side of the chart, hearing loss is measured in decibels (dB). Decibels are an indication of loudness or intensity. The range of normal hearing is between 0 dB and 90 dB. For example, a barely audible whisper can be heard at 0 dB; at 50 dB, the sound of an automobile ten feet away can be heard.

Pitch

Frequency of sound waves, hertz (Hz), is measured along the horizontal axis of an audiogram. Frequency is sometimes referred to as pitch. The human ear can detect very low pitch, at about 125 Hz, and very high pitch, at about 8,000 Hz. Speech is in the range of 250–4,000 Hz. Each ear is tested separately. On an audiogram an O indicates the right ear and an X indicates the left ear.

Bone Conduction

The determination of sensorineural loss is accomplished with bone conduction audiometry.

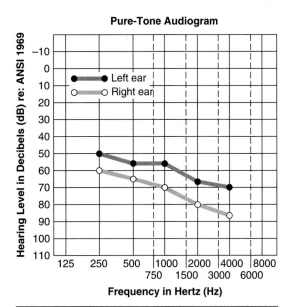

Pure-Tone Audiogram

FIGURE 16.3

Chad's audiogram

Source: Cohen, Libby G., and Loraine J. Spenciner (1994). *Assessment of Young Children.* White Plains, N.Y.: Longman Publishers. Reprinted with permission.

The bones in the skull can be made to vibrate by a bone-conduction vibrator; this vibration causes electrochemical activity in the inner ear as well as changes in the inner and outer ear. The examiner tests each ear separately. A vibrator is placed on the mastoid bone behind the individual's ear or on the forehead. Testing proceeds as in air conduction, and the results of the bone conduction are reported on the audiogram.

Speech Audiometry

Pure-tone audiometry and bone conduction audiometry yield limited facts about an individual's ability to hear. Speech audiometry provides information about the ability to *use* audition, or the act or power of hearing. How well an individual is able to understand speech is more important than the ability to hear pure tones. In speech audiometry, the individual wears earphones and the evaluator speaks into a microphone (a tape recording can also be used). Depending on the individual's age and abilities, the student is asked to repeat the words, point to pictures, or to write the words (Madell, 1990; Roeser and Price, 1981).

Immittance Audiometry

Martin (1991) writes that immittance audiometry, also referred to as impedance audiometry, should be conducted on individuals who are suspected of having a hearing loss. A student can have a middle ear disorder yet pass the audiological evaluation. Immittance audiometry is used to identify the presence of fluid in the middle ear and other abnormalities in the outer ear and middle ear.

This procedure customarily uses three measures: tympanometry, which evaluates how well the ear transmits energy as air pressure in the ear canal changes; static immittance,

which measures the tympanic membrane and the middle ear cavity; and acoustic reflex thresholds, which measure the intensity of the contraction of the stapedius muscle in the middle ear (Ross, Brackett, and Maxon, 1991). The results of immitance screening are plotted on a tympanogram (Figure 16.4). The graph of this tympanogram shows that the left ear has some otitis media, or inflammation of the middle ear; the right ear appears normal.

CATEGORIES OF HEARING IMPAIRMENTS

Although there is some disagreement in the literature, general categories for describing hearing loss have been established (Northern and Downs, 1991, pp. 13–15). Losses 15 to 30 dB are considered mild, 30 to 50 dB are moderate, 50 to 70 dB are severe, and 70 dB or greater are profound. Students with a mild (15 to 30

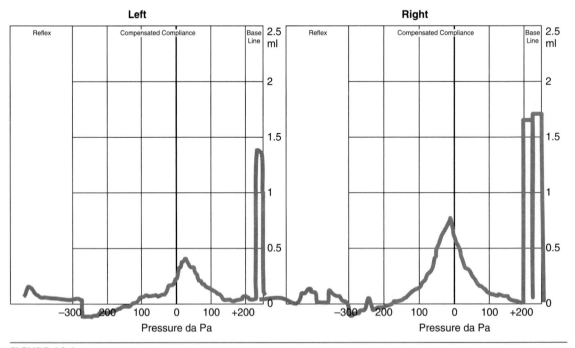

FIGURE 16.4

A Tympanogram

dB) hearing loss can hear vowel sounds clearly but voiceless consonants may be missed. Students with a moderate (30 to 50 dB) hearing loss miss almost all the speech sounds at conversational level. These students may show inattention and difficulty with grammatical rules of language. Prepositions and word endings (-s, -ed) are difficult to hear. Hearing aid amplification may help. Students with a severe (50 to 70 dB) hearing loss cannot hear sounds or normal conversation without amplification. With the use of a hearing aid, the student can discern vowel sounds and differences in manner of articulation. The term *deaf* is used to refer to hearing losses that are severe or profound.

Categorizing students on the basis of an audiogram is problematic because so many factors can affect the ability to hear. Describing a student's hearing loss based on an unaided audiogram is misleading and inaccurate. The report, rather, must describe how well a student's hearing functions under normal listening conditions (Moores, 1987).

ASSESSMENTS SPECIFIC FOR STUDENTS WITH HEARING IMPAIRMENTS

A complete assessment battery for a student with a hearing impairment consists of evaluations of communications skills, cognitive functioning, academic achievement, and social-emotional skills (Mayer, 1996). If the examiner does not know how to communicate with a student who has a hearing loss, the results of the testing may be of little use. Frequently, examiners will modify administration and response procedures to accommodate the needs of the student. However, any modifications should be made carefully and interpretation of performance rendered with due caution. A variety of assessment approaches is required for planning the program and in monitoring student progress. The Individuals with Disabilities Education Act Amendments of 1997 state that the IEP team must consider (for the student who is deaf or hard of hearing) the student's language and communication needs including opportunities for direct communication with peers and professional personnel in the student's language and communication mode, academic level, and opportunities for direct instruction in the student's language and communication mode. Beginning at age 14 the IEP team must consider transition service needs.

Standardized Instruments

The use of standardized tests that assess developmental, cognitive, and communication readiness, as well as academic areas to evaluate students who have a hearing loss can be problematic. Many commercially published standardized measures do not systematically include students who are deaf or hard of hearing in the standardization sample. When a student who has a hearing loss is given a test that has not been normed on students with hearing losses, the results of the tests have limited use.

There are some tests that have been normed on students who are deaf or have a hearing impairment. These are listed in Table 16.5.

PREFERRED PRACTICES

Since sensory impairments are low-incidence disabilities, many classroom teachers have had little exposure to working with students who are deaf or who have a hearing impairment. Team meetings should be scheduled and planned carefully to include professionals who work outside of the school community but who can be helpful in answering questions and in planning the student's individualized education program. For example, the audiologist can help interpret assessment results and alert teachers to any changing conditions.

TABLE 16.5   Selected Tests Standardized on Students with Hearing Impairments

Test	Skills	Grade/Age
Achievement		
Kaufman Assessment Battery for Children (Kaufman and Kaufman, 1983)	Simultaneous processing, sequential processing, achievement	2 years, 6 months to 12 years, 5 months
Stanford Achievement Test (Gardner, Rudman, Karlsen, and Merwin, 1982)	Reading, vocabulary, arithmetic, spelling	Kindergarten to grade 12
Test of Early Reading Ability—Deaf or Hard of Hearing (Reid, Hresko, Hammill, and Wiltshire, 1991)	Reading	3 years to 13 years, 11 months
Uniform Performance Assessment System (White, Haring, Edgar, Affleck, and Hayden, 1981)	Preacademic communication, social, self-help, gross and fine motor development	Birth to 6 years
Cognition		
Nebraska Test of Learning Aptitude (Hiskey, 1966)	Intelligence	3 to 16 years
Communication		
Carolina Picture Vocabulary Test (Layton and Holmes, 1985)	Vocabulary	5 to 12 years
Grammatical Analysis of Elicited Language	Grammar	
Pre-Sentence Level (Moog, Kozak, and Geers, 1983)		3 to 6 years
Simple Sentence Level (Moog and Geers, 1985)		5 to 9 years
Complex Sentence Level (Moog and Geers, 1980)		8 to 12 years
Rhode Island Test of Language Structure (Engen and Engen, 1983)	Syntax	3 to 20 years
Test of Expressive Language Ability (Bunch, 1981a)	Expressive language	7 to 12 years
Test of Receptive Language Ability (Bunch, 1981b)	Receptive language	6 to 12 years
Total Communication Receptive Vocabulary Test (Scherer, 1981)	Receptive language	3 to 12 years
Adaptive Development		
Vineland Adaptive Behavior Scales (Sparrow, Balla, and Cicchetti, 1984) Expanded Form Survey Form	Adaptive development	Birth to 18 years

Cohen, Libby G., and Loraine J. Spenciner (1994). *Assessment of Young Children.* White Plains, N.Y.: Longman. Reprinted by permission.

SNAPSHOT

Chad

Chad is an 8-year-old, happy, well-adjusted child who is experiencing moderate to severe developmental delays. He was born after a normal pregnancy and reached the childhood milestones at average ages. He sat alone at 6 months, crawled at 8 months, and walked at 12 months. His speech and language development was typical.

When Chad was 4 years old he had a high temperature and a seizure that lasted for several hours. The blood oxygen supply to his brain was interrupted during the seizure. After the seizure, there was a noticeable regression in Chad's development.

He stopped using speech and chose to crawl rather than walk. This was of great concern to Chad's mother and his pediatrician. He was referred for speech, language, and hearing testing and a severe bilateral hearing loss was discovered. Chad's audiogram can be found in Figure 16.3.

Today, Chad receives special education services in the regular classroom. A sign language interpreter works directly with Chad in his classroom and is also available to consult with Chad's teachers. A therapeutic recreation specialist works with Chad on a biweekly basis and assists in his adaptive physical education program.

S E C T I O N   3

Identifying and Assessing Students with Physical Disabilities

SECTION OBJECTIVES

After completing this section, you should be able to:

Identify and define specialized terms used in assessing motor development.

Describe several warning signs of motor problems.

Discuss key models in the assessment and treatment of students with motor delays.

UNDERSTANDING DIFFICULTIES AND DISABILITIES IN MOTOR DEVELOPMENT

Students with motor difficulties experience problems in one or more of the following areas: muscle development, bones or joints, absence or malformation or a limb or structure, or trauma to the head, neck, or spinal cord. The most common types of difficulty that can be observed involve muscle deficits. These include:

- Deficits in **muscle tone.** Muscle tone refers to the amount of tension that is present in a resting muscle. Muscles that have too little tone appear limp, or **hypotonic;** whereas muscles which are constantly tensed or stretched are referred to as **hypertonic.**
- Deficits in muscle control. Problems in muscle control are seen as jerky, involuntary movements of the arms and legs, called **tremors.**

TABLE 16.6   Common Disorders Associated with Motor Disabilities

Disorder	Description	Prognosis
Cerebral palsy	A group of disorders that result from intracranial lesions	Nonprogressive
Juvenile rheumatoid arthritis	Inflammation and swelling of the joints	Remission with possible recurrence
Muscular dystrophy	Degeneration of the voluntary muscles	Progressive
Spina bifida	Congenital malformation of the spinal cord	Nonprogressive, but spinal curvature may develop
Spinal cord injuries	Trauma to the spinal cord	Nonprogressive with therapy
Traumatic brain injury (TBI)	Severe injuries to the head that may include shearing or tearing of brain tissue. Severe TBI results in a coma.	Some individuals will recover some skills, but for others damage is permanent.

- Deficits in muscle strength. The student may differ noticeably in muscle strength on the right and left sides of the body or between the limbs. A muscle weakness is referred to as **paresis;** an inability to move is denoted with the combining form *-plegia*. Thus hemiplegia is an inability to move one side of the body

There are many disorders that cause motor impairments; Table 16.6 lists and briefly describes the most common ones.

SIGNALS OF MOTOR DIFFICULTIES

Good observational skills and knowledge of early signs of motor difficulties are instrumental in the early identification of motor problems. Table 16.7 indicates several early signs that may indicate motor difficulties.

In some progressive disorders such as muscular dystrophy, children experience a decrease in motor coordination. There may also be concerns about equilibrium and posture.

TABLE 16.7   Early Signs of Motor Difficulties

1. Abnormal positioning of arms or legs during play or at rest

2. Tremor in hands or arms when performing an activity

3. Major difference in strength between the left and right sides of the body

4. Poor balance and equilibrium

5. Difficulty in visual tracking

6. Weakness, low muscle tone, and fatigue in gross motor activities

7. Poor coordination during gross and fine motor activities

8. Poor muscle control of lips and tongue

9. Jerking or twitching movements

Adapted from Cook, R. E., A. Tessier, and M. D. Klein (1996). *Adapting Early Childhood Curricula for Children in Inclusive Settings*, 4th ed., p. 283.

COMMON ASSUMPTIONS CONCERNING MOTOR DEVELOPMENT

Common assumptions and beliefs about development provide the basis for assessing and working with students with motor delays and deficits. These assumptions are:

1. Motor development is one aspect in an integral picture of a student's development and should not be viewed in isolation. Motor, cognitive, and communication skills are interdependent. Delays in motor development can affect cognitive development and language or communication functioning.
2. Typical motor development follows a predictable skill sequence, and later skill development is usually dependent upon mastery of earlier skills. Atypical motor development may show a pattern of prolonged stays at an immature stage or acquisition of partial skills that do not fit into any one particular stage. Students who have experienced trauma to the head, neck, or spinal cord have an arrested motor development.

WHAT SHAPES OUR VIEWS

There are several different approaches that form the basis of assessment and treatment procedures for students experiencing neuromuscular disorders (Table 16.6). The most common approaches are the neurodevelopmental treatment approach, proprioceptive neuromuscular facilitation, sensorimotor approach (Rood technique), and sensory integration programming. Each of these perspectives has a fairly narrow focus on the entire assessment and treatment spectrum (Kottke, 1982).

Several of these perspectives were developed from work with particular populations of students; for example, the neurodevelopmental treatment approach was first developed for

use with children with cerebral palsy, and sensory integration was developed for use with students with learning disabilities. In fact, certain individual characteristics can influence which approach will be more effective (Guess and Noonan, 1982). Conventionally, practitioners will use a combination of approaches in their assessment and treatment procedures.

Neurodevelopmental Treatment

The basic principle behind the **neurodevelopmental treatment** (NDT) approach is to facilitate the child's normal, natural movement and to allow the child to experience that feeling through typical activities. NDT utilizes reflex facilitation to reinforce postural activities and works on inhibiting primitive reflexes to facilitate more mature responses. This approach was developed by Karel and Berta Bobath (1972) and emphasizes the need to inhibit hypertonia before beginning therapy. Physical therapists often recommend neurodevelopmental therapy for students with cerebral palsy.

Proprioceptive Neuromuscular Facilitation and the Rood Technique

Methods such as **proprioceptive neuromuscular facilitation** (PNF), developed by Margaret Knott and Dorothy E. Voss (1968) and the Rood technique (Tiffany and Huss, 1988) assume that as the voluntary activity becomes stronger, there will be a fading of incoordination (Kottke, 1982). Various techniques are used to induce muscle relaxation and to increase range of motion. PNF has been found to be successful in patients with ligament reconstruction and in other rehabilitative situations (Lutz and Stuart, 1990; Osternig, Robertson, Troxel, and Hansen, 1987).

Sensory Integration

Sensory integration (SI) was originally developed by Jean Ayres who had been working with children with learning and behavior disabilities. The theory of sensory integration focuses on the importance of the organization of sensory input, without which sensory information may either be lost or not fully utilized. During the learning process, the student receives information through the many sensory systems, and the brain takes in, sorts, organizes, and integrates this knowledge with stored information from past experiences. Sensory input comes not only from the five common senses of vision, hearing, taste, smell, and touch but from several other sources as well. Young (n.d.) identified these sources as including:

1. balance or vestibular (from the inner ear) sensation
2. kinesthesia-proprioception—a conscious awareness of one's body position
3. temperature
4. pain
5. chemical receptors in body organs
6. vital receptors to pressure

The theory of sensory integration is based in the importance of the brain being able to accept some and reject other stimuli and then to send the information on to one or more processing centers for integration. This theoretical framework needs empirical research to evaluate its effectiveness.

ASSESSMENTS SPECIFIC FOR STUDENTS WITH PHYSICAL DISABILITIES

Team members, including speech and language pathologists, occupational therapists, and physical therapists, need to collect data from a variety of areas in planning and monitoring the programs of students with physical disabilities. Teachers, parents, and other team members provide assistance. Information will need to be collected about the student's receptive and expressive language abilities and, for students who do not have intelligible speech, information concerning the augmentative/alternative communi-

cation system (discussed in Chapter 10). Assessment will also include details about gross and fine motor skills, the positioning of the student in order to function in the classroom, and assistive technology needed to complete assignment and classroom activities. The Individuals with Disabilities Act Amendments of 1997 state that the IEP team must consider whether a student with disabilities requires assistive technology devices and services. Beginning at age 14 the IEP team must consider transition service needs.

Observation

Therapists, teachers, and family members can gather much information about a student's motor skills through observation. This information can include both quantitative measures of movement as well as information about the quality of movement. Neisworth and Bagnato (1987) identify the following questions to consider in observing and appraising patterns of neuromotor development:

1. How does the child's posture and muscle tone change under different conditions and in different positions?
2. Which parts of movement are absent and which contribute to the child's delay in gaining motor milestones?
3. In which positions is the child's postural tone most normal?
4. Which position helps the child to perform the greatest number of voluntary, self-initiated movements?
5. How does the child gather information from his/her surroundings? (p. 336)

Observation recording sheets are helpful in monitoring the student's daily progress (Hanson and Harris, 1992). Figure 16.5 shows an observation data sheet for a period of ten days. The target skill is crossing midline and each of the student's successes are recorded as pluses; nonattempts are recorded as minuses. The total number of pluses for each day is circled. Thus the teacher or therapist can readily create a profile of the student's skill.

GOAL:

Brings hands to mid-line when prompted (facilitated) to assume sitting position.

	Week 1							Week 2						
Date:	2-9	2-10	2-11	2-12	2-13	2-14	2-15	2-16	2-17	2-18	2-19	2-20	2-21	2-22
	+10	−10	−10	−10	+10	+10	−10	+10	+10	+10	+10	+10	+10	+10
	+9	−9	−9	−9	+9	−9	+9	−9	+9	−9	+9	+9	+9	+9
	+8	−8	+8	+8	−8	−8	−8	+8	+8	+8	−8	+8	+8	+8
	−7	+7	−7	+7	+7	−7	−7	+7	+7	+7	−7	+7	+7	+7
	−6	−6	+6	−6	−6	+6	+6	+6	−6	−6	+6	+6	+6	+6
	−5	+5	−5	−5	+5	+5	+5	−5	+5	+5	+5	+5	+5	+5
	+4	−4	−4	+4	−4	−4	+4	+4	−4	+4	+4	+4	+4	+4
	+3	−3	+3	+3	+3	−3	+3	+3	−3	+3	+3	+3	+3	+3
	−2	−2	+2	−2	+2	+2	+2	+2	+2	+2	+2	+2	+2	+2
	−1	−1	−1	+1	−1	+1	+1	+1	+1	+1	+1	+1	+1	+1
	0	0	0	0	0	0	0	0	0	0	0	0	0	0

FIGURE 16.5

Data Sheet for Recording Observations

Source: From *Teaching the Young Child with Motor Delays* by Marci J. Hanson and Susan R. Harris. Austin, TX: PRO-ED, Inc., 1986.

Standardized Instruments

Young children suspected of having motor problems can be assessed by standardized screening instruments such as the *Denver Developmental Screening Test II* or the *AGS Early Screening Profiles* discussed in Chapter 2. Other instruments that have been designed to specifically assess motor functioning include the *Bruininks-Oseretsky Test of Motor Proficiency* and the *Peabody Developmental Motor Scales and Activity Cards.*

Bruininks-Oseretsky Test of Motor Proficiency

The *Bruininks-Oseretsky Test of Motor Proficiency* (Bruininks, 1978) assesses motor functioning of students from 4.6 to 14.6 years of age. The test was designed to assess motor development for the purposes of 1) making decisions about educational placement (such as physical education programming), 2) assessing gross and fine motor skills, and 3) developing and evaluating motor training programs. This instrument consists of two forms: the Short Form of 14 items from the Complete Battery, and the Complete Battery, which consists of eight subtests with a total of 46 items. The subtests include:

1. Running Speed and Agility
2. Balance
3. Bilateral Coordination
4. Strength
5. Upper-limb Coordination
6. Response Speed
7. Visual-Motor Control
8. Upper-limb Speed and Dexterity

This standardized instrument is norm-referenced, and a student's raw score can be reported as a standard score, a percentile rank, or a stanine. The norms, however, are dated,

SNAPSHOT

Richie

Richie is 10 years old and attends fourth grade. He has an extensive medical history with a suspected partial chromosomal condition. An occupational therapist who consults for the program recently completed the following assessment to help the team in planning Richie's program.

I. *Sensorimotor Functioning:* During movement activities, Richie stiffens his body and lower trunk area (anterior tilt), which results in difficulties in balance and maintaining his body position in space. He compensates by protective extension (out stretched arms). Richie is also tactile defensive to soft materials. He refuses to handle soft materials, including cheese or fruit. He will not par-

ticipate in art activities that include working with clay or finger paints.

II. *Gross Motor:* Richie can hop on two feet but has difficulty in walking along a taped line. He can catch a ball at three feet.

III. *Fine Motor:* Richie shows a strong preference for using his right hand. He has some difficulty with using a pincer grasp for small objects. Richie uses a palmar grasp when holding a pencil and a "hunt and peck" method in keyboarding.

IV. *Adaptive:* Mother reports that Richie is learning to dress himself but needs some assistance with pulling his shirt over his head.

---

and reliability and validity studies are limited. Use of this instrument requires caution.

Peabody Developmental Motor Scales and Activity Cards

The *Peabody Developmental Motor Scales and Activity Cards* (Folio and Fewell, 1983) includes both a standardized test and an instructional packet of activity cards. The test measures fine and gross motor skills in children 1 month to 83 months (7 years of age). According to the manual, this instrument may be used with children with disabilities who are chronologically older than 7 but with motor development in the birth to 7 developmental age range. The *Peabody Developmental Motor Scales* includes the assessment of fine motor skills (112 items) grouped into four skill clusters:

1. Grasping
2. Hand Use

3. Eye/Hand Coordination
4. Manual Dexterity

Gross motor skills (170 items) are grouped into five skill clusters:

1. Reflexes
2. Balance
3. Nonlocomotor
4. Locomotor
5. Receipt and Propulsion

The standard scores of this test should be used with caution since the norms were developed on a relatively small sample of children. Additional research would be helpful in verifying some of the preliminary information regarding reliability and validity. The detailed information about a child's fine and gross motor development and the instruction packet of activity cards related to the test items are potentially helpful in program planning.

ASSESSMENT OF ACADEMIC AND SOCIAL SKILLS

A variety of assessment approaches are needed in assessing academic and social skills. To choose an approach, the teacher or examiner will need to consider the accommodations needed by the particular student and ensure that these specific modifications to accommodate the student's limited response mode are incorporated into the selected assessment approach (Gleckel and Lee, 1996). Fairness in the assessment approach is critical.

The use of standardized instruments with students with limited motor abilities presents problems. Students may be penalized in two ways: First, students cannot demonstrate motoric responses to questions or to tasks, and second, students with limited ability to speak may be viewed as mentally retarded when they understand but are unable to convey or express that understanding (Gleckel and Lee, 1996).

PREFERRED PRACTICES

In assessing students, teachers and therapists must be alert to test items that require motor responses that the student is unable to produce, thus adversely affecting the total test score. Information gathered through observation is a necessary addition to the use of standardized instruments. Home video recordings are an important supplement as well as a means of involving the parent(s) in monitoring their child's progress.

EXTENDING LEARNING

16.1 Many states have an educational consultant for students with visual impairments. Contact your state agency to learn about available resources for teachers who have a student with a visual impairment in their classroom.

16.2 Visit a speech clinic and observe an audiological exam—or have your own hearing tested. What tests were included in the examination? What conclusions would you draw based on the audiogram?

16.3 Locate one or two of the standardized assessment instruments discussed in this chapter. Compare the technical characteristics of the instruments. For what purpose would you recommend using (or not using) each of the instruments? Why?

16.4 Arrange to visit with an occupational or physical therapist in a hospital, clinic, or school setting. What types of assessment procedures are used?

16.5 Observe a student with a visual, auditory, or motor disability in school. Interview the classroom teacher and the special education consultant about the modifications that were made. Were any adaptations made for testing and assessment?

REFERENCES

Anderson, S., K. Davis, and S. Boigion (1991). *The oregon project for visually impaired and blind preschool children.* 5th ed. Medford, Ore: Jackson Educational Service District.

Barraga, N. C., and J. N. Erin (1992). *Visual handicaps & learning.* Austin, Tex.: Pro-Ed.

Bobath, K., and B. Bobath (1972). Cerebral palsy. In *Physical therapy services in the developmental disabilities,* eds. P. H. Peterson, and C. E. Williams, Springfield, Ill.: Charles C. Thomas.

Bradley-Johnson, S., and L. D. Evans (1991). *Psychoeducational assessment of hearing-impaired students.* Austin, Tex.: Pro-Ed.

Brigance, A. H. (1983). *Brigance® comprehensive inventory of basic skills.* No. Billerica, Mass: Curriculum Associates.

Bruininks, R. H. (1978). *Bruininks-Oseretsky test of motor proficiency.* Circle Pines, Mn: AGS.

Cohen, L. G., and L. J. Spenciner (1994). *Assessment of Young Children.* White Plains, NY: Longman.

Cook, R. E., A. Tessier, and M. D. Klein (1996). *Adapting early childhood curricula for children in inclusive settings.* 4th ed. Englewood Cliffs, N.J.: Merrill, an imprint of Prentice Hall.

Ferrell, K. A. (1986). Infancy and early childhood. In *Foundations of education for blind and visually handicapped children,* ed. G. T. Scholl, 119–135. New York: American Foundation for the Blind.

Folio, M. R., and R. Fewell (1983). *Peabody developmental motor scores and activity cards.* Chicago, Ill.: Riverside.

Gleckel, L. K., and R. L. Lee (1996). Children with physical disabilities. In *Exceptional Children in Today's Schools,* 3d ed., ed. E. L. Meyen, 399–432. Denver, Col.: Love.

Guess, D., and M. J. Noonan (1982). *Evaluating neurodevelopmental theory and training with cerebral palsied, severely handicapped students. Final report.* Lawrence: University of Kansas, Department of Special Education.

Hanson, M. J., and S. R. Harris (1986). *Teaching the young child with motor delays.* Austin, Tex.: Pro-Ed.

Harcourt Brace Educational Measurement (1996). *Stanford achievement test.* 9th ed. San Antonio, Tex.: Harcourt Brace Jovanovich.

Hill, E. (1992). Instruction in orientation and mobility skills for students with visual handicaps. *DVH Quarterly* 37(2): 25–26.

Hoover, H. D., A. N. Hieronymous, D. A. Frisbie, and S. B. Dunbar (1993) *Iowa tests of basic skills.* Chicago: Riverside.

Huss A. J. (1988). Sensorimotor and neurodevelopmental frames of reference. In *Willard and spackman's occupational therapy,* 7th ed., eds. H. L. Hopkins and H. D. Smith, 114–127. Philadelphia: Lippincott.

Knott, M., and D. E. Voss (1968). *Proprioceptive neuromuscular facilitation: Patterns and techniques.* 2d ed. New York: Harper & Row.

Kottke, F. J. (1982). Therapeutic exercise to develop neuromuscular coordination. In *Krusen's handbook of physical medicine and rehabilitation,* eds. F. J. Kottke, G. K. Stillwell, and J. F. Lehmann, 218–252. Philadelphia: W. B. Saunders.

Lighthouse Low Vision Services (1970). *New York Lighthouse symbol flash cards.* Available from the New York Lighthouse, 111 East 59th St., N.Y., N.Y. 10022.

Lutz, G. E., and M. J. Stuart (1990). Rehabilitative techniques for athletes after reconstruction of the anterior cruciate ligament. *Mayo Clinic Proceedings* 65: 1322–1329.

Madell, J. R. (1990). Audiological evaluation of the mainstreamed hearing-impaired child. In *Hearing-impaired children in the mainstream,* ed., M. Ross, 27–44. Baltimore, Md.: York.

Martin, F. N. (1991). *Introduction to audiology.* 4th ed. Englewood Cliffs, N.J.: Prentice Hall.

Mayer, M. H. (1996). Children who are deaf or hard of hearing. In *Exceptional Children in Today's Schools,* 3d ed., ed. E. L. Meyen, 315–350. Denver, Col.: Love.

Moores, D. (1987). *Educating the deaf: Psychology, principles, and practices.* 3d ed. Boston: Houghton Mifflin.

National Society to Prevent Blindness (1991). *Home eye test for preschoolers.* Schaumburg, Ill.: National Society to Prevent Blindness, 500 East Remington Road 60173-5611.

Neisworth, J. T., and S. J. Bagnato (1987). *The young exceptional child.* New York: Macmillan.

Northern, J. L., and M. P. Downs (1991). *Hearing in children.* 4th ed. Baltimore: Williams & Wilkins.

Osternig, L. R., R. Robertson, R. Troxel, and P. Hansen (1987). Muscle activation during proprioceptive neuromuscular facilitation (PNF) stretching techniques. *American Journal of Physical Medicine* 66(5): 298–307.

Pawelski, C. (1992). Personnel communication with Christine Pawelski, Early Childhood Consultant, American Foundation for the Blind, June.

Roeser, R. J., and D. R. Price (1981). Audiometric and impedance measures: Principles and interpretation. In *Auditory disorders in school children,* eds. R. J. Roeser and M. P. Downs, 71–101. New York: Thieme-Stratton.

Ross, M., D. Brackett, and A. B. Maxon (1991). *Assessment and management of mainstreamed hearing-impaired children.* Austin, Tex.: Pro-Ed.

Silberman, R. K. (1996). Children with visual impairments. In *Exceptional Children in Today's Schools,* 3d ed., ed. E. L. Meyen, 351–398. Denver, Col.: Love.

Young, M. H. (n.d.). Sensory integration programming. In *Topics in therapeutic programming for students with severe handicaps* (sensory integration programming instructional module), ed. P. H. Campbell. Akron, Ohio: Children's Hospital Medical Center of Akron.

Youth in Transition

OVERVIEW

The provision of transition services is critical in assisting students with disabilities prepare for adult life. Although students with disabilities continue to fall behind their typical peers in post-school employment, wages, postsecondary education, and residential independence, gains have been made. The federal commitment to supporting transition activities once students leave school has contributed to these improvements (Blackorby and Wagner, 1996). The federal government mandates that students with disabilities be provided with services that will facilitate their transition from school to post-school activities, including postsecondary education, vocational training, integrated employment (including supported employment), continuing and adult eduction, adult services, independent living, and community participation.

The Individuals with Disabilities Education Act amendments of 1997 (IDEA) requires that individual transition planning be based on present levels of performance. Transition planning is an *outcome-oriented* process in which the focus is on the attainment of prespecified performance objectives. Assessment of students' transition needs and preferences is an important part of the transition process and should include assessment of vocational, career, academic, personal, social, and living needs. A variety of approaches are required for comprehensive transition assessment, and because transition planning is a process that occurs over a long period of time, transition assessment and the monitoring of transition plans should be conducted periodically.

CHAPTER OBJECTIVES

After completing this chapter you should be able to:

Define the concept of transition.

Explain the purposes of transition assessment.

Describe the ways in which students' transition needs and preferences are assessed.

Compare several approaches to transition assessment.

WHAT SHAPES OUR VIEWS

Transitions occur across the life span. Major transitions occur as individuals with disabilities receive services, begin school, leave school, move from separate settings to inclusive ones, and move from school to the community, further education, employment, and independent living (Blalock and Patton, 1996). The Division of Career Development and Transition of the Council for Exceptional Children has adopted the following definition when referring to youth who are in transition:

> Transition refers to a change in status from behaving primarily as a student to assuming emergent adult roles in the community. These roles include employment, participating in postsecondary education, maintaining a home, becoming appropriately involved in the community and experiencing satistfactory personal and social relationships. The process of enhancing transition involves the participation and coordination of school programs, adult agency services, and natural supports within the community. The foundations for transition should be laid during the elementary and middle school years, guided by the broad concept of career development. Transition planning should begin no later than age 14, and students should be encouraged, to the full extent of their capabilities, to assume a maximum of responsibility for such planning. (Halpern, 1994, p.117)

Three laws provide the authorization and the focus for transition services. These laws are the School-to-Work Opportunities Act of 1994 (P.L. 103–239), the Carl D. Perkins Vocational and Applied Technology Act of 1990 (P.L. 99–457), and the Individuals with Disabilities Education Act amendments of 1997 (IDEA) (P.L. 105–17).

The School-to-Work Opportunities Act of 1994 (P.L. 103–239) provides for a national framework (Krieg, Brown, and Ballard, 1995) that supports school-to-work opportunities. The implementation of the school-to-work opportunities system is determined by each state and the ultimate goal is to link youth to productive employment. Because the implementation of this legislation is determined by each state, the participation of students with disabilities varies from one state to the next.

The Carl D. Perkins Vocational and Applied Technology Act of 1990 (P.L. 99–457) guarantees equal access to vocational education programs and opportunities for all students. Students who are eligible to receive services under the Perkins Act include students who are economically disadvantaged, educationally disadvantaged, disabled, have limited English proficiency, are trying to enter a field not usually associated with their gender (e.g., a female construction worker), or are in correctional institutions. The Perkins Act links students with disabilities to transition services by mandating that each student who has a disability and who participates in vocational education:

- has equal access to vocational activities,
- is assessed regarding vocational interests, abilities, and special needs,
- be provided with special services, and
- be provided with guidance, career, and transition counseling.

TRANSITION SERVICES

The Individuals with Disabilities Education Act Amendments of 1997 is the major legislation that mandates **transition services**. The focus is on assisting the individual with a disability to make a smooth transfer from the school to independent adult life.

. . . . transition services means a coordinated set of activities for a student, designed within an outcome-oriented process, that promotes movement from school to post-school activities, including postsecondary education, vocational training, integrated employment (including supported employment) continuing and adult education, adult sevices, independent living, and community participation (sec. 300.18).

The coordinated set of activities that are described in the preceding paragraph must:

1. Be based upon the individual student's needs, taking into account the student's preferences and interests; and
2. Include:
   a. Instruction,
   b. Community experiences,
   c. The development of employment and other post-school adult living objectives, and
   d. If appropriate, acquisition of daily living skills and functional vocational evaluation [20 U.S.C. 1401 (a) (19)].

A coordinated set of activities means that all transition activities must meet the student's needs and complement, not duplicate, each other. Many individuals and agencies are involved in the transition process. The coordinated set of transition activities must include:

• instruction
• community experiences
• developing employment objectives
• developing adult living objectives

The following transition activities may be included if they are appropriate:

• daily living skills
• functional vocational evaluation

Age at Which Transition Services Should Begin

Beginning at age 14, and updated annually, the IEP team must develop a statement of transi-

Postsecondary Education	Community college College or university Other postsecondary education
Vocational Training	Vocational technical center Rehabilitation facility Community-based education and training Other vocational training
Continuing and Adult Education	Adult basic education Community college Other continuing/adult education
Employment	Competitive employment Supported employment Sheltered employment Volunteer work Other employment
Community Participation	Specialized recreation/ social activities Sports or social clubs Community center programs Parks and recreation programs Hobby clubs Independent activities Other community participation
Independent Living	Financial and income Living arrangements Medical services and resources Personal management Transportation Advocacy and legal services

FIGURE 17.1

Post-School Outcomes and Activities

Source: Adapted from Love, L. (1993). *Developing and Including Transition Services in the IEP.* Phoenix, Ariz.: Arizona Department of Education.

tion service needs of the student that focuses on the student's courses of study. At age 16, transition services must be discussed and documented at every IEP meeting until the student leaves school. Figure 17.1 can assist in planning for post-school outcomes and transition services. Figures 17.2, 17.3, and 17.4 are questionnaires designed to assess the need for transition services.

Transition Planning Assessment
Elementary School

Student's name: _____   Date: _____

| Postsecondary Education | Does the student express interest in postsecondary education? |

Employment/Career Awareness
Can the student explain parent(s) jobs?
Can the student name several types of jobs?
Can the student explain how his/her skills could relate to a job?
Does the student express interest in 2 to 3 different jobs?

Community Participation
Does the student go to restaurants, movies, or library?
Does the student participate in sports activities?
Does the student negotiate his/her neighborhood easily?
Which community activities does the student participate in?
What activities does the student participate in during leisure time?

Independent Living

Financial and Income
Does the student receive an allowance?
Does the student receive Social Security income?
Does the student spend his/her money responsibly?

Living Arrangements
Can the student discuss various types of living arrangements (homes, apartments, etc.)?

Medical Services and Resources
Can the student describe his/her medical needs?
Can the student take medication independently?
Can the student state his/her doctor's name?
Will there be a need for ongoing medical care?

Personal Management
Does the student choose her/his clothes and dress herself/himself?
Does the student perform personal hygiene tasks independently?
Does the student follow safety rules?
Does the student have chores at home?

Socialization and Friendships
Does the student have age-appropriate friends?
Does the student have opportunities to develop friendships?
Does the student participate in activities with friends?

Transportation
Can the student negotiate his/her neighborhood?
Can the student negotiate her/her way around the school independently?

Advocacy
Will the student be in need of advocacy or legal services in the future?

Self-Advocacy
Does the student communicate her/his needs effectively?
Does the student ask for help when needed?
Does the student use communication devices effectively?
Does the student resolve conflicts with others effectively?

FIGURE 17.2

Transition Planning Assessment: Elementary School

Source: Adapted from Love, L. (1993). *Developing and Including Transition Services in the IEP.* Phoenix, Ariz.: Arizona Department of Education.

```
┌─────────────────────────────────────────────────────────────────────────────────┐
│                          Transition Planning Assessment                           │
│                           Middle School/Junior High School                        │
│  Student's name:                                              Date:               │
│                                                                                   │
│  Postsecondary Education      Can the student describe types of training (e.g., community college, vocational │
│                                 training, etc.) for postsecondary careers?        │
│                               Does the student express interest in postsecondary education? │
│                                                                                   │
│  Employment/Career Awareness  Does the student have opportunities to try out different jobs? │
│                               Does the student know where to find information on different types of jobs? │
│                               Can the student evaluate his/her skills in relation to a job? │
│                               Does the student make realistic decisions in planning for a future job? │
│                                                                                   │
│  Community Participation      Does the student demonstrate ability to go to restaurants, movies, or library? │
│                               Does the student identify and participate in leisure activities? │
│                               Does the student negotiate his/her neighborhood easily? │
│                               Does the student know where to find information about leisure activities? │
│                               Does the student participate in individual and group leisure/recreation activities? │
│                                                                                   │
│  Independent Living           Financial and Income                                │
│                               Does the student receive an allowance?              │
│                               Does the student earn money from jobs (e.g., babysitting)? │
│                               Does the student receive Social Security income?    │
│                               Does the student spend his/her money responsibly?   │
│                               Does the student make her/his own purchases?        │
│                               Living Arrangements                                 │
│                               Does the student express an interest for a certain type of living arrangement? │
│                               Medical Services and Resources                      │
│                               Does the student demonstrate a basic understanding of different types of │
│                                 medical care?                                     │
│                               Can the student take medication independently, if needed? │
│                               Does the student realistically express her/his medical needs and limitations? │
│                               Will the student need ongoing medical assistance?   │
│                               Personal Management                                 │
│                               Does the student choose her/his clothes and dress herself/himself? │
│                               Does the student perform personal hygiene tasks independently? │
│                               Does the student follow safety rules?               │
│                               Does the student have chores at home?               │
│                               Socialization and Friendships                       │
│                               Does the student have age-appropriate friends?      │
│                               Does the student have opportunities to develop friendships? │
│                               Does the student participate in activities with friends? │
│                               Transportation                                      │
│                               Can the student negotiate his/her neighborhood?     │
│                               Can the student negotiate his/her way around the school independently? │
│                               Advocacy                                            │
│                               Will there be a need for ongoing advocacy or legal services? │
│                               Self-Advocacy                                       │
│                               Does the student participate in the IEP meeting?    │
│                               Does the student communicate her/his needs effectively? │
│                               Does the student express desires effectively?       │
│                               Does the student have opportunities to make choices and decisions? │
│                               Does the student communicate effectively with peers and adults? │
└─────────────────────────────────────────────────────────────────────────────────┘
```

FIGURE 17.3

Transition Planning Assessment: Middle/Junior High School

Source: Adapted from Love, L. (1993). *Developing and Including Transition Services in the IEP.* Phoenix, Ariz.: Arizona Department of Education.

Transition Planning Assessment
High School

Student's name: Date:

Postsecondary Education
Does the student want or need postsecondary education or training?
Does the student need assistance from an adult agency?
Does the student need assistance in selecting and applying to postsecondary education or training?

Employment/Career Awareness
Does the student demonstrate an understanding of her/his employment options?
Does the student demonstrate the skills, aptitudes, and behaviors to reach his/her goals?
Can the student evaluate his/her skills in relation to a job?
Does the student need help finding a job?
Does the student need help keeping a job?

Community Participation
Does the student demonstrate how to locate and use shopping malls, theaters, library, and community services?
Does the student use transportation?
Does the student negotiate his/her neighborhood easily?
Does the student know where to find information about leisure activities?
Does the student participate in individual and group leisure/recreation activities?

Independent Living
Financial and Income
Does the student have a source of income?
Does the student know how to budget her/his money?
Does the student know how to use bank accounts?
Does the student make her/his own purchases?
Living Arrangements
Does the student need assistance in selecting living arrangements?
Does the student need assistance in independent living?
Medical Services and Resources
Does the student realistically express her/his medical needs and limitations?
Will the student need ongoing medical assistance?
Can the student manage her/his own medical needs independently?
Personal Management
Does the student choose her/his clothes and dress herself/himself?
Does the student perform personal hygiene tasks independently?
Does the student perform routine household tasks?
Does the student have chores at home?
Does the student manage money effectively?
Socialization and Friendships
Does the student have age-appropriate friends?
Does the student have opportunities to develop friendships?
Does the student participate in activities with friends?
Transportation
Can the student negotiate his/her neighborhood and community?
Does the student know how to find and use transportation?
Does the student have a driver's license?
Advocacy
Does the student demonstrate an understanding of her/his rights and responsibilities?
Does the student need ongoing advocacy support?
Does the student need ongoing guardian support?
Self-Advocacy
Does the student participate in the IEP meeting?
Does the student communicate her/his needs effectively?
Does the student have opportunities to make choices and decisions?
Does the student communicate effectively with peers and adults?

FIGURE 17.4

Transition Planning Assessment: High School

Source: Adapted from Love, L. (1993). *Developing and Including Transition Services in the IEP.* Phoenix, Ariz.: Arizona Department of Education.

Individual Transition Plan

According to the Individual with Disabilities Act Amendments of 1997, beginning at age 14, and updated annually, a statement of transition service needs of the student that focus on the student's courses of study must be developed. Beginning at age 16 (or younger), a statement of the needed transition services for the student including a statement of the interagency responsi-bilities must be added to the student's transition plan. If transition services are required, a special IEP is often developed. Although the terminology is not mandated by law, this special IEP is sometimes called an **individual transition plan** (ITP). The ITP must include descriptions of services and the responsibilities of the school and participating agencies in the transition of the student from school. Figure 17.5 is an example of a school to post-school transition plan.

Student Name _____ Birthdate _____ Date of IEP _____ Page ____ of ____

Transition Services

School to Post-School Transition Plan

Student preferences and interests for transition services:

Post-school outcomes to be considered:

[ ] Postsecondary Education	[ ] Vocational Training
[ ] Employment	[ ] Continuing & Adult Education
[ ] Independently Living	[ ] Adult Services
[ ] Community Participation	[ ] Other (Specify) _____

Coordinated Set of Activities from School to Post-school Outcomes

Transition Service Area	Year 1	Year 2	Year 3	Year 4	Year 5
1. INSTRUCTION					
2. COMMUNITY EXPERIENCES					
3. EMPLOYMENT					
4. ADULT LIVING					
5. DAILY LIVING SKILLS					
6. VOCATIONAL EVALUATION					

continued

FIGURE 17.5

School to Post-School Transition Plan

Source: Adapted from Love, L. (1993). *Developing and Including Transition Services in the IEP.* Phoenix, Arizona: Arizona Department of Education. Reprinted with permission.

FIGURE 17.5   (Continued)

Student Name_____ Birthdate _____ Date of IEP _____Page ____ of ____

Transition Services

Student preferences and interests for transition services:

Post-school outcomes to be considered: *(Refer to "School to Post-school Transition Plan")*

[ ] Postsecondary Education   [ ] Vocational Training
[ ] Employment   [ ] Continuing & Adult Education
    (including Supported Employment)   [ ] Adult Services
[ ] Independent Living   [ ] Community Participation
[ ] Other (Specify) _____

Student present level of development or educational performance:

Statement of current transition services:

1. INSTRUCTION

2. COMMUNITY EXPERIENCES

3. EMPLOYMENT

4. ADULT LIVING

5. DAILY LIVING SKILLS

6. FUNCTIONAL VOCATIONAL EVALUATION

Student Name_____ Birthdate _____ Date of IEP _____Page ____ of ____

Transition Services

Local Education Agency & Participating Agency Responsibility

Service or Responsibility	Responsible Agency	Start Date	End Date

Additional discussion of transition services:

PURPOSES OF TRANSITION ASSESSMENT

In order to develop an IEP or ITP, information about present levels of performance is gathered, using transition assessment, in the areas of vocational, career, academic, personal, social, and living needs. Transition assessment has multiple purposes, including (Brandt, 1994; Krieg, Brown, and Ballard, 1995; Leconte, Castleberry, King, and West, 1994–1995):

- recognizing levels of career development
- identifying self-concept

SNAPSHOT

Tiffany[1]

Tiffany is 14 years old and is in seventh grade. She is currently identified as having a language disability, mental retardation, and a behavior disorder. Tiffany's language skills are well below the average range for a 14-year-old.

In a conversation with her special education teacher, Tiffany noted that she often experiences feelings of sadness and depression. She said that when she feels this way, she retreats into her closet. She also reported that she experiences difficulties with anxiety and stated that she sometimes gets "the shakes." Tiffany did admit to having entertained thoughts about hurting herself in the past. When asked to explain this, she stated that it was due to "all my stress."

Tiffany described herself as a member of a family of two children. She did not know her birth date and did not know how old her sister is. When asked if the sister is younger or older, Tiffany responded, "Mom didn't tell me." While she appeared resentful of her mother's interference, she also appeared to be very dependent upon her mother for direction and guidance.

When asked about possible career choices, Tiffany indicated that she did not know what she would like to do following high school. She then added that she liked "police work" and might want to be a "policeman" following school. Regarding school, Tiffany indicated that she felt that she was failing her classes. She noted that she does not have any friends and thought that many other students disliked her.

In an interview with Tiffany's mother, great concern was expressed regarding her daughter's future. She noted that Tiffany is "very immature," has literally "no friends in the neighborhood," and prefers to play with her 6-year-old sister. Ms. S. stated that Tiffany was "generally irresponsible," and the mother is "afraid" to leave Tiffany alone for more than an hour at a time. Ms. S. admits to not letting Tiffany do much independently because "Tiffany always makes a mess of things." Ms. S. is also concerned about Tiffany's emotional state and notes that Tiffany has threatened to hurt herself in the past, although there has never been any self-abusive behavior observed. Tiffany's mother believes that Tiffany would be able to get a job at a local motel as a chambermaid. She does admit, however, that Tiffany has generally low levels of skill in this area.

The special educator has suggested that the team convene and begin to plan for Tiffany's transition.

---

[1]Brandt, J. E. (1994). *Assessment and transition planning: A curriculum for school psychologists and special educators.* Biddeford, Maine: University of New England. Adapted with permission.

- evaluating academic, vocational, and career preferences and training needs
- determining life supports
- identifying abilities, interests, strengths, and needs
- matching interests and abilities with training and employment
- analyzing the results of information from previous assessments
- taking part in activities that promote self-discovery of vocational and career interests
- assessing work-related behaviors, skills, and aptitudes
- recognizing the need for continuing education and adult services
- identifying needs for supported employment.

PUBLISHED INSTRUMENTS

Work-Related Behaviors, Skills, and Aptitudes

Living Skills Checklist

The *Living Skills Checklist* (Brandt, 1994) is an informal checklist that assesses skills for daily living in the areas of personal hygiene/grooming, housekeeping, laundry/clothing care, time, numbers, writing, money, reading, personal/social skills, food preparation/cooking, mobility, and health and safety. This instrument is useful for informally assessing an individual's strengths and needs or to document progress. Figure 17.6 illustrates this checklist.

Test of Practical Knowledge

The *Test of Practical Knowledge (TPK)* (Wiederholt and Larsen, 1983) is a group-administered test of 100 items of everyday knowledge the authors believe that high school students should know. It is designed to measure personal knowledge, social knowledge, and occupational knowledge with students ages 12 years, 11 months through 18 years.

Administration

The *TPK* requires that students read silently and then mark the correct answer in a multiple-choice format. The first five items serve more than one purpose: They can be used to teach students how to respond to the test items, and they function as a screening device to identify students who do not understand the directions or who lack the ability to respond to the questions.

Scoring

The test is hand scored using a template that is placed on top of the student's responses. Raw scores can be converted to stanines and percentiles. The total score, called the Practical Knowledge Quotient (PKQ), has a mean of 100 and a standard deviation of 15.

Standardization

The standardization sample consisted of 1,398 students from 11 states who were in grades 8 through 12, selected on the basis of region of the country, gender, ethnicity, and urban or rural residence.

Reliability

Internal consistency and test-retest reliability were established. The coefficients range from .76 to .90, with most of the coefficients ranging from .80 to .90. These coefficients are within acceptable guidelines.

Validity

A number of comparisons are made between the *TPK,* the *SRA Achievement Series,* and the *Iowa Tests of Educational Development.* The correlations were moderate, indicating that there is some relationship between the items on the *TPK* and those on the achievement tests. Correlations between the *TPK* and the *Wechsler Intelligence Scale for Children (WISC)* ranged from .23 to .60, indicating that there is some relationship between intelligence and practical knowledge. One validity study was conducted using the *WISC* with students who were identi-

Living Skills Checklist

Student: _____

Date: _____ Completed by: _____

For each item indicate either: A = Asset L = Limitation U = Unknown

PERSONAL HYGIENE/GROOMING

1. Washes hands
2. Washes hair
3. Washes body
4. Uses deodorant
5. Combs/brushes hair
6. Brushes teeth
7. Shaves using razor
8. Cleans/clips fingernails
9. (Female) Handles feminine hygiene
10. Uses tissue/handkerchief

HOUSEKEEPING

1. Dry-mops/sweeps floor
2. Wet-mops floor
3. Cleans bathroom
4. Washes dishes
   a) uses sink
   b) uses dishwasher
5. Dries dishes
6. Stores dishes/pans/utensils in proper place
7. Cleans countertop
8. Disposes of garbage in disposal or garbage container

LAUNDRY/CLOTHING CARE

1. Sorts clothes (light/white, dark/colored)
2. Uses regular washer
3. Uses regular dryer
4. Folds/hangs clothes
5. Mends clothes (buttons, hems, seams)

TIME

1. Distinguishes units of time
   a) day/night
   b) morning/evening/afternoon
2. Distinguishes a.m./p.m.
3. Distinguishes workdays/nonworkdays
4. Tells time by hour and half hour
5. Sets/uses alarm clock
6. Arrives on time: work, appointments
7. Identifies date: day, month, year
8. Identifies numbers of days of week
9. Uses calendar
10. Estimate amount of time to do task:
    a) cleaning
    b) shopping
    c) cooking
    d) leisure activity
    e) shower/bath
    f) errands

continued

FIGURE 17.6

Living Skills Checklist

Source: Adapted from Brandt, J. (1994). *Assessment and Transition Planning.* Biddeford, Maine: University of New England.

FIGURE 17.6 (Continued)

NUMBERS

1. Recognizes numerals:
   a) 0 to 12
   b) above 12
2. Copies numerals:
   a) 0 to 12
   b) above 12
3. Counts objects:
   a) 0 to 12
   b) above 12
4. Uses calculator to add, subtract, multiply, divide
5. Uses measuring cups and spoons
6. Uses ruler and tape measure

WRITING

1. Writes/copies full name in manuscript or cursive
2. Writes/copies:
   a) address
   b) Social Security number
   c) telephone number
   d) date of birth
3. Writes/copies sentences/letter
4. Addresses envelope
5. Mails letter
6. Fills out job application

MONEY

1. Gives correct coin amounts for:
   a) five cents
   b) ten cents
   c) fifteen cents
   d) twenty-five cents
   e) fifty cents
2. Uses coins/coin combination for:
   a) food purchase at lunch
   b) vending machine
   c) pay telephone
3. Identifies/gives correct bill(s) for:
   a) one dollar
   b) five dollars
   c) ten dollars
4. Uses concepts of "more than"/"less than"
5. Estimates cost of purchase
6. Uses checkbook
7. Carries own money—performs cash transactions—waits for change as necessary

READING

1. Reads own name
2. Reads important signs/functional words
3. Reads newspapers
   a) locates want ad
   b) uses want ad to find job

PERSONAL/SOCIAL SKILLS

1. Carries identification (ID) card
2. Responds when spoken to

FIGURE 17.6 (Continued)

3. Communicates basic needs: verbally, nonverbally
4. Communicates full name: verbally, using ID, written
5. Communicates address, phone number: verbally, using ID, written
6. Communicates school, or place of work: verbally: using ID, written
7. Uses names of others when interacting
8. Uses "please," "thank you," etc.
9. Expresses anger in acceptable manner
10. Expresses fear in acceptable manner
11. Expresses affection in acceptable manner: same sex, opposite sex
12. Expresses dislike in acceptable manner
13. Apologizes
14. Initiates interaction with:
   a) staff
   b) peers
   c) visitors
   d) sales person/wait person
15. Converses with:
   a) staff
   b) peers
   c) visitors
16. Refrains from talking to stangers unless necessary
17. Uses telephone
18. Answers door in acceptable manner
19. Practices acceptable manners in/at:
   a) restaurant
   b) theater/spectator event
   c) party/dance
   d) church/religious center
   e) doctor
   f) dentist
20. Practices acceptable manners as:
   a) customer
   b) guest
   c) host
21. Demonstrates a complying attitude:
   a) follows directions from staff
   b) follows activity schedule
   c) performs duties
   d) works on training objective
22. Demonstrates trustworthiness:
   a) conduct can be trusted in unsupervised situations
   b) tells the truth
   c) takes responsibility for personal actions and decisions
   d) asks permission to use property of others
23. Accepts/adjusts to situations that are contrary to own will or desire
24. Abides by group decisions
25. Accepts/adjusts to staff change
26. Accepts/adjusts to novel situations: visitors, schedule changes
27. Uses acceptable table manners
28. Engages in passive activity: TV, radio, stereo, movie
29. Engages in solitary games
30. Engages in games with others
31. Engages in hobby/craft activity
32. Engages in active socialization with friends, family groups, parties, members of the opposite sex, social clubs

continued

FIGURE 17.6 (Continued)

FOOD PREPARATION/COOKING

1. Identifies kitchen utensils/cookware: table knife, spoon, fork, etc.
2. Identifies dishes: plate, cup, cereal bowl, soup bowl, glass, cup, etc.
3. Identifies appliances such as stove, oven, refrigerator, etc.
4. Can use basic kitchen utensils: knife, etc.
5. Can prepare simple meal: sandwiches, etc.
6. Can operate cooking equipment: stove, microwave, etc.
7. Can prepare simple food requiring cooking, coffee, tea, etc.
8. Can prepare/cook complete meal

MOBILITY

1. Walks
2. Rides bicycle
3. Rides public transportation
4. Can successfully travel to:
   a) store
   b) laundromat
   c) bus stop
   d) shopping mall
   e) church/religious center
   f) doctor/dentist office
   g) parents' home
   h) friend's home
5. Identifies/reads street signs
6. Identifies/reads house numbers
7. Identifies appropriate place to go if lost

HEALTH/SAFETY

1. Treats simple health problems
   a) cuts/scrapes
   b) slivers/splinters
   c) upset stomach
   d) cold
2. Treats more serious medical problem independently or contacts others for assistance
3. Takes medication
4. Refills prescription
5. Uses telephone to call in sick
6. Recognizes importance of not using alcohol with medications
7. Has basic understanding of human sexuality
8. Follows fire safety procedures
9. Follows safety protocols (e.g., uses safety goggles, etc.)

fied as "normal" and students who were identified as learning disabled. As predicted, the students with learning disabilities had lower scores on the *TPK* than students who were identified as normal.

Summary

The *Test of Practical Knowledge* is a measure that focuses on the practical knowledge needed by adolescents. The standardization sample needs to be updated. Adequate reliability is demonstrated, but further evidence of content and construct validity is needed.

BRIGANCE® Diagnostic Inventories

The *BRIGANCE® Diagnostic Inventories* are criterion-referenced tests that are similar in purpose, scoring, administration, and interpretation. The inventories are useful in program planning and in monitoring programs. Table 17.1 summarizes each of the inventories.

A summary of instruments that assess work-related behaviors, skills, and aptitudes can be found in Table 17.2.

Vocational Interests

A summary of interest inventories is available in Table 17.3.

Reading-Free Vocational Interest Inventory—Revised

The *Reading-Free Vocational Interest Inventory–Revised (R-FVII)* (Becker, 1988) is a vocational interest inventory for students who are mentally retarded or learning disabled. The tests consists of 55 sets of three pictures. The pictures are black and white drawings that depict women and men in work activities.

Administration

The *R-FVII* can be administered to individuals or to groups of students. The directions are read to the test taker and the test taker circles the drawings that depict the work that he or she prefers to do. No reading is required by the students.

Scoring

The consummable student booklets are hand scored. Raw scores are transformed to T-scores, percentiles, and stanines. Scores that fall above the 75th percentile indicate areas of high interest; scores falling below the 25th percentile indicate areas of low interest.

Standardization

The *R-FVII* was standardized on over 8,000 students with mild mental retardation or learning disabilities in grades 7 through 12. In addition, adult norms were based on the test performance of over 3,000 adults who were mentally retarded and economically or environmentally disadvantaged. Although the test manual describes a study of students in grades 7 through 12 who were moderately mentally retarded, the norms tables do not incorporate this information. However, the manual suggests that the norms are appropriate for students who are moderately mentally retarded (Miller, 1992).

Reliability

Test-retest and internal consistency reliability is adequate, with coefficients generally in the .70s and .80s.

Validity

Although the manual states that the items were reviewed by experts, the description of content validity is sketchy. Concurrent validity was determined by comparing the *R-FVII* with the

TABLE 17.1 Brigance® Inventories

Name	Ages/grades	Transition related skills
BRIGANCE® Diagnostic Inventory of Basic Skills (Brigance, 1977)	Grades K through 6	1. Readiness 2. Word Recognition 3. Word Analysis 4. Vocabulary 5. Handwriting 6. Grammar and Mechanics 7. Spelling 8. Reference Skills 9. Math Placement 10. Number Sequences 11. Operations 12. Measurement 13. Geometry
BRIGANCE® Diagnostic Inventory of Essential Skills (Brigance, 1981)	Grades 4 through 12	1. Word Recogniton 2. Oral Reading 3. Reading Comprehension 4. Functional Word Recognition 5. Word Analysis 6. Reference Skills 7. Schedules and Graphs 8. Writing 9. Forms 10. Spelling 11. Numbers 12. Number Facts 13. Computation of Whole Numbers 14. Fractions and Mixed Numbers 15. Decimals 16. Percents 17. Measurement 18. Metrics 19. Math Vocabulary 20. Money and Finance
BRIGANCE® Comprehensive Inventory of Basic Skills (Brigance, 1983)	Grades K through 9	1. Readiness 2. Speech 3. Word Recognition 4. Oral Reading 5. Reading Comprehension 6. Word Analysis 7. Word Recognition 8. Listening 9. Spelling 10. Writing 11. Reference Skills 12. Graphs and Maps

TABLE 17-1 (Continued)

Name	Ages/grades	Transition related skills
		13. Math Grade Placement
		14. Numbers
		15. Number Facts
		16. Computation of Whole Numbers
		17. Fractions and Mixed Numbers
		18. Decimals
		19. Percents
		20. Measurement
		21. Metrics
		22. Math Vocabulary
BRIGANCE® Assessment of Basic Skills–Spanish Edition (Brigance, 1984)	Grades K through 6	1. Readiness 2. Word Recognition 3. Word Analysis 4. Vocabulary 5. Handwriting 6. Grammar and Mechanics 7. Spelling 8. Reference Skills 9. Math Placement 10. Number Sequences 11. Operations 12. Measurement 13. Geometry
BRIGANCE® Life Skills Inventory (Brigance, 1994)	Vocational Secondary Adult education	1. Speaking and Listening Skills 2. Functional Writing Skills 3. Common Signs and Warning Labels 4. Telephone Skills 5. Money and Finance 6. Food 7. Clothing 8. Health 9. Travel and Transportation 10. Health Practices and Attitudes 12. Self-Concept 13. Auto Safety
BRIGANCE® Employability Skills Inventory (Brigance, 1995)	Vocational Secondary Adult education Job training	1. Reading 2. Career Awareness and Self-Understanding 3. Job Seeking Skills 4. Self-Concept 5. Motor Coordination 6. Responsibility 7. Speaking and Listening Skills 8. Preemployment Writing 9. Math Skills and Concepts

TABLE 17.2   Tests of Work-Related Behaviors, Skills, and Aptitudes

Instrument	Individuals	Characteristics
BRIGANCE® Employability Skills Inventory (Brigance, 1995)	All disabilities	Criterion-referenced
Kaufman Functional Academic Skills Test (K-FAST) (Kaufman and Kaufman, 1995)	Mild cognitive disabilities Behavioral disabilities	Norm-referenced, standardized test; assesses performance in reading and mathematics applied to daily life situations
LCCE (Life-Centered Career Education) Knowledge Battery (Brolin, 1992)	Mild cognitive disabilities Behavioral disabilities	Curriculum-based assessment associated with the LCCE Curriculum
LCCE (Life-Centered Career Education) Performance Battery (Brolin, 1992)	Mild cognitive disabilities Behavioral disabilities	Criterion-referenced assessment associated with the LCCE Curriculum
Living Skills Checklist (Brandt, 1994)	All disabilities	Informal checklist Assesses skills for daily living
Quality of Life Questionnaire (Schalock and Keith, 1993)	Mild to severe cognitive disabilities Ages 18+	Assesses levels of satisfaction, productivity, independence, community integration Interview
Quality of Student Life Questionnaire (Keith and Schalock, 1995)	All disability groups Ages 14 through 25	Assesses levels of satisfaction, well-being, social belonging, and control Interview

1964 revision of the *Geist Picture Interest Inventory* (Geist, 1964). The descripton of construct validity is limited.

Summary

The *Reading-Free Vocational Interest Inventory–Revised* is designed to measure the vocational interests of students with mild mental retardation or learning disabilities who are in grades 7 through 12. The norms should be updated to reflect recent census figures. Reliability is adequate; validity is limited. Evidence of predictive validity should be provided so that predictions can be made about vocational interests and actual vocations that are pursued.

Social and Prevocational Information Battery—Revised

The *Social and Prevocational Information Battery–Revised (SPIB-R)* (Halpern and Irvin, 1986) is composed of a set of nine subtests that assess knowledge in the following areas: employability, economic self-sufficiency, family living,

TABLE 17-2   (Continued)

Instrument	Individuals	Characteristics
Social and Prevocational Information Battery–Revised (Halpern, Irvin, and Munkres, 1986)	Mild disabilities	Assesses skills related to banking, budgeting, job-related skills and behaviors, home management, health, personal care Administered verbally
Test of Practical Knowledge (Wiederholt and Larsen, 1983)	Mild disabilities	Measures personal knowledge, social knowledge, occupational knowledge
Transition Behavior Scale (McCarney, 1986)	All disabilities	Assesses work-related behaviors, interpersonal skills, social and community expectations Rated by at least 3 individuals
Transition Planning Inventory (Clark and Patton, 1995)	All disabilities	Assesses skills related to employment, education, daily living, leisure, community integration, health, communication, interpersonal relationships Rating scale completed by student, parent/guardian, and school personnel

Source: Adapted from Clark (1996).

personal habits, and communication. The complete test consists of 277 items, with each subtest containing between 26 to 36 items.

Administration

All of the 277 items are administered orally to small groups of junior high school and high school–age students. The ability to read is not required. Students indicate the correct response by pointing to the correct picture or by marking items true or false. Sample items are presented to the students at the beginning of the test to ensure that they understand the items that will be administered. The authors advise that testing occur in three sessions within one week.

Scoring

Items are scored as either correct or incorrect. Percentile ranks and percentage correct are compared for junior high school and senior high school reference groups. The derived scores are based on the original test, not on the revised version.

TABLE 17.3 Interest Inventories

Instrument	Grade level	Reading level	Administration time
APTICOM Occupational Interest Inventory (JEVS, 1985)	Grade 9 through adult	Grade 4	20 minutes
Career Assessment Inventory–Enhanced (Johansson, 1986)	Grade 8 through adult	Grade 8	40 minutes
Career Assessment Inventory–Vocational (Johansson, 1982)	Grade 8 through adult	Grade 6	25 minutes
Gordon Occupational Checklist II (Gordon, 1980)	Grade 8 through adult	Not reported	50 minutes
Kuder General Interest Survey–Form E (Kuder, 1988)	Grade 6 through 12	Grade 6	40 minutes
Kuder Occupational Interest Survey–Form DD (Kuder, 1985)	Grade 10 through adult	Grade 6	60 minutes
Kuder Preference Record–Vocational (Kuder, 1978)	Grade 9 through 12	Grade 9	30 minutes
Occupational Aptitude Survey and Interest Schedule (2nd ed.) (OASIS-2) (Parker, 1991)	Grade 8 through 12	Not reported	30 minutes
Reading-Free Vocational Interest Inventory–Revised (Becker, 1988)	Grade 9 through adult	No reading required	20 minutes
Social and Prevocational Information Battery–Revised (Halpern and Irvin, 1986)	Grade 7 through 12	No reading required	approx. 60 minutes
Strong-Campbell Interest Inventory (Campbell and Hansen, 1985)	Grade 8 through adult	Grade 8	60 minutes
Wide Range Employability Sample Test (Jastak and Jastak, 1990)	Age 16 through 54	No reading required	60 minutes
Wide Range Interest-Opinion Test (WRIOT) (Jastak and Jastak, 1979)	Grade 7 through adult	No reading required	approx. 30 to 60 minutes

Standardization

Normative data for the *SPIB* are provided, but not for the revised version, *SPIB-R*. The sample consisted of approximately 900 students with mental retardation from Oregon. The overwhelming majority of the standardization sample was white. No attempt was made to select a standardization sample representative of ethnic or racial groups. The original sample included students from grades 7 through 12.

Reliability

Reliability data for the original *SPIB* are presented in the manual. Internal consistency reliability coefficients ranged from .65 to .82 for the subtests. The total test reliability coefficients were .93 and .94. Test-retest reliability coefficients for the subtests ranged from .62 to .79, and total test reliability coefficients ranged from .91 to .94.

Validity

The discussion of content validity in the manual is only relevant for the original *SPIB*. Content validity was established by reviewing curriculum guides and research studies. Predictive validity was determined using a 1972-1973 version of the test. No evidence of predictive validity for the *SPIB-R* is presented. Additional validity studies have been conducted by the authors (Stinnett, 1992), and they demonstrate that the *SPIB-R* has limited validity.

Summary

The *Social and Prevocational Information Battery–Revised* is designed to evaluate the skills necessary for community adjustment of junior high and high school students with mental retardation. The norms, reliability, and validity are based on the original version, and the standardization sample is too restrictive to be useful. This instrument should be used in conjuction with other measures.

Adaptive Behavior and Life Skills

Responsibility and Independence Scale for Adolescents

The *Responsibility and Independence Scale for Adolescents (RISA)* (Salvia, Neisworth, and Schmidt, 1990) is a norm-referenced measure of adolescent adaptive behavior intended to be used with students who are between the ages of 12.0 and 19.11 years. This instrument was described in Chapter 14.

BOX 17.2

SOCIAL AND PREVOCATIONAL INFORMATION BATTERY–REVISED

Publication Date: 1986

Purposes: Assesses prevocational skills and daily functioning

Age/Grade Levels: Junior high school and high school–age students

Time to Administer: Approximately 20 minutes for each of the nine subtests

Technical Adequacy: The standardization sample, reliability, and validity are less than adequate.

Suggested Uses: Cautiously use with students to determine ability to demonstrate prevocational skills and daily functioning. Should be used in combination with at least one other instrument. Does not require that the student is able to read.

Work Samples

Work samples assess students' skills, aptitudes, job preferences, and ability to profit from vocational training. Work sampling evaluates abilities on tasks that simulate actual job tasks. Most commercial work sample systems are based on the *Dictionary of Occupational Titles* (DOT) (U.S. Department of Labor, 1991), a system developed by the U.S. Department of Labor that classifies occupations. Work samples can also be used to evaluate the progress a student makes in a vocational training program.

In addition to commercial systems, evaluators can construct their own work samples and job simulations. Evaluators must conduct observations of students during vocational training and while working in actual jobs, and information is also collected from interviews with job supervisors and written evaluations. Table 17.4 describes commercial work sample systems.

TABLE 17.4 Work Evaluation Systems

Instrument	Group/individual administration	Time
Singer Vocational Evaluation System (Singer Educational Division, Career Systems, 1982)	Small group/individual	3 to 5 days
Valpar Component Work Sample System (Brandon, Balton, Rup, and Rasiter, 1974)	Small group/individual	Various times
Vocational Information and Evaluation Work Samples (Mandlebaum, Rosen, and Miller, 1977)	Small group/individual	14 to 18 hours
Wide Range Employability Sample Test (Jastak and Jastak, 1980)	Small group/individual	2 hours

CONNECTING INSTRUCTION WITH ASSESSMENT

Curriculum-Based Vocational Assessment

Curriculum-based vocational assessment (CBVA) is a type of curriculum-based assessment used in planning and developing vocational education opportunities for students with disabilities (Albright and Cobb, 1988). Conceptually, CBVA is different from traditional vocational assessment, which focuses on occupational areas and consists of formal, standardized measures. Albright and Cobb (1988) describe CBVA as an integral aspect of the three different stages of a student's program and list the types of questions on which the assessment should focus at each stage. For example, the first stage of the assessment process occurs prior to and during the first weeks of a student's participation in a vocational program. The sample questions at this stage are: "Which vocational program is most appropriate for the student? What are the special service needs of the student in this particular program? What will be the criteria used to determine student success?" (p. 16).

The second stage of assessment is an ongoing process of evaluation as the student progresses in the vocational education program. The sample questions include: "How is the student performing in the vocational setting? What changes are needed in the student's program?" (p. 16).

The third stage of the assessment process begins when the student exits the program. The sample questions include: "What are the special services needed to help the student transition into employment and/or postsecondary education? Which adult service agencies need to be linked up to the student? How will student adjustment be monitored?" (p. 16).

Another approach to CBVA was developed by Lomard, Larsen, and Westphal (1993). The Teach Prep Assessment Model consists of five steps named MAGIC. The first step (*M*) is *M*aking a prediction for the student's future. Informal assessment in this phase involves gathering information about the student's needs, preferences, and interests, and formal assessment consists of the evaluation of occupational interests, vocational aptitude, academic skills, and learning style. The second step (*A*) is *A*ssess entry level skills. During this step CBVA is conducted. In the third step (*G*), or *G*uide skill acquisition to skill mastery, teachers and other personnel conduct a discrepancy analysis between the student's current skills and the entry level target skills. Goals and objectives are developed. The fourth step (*I*) is *I*nstruct for generalization, and it focuses on using skills in multiple settings. The final step (*C*) is *C*onduct maintenance checks. During this last step, there is ongoing assessment to monitor student performance as well as the curriculum and instruction. The final step includes evaluation of both student and program.

Students or employees can assist in monitoring their own demonstration of work-related behaviors and skills. A simple checklist that uses icons can be used for this purpose (Figure 17.7).

Performance-Based Assessment

In Chapter 7, portfolio assessment was described as the deliberate collection of the products of a student's work to demonstrate the student's efforts, progress, and achievement. When applied to transition assessment, portfolios are used to document the transition needs and preferences of students. Documentation of

Name: _____		
Observer: _____ Date: _____		
	☐ Yes	☐ No
1. I can use the mop.		
2. I can check the iron.		
3. I can find the exit.		
4. I can set the table.		
5. I can tell the time to go to work.		

FIGURE 17.7
A Picture/Symbol Checklist

a student's transition needs can include work samples, audiotapes, videotapes, inventories, checklists, observations, and self-reports.

A portfolio used to document transition needs and preferences produces a rich, detailed portrait of the student. It depicts the student in natural work and living environments and provides continuous information, feedback, and growth toward transition needs and goals. Further, portfolio assessment can link interventions directly to the student's activities.

In addition to the assessment tools described in this chapter, the assessment of transition needs can include many of the procedures that have been described in previous chapters, including:

- oral descriptions
- written descriptions
- checklists
- questionnaires
- interviews
- conferences
- student journals and notebooks
- discussions between students, parents, and teachers.

PREFERRED PRACTICES

The overall intent of transition assessment is to assist students in making a transition from school to post-school activities, including post-secondary education, vocational training, integrated employment (including supported employment), continuing and adult eduction, adult services, independent living, and community participation. Transition assessment must include the evaluation of vocational, career, academic, personal, social, and living needs. The assessment of transition needs and preferences is an outcome-oriented process that begins when the child is young and takes place over a period of time.

Cooperation between experts and interagency collaboration are essential to the assessment process. The assessment of transition needs and preferences should be conducted by professionals who come from a variety of disciplines and incorporate input from parents, caregivers, and the student. Collaboration is important to the success of a student's transition.

A variety of assessment tools are used to conduct transition assessment. These include standardized instruments, curriculum-based assessment, authentic assessment tools, direct observation, checklists, and informal approaches. Much more experimentation with various assessment methods, especially in how and when to use them, is needed in order to continue to develop approaches that can be used with confidence.

EXTENDING LEARNING

17.1 After reviewing the purposes of transition assessment, identify specific assessment tools that fit these purposes.

17.2 Ideally, at what age should transition assessment begin. Why?

17.3 After reading the Snapshot, use the assessment data to develop an individual transition plan.

17.4 How can performance-based assessment contribute to the assessment of transition needs and preferences?

17.5 Visit a local school and interview a special education teacher who is involved with providing transition services. What types of assessment instruments are used with students in transition planning? Share your findings with the class.

17.6 Interview a school guidance counselor or a rehabilitation counselor regarding transition services offered to students and asssessment approaches. Share your findings with the class.

REFERENCES

Albright, L., and R.B. Cobb (1988). Curriculum based vocational assessment: A concept whose time has come. *Journal for Vocational Special Needs Education* 10(2), 13–16.

Becker, R. L. (1988). *Reading-free vocational interest inventory–Revised.* Columbus, Ohio: Elbern.

Blackorby, J., and M. Wagner (1996). Longitudinal post-school outcomes of youth with disabilities: Findings from the national longitudinal transition study. *Exceptional Children* 62: 399–413.

Blalock, G., and J. R. Patton (1996). Transition and students with learning disabilities: Creating sound futures. *Journal of Learning Disabilities* 29: 7–16.

Brandon, T., D. Balton, D. Rup, and C. Rasiter (1974). *Valpar component work sample system.* Tuscon, Ariz.: Valpar Corporation.

Brandt, J. E. (1994). *Assessment and transition planning: A curriculum for school psychologists and special educators.* Biddeford, Maine: University of New England.

Brigance, A. H. (1977). *BRIGANCE® diagnostic inventory of basic skills.* No. Billerica, Mass.: Curriculum Associates.

Brigance, A. H. (1981). *BRIGANCE® diagnostic inventory of essential skills.* No. Billerica, Mass.: Curriculum Associates.

Brigance, A. H. (1983). *BRIGANCE® comprehensive inventory of basic skills.* No. Billerica, Mass.: Curriculum Associates.

Brigance, A. H. (1984). *BRIGANCE® assessment of basic skills–Spanish edition.* No. Billerica, Mass.: Curriculum Associates.

Brigance, A. H. (1994). *BRIGANCE® life skills inventory.* No. Billerica, Mass.: Curriculum Associates.

Brigance, A. H. (1995). *BRIGANCE® employability skills inventory.* No. Billerica, Mass.: Curriculum Associates.

Brolin, D. E. (1993a). *Life-centered career education (LCCE) knowledge and performance batteries.* Reston, Va.: The Council for Exceptional Children.

Brolin, D. E. (1993b). *Life-centered career education: A competency-based approach.* 4th ed. Reston, Va.: The Council for Exceptional Children.

Bruinicks, R. H., R. W. Woodcock, R. F. Weatherman, and B. K. Hill (1984). *Scales of independent behavior: Woodcock-Johnson psychoeducational battery–Part four.* Allen, Tex.: DLM.

Campbell, D. P., and J. Hansen (1985). *Strong-Campbell interest inventory.* Stanford, Calif.: Stanford University Press.

Carl D. Perkins Vocational and Applied Technology Act (P.L. 99–457). (1990). Washington, D.C.: U.S. Government Printing Office.

Clark, G. (1996). Transition planning assessment for secondary-level students with learning disabilities. *Journal of Learning Disabilities* 29: 79–92.

Clark, G. M., and J. R. Patton (1995). *Transition planning inventory.* Austin, Tex.: PRO-ED.

Geist, H. (1964). *Geist picture interest inventory–revised.* Beverly Hills, Calif.: Western Psychological Services.

Gordon, L. V. (1980). *Gordon occupational checklist.* San Antonio, Tex.: The Psychological Corporation.

Halpern, A. S. (1994). The transition of youth with disabilities to adult life: A position statement of the division on career development and transition, the Council for Exceptional Children. *Career Development for Exceptional Individuals* 17: 115–124.

Halpern, A. S., and L. K. Irvin (1986). *Social and prevocational information battery–Revised* (SPIB-R). Monterey, Calif.: CTB Macmillan/McGraw Hill.

Hsu, L. M. (1985). Review of wide range interest-opinion test. *Mental Measurements Yearbook* Vol. 9: 1737–1738. Lincoln: University of Nebraska.

Individuals with Disabilities Education Act Amendments (P.L. 101–476) (October 7, 1991). Washington, D.C.: U.S. Government Printing Office.

International Center for the Disabled (n.d.). *TOWER system.* New York: ICD Rehabilitation and Research Center, International Center for the Disabled.

Jastak, J. F., and S. R. Jastak (1979). *Wide range interest-opinion test.* Wilmington, Del.: Jastak Associates.

Jastak, J. F., and S. R. Jastak (1980). *Wide range employability sample test.* Wilmington, Del.: Jastak Associates.

Jewish Employment and Vocational Service (n.d.). *Philadelphia Jewish employment and vocational service work sample system.* Philadelphia: Author.

Johansson, C. B. (1982). *Career assessment inventory–vocational.* Minneapolis: NCE Interpretive Scoring Systems.

Johansson, C. B. (1986). *Career assessment inventory–enhanced.* Minneapolis: NCE Interpretive Scoring Systems.

Kaufman, A. S., and N. L. Kaufman (1995). *Kaufman functional academic skills test* (K-FAST). Circle Pines, Minn.: American Guidance Service.

Krieg, F. J., P. Brown, and J. Ballard (1995). *Transition: School to work.* Bethesda, Md.: National Association of School Psychologists.

Kuder, G. F. (1978). *Kuder preference record–Vocational.* Chicago: Science Research Associates.

Kuder, G. F. (1985). *Kuder occupational interest survey–Form DD.* Chicago: Science Research Associates.

Kuder, G. F. (1988). *Kuder general interest inventory–Form E.* Chicago: Science Research Associates.

Leconte, P. J., M. Castleberry, S. King, and L. West (1994–95). Critical issues in assessment: Let's take the mystery out of assessment for vocational preparation, career development, and transition. *Diagnostique* 20(1–4): 33–51.

Lomard, R. C., K. A. Larsen, and S. E. Westphal (1993). Validation of vocational assessment services for special populations in tech-prep: A model for translating the Perkins assurances into practice. *Journal for Vocational Special Needs Education* 16(1): 14–22.

Love, L. (1993). Developing and including transition services in the IEP: Transition services program. Phoenix: Arizona Department of Education. (ERIC Document No. 380 964)

Mandelbaum, B. L., G. Rosen, and M. Miller (1977). *Vocational information and evaluation work samples.* Philadelphia: Vocational Research Institute.

McCarney, S. B. (1989). *Transition behavior scale.* Columbia, Mo.: Hawthorne Educational Service.

Miller, R. J. (1992). Review of the reading-free vocational interest inventory–Revised. *Mental Measurements Yearbook* Vol. 11: 752–753. Lincoln: University of Nebraska Press.

Parker, R. (1983). *Occupational aptitude survey and interest schedule.* 2d ed. Austin, Tex.: PRO-ED.

Salvia, J., J. T. Neisworth, and M. W. Schmidt (1990). *Responsibility and independence scale for adolescents.* Allen, Tex.: DLM.

Schalock, R. L., and K. D. Keith (1993). *Quality of life questionnaire.* Worthington, Ohio: IDS.

Schalock, R. L., and K. D. Keith (1995). *Quality of student life questionnaire.* Worthington, Ohio: IDS.

Singer Company Career Systems (1982). *Singer vocational evaluation system.* Rochester, N.Y.: Singer Eductional Division, Career Systems.

Sparrow, S., D. Balla, and D. Cicchetti (1984). *Vineland adaptive behavior scales.* Circle Pines, Minn.: American Guidance Service.

Stinnett, T. A. (1992). Review of the social and prevocational information battery–Revised. *Mental Health Measurements Yearbook* Vol. 12: 836–838. Lincoln: University of Nebraska Press.

U.S. Department of Labor (1991). *Dictionary of occupational titles.* (4th ed.). Washington, D.C.: U.S. Government Printing Office.

Wiederholt, J. L., and S. C. Larsen (1983) *Test of practical knowledge.* Austin, Tex.: PRO-ED.

Interpreting Tests and Writing Reports

OVERVIEW

Synthesizing and interpreting assessment information is the culmination of the assessment process. The assessment report is used to communicate what has been learned about the student and to make recommendations based on the assessment results. This chapter is a discussion of how to synthesize and interpret assessment information and how to complete an effective written report.

CHAPTER OBJECTIVES

After completing this chapter, you should be able to:

Discuss the process of interpreting assessment results.

Explain the general principles that guide the development of assessment reports.

Describe the components of an assessment report.

Explain considerations in sharing reports with the student and with family members.

Discuss the use of computer-generated test results and reports.

WHAT SHAPES OUR VIEWS

The interpretation of assessment results involves the practioner in a series of analyses, in examining the assessment data, explaining the results, and clarifying the information. In interpreting results, the examiner focuses on the assessment questions to give meaning to the information. Interpretation begins with an examination of the student's overall performance and then moves to a consideration of each of the appropriately measured behaviors, skills, and abilities.

Interpreting data takes practice and skill. Cohen, Stern, and Balaban (1983) suggest the following questions: "Can we verify every statement we make? Do we have evidence for our hunches and our guesses?" (p. 202). The more you use a test or conduct an observation or complete an interview, the more you will come to understand the information that can be gathered and how it can be interpreted. One method of interpreting results is a process called hypothesis generation.

Generating a Hypothesis

When interpreting the results of testing, we prefer the process described as hypothesis generation (Kaufman, 1979, 1994; McGrew, 1986, 1994) or integrative interpretation (Kamphaus, 1993). In test interpretation, a hypothesis is an explanation of a student's performance and behavior based on the assessment data that have been collected.

As the assessment information is reviewed, several hypotheses will emerge. One hypothesis will relate to the referral questions; other hypotheses may relate to levels of achievement, behavior, cognitive ability, communication, development, functioning, motor development, or sensory functioning.

The test data (i.e., the results of the various assessment approaches, including standard-ized testing, curriculum-based assessment, performance-based assessment, observations, interviews, and so on) will be used to support one or more hypotheses. For example, information obtained from interviews with teachers, therapists, support staff, the student, and family members is integrated with information obtained from behavioral observations of the student to support the determination of attention-deficit hyperactivity disorder.

Kaufman, discussing his approach to test interpretation, cautions examiners to remember that hypotheses "are not facts and may indeed prove to be artifacts" (Kaufman, 1979, p. 177). Hypotheses are informed assumptions; when hypotheses cannot be substantiated by evidence, further investigation is warranted. The test data may need to be reanalyzed, or additional data may have to be collected to generate new or modified hypotheses.

Examiner Bias

Examiner bias can arise in the interpretation of assessment results. Examiners need to be aware of the types of biases in order to identify and control them. Bias colors how the data will be viewed and interpreted.

Bentzen (1993) describes two levels of potential bias. At one level is the personal bias and perspective of the examiner; the examiner brings individual experiences, abilities, attitudes, and knowledge to the interpretation process. Examiners need to take precautions in not letting personal bias interfere with the careful, objective interpretation of information. The second level of bias is the result of formal training and includes bias shaped by theory, conceptual framework, or philosophy. These biases affect how you interpret a situation, event, or behavior.

Using Professional Knowledge

To interpret test results, the examiner must understand the purpose of the test itself, how it is administered, and what the test scores mean. In our discussion of norm-referenced tests and standardization samples in Chapter 4, you learned that a standardized test can be administered to students with characteristics that are similar to the norm group and that the student's score can be compared with those of the norm group. In interpreting test results, the examiner must consider the norm sample of a test instrument; if the characteristics of the student tested are not similar to those of the norm group, the examiner will need to explain how the test scores are affected. The test scores of students who have characteristics different from the norm sample cannot be compared with the test scores of the students who participated in the standardization of the instrument.

Examiners need to understand the test scores and be able to explain them to others. For example, an examiner may be called upon to explain the difference between a percentile rank and a percentage-correct score or to clarify misperceptions about a grade equivalent score or standard score.

In interpreting assessment information, the examiner must be a keen observer of behavior and of environmental conditions that adversely affect student performance. In previous chapters we have examined the effects of the physical, learning, and social environments on performance. Observations of the environment and of the student will add valuable information. As the examiner synthesizes assessment results, the observations may corroborate information obtained during formal testing, or these observations may help to explain why a student's score was unexpectedly low.

Interpreting assessment information requires a wide range of knowledge concerning child and adolescent growth and development as well as disability. Examiners need professional knowledge of classroom curriculum and pedagogy, and a solid understanding of statistics is essential in interpreting test scores. Knowledge of special education, related ser-

vices, state regulations, and federal law is essential in clarifying the information.

RESPONDING TO DIVERSITY

In previous chapters we have discussed problems of test bias regarding students who come from diverse cultural, ethnic, racial and linguistic backgrounds, geographic regions of origin, and gender, disability, and economic groups. Examiners must be aware not only that standardized instruments but other assessment approaches can be biased. For example, in Chapter 7 we examined how portfolio assessments are, for the most part, biased toward students who attend school infrequently.

We know that the purpose for one of the assessment steps, determining eligibility, is to identify students with disabilities who need special education services. Lyman (1986) describes these instruments:

> Any test that is worthwhile must *discriminate;* after all, this is just another way of saying that it will "reveal individual differences." But the intended discrimination should be on the basis of the trait being measured, not on the basis of racial or ethnic background. (pp. 7–8)

GENERAL PRINCIPLES FOR REPORT WRITING

The following general principles guide the development of a well-written report.

Organize the Information

Organize the information systematically. Information should be presented in sections with appropriate headings. Discuss conclusions and recommendations at the end of the report; do not insert them in the body of the document.

Relate Only the Facts

Report only factual information. Do not include unsubstantiated information. When including information from other sources, such as other assessment reports, mention the date and name of the sources.

Include Only Essential Information

Write about the facts, but avoid extraneous information about the student or family. Although your report must be comprehensive, some information is not essential; you will need to make judgments about whether what you have learned is appropriate for inclusion. Use only information that contributes to the understanding of the student, the test results, and recommendations.

Be Aware of Bias

Avoid generalizations that can bias the report. Be careful about stereotyping groups. Critically review your report before submitting it.

Present Accurate Information

Make sure that the information is accurate. Review the information to check for accuracy. When calculating test scores on the test form, be sure to double-check your work. Some tests require scores of several different types, and it is easy to make errors converting from one type of test score to another. The examiner must always verify that the test scores were copied correctly from the test to the report. Be sure that there are no misinterpretations about performance due to inaccurate calculations or inaccurate copying.

Include Any Reservations

Incorporate, and discuss fully, any reservations about the assessment process and its effect on the results. Reservations may include observations of the student that indicate the results are not accurate or do not reflect the student's best abilities. Record any interruptions or other disturbances in the environment that may have affected the results, and note the limitations in technical adequacy of the instrument(s) for students with characteristics not represented by the norming sample.

Avoid Technical Jargon

Use clear, understandable language; technical jargon can make the report confusing or ambiguous. A discussion of the formulas used to measure discrepancies or of the theoretical perspectives of various experts is avoided. How could the language in the following excerpt be simplified?

> Tony has dual diagnostic deficits that affect expressive and receptive language, articulation, internal regulation, and cognition. A coexisting diagnosis can be made of Attention-Deficit Hyperactive Disorder and mental retardation. This diagnosis is strongly suggested by biological maternal history of ethanol abuse, apparently during the gestational period and Tony's striking physiognomy.

Write Clearly

Work to develop report-writing skills. Use the writing process to create a working draft. Reread and rewrite the working draft. Check the draft for grammatical mistakes and punctuation errors. Use the spell check feature of your word processing program. Avoid ambiguous language. Use a checklist like that found in Table 18.1 later in this chapter to ensure that you have included all the necessary information.

TYPES OF ASSESSMENT REPORTS

Assessment reports are written for a variety of purposes, and the information they contain varies accordingly. Reports are written to 1) summarize a series of observations and synthesize the observational data, 2) report student progress over a period of time, 3) describe the results of administering an individual test, and 4) integrate and interpret the results of a comprehensive assessment.

Reports of Observations

A teacher customarily writes a report on the observations conducted on a student in one or more settings. We have discussed the importance of conducting multiple observations to obtain an accurate sample of student behavior. The written report organizes the information collected from all the observations.

How to Write an Observation Report

A written observation report should be completed as soon as possible after the final observation. Observation reports include the following information:

1. Student information, including name, date of birth, age, grade, and teacher's name.
2. Dates of observations.
3. Purpose(s) for conducting the observations. The observations may focus on the environment or on the student. The purpose of the observations should be clearly stated and the events or behaviors should be defined in observable terms.
4. Setting(s) in which the observations were conducted.
5. Description of the environments, including the physical, learning, and social aspects.

6. Behavioral observations. Be sure to relate only information observed. Do not interpret or make judgments.
7. Discussion. Summarize your observations of the environment and the student's behavior. Include your interpretation of the assessment data.
8. Recommendations. State realistic suggestions that can be implemented.

How to Represent Information Graphically

Graphs allow us to illustrate information not readily available in a text format or on a data sheet. Graphs permit the viewer to think about the substance of the data and encourage the eye to compare different data (Tufte, 1983). Data that are displayed graphically enhance understanding and serve to highlight findings that may be embedded in the observation forms and not apparent on examination of the forms (Nicolson and Shipstead, 1994). Two types of graphs are commonly used.

1. Pie Charts: Pie charts are most useful in displaying percentages of data when the examiner wants to illustrate parts of a whole.
2. Bar Graphs: Bar graphs are most useful in displaying frequency counts or plotting trends over time.

Let's examine these two methods within the context of an assessment question: "During math class, how much time is Cindy actively engaged in math-related activities?" Math-related activities are defined as looking at the teacher during the class lesson, working with paper and pencil on math problems, and discussing solutions to the math problems with peers. The observer collected data over a period of three days. The data analysis indicated that Cindy engaged in several behaviors during the class period: she was out of her seat, out of the classroom, looking around the room, and engaged in math-related activities.

The three pie charts in Figure 18.1 allow comparison of Cindy's behavior on each day of

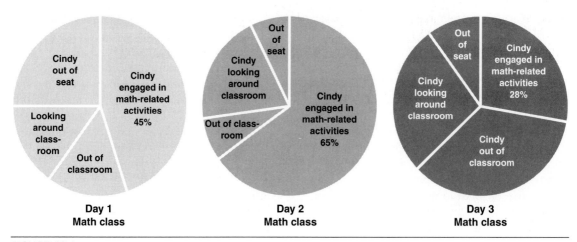

FIGURE 18.1

Data Presentation in Pie Charts

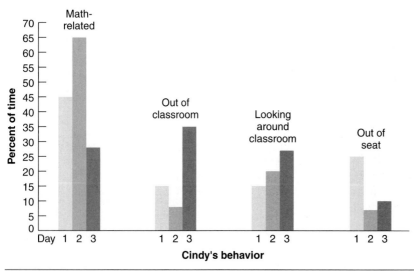

FIGURE 18.2

Data Presentation in a Bar Chart

the observation. The same data can be represented in bar graphs, as in Figure 18.2. The discussion in the assessment report could center on the types of teaching and learning strategies that were used on the different days or on the reasons why Cindy was out of her seat or out of the classroom. The pie chart allows us to see the whole period of time available for mathematics and how Cindy spent this time over the period observed.

The bar graph allows us to see the percentage of time Cindy was out of her seat, out of the classroom, looking around, and engaged in a math activity over the three-day period by activity. The discussion in the assessment report could compare Cindy's behaviors over the observation period. Which type of graph do you think best displays the data in answer to the observation question? (The answer is found at the end of the activities in Extending Learning.)

In earlier chapters we discussed the need to compare the target student with one or more other students about whom the teacher had no concern. Variations of bar graphs allow us to compare several students and provide additional information regarding whether or not the target student's (Cindy's) behavior is atypical (Figure 18.3).

Progress Reports

Progress reports are a summary of the advances a student makes during a specific time period and provide a link to the IEP, which requires periodic monitoring of the student's progress. Progress reports must relate information about the student with reference to these goals and intended outcomes of the IEP. These reports can be prepared to accompany a report card at the end of the marking period or to provide an update of information to family and other team members. One example of a progress report is a checklist (Figure 18.6).

Individual Test Reports

Individual test reports describe the test results and the examiner's interpretation of the student's performance. Usually, these reports are shared at the team meeting and become part of the student's permanent record. Individual reports of tests present a limited account of a student's performance, thus they may be combined later into a comprehensive assessment report to provide more complete information on the student.

A written test report must be completed by each member of the team who conducts an assessment of the student. At the team meeting, reports by the several examiners—the special education teacher, the school psychologist, the physical or occupational therapist, or the speech and language pathologist—are considered.

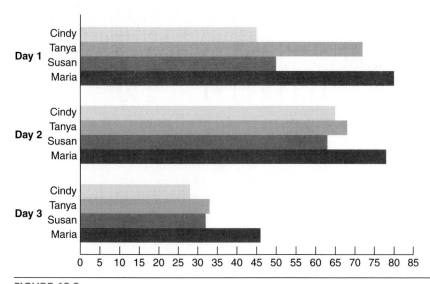

FIGURE 18.3

Percent of Engagement in Math-Related Activity for Four Students Over Three Days

SNAPSHOT

Observation Report on John Diamond

The special education consultant, Marilyn Fillbrick, was asked to observe an eighth grade student, John, in his regular classroom. At the time, John was receiving speech therapy and had been referred to the school psychologist because the team was concerned with John's aggressive behavior. According to the eighth grade teacher, "He is always in motion. He frequently hits and pushes other students, and he is verbally abusive."

Marilyn met with John's teacher to discuss John's problem behaviors more fully. The meeting helped to clarify the behaviors that were of concern and to plan the best time and place to conduct the observations. Marilyn decided to develop her own observation instrument based on an interval recording method described in Chapter 5.

After completing her observations, Marilyn wrote an observation report that summarized the findings. She also developed a graph to help explain the observation data. A copy of one of her data sheets (Figure 18.4) and the graph (Figure 18.5) that she developed to help explain her data follow her written report.

Observation Report

Name: John Diamond

Birth Date: 9/21/xx

Age: 13 years, 2 months

Grade: 8

Teacher: Dara Hall

Dates of Observations: 11/1/xx; 11/4/xx; 11/8/xx

Observer: Marilyn Fillbrick

Purpose of Observations: The assessment team requested classroom observations because of concerns regarding John's behavior problems. Specific concerns include: his out-of-seat behavior, hitting and pushing other students, and verbally abusing others. The purpose of the observations was to determine the degree to which John actually engages in the behaviors of concern.

Setting: Students change classes for each subject. Three observations were conducted over a two-week period; John was observed in mathematics and language arts classes and during the lunch period. Each observation consisted of 30 minutes and took place between 9:00 and 11:00 a.m.

Observations of the Environment: The classrooms are designed for small group work with student desks clustered in groups of four. Students are not assigned a particular desk but are free to choose where to work. The classrooms consisted of 20–23 students with one teacher and occasional other support staff.

Behavioral Observations: Results of the observations indicate that John did indeed display many aggressive behaviors. John pushed and poked other students 5–6 times during each of the observations; less frequently (3–4 times each observation), he hit and swore at other students and occasionally (2 times each observation) swore at the teacher. These behaviors usually occurred when students were changing classes.

At other times (5–6 times each observation), John joined the other students in laughter, volunteered answers, helped a

Name: John					Date: November 1

Two-minute interval	Behavior: p = push, h = hit, s = swear	Total behaviors			Comments
		p	h	s	Math class
00–02					Teacher goes over assignment for following day. John asks questions to clarify.
02–04					
04–06		||		IIII	Class changes at 9:05 Behavior occurs during transition and in hallway.
06–08		||	||||		Hits and pokes the boy behind him.
08–10					Other occurrences? –unable to follow John closely during this period.
10–12			||		Language arts class begins at 9:12.
12–14					Helps student find materials.
14–16		I			Volunteers to assist teacher.
28–30					

FIGURE 18.4

Teacher-Developed Data Sheet

student who was having difficulty with finding materials, and participated in activities willingly.

Discussion: John engages in pushing, hitting, and poking other students as well as swearing at others, including the teacher. These observations indicate that the teacher continually has to watch him closely, and frequently has to intervene on behalf of the other students.

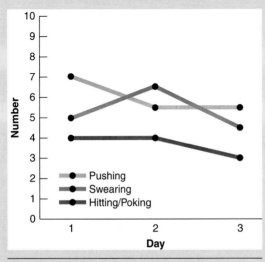

FIGURE 18.5

Teacher-Developed Graphs

John's problem behaviors are most apparent when he is listening without being able to be active, when the general noise level in the classroom begins to escalate, and when he is anticipating transition.

Aggression was especially high during transition, with no instances occurring during a spelling activity in which the teacher directed the whole class and each student was actively engaged. Few aggressive behaviors occurred during small group math manipulative activities. Both spelling and math were structured and required him to be more involved.

John appears to be a happy youngster, laughing and participating in activities willingly, but shows little self-control or regard for his effects on others.

Recommendations: John appears to benefit from structured learning activities that include active student participation. Classroom noise should be monitored, as this may have an adverse effect on his behavior. Positive behavior management strategies should be shared with his teacher and other support staff in the classroom.

Second marking period	In Progress	Mastered
1. Uses correct punctuation to end a sentence.		X
2. Uses correct form of *you're* and *your*.	X	
3. Uses correct form of *their, there,* and *they're*.	X	
4. Uses commas in a series correctly.		X
5. Uses correct form of adjectives.	X	
6. Correctly places apostrophe in contractions and possessives.	X	

FIGURE 18.6

Progress Report

COMPREHENSIVE ASSESSMENT REPORTS

A comprehensive assessment report is usually extensive; it summarizes what we know about the student and what we have learned based on the results of a thorough assessment. Typically, a comprehensive report relies on the many sources of assessment information that we have described in this book.

WRITING THE REPORT

Individual test reports and comprehensive test reports should be organized by the following areas.

1. Identifying data
2. Reason for referral
3. Background information
4. Family involvement
5. Observations of the environment
6. Behavioral observations
7. Tests, interviews, and performance-based assessment
8. Discussion of the results
9. Summary
10. Recommendations

Each area should be a separate section. Use appropriate subheadings to help organize the report, as suggested by the lists in the sections that follow.

Identifying the Data

Information in the first section of the report identifies the student, the parents, the school, the test, and the examiner:

1. About the student: include the student's name, address, phone number, chronological age in years and months, birth date, and gender.
2. About the family: include the names and addresses of family members.

3. About the school: include the student's grade level, school's name, address, phone number, director or principal's name, and teacher's name.
4. About the testing: include the name of the examiner, the date of testing, and the date the report was written.

School records, the referral form, interviews with family members or teachers, records of administered tests, and so forth are standard sources for this information.

Reason for Referral

The second section contains a summary of the reasons for referral and the name of the person who initiated the referral. Throughout the report, be sure that the reasons for referral are directly addressed and that the conclusions and recommendations refer to them. As the report is developed, one of its central themes will be the grounds for the referral and the extent to which the testing addressed these issues. This information can be obtained from the referral form and from interviews with family members, teachers, and staff.

Background Information

Information about the student's background—the student's education, family history, medical care, and previous assessment results—should be briefly summarized.

Medical history can include a description of any unusual medical problems, diagnoses, extended hospital stays, continuing medical care, general health, and results of vision and hearing testing. Some students have experienced early and prolonged medical interventions; some of these students may have had extended hospital stays and received extensive care for genetic abnormalities or other conditions. Their medical folders can be quite lengthy, and the examiner will need to judge which information is pertinent to the reason for referral. Extensive discussion of a student's medical history may bias the reader to think that the child is severely disabled or may be unusually difficult to manage.

Facts such as dates of attendance, regularity of attendance, type of placement or services provided, performance, interventions tried, and results of previous educational testing can be obtained from school records, interviews, and home visits. A summary of child care experiences, depending on the age of the student, is also important.

Details of familial and/or cultural background can be useful, but this type of information should be used carefully and judiciously. Use it only when it is relevant and helps to explain the behavior of the student or the results of testing. Knowledge about the family and cultural background is customarily obtained from interviews with the student, family members, teachers, and other professionals, and through a home visit.

Family Involvement

As members of the assessment team, parents can assist in identifying strengths and needs of their child and in gathering information by keeping logs, checklists, and other written documents. They also make observations or collect information by tape-recording or videotaping their child. In addition, family members contribute description and understanding through the interview process. The information collected or contributed by family members should be noted in the written report.

Observations of the Environment

The description of the classroom environment includes the physical setting and the learning and social environments. In several previous chapters we have discussed important environmental factors and have suggested ways to

gather information about these aspects of the classroom.

Behavioral Observations

The report includes a description of the student's behavior during testing. The examiner will want to observe whether the student was cooperative, distractible, attentive, tired, or shy, or exhibited other types of behavior. How did the student approach the testing situation? What was the student's behavior at the beginning of the testing? During the testing? At the end? This section reports any observations conducted in the classroom, playground, cafeteria, or other setting.

As discussed in Chapter 5, systematic observations can be an important source of data. Methodical observations help us to understand the student's behavior and learning strategies and can also inform us about intervention strategies. Nevertheless, observations about behavior in the testing situation may not be generalizable to other settings. During testing, a narrow sample of behavior is assessed. To a certain extent, the testing situation is artificial, and this must be considered when interpreting results and drawing conclusions about a student's behavior (Sattler, 1990). A student's behavior can vary in different settings and with different examiners.

In writing the report, use the following list of behaviors as a starting point for discussion (Sattler, 1990):

- Physical appearance
- Reactions to test session and to the examiner
- General behavior
- Typical mode of relating to the examiner
- Language style
- General response style
- Response to failures
- Response to successes
- Response to encouragement
- Activity level
- Attitude toward self

- Attitude toward the examiner and the testing process
- Visual-motor ability
- Unusual habits, mannerisms, or verbalizations
- Examiner's reaction to the student.
  (p. 728)

Tests, Interviews, and Performance-Based Assessment

The report includes a list of the tests and assessments, both formal and informal, and the interviews that were conducted to collect the assessment data.

Discussion of Results

In listing the results of the assessment instruments, use the same types of scores throughout the section. Standard scores, percentiles, or stanines are preferred. Two or more types of scores, such as standard scores and percentiles, may be reported. Always include the confidence intervals when reporting standard scores. Some examiners like to report scores in a table format within the discussion of the results.

This section of the report includes the interpretation of the assessment results. Hypothesis generation, discussed earlier in this chapter, is included in the results section. Each test should be analyzed separately, and then the results synthesized. The following steps for test interpretation are adapted from the works of Kamphaus (1993), Kaufman (1979, 1994), and McGrew (1986, 1994):

Step 1: Interpret overall performance. Describe the overall performance of the student on the tests, and supply an interpretation of the full-scale or total score performances.

Step 2: Determine relative strengths and needs in each area tested. Make a list of the subtests in each test that represent relative strengths and relative weaknesses. Determine the abilities that are represented by each of the subtests.

Step 3: Compare the subtests on all the tests. Consider each subtest and the abilities it measures. Compare the shared abilities across the test data. If relative strengths and weaknesses do not emerge across the data, then interpret unique abilities.

Step 4: Integrate the relative strengths and needs. Identify relative strengths and weaknesses by comparing all the test data, including the results of formal and informal testing, interviews, observations, and background information about the student.

Summary

This section should be brief. Summarize the major points that have been discussed and synthesize the results. Report the current level of functioning and indicate areas of relative strength and need. Answer the referral questions. Restate the themes that have emerged.

Recommendations

An assessment is conducted chiefly to answer the referral questions about the student and to develop recommendations. The recommendations should logically be based on the information that is contained in the assessment report. Suggest realistic, practical recommendations that can be implemented. Recommendations can be developed for the students in a variety of settings, including school, home, and community. Specific goals and objectives should not be included in the assessment report; these are to be written in the IEP or IFSP during the team meeting. An example of a comprehensive assessment report is illustrated in the following snapshot.

SNAPSHOT

Gina's Comprehensive Assessment Report

Larry Kahn is one of the special education consultants for the Allen School District. He recently completed a comprehensive assessment of Gina A., a kindergarten student. Gina was referred to the assessment team by her teacher, Maria Gordon, who was troubled about her high level of activity and her lack of skills, among other concerns. The assessment report follows:

Office of Special Services

14 Main Street

Allen, _____

Telephone: 200-299-2000

Name: Gina A.

Address: 1 Hill Road
Allen, _____

Birth Date: March 4, 19xx

Age: 5 years, 2 months

Sex: female

Foster Parent: C. B.

Address: 1 Hill Road
Allen, _____

Telephone: xxx-xxx-xxxx

Date: May 10, 19xx

Date of testing: May 6, 19xx

Examiner: L. A. Kahn

School: Allen Elementary School

Principal: L. Lindly

Teacher: M. Gordon

Grade: K

Reason for Referral

Gina was referred by her teacher because of problems of extreme activity within the classroom, developmental concerns, and a history of physical abuse.

Background Information

An evaluation by the E. C. Medical Center on 2/23/xx stated that Gina presented evidence of fetal alcohol syndrome. In at least four or five evaluations over the years, this child was identified as having a mild developmental delay. Efforts to secure early intervention services have been made off and on since infancy. However, because Gina's biological mother moved frequently, Gina received limited services. Dr. Jones on 10/10/xx indicated a Stanford-Binet score of 62 and "functioning well below her chronological age in language, cognitive, and motor skills areas."

Gina has been in foster care since the age of four, when she was exposed to inappropriate sexual behaviors at home, neglect, and abuse. Her biological mother, who has a history of physical and sexual abuse, is completing a prison sentence. Her brother, Paul, is living with a paternal grandmother. Her father has infrequent contact with the family. Her foster care family wants to help Gina, and the family has been very involved in the assessment process.

Family Involvement

Mr. and Mrs. B., Gina's foster family, have been in frequent contact with the assessment team. Several team members visited the home, where Mr. and Mrs. B. shared their concerns about Gina and volunteered to participate with the team in identifying Gina's strengths and needs.

Observations of the Environment

Gina is currently in an inclusive kindergarten, that is, the classroom includes some children who have disabilities and some children who do not. There are 18 children in the classroom, with a teacher and an aide. In addition, an occupational therapist and a speech and language pathologist work with some of the children in the classroom on a weekly basis. The therapists are available to consult with the teacher during a weekly planning time.

The classroom is divided into four learning centers: math, science, reading, and community studies. There is much activity in the room as the children, teacher, aide, and related service personnel move about. Children's pictures and drawings cover the walls. The room appears to be stimulating and busy.

Behavior Observations

Informal testing and achievement testing were begun in a quiet corner of the classroom so that Gina could get used to the examiner before going to the examiner's office for further testing. The child was very reluctant to participate in the testing, and her behavior was consistently negative during the testing session. Gina repeatedly questioned why she was being asked to complete test items and several times she refused to try an item. Testing sessions were very brief because of her refusal to participate compounded by her short attention span. She could attend to a task for a few seconds but then was distracted by pictures on the wall, sounds from the radiator, and other background noise. She had to be coaxed to focus on the tasks. She was very distracted by all the test materials and touched everything throughout the session.

Tests and Interviews

The following tests were administered: Kaufman Assessment Battery for Children (K-ABC), Peabody Picture Vocabulary Test-III, and the Child Behavior Checklist. Gina was observed three different times in her classroom. Interviews were conducted with Gina's foster parent and with her teacher.

Discussion of Results

On the Kaufman Assessment Battery for Children Gina's mental processing composite score was a percentile rank of 2; the achievement score was a percentile rank of 1. Relative strengths on the cognitive and achievement batteries were Hand Movements (motor planning, perceptual organization) and Gestalt Closure (recall, alertness to the environment). Significant weaknesses on the cognitive and achievement batteries were Number Recall (short-term auditory memory, reproduction of a model), Riddles (word knowledge/recall), Word Order (verbal/auditory comprehension), Photo Series (visual sequencing, visual perceptual organization), Arithmetic (quantitative concepts, applied school-related skills, reasoning, verbal comprehension), Reading/Decoding (applied school-related skills, early language development, long-term memory, reasoning).

On the Peabody Picture Vocabulary Test-III, Gina received a standard score of 45 with her true

score following within the range of 45–57. The score indicates performace at the 1st percentile rank. Her performance remains consistent in terms of her overall standard score, indicating that her understanding of single words is commensurate with her cognitive ability.

On the Child Behavior Checklist, Gina scored in the high range of externalizing behaviors: attention problems, 80th percentile; delinquent behavior, 70th percentile; and aggressive behavior, 77th percentile.

Overall, it appears that Gina's short attention span and distractibility interfere with the formal
testing. Observations confirmed that Gina performs somewhat better in the classroom than
on the formal testing. However, when Gina's performance is compared with typical children
in the kindergarten classroom, she performs well below her age peers. Classroom observations also indicate that Gina is reluctant to comply with requests made by her teacher and
that she rarely cooperates with other children. She has a constant need for limit setting.

Summary

Gina is a child who has been diagnosed as having fetal alcohol syndrome. The results of formal testing, observations, and interviews indicate that she has a developmental delay, has a
short attention span, is distractible, and has many negative behaviors. Her concept and language development are well below that of her age peers.

Recommendations

Gina is certainly in need of special education services to address her broad-based developmental delays. She will need intensive intervention services, consistent setting of limits, expectations for more age-appropriate behavior, and an environment with a great deal of structure.

Counseling and behavior management strategies should be offered to the foster family to
help them deal with the negative behaviors, attention span, and distractibility.

After completing the written report, Larry contacted Gina's foster parents to arrange for a convenient time to share the report with them. He wanted an opportunity to go over the report prior to the team meeting to allow the family an opportunity to ask questions and to discuss specific areas in more detail. During Gina's team meeting he will present the results and recommendations contained in the report, then file a copy of the report in the office of student records.

EVALUATING THE REPORT

Writing an assessment report is an important way to communicate test findings. A report helps you to organize the results of testing systematically, to analyze a student's performance, and to make recommendations. Reports must be written clearly using correct grammar and spelling. Table 18.1 illustrates a checklist that can be used to review the adequacy of assessment reports.

SHARING ASSESSMENT RESULTS WITH OTHERS

Family Members

Assessment results and recommendations should be shared with family members as soon as possible after the report has been completed. Look over the test results and make sure that you can explain the test scores. You will want to be careful that your words are not

TABLE 18.1   A Checklist for Evaluating an Assessment Report

Report section	Yes	No
A. Identifying Information		
1. Is the information complete?	_____	_____
2. Is the information accurate?	_____	_____
B. Reason for Referral		
1. Is the reason for referral clearly described?	_____	_____
2. Is the source of the referral included?	_____	_____
3. Does the reason for referral provide a reason for conducting the assessment?	_____	_____
C. Background Information		
1. Is this section complete?	_____	_____
2. Are any of the descriptions vague?	_____	_____
3. Can some information be omitted?	_____	_____
D. Behavioral Observations		
1. Are the observations clearly described?	_____	_____
2. Are any of the descriptions vague?	_____	_____
3. Does this section help the reader to visualize the student's behavior?	_____	_____
E. Assessment Approaches Used		
1. Are the sources of information identified?	_____	_____
F. Discussion of Results		
1. Does the discussion relate to the referral questions?	_____	_____
2. Is this section organized around themes?	_____	_____
3. Are the themes discussed separately, including references to appropriate tests and assessment procedures?	_____	_____
4. Are strengths and needs described?	_____	_____
G. Summary		
1. Does this section restate the major themes and how the testing addressed the reasons for referral?	_____	_____
2. Is this section too long?	_____	_____

continued

TABLE 18-1 (Continued)

Report section	Yes	No
H. Recommendations		
1. Do the recommendations logically follow from the rest of the report?	_____	_____
2. Can the recommendations be implemented?	_____	_____
3. Are recommendations for a variety of settings included?	_____	_____
4. Are the recommendations understandable?	_____	_____
I. General Evaluation		
1. Is the writing clear?	_____	_____
2. Has the report been proofread?	_____	_____
3. Have the spelling, grammar, and punctuation been checked?	_____	_____
4. Are the sections of the report identifiable?	_____	_____
5. Has technical language been minimized?	_____	_____
6. Is there any bias?	_____	_____

misunderstood, as family members may be very anxious about the assessment outcome. It is good practice to plan the topics to be covered and what you want to say. Using descriptive terms to interpret test scores is helpful for parents and other team members. Lyman (1986) suggests the following scale:

Percentile ranks	Descriptive terms
96 or above	Very high; superior
85–95	High; excellent
75–85	Above average; good
25–75	About average; satisfactory or fair
15–25	Below average; fair or slightly weak
5–15	Low; weak
5 or below	Very low; very weak (p. 136)

The Family Educational Rights and Privacy Act

In Chapter 1 we discussed the Family Educational Rights and Privacy Act (also known as the Buckley amendment). The Buckley amendment allows families access to their records held at any educational agency that accepts federal money, including a public school. Family members have a right to all assessment information, and you should provide a copy of the report to the family members that they can take with them, as is their choice.

The Buckley amendment also protects students and families from the illicit sharing of assessment information. Before assessment information can be released to other agencies or individuals outside of the school system, the parent must sign a written consent form. The consent form specifies which records are to be released, to whom, and the reason for the release. A copy of the records to be released must be sent to the student's parents.

The Student

Students usually are anxious to know, "How did I do?" When students pose this question during the test, the examiner should offer a

Compuscore for the WJ-R
Wednesday, June 23, 19_ _
Norms Based On Age 12–7

Name: Amy Budd
ID:
Sex: f

Examiner: Albert
School/Agency:
Teacher/Department:
City: State:

Testing Date: 4/3/xx
Birth Date: 9/13/xx
Age: 12 years 7 months

Adult Subjects
  Education:
  Occupation:

Grade Placement: 6.0
Years Retained:
Years Skipped:
Years of Schooling: 6.0

Other Info:
Glasses?   Used during testing
Hearing Aid?   Used during testing

Test Name	Raw Score	W	Age Equiv.	Grade Equiv.	RMI		SS	PR
1. Memory for Names	44-C	490	6–7	1.1	71/90		83	13
			(E) 4–2	K.0[26]		–1 SEM	79	8
			(D) 11–0	5.1		+1 SEM	87	19
2. Memory for Sentences	45	498	9–6	4.6	79/90		93	32
			(E) 7–9	2.3		–1 SEM	87	19
			(D) 13–4	7.6		+1 SEM	99	47
3. Visual Matching	34	488	9–0	3.6	34/90		74	4
			(E) 8–1	2.6		–1 SEM	68	2
			(D) 10–1	4.7		+1 SEM	80	9
4. Incomplete Words	23	489	6–7	1.3	66/90		78	7
			(E) 5–6	K.3		–1 SEM	70	2
			(D) 9–11	4.6		+1 SEM	86	18
5. Visual Closure	31	494	9–0	3.4	75/90		86	17
			(E) 6–8	1.2		–1 SEM	77	6
			(D) 12–6	6.6		+1 SEM	95	37
6. Picture Vocabulary	31	494	9–0	3.5	55/90		83	13
			(E) 7–7	2.1		–1 SEM	78	7
			(D) 10–10	5.4		+1 SEM	88	21
7. Analysis-Synthesis	20-F	494	8–8	3.4	68/90		88	21
			(E) 7–3	2.0		–1 SEM	82	12
			(D) 11–5	6.1		+1 SEM	94	34
BROAD COGNITIVE ABILITY (E Dev)	---	493	8–5	2.9	71/90		79	8
			(E) 6–4	1.0		–1 SEM	75	5
			(D) 11–5	5.9		+1 SEM	83	13
BROAD COGNITIVE ABILITY (Std)	---	492	8–6	3.1	63/90		74	4
			(E) 6–11	1.5		–1 SEM	70	2
			(D) 10–10	5.5		+1 SEM	78	7

FIGURE 18.7

Sample Computer Printout from the WJ-R Test

Source: Copyright © 1995, by The Riverside Publishing Company. Reproduced from *Compuscore for the WJ-R (Macintosh version),* by Richard W. Woodcock and M. Bonner Johnson, with permission of the publisher.

neutral response. For example, "I can see that you are trying hard."

Once the assessment has been completed, you are often asked or expected to explain some of the general results, depending on the age of the student, the student's interest in the testing situation, and your knowledge of the student. In some instances, your explanation may need to be a delicate balance between not discouraging the student on the one hand and helping the older student accept certain limitations and appreciate what can be accomplished on the other. Thus, you might say, "You may have to study harder and longer than some boys and girls do to get good grades" (Lyman, 1986, p. 135).

COMPUTER-GENERATED REPORTS

Test publishers frequently offer test software that not only computes test scores but also generates reports. For most computer scoring programs, the examiner enters the identifying information and the raw scores. Raw scores are computed, and the results can be printed in a variety of formats (Figure 18.7).

TABLE 18.2   Considerations for Evaluating Test-Scoring and Report Software

1. Name of software:

2. System requirements:

3. Ease of use:

    Is program easily installed and user friendly?

    Is there a telephone hotline?

    Is the documentation easy to use?

4. Does the program allow information to be entered by a scanner?

5. Does the program allow cross-referencing:

    To student's IEP?

6. What test scores does the program yield?

    Standard scores   Stanines   Percentiles   Other

7. Does the program generate confidence intervals (with standard scores)?

8. Quality of the report:

    Does the report contain technical jargon?

    Does the report contain any generalizations that may bias the report?

Test-scoring software and computer-generated reports help to minimize scoring and computation errors and can be helpful in producing an individual test report. These programs should be carefully selected and used. Table 18.2 provides a software review checklist for evaluating test scoring and computer-generated reports.

Since most of these programs yield a report based on a single test, they do not integrate information from other sources, such as additional assessments, observations and interviews. Perhaps, more importantly, computer-generated reports do not provide the quality of interpretation that an experienced professional, using a variety of sources, can produce.

PREFERRED PRACTICES

Interpreting and writing assessment reports takes practice and a solid base of professional knowledge. Beginning teachers should have the opportunity to work with a mentor during the assessment process. A mentorship must include time to discuss interpretations of assessment information and to review and examine drafts of the assessment report.

Care needs to be taken when interpreting low scores. We know that students often live up—or down—to our expectations. The report that we share with family members and later file in the student's records can have an impact on how the family and teachers perceive the student in years to come.

The role of technology in assessment continues to evolve and will provide many exciting options in the future. We will need to keep abreast of these new developments and be prepared to learn new skills. The use of technology in interpreting and reporting assessment information may offer different promises tomorrow. Our challenge will be to use both our skills as professionals and our skills as thoughtful human beings to determine what is appropriate and what is not!

EXTENDING LEARNING

18.1 Working with others in a small group, prepare an explanation of the purposes of assessment reports. Exchange papers with another group and compare your work.

18.2 Discuss how the hypothesis generation approach can be useful in interpreting test performance.

18.3 Make plans to conduct a series of observations in a classroom. Working with a small group of students, identify the purpose of your observations and what you will be observing. You may want to refer to Chapter 5 for the steps in planning an observation. After you have completed the observations, write an observation report. Be sure to keep your original data collection forms. Share your report with others in your group. Could the information in your report be enhanced? How could your observation data be displayed graphically? Use your small group to discuss ways to represent the data.

18.4 Use the checklist for evaluating an assessment report to critique Larry Kahn's report on Gina. Can you make any suggestions for improvement?

18.5 Obtain a computer program related to testing. Using the criteria presented in this chapter, evaluate the usefulness of this program. What additional criteria would you add to our list?

(Answer to Cindy's math class observation data from page 484: The pie chart is the best way to display data in answer to the observation question because it allows the viewer to see how Cindy spends her time during the entire math class. If the observation question had been concerned with increasing or decreasing a behavior, then the bar graph would have been the best choice.)

REFERENCES

Bentzen, W. R. (1993). *A guide to observing and recording behavior.* 2d ed. Albany, N.Y.: Delmar.

Cohen, D. H., V. Stern, and N. Balaban (1983). *Observing and recording behavior of young children.* 3d ed. New York: Teachers College Press.

Kamphaus, R. W. (1993). *Clinical assessment of children's intelligence.* Boston: Allyn & Bacon.

Kaufman, A. (1979). *Intelligent testing with the WISC-R.* New York: Wiley.

Kaufman, A. (1994). *Intelligent testing with the WISC-III.* New York: Wiley.

Lyman, H. B. (1986). *Test scores and what they mean.* 4th ed. Englewood Cliffs, N.J.: Prentice Hall.

McGrew, K. S. (1986). *Clinical interpretation of the Woodcock-Johnson tests of cognitive ability.* Orlando, Fla: Grune & Stratton.

McGrew, K. S. (1994). *Clinical interpretation of the Woodcock-Johnson Tests of cognitive ability–Revised.* Boston: Allyn & Bacon.

Nicolson, S., and S. G. Shipstead (1994). *Through the looking glass.* New York: Merrill.

Sattler, J. (1990). *Assessment of children.* 3d ed. San Diego: Jerome M. Sattler.

Tufte, E. R. (1983). *The visual display of quantitative information.* Cheshire, Conn.: Graphics Press.

Implementing Program Evaluation

OVERVIEW

Program evaluation is a critical aspect of our work with students and their families. In this chapter we will explore the evaluation process at three different programmatic levels. First, we will examine ways of gathering, on an ongoing basis, information about the student. This, you will recall, is the monitoring step. We will need to evaluate and document advancement toward the goals and objectives developed in the IEP. As a result of monitoring a student's progress, we often decide to make changes in instruction and in the services. In a review of the literature, Gallagher and Desimone (1995) found that the process of monitoring IEPs is largely neglected. This is a disturbing finding, given the critical need to carefully review services as they are being provided and the lost opportunity to make necessary changes when they are identified during the monitoring process.

At another level, we will want to evaluate the student's overall program after a period of time. This level is the evaluation step in the assessment process and is conducted annually for students with IEPs. Does the student continue to need special education services?

Third, we should evaluate the services that our school or agency offers. We can gather information from several different sources for this kind of inquiry. Teachers can provide administrators with information regarding work conditions, equipment needs, or training priorities. Many programs that have a high staff turnover can gain valuable feedback through regular program evaluation. We will want to gather information from parents or other family members. Are they satisfied with their child's education program? Do they feel that the teachers are responsive to their questions and concerns? Are they involved in the process of making educational decisions? We can also aggregate information about the progress of groups of students in order to examine a program's success and benefits. If the program is funded by public monies, then an evaluation must be conducted periodically to demonstrate accountability for funds expended.

CHAPTER OBJECTIVES

After completing this chapter, you should be able to:

Define the term *evaluation* and describe a rationale for conducting evaluations.

Compare and contrast different models of evaluation.

Contrast the process of review and evaluation of the IFSP and an IEP.

Describe important areas to address in conducting program evaluation.

INTRODUCTION TO EVALUATION

Evaluation is a process that we all undertake frequently, especially as college and university students. We compare instructors, "Dr. Di-Matina is so much more interesting than Dr. Doyle." We rate the exams, "That exam was terrible—it didn't cover what I had studied." Or we measure classroom learning activities: "That small-group exercise in class really helped me understand the different group dynamics involved in teamwork."

In terms of an overall course evaluation, we could provide our instructor with several different types of information. We could provide feedback on lectures: Are they interesting? Are they delivered too quickly? Or on the classroom climate, both physical and social: Is it too cold? Is the seating comfortable? Is there a feeling of support and encouragement? Or on the assignments: Are there too many? Do they relate to the course objectives stated in the syllabus? The results of our evaluation will be helpful to our instructor. Perhaps some changes will be made before the next term!

There are many different ways of "evaluating." In fact, there are many different definitions of **evaluation.** We will use the definition developed by Smith and Glass (1987), which states that evaluation is the process of establishing a value judgment based on the collection of actual data.

In 1981, the Joint Committee on Standards for Education Evaluation, which represented major educational organizations, published a list of standards. According to the Joint Committee (1981), a good evaluation must satisfy four important criteria:

- Utility: An evaluation should be informative and useful as well as timely.
- Feasibility: An evaluation should be appropriate to the setting and cost effective.
- Propriety: The rights of individuals affected by the evaluation must be protected.
- Accuracy: The evaluation instrument should be valid and reliable.

The field of evaluation has its own terms for the individuals who are involved in the evaluation process. **Stakeholders** are individuals who are interested in the results of the evaluation. An evaluation of the effectiveness of the program at Wentworth School will have several different groups, or stakeholders, who are interested in the findings. The teachers, therapists, and other staff at the school will want to know the results of the evaluation as well as the parents and administrators. On the other hand, an evaluation of the cost-effectiveness of the same program may be of primary interest to the school board members and administrators.

The evaluation should be conducted by an individual with a background in research design, measurement, and evaluation. The person may be an **internal evaluator,** such as a teacher or administrator who is trained in these skills, or from the outside, an **external evaluator** who is hired specifically for the purpose of completing the evaluation. There are advantages as well as disadvantages in using an inside or outside evaluator. Which of the following aspects are considered to be an advantage in hiring an inside evaluator? an outside evaluator? (The answer is found at the end of the section on Extending Learning.)

- Nonbiased
- Knowledge of special education programs
- Time to complete evaluation
- Cost savings
- Knowledge of questions to ask
- Knowledge of effective strategies for evaluation

The evaluator is hired by the client who has requested the evaluation. The client may be one person, such as the administrator of the program, or the client may be a group of people, such as an advisory board, parent group, or state education department.

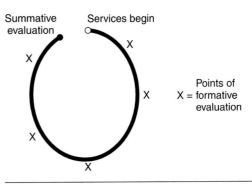

FIGURE 19.1

Evaluation as an Ongoing Process

Source: Cohen, Libby G., and Loraine J. Spenciner (1994). *Assessment of Young Children.* White Plains, N.Y.: Longman Publishers. Reprinted with permission.

WHEN DOES EVALUATION HAPPEN?

Formative Evaluation

An evaluation that is ongoing during the period of program implementation is called a **formative evaluation.** Formative evaluation is very useful to teachers and therapists who are providing direct services because, by examining the data, adjustments and changes can be made before the end of the program cycle. This process is seen in Figure 19.1.

In this example, practitioners conduct an evaluation to monitor the student's progress. If the data indicate a need to adjust the program substantially from what is described in the education program, an IEP team meeting must be called and parents must approve these changes.

Summative Evaluation

An evaluation that is completed at the end of the cycle is called a **summative evaluation.** Summative evaluations can be completed on

an individual student's program plan. For example, a summative evaluation is completed during the annual review of the IEP.

Summative evaluations can be conducted on entire programs too. Depending on the focus, these evaluations provide administrators with a variety of information, including accountability and cost-effective data, parent or staff satisfaction data, or program effectiveness data.

WHAT SHAPES OUR VIEWS

One of the most well known models for evaluating special education services was developed by Tyler (1950), one of the founders of educational evaluation. This model—called objectives-based evaluation—has long been used by teachers and administrators in special education in several different ways:

1. to evaluate a student's ongoing progress toward the objectives described in the IEP;
2. to evaluate the student's program at the end of a time period or unit of study; or
3. to evaluate the overall program of the school.

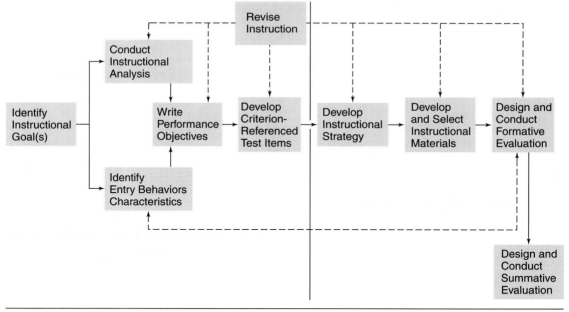

FIGURE 19.2

The Dick and Carey Systems Approach Model for Designing and Evaluating Instruction

Source: From *Systematic Design of Instruction,* Second Edition, by Walter Dick and Lou Carey. Copyright © 1985, 1978 by Scott, Foresman and Company. Reprinted by permission of HarperCollins Publisher.

The first step in conducting an *objectives-based evaluation* begins with identifying the set of objectives that will be measured. Next, the procedures or instruments to assess these objectives are identified or developed. Teachers and therapists who are monitoring IEP progress collect products of the student's work, use portfolios, make periodic videotapes of the student, administer tests, or develop their own instruments for measuring progress. Products and test data are then collected and analyzed to ascertain whether or not the objectives have been met. Tyler described this approach as a recurring sequence that should be conducted on a regular, ongoing basis.

Dick and Carey (1985) have described a similar model, which stresses the identification of student skills and the collection of data in order to revise instruction. This approach, like Tyler's, is an example of an objectives-oriented model. The various steps in using this *systems approach model* are seen in Figure 19.2.

PLANNING AN EVALUATION OF A SPECIFIC STUDENT'S PROGRAM

Teachers and other professionals who provide special education and related services must evaluate the education program periodically. The IDEA Amendments of 1997 state that the IEP and IFSP must be reevaluated at least once a year. In addition, families receiving services under an IFSP must be provided a *review* of the plan at least every six months, or more often if appropriate, based on child or family needs. This review is important because services that were originally identified during the team meeting may need to be altered or adjusted. (A note about terminology: We will be using the term *review* to address the process of examining the IEP and IFSP and the term *monitor* to address the ongoing process undertaken by teachers and therapists for evaluating a student's daily or weekly progress.)

Steps to Reviewing and Evaluating the IFSP for Young Children

Step 1: Identifying Outcomes

In Chapter 1 we discussed the fact that IFSPs are written with outcome statements, rather than goals, and in Chapter 2 we explained how outcome statements are developed during the early childhood team meeting. IFSP outcome statements are developed based on family concerns, resources, and priorities as they relate to the child's development or family life that is related to the developing child. The strategies and activities follow outcome statements and include the following:

Who will do what?

When will they do it?

How will we know if there is progress?

Step 2: Agreeing on Evaluation Criteria

The team will need to decide on the criteria for evaluating the outcome statements. How will we know if the outcome statement has been achieved? Not only should family members identify the outcomes of the intervention services, but they should define how the success of the outcome will be measured (Kramer, McGonigel, and Kaufman, 1991).

Step 3: Meeting Time Lines: IFSP Review and Evaluation

The team member who is acting as service coordinator is responsible for ensuring that the family is provided a review of the IFSP every six months. The purpose of the review is to determine the degree to which progress is being made toward achieving the outcomes and to decide whether modifications or revisions are necessary.

SNAPSHOT

The Nelson Early Childhood Team

The four members of the team are seated around the Nelson's living room floor. Jane Skinner, the early intervention specialist and family service coordinator, is taking notes as Joe Lewis, the speech therapist, summarizes the team members' observations. Margaret Nelson, Brian's mother, smiles as Doris Smith, the preschool teacher, describes Brian's creative use of gestures and sounds. Mrs. Nelson states that she would like to know what Brian is trying to tell her. From their

discussion the following outcome is defined:

Brian will increase his attempts in using language in order to make his needs known and to communicate with others.

As the outcomes for services are defined, Jane asks Ms. Nelson if she would be willing to assist in the review process by observing and noting Brian's attempts at communication. The team decides to review Brian's progress every three months.

The family service coordinator is also responsible for ensuring that the IFSP is evaluated at least once a year. The purpose of the reevaluation is to review the outcomes and current information, to revise outcomes, if necessary, and to write a new IFSP. How does all of this work? In the Snapshot on page 505 we can sit in on the last few minutes of a team that is planning early intervention services for 3-year-old Brian, a little boy with Down syndrome.

Steps to Monitoring and Evaluating the IEP

Step 1: Identifying Annual Goals and Evaluation Criteria

Measurable annual goals are written for each area in which the student will receive services. These goals need to be written to describe gains that could reasonably be achieved during the program year. How these goals will be evaluated should also be stated. Examples of an annual goal might be:

> Written language: By June, Raymond will demonstrate improvement in written language by his ability to write a three-paragraph story with 90 percent accuracy in grammar.

or

> Adaptive: Alexandra will eat lunch independently in the school cafeteria by the end of the program year.

Step 2: Identifying Short-term Objectives and Evaluation Criteria

Specific objectives, or benchmarks, are written to help the student meet the annual goal. These statements must be written so that a teacher can readily identify whether or not the objectives are being met. Objectives that are written in this manner are called *behavioral objectives* because they describe a student's behavior and are not left to a chance interpretation.

Objectives include the criteria as to how an observer will decide whether the objective has been achieved, the evaluation procedures, and when the objective will be reviewed. Thus, objectives have the following components:

1. the behavior is described in terms that can be observed;
2. the criteria for successful performance is stated;
3. the method of evaluating the behavior is described;
4. the time period for review is indicated.

There are many different styles used in writing objectives. The following examples illustrate two different styles of writing objectives with criteria for evaluation.

> Given ten computational problems in mathematics (sums to 10) and a set of manipulatives (e.g., blocks or sticks), Robin will calculate the correct answer with 100 percent accuracy as measured by teacher observation. To be reviewed: June 19xx

> By June, Robin will compute correctly ten mathematical problems (sums to 10) using a calculator as measured by the *BRIGANCE® Comprehensive Inventory of Basic Skills.*

Step 3: Monitoring Progress

A student's progress should be monitored on an ongoing basis. Teachers and therapists will want to review objectives each marking period, or sooner, in order to monitor progress. Some of the questions that might be asked include: Is the student making progress toward this objective? Is this objective still appropriate, or have conditions changed? This provides an opportunity to make adjustments, if necessary. Best practice dictates that parents be provided with a copy of the review.

Graphing is an excellent way of monitoring progress, and there are many different types

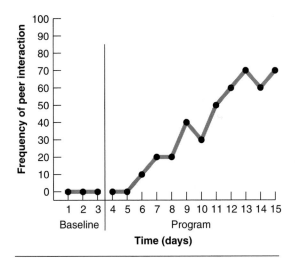

FIGURE 19.3

Charting a Student's Progress

Source: From *A Practical Guide to Solving Preschool Behavior Problems* by Eva L. Essa, Ph.D. Delmar Publishers Inc., Albany, NY; copyright 1990.

and formats. An easy method of monitoring progress is described by Essa (1995).

Figure 19.3 is used to record a student's frequency of interaction with peers before the beginning of the intervention (baseline) and during implementation of the program. Graphs similar to this one allow continuous monitoring of the student's progress and present a profile of progress over a time. Figure 19.3 represents progress over a two-week span. One of the disadvantages to graphing is that the adult must find time to record the information.

Students may take responsibility for graphing their progress. In fact, students can increase their independence by being able to record their own behavior through self-monitoring. Even preschool children with disabilities have been shown to increase appropriate behaviors through self-monitoring (Sainato, Strain, Lefebvre, and Rapp, 1990). McGinnis and Goldstein (1984) describe a method for helping elementary children and older adoles-

cents with behavior problems in which students use a self-scoring report sheet after each activity. Figure 19.4 illustrates a self report.

Self-monitoring techniques help students with disabilities to increase opportunities for success in regular classroom settings. Dunlap, Dunlap, Koegel, and Koegel (1991) describe several examples of using self-monitoring for increasing on-task time, increasing responsivity to questions for a child with autism, and increasing accuracy on subtraction problems.

Step 4: Evaluation

The Individuals with Disabilities Act amendments of 1997 state that the IEP team must review existing evaluation data. On the basis of the review and input from the student's parents, the team identifies what additional data is needed. During this reevaluation, the team will consider whether the student continues to need services, the present level of performance and educational needs of the student, whether changes are needed in the type of services, or whether the amount of service time should be changed.

RESPONDING TO DIVERSITY

Evaluations designed to include family members have to be responsive to family diversity. To encourage family participation, you will need to consider the following questions: What family members should be contacted? What are the preferences for communication? Should I send written materials? If so, are there alternative formats (such as braille) or translations that will be necessary? Evaluation procedures and the evaluation questions should be designed so that the family members will be encouraged to contribute information. The Snapshot on page 509 illustrates a case in point.

Student: _Michelle_   Date: _Sept. 30_

Skill: _Staying out of fights_

Steps:

1. Stop and count to 10.
2. Decide what the problem is.
3. Think of other ways to deal with the problem.
   a. walk away for now.
   b. talk to the person in a friendly way.
   c. ask someone for help.
4. Act out your best choice.

When I Practiced   How did I do?

on the bus

morning recess

music

after school

FIGURE 19.4

A Self Report: Staying Out of Fights

Source: From *Skillstreaming the Elementary School Child: A Guide for Teaching Prosocial Skills* (p. 93) by E. McGinnis and A. P. Goldstein, 1984, Champaign, Ill.: Research Press. Copyright 1984 by the authors. Adapted by permission.

PLANNING AN EVALUATION OF A PROGRAM

Identifying the Focus

An evaluation of an overall program, such as special education transition services provided to students in high school or a specialized reading program for students with disabilities, generates much useful information to advisory boards, administrators, staff, and parents. Borg and Gall (1983) identified four general categories that may be the focus in a program evaluation. These include:

1. Program goals: What are the goals of the program? Does the program achieve the goals through the various services and activities? "A goal is the purpose, effect, or end-point that the program is attempting

SNAPSHOT

Reaching Out to Family Members

Iliana Hernandez (1996) talks about her work with parents.

"I don't look Hispanic, but I am 100 percent born in Cuba, of Spanish descent. . . . I helped found Parent to Parent of Miami. My first attempt inviting parents to a Spanish-speaking meeting was a translated flyer. Guess what happened? Nobody showed up. That's when I said, 'Well, if I want to start helping my people, I have to know my people. . . . We needed more than language. We needed cultural understanding.'

For instance, something I realized is the impact of the grandmother. There is nothing more powerful in a Hispanic family than the grandmothers. That old lady is the one who sets the rules of the house.

Another thing that works well with Hispanic families is one-to-one support. We work more effectively on a personal basis. We hate papers. Parents tell me, 'I don't want to read it. I want you to tell me what you have for me . . . .'" (p. 6)

to achieve" (Borg and Gall, 1983, p. 743). Some programs may have goals that are very specific; other programs may have more general goals. However, goals are critical to the worth of the program.

2. Program resources: What are the program resources? Are they sufficient to meet the program goal(s)? Program resources may include a variety of areas, such as personnel, volunteers, transportation, materials, equipment, and space.
3. Program procedures: What are the procedures used to achieve the program goal(s)? Procedures may include teaching techniques and strategies or arrangements of the environment.
4. Program management: How are resources and procedure monitored? Is the management as efficient as it can be?

The focus of the evaluation is usually determined by the program director, administrator, or through discussion in a staff meeting, although common concerns could be voiced by an advisory board or staff members. These individuals in consultation with the evaluator will determine the evaluation procedures. For ex-

ample, a special education director is interested in evaluating the efficiency and cost effectiveness of special education services in the school district. However, more often than not, several different areas of concern or global questions regarding the program may have been raised.

Developing a Needs Assessment Questionnaire

Sometimes administrators need assistance in specifying an area for evaluation. An informal survey or needs assessment questionnaire is an excellent way of identifying the area(s) of greatest need. There are several considerations in developing a questionnaire.

- Questionnaires should be fairly short and questions simply stated.
- Items that can be checked are easy to complete.
- Including some open-ended questions allows individuals to respond to areas that may have been overlooked.
- Questionnaires that are brief and easy to complete are much more likely to be filled in and returned. Remember, a key issue in

SNAPSHOT

An Informal Method for Identifying Needs at the Waverly School District

The faculty at the Waverly School District used the following steps to identify and prioritize their needs. Laurel Fuller, special education director, solicited input from teachers and teaching assistants at a district-wide meeting by distributing sheets of paper and asking the educators to identify four areas that they felt needed attention and to number them in order of priority.

The papers were collected and priorities were assigned points from 4 to 1. (The highest number was assigned to the first priority listed.) The total number of points was then calculated for each of the items listed and the top-priority item was identified. Through this informal needs assessment, Dr. Fuller was able to utilize information solicited from each member of the staff.

evaluation is obtaining as many responses as possible from all the relevant parties.

The design and development of questionnaires is beyond the scope of this book. The interested reader is encouraged to refer to resources specific to the development of questionnaires and surveys.

In the Snapshot above, a needs assessment was conducted to determine a schedule of in-service training. The special education director wanted to identify the content areas that would be most beneficial to the teachers. This needs assessment was designed to solicit input from all the teachers and to prioritize training needs.

Identifying the Informants

There are a number of individuals, or informants, who may provide information, including students, parents and other family members, teachers and support staff, administrators, and community members. The questions to be answered by the program evaluation must be considered in deciding whom to include in completing the evaluation. Generally

speaking, program evaluations should include information from the consumers of services.

Collecting Information

Evaluation data may be collected in a variety of ways depending on the evaluation model adopted. Both quantitative data as well as qualitative data can be assembled.

Quantitative Data

Quantitative data are information that can be assigned a number or score. Program evaluations often include pretest and posttest scores. Data collection includes the use of surveys or questionnaires on which individuals rate different statements. Surveys and rating scales can be completed by family members as well as teachers and students. The rating forms the basis of quantitative data. Quantitative data is used to provide statistical information and analyses.

Qualitative Data

Qualitative data are descriptive rather than numeric. Information is gathered through interviews, discussions, observations, written answers, or students' work. Products that students have produced from work and play activities, video- and audiotape recordings are all examples of qualitative data. Products of the program such as newsletters or monthly calendars of activities are good sources. Anecdotal and running records as well as specimen records are other excellent sources. Although qualitative data are more difficult to synthesize, this type of data often provides helpful and, sometimes, unexpected findings.

Focus Groups

Focus groups also provide an informal way of collecting information. Focus groups can be small gatherings of individuals from similar constituencies or from different backgrounds, and the group may respond to specific questions or simply offer informal feedback to the group facilitator regarding the program.

A parent focus group can involve several family units; individual members may include mothers, fathers, grandparents, aunts, and other important individuals. Some groups include a deliberate mix of family members to encourage dialogue. Usually, focus groups are preferred by families because of their informal nature. Through group interaction, preferences and satisfaction with programs and services are determined.

Teacher-Developed Program Evaluation Instruments

Teachers and administrators often develop their own forms, tailored to meet the needs of the evaluation. Figure 19.5 illustrates a teacher-developed form that focused on the school's IEP team process. This form was developed as the result of a schoolwide effort to increase home-school partnerships. During the schoolwide meeting of all teachers, the special education staff decided to look at the IEP process. Some of the questions that they wanted to answer included: Do parents feel welcome at the IEP team meetings? Do parents feel that we

Question	Please circle the appropriate number: 1 = always, 2 = usually, 3 = sometimes, 4 = rarely.				Additional comments
1. Were you given adequate notice of the team meeting?	1	2	3	4	
2. Did you feel welcome at the team meeting?	1	2	3	4	
3. Did you feel that other team members were interested in your comments during the meeting?	1	2	3	4	
4. Did you feel that your questions or concerns were addressed adequately during the meeting?	1	2	3	4	
5. Did you feel satisfied with the outcome of the team meeting?	1	2	3	4	

FIGURE 19.5

A Teacher-Developed Form: Parent Satisfaction with the IEP Team Process

value their contributions? Are there areas that we could improve?

Standardized Instruments

Several evaluation instruments have been developed for programs that serve young children. The *Parent Satisfaction Survey* (as cited in McGonigel, Kaufman, & Johnson, 1991) and the *Family-Focused Intervention Scale* (Mahoney, O'Sullivan, and Dennebaum, 1990) solicit information from family members regarding their satisfaction with their children's early education programs and intervention services. The *Family-Centered Program Rating Scale* (Murphy and Lee, 1991) provides an opportunity for program evaluation by both family members as well as service providers in order to assist the program to become more family-centered.

Comprehensive Assessment of School Environments

The *Comprehensive Assessment of School Environments (CASE)* (Halderson, Kelley, Keefe, Berge, Glover, Sorenson, Speth, Schmitt, and Loher, 1989) is a comprehensive instrument designed for use in junior and senior high schools. The *CASE* is comprised of four surveys: Parent Satisfaction Survey, Teacher Satisfaction Survey, Student Satisfaction Survey, and School Climate Survey, which alone is administered to parents, teachers, and students alike.

Parents are asked to complete both the School Climate Survey and the Parent Satisfaction Survey, which consists of the following areas: parent involvement, curriculum, student activities, teachers, support services, school building/supplies/maintenance, student discipline, school administrators, and school information services. Further evidence of reliability and validity is needed before this instrument can be used with confidence.

Effective School Battery

The *Effective School Battery (ESB)* (Gottfredson, 1991) is a survey designed for use in Grades 7–12. According to the publisher, the survey may be used to identify areas of excellence as well as problem areas. The *ESB* can be utilized to promote effective planning and program development and to monitor progress.

The instrument consists of teacher and student survey booklets. Teachers and students provide information about their perceptions, behavior, and attitudes related to school safety, staff morale, administrative leadership, fairness and clarity of school rules, respect for students, classroom orderliness, academic climate, school rewards, and so on.

The normative data consisted of over 14,000 students from urban high schools where a high majority of the students were African American (44%). Other sample students were Spanish American (29%), Asian American (1%), Native American (2%), and White (22%).

Teachers considering the use of this instrument must carefully study the manual regarding the demographics of the schools that were involved in the development of this instru-

---

BOX 19.1

FAMILY-CENTERED PROGRAM RATING SCALE

Publication Date: 1991

Purposes: Evaluates an early childhood education program in terms of the program, the staff, and the families

Age/Grade Levels: Programs serving young children and families

Time to Administer: Approximately 15 minutes

Technical Adequacy: Adequate reliability and validity

Suggested Use: Assesses the degree of family-focused practices in an early childhood program. This scale is available in both English and Spanish.

ment. Original samples (from 1981–1983) consisted of 52–61 schools in St. Paul, Minnesota, Chicago, Baltimore, East Harlem in New York City, and areas of Wisconsin. According to the manual, the samples differ from year to year and the data from some schools were not available in time to be used in the analyses. The instrument should be updated and additional studies need to be completed using a more comprehensive sample.

Costs Involved

The final step in planning an evaluation is examining the costs involved. Typical cost items are consultant fees, including mileage, lodging, and meals; telephone; postage; computer time, including graphics production and supplies; copying, and so on.

Of course, costs do not only have to do with money. Other cost considerations include: How much time is involved? How much staff time will be allocated? Will additional costs of staffing substitutes be incurred? What are the potential "costs" in terms of psycho-social is-

sues to the staff? to the students? to the parents and other family members?

ISSUES IN DESIGNING AND CONDUCTING EVALUATIONS

In planning locally developed program evaluations, teachers and administrators must carefully consider the best methods for collecting evaluation information. In the preceding example (Figure 19.5) the teachers and administrators were interested in gathering information about parents' feelings regarding the team process. Notice that items in the questionnaire are worded so as to gather information from the individual's perception.

In another school the special education administrator and teachers needed to know if the transition program at the high school was successful. The evaluation plan was to examine student test scores and to survey parents and students. Several school faculty members volunteered to work with the administrator in developing a draft student questionnaire (Figure 19.6).

After reading the draft, one of the teachers made the observation that there is only one question in this survey worded appropriately to gather information from the students' perspective. Which question is this? Instead of a survey, what ways can be used to gather information regarding some of the other questions? Would these ways be advantageous? Why?

BOX 19.2

EFFECTIVE SCHOOL BATTERY

Publication Date: 1991

Purposes: Assesses teacher and student perceptions, behavior, and attitudes related to the school environment

Age/Grade Levels: 7 through 12

Time to Administer: Approximately 20 minutes

Technical Adequacy: This battery is best used as a guide since its technical adequacy is weak.

Suggested Use: Evaluates a school's strengths and areas of weakness. May be used to monitor improvement.

PARTICIPATING IN AN EVALUATION OF YOUR PROGRAM BY OTHERS

The IDEA Amendments of 1997 provide for the regular evaluation of local educational agencies, such as public schools, that serve students with disabilities. In fact, each state department of education in the US must submit a plan to

Section I. (Organization)

1. I write down the due date of my assignments.

_____always _____usually _____sometimes _____never

2. I use the Study Skills Outline to plan my week.

_____always _____usually _____sometimes _____never

3. I remember to bring home the materials needed to finish my homework.

_____always _____usually _____sometimes _____never

Section II. (Survival Skills)

4. I can locate information in an appliance manual (for example a manual for a VCR).

_____always _____usually _____sometimes _____never

5. I can use my calculator to compute the correct amount of money at the shopping center.

_____always _____usually _____sometimes _____never

6. I can use a computer to search for information.

_____always _____usually _____sometimes _____never

Section III. (School/Work)

7. I feel that this job allows me to practice my skills.

_____always _____usually _____sometimes _____never

FIGURE 19.6

A Poorly Designed Evaluation?

Washington that includes, in part, a description of their plan for evaluation. This plan must assess the effectiveness of a sample of programs in the state that are serving individuals with disabilities. The state evaluation must also address the effectiveness of the IEPs for individual students as well as the overall effectiveness of their program. The Snapshot on page 515 illustrates one way staff in a state department of education can choose to conduct their evaluation.

PREFERRED PRACTICES

Program evaluation must be a routine aspect of all programs. Evaluations are addressed at different levels: from the student's (and family's) perspective and from the perspective of the overall program. The most useful program evaluations include data from a variety of sources and it is both quantitative and qualitative data. When conducting analyses of quantitative data, caution is always used in interpreting scores that reflect change.

As funding continues to be an issue in the types of services that are offered, programs will be under more and more pressure to demonstrate effectiveness and accountability. Implementing program evaluation is an important component in the assessment process and should not be left to chance or excess funding at the end of a program cycle! As our field continues to grow and develop, we will need to continue the search for adequate methods and approaches with which to measure our work with students and their families.

SNAPSHOT

Evaluating Special Education Services at Sandy Brook Public School

Three months ago the Director of Special Education Services, Josh Liebermann, at Sandy Brook Public School received a form letter from the State Department of Education. The letter described the federal requirement that each local education agency that receives federal monies for the education of students with disabilities must be evaluated periodically by members of the State Education Department Program Review Team. Josh scanned the names of the individuals who were on the Department of Education team. There were four people who would be arriving: two consultants from the state education department, a special education director from a nearby school district, and an administrator from a school district in the southern part of the state. The letter described a tentative schedule for the visit and the items that the team would like to review.

The letter contained a clear description of what the team would need. They wanted to review several different IEPs, and they wanted to talk with several of the parents as well as teachers in the building. Later, the team would send a report summarizing their findings and recommendations for improvement, if necessary.

EXTENDING LEARNING

19.1 Describe the different levels of program evaluation.

19.2 What are the federal requirements for evaluating the IFSP? the IEP?

19.3 Research other models of evaluation. For example, you might look at consumer-oriented or naturalistic models.

19.4 Make an appointment to talk to the special education administrator at your local school. How are special services evaluated?

19.5 You are interviewing for a job as special education teacher at the Riley School. The assistant principal asks you, "How would you monitor and evaluate progress of students in your program?" Prepare a response to the question.

(Answer to question on p. 503: Which of the following aspects are considered to be an advantage in hiring an outside evaluator? an inside evaluator?

Advantages to hiring an outside evaluator are that the person is nonbiased, knows the type of evaluation questions to ask, and has the time to complete the evaluation. On the other hand, the cost of using someone "in house," an inside evaluator, will be less; and there is an assurance that the individual has a knowledge of special education programs.)

REFERENCES

Borg, W. R., and M. D. Gall (1983). *Educational research an introduction.* New York: Longman.

Cohen, L. G., and L. J. Spenciner (1994). *Assessment of Young Children.* White Plains, NY: Longman.

Dick, W., and L. Carey (1985). *The systematic design of instruction.* Glenview, Ill.: Scott Foresman.

Dunlap, L. K., G. Dunlap, L. K. Koegel, and R. L. Koegel (1991). Using self-monitoring to increase independence. *Teaching Exceptional Children* 23(3): 17–22.

Essa, E. (1995). *A practical guide to solving preschool behavior problems.* 3d ed. Albany, N.Y.: Delmar Publishers.

Federal Register 57 (189): 44794–44852. Washington, D.C.: U.S. Government Printing Office, September 19, 1992.

Gallagher, J., and L. Desimone (1995). Lessons learned from implementation of the IEP: Applications to the IFSP. *Topics in Early Childhood Special Education* 15(30): 353–378.

Gottfredson, G. D. (1991). *Effective school battery.* Odessa, Fla.: Psychological Assessment Resources.

Halderson, C., E .A. Kelley, J. W. Keefe, P. S. Berge, J. A. Glover, C. Sorenson, C. Speth, N. Schmitt, and B. Loher (1989). *Comprehensive assessment of school environments.* National Association of Secondary School Principals.

Hernandez, I. (1996). Reaching underserved populations. *Families and Disabilities Newsletter* 7(1): 6.

Joint Committee on Standards for Educational Evaluation (1981). *Standards for evaluation of educational programs, projects, and materials.* New York: McGraw-Hill.

Kramer, S., M. J. McGonigel, and R. K. Kaufman, (1991). Developing the IFSP: Outcomes, strate-gies, activities, and services. In *Guidelines and recommended practices for the individualized family service plan,* eds. M. J. McGonigel, R. K. Kaufman, and B. H. Johnson, 57–66. Bethesda, Md.: Association for the Care of Children's Health.

Mahoney, G., P. O'Sullivan, and J. Dennebaum (1990). Maternal perceptions of early intervention services: A scale for assessing family-focused intervention. *Topics in Early Childhood Special Education* 10(1): 1–15.

McGinnis, E., and A. P. Goldstein (1984). *Skillstreaming the elementary school child.* Champaign, Ill.: Research Press.

McGonigel, M. J., Kaufmann, R. K., and Johnson, B. H. eds. (1991). *Guidelines and recommended practices for the individualized family service plan.* Bethesda, Md.: Association for the Care of Children's Health.

Murphy, D. L., and I. M. Lee (1991). *Family-centered program rating scale.* Lawrence Beach Center on Families and Disability, University of Kansas.

Sainato, D. M., Strain, P. S., Lefebvre, D., and Rapp, N. (1990). Effects of self-evaluation on the independent work skills of preschool children with disabilities. *Exceptional Children* 56(4): 540–549.

Smith, M. L., and G. V. Glass (1987). *Research and evaluation in education and the social sciences.* Englewood Cliffs, N.J.: Prentice Hall.

Tyler, R. W. (1950). *Basic principles of curriculum and instruction.* Chicago: University of Chicago Press.

Glossary

achievement testing The assessment of past learning.

adaptive behavior Refers to "the quality of everyday performance in coping with environmental demands" (Grossman, 1983, p. 42).

adaptive development The young child's self-help skills, such as dressing, toileting, and grooming.

adaptive skills An individual's general competence in coping with the everyday demands of the environment. These skills include communication, self-care, home living, social skills, community use, self-direction, health and safety, functional academics, leisure, and work (American Association on Mental Retardation, 1992).

alternate form reliability An estimate of the correlation of scores between two forms of the same test.

analytic scoring A type of scoring in which an independent score is reported for each area of the scoring rubric. This type of scoring provides diagnostic information. Individual scores indicate areas of strengths and areas that need improvement.

anchor papers Student papers that represent writing at different levels of performance.

anecdotal record A brief narrative description of an event or events that the observer felt was important to record.

assessment An evaluation process that includes observing, collecting, recording, and interpreting information to answer questions and make legal and instructional decisions about students.

assistance team A school-based team that consists of both regular and special education teachers who work together to solve problems and to offer suggestions to other teachers before the student is referred to the IEP team. This team may be known by other terms, such as **student assistance team, teacher assistance team,** or **intervention assistance team.**

augmentative/alternative communication (AAC) A method or device used by a person with a communication disability in order to communicate.

authentic assessment The student completes or demonstrates knowledge, skills, or behavior in a real-life context; real-world standards are used to measure the student's knowledge, skills, or behavior.

basal level The point below which the examiner assumes that the student could obtain all correct responses and at which the examiner begins testing.

benchmarks Examples of student work that illustrate each scoring level on the assessment scale.

category recording A system of recording behavior by discrete groupings.

ceiling level The point above which the examiner assumes that the student would obtain all incorrect responses if the testing were to continue and the point at which the examiner stops testing.

checklist A list of characteristics or behaviors arranged in a consistent manner that allows the evaluator to record the presence or absence of individual characteristics, events, or behaviors.

Child Find A series of activities that increase public awareness and provide information about screening, programs, and early intervention or special education services. These services and activities help in locating children with special needs.

collaborating A cooperative process conducted by two or more individuals for the purpose of working together to address common interests and issues.

concurrent validity The extent to which two different tests administered at about the same time correlate with each other.

conferencing A process conducted by two or more individuals for the purpose of sharing information, concerns, and ideas regarding common issues.

confidence interval The range within which the true score can be found; frequently called the band of error or confidence level.

consequential validity The extent to which an assessment instrument promotes the intended consequences.

construct validity The extent to which a test measures a particular construct or concept.

content validity The extent to which the test items reflect the content it is designed to cover.

correlation The extent to which two or more scores vary together.

correlation coefficient A statistical technique for determining the direction and strength of the relationship between scores or among groups of scores.

criterion-referenced test (CRT) A test that measures a student's test performance with respect to a well-defined content domain.

criterion-related validity The extent that test scores obtained on one test or another measure are related to scores obtained on another test or another outcome.

curriculum-based assessment (CBA) A broad approach to linking instruction with assessment.

curriculum-based measurement (CBM) A type of curriculum-based assessment that emphasizes repeated, direct measurement of student performance.

curriculum-based vocational assessment (CBVA) A type of curriculum-based assessment used in planning and developing vocational educational opportunities for students with disabilities.

derived scores The result of transforming raw scores to other types of scores.

descriptors Written descriptions included in a rubric that explain each of the levels of achievement.

determining eligibility A process used to determine if a student meets the eligibility criteria for services according to federal and state definitions. Determining eligibility represents step 3 of the assessment process.

developmental delay A term used to identify infants and toddlers so that they can receive early intervention services without being labeled for a specific disability. The Individuals with Disabilities Act Amendments of 1997 state that at the discretion of an individual state, the term *developmental delay* may be used with children ages 3 through 9 so that young children can receive special education services without being labeled for a specific disability category.

developmental scores Raw scores that have been transformed to reflect the average performance at age and grade levels.

developmental quotient An estimate of the rate of development.

deviation IQ scores A standard score with a mean of 100 and a standard deviation of 15 or 16.

domain A specific range of test items.

direct observation The systematic process of gathering information by looking at students and their environments.

due process A set of safeguards to be followed during the assessment process and the delivery of services described in the Individuals with Disabilities Education Act (IDEA) Amendments of 1997. Due process ensures that the rights of families and their children are not violated.

duration recording A method of recording that measures the length of time a specific event or behavior persists.

early childhood team A team that consists of the parents, the family service coordinator, and representatives of various disciplines who assess and implement early intervention services. The team makes decisions regarding eligibility and services for children birth through age 2 and, in some states, for children ages 3 to 5.

error analysis A technique that identifies patterns of errors in students' work.

evaluating the program A process used to assess (1) the progress the student has made in the individualized education program and (2) the overall quality of the school program. Evaluating the program represents step 6 in the assessment process.

event recording The recording of a behavior each time it occurs during an observation period.

expansion A restatement of the student's verbal language that adds words or more complex phrases.

expressive language The ability to use language to communicate information, thoughts, feelings, and ideas.

exhibition A display of a student's work that demonstrates knowledge abilities, skills, and attitudes.

externalizing behaviors A broad array of behaviors directed outward that include disruptive and antisocial behaviors.

extrapolation The process used when estimates of the performance of students outside the normative sample are made.

face validity The extent to which a test looks valid.

false negative The type of error that is made when a student is not referred by the screening but should have been.

false positive The type of error that is made when a student is referred by the screening but should not have been.

family A unit of two or more individuals who may or may not be related but who have extended commitments to each other.

family-directed assessment A type of assessment that focuses on information family members choose to share with other team members regarding family resources, priorities, and concerns. Family-directed assessment relates to children ages birth through 2 and, in some states, to children ages 3 to 5.

Family Educational Rights and Privacy Act (FERPA) The Family Rights and Privacy Act (P. L. 93–380), which was passed by Congress in 1974, gives the family the right to review all records kept on their child as well as the right to challenge any of the information within the records.

family-focused philosophy This approach to working with families emphasizes the importance of enabling family members to mobilize their own resources in order to promote child and family functioning.

frequency distribution A way of organizing test scores based on how often they occur.

grapheme The written equivalent of a phoneme.

graphophonics Knowledge of letters and their associated sounds.

holistic scoring A type of scoring in which the teacher assigns a single score based on a scoring rubric. This type of scoring lacks the depth of information found in analytic scoring; however, it may be easier to design and conduct than analytic scoring.

Individuals with Disabilities Education Act (IDEA) Amendments of 1997 A federal law that focuses on the education of children and youth with disabilities; it specifies special education services under two parts: Part B describes special education services for children and youth ages 3 through 21; Part C describes early intervention services for infants and toddlers, birth through age two. Part B and Part C of the IDEA Amendments of 1997 mandate specific requirements relating to the assessment process that teachers and test examiners must know and understand.

individualized education program (IEP) The IDEA Amendments of 1997 mandate that all students with disabilities ages 3 through 21 have an individualized education program (IEP). This written plan specifies the special education and related services that must be provided.

individualized family service plan (IFSP) The IDEA Amendments of 1997 mandate that all young children (birth through 2 years) and their families have an individualized family service plan (IFSP). Children ages 3 to 5 may receive services provided by an IFSP or an IEP. The IFSP is a written document that specifies the plan for services and is guided by the family's concerns, priorities, and resources.

individualized transition plan (ITP) A plan that describes the transition service and needs of the student and responsibilities for the school and participating agencies in the transition of the student from school to post-school activities including education, training, employment, and independent living. This plan is written for students beginning at age 14.

IEP team A multidisciplinary team consisting of the parents, school personnel, and, when possible, the student, that has the responsibility to make decisions regarding assessment procedures as defined by IDEA. This team may be known as the **special services team** or other term as defined by state regulation.

informal testing A broad category of assessment approaches that do *not* include standardized tests.

informant An individual who knows the student well and who can provide information about that student.

inner language The language used during thinking, planning, and other mental processes.

intensity recording A measure of the strength of a behavior.

internal consistency reliability An estimate of the homogeneity or interrelatedness of responses to test items.

internalizing behaviors Behaviors that are inner-directed and include social withdrawal, anxious or inhibited behaviors, or somatic problems.

interpolation The process used when scores are estimated within the ages and grades that were tested.

interscorer/interrater/interobserver reliability An estimate of the extent to which two or more scorers, observers, or raters agree on how a test should be scored or behaviors should be observed.

interval recording A recording of specific events or behaviors during a prespecified time interval.

interval scale A scale in which the items are the same distance apart; the scale does not have an absolute zero.

intervention assistance team *See* **assistance team.**

language disorder A difficulty or inability in decoding or encoding the set of symbols used in language or an inability to effectively use inner language. *See also* **speech disorder.**

language probe A diagnostic technique in which instruction is modified to elicit specific information about a student's receptive or expressive language.

language sample A recording of a student's oral language that yields information regarding vocabulary, syntax, semantics, and articulation.

latency recording A measure of the amount of time elapsed between a behavior or event (or request to begin the behavior) and the beginning of the prespecified behavior.

maladaptive behaviors Behaviors that include antisocial behaviors, aggression, withdrawal behavior, delayed social skills, and difficulties with interpersonal relationships.

mean The average score.

median The point on a scale above which and below which 50 percent of the cases occur. A point or score that separates the top 50 percent of students who took the test from the bottom 50 percent of students.

miscues Patterns of errors. According to Goodman (1984, 1989) these are "natural" errors rather than mistakes.

mode The score that occurs most often in a group of scores. The mode is the most commonly occurring test score.

monitoring individual progress A process used to determine if the student is making progress by examining the student's work, accomplishments, and achievements. Monitoring individual progress represents step 5 of the assessment process.

morpheme The single unit of letters that comprise a unit of meaning. A morpheme may be a whole word, prefix, or a suffix.

morphology The study of the single units of letters that represent a unit of meaning.

multidisciplinary team Professionals from two or more disciplines or professions who are involved in the provision of integrated and coordinated services including assessment activities.

nominal scale The items on the scale represent names; the values assigned to the names do not have any innate meaning or value.

normal curve A symmetrical bell-shaped curve.

normal curve equivalent (NCE)   A standard score with a mean of 50 and a standard deviation of 21.06.

norm-referenced test   A test that compares a student's test performance with that of similar students who have taken the same test.

norms   The scores obtained by the standardization sample; the scores to which students are compared when they are administered a test.

obtained score   The score that an individual receives on a test.

ordinal scale   The items on the scale are listed in rank order.

outcome-oriented process   A process in which the focus is on the attainment of prespecified performance objectives.

percentage score   The percent of test items that were answered correctly.

percentile rank   The point in a distribution at or below which the scores of a given percentage of students fall.

performance-based assessment   The demonstration of knowledge, skills, or behavior.

phoneme   The smallest unit of sound that has meaning in a language.

phonology   The study of speech sounds.

population   The large group from which the sample of individuals is selected and to which individual comparisons are made regarding test performance.

portfolio   A systematic collection of a student's work, assembled over a period of time, that demonstrates the student's efforts, progress, and achievement.

pragmatics   The study of the use of language in social situations.

predictive validity   The extent to which one measure predicts later performance or behavior.

prereferral   A process in which questions and concerns about a student are raised and discussed. Prereferral procedures are not required by law and not all schools have a prereferral process.

probe   A diagnostic technique in which instruction is modified in order to determine whether an instructional strategy is effective.

program evaluation   A process used to assess (1) the progress the student has made in the individualized education program and (2) the overall quality of the school program. Evaluating the program represents step 6 in the assessment process.

program planning   The process of determining the student's current level of functioning and planning the instructional program. Program planning is step 4 of the assessment process.

questionnaire   A set of questions designed to gather information.

ratio scale   The items on the scale are the same distance apart; the scale does have an absolute zero.

raw scores   The number of items correct without adjustment for guessing.

referral   A process in which questions and concerns about a student are raised and referred to the IEP team. The referral may come from a teacher, parent, or the student. Referral represents step 2 of the assessment process.

reliability   Indicates the consistency or stability of test performance.

receptive language   The ability to understand spoken language.

running record   A description of the events that is written as the events occur.

sample   A subgroup of a large group that is representative of the large group. This subgroup is the group that is actually tested.

schema   An "interlocking knowledge network" (Rhodes and Shanklin, 1993, p. 151).

screening   A process used to identify students who may have a disability and who will be referred for further assessment. Screening is step 1 of the assessment process.

semantics   The study of word meanings.

shaping   A term that refers to reinforcing successive approximations of the target or goal behavior. In reference to the development of language, the verbal response is reinforced as the sound or word being produced more and more closely approximates the sound or word in the language.

skewed distribution   A curve in which most of the scores are at the low end or the high end of the curve.

special services team   *See* **IEP team.**

speech   The production of oral language for the purpose of expression.

split-half reliability   An estimate of the correlation of scores between two halves of a test.

standard deviation (SD)   A measure of the degree to which various scores deviate from the mean, or average score.

standard error of measurement (SEM)   The amount of error associated with individual test scores, test items, item samples, and test times.

standardization sample   The individuals who are actually tested during the process of test development.

standardized test   A test in which the administration, scoring and interpretation procedures are prescribed in the test manual and must be strictly followed. A standardized test is usually norm referenced.

standard scores   Raw scores that have been transformed so that they have the same mean and the same standard deviation.

stanine   A type of standard score that has a mean of 5 and a standard deviation of 2; a distribution of scores can be divided into 9 stanines.

student assistance team   *See* **assistance team.**

supports   "Resources and strategies that promote the interests and causes of individuals with or without disabilities; that enable them to access resources, information, and relationships inherent within integrated work and living environments; and that result in their enhanced interdependence/intradependence, productivity, community integration, and satisfaction" (American Association on Mental Retardation, 1992, p. 101).

syntax   A system of rules that dictates how words are combined into meaningful phrases and sentences.

task analysis   The division of a skill into small, discrete, sequential steps.

teacher assistance team   *See* **assistance team.**

testing   Administering a set of questions to an individual or group in order to determine knowledge or skills. Results are reported in one or more types of scores.

test-retest reliability   An estimate of the correlation between scores when the same test is administered two times.

transition   Moving from one system of services to another.

transition services   A coordinated set of activities for a student, designed within an outcome-oriented process, that promotes movement from school to post-school activities, including postsecondary education, vocational training, integrated employment (including supported employment), continuing and adult education, adult services, independent living, and community participation.

triangulation   Conclusions about student performance that are based on multiple sources of information.

true score   The score an individual would obtain on a test if there were no measurement errors.

validity   The extent to which a test measures what it says it measures.

voice output communication aid (VOCA)   A communication device that uses a synthesized speech system for the purpose of communication.

young children   Children ages birth through age 8.

Index

AAC (augmentative/alternative communication), 275–276, 448

AALIPS (Arthur Adaptation: Leiter International Performance Scale), 340

AAMR (American Association on Mental Retardation), 381–384, 386

ABACUS (Arizona Basic Assessment and Curriculum Utilization System), 324

ABC approach to assessing behavior, 250, 401–402, 408, 426

ABI (Adaptive Behavior Inventory), 385–386

ABIC (Adaptive Behavior Inventory for Children), 386

ABI-Short (Adaptive Behavior Inventory–Short Form), 386

ABS (Adaptive Behavior Scales), 386–388

ABS-RC:2 (Adaptive Behavior Scales–Residential and Community:2), 387

ABS-S:2 (Adaptive Behavior Scales–School Edition:2), 386–389

Achenbach, T. M., 35, 43, 414

Achievement test (definition), 129

Achromatopsia, 431

Acoustic reflex threshold, 442

ACTeRS (ADD-H: Comprehensive Teacher's Rating Scale–Second Edition), 413

Adaptive behavior (definition), 381

Adaptive Behavior Inventory (ABI), 385–386

Adaptive Behavior Inventory for Children (ABIC), 386

Adaptive Behavior Inventory–Short Form (ABI-Short), 385–386

Adaptive Behavior Scales (ABS), 386–388

Adaptive Behavior Scales–Residential and Community:2 (ABS-RC:2), 387

Adaptive Behavior Scales–School Edition:2 (ABS-S:2), 386–389

Adaptive development, 5, 8, 311, 318, 322

Adaptive Living Skills Curriculum (ALSC), 388–389

Adaptive skills (definition), 381

ADD (attention-deficit disorder), 14, 492

ADDES-HV (Attention-Deficit Disorders Evaluation Scales–Home Version), 412–413

ADDES-SV (Attention-Deficit Disorders Evaluation Scales–School Version), 412–413

ADD-H: Comprehensive Teacher's Rating Scale (ACTeRS–Second Edition), 413

ADHD (attention-deficit hyperactivity disorder), 145–146, 379, 386, 409–410, 413–415, 422, 480, 482

Adventitious visual impairment, 430

AEPS (Assessment, Evaluation, and Programming System for Infants and Children), 387

AERA (American Educational Research Association), 19–20, 56–57, 59–61, 63–64, 81–82

Affleck, J. Q., 444

Age equivalent, 76, 79, 256

AGS Early Screening Profiles, 32–35, 319, 385, 387

Airasian, P. W., 172, 183

Alberto, P. A., 400

Albinism, 430

Albright, L., 474

Alessi, G. J., 100–101, 121–123, 146, 151

Algozzine, B., 341

Allman, T., 385, 387

Almond, P. J., 413

Alnot, S. D., 134

Alper, S. K., 26

Alpern, G., 387

Alpert, C. L., 255

ALSC (Adaptive Living Skills Curriculum), 388–389

Alternate form reliability, 57–58

Amblyopia, 430–432

American Association on Mental Retardation (AAMR), 381–384, 386

American Educational Research Association (AERA), 19–20, 56–57, 59–61, 63–64, 81–82

American Psychological Association (APA), 1, 19–20, 56–57, 59–61, 81–82, 409

Analytic scoring, 179, 182, 242–243

Anastasi, A., 57, 61, 70, 75–77, 151, 295, 339, 347, 358, 367, 378

Ancess, J., 174

Anchor papers, 244

Anderson, J. L., 388–389

Anderson, S., 437

Anecdotal record, 91, 93–96, 132, 151, 162, 512

Annual review, 17, 40, 118, 172, 177, 503

Ansley, T. N., 134

Antecedent-behavior-consequence approach to assessing behavior (ABC approach), 250, 401–402, 408, 426

APA (American Psychological Association), 1, 19–20, 56–57, 59–61, 81–82, 409

Applied behavior analysis, 401–402

Aprenda: La Prueba de Logros en Español, 134

Approaches to assessing development
behavioral, 323, 401, 406, 408, 480, 483, 485, 489–490
biological, 323, 402
functional, 323, 382
Piagetian, 321

Approaches to teaching reading
cognitive, 197
direct instruction, 197
explicit instruction, 197
instructor variables, 197
whole language, 197

APTICOM Occupational Interest Inventory, 472

Arik, J. R., 413

Arizona Basic Assessment and Curriculum Utilization System (ABACUS), 324

Arter, J. A., 184

Arthur, G., 340

Arthur Adaptation: Leiter International Performance Scale (AALIPS), 340

Articulation, 4, 32, 253, 255, 260, 272, 294, 319, 443, 482

Aschbacher, P. R., 168

Ashlock, R. B., 298

ASIEP-2 (Autism Screening Instrument for Educational Planning–Second Edition), 413

Assessment
definition of, 2, 8
group, 133–134
peer, 129, 154, 158–159, 162, 217–218, 225, 235, 245–246, 294, 303–305
self, 129, 154, 162, 171, 177, 217, 225, 235, 245, 294, 304
transition, 8, 311, 332–334, 438, 453, 461, 475–476

Assessment, Evaluation, and Programming System for Infants and Children (AEPS), 387

Assessment process
determining eligibility (step 3), 9–11, 14–16, 92, 132–133, 235, 286, 313, 334, 382, 395, 481
evaluating the program (step 6), 17, 40, 47, 109, 227, 425, 449, 503
making a referral (step 2), 6, 9–11, 14–15, 26, 28–30, 38, 41–43, 92, 124, 251, 253–254, 311, 321, 323, 409, 440, 480, 489, 492, 494
monitoring the program (step 5), 9, 10–14, 17, 36, 38, 41–42, 45, 92, 96, 130–133, 152, 228–229, 235, 257–258, 281–282, 314–315, 326, 329–330, 377, 382, 388, 402, 408, 410–411, 425, 443, 448, 451, 453, 467, 475, 485, 501, 504, 506–508
planning the program (step 4), 9, 10–13, 16–17, 33, 92, 101, 130–133, 155–158, 178, 228–229, 235, 237–238, 240–242, 249, 251–258, 281–282, 299–301, 303, 314–315, 326, 382, 395, 410–411, 436, 443, 450, 467
screening (step 1), 9–14, 22, 31, 40, 61, 92, 132–133, 156–157, 167, 228–229, 235, 237, 251, 257–258, 281–282, 286, 299, 311, 313–315, 318, 321, 323, 326, 334–335, 410–411, 431–432, 442, 448, 462

Assessment team, 6, 127, 251, 253–254, 312, 318, 321, 326, 423, 438, 485, 490, 493, 495

Assistance team, 6, 14, 41–42, 94, 405, 407

Assistive technology (AT), 38, 275, 291, 448

Association of Persons with Severe Handicaps, The (TASH), 334

Asthma, 4

Astigmatism, 431

AT (assistive technology), 38, 275, 291, 448

Atkinson, R., 48

Attention-deficit disorder (ADD), 14, 413–415, 492

Attention-Deficit Disorders Evaluation Scale–Home Version (ADDES-HV), 412–413

Attention-Deficit Disorders Evaluation Scale–School Version (ADDES-SV), 412–413

Attention deficit hyperactivity disorder (ADHD), 145–146, 379, 386, 409–410, 413–415, 422, 480, 482

Attention-Deficit/Hyperactivity Disorder Test, 413

Attermeier, S. M., 324, 387

Attridge, C., 122

Audiogram, 441, 443, 451

Audiologist, 16, 429, 440, 443

Audiometer, 441

Audiometry

    bone conduction, 441

    immittance, 441–442

    pure tone, 441

    speech, 441–442

Auger, C., 313

Augmentative/alternative communication (AAC), 275–276, 448

Ault, M. H., 408

Aurbach, E., 176–177

Autism, 4, 119, 276, 410–411, 413, 508

Autism Screening Instrument for Educational Planning–Second Edition (ASIEP-2), 413

Average score, 73–74

Ayres, A. J., 447

Bagnato, S. J., 325, 448

Bailey, D. B., 76, 146, 313

Baker, E. L., 61–62, 183

Balaban, N., 480

Balla, D. A., 386, 392, 444

Ballard, J., 454, 461

Balow, I. H., 134

Balton, D., 474

Band of error, 67, 79, 81–82, 84, 86, 90, 492

Bandura, A., 250

Banikowski, A. K., 200, 230, 287

Bankson, N. W., 260

Bankson Language Test–Second Edition, 260

Barkley, R. A., 411

Baroody, A. J., 286, 291–293

Barraga, N. C., 438

Basal

    level, 80–81

    rule, 80–81, 84

    score, 80–81, 84

BASC (Behavior Assessment for Children), 414

Basic Achievement Skills Individual Screener (BASIS), 1, 135–137, 200, 230, 287

BASIS (Basic Achievement Skills Individual Screener), 1, 135–137, 200, 230, 287

Batería-R Tests of Cognitive Ability–Spanish Form, 135, 340, 342, 350

Batería-R Tests of Achievement–Spanish Form, 135, 342

Batería Woodcock Psico-Educativa en Español, 135

Battelle Developmental Inventory (BDI), 35, 80, 319, 324, 326, 385, 387, 397

Bayley, N., 35, 324, 326

Bayley Scales of Infant Development–Second Edition, 35, 324, 326

BDI (Battelle Developmental Inventory), 35, 80, 319, 324, 326, 385, 387, 397

Beaty, J., 94–95, 97, 103–104

Becker, R. L., 467, 470, 472

Behavioral approach to assessing development, 323, 401, 406, 408, 480, 483, 485, 489–490

Behavioral theory of the development of oral language, 250

Behavior Assessment for Children (BASC), 414

Behavior Evaluation Scale–Second Edition (BES-2), 414, 417

Behavior Rating Profile-2, 35, 414

Behavior rating scale, 403, 411–412

Bell-shaped curve, 72

Benchmark, 181–182

Bentzen, W. R., 180

Berge, P. S., 512

Berk, R. A., 70, 151, 295

Berman, B., 298

BES-2 (Behavior Evaluation Scale–Second Edition), 414, 417

Bijou, S. W., 408

Binet, A., 369

Biological approach to assessing development, 323, 402

Birch, H. G., 403

Blackorby, J., 453

Blalock, G., 454

Bliem, C. L., 172

Blind Learning Aptitude Test, 340

Bobath, B., 447

Bobath, K., 447

Boigion, S., 437

Boll, T., 387

Bone conduction audiometry, 441

Bonilla-Bowman, C., 178

Borg, W. R., 509–510

Bos, C. S., 324

Boykin, R. R., 286

Brackett, D., 439–440, 442

Bradley-Johnson, S., 439–440

Brahier, D. J., 280

Braille Literacy Plan, 437–438

Brandon, T., 387

Brandt, J. E., 461–462, 470

Brandt, R., 168

Brazelton, T. B., 404

Bredekamp, S., 20, 39, 326

Brengelman, S. U., 159

Bricker, D., 387

Brigance, A. H., 33, 70, 152–153, 200, 206, 230,
    236, 260, 287, 295–297, 319, 466–470, 506

BRIGANCE® Assessment of Basic Skills–Spanish Edition,
    152–153, 200, 206, 230, 287, 297, 469

BRIGANCE® Comprehensive Inventory of Basic Skills,
    152–153, 200, 206, 230, 260, 287, 296,
    468–469, 506

BRIGANCE® Diagnostic Employability Skills Inventory,
    152–153, 206, 287

BRIGANCE® Diagnostic Inventory of Basic Skills,
    152–153, 200, 206, 230, 236, 287, 296, 468

*BRIGANCE® Diagnostic Inventory of Early
    Development–Revised*, 152–153, 260, 287,
    297, 385

BRIGANCE® Diagnostic Inventory of Essential Skills,
    70, 152–153, 200, 206, 230, 296, 468

BRIGANCE® Diagnostic Life Skills Inventory, 152, 206,
    287, 297

BRIGANCE® Early Preschool Screen, 33

BRIGANCE® Employability Skills Inventory, 153, 206,
    297, 469–470

BRIGANCE® Life Skills Inventory, 206, 469

*BRIGANCE® Preschool Screen for Three- and Four-
    Year-Old Children*, 33, 319

British Ability Scales, 355

Brolin, D. E., 470

Brown, J. I., 199, 201–202

Brown, L., 35, 341, 375, 385–386, 409

Brown, P., 454, 461

Brown, R. T., 414

Brown, V. L., 231, 261, 269, 286, 293–294

Browning, K. G., 33

Bruininks, R. H., 32–35, 385–386, 388–389, 391,
    393, 448–449

Bruininks-Oseretsky Test of Motor Proficiency,
    448–449

Brusca, R., 120

Bryant, B. R., 135, 152, 199–200, 230, 233, 287,
    340, 352

Buckley Amendment, 1974 (Family Educational
    Rights and Privacy Act/FERPA/PL 93–380), 8,
    22, 497

Bunch, G. O., 444

Bursuck, W., 159

CAAS (*Children's Attention and Adjustment Survey*),
    414

Cahill, E., 298

California Achievement Tests/5, 134

CALS (*Checklist of Adaptive Living Skills*), 386,
    388–389

Campbell, D. P., 472

Campbell, J. R., 193–194

Campbell, P. H., 452

Campbell, S. B., 427

Career Assessment Inventory–Enhanced, 472

Career Assessment Inventory–Vocational, 472

Carey, L., 504

Carl D. Perkins Vocational and Applied Technology
    Education Act Amendments, 1990 (PL
    101–392), 454

*Carolina Curriculum for Infants and Toddlers with
    Special Needs–Second Edition* (*CCITSN*), 385,
    387

*Carolina Curriculum for Preschoolers with Special
    Needs* (*CCPSN*), 324, 385, 387

Carolina Picture Vocabulary Test, 444

Carrow-Woolfolk, E., 69, 230, 251, 260, 264

CARS (Childhood Autism Rating Scale), 413

CASE (Comprehensive Assessment of School Environments), 512

Castleberry, M., 461

Cataracts, 430–431

Category recording, 91, 93, 101–102

Cattell, J., 342, 347

Catterson, J., 199

CBA (curriculum-based assessment), 12, 129–132, 150–151, 162, 194–195, 204–205, 223, 228, 247, 257–258, 281–282, 314–315, 410–411, 437–438, 454, 470, 474, 476, 480

CBCL (Child Behavior Checklist), 35, 43–44, 414, 417–419, 422

CBM (curriculum-based measurement), 204–205, 235

CBVA (curriculum-based vocational assessment), 454, 474

CCITSN (Carolina Curriculum for Infants and Toddlers with Special Needs, Second Edition), 385, 387

CCPSN (Carolina Curriculum for Preschoolers with Special Needs), 324, 385, 387

CEC (Council for Exceptional Children), 1, 20, 114, 312

Ceiling
  level, 80–81
  rule, 80–81, 84
  score, 80–81, 84

CELF-P (Clinical Evaluation of Language Fundamentals–Preschool), 263

CELF-R (Clinical Evaluation of Language Fundamentals–Revised), 232, 256, 263, 265, 268

CELF-Spanish (Clinical Evaluation of Language Fundamentals–Spanish Edition), 258

CELF-3 (Clinical Evaluation of Language Fundamentals–Third Edition), 256, 258–260, 263

Center for Research on Evaluation, Standards, and Student Teaching (CRESST), 87

Central tendency, measures of, 72–75, 90

Cerebral palsy, 4, 275, 375, 446–447

C.F. ("counts fingers"; measurement of visual acuity), 435

Chafin, A. E., 184

Chandler, L., 333

Checklist of Adaptive Living Skills (CALS), 386, 388–389

Chess, S., 403

Child Behavior Checklist (CBCL), 35, 43–44, 414, 417–419, 422

Child Behavior Checklist/4–18, 403, 417

Child Behavior Checklist/2–3, 417

Child Development Inventory, 35, 325

Child Find, 3, 9, 32, 314, 321

Childhood Autism Rating Scale (CARS), 413

Children's Attention and Adjustment Survey (CAAS), 414

Choate, J. S., 150, 171

Chomsky, N., 251

Christenson, S. L., 111–113

Chronological age, 77, 84–85, 275, 489, 494

Cicchetti, D. V., 32–35, 386, 392, 444

Clark, G. M., 471

Classroom Ecological Inventory, 113–115

Classroom Reading Miscue Assessment (CRMA), 209–210

Claus, A. S., 280

Clifford, R. M., 107–109

Clinical Evaluation of Language Fundamentals–Preschool (CELF-P), 263

Clinical Evaluation of Language Fundamentals–Revised (CELF-R), 232, 256, 263, 265, 268

Clinical Evaluation of Language Fundamentals–Spanish Edition (CELF-Spanish), 258

Clinical Evaluation of Language Fundamentals–Third Edition (CELF-3), 256, 258–260, 263

Cloze technique, 136, 207, 209

Clubfoot, 4

Cobb, R. B., 474

Coffman, W. E., 358

CogAT (Cognitive Abilities Test), 340, 343

Cognitive Abilities Test (Form 5) (CogAT), 340, 343

Cognitive approach to teaching reading, 197

Cognitive stages of development (Piagetian)
  concrete operations, 322
  formal operations, 322, 360
  preoperational thought, 322
  sensorimotor intelligence, 322

Cohen, D. H., 480

Cohen, L. G., 47, 316, 412, 441, 444, 503

Cohen, P., 169

Cole, D. J., 172, 174–175

Coles, C. D., 409

Collaborating, 3, 91–92, 115, 125–126, 128, 152, 170, 172, 228–229, 236, 303, 409, 476

Color vision, 430, 435

Colson, S. E., 200, 230, 287

Comprehensive Assessment of School Environments (CASE), 512

Comprehensive Receptive and Expressive Vocabulary Test (CREVT), 260

Comprehensive Test of Nonverbal Intelligence (CTONI), 340, 343–345

Concrete operations stage (Piagetian), 322

Concurrent validity, 60–61

Conductive hearing loss, 439–440

Cone, J. D., 389–390

Conference, 12–13, 49–51, 91, 111, 115, 130–131, 154–157, 172, 194–195, 207, 215–216, 228–229, 235, 237–238, 251, 257–258, 272, 281–282, 295, 301, 314–315, 395, 410–411, 476

Confidence band, 67, 79, 81–82, 84, 86, 90, 492

Confidence interval, 67, 79, 81–82, 84, 86, 90, 492

Congenital
  anomaly, 4
  deafness, 439
  visual impairment, 430

Conners, C. K., 35, 403, 415, 418–422

Conners' Parent Rating Scale–Revised (CPRS-R), 35, 419, 422

Conners' Rating Scales (CRS), 418, 422

Conners' Rating Scales–Revised (CRS-R), 403, 415, 419–422

Conners' Teacher Rating Scale–Revised (CTRS-R), 419–421

Connolly, A. J., 133, 139, 141, 203, 286–291

Conoley, J. C., 79

Consent, right of, 29–30

Consequential validity, 61–62, 183

Construct validity, 59, 61–62

Content validity, 59, 227–228

Continuous record, 91–93, 95–96, 512

Cook, R. E., 446

Correa, V. I., 331

Correlation
  definition of, 53–54
  direction of, 54
  split-half, 58
  strength of, 54

Correlation coefficient (r), 54, 56, 59

Cortical blindness, 430

Costantino, G., 415

Council for Educational Diagnostic Services, 20–21

Council for Exceptional Children (CEC), 1, 20, 114, 312

CPRS-R (Conners' Parent Rating Scale–Revised), 35, 419, 422

CRESST (Center for Research on Evaluation, Standards, and Student Teaching), 87

CREVT (Comprehensive Receptive and Expressive Vocabulary Test), 260

Criterion-referenced assessment, 12–13, 129–132, 162, 194–195, 223, 228–229, 235, 247, 257–258, 281–282, 295, 314–315, 323, 410–411

Criterion-referenced test (CRT), 12–13, 17, 70, 75, 151–152, 162, 205–206, 235, 295, 309, 327

Criterion-related validity, 60

Critical period, 401, 404

CRMA (Classroom Reading Miscue Assessment), 209–210

Cronbach, L. J., 59

Cronin, M. E., 286, 293–294

CRS (Conners' Rating Scales), 418, 422

CRS-R (Conners' Rating Scales–Revised), 403, 415, 419–422

CRT (criterion-referenced test), 12–13, 17, 70, 75, 151–152, 162, 205–206, 235, 295, 309, 327

CTONI (Comprehensive Test of Nonverbal Intelligence), 340, 343–345

CTRS-R (Conners' Teacher Rating Scale–Revised), 419–421

Curriculum-based assessment (CBA), 12, 129–132, 150–151, 162, 194–195, 204–205, 228, 247, 257–258, 281–282, 314–315, 410–411, 437–438, 454, 470, 474, 476, 480

Curriculum-based measurement (CBM), 204–205, 235

Curriculum-based vocational assessment (CBVA), 454, 474

Cushman, P., 170

DAB-2 (*Diagnostic Achievement Battery–Second Edition*), 135–138, 200, 230

Darling-Hammond, L., 174

Das, J. P., 347, 355

DAS (*Differential Ability Scales*), 340, 347–351

Data, qualitative, 404, 511–512, 515

Data, quantitative, 370, 448, 511, 515

DATA-2 (*Diagnostic Achievement Test for Adolescents–Second Edition*), 135, 200, 230

Davidson, P. S., 154, 282, 294

Davis, C., 341

Davis, K., 437

DDST-II (*Denver Developmental Screening Test II*), 268, 319, 327, 448

Deal, A., 47

Deaf-blindness, 4

Deafness, 4

DEC (Division for Early Childhood), 312, 334

Delaney, E. A., 361

Dennebaum, J., 39, 512

Dennis, R. E., 19

Denver Developmental Screening Test II (DDST II; Denver II), 268, 319, 327, 448

Denver II (Denver Developmental Screening Test II), 268, 319, 327, 448

Derived score, 76, 79, 86

Descriptor, 80, 100, 102–103, 105, 176, 179, 182

Desimone, L., 501

Detroit Tests of Learning Aptitude–Primary: Second Edition (DTLA-P:2), 340, 344–346

Detroit Tests of Learning Aptitude–Third Edition (DTLA-3), 340, 346–348

DeVellis, R. F., 58, 148

Developmental
    approach to assessing behavior, 401, 404
    delay, 3, 5, 312–314, 326, 334, 443, 494
    perspective, 404
    quotient, 77
    score, 76–77, 86

Developmental Indicators for the Assessment of Learning–Revised (DIAL-R), 320

Developmental Profile II (DP-II), 387

Devereux Behavior Rating Scales, 415

Deviation IQ score, 80

Diabetes, 4

Diagnostic Achievement Battery–Second Edition (DAB-2), 135–138, 200, 230

Diagnostic Achievement Test for Adolescents–Second Edition (DATA-2), 135, 200, 230

Diagnostic and Statistical Manual IV (DSM-IV), 409

Diagnostic Reading Scales, 199

Diagnostic Screening Tests: Math (DSTM), 286

DIAL-R (*Developmental Indicators for the Assessment of Learning–Revised*), 320

Diana v. State Board of California (1970), 20

Dick, W., 504

Dick and Carey Systems Approach model of evaluation, 504

Dictionary of Occupational Titles (DOT), 473

Diez, M. E., 169

Differential Ability Scales (DAS), 340, 347–351

Digital Portfolio, 176

Direct instruction approach to teaching reading, 197

Direct observation, 92, 118–120, 122, 409, 476

Distance visual acuity, 435

Distribution
    frequency, 72
    negatively skewed, 72
    normal, 73–74, 78
    positively skewed, 73
    skewed, 72–73

Division for Early Childhood (DEC), Council for Exceptional Children (CEC), 312, 334

Dodds, J. B., 268, 319, 327, 448

Domain, 6, 33, 70, 151, 249, 295

Donahue, P. L., 193–194

DOT (*Dictionary of Occupational Titles*), 473

Downs, M. P., 442

Down syndrome (Trisomy 21), 330, 506

DP-II (*Developmental Profile II*), 387

Dresser, N., 405

DSM-IV (*Diagnostic and Statistical Manual IV*), 409

DSTM (*Diagnostic Screening Tests: Math*), 286

DTLA-P:2 (*Detroit Tests of Learning Aptitude–Primary: Second Edition*), 340, 344–346

DTLA-III (*Detroit Tests of Learning Aptitude–Third Edition*), 340, 346–348

Due process, 3, 5, 21, 29, 51

Dunbar, S. B., 134, 438

Dunlap, G., 508

Dunlap, L. K., 508

Dunn, L. M., and L. M. Dunn, 261, 266–268

Dunst, C., 47

Duration recording, 91, 93, 98–99, 116, 121, 127

Durrell, D., 199

Durrell Analysis of Reading Difficulty, 199

Early Childhood Environmental Rating Scale (ECERS), 107–109

Early childhood team, 5–6, 32–33, 36, 330, 505–506

Early Screening Inventory (ESI), 33, 320

Early Screening Inventory-3 (ESI-3), 33

Eaves, R. C., 341

ECERS (Early Childhood Environmental Rating Scale), 107–109

Ecological approach to assessing behavior, 401

Edgar, E. B., 444

Education for All Handicapped Children Act, The, 1975 (PL 94–142), 2, 312

Education of the Handicapped Act Amendments, The, 1986 (PL 99–457), 6–7, 312

Effective School Battery (ESB), 512–513

Eisert, D., 416

EIWN-R (Escala de Inteligencia Wechsler Para Niños–Revisada), 340

EIWN-R PR (Escala de Inteligencia Wechsler Para Niños–Revisada de Puerto Rico), 340

Electronic Portfolio, 176

Eligibility, determining (step 3 of the assessment process), 9–11, 14–16, 92, 132–133, 235, 286, 313, 334, 382, 395, 481

Elliott, C. D., 340, 347–351

Elliott, S. N., 415

Emotional disturbance, serious, 4

Engen, E., 444

Engen, T., 444

Enright, B. E., 150, 286, 295–296

Enright Diagnostic Inventory of Basic Arithmetic Skills, 286, 295–296

Environment

   learning, 92, 101, 104, 109, 115–116, 129, 159–160, 162–163, 183, 217–218, 220–221, 225, 246, 249, 272, 274, 276–277, 305, 307, 309, 314, 399, 403–405, 407–408, 481, 490

   physical, 104–107, 129, 159–161, 217–219, 225, 246, 249, 272, 274, 276, 305–306, 314, 399, 403, 405, 407–408, 481, 490

   social, 92, 104, 115–116, 129, 159, 162, 164, 183, 217–218, 222, 225, 246, 249, 272, 274, 276, 305, 308, 314, 399, 401, 403–405, 407–408, 481, 490

Environmental observation, 104–109

Environmental rating scale, 101, 106

Epilepsy, 4

Epstein, M. J., 159

Equivalent

   age, 76–77, 134, 229–230, 256

   grade, 76–77, 79, 134, 229–230, 481

Equivalent form reliability, 57–58

Erford, B. T., 286

Erikson, E., 404

Erin, J. N., 438

Error

   analysis, 12–13, 130–131, 153–155, 194–195, 207–210, 228–229, 235–236, 257–258, 281–282, 295, 298, 314–315, 403

   of commission, 118–119

   of omission, 118–119

   of transmission, 118–119

   score, 56

ESB (Effective School Battery), 513–514

Escala de Inteligencia Wechsler Para Niños–Revisada (EIWN-R), 340

Escala de Inteligencia Wechsler Para Niños–Revisada de Puerto Rico (EIWN-R PR), 340

Escalas de Conducta Independiente (Spanish Form of Scales of Independent Behavior), 386

ESI (Early Screening Inventory), 33, 320

ESI-3 (Early Screening Inventory-3), 33

Essa, E., 507

Estes, J. J., 293

Estes, T. H., 293

Estes Attitude Scales, 293

European American English, 253–254

Evaluating the program (step 6 of the assessment process), 17, 40, 47, 109, 227, 425, 449, 503

Evaluation

   formative, 503

right of, 30
student, 17
summative, 503
triennial, 17, 47, 508
Evans, L. D., 439–440
Event recording, 91, 93, 95–102, 116, 121, 127
EVT (Expressive Vocabulary Test), 260, 263–264
Examiner bias, 377, 480
Exhibition, 12–13, 70, 130–132, 153–154, 178, 184, 194–195, 207, 217, 228–229, 235, 242, 247, 281–282, 295, 303, 314–315, 410–411
Expansion technique, 250–251, 273–274
Explicit instruction approach to teaching reading, 197
Expressive language, 251, 254–255, 271, 276, 326, 382, 448, 482
Expressive One-Word Picture Vocabulary–Revised (English and Spanish Forms), 261, 294
Expressive Vocabulary Test (EVT), 260, 263–264
External evaluator, 502, 516
Externalizing behaviors, 400, 414–415, 494
Extrapolation, 77

Face validity, 61
Fahrenheit, D., 72
Falek, A., 409
Falk, B., 174
False negative, 321
False positive, 321
Family (definition), 24
Family-Centered Program Rating Scale, 39, 512
Family-directed assessment, 7, 33, 35–36, 314–315, 328
Family Educational Rights and Privacy Act, 1974 (FERPA/Buckley Amendment/PL 93–380), 8, 22, 497
Family-Focused Intervention Scale, 39, 513
Family-focused philosophy, 31
Family Information Summary, 36–37
Family systems model, 24, 51
FAPE (free appropriate public education), 3, 313
Farr, R. C., 134, 190, 215, 241
Feldt, L. S., 134
Ferguson, D. L., 126
Fernstrom, P., 113–115

FERPA (Family Educational Rights and Privacy Act, 1974/Buckley Amendment/PL 93–380), 8, 22, 497
Fewell, R., 449
FirstSTEP: Screening Test for Evaluating Preschoolers, 33, 316–317, 320, 385, 387
Fishco, V. V., 199
Flagler, S., 325
Flowers, J., 408
Focus group, 512
Folio, M. R., 449–450
Ford, K. L., 172
Formal operations stage (Piagetian), 322
Formal Reading Inventory, 199
Formative evaluation, 503
Forsyth, R. A., 134
Fowler, S. A., 330
Frankenburg, W. K., 268, 319, 327, 448
Free appropriate public education (FAPE), 3, 313
Frequency
    distribution, 72
    of behavior, 103, 118, 140, 146, 152, 400, 507–508
    of sound waves, 441
    polygon, 72
    recording, 96–97
French, J. L., 341
Frick, T., 121
Friederwitzer, F. J., 298
Frisbie, D. A, 134, 438
Fuchs, D., 113–115
Fuchs, L., 113–115, 178
Functional approach to assessing development, 323
Functional vision, 430, 435–439
Furuno, S., 325, 385, 387

Gall, M. D., 509–510
Gallagher, J., 501
Gallucci, C., 409
Gardner, E. F., 444
Gardner, H., 169, 176, 376–377
Gardner, M. F., 261, 294
Gates, A. I., 199
Gates-MacGinitie Reading Tests–Third Edition, 199
Gates-McKillop-Horowitz Reading Diagnostic Tests, 199

Gay, L. R., 73

Geers, A. E., 444

Geist, H., 470

Geist Picture Interest Inventory–Revised, 470

Gersten, R., 158–159

Giangreco, M. F., 19

Gillespie, C. S., 172, 190

Gillespie, R. D., 172, 190

Gilliam, J. E., 413

Gilliam Autism Rating Scale, 413

Gilman, C. J., 385, 388–389

Ginsburg, H. P., 286, 291–293

Glass, G. V., 502

Glaucoma, 430–431

Gleckel, L. K., 450

Glover, J. A., 512

Gnagey, T. D., 286

Goldenberg, D. S., 320

Goldstein, A. P., 508

Gonder, P., 184

Goodman, K. S., 155, 195

Gordon, E. W., 178

Gordon, L. V., 472

Gordon Occupational Checklist-II, 472

GORT-R (Gray Oral Reading Tests–Revised), 198, 200

GORT-III (Gray Oral Reading Tests–Third Edition), 198, 200

Gottfredson, G., D., 512

Grade equivalent, 76–77, 79, 134, 229–230, 481

Grady Profile, The, 176–177

Grammatical Analysis of Elicited Language, 444

Grapheme, 255

Graphic rating scale, 112, 148

Graphophonics, 196

Gray Oral Reading Tests–Revised (GORT-R), 198, 200

Gray Oral Reading Tests–Third Edition (GORT-3), 198, 200

Greenberg, L., 416

Greenspan, S. I., 318, 404

Gresham, F. M., 415

Griffiths, R., 340

Griffiths Mental Development Scales, 340

Gronlund, N. E., 76, 79, 94, 103, 148

Grossman, H., 381

Group test, 133–134

Guaranteed rights of parents and guardians, 29

Guess, D., 447

Guidubaldi, J., 319, 324

Gunter, P. L., 408

Guskey, T. R., 160, 302

Hacker, B. J., 324, 367

Hagen, E. P., 340, 343, 360–364

Hains, A. H., 330

Halderson, C., 512

Hall, A., 437

Halpern, A. S., 454, 470–473

Hammill, D. D., 35, 199, 201–202, 231, 233–234, 260–261, 269–270, 292, 340, 343–348, 414, 444

Haney, M., 25

Haney, W., 178

Hanna, G. S, 199

Hansen, J., 472

Hansen, P., 699

Hanson, M. J., 25, 29, 448–449

Hard-of-hearing (definition), 439–440

Haring, N. G., 400, 444

Harms, T., 107–109

Harris, L., 49

Harris, S. R., 448–449

Harrison, P. L., 33–35, 319, 387, 392

Hartsough, C., 414

Hawaii Early Learning Profile (HELP), 385, 387

Hawaii Early Learning Profile for Preschoolers (HELP for Preschoolers), 323, 325, 385

Hawaii Early Learning Profile for Special Preschoolers (HELP for Special Preschoolers), 385, 387

Hayden, A. H., 444

Hearing impairment, 4

HELP (Hawaii Early Learning Profile), 385, 387

HELP for Preschoolers (Hawaii Early Learning Profile for Preschoolers), 323, 325, 385

HELP for Special Preschoolers (Hawaii Early Learning Profile for Special Preschoolers), 385, 387

Hemophilia, 4

Henderson, L. W., 33

Herbert, J., 122

Herman, J. L., 168

Hernandez, I., 509

Herron, S. R., 231–232

Heward, W. L., 126

Hewitt, G., 175, 179, 182

Hieronymous, A. N., 134, 482

High-stakes testing, 313, 318, 182, 190, 333

Hill, B. K., 386, 391, 393

Hill, E., 438

Hiskey, M. S., 341, 444

Hogan, T. P., 134

Hoge, R. D., 122

Holistic scoring, 179, 181–182, 242–243

Holmes, D. W., 444

Hoover, H. D., 134, 438

Hopkins, H. L., 447

Hopkins, T. F., 361

Horn, R., 342, 247, 354, 373, 376

Horn-Cattell model of intelligence, 342, 347, 354, 373, 376

Horowitz, E. C., 199

Hosaka, C. M., 385, 387

Hough, O. M., 134

Howell, K. W., 131

H.M. ("hand movement"; measurement of visual acuity), 435

Hresko, W. P., 199, 231–232, 261, 292, 444

Hudson, F. G., 200, 230, 287

Hudson Education Skills Inventory, 200, 230, 287

Humanistic approach to assessing behavior, 401, 404

Huss, A. J., 447

Hymes, D. L., 184

Hypertonic, 445, 447

Hypothesis generation, 480, 492, 499

Hypotonic, 445

IDEA, 1990 (Individuals with Disabilities Education Act/PL 101–476), 2, 3, 8, 15, 17, 22, 30, 32, 38, 43, 142, 275, 291, 312–313, 417, 504, 514

IDEA Amendments, 1991 (Individuals with Disabilities Education Act Amendments, PL 102–119), 6–7, 312, 453

IDEA Amendments, 1997 (Individuals with Disabilities Education Act Amendments, PL 105–17), 2–3, 5, 17, 29, 32, 133, 275, 312, 409, 438, 443, 448, 453–454, 459, 504, 513

Idol, L., 204–205

Idol, Nevin, Paolucci-Whitcomb Model of Curriculum-Based Assessment, 204–205

IEP (individualized education program), 5–8, 12–14, 16, 17, 36, 42, 45–47, 49, 51, 95–96, 99, 117–118, 130–131, 133, 146, 152, 173, 177, 194–195, 228–229, 253, 257–258, 272, 281–282, 290, 314–315, 409–411, 438, 455, 459, 461, 485, 492, 501–506, 511–512, 515–516

IEP team, 6–8, 14, 17, 42, 45, 96, 99, 118, 177, 290, 409, 455, 512

IFSP (individualized family service plan), 6, 7, 14, 30, 36–37, 39–40, 51, 314–315, 330, 328, 492, 502, 504–506, 516

Ilmer, S., 32–35, 319, 385, 387

Immittance audiometry, 441–442

Impedance audiometry, 442

Inatsuka, T. T., 385, 387

Independent evaluation, right to, 30

Individualized education program (IEP), 5–8, 12–14, 16, 17, 36, 42, 45–47, 49, 51, 95–96, 99, 117–118, 130–131, 133, 146, 152, 173, 177, 194–195, 228–229, 253, 257–258, 272, 281–282, 290, 314–315, 409–411, 438, 455, 459, 461, 485, 492, 501–506, 511–512, 515–516

Individualized family service plan (IFSP), 6, 7, 14, 30, 36–37, 39–40, 51, 314–315, 330, 328, 492, 502, 504–506, 516

Individualized transition plan (ITP), 7–8, 459, 461, 476

Individuals with Disabilities Education Act, 1990 (IDEA/PL 101–476), 2, 3, 8, 15, 17, 22, 30, 32, 38, 43, 142, 275, 291, 312–313, 417, 504, 514

Individuals with Disabilities Education Act Amendments, 1991 (IDEA Amendments/PL 102–119), 6–7, 312, 453

Individuals with Disabilities Education Act Amendments, 1997 (IDEA Amendments/PL 105–17), 2–3, 5, 17, 29, 32, 133, 275, 312, 409, 438, 443, 448, 453–454, 459, 504, 513

Infant-Preschool Play Assessment Scale, 325

Informal test, 70, 86, 152, 492, 495. *See* also Performance-based assessment, Portfolio, Exhibition

Informant, 384, 511

Inner language, 251

Inside evaluator, 502, 516

Instructional Environment System, The (Second Edition) (TIES-2), 111–113

Instructor variables in approach to teaching reading, 197

Integrative interpretation, 93, 480

Intelligence quotient (IQ), 54, 72, 74, 80, 378

Intensity recording, 91, 99, 101, 119

Internal consistency reliability, 57–59

Internalizing behavior, 400, 414–415

International Reading Association (IRA), 196–197, 203–204, 234

Interpolation, 77

Interscorer/interobserver/interrater reliability, 57–58, 102, 104, 120–121, 179, 182

Interval recording, 91, 93, 100–102, 116, 146, 485

Interval scale, 71–72

Intervention assistance team, 14

Iowa Tests of Basic Skills, 133–134, 343, 438

Iowa Tests of Educational Development, 134

IQ (intelligence quotient, 54, 72, 74, 80, 378

IRA (International Reading Association), 196–197, 203–204, 234

Ireton, H. R., 35, 325

Irvin, L. K., 471–473

ITP (individualized transition plan), 7–8, 459, 461, 476

Jacks, R., 39

Jaeger chart numbers, 435

Jastak, J. F., 472

Jastak, S. R.., 472

Jayanthi, J., 159

Jens, K. G., 387

Johansson, C. B., 472

Johnsen, S. K., 341, 364–366

Johnson, B. H., 512

Johnson, M. B., 69–70, 81, 135, 139, 141, 148–150, 199–200, 202–204, 231, 262, 265, 271, 287, 290, 341–342, 373–376, 386, 393, 497

Johnson-Martin, N. M., 324, 387

Joint Committee on Standards for Educational Evaluation, 502

Journal, student, 12–13, 130–131, 153–154, 157, 162, 194–195, 207–208, 215, 225, 228–229, 235, 240, 242, 257–258, 281–282, 294–295, 301, 303, 314–315, 410–411, 424, 276

Julia, M. C., 25

Juvenile rheumatoid arthritis, 446

K-ABC (Kaufman Assessment Battery for Children), 70, 138, 140, 200, 265, 287, 341, 355–358, 360, 372–373, 495

Kaiser, A. P., 255

KAIT (Kaufman Adolescent and Adult Intelligence Test), 341, 351–355, 360–364

Kamphaus, R. W., 414, 480, 492

Karlsen, B., 444

Kaufman, A. S., 32–35, 70, 82–84, 135, 138–141, 200, 203, 230, 232, 260, 265, 287, 290, 325, 341, 351–364, 372–373, 470, 480, 492, 495

Kaufman, N. L., 32–35, 70, 82–84, 135, 138–141, 200, 203, 230, 232, 260, 265, 287, 290, 325, 341, 351–364, 372–373, 470, 495

Kaufman Adolescent and Adult Intelligence Test (KAIT), 341, 351–355, 360–364

Kaufman Assessment Battery for Children (K-ABC), 70, 138, 140, 200, 265, 287, 341, 355–358, 360, 372–373, 495

Kaufman Brief Intelligence Test (K-BIT), 232, 265, 341, 354, 358–360

Kaufman Functional Academic Skills Test (K-FAST), 470

Kaufmann, R. K., 505, 512

Kaufman Survey of Early Academic and Language Skills (K-SEALS), 325

Kaufman Test of Educational Achievement (K-TEA), 82–84, 135, 138–141, 200, 203, 230, 232, 260, 265, 287, 290

Kaye, J. H., 100–101, 121–123, 146, 151

K-BIT (Kaufman Brief Intelligence Test), 232, 265, 341, 354, 358–360

Keefe, J. W., 512

Keeves, J. P., 61, 70, 151, 295

Keith, K. D., 470

Kelley, E. A., 512

KeyMath-R (KeyMath Revised: A Diagnostic Inventory of Essential Mathematics), 133, 139, 141, 203, 286–291

KeyMath Revised: A Diagnostic Inventory of Essential Mathematics (KeyMath-R), 133, 139, 141, 203, 286–291

K-FAST (Kaufman Functional Academic Skills Test), 470

Kick, F., 172, 174–175

Kilian, L., 298

King, R. P., 172

King, S., 461

Klein, M. D., 446

Knott, M., 447

Knowledge-acquisition components (triarchic theory of intelligence), 377

Knox, V., 25

Koegel, L. K., 508

Koegel, R. L., 508

Kopp, C., 404

Kovach, J., 39

Kramer, S., 505

Kreitzer, A., 178

Krieg, F. J., 454, 461

Krug, D. A., 413

K-SEALS (Kaufman Survey of Early Academic and Language Skills), 325

K-TEA (Kaufman Test of Educational Achievement), 82–84, 135, 138–141, 200, 203, 230, 232, 260, 265, 287, 290

Kuder, G. F., 472

Kuder General Interest Survey (Form E), 472

Kuder Occupational Interest Survey (Form DD), 472

Kuder Preference Record–Vocational, 472

Kuder-Richardson formulas, 58

Kugler, J. F., 339

Kuhn, M. R., 196–197, 226

Kulm, G., 156–157, 299–301, 303

Lambert, N., 386–389, 414

Langer, J. A., 193–194

Language
   acquisition device, 251
   disorders, 251, 254, 257–258
   probe, 272
   sample, 172, 255–256, 272, 277

LAP (Learning Accomplishment Profile), 385, 387

Larry P. v. Riles (California, 1979), 20

Larsen, K. A., 474

Larsen, S. C., 233–234, 261, 269, 462, 466–467, 471

Latency recording, 91, 100, 116, 119

Layton, T. L., 444

LCCE (Life-Centered Career Education) (Knowledge Battery), 470

LCCE (Life-Centered Career Education) (Performance Battery), 470

Lead poisoning, 4

Leal, D., 116–117

Learning Accomplishment Profile (LAP), 385, 387

Leavell, A. G., 172

LeBuffe, P. A., 415

Leconte, P. J., 461

Lee, I. M., 37, 39, 512

Lee, R. L., 450–451

Lefebvre, D., 508

Lefever, D. W., 134

Lehmann, I. J., 58, 70, 151

Leigh, J. E., 385–386, 414, 417

Leland, H., 386–389

Leukemia, 4

Lewis, J. F., 386

Life-Centered Career Education (LCCE) (Knowledge Battery), 470

Life-Centered Career Education (LCCE) (Performance Battery), 470

Linn, R. L., 61–62, 76, 79, 94, 103, 148, 183

Living Skills Checklist, 462–466, 470

Livingston, R., 358

Loher, B., 512

Lloyd, B. H., 134

Lomard, R. C., 474

Long-term memory, 196

Lorge-Thorndike Intelligence Tests, 351

Love, L., 455–460

L.P. ("light perception"; measurement of visual acuity), 435

Lugo, D. E., 261, 266

Lund, K. A., 324

Luria, A., 355

Luria-Nebraska System of Neuropsychological Assessment, 351

Lutz, G. E., 447

Lyman, H. B., 80, 481, 497, 499

Lynch, E. W., 25

McCarney, S. B., 412–413, 417, 471
McCarthy, D., 341, 371, 373
McCarthy, J. M., 324
McCarthy Scales of Children's Abilities, 341, 371, 373
McConeghy, J., 159
McConnell, S. R., 416
McCormick, K., 3, 313
McEntire, E., 286, 293–294
McEvoy, M., 3, 313
McGhee, R., 231, 233
McGinnis, E., 508
MacGinitie, R. K., 199
MacGinitie, W. H., 199
McGonigel, M. J., 505, 512
McGrew, K. S., 480, 492
McKillop, A. S., 199
McLean, M., 3, 76, 146, 313
Madaus, G. F., 178
Madell, J. R., 442
Mahoney, G., 39, 512
Maladaptive behavior, 381, 384–385, 409
Malgady, R. G., 415
Mandelbaum, B. L., 474
Mann, L., 341
Mardell-Czudnowski, C., 320
Markwardt, F. C., Jr., 133, 135, 139–143, 200, 203, 231–232, 287, 290
Marolda, M. R., 154, 282, 294
Marsden, D. B., 33
Marston, D., 204–205, 298
Martin, F. N., 442
Maxon, A. B., 439–440, 442
Mayer, M. H., 443
Mayer, R. G., 93
Mean length of utterance (MLU), 255
Mean score, 73–75, 78–80, 82, 90
Measurement, scales of, 70–72
Measures of central tendency
    mean, 73–75, 78–80, 82, 90
    median, 73–75, 77–78, 90
    mode, 73–75, 90
Mecham, M. J., 262
Median score, 73–75, 77–78, 90
Medina, A., 19
Mehrens, W. A., 58, 70, 73, 151
Mehring, T. A., 159, 200, 230, 287, 315, 318, 320, 333

Meisels, S. J., 33, 315, 318, 320, 333
Mental Measurements Yearbooks (MMY), 87, 89
Mental retardation, 4
Mercer, J. R., 386
Merrell, K. W., 125, 426
Merrill, M. A., 360
Merwin, J. C., 444
Merz, W. R., 358
Mesulam, M., 403
Metacomponents (triarchic theory of intelligence), 377
Metropolitan Achievement Informal Tests, 70
Metropolitan Achievement Tests–Seventh Edition, 134
Meyer, C. A., 170
MI (multiple intelligences), 176, 376
Miller, L. J., 33, 150, 318, 320
Miller, M., 474
Miller, R. J., 467
Miscue analysis, 155, 195, 207–210
Mixed hearing loss, 440
MLU (mean length of utterance), 255
MMY (Mental Measurements Yearbooks), 87, 89
Mode score, 73–75, 90
Modeling, 250–251, 273, 285
Monitoring the program (step 5 of the assessment process), 9, 10–14, 17, 36, 38, 41–42, 45, 92, 96, 130–133, 152, 228–229, 235, 257–258, 281–282, 314–315, 326, 329–330, 377, 382, 388, 402, 408, 410–411, 425, 443, 448, 451, 453, 467, 475, 485, 501, 504, 506–508
Moog, J. S., 444
Moon, C. J., 169
Moores, D., 443
Moran, M. R., 254, 272
Moreau, L. E., 386, 388–389
Morpheme, 255, 272
Morphology, 255–256
Mullen, E. M., 325
Mullen Scales of Early Learning, 325
Mullis, I. V. S., 193–194
Multidisciplinary team, 5, 15–16, 21, 29–30, 37
Multiple disabilities, 4
Multiple intelligences (MI), 176, 376
Munkres, A. W., 471
Muñoz-Sandoval, A. F., 262, 342
Murphy, D. L., 37, 39, 512
Muscular dystrophy, 446

Myopia, 431

NAEYC (National Association for the Education of Young Children), 1, 312, 326, 334, 339–341
Naglieri, J. A., 415
Naslund, R. A., 134
National Association for the Education of Young Children (NAEYC), 1, 312, 326, 334, 339–341
National Association of Test Directors, 88
National Council on Measurement in Education (NCME), 19–20, 56–57, 59–61, 81–82
National Council of Teachers of Mathematics (NCTM), 169–170, 176, 279–280, 282–285, 288, 290–291, 294, 299–301, 305
National Forum on Assessment, 62, 65
National Research Council, 303
National Society to Prevent Blindness, 432
NCE (normal curve equivalent), 80, 256
NCME (National Council on Measurement in Education), 19–20, 56–57, 59–61, 81–82
NCTM (National Council of Teachers of Mathematics), 169–170, 176, 279–280, 282–285, 288, 290–291, 294, 299–301, 305
NDT (neurodevelopmental treatment), 447
Near visual acuity, 432–435
Nebraska Test of Learning Aptitude, 341, 444
Needs assessment questionnaire, 510–511
Neiminen, G. S., 120
Neisworth, J. T., 325, 390–392, 448, 473
Nelson-Denny Reading Test, 199
Nephritis, 4
Neumann, S. B., 193–194
Neurobiological approach to assessing behavior, 346, 401, 403
Neurodevelopmental treatment (NDT), 447
Nevin, A., 204–205
Newborg, J., 35, 319, 324, 387
Newcomer, P. L., 135–137, 199–200, 230, 261, 270, 287
Newland, T. E., 340
New York Lighthouse Symbol Flash Card Vision Test, 432
Nicolson, S., 483
Niguidula, D., 176
Nihira, K., 386–389
Nitko, A. J., 56, 124, 133, 185–189

N.L.P. ("no light perception"; measurement of visual acuity), 435
Nominal scale, 70–71
Noonan, M. J., 447
Norm
    group, 122, 131, 295, 481
    sample, 68, 70, 73, 90, 122, 318, 481
    tables, 86, 132
Normal curve, 72–73, 78, 80
Normal curve equivalent (NCE), 80, 256
Normal distribution, 73–74, 78
Normative sample, 68, 70, 73, 90, 122, 318
Norm-referenced test (NRT), 5, 12–13, 16–17, 59, 67–68, 70, 80, 86, 89–90, 129, 132–134, 151–152, 167, 194–195, 203–204, 206, 223, 225, 227–229, 234, 246–247, 256–258, 281–282, 286, 294–295, 309, 314–315, 318, 410–411, 437–438
Northern, J. L., 442
Notice, right of, 29–30
NRT (norm-referenced test), 5, 12–13, 16–17, 59, 67–68, 70, 80, 86, 89–90, 129, 132–134, 151–152, 167, 194–195, 203–204, 206, 223, 225, 227–229, 234, 246–247, 256–258, 281–282, 286, 294–295, 309, 314–315, 318, 410–411, 437–438
Numerical scale, 148
Nystagmus, 431

O&M (orientation and mobility), 116, 430, 436–438
OASIS-2 (Occupational Aptitude Survey and Interest Schedule–Second Edition), 472
Observation
    direct, 92, 118–122, 194–195, 409, 476
    environmental, 104–109
    systematic, 86, 132, 146, 162, 490
Observer
    bias, 95
    drift, 120
    expectancy, 120
Obtained score, 56, 81, 86
Occupational Aptitude Survey and Interest Schedule–Second Edition (OASIS-2), 472
O.D. ("oculus dexter" or "right eye"; used in reporting visual acuity), 435
Olinger, E., 120
Olson, K. A., 33

Ophthalmologist, 431–432, 436

Optometrist, 431

Oral description, 6, 130–131, 154–156, 176,
    194–195, 207, 213, 228–229, 235, 237,
    257–258, 281–282, 290, 295, 299, 314–315,
    410–411, 476

Oral and Written Language Scales (OWLS), 69,
    230–232, 251, 261, 264–265, 267

Oral language, theories regarding the development
    of
    behavioral approach, 250
    psycholinguistic approach, 195, 250–251
    social learning theory approach, 250–251

Ordinal scale, 70–72

*Oregon Project for Visually Impaired and Blind
    Preschoolers–Fifth Edition*, 437

O'Reilly, K. A., 385, 387

Orientation and mobility (O&M), 116, 430,
    436–438

Orthopedic impairment, 4

O.S. ("Oculus sinister" or "left eye"; used in
    reporting visual acuity), 435

Osternig, L. R., 447

O'Sullivan, P., 39, 512

Other health impairment, 4

Otitis media, 439, 442

Otolaryngologist, 440

Otologist, 440

O.U. ("oculus uterque" or "both eyes"; used in
    reporting visual acuity), 435

Outcome-oriented process (definition), 476

Overton, T., 81

OWLS (Oral and Written Language Scales), 69,
    230–232, 251, 261, 264–265, 267

Padilla, A. M., 19

Padilla, E. R., 261, 266

Page, E. B., 358

Palombaro, M. M., 409

Paolucci-Whitcomb, P., 204–205

Parallel form reliability, 57–58

Parent Satisfaction Survey, 39, 512

*Parents in Action on Special Education (PASE) v.
    Hannon* (Illinois, 1980), 20

Paresis, 445

Parker, R., 472

Patton, J. R., 454, 471

Pawelski, C., 437

PDD (pervasive developmental disorder), 276

*Peabody Developmental Motor Scales and Activity
    Cards*, 449–450

Peabody Individual Achievement Test (PIAT), 140,
    142

*Peabody Individual Achievement Test–Revised (PIAT-
    R)*, 133, 135, 139–143, 200, 203, 231–232,
    287, 290

Peabody Picture Vocabulary Test (PPVT), 269, 292

Peabody Picture Vocabulary Test–Revised (PPVT-R),
    142, 232, 265, 354

*Peabody Picture Vocabulary Test–Third Edition
    (PPVT-III)*, 259, 261, 264, 266–268, 493, 395

Peak, P. K., 231–232

Pearson, N. A., 340, 343–345

Peck, C. A., 409

Peer assessment, 129, 154, 158–159, 162,
    217–218, 225, 235, 245–246, 294, 303–305

Percentage
    correct, 77, 481
    duration rate, 98–99
    of agreement, 121
    of occurrences of behavior, 146, 256
    score, 75–76

Percentile
    rank, 77–80, 481, 497
    score, 76–79, 86–87, 134, 229, 395, 492

Performance-based assessment, 61–62, 70, 86,
    129–130, 153–154, 157, 167–169, 182–184,
    190, 194–195, 215, 235, 240, 247, 295, 301,
    437–438, 475–476, 480, 489, 492

Performance components (triarchic theory of
    intelligence), 377

Perkins, Carl D., Vocational and Applied Technology
    Education Act Amendments, 1990 (PL
    101–393), 454

Perkins-Binet Tests of Intelligence for the Blind, 341

Persky, H. R., 193–194

Perspectives on assessing behavior
    behavioral, 323, 401, 406, 408, 480, 483, 485,
        489–490
    biological, 323, 401–402
    developmental, 401, 404
    ecological, 401

emotional, 401
  humanistic, 401, 404
  neurobiological, 401, 403
  psychoanalytic, 401
  psychoeducational, 401
  temperament, 312, 323, 401, 403–404, 426
Pervasive developmental disorder (PDD), 276
Peterson, D. R., 35, 404, 415, 422
Peterson, R. F., 408
Pfeiffer, S. I., 415
Phelps-Gunn, T., 262
Phelps-Ternski, D., 262
Phonation, 251, 253
Phoneme, 255–256, 272
Phonology, 255
Piaget, J., 322
PIAT (Peabody Individual Achievement Test), 140, 142
PIAT-R (Peabody Individual Achievement Test–Revised), 133, 135, 139–143, 200, 203, 231–232, 287, 290
Pictorial Test of Intelligence, 341
PL 94–142, 1975 (The Education for All Handicapped Children Act), 2, 312
PL 99–457, 1986 (The Education of the Handicapped Act Amendments), 6–7, 312
PL 93–380, 1974 (Family Educational Rights and Privacy Act/FERPA/Buckley Amendment), 8, 22, 497
PL 105–17, 1997 (Individuals with Disabilities Education Act Amendments/IDEA Amendments), 2–3, 5, 17, 29, 32, 133, 275, 312, 409, 438, 443, 448, 453–454, 459, 504, 513
PL 101–476, 1990 (Individuals with Disabilities Education Act/IDEA), 2, 3, 8, 15, 17, 22, 30, 32, 38, 43, 142, 275, 291, 312–313, 417, 504, 514
PL 101–392, 1990 (Carl D. Perkins Vocational and Applied Technology Education Act Amendments), 454
PL 103–239, 1994 (School-to-Work Opportunities Act), 454
PL 102–119, 1991 (Individuals with Disabilities Education Act Amendments/IDEA Amendments), 6–7, 312, 453
Plake, B. S., 79

Planning the program (step 4 of the assessment process), 9, 10–13, 16–17, 33, 92, 101, 130–133, 155–158, 178, 228–229, 235, 237–238, 240–242, 249, 251–258, 281–282, 299–301, 303, 314–315, 326, 382, 395, 410–411, 436, 443, 450, 467
Plante, L., 159
Platzman, K. A., 409
-plegia, 445
PLS-R (Preschool Language Scale–Revised), 268
PLS-3 (Preschool Language Scale–3), 261, 267–269, 292
PLS-3, Spanish Edition (Preschool Language Scale–3, Spanish Edition), 268
PNF (proprioceptive neuromuscular facilitation), 447–448
Poliomyelitis, 4
Polloway, E. A., 159, 255, 272
Pond, R. E., 267–269, 292
Portfolio
  benefits of a, 172
  cautions about using a, 178, 183–184, 190
  contents of a, 172–173
  organization of a, 173–177, 216–217, 303
  purposes of a, 172
  rubric for scoring of a, 179, 182
Portfolio assessment, 12–13, 62–63, 70, 86, 130–132, 153–154, 157–158, 167, 172, 183, 190, 194–195, 207, 215–217, 235, 241–242, 247, 257–258, 272, 281–282, 295, 301–303, 314–315, 410–411, 424, 475–476, 481, 504
Portfolio Assessment Kit, 176
Poteet, J. A., 150, 171
Power test, 59
PPVT (Peabody Picture Vocabulary Test), 269, 292
PPVT-R (Peabody Picture Vocabulary Test–Revised), 142, 232, 265, 354
PPVT-III (Peabody Picture Vocabulary Test–Third Edition), 259, 261, 264, 266–268, 493, 395
Pragmatics, 196, 256, 272
Predictive validity, 59–61, 333
Preoperational thought stage (Piagetian), 322
Prereferral
  decision, 6, 10–11, 14
  model, 6, 41, 92
Preschool Language Scale–Revised (PLS-R), 268

Preschool Language Scale-3 (PLS-3), 261, 267–269, 292

Preschool Language Scale-3, Spanish Edition (PLS-3, Spanish Edition), 268

Prescriptive Reading Inventory, 199

Price, D. R., 442

Probe, 12–13, 130–131, 153–155, 194–195, 207, 209, 211, 228–229, 235–236, 256–258, 272, 281–282, 295–298, 314–315, 410–411

Program

    evaluation (step 6 of the assessment process), 17, 40, 47, 109, 227, 425, 449, 503

    monitoring (step 5 of the assessment process), 9, 10–14, 17, 36, 38, 41–42, 45, 92, 96, 130–133, 152, 228–229, 235, 257–258, 281–282, 314–315, 326, 329–330, 377, 382, 388, 402, 408, 410–411, 425, 443, 448, 451, 453, 467, 475, 485, 501, 504, 506–508

    planning (step 4 of the assessment process), 9, 10–13, 16–17, 33, 92, 101, 130–133, 155–158, 178, 228–229, 235, 237–238, 240–242, 249, 251–258, 281–282, 299–301, 303, 314–315, 326, 382, 395, 410–411, 436, 443, 450, 467

Project Dakota Parent Satisfaction Survey, 39

Proprioceptive neuromuscular facilitation (PNF), 447–448

Prueba del Desarrollo Inicial del Lenguaje, 261

Psychoanalytic approach to assessing behavior, 401

Psychoeducational approach to assessing behavior, 401

Psycholinguistic theory of the development of oral language, 195, 250–251

Pure-tone audiometry, 441

Pyramid Scales, 389–390

Qualitative data, 511–512, 515

Quality of Life Questionnaire, 470

Quality of Student Life Questionnaire, 470

Quantitative data, 448, 511, 515

Quay, H. C., 35, 403–404, 15, 422–423

Questionnaire, 18, 32, 34, 47, 51, 91, 113, 115, 153–154, 156–157, 207, 213, 235, 237–238, 245, 272, 295, 299, 455, 457–458, 476, 510–511, 514

r (reliability coefficient), 56, 59, 121

Rakes, T. A., 150

Rank, percentile, 77–80, 481, 497

Rankin, R. J., 358

Rapp, N., 508

Rasmussen, S. K., 408

Rastler, C., 474

Rating

    recording, 121

    scale, 18, 36, 43, 51, 72, 91, 93, 101–106, 116, 122, 148, 223, 247, 309, 332, 339, 402–403, 411–412, 423, 511

Ratio scale, 72, 75–76, 80–82, 84, 86, 499

Raw score, 133, 141–142, 150, 152, 154, 156, 159

RBPC (Revised Behavior Problem Checklist), 35, 403–404, 415, 418, 422–423

Reactivity, 120

Readiness

    reading, 333

    school, 311, 332–333, 443

Reading-Free Vocational Interest Inventory-Revised (R-FVII), 467, 470, 472

Reading readiness, 333

Reading theories

    psycholinguistic, 195, 250–251

    schema, 195–196

    socio-psycholinguistic, 196

    transactional, 196

Receptive language, 16, 251, 255–256, 263, 271–272, 276, 326, 382, 448, 482

Recording interval, 100–102

Referral, making a (step 2 of the assessment process), 6, 9–11, 14–15, 26, 28–30, 38, 41–43, 92, 124, 251, 253–254, 311, 321, 323, 409, 440, 480, 489, 492, 494

Reichler, R. J., 413

Reid, D. K., 199, 261, 444

Reisman, F. K., 286

Relative standing, scores of, 76–77, 86

Reliability

    alternate form, 57–58

    definition of, 55

    equivalent form, 57–58

    internal consistency, 57–59

interscorer/interobserver/interrater, 57–58, 102, 104, 120–121, 179, 182
    parallel form, 57–58
    split-half, 57–58
    test-retest, 57–59
Reliability coefficient (*r*), 56, 59, 121
Renner, B. R., 413
Repetto, J. B., 331
Repp, A. C., 120
Residual vision, 437
Resonation, 253
Respiration, 251
Responsibility and Independence Scale for Adolescents (RISA), 390–392, 473
Retelling, 207, 211, 213
Retinopathy of prematurity (ROP), 430
Revised Behavior Problem Checklist (RBPC), 35, 403–404, 415, 418, 422–423
R-FVII (Reading-Free Vocational Interest Inventory–Revised), 467, 470, 472
Rheumatic fever, 4
Rhode Island Test of Language Structure, 444
Rhodes, L. K., 194–198, 203–204, 208–211, 214, 216, 226, 234, 236, 238–240
Richards, H. C., 293
Right
    of consent, 29–30
    of evaluation, 30
    of notice, 29–30
    to an independent evaluation, 30
RISA (Responsibility and Independence Scale for Adolescents), 390–392, 473
Risinger, C. F., 134
Rivera, D. M., 231, 233
Rivera, D. P., 152
Robertson, R., 447
Roeser, R. J., 442
Roettger, D., 293
Rogers, C. R., 404
Rogler, L. H., 415
Rood technique (sensorimotor approach), 447
ROP (retinopathy of prematurity), 430
Rosegrant, T., 20
Rosen, G., 474
Rosenblatt, L., 196

Rosenkoetter, S. E., 330
Ross, M., 439–440, 442
Rubric, 154, 167, 176, 179, 190, 235, 242–244, 294, 302–303
Rudman, H. C., 444
Rudner, L. M., 79
Rueda, R., 130–131
Running record, 91–93, 95–96, 512
Rup, D., 474
Ryan, C. W., 172, 174–175, 298
Rynders, J., 32–35

Sainato, D. M., 508
Salisbury, C. L., 409
Salvia, J., 59, 62, 64, 70, 125, 347, 354–355, 390–392, 473
Sandoval, J., 414
Sanford, A. R., 387
SAT (Scholastic Aptitude Test), 72
SAT (student assistance team), 6, 14, 41–42, 94
Sattler, J. M., 19, 58, 76–77, 86–87, 94, 97–98, 102, 121–122, 135, 146, 339–341, 360–364, 378, 490
Sawyer, C., 275
Scale
    interval, 71–72
    nominal, 70–71
    numerical, 148
    ordinal, 70–72
    ratio, 72, 75–76, 80–82, 84, 86, 499
    semantic differential, 108, 148
Scales of Independent Behavior (SIB), 391
Scales of Independent Behavior–Revised (SIB-R), 386, 391, 393
Scales of measurement, 70–72
Scan-check method for developing informal norms, 122
Scannell, D. P., 134
Schakel, J., 3, 313
Schalock, R. L., 470
Schema theory of the development of oral language, 195–196
Scherer, P., 444
Schizophrenia, 4
Schloss, C. N., 26

Schloss, P. J., 26

Schmidt, M. W., 390–392, 473

Schmitt, N., 512

Scholastic Aptitude Test (SAT), 72

Scholl, G. T., 437

School assistance team, 405, 407

School readiness, 311, 332–333, 443

School-to-Work Opportunities Act, 1994 (PL 103–239), 454

Schopler, E., 413

Score
  average, 73–74
  basal, 80–81, 84
  ceiling, 80–81, 84
  derived, 76, 79, 86
  developmental, 76–77, 86
  deviation IQ, 80
  error, 56
  mean, 90
  median, 73–74, 77–78, 90
  mode, 73–74, 90
  obtained, 56, 81, 86
  of relative standing, 76–77, 86
  percentage, 75–76
  percentile, 76–79, 86–87, 134, 229, 395, 492
  raw, 133, 141–142, 150, 152, 154, 156, 159
  standard, 76, 78–79, 80–82, 86–87, 134, 229
  T, 80, 359
  true, 53, 56, 81–82, 86
  z, 80

Scoring
  analytic, 179, 182, 242–243
  holistic, 179, 181–182, 242–243

Scott, S., 113–115

Screening (step 1 of the assessment process), 9–14, 22, 31, 40, 61, 92, 132–133, 156–157, 167, 228–229, 235, 237, 251, 257–258, 281–282, 286, 299, 311, 313–315, 318, 321, 323, 326, 334–335, 410–411, 431–432, 442, 448, 462

Screening task, 321

Script-implicit (SI), 205

SD (standard deviation), 74, 79–80, 313

S-DMS (Slosson-Diagnostic Math Screener), 286

SDMT4 (Stanford Diagnostic Mathematics Tests–Fourth Edition), 286, 290–291

SDRT4 (Stanford Diagnostic Reading Tests–Fourth Edition), 199, 201

Secord, W., 255–256, 258–260, 263

Self-assessment, 129, 154, 162, 171, 177, 217, 225, 235, 245, 294, 304

SEM (standard error of measurement), 81–82

Semantic differential scale, 108, 148

Semantics, 196, 238, 255, 272–273, 346

Semel, E., 255–256, 258–260, 263

Semmel, M. I., 121

Sensorimotor approach (Rood technique), 447

Sensorimotor intelligence stage (Piagetian), 322

Sensorineural hearing loss, 440–441

Sensory integration (SI), 698

Sequential Assessment of Mathematics Inventories–Standardized Inventory, 286

Serious emotional disturbance, 4

Severson, H. H., 404, 415, 423–425

S-FRIT (Slosson Full-Range Intelligence Test), 341

Shank, M., 116–117

Shanklin, N. L., 194–198, 203–204, 216, 226, 234, 238–240

Shaping, 250

Shapiro, J., 27

Shearer, M., 386

Shelton, T. L., 411

Shepard, L., 17, 172, 333–334

Sherbenou, R. J., 341, 364–366

Shipstead, S. G., 483

Shores, R. E., 408

Short-term memory, 196

SI (script-implicit), 205

SIB (Scales of Independent Behavior), 391

SIB-R (Scales of Independent Behavior–Revised), 386, 391, 393

Sickle cell anemia, 4

Silberman, R. K., 437–438

Simon, T., 360

Singer Vocational Evaluation System, 474

SIT (Slosson Intelligence Test), 341, 360

SIT-R (Slosson Intelligence Test–Revised), 341

Skewed distribution, 73

Sleator, E. K., 413

Slosson, R., 341, 360

Slosson-Diagnostic Math Screener (S-DMS), 286

Slosson Full-Range Intelligence Test (S-FRIT), 341

Slosson Intelligence Test (SIT), 341, 360

Slosson Intelligence Test–Revised (SIT-R), 341

SLP (speech and language pathologist), 16, 251, 253, 255, 272, 275–277, 290, 318, 326, 330, 368, 448, 485, 495

Smith, B. J., 3, 313

Smith, F., 196

Smith, I. E., 409

Smith, M. L., 502

Smith, T. E. C., 255, 272

Snapshot (a limitation of the screening process), 321

Snyder, P., 313

Social and Prevocational Informational Battery–Revised (SPIB-R), 470–473

Social learning theory of the development of oral language, 195, 250–251

Social Skills Rating System (SSRS), 415

Socio-psycholinguistic theory of the development of oral language, 196

Sonnenschein, J. L., 135–136, 200, 230, 283–285, 287

Sorenson, C., 512

Spache, G. D., 199

Spandel, V., 184, 243

Sparrow, S. S., 32–35, 386, 392–395, 444

Specific learning disability, 4

SPECS (System to Plan Early Childhood Services), 325

Speech and language pathologist (SLP), 16, 251, 253, 255, 272, 275–277, 290, 318, 326, 330, 368, 448, 485, 495

Speech audiometry, 441–442

Speech disorders, 251, 253

Speech or language impairment, 4

Speech production
    articulation, 4, 32, 253, 255, 260, 272, 294, 319, 443, 482
    phonation, 251, 253
    resonation, 253
    respiration, 251

Speer, W. R., 280

Spenciner, L. J., 47, 316, 412, 441, 444, 503

Speth, C., 512

SPIB-R (Social and Prevocational Informational Battery–Revised), 470–473

Spina bifida, 446

Split-half reliability, 57–58

Sprague, R. L., 413

SRA Achievement Series, 134, 462

SSBD (Systematic Screening for Behavioral Disorders), 404, 415

SSBD-2 (Systematic Screening for Behavioral Disorders–Second Edition), 423–425

SSRS (Social Skills Rating System), 415

Stahl, S. A., 196–197, 226

Stakeholder, 182, 502

Standard deviation (SD), 74, 79–80, 313

Standard error of measurement (SEM), 81–82

Standardization sample, 60, 63–64, 68–69, 77, 86, 90, 132, 287, 443, 481

Standardized Reading Inventory, 199

Standardized test, 32, 62, 68, 70, 80, 82, 86–87, 102, 129–134, 151–152, 172–173, 178, 223, 225, 227, 229–230, 234, 239–240, 246–247, 249, 256, 271, 277, 282, 309, 339, 443, 480–481

Standards for Educational and Psychological Testing, 56, 59–60, 64, 81

Standard score, 76, 78–79, 80–82, 86–87, 134, 229

Stanford Achievement Test–Ninth Edition, 134, 438

Stanford-Binet Intelligence Scale: Form L-M, 360

Stanford-Binet Intelligence Scale–Fourth Edition, 360–364, 371

Stanford Diagnostic Mathematics Test–Fourth Edition (SDMT4), 286, 290–291

Stanford Diagnostic Reading Test–Fourth Edition (SDRT4), 199, 201

Stanine, 76, 80, 86–87, 134, 256, 492

Static immittance, 442

Steiber, S., 416

Steiner, V. G., 261, 267

Stern, V., 480

Sternberg, R., 346, 397

Stewart, S. C., 171

Stiggins, R. J., 243

Stock, J. R., 35, 80, 319, 324, 326, 387, 397

Stoy, M. R., 409

Strabismus, 430

Strain, P. S., 508

Strong-Campbell Interest Inventory, 472

Stuart, M. J., 447

Student assistance team (SAT), 6, 14, 41–42, 94
Student
 evaluation, 17
 journal, 12–13, 130–131, 153–154, 157, 162,
  194–195, 207–208, 215, 225, 228–229, 235,
  240, 242, 257–258, 281–282, 294–295, 301,
  303, 314–315, 410–411, 424, 276
 rating scale, 102
 work sample, 235, 238, 240
Sulzer-Azaroff, B., 93
Summative evaluation, 503
Survey, 12–13, 130–131, 194–195, 228–229,
  257–258, 281–282, 314–315, 410–411
Sutherland, D., 298
Suzuki, L. A., 339
Sviniski, J., 324
Swallow, R. M., 437
Swicegood, P., 172
Syntax, 196, 250–251, 255–256, 272–273
Synthesized speech, 249, 275
Systematic Screening for Behavioral Disorders (SSBD),
  404, 415
*Systematic Screening for Behavioral Disorders–
  Second Edition (SSBD-2)*, 404, 415, 423–425
System to Plan Early Childhood Services (SPECS),
  325

Tacetta, D., 298
Tally, 96
Tanchak, T. L., 275
Target behavior, 100, 250, 402
TASH (The Association of Persons with Severe
  Handicaps), 334
Task analysis, 250, 401–402
Taylor, R. L., 152, 378
TBI (traumatic brain injury), 4, 410–411, 446
TE (text-explicit), 205
Teacher assistance team, 14
Teach Prep Assessment Model, 474
Team
 early childhood, 5–6, 32–33, 36, 330,
  505–506
 multidisciplinary, 5, 15–16, 21, 29–30, 37
*TELD-2 (Test of Early Language Development–Second
  Edition)*, 261, 292

*TEMA-2 (Test of Early Mathematics Ability–Second
  Edition)*, 286, 291–293
Temperament approach to assessing behavior, 312,
  323, 401, 403–404, 426
Terman, L. M., 360
Tessier, A., 446
Test Critiques, 87, 89
Test de Vocabulario en Imágenes Peabody (TVIP),
  261, 266–267
*Test for Auditory Comprehension of
  Language–Revised*, 265
Testing, high-stakes, 313, 318, 182, 190, 333
*Test of Adolescent and Adult Language–Third Edition
  (TOAL-3)*, 231, 261, 269–270
*Test of Early Language Development–Second Edition
  (TELD-2)*, 261, 292
*Test of Early Mathematics Ability–Second Edition
  (TEMA-2)*, 286, 291–293
*Test of Early Reading Ability—Deaf or Hard of
  Hearing*, 444
Test of Early Reading Ability–Second Edition, 199
Test of Early Written Language (TEWL), 232–233
*Test of Early Written Language–Second Edition
  (TEWL-2)*, 231–233
Test of Expressive Language Ability, 444
*Test of Language Development–Intermediate: Second
  Edition (TOLD-I:2)*, 261, 269
*Test of Language Development–Primary: Second
  Edition (TOLD-P:2)*, 261, 270–271, 292
*Test of Mathematical Abilities–Second Edition
  (TOMA-2)*, 286, 293–294
*Test of Nonverbal Intelligence–Second Edition
  (TONI-2)*, 341, 360, 364–366
Test of Phonological Awareness, 199
Test of Practical Knowledge (TPK), 462, 466–467,
  471
Test of Pragmatic Language, 262
Test of Reading Comprehension (TORC), 202
*Test of Reading Comprehension–Third Edition
  (TORC-3)*, 199, 201–202
Test of Receptive Language Ability, 444
*Test of Variables of Attention (TOVA)–Auditory
  Version*, 416
Test of Variables of Attention (TOVA)–Visual Version,
  416

Test of Written Expression (TOWE), 231, 233

Test of Written Language–Second Edition (TOWL–2), 269

Test of Written Language–Third Edition (TOWL–3), 231, 233–234

Test of Written Spelling–Third Edition (TWS–3), 231, 234

Test-retest reliability, 57–59

Tests in Print, 87, 89

Tests of Achievement and Proficiency, 134

TEWL (Test of Early Written Language), 232–233

TEWL–2 (Test of Early Written Language–Second Edition), 231–233

Text-explicit (TE), 205

Text-implicit (TI), 205

Think-aloud, 207, 209, 211

Thomas, A., 403

Thorndike, R. L., 340, 343, 360–364

Thorpe, L. P., 134

Thurlow, M., 385

TI (text-implicit), 205

TIES-II (Instructional Environment System, The, Second Edition), 111–113

Tiffany, E. G., 447

Tindal, G. A., 298

TOAL–3 (Test of Adolescent and Adult Language), 231, 261, 269–270

TOLD-I:2 (Test of Language Development–Intermediate: Second Edition), 261, 269

TOLD-P:2 (Test of Language Development–Primary: Second Edition), 261, 270–271, 292

TOMA–2 (Test of Mathematical Abilities–Second Edition), 286, 293–294

Tone, B., 190, 215, 241

TONI–2 (Test of Nonverbal Intelligence–Second Edition), 341, 360, 364–366

TORC (Test of Reading Comprehension), 202

TORC–3 (Test of Reading Comprehension–Third Edition), 199, 201–202

Torgeson, J. K., 199

Total Communication Receptive Vocabulary Test, 444

Tourette's syndrome, 405

TOVA (Test of Variables of Attention) (Auditory Version), 416

TOVA (Test of Variables of Attention) (Visual Version), 416

TOWE (Test of Written Expression), 231, 233

TOWL–2 (Test of Written Language–Second Edition), 269

TOWL–3 (Test of Written Language–Third Edition), 231, 233–234

TPK (Test of Practical Knowledge), 462, 466–467, 471

Trafton, P. R., 280

Transactional theory of the development of oral language, 196

Transition assessment, 8, 311, 332–334, 438, 453, 461, 475–476

Transition Behavior Scale, 471

Transition Planning Inventory, 471

Traumatic brain injury (TBI), 4, 410–411, 446

Tremor, 445

Triangulation, 198, 227, 480

Triarchic theory of intelligence

    knowledge-acquisition components, 377

    metacomponents, 377

    performance components, 377

Triennial evaluation, 17, 47, 508

Trisomy 21 (Down syndrome), 330, 506

Trivette, C., 47

Troutman, A. C., 400

Troxel, R., 447

True score, 53, 56, 81–82, 86

T-score, 80, 359

Tuberculosis, 4

Tufte, E. R., 483

Turbiville, V., 37

Turnbull, A. P., 24, 26, 37, 49, 116–117

Turnbull, H. R. III, 24, 26, 49, 116–117

TVIP (Test de Vocabulario en Imágenes Peabody), 261, 266–267

TWS–3 (Test of Written Spelling–Third Edition), 231, 234

Tyler, R. W., 503–504

Tympanogram, 442

Tympanometry, 442

Ullmann, R. K., 413

Uniform Performance Assessment System, 444

Utah Test of Language Development–Third Edition, 262

VABS (Vineland Adaptive Behavior Scales), 386, 390, 393–397, 444
Valencia, R. R., 358
Validity
    concurrent, 60–61
    consequential, 61–62, 183
    construct, 59, 61–62
    content, 59, 227–228
    criterion-related, 60
    definition of, 59
    face, 61
    predictive, 59–61, 333
Valpar Component Work Sample System, 474
Vance, H. R., 341
Vandermeer, L., 113–115
Vaughn, S., 158–159
Vermont Analytic Assessment Scale, 179–180
Vineland Adaptive Behavior Scales (VABS), 386, 390, 393–397, 444
Visual analog scale, 114, 148
Visual field, 430, 435
Visual impairment
    adventitious, 430
    congenital, 430
Visual impairment including blindness, 4
VOCA (voice output communication aid), 275
Vocational Information and Evaluation Work Samples, 474
Voice output communication aid (VOCA), 275
Voss, D. E., 447
Vraniak, D. A., 339

Wagner, M., 710
WAIS-R (Wechsler Adult Intelligence Scale–Revised), 354, 360
Walker, H. M., 404, 415–416, 423–425
Walker-McConnell Scale of Social Competence, 416
Wallace, G., 260
Waltman, G. H., 25
Warren, S. F., 255
Wasik, B. A., 315
Wayman , K. I., 25–26
Weatherman, R. F., 386, 391, 393

Wechsler, D., 74, 80, 133, 135, 142–147, 200, 231–232, 263, 265, 287, 290, 294, 341, 347, 354, 359–360, 363, 365–373, 462
Wechsler Adult Intelligence Scale–Revised (WAIS-R), 354, 360
Wechsler Individual Achievement Test (WIAT), 80, 133, 135, 142–147, 200, 231, 287
Wechsler Intelligence Scale for Children (WISC), 365, 462
Wechsler Intelligence Scale for Children–Revised (WISC-R), 294, 354, 359–360, 363, 365, 368–369, 372–373
Wechsler Intelligence Scale for Children–Third Edition (WISC-III), 74, 80, 232, 263, 265, 290, 341, 359, 365–371
Wechsler Preschool and Primary Scale of Intelligence (WPPSI), 294, 371
Wechsler Preschool and Primary Scale of Intelligence–Revised (WPPSI-R), 341, 366, 369, 371–373
Welch, D. L., 200, 230, 287
Wesson, C. L., 172
West, L., 461
Westphal, S. E., 474
White, B., 400, 404
White, O. R., 444
Whole language approach to teaching reading, 197
WIAT (Wechsler Individual Achievement Test), 80, 133, 135, 142–147, 200, 231, 287
Wide Range Achievement Test (WRAT), 140
Wide Range Achievement Test–Third Edition (WRAT-3), 135, 146, 148, 200, 231, 287
Wide Range Employability Sample Test, 472, 474
Wide Range Interest-Opinion Test (WRIOT), 472
Wiederholt, J. L., 231, 261, 269, 340, 343–345, 462, 466–467, 471
Wiederholt, L., 198–202
Wiggins, G., 168
Wiig, E. H., 255–256, 258–260, 263
Wilde, S., 236
Wilkinson, G., 135, 146, 148, 200, 231, 287
Williams, K. T., 260, 263
Willis, S., 242
Wiltshire, S., 444
Winters, L., 168

WISC (*Wechsler Intelligence Scale for Children*), 365, 462

WISC-R (*Wechsler Intelligence Scale for Children-Revised*), 294, 354, 359–360, 363, 365, 368–369, 372–373

WISC-III (*Wechsler Intelligence Scale for Children-Third Edition*), 74, 80, 232, 263, 265, 290, 341, 359, 365–371

Wiske, M. S., 33, 320

WJ-R (*Woodcock-Johnson Psychoeducational Battery-Revised*), 69–70, 81, 135, 148–150, 200, 203, 231, 287, 341–342, 373–376

WJ-R ACH (*Woodcock-Johnson Psychoeducational Battery-Revised, Tests of Achievement*), 135, 148–150, 373

WJ-R COG (*Woodcock-Johnson Psychoeducational Battery-Revised, Tests of Cognitive Ability*), 148, 373–376

Wnek, L., 35, 319, 324, 387

Wolery, M., 76, 146

Wolf, D., 178

Woodcock, R. W., 69–70, 81, 135, 139, 141, 148–150, 199–200, 202–204, 231, 262, 265, 271, 287, 290, 341–342, 373–376, 386, 391, 393, 497

Woodcock-Johnson Psychoeducational Battery-Revised (WJ-R), 69–70, 81, 135, 148–150, 200, 203, 231, 287, 341–342, 373–376

Woodcock-Johnson Psychoeducational Battery-Revised, Tests of Achievement (WJ-R ACH), 135, 148–150, 373

Woodcock-Johnson Psychoeducational Battery-Revised, Tests of Cognitive Ability (WJ-R COG), 148, 373–376

Woodcock Language Proficiency Battery-Revised (English Form), 262, 271

Woodcock Language Proficiency Battery-Revised (Spanish Form), 262

Woodcock-Muñoz Language Survey (English and Spanish Forms), 262

Woodcock Reading Mastery Test-Revised (WRMT-R), 139, 141, 199, 202–204, 265, 290

WPPSI (*Wechsler Preschool and Primary Scale of Intelligence*), 294, 371

WPPSI-R (*Wechsler Preschool and Primary Scale of Intelligence-Revised*), 341, 366, 369, 371–373

WRAT (*Wide Range Achievement Test*), 140

WRAT-3 (*Wide Range Achievement Test-Third Edition*), 135, 146, 148, 200, 231, 287

WRIOT (*Wide Range Interest-Opinion Test*), 472

Written description, 12–13, 130–131, 154, 156, 179, 228–229, 235, 237, 257–258, 272, 281–282, 295, 299, 314–315, 410–411, 476

WRMT-R (*Woodcock Reading Mastery Test-Revised*), 199, 202–204

Young, M. H., 447

Young children (definition of), 312

Ysseldyke, J., 59, 62, 64, 70, 111–113, 125, 347, 354–355

Zaslovsky, C., 286

Zeisloft-Falbey, B., 385–387

Zeller, R. A., 61

Zelman, J. G., 387

Zimmerman, I. L., 261, 267–269

z-score, 80